Gleim Publications, Inc., offers five university-level study systems:

Auditing & Systems Exam Questions and Explanations with Test Prep CD-Rom
Business Law/Legal Studies Exam Questions and Explanations with Test Prep CD-Rom
Federal Tax Exam Questions and Explanations with Test Prep CD-Rom
Financial Accounting Exam Questions and Explanations with Test Prep CD-Rom
Cost/Managerial Accounting Exam Questions and Explanations with Test Prep CD-Rom

The following is a list of Gleim certification examination review systems:

CIA Review: Part I, Internal Audit Role in Governance, Risk, and Control
CIA Review: Part II, Conducting the Internal Audit Engagement
CIA Review: Part III, Business Analysis and Information Technology
CIA Review: Part IV, Business Management Skills

CMA Review: Part 1, Business Analysis
CMA Review: Part 2, Management Accounting and Reporting
CMA Review: Part 3, Strategic Management
CMA Review: Part 4, Business Applications

CPA Review: Financial
CPA Review: Auditing
CPA Review: Business
CPA Review: Regulation

EA Review: Part 1, Individuals
EA Review: Part 2, Businesses
EA Review: Part 3, Representation, Practice, and Procedures

An order form is provided at the back of this book, or contact us at www.gleim.com or (800) 87-GLEIM (800-874-5346).

REVIEWERS AND CONTRIBUTORS

Garrett W. Gleim, B.S., CPA (not in public practice), is a graduate of The Wharton School at the University of Pennsylvania. Mr. Gleim coordinated the production staff, reviewed the manuscript, and provided production assistance throughout the project.

Grady M. Irwin, J.D., is a graduate of the University of Florida College of Law and has taught in the University of Florida College of Business. Mr. Irwin provided substantial editorial assistance throughout the project.

Scott Lawton, B.S., is a graduate of Brigham Young University-Idaho and Utah Valley University. He has passed the EA exam and has been employed by the Utah State Tax Commission.

John F. Rebstock, B.S.A., is a graduate of the Fisher School of Accounting at the University of Florida. He has passed the CIA and CPA exams. Mr. Rebstock reviewed portions of the manuscript.

Stewart B. White, B.M., *Cum Laude*, University of Richmond, B.S., Virginia Commonwealth University, has passed the CPA and CISA exams and has worked in the fields of retail management, financial audit, IT audit, COBOL programming, and data warehouse management.

A PERSONAL THANKS

This manual would not have been possible without the extraordinary effort and dedication of Jacob Brunny, Kyle Cadwallader, Julie Cutlip, Mumbi Ngugi, Eileen Nickl, Teresa Soard, and Joanne Strong, who typed the entire manuscript and all revisions, and drafted and laid out the diagrams and illustrations in this book.

The authors also appreciate the production and editorial assistance of Christine Bertrand, Ellen Buhl, Katherine Goodrich, James Harvin, Jean Marzullo, Shane Rapp, Victoria Rodriguez, Laura Ter Keurst, and Martha Willis.

The authors also appreciate the critical reading assistance of Corinne Contento, Margaret Curtis, Ellie Gonzalez, and Holly Johnson.

Finally, we appreciate the encouragement, support, and tolerance of our families throughout this project.

THIRTEENTH EDITION

PART II

CONDUCTING THE INTERNAL AUDIT ENGAGEMENT

by

Irvin N. Gleim, Ph.D., CPA, CIA, CMA, CFM

with the assistance of
Grady M. Irwin, J.D.

ABOUT THE AUTHOR

Irvin N. Gleim is Professor Emeritus in the Fisher School of Accounting at the University of Florida and is a member of the American Accounting Association, Academy of Legal Studies in Business, American Institute of Certified Public Accountants, Association of Government Accountants, Florida Institute of Certified Public Accountants, The Institute of Internal Auditors, and the Institute of Management Accountants. He has had articles published in the *Journal of Accountancy*, *The Accounting Review,* and *The American Business Law Journal* and is author/coauthor of numerous accounting and aviation books and CPE courses.

Gleim Publications, Inc.
P.O. Box 12848
University Station
Gainesville, Florida 32604
(800) 87-GLEIM or (800) 874-5346
(352) 375-0772
FAX: (352) 375-6940
Internet: www.gleim.com
Email: admin@gleim.com

This is the first printing of the thirteenth edition of *CIA Review: Part II, Conducting the Internal Audit Engagement*. Please email update@gleim.com with **CIA II 13-1** included in the subject or text. You will receive our current update as a reply. Updates are available until the next edition is published.

EXAMPLE:

To: update@gleim.com
From: *your email address*
Subject: **CIA II 13-1**

ISSN: 1547-805X

ISBN: 978-1-58194-632-1

ACKNOWLEDGMENTS FOR PART II

The author is grateful for permission to reproduce the following materials copyrighted by The Institute of Internal Auditors: Certified Internal Auditor Examination Questions and Suggested Solutions (copyright © 1980 - 2007), excerpts from *The Practice of Modern Internal Auditing* and from *Sawyer's Internal Auditing* (5th ed.), The IIA Code of Ethics, *International Standards for the Professional Practice of Internal Auditing*, and Practice Advisories.

The authors also appreciate and thank the Institute of Certified Management Accountants for permission to use questions from past CMA examinations, copyright © 1982 - 2007 by the Institute of Management Accountants.

Visit our website (www.gleim.com) for the latest updates and information on all of our products.

This publication is designed to provide accurate and authoritative information with regard to the subject matter covered. It is sold with the understanding that the publisher is not engaged in rendering legal, accounting, or other professional service.

If legal advice or other expert assistance is required, the services of a competent professional person should be sought.

(From a declaration of principles jointly adopted by a Committee of the American Bar Association and a Committee of Publishers.)

TABLE OF CONTENTS

CIA Complete System

PREFACE

The purpose of this book is to help **you** prepare **yourself** to pass Part II of the CIA examination. The overriding consideration is to provide an inexpensive, effective, and easy-to-use study program. This manual

1. Defines topics tested on Part II of the CIA examination.

2. Includes all recent changes in Part II of the CIA program.

3. Explains how to optimize your grade by analyzing how the CIA exam is constructed and graded.

4. Suggests exam-taking techniques to help you maximize your exam score.

5. Outlines all of the subject matter tested on Part II of the CIA exam in 10 easy-to-use study units, including all relevant authoritative pronouncements.

6. Reorganizes past exam questions according to the subunits within each of the 10 study units and presents an intuitively appealing explanation of each objective question answer.

7. Provides an opportunity for professional accountants to obtain CPE credit while preparing to pass the CIA exam. See the following page for more information.

The outline format and spacing and the question and answer formats are designed to facilitate learning, understanding, and readability. Please read the Introduction of this book carefully.

Even though Gleim's four-volume *CIA Review* constitutes a complete self-study program for the CIA exam, candidates may consider enrolling in a formal review program. Local IIA chapters throughout the world have, in the past, coordinated their CIA review programs with our materials. All candidates should invest in our *CIA Complete System with Gleim Online*, which is designed to maximize your limited studying time. Our *System* includes our *CIA Test Prep* CD-Rom, which is a powerful supplemental study aid. Also, our *System* includes our audio series, books, and online review course. If you have not already purchased our *CIA Complete System with Gleim Online*, you may call us at (800) 874-5346 to purchase the remaining components at a reduced price.

Thank you for your interest in our materials. We deeply appreciate the thousands of letters and suggestions we have received from CIA, CMA, CPA, and EA candidates and accounting students and professors during the last four decades.

Please send us your suggestions, comments, and corrections concerning *CIA Review: Part II*. The last page in this book has been designed to help you note corrections and suggestions throughout your study process. It is imperative that we receive your feedback after you take the CIA exam. We pledge to continue to improve the product (with your suggestions, we hope) in subsequent editions.

To continue providing our customers with first-rate service, we request that questions about our materials be sent to us via <u>mail</u>, <u>email</u>, or <u>fax</u>. The appropriate staff member will give each question thorough consideration and a prompt response. Questions concerning orders, prices, shipments, or payments will be handled via telephone by our competent and courteous customer service staff.

Good Luck on the Exam,

Irvin N. Gleim

February 2008

EARN CPE CREDITS WHILE STUDYING FOR THE CIA EXAM

The Gleim approach to CPE is both interactive and intense. You should be continually challenged to answer each question correctly. When you answer a question incorrectly or have difficulty, you should pursue a complete understanding by reading the answer explanation and consulting reference sources as necessary.

We offer CPE credit online that correlates with this Thirteenth Edition text. Please call us at 800-87-GLEIM (800-874-5346) for more information.

Most of the questions in the study guide were taken from various professional examinations. Each question is revised, adapted, etc., to provide broader, up-to-date coverage of the internal auditing body of technical knowledge. In addition, publisher questions cover material added since examinations became "closed."

To continue providing our customers with first-rate service, we request that questions about our materials be sent to us via mail, email, or fax. The appropriate staff member will give each question thorough consideration and a prompt response. Questions concerning orders, prices, shipments, or payments will be handled via telephone by our competent and courteous customer service staff.

Thank you for your interest, and we look forward to hearing from you.

Best Wishes in Your CPE Endeavors,

Irvin N. Gleim

February 2008

PREPARING FOR AND TAKING THE CIA EXAM

ABOUT THE CIA EXAM

Introduction

CIA is the acronym for Certified Internal Auditor. The CIA designation is international, with the examination administered in numerous countries. The CIA exam has been administered by The Institute of Internal Auditors (The IIA) since 1974. The exam consists of four 3-hour parts that are given on demand throughout the year. Each part consists of 100 four-answer multiple-choice questions.

Computer-Based Testing

The CIA exam is computerized to facilitate easier testing. The computerized environment allows you more freedom in choosing when and where to take the test and ensures that your score is available to you immediately at the conclusion of your test. Additionally, the risk of committing mistakes when transferring answers to a booklet is eliminated with computer-based testing.

Part I	The Internal Audit Activity's Role in Governance, Risk, and Control	3 hours
Part II	Conducting the Internal Audit Engagement	3 hours
Part III	Business Analysis and Information Technology	3 hours
Part IV	Business Management Skills	3 hours
		12 hours

Each part consists of 100 questions, and testing lasts 2 hours and 45 minutes with 15 minutes given for tutorials and a survey. Pearson VUE, the testing company that The IIA contracts to proctor the exams, has over 400 testing centers worldwide, and candidates can choose test dates throughout the year. The Gleim Test Prep CD-Rom and Gleim Online provide tutorials and exact exam emulations of the Pearson VUE computer screens and procedures to prepare you to PASS. The exam application fee is $60. The price to register per part is $130 for members and $160 for non-members.

Please note as you read through this introduction that CIA program rules and prices are subject to change. Please visit Gleim's CIA Candidate Forum at www.gleim.com/account/forum/CIA for the most up-to-date information.

Development of Internal Auditing

Internal auditing is a management-oriented discipline that has evolved rapidly since World War II. Once a function primarily concerned with financial and accounting matters, internal auditing now addresses the entire range of operating activities. Thus, it performs a correspondingly wide variety of **assurance** and **consulting** services. The development of internal auditing was fostered by the increased size and decentralization of organizations and the greater complexity and sophistication of their operations. The result is a need for an independent, objective means of evaluating and improving risk management, control, and governance processes. Accordingly, The IIA's **definition of internal auditing** is as follows:

> *Internal auditing is an independent, objective assurance and consulting activity designed to add value and improve an organization's operations. It helps an organization accomplish its objectives by bringing a systematic, disciplined approach to evaluate and improve the effectiveness of risk management, control, and governance processes.*

Public policy considerations have contributed to the improved status and broadened scope of internal auditing. For example, U.S. organizations are expected to maintain reasonably detailed and accurate accounting records and a reasonably effective system of internal accounting control. Moreover, U.S. public companies must have an internal audit activity and an audit committee composed of nonmanagement directors.

The Institute of Internal Auditors (IIA)

The IIA was organized in 1941 to develop the professional status of internal auditing. The organization's headquarters was in New York City until 1972, when it moved to Altamonte Springs, about 5 miles north of Orlando, Florida.

The IIA has an annual budget of approximately $17 million and employs a full-time staff of 100+. Presently, over 60,000 individuals have attained The Institute of Internal Auditors' CIA designation.

The IIA has chapters in more than 200 metropolitan areas and has affiliated national institutes in many countries around the world. The chapters and institutes hold regular meetings, seminars, and conferences that encourage members to network with peers, develop professional contacts, and stay informed about current issues and practices in internal auditing.

The Institute of Internal Auditors' mission is to be the primary international professional association, organized on a worldwide basis, dedicated to the promotion and development of the practice of internal auditing.

The IIA is committed to:

- Providing, on an international scale, comprehensive professional development activities, standards for the practice of internal auditing, and certification.
- Researching, disseminating, and promoting to its members and to the public throughout the world, knowledge and information concerning internal auditing, including internal control and related subjects.
- Establishing meetings worldwide in order to educate members and others as to the practice of internal auditing as it exists in various countries throughout the world.
- Bringing together internal auditors from all countries to share information and experiences in internal auditing and promoting education in the field of internal auditing.

The IIA's annual dues in the United States, Canada, and Caribbean nations:

1.	Regular Member	$130	4.	Life Member	$2,100
2.	Government Audit Program	$65	5.	Retired Member	$30
3.	Educational Member	$65	6.	Student Member	$30

For non-Chapter members outside the United States, Canada, and the Caribbean nations, dues are $115. These members are also required to pay a $30 bank collection charge for drafts drawn on banks outside the U.S., Canada, and the Caribbean. All applicants except students also must pay a membership application fee of $25.

CIA Board of Regents

The Board of Regents is a special committee of The Institute of Internal Auditors established to direct the certification program for internal auditors as established or modified by The IIA's Board of Directors.

The Board of Regents consists of at least nine regents. The regents are appointed by the Chairman of the Board of Directors to serve 3-year terms. Membership on the Board of Regents rotates, with two or three regents being appointed each year. The responsibilities of the Board of Regents include:

a.   Defining the common body of knowledge for the Certified Internal Auditor examination and other Institute certification examinations

b.   Defining the education, experience, character, examination, and other program requirements relating to The Institute certifications

c.   Defining continuing professional education (CPE) requirements for Institute certifications

d.   Maintaining the quality and security of examinations

e.   Promoting The Institute's certifications globally

CIA Program

The following is the official statement of The IIA Board of Directors regarding the CIA program:

Professional Qualifications

To assist in achieving the goals and objectives of The Institute, the Certified Internal Auditor (CIA) Program was established. The Board of Directors will develop, approve and modify as necessary, such policies and procedures as may be required to stimulate and encourage this program.

While "Certified Internal Auditor" is intended to be the worldwide designation of qualified internal audit professionals, it is recognized for various reasons other professional organizations of internal auditors may develop similar designations. The Board of Directors will develop, approve and modify as necessary, such procedures as may be deemed desirable to recognize those designations.

The Board may also approve additional certifications as appropriate.

The IIA Certification Department

The Vice Presidents of the Learning Center and the Certification Department staff, who are located in The IIA's Florida offices, administer the program. They undertake all of the day-to-day work with respect to the Board of Regents' responsibilities.

The chair of the Board of Regents divides the members into subcommittees. Each subcommittee is responsible for one part of the exam; i.e., each subcommittee makes the initial recommendations concerning the content and grading of its part of the examination to the Board of Regents as a whole.

Well-Planned Evolution Rather than Abrupt Change

One of the responsibilities of The IIA Board of Regents is to continually update and enhance the sources of exam questions, which in their entirety constitute the **common body of knowledge**.

At the same time, the scope and content of the CIA exam appear to evolve so as to be predictable to CIA candidates. Addition of new topics and deletion of currently tested topics are announced at least one year in advance so that candidates may plan and prepare accordingly. The **common body of knowledge**, referred to in The IIA's materials, is reflected in this edition of *CIA Review*.

Pass rates on the exam are low enough to give the examination credibility relative to the CMA and CPA exams but are high enough to encourage accounting and auditing professionals to participate in the CIA certification program. Everyone, including The IIA Board of Directors, the Board of Regents, the certification staff, CIAs, noncertified internal auditors, and the accounting/auditing profession in general, is interested in the continual upgrading and improvement of the CIA exam.

Objectives and Content of the CIA Examination

The CIA exam tests a candidate's knowledge and ability regarding the current practice of internal auditing. It enables candidates and prospective managers to adapt to professional changes and challenges by

- Addressing nearly all management skills
- Focusing on the principles of management control
- Measuring a candidate's understanding of risk management and internal controls

---

THE IIA'S CIA CONTENT SPECIFICATION OUTLINES

Part I: The Internal Audit Activity's Role in Governance, Risk, and Control

A.	Comply with The IIA's Attribute Standards	20%
B.	Establish a risk-based plan to determine the priorities of the internal audit activity	20%
C.	Understand the internal audit activity's role in organizational governance	15%
D.	Perform other internal audit roles and responsibilities	5%
E.	Governance, risk, and control knowledge elements	20%
F.	Plan Engagements	20%

Part II: Conducting the Internal Audit Engagement

A.	Conduct Engagements	30%
B.	Conduct Specific Engagements	30%
C.	Monitor Engagement Outcomes	10%
D.	Fraud Knowledge Elements	10%
E.	Engagement Tools	20%

Part III: Business Analysis and Information Technology

A.	Business Processes	20%
B.	Financial Accounting and Finance	20%
C.	Managerial Accounting	15%
D.	Regulatory, Legal, and Economics	10%
E.	Information Technology (IT)	35%

Part IV: Business Management Skills

A.	Strategic Management	25%
B.	Global Business Environments	20%
C.	Organizational Behavior	20%
D.	Management Skills	25%
E.	Negotiating	10%

See Appendix A for complete details and cross references to this book.

The IIA publishes a Content Specification Outline (CSO), also known as a Content Syllabus, to outline topics covered on each part of the CIA exam. The percentage coverage of each exam part is indicated to the right of each topic. (Note that The IIA "percentage coverage" is given in ranges, e.g., 15-25%, as presented in Appendix A. Above, we present the midpoint of each range to simplify and provide more relevant information to CIA candidates, e.g., 20% instead of 15-25%.) In other words, the percentages listed are plus or minus 5% of the percentage coverages you can expect to encounter during the actual exam. We continually adjust the content of our materials to changes in The IIA's CSOs and changes to CIA exam questions.

Appendix A contains the CSOs in their entirety as well as cross references to the subunits in our text where topics are covered. Remember that we have studied and restudied the CSOs in developing our *CIA Review* materials. Accordingly, you do not need to spend time with Appendix A. Rather, it should give you confidence that Gleim's *CIA Review* is the best review source available to help you PASS the CIA exam. The CSOs refer to proficiency and awareness levels. The IIA definitions of these levels are presented below.

Proficiency -- *Candidate is able to exhibit the competency in understanding and applying the subject matter in the workplace on a regular basis with skill and expertise.*

Awareness -- *Candidate exhibits awareness and knowledge. Candidate is able to define terms, recognize issues, and recall facts about the issues.*

Gleim Study Unit Listing

We believe our 10 study unit titles better describe the content of each part of the CIA exam. Our study unit titles and content also reflect feedback from CIA candidates. Please use the last page in this book to give us feedback after each exam. Thank you.

LISTING OF GLEIM STUDY UNITS

Part I: Internal Audit Role in Governance, Risk, and Control

1. Standards and Proficiency
2. Charter, Independence, and Objectivity
3. Internal Audit Roles I
4. Internal Audit Roles II
5. Control I
6. Control II
7. Planning and Supervising the Engagement
8. Managing the Internal Audit Activity I
9. Managing the Internal Audit Activity II
10. Engagement Procedures, Ethics, and Fraud

Part II: Conducting the Internal Audit Engagement

1. Engagement Information
2. Communicating Results and Monitoring Progress
3. Specific Engagements I
4. Specific Engagements II
5. Information Technology I
6. Information Technology II
7. Specific IT Engagements
8. Statistics and Sampling
9. Other Engagement Tools
10. Ethics and Fraud

Part III: Business Analysis and Information Technology

1. Business Performance
2. Managing Resources and Pricing
3. Financial Accounting I
4. Financial Accounting II
5. Finance
6. Managerial Accounting
7. Regulatory, Legal, and Economic Issues
8. Information Technology I
9. Information Technology II
10. Information Technology III

Part IV: Business Management Skills

1. Structural Analysis and Strategies
2. Industry and Market Analysis
3. Industry Environments
4. Strategic Decisions
5. Global Business Issues
6. Motivation and Communications
7. Organizational Structure and Effectiveness
8. Managing Groups
9. Influence and Leadership
10. Time Management, Conflict, and Negotiation

Admission to the CIA Program

Anyone who satisfies these character, educational, and professional requirements may sit for the examination.

1. **Bachelor's degree or equivalent.** Candidates must have an undergraduate (4-year) degree or its equivalent from an accredited college-level institution.

    a. Educational programs outside the United States and the qualifications of candidates who have completed most but not all of a degree program are evaluated by The IIA's Board of Regents to determine equivalency.

    b. The IIA's affiliates have been given the authority to recommend educational and experience criteria for their countries to ensure adequate consideration of cultural and societal differences around the world. In addition, certain international professional designations (such as Chartered Accountant) may be accepted as equivalent to a bachelor's degree.

    c. A major in accounting is not required.

2. **Character reference.** CIA candidates must exhibit high moral and professional character and must submit a character reference from a responsible person such as a CIA, supervisor, manager, or educator. The character reference must accompany the candidate's exam application.

3. **Work experience.** Candidates are required to have 24 months of internal auditing experience (or the equivalent) prior to receiving the CIA certificate. A candidate may sit for the exam before completing the work experience requirements, but (s)he will not be certified until the experience requirement is met.

    a. An advanced academic degree beyond the bachelor's or work experience in related business professions (such as accounting, law, or finance) can be substituted for one year of work experience (1-year maximum).

    b. Equivalent work experience means experience in audit/assessment disciplines, including external auditing, quality assurance, compliance, and internal control.

    c. Full-time college or university-level teaching in the subject matter of the examination is considered equivalent to work experience. Two years of teaching equals one year of internal auditing work experience.

    d. Work experience must be verified by a CIA or the candidate's supervisor. An Experience Verification Form is available on The IIA's website or in the CIA brochure for use in verifying professional experience. This may accompany the candidate's application or be submitted later when criteria have been met.

If you have questions about the acceptability of your work experience, contact The IIA Certification Department at certification@theiia.org or by fax at (407) 937-1101. If you do not possess a bachelor's degree and are unsure whether your educational achievements or professional designation qualify as equivalents to a bachelor's degree, you should submit related educational/professional information with your exam application and include a cover letter requesting review by the Board of Regents. Include a complete description of your situation. Please submit these materials to:

IIA Certification
The Institute of Internal Auditors
247 Maitland Avenue
Altamonte Springs, FL 32701-4201

You will receive a response from The IIA as soon as the certification staff or the Board of Regents evaluates your request. Applicants for equivalency may be registered for the exam pending review but should expect a separate letter regarding the outcome of the review. Applicants who do not receive an equivalency status letter within four weeks of submission of the application and equivalency request should contact The IIA.

Application/Registration for the CBT Exam

Our initial information on applying/registering for the CBT CIA exam includes the following:

1. The application/registration process for the CBT CIA exam will be available online in most countries. Go to www.theiia.org for information on how to apply in countries where an online application is not available.

2. Once you have registered for a part of the exam, you will have 6 months to sit for that part.

3. You may register to take as many parts as you wish in the same time period.

4. If you have previously passed any part(s) of the the CIA exam in the paper and pencil format, you will be able to retain the credit you received for those parts. You will take any remaining parts in the CBT format.

5. A candidate has an initial eligibility period of two years (five examinations) after his/her first registration is approved. The eligibility period is subsequently extended for two years each time a candidate sits for a part. A candidate's eligibility will expire only if the candidate does not take a single exam part within any two-year period. If eligibility expires, the candidate loses credit for any part or parts previously passed and must reregister for consideration as a candidate for future examinations.

6. If you fail an exam part, you must wait 90 days to retake that part.

For more information on the registration process for the CBT exam as it is released by The IIA, check Gleim's CIA Candidate Forum at www.gleim.com/account/forum/CIA.

Professional Recognition Credit for Part IV

The IIA offers a Part IV Professional Recognition Credit for qualified professional certifications. Registered candidates and new CIA candidates who have successfully completed the examination requirements for many designations are eligible to receive credit for Part IV of the CIA exam. In the U.S., these designations include

CBA	CCSA	CFIRS	CISA	CPEA
CBM	CDFM	CGAP	CISSP	CPA
NCCO	CFSA	CGFM	CIDA	CRCM
CCBIA	CFE	CHFP	CMA	CRP

Please visit The IIA's website (www.theiia.org) for a complete list of certifications approved for credit in other countries. Hence, candidates who attain the credit for Part IV and pass Parts I, II, and III satisfy the examination requirement for the CIA designation.

Nondisclosed Exam

The CIA exam is a **nondisclosed** exam. **Nondisclosed** means that exam questions and solutions are NOT released after each examination. You will be asked to read and sign the Non-Disclosure Agreement prior to taking the CIA exam.

In order to keep our materials up to date and relevant to CIA candidates, we request feedback after each CIA exam. We need to know what topics need to be added or enhanced in our *CIA Review* materials. Note that we are not asking for information about CIA questions. Rather, we are asking for feedback on our outlines, questions, and answer explanations. This approach has been approved by The IIA.

CIA Exam Fees

Fees	IIA Members	Nonmembers	Professors/ Full-Time Students
Exam Application (initial nonrefundable fee)	US $60	US $75	US $30
Exam Parts Registration (per part/per sitting)	US $130	US $160	US $85
Part IV Professional Recognition Credit (PRC-IV) (non-refundable fee; waived for CCSAs, CGAPs and CFSAs)	US $130	US $160	US $85
Canadian Exam Site Tax (*percent of total exam part fees paid, including PRC-IV credit)	GST 6%* HST 14%*	GST 6%* HST 14%*	GST 6%* HST 14%*
Deferrals/Cancelations/Changes			
...by the application deadline (without exam fee refund)	US $0	US $0	US $0
...by the application deadline (with exam fee refund)	US $25	US $25	US $25
...after the application deadline	US $35	US $35	US $35
...beginning Wednesday of week before exam or no-shows	US $85	US $110	US $35

Special Professor and Student Examination Fee

The exam application fee is the charge for enrolling candidates in the CIA program. The CIA examination is available to professors and full-time students at reduced fees. For them, the exam application fee is $30 (instead of $60), plus an exam registration fee of $85 (instead of $130) per part. Professors and students may sit for each part at this special rate one time only.

1. To be eligible for the reduced rate, a student must

    a. Be enrolled as a senior in an undergraduate program or as a graduate student

    b. Be a full-time student as defined by the institution in which the student is enrolled (a minimum of 12 semester hours or its equivalent for senior-level undergraduate students and 9 semester hours for graduate students)

    c. Register for and take the CIA exam while enrolled in school

2. In addition to the requirements above, the following items should be submitted to the Certification Department of The Institute of Internal Auditors while the student is still enrolled in school:

    a. A Certified Internal Auditor Examination Registration/Application Form *(with school address substituted for business address)*

    b. A completed and signed Full-Time Student Status Form in lieu of a transcript

    c. A completed and signed Character Reference Form

    d. Payment for the $30 exam application fee and the $85 exam registration fee for each part

Maintaining Your CIA Designation

After certification, CIAs are required to maintain and update their knowledge and skills. Practicing CIAs must complete and report 80 hours of Continuing Professional Education (CPE) every two years. Every February, CIAs who are required to report in the current year will receive reporting forms and instructions from The IIA. Completed forms should be filed with The IIA by May 31 of the required reporting year. Each July, participants in the current year's CPE program will receive a status report acknowledging acceptance of the number of hours reported. Even-numbered certificates report in even years and odd-numbered certificates in odd years.

Examination Sites

The CBT CIA examinations are administered at Pearson VUE testing centers, which are located in the United States, the United Kingdom, India, Japan, and China. A complete list of these test centers, addresses, and driving directions can be found at www.pearsonvue.com. Click on the "Locate a Test Center" link at the top of the screen, and then choose the country and region in which you would like to take your exam.

If you require testing accommodations because of a special need, call a Pearson VUE agent at the time of registration for assistance.

PREPARING TO PASS THE CIA EXAM

Control: How To Be In

You have to be in control to be successful during exam preparation and execution. Control can also contribute greatly to your personal and other professional goals. The objective is to be confident that the best possible performance is being generated. Control is a process whereby you

1. Develop expectations, standards, budgets, and plans
2. Undertake activity, production, study, and learning
3. Measure the activity, production, output, and knowledge
4. Compare actual activity with expected and budgeted activity
5. Modify the activity, behavior, or study to better achieve the desired outcome
6. Revise expectations and standards in light of actual experience
7. Continue the process or restart the process in the future

Every day you rely on control systems implicitly. For example, when you groom your hair, you use a control system. You have expectations about the desired appearance of your hair and the time required to style it. You monitor your progress and make adjustments as appropriate. The control process, however, is applicable to all of your endeavors, both professional and personal. You should refine your personal control processes specifically toward passing the CIA exam.

In this book, we suggest explicit control systems for

1. Preparing to take the CIA exam
2. Studying an individual Gleim study unit
3. Answering individual multiple-choice questions

Most endeavors will improve with explicit control. This is particularly true of the CIA examination.

1. Develop an explicit control system over your study process.

2. Practice your question-answering techniques (and develop control) as you prepare solutions to recent CIA questions during your study program.

3. Prepare a detailed plan of steps you will take at the CIA exam.

How Many Parts to Take

The CIA examination consists of four parts: Parts I and II cover internal auditing subject matter, whereas Part III, Business Analysis and Information Technology, and Part IV, Business Management Skills, cover a wide variety of material.

According to The IIA, you may choose to take only one part at each sitting, which is what Gleim recommends for the CBT exam. Unless you have a strong preference to do otherwise, it is best to take the parts in numerical order, from Part I to Part IV.

Candidates have an initial eligibility period of 2 years from the first exam after their registration is approved. In addition, each time a candidate sits for an exam part, the candidate's eligibility period is extended 2 years from the date of the last exam part taken. A candidate's eligibility expires only if the candidate does not take a single exam part within any 2-year period. If a candidate's eligibility expires, the candidate loses credit for any part or parts passed and must submit a new CIA Exam Application Form and appropriate fees in order to take future examinations.

Study Plan, Time Budget, and Calendar

Complete one *CIA Review* study unit at a time. Initially, budget 3 to 4 hours per study unit (1 to 2 hours studying the outline and 1 to 2 minutes each on all the multiple-choice questions). Depending on your background, your time to prepare will vary.

This Introduction	2	Hours
10 study units at 3.5 hours each	35	
Review	10	
Total	47	Hours

Each week, you should evaluate your progress and review your preparation plans for the time remaining prior to the exam. Marking a calendar will facilitate your planning. Note the exam dates and the weeks to go before the exam. Review your commitments, e.g., out-of-town assignments, personal responsibilities, etc., and note them on your calendar to assist you in keeping to your schedule.

Core Concepts

Core concepts are included at the beginning of each study unit. The core concepts provide an overview of the key points that serve as the foundation for learning. In many cases, the core concepts are concise statements of attribute, performance, and implementation standards. As part of your review, you should make sure that you understand each of them.

Study Unit Summaries

Study unit summaries also are included in each study unit. These summaries are similar to the core concepts, but they provide more in-depth synopses of the material. They should help reinforce the main points within each of the study units.

Practice Advisory Summaries

Gleim *CIA Review* also provides the summarization of practice advisories (PA). Each PA is followed by a synopsis of its crucial aspects. The PA summaries provide the reinforcement of key issues that The IIA expects CIA candidates to know.

How to Study a Study Unit Using Gleim's Complete System

To ensure that you are using your time effectively, we recommend that you follow the steps listed below when using all of the materials together (books, CD-Rom, audios, and Gleim Online):

1. (25-30 minutes) In the *CIA Gleim Online* course, complete Multiple-Choice Quiz #1 in 20-25 minutes (excluding the review session). It is expected that your scores will be low on the first quiz.

    a. Immediately following the quiz, you will be prompted to review the questions you marked and/or answered incorrectly. For each question, analyze and understand why you marked it or answered it incorrectly. This step is an essential learning activity.

2. (15-30 minutes) Use the audiovisual presentation for an overview of the study unit. The Gleim *CIA Review Audios* can be substituted for audiovisual presentations and can be used while driving to work, exercising, etc.

3. (30-45 minutes) Complete the 30-question True/False quiz. It is interactive and most effective if used prior to studying the Knowledge Transfer Outline.

4. (60 minutes) Study the Knowledge Transfer Outline, specifically the troublesome areas identified from the multiple-choice questions in the Gleim Online course. The Knowledge Transfer Outlines can be studied either online or from the books.

5. (25-30 minutes) Complete Multiple-Choice Quiz #2 in the Gleim Online course.

    a. Immediately following the quiz, you will be prompted to review the questions you marked and/or answered incorrectly. For each question, analyze and understand why you marked it or answered it incorrectly. This step is an essential learning activity.

6. (40-50 minutes) Complete two 20-question quizzes while in Test Mode from the *CIA Test Prep* CD-Rom.

When following these steps, you will complete all 10 units in about 30-40 hours. Then spend about 5-10 hours using the *CIA Test Prep* CD-Rom to create customized tests for the problem areas that you identified. To review the entire part before the exam, use the *CIA Test Prep* CD-Rom to create 20-question quizzes that draw questions from all ten study units. Continue taking 20-question quizzes until you approach your desired proficiency level, e.g., 75%+.

CIA Gleim Online

Gleim's *CIA Gleim Online* is a versatile, interactive, self-study review program delivered via the Internet. With *CIA Gleim Online*, Gleim guarantees that you will pass the CIA exam on your first sitting. It is divided into four courses (one for each part of the CIA exam).

Each course is broken down into 10 individual, manageable study units. Completion time per study unit will vary from 3-5 hours. Each study unit in the course contains an audiovisual presentation, 30 true/false study questions, 10-20 pages of Knowledge Transfer Outlines, and two 20-question multiple-choice quizzes.

CIA Gleim Online provides you with a Personal Counselor, who will provide support to ensure your competitive edge. Gleim Online is a great way to get confidence as you prepare with Gleim. This confidence will continue during and after the exam.

Gleim Books and Test Prep CD-Rom

Twenty-question tests in the **CIA Test Prep** CD-Rom will help you focus on your weaker areas. Make it a game: How much can you improve?

Our *CIA Test Prep* CD-Rom forces you to commit to your answer choice before looking at answer explanations; thus, you are preparing under true exam conditions. It also keeps track of your time and performance history for each study unit, which is available in either a table or graphical format.

Simplify the exam preparation process by following our suggested steps listed below. DO NOT omit the step in which you diagnose the reasons for answering questions incorrectly; i.e., learn from your mistakes while studying so you avoid making similar mistakes on the CIA exam.

1. In test mode, answer a 20-question diagnostic test from each study unit before studying any other information.

2. Study the Knowledge Transfer Outline for the corresponding study unit in your Gleim book. Place special emphasis on the weaker areas that you identified with the initial diagnostic quiz in Step 1.

3. Take two or three 20-question tests in test mode after you have studied the Knowledge Transfer Outline.

4. Immediately following the quiz, you will be prompted to review the questions you marked and/or answered incorrectly. For each question, analyze and understand why you answered it incorrectly. This step is an essential learning activity.

5. Continue this process until you approach a predetermined proficiency level, e.g., 75%+.

6. Modify this process to suit your individual learning process.

   a. Learning from questions you answer incorrectly is very important. Each question you answer incorrectly is an **opportunity** to avoid missing actual test questions on your CIA exam. Thus, you should carefully study the answer explanations provided to understand why you chose the incorrect answer so you can avoid similar errors on your exam. This study technique is clearly the difference between passing and failing for many CIA candidates.

b. You **must** determine why you answered questions incorrectly and learn how to avoid the same error in the future. Reasons for missing questions include:

1) Misreading the requirement (stem)
2) Not understanding what is required
3) Making a math error
4) Applying the wrong rule or concept
5) Being distracted by one or more of the answers
6) Incorrectly eliminating answers from consideration
7) Not having any knowledge of the topic tested
8) Employing bad intuition (WHY?) when guessing

c. It is also important to verify that you answered correctly for the right reasons. Otherwise, if the material is tested on the CIA exam in a different manner, you may not answer it correctly.

d. It is imperative that you complete your predetermined number of study units per week so you can review your progress and realize how attainable a comprehensive CIA review program is when using Gleim's Complete System. Remember to meet or beat your schedule to give yourself confidence.

> Avoid studying Gleim questions to learn the correct answers. Use Gleim questions to help you learn how to answer CIA questions under exam conditions. Expect the unexpected and be prepared to deal with it. Become an educated guesser when you encounter questions in doubt; you will outperform the inexperienced exam taker.

Gleim Audio Reviews

Gleim *CIA Review* audios provide a 15- to 40-minute introductory review for each study unit. Each review provides a comprehensive overview of the outline in the *CIA Review* book. The purpose is to get candidates "started" so they can relate to the questions they will answer before reading the study outlines in each study unit.

The audios are short and to the point, as is the entire Gleim System for Success. We are working to get you through the CIA exam with minimum time, cost, and frustration.

If You Failed One or More Parts

The pass rate on each part of the CIA exam averages about 45%. Thus, you may not pass all parts attempted. If you failed a part, you must wait at least 90 days to retake it.

1. Once you have put the reaction to the bad news behind you, you should regroup and begin implementing the suggestions in this introduction. The Gleim system really works! Avoid thinking "I knew that" or "I don't have to study that again." What you knew and how you took the exam last time did NOT work. Develop new and improved perspectives.

2. Avoid failure on the next exam by **identifying**, **correcting**, and **understanding** your mistakes as you practice answering multiple-choice questions during your study sessions. Use the Gleim system as described on the previous pages. This methodology applies to all CIA candidates. Understand your mistakes while you study so you can avoid them on the exam.

As you practice answering multiple-choice questions under exam conditions, it is imperative that you re-study each question you answer incorrectly.

Multiple-Choice Question-Answering Technique

The following suggestions are to assist you in maximizing your score on each part of the CIA exam. Remember, knowing how to take the exam and how to answer individual questions is as important as studying/reviewing the subject matter tested on the exam.

1. **Budget your time.**

   a. We make this point with emphasis. Just as you would fill up your gas tank prior to reaching empty, so too should you finish your exam before time expires.

   b. You have 165 minutes to answer 100 questions, i.e., 1.65 minutes per question. We suggest you attempt to answer eight questions every 10 minutes, which is 1.25 minutes per question. This would result in completing 100 questions in 125 minutes to give you almost 40 minutes to review questions that you have flagged.

   c. Use the wipeboard provided by Pearson VUE for your Gleim Time Management System at the exam. List the question numbers for every 20 questions (i.e., 1, 21, 41, etc.) in a column on the left side of the wipeboard. The right side of the wipeboard will have your start time at the top and will be used for you to fill in the time you have remaining at each question checkpoint. Stay consistent with 1.25 minutes per question.

2. **Answer the items in numerical order.**

   a. Do **not** agonize over any one item. Stay within your time budget.

   b. Note any items you are unsure of by clicking the "Flag for Review" button in the upper-right corner of your screen, and return to them later if time allows. Plan on going back to all the questions you flagged.

3. **For each item,**

   a. **Read the question** stem carefully (the part of the question that precedes the answer choices) to determine the precise requirement.

      1) Focusing on what is required enables you to ignore extraneous information and to proceed directly to determining the correct answer.

         a) Be especially careful to note when the requirement is an **exception**; e.g., "Which of the following is **not** an indication of fraud?"

   b. **Determine the correct answer** before reading the answer choices. The objective is to avoid allowing the answer choices to affect your reading of the question.

      1) **Cover up the answer choices** by scrolling to view only the question or, if necessary, with your hand. Do not allow the answer choices to affect your reading of the item stem.

      2) When four answer choices are presented, three of them are incorrect. They are called distractors for a very good reason.

      3) Read each answer choice with close attention.

         a) Even if answer (A) appears to be the correct choice, do not skip the remaining answer choices. Answer (B), (C), or (D) may be better.

         b) Treat each answer choice as a true/false question.

   c. **Select the best answer.** Select the most likely or best answer choice. If you are uncertain, make an educated guess.

      1) The CIA exam does not penalize guessing, because your score is determined by the number of correct responses. Thus, you should answer every question.

If You Don't Know the Answer

Guess, but make it an educated guess, which means select the best possible answer. First, rule out answers that you feel are obviously incorrect. Second, speculate on The IIA's purpose and/or the rationale behind the question. These steps may lead you to the correct answer. Third, select the best answer, or guess between equally appealing answers. Flag the question in case you have time to return to it for further analysis. However, unless you made an obvious mistake or computational error, try to avoid changing answers at the last minute. Your first guess is usually the most intuitive.

If you cannot make an educated guess, read the item and each answer and pick the best or most intuitive answer. Never leave a question unanswered.

Do **not** look at the previous answer to try to detect an answer. The answers are random, but it is possible to have four or more consecutive questions with the same answer letter, e.g., answer B.

NOTE: Do not waste time beyond the amount budgeted. Move ahead and stay on or ahead of schedule.

CBT Exam Components

Time and Progress

The upper-right corner of the screen will continually display the time you have remaining in your exam. Below the time remaining, the question number you are currently working on is displayed in contrast to how many total questions there are on the exam (e.g., 14 of 100).

You can choose to allow these reminders to show during the exam, or you can minimize them by clicking on their icons. If you minimize the time remaining, it will automatically reappear when you have 5 minutes left.

Navigation

The following Navigation buttons will be available at the bottom of every screen during your exam:

Previous – Moves you back to the preceding screen
Next – Moves you forward to the following screen

Using the Scroll Bar

If you encounter a question that does not fit on the screen in its entirety, use the scroll bar that will appear along the side of the screen. To scroll down, you can either click on the scroll bar and drag it down or click on the arrow at the bottom of the scroll bar. To show the top part of the question again, either click and drag the scroll bar back up or click on the arrow at the top of the scroll bar.

Make certain that you have seen the entire question by always checking to see if the scroll bar appears. If you attempt to complete a question without scrolling to the bottom of the screen, a prompt may appear to remind you to scroll down.

English Display Screen

If you are taking the CIA exam in a language other than English, you may choose to view an English translation of any question on the exam.

To view the translation, click on the English button below the question. A separate screen will open and display the English translation of the current question. Close the translation when you are finished with it by clicking on the X in the lower-right corner of the translation screen.

Calculator

There will be an online calculator available for every question on the CIA exam. To use the calculator, click on the Calculator button in the upper-left corner of the screen. To enter numbers, you can either use your mouse to click the numbers on the calculator display or use the number keypad on your keyboard. Close the calculator when you are finished with it by clicking on the X in the upper-right corner of the calculator display screen.

Flag for Review

To flag a question so you can go back and review it later, click the Flag for Review button in the upper-right corner of the question screen. A flag image will appear in the flag icon on the question screen and to the left of that question number on the review screen. You can flag both answered and unanswered questions for review, but you must complete your review of flagged questions (and answer any unanswered questions) in the allotted exam time.

To unflag a flagged question, click on the Flag for Review button again.

The CIA's Review Screen

Once you get to the end of the exam, the Review Screen will be displayed. Each question is displayed with the status of that question: answered, flagged for review, or incomplete (unanswered).

You will be able to review your questions by choosing to either

> **Review All** questions and answers
> **Review Incomplete** questions and answers only
> **Review Flagged** questions and answers only

The computer will then generate your review based on which questions you chose to be included. During this review, you will be able to go back to your main Review Screen by selecting the Review Screen button. Once you are done with your review, you will click on the End Review/Exam button and then confirm that you are, in fact, done with the review/exam. Once you have clicked Yes on this screen, you will no longer be able to return to your review/exam.

TAKING THE CIA EXAM

CIA Examination Preparation Checklist

1. **Apply online** to the exam program (see page 8).
2. **Register online** for the desired part on the same application form (for the initial application and registration), or file the reapplication form.
   a. As soon as your examination location is confirmed, make travel and lodging reservations if necessary.
3. Acquire your study materials. Rely on our *CIA Complete System with Gleim Online* as your primary study source.
4. Plan your study program.
5. Locate a suitable place to study.
6. Implement your study program.
7. Periodically review, reassess, and revise your study program as needed.
8. Recognize that an orderly, controlled study program builds confidence, reduces anxiety, and produces success!
9. **Pass the examination!**

Exam Psychology

Plan ahead for the exam and systematically prepare for it. Go to the exam and give it your best. Neither you nor anyone else can expect more. If you have undertaken a systematic preparation program, you will do well.

Maintain a positive attitude and do not become anxious or depressed if you encounter difficulties before or during the exam. An optimist will usually do better than an equally well-prepared pessimist. Remember, you are not in a position to be objective about your results during the exam. Many well-prepared examination candidates have been pleasantly surprised by their scores. Indeed, you should be confident because you are competing with many less-qualified persons who have not prepared as well as you. Optimism and a fighting spirit are worth points on every exam; fear, anxiety, and depression tend to impair performance.

Proper exercise, diet, and rest during the weeks before the exam are very important. High energy levels, reduced tension, and a positive attitude are among the benefits. A good aerobic fitness program, a nutritious and well-balanced diet, and a regular sleep pattern will promote your long-term emotional and physical well-being as well as contribute significantly to a favorable exam result. Of course, the use of health-undermining substances should be avoided.

CBT Preparation

Your examination will be taken on a computer at the Pearson VUE testing center. You do not need any computer experience or typing skills to take your examination. Before you start the examination, you will be able to take a tutorial on the testing system if you wish. If you have used the Gleim *CIA Test Prep* CD-Rom and Gleim Online, you will be completely familiar and comfortable with the CBT format.

Examination Tactics

1. Arrive 15-30 minutes before your scheduled appointment. This early check-in allows time for you to sign in and for staff to verify your identification.

2. Before you are allowed to enter the testing room, you will be required to show 2 forms of identification, including one government-issued photo identification. Both must have signatures.

3. Dressing for exam success means emphasizing comfort, not appearance. Be prepared to adjust for changes in temperature, e.g., remove a sweater or put on a coat. Do not bring notes, this text, other books, etc., to the exam. You will only make yourself nervous and confused by trying to cram during the last 5 minutes before the exam. Books are not allowed in the exam room anyway.

4. Read the exam instructions carefully.

5. Answer the 100 questions in chronological order. Flag any questions that you are leaving for later or you wish to review.

6. You have 165 minutes (2 hours 45 minutes) to answer 100 questions. If you allocate 1.25 minutes per question, you will use only 125 minutes, leaving 40 minutes to complete Steps 7 and 8. If you use the Gleim Time Management System to pace yourself during the exam, you will have adequate time to complete each part.

7. After you worked through all 100 questions, you should return to the questions you flagged and make a final selection, i.e., your best answer.

    a. Review each question carefully. If you made an obvious mistake, e.g., misread the question, make the correction. DO NOT, however, begin changing answers and second guessing yourself. Your first answer to each question should be based on the systematic question-answering technique that you have practiced throughout your preparation program.

8. As soon as you return home from your exam, please email, fax, or write to us with your comments on our materials. We are particularly interested in which topics need to be added or expanded. We are NOT asking about specific CIA questions. Rather, we are asking for feedback on our materials. Use the last two pages in each Gleim book to send us your comments. This approach is approved by The IIA.

9. Re-review this tactics list and be confident in maximizing your score.

STUDY UNIT ONE
ENGAGEMENT INFORMATION

(33 pages of outline)

Internal auditing work includes (1) engagement planning; (2) identifying, analyzing, evaluating, and recording information; (3) communicating results; and (4) monitoring progress in accordance with The IIA Professional Practices Framework and any other standards that may apply. This study unit addresses identifying, analyzing, and evaluating information, a process that involves executing the **engagement work program**. It also addresses the kinds of information identified and the procedures used. These classifications help the internal auditor determine what role each piece of information plays in providing a sound basis for engagement **observations, conclusions, and recommendations**. Recording information to document the engagement in the **working papers** is covered in the final subunits.

The basic pronouncement is **General Performance Standard 2300 – Performing the Engagement**.

> *Internal auditors should identify, analyze, evaluate, and record sufficient information to achieve the engagement's objectives.*

Core Concepts

- Internal auditors identify, analyze, evaluate, and record sufficient information to achieve their objectives.
- Information should be sufficient, reliable, relevant, and useful.
- Conclusions and results should be based on appropriate analyses and evaluations.
- Internal auditors should be collectively and individually proficient and exercise due professional care.
- Internal auditors must determine the extent to which management has established adequate criteria for evaluating whether objectives have been accomplished.
- Information gathering should be adequately supervised.
- Engagement observations, conclusions, and recommendations should be sufficiently supported by the body of information gathered.
- Internal auditors should record relevant information to support conclusions and results.
- Working papers documenting the engagement are prepared by internal auditors and reviewed by IAA management.
- Use of computer and telecommunications technology for conducting the engagement raises special security concerns.
- Working papers should be subject to supervisory review.
- The CAE should control access to working papers and develop retention requirements.

1.1 IDENTIFYING INFORMATION

1.   This subunit concerns the identification and collection of information to support the engagement objectives. One typical method is the use of analytical auditing procedures. This subunit also defines the desirable characteristics of information. These matters are addressed by one General Performance Standard, one Specific Performance Standard, and three Practice Advisories.

2.   Internal auditors must follow the guidance on audit evidence contained in the Standards. The Practice Advisory on the audit evidence requirement for information systems (IS) auditing adapts that guidance to a specific context. However, the basic principles apply to all evidence gathering.

3.   ***2100   Nature of work*** – *The internal audit activity evaluates and contributes to the improvement of risk management, control, and governance systems.*

    a.   ***PEACTICE ADVISORY 2100-14: AUDIT EVIDENCE REQUIREMENT***

        1.   ***PLANNING***

            Types of Audit Evidence

            *When planning IS audit work, the auditor should take into account the **type** of audit evidence to be gathered, its **use** as audit evidence to meet audit objectives, and its varying levels of **reliability**. Among the things to be considered are the **independence and qualifications of the provider** of the audit evidence. For example, **corroborative audit evidence** from an independent third party can be more reliable than audit evidence from the organization being audited. **Physical audit evidence** is generally more reliable than the representations of an individual.*

            *The various **types of audit evidence** that the auditor should consider using include*

- *Observed processes and existence of physical items*
- *Documentary audit evidence*
- *Representations*
- *Analysis*

            Observed processes and existence of physical items *can include observations of activities, property, and information systems functions, such as*

- *An inventory of media in an offsite storage location*
- *A computer room security system in operation*

            Documentary audit evidence, *recorded on paper or other media, can include*

- *Results of data extractions*
- *Records of transactions*
- *Program listings*
- *Invoices*
- *Activity and control logs*
- *System development documentation*

            Representations *of those being audited can be audit evidence, such as*

- *Written policies and procedures*
- *System flowcharts*
- *Written or oral statements*

            *The **results of analyzing information** through comparisons, simulations, calculations, and reasoning can also be used as audit evidence. Examples include*

- *Benchmarking IS performance against other organizations or past periods*
- *Comparison of error rates among applications, transactions, and users*

Availability of Audit Evidence

*The auditor should consider the time during which information exists or is available in determining the **nature, timing, and extent of substantive testing** and, if applicable, **compliance testing**. For example, audit evidence processed by Electronic Data Interchange (EDI), Document Image Processing (DIP), and dynamic systems, such as spreadsheets, may not be retrievable after a specified period of time if changes to the files are not controlled or the files are not backed up.*

Selection of Audit Evidence

*The auditor should plan to use the **best audit evidence attainable** consistent with the importance of the audit objective and the time and effort involved in obtaining the audit evidence. If audit evidence obtained in the form of oral representations is critical to the audit opinion or conclusion, the auditor should consider obtaining documentary confirmation of the representations, either on paper or on other media.*

2. **PERFORMANCE OF AUDIT WORK**

Nature of Audit Evidence

*Audit evidence should be **sufficient, reliable, relevant, and useful** in order to form an opinion or support the auditor's findings and conclusions. If, in the auditor's judgment, the audit evidence obtained does not meet these criteria, the auditor should obtain **additional audit evidence**. For example, a program listing may not be adequate audit evidence until other audit evidence has been gathered to verify that it represents the actual program used in the production process.*

Gathering Audit Evidence

*Procedures used to gather audit evidence vary depending on the information system being audited. The auditor should select the **most appropriate procedure for the audit objective**. The following procedures should be considered:*

- *Inquiry*
- *Observation*
- *Inspection*
- *Confirmation*
- *Reperformance*
- *Monitoring*

*The above can be applied through the use of **manual audit procedures**, **computer-assisted audit techniques**, or a combination of both. For example,*

- *A system that uses manual control totals to balance data entry operations might provide audit evidence that the control procedure is in place by way of an appropriately reconciled and annotated report. The auditor should obtain audit evidence by reviewing and testing this report.*
- *Detailed transaction records may only be available in machine-readable format requiring the auditor to obtain audit evidence using computer-assisted audit techniques.*

Audit Documentation

Audit evidence gathered by the auditor should be appropriately documented and organized to support the auditor's findings and conclusions.

3.   **REPORTING**

*When the auditor believes **sufficient audit evidence cannot be obtained**, the auditor should disclose this fact in a manner consistent with the communication of the audit results.*

PA Summary

- When **planning** information systems (IS) audit work, the auditor considers the **type** of evidence, its **use**, its **reliability**, and the **independence** and **qualifications** of the provider. For example, **corroborative evidence** from an independent third party can be more reliable than evidence from the auditee, and **physical evidence** is generally more reliable than representations.

- **Types** of evidence include observations, documentation, representations, and analysis. **Observations** may be made of activities, property, and information systems functions. **Documentary evidence** is recorded on paper or other media. **Representations** are made by those being audited. The **results of analyzing information** arise from comparisons, simulations, calculations, and reasoning.

- The auditor considers the time when evidence is **available or exists** to determine the nature, timing, and extent of **substantive testing** and **compliance testing**.

- The auditor should plan to use the **best evidence attainable** consistent with the audit objective and the effort required. If oral representations are critical to the opinion or conclusion, the auditor should consider documentary confirmation in some medium.

- Evidence should be **sufficient**, **reliable**, **relevant**, and **useful**. If it does not meet the criteria, the auditor should obtain **additional audit evidence**.

- Procedures vary with the information system audited. Procedures should be those most appropriate for the audit objective. They include (1) inquiry, (2) observation, (3) inspection, (4) confirmation, (5) reperformance, and (6) monitoring.

- Procedures may be **manual, computer-assisted**, or a combination.

- Evidence should be appropriately **documented** and organized to support findings and conclusions.

- The auditor should make **appropriate disclosures** when sufficient evidence cannot be obtained.

---

4.   **2310**   *Identifying Information* – *Internal auditors should identify sufficient, reliable, relevant, and useful information to achieve the engagement's objectives.*

a.   **PRACTICE ADVISORY 2310-1: IDENTIFYING INFORMATION**

1.   *Information should be collected on all matters related to the **engagement objectives** and **scope of work**. Internal auditors use analytical auditing procedures when identifying and examining information. **Analytical auditing procedures** are performed by studying and comparing relationships among both financial and nonfinancial information. The application of analytical auditing procedures for identifying information to be examined is based on the premise that, in the absence of known conditions to the contrary, relationships among information may reasonably be expected to exist and continue. Examples of contrary conditions include unusual or nonrecurring transactions or events; accounting, organizational, operational, environmental, and technological changes; inefficiencies; ineffectiveness; errors; irregularities; or illegal acts.*

2. *Information should be **sufficient, reliable, relevant, and useful** to provide a sound basis for engagement observations, conclusions, and recommendations. **Sufficient** information is factual, adequate, and convincing so that a prudent, informed person would reach the same conclusions as the internal auditor. **Reliable** information is competent and the best attainable through the use of appropriate engagement techniques. **Relevant** information supports engagement observations and recommendations and is consistent with the objectives for the engagement. **Useful** information helps the organization meet its goals.*

PA Summary

- Information is collected on all matters related to **engagement objectives** and **scope of work**.
- **Analytical procedures** are used to identify and examine information. They are used to study and compare relationships among financial and nonfinancial information. Their application is based on the premise that, absent known contrary conditions, these relationships may reasonably be expected to exist and continue.
- The PA defines **sufficiency, reliability, relevance, and usefulness** of information.

---

5. Determining **whether information is adequate** for the internal auditor's purposes is a matter of judgment that depends on the particular situation.

   a. Although the judgment is supposed to be objective, it will inevitably vary with the internal auditor's training, experience, and other personal traits.

   b. Furthermore, the decision about the adequacy of information is not readily quantifiable.

6. The **sufficiency** criterion is explicitly defined in objective terms. The conclusions reached should be those of a prudent, informed person.

   a. For example, **objectivity** is enhanced when samples are chosen using standard statistical methods.

   b. The basic issue is whether the information has the degree of **persuasiveness** needed in the circumstances.

      1) Thus, persuasiveness must be greater in a fraud investigation of a senior manager than in an engagement involving petty cash. The difference in risk determines the quality and quantity of information.

7. **Reliable** information is competent and the best attainable using appropriate methods.

   a. Information is reliable when the internal auditor's results can be verified by others.

      1) Reliable information is valid. It accurately represents the observed facts.

   b. Information should consist of what may be collected using reasonable efforts subject to such **inherent limitations** as the **cost-benefit** constraint.

      1) Accordingly, internal auditors employ efficient methods, e.g., statistical sampling and analytical auditing procedures.

   c. Evidence is more reliable if it is

      1) Obtained from sources **independent** of the engagement client, such as confirmations of receivables or expert appraisals that are timely and made by a source with no connection to the auditee

      2) **Corroborated** by other information

      3) **Direct**, such as the internal auditor's personal observation, rather than indirect, such as hearsay

      4) An **original** document, not a copy

8. The definition of **relevance** emphasizes the need for work to be restricted to achieving objectives. However, information also should be gathered on "all matters" within the engagement's scope.

   a. Relevant information has a **logical relationship** to what it purports to prove.

      1) For example, **vouching** journal entries to the original documents does not support the completeness assertion about reported transactions. Instead, **tracing** transactions to the accounting records would provide relevant information.

9. Information is **useful** when it "helps the organization meet its goals."

   a. The organization's ultimate goal is to create value for its owners, other stakeholders, customers, and clients. Hence, this characteristic of information is consistent with the definition of internal auditing. It should add value, improve operations, and help an organization achieve its objectives.

   b. Furthermore, the identification of information that is useful to the organization is the ultimate justification for the existence of an internal audit activity.

10. **Engagement client feedback** is valuable in the internal auditor's determination of whether the information supports the engagement observations, conclusions, and recommendations.

    a. If the engagement observations are negative, the client has a natural incentive to find the flaws in the internal auditor's information and reasoning. Constructive feedback of this kind helps the internal auditor strengthen the evidential base of the engagement communications.

       1) The client's tendency to be critical of negative observations means that agreement lends substantial credibility to the internal auditor's position.

       2) However, agreement with positive observations may represent client self-interest rather than useful feedback.

11. Stop and review! You have completed the outline for this subunit. Study multiple-choice questions 1 through 11 beginning on page 53.

1.2 ANALYSIS AND EVALUATION

1. This subunit is devoted to the **analytical auditing procedures** used by the internal auditors to assess and evaluate the information identified. These procedures are used not only in planning the engagement but also during the conduct of the engagement. Analysis and evaluation are addressed in one Specific Performance Standard and one Practice Advisory. Study Unit 8, "Statistics and Sampling," is also relevant.

2. *2320*   *Analysis and Evaluation* – *Internal auditors should base conclusions and engagement results on appropriate analyses and evaluations.*

   a. *PRACTICE ADVISORY 2320-1: ANALYSIS AND EVALUATION*

      1. *Analytical auditing procedures provide internal auditors with an efficient and effective means of **assessing and evaluating information** collected in an engagement. The assessment results from comparing information with expectations identified or developed by the internal auditor. Analytical auditing procedures are useful in identifying, among other things,*

         - *Differences that are not expected*
         - *The absence of differences when they are expected*
         - *Potential errors*
         - *Potential irregularities or illegal acts*
         - *Other unusual or nonrecurring transactions or events*

2. *Analytical auditing procedures may include*

- *Comparison of current period information with similar information for prior periods*
- *Comparison of current period information with budgets or forecasts*
- *Study of relationships of financial information with the appropriate nonfinancial information (for example, recorded payroll expense compared with changes in average number of employees)*
- *Study of relationships among elements of information (for example, fluctuation in recorded interest expense compared with changes in related debt balances)*
- *Comparison of information with similar information for other organizational units*
- *Comparison of information with similar information for the industry in which the organization operates*

3. *Analytical auditing procedures may be performed using monetary amounts, physical quantities, ratios, or percentages. **Specific analytical auditing procedures** include, but are not limited to, ratio, trend, and regression analysis; reasonableness tests; period-to-period comparisons; and comparisons with budgets, forecasts, and external economic information. Analytical auditing procedures assist internal auditors in **identifying conditions that may require subsequent engagement procedures**. Internal auditors should use analytical auditing procedures in **planning** the engagement in accordance with the guidelines contained in Section 2200 of the Standards (Practice Advisory 2210-1: Engagement Objectives).*

4. *Analytical auditing procedures should also be **used during the engagement** to examine and evaluate information to support engagement results. Internal auditors should consider the **factors** listed below in determining the **extent to which analytical auditing procedures should be used**. After evaluating these factors, internal auditors should consider and use additional procedures, as necessary, to achieve the engagement objective.*

- *The significance of the area being examined*
- *The adequacy of the system of internal control*
- *The availability and reliability of financial and nonfinancial information*
- *The precision with which the results of analytical auditing procedures can be predicted*
- *The availability and comparability of information regarding the industry in which the organization operates*
- *The extent to which other engagement procedures provide support for engagement results*

5. *When analytical auditing procedures identify **unexpected results or relationships**, internal auditors should examine and evaluate such results or relationships. The examination and evaluation of unexpected results or relationships from applying analytical auditing procedures should include **inquiries of management and the application of other engagement procedures** until internal auditors are satisfied that the results or relationships are sufficiently explained. **Unexplained results or relationships** from applying analytical auditing procedures may be indicative of a significant condition, such as a potential error, irregularity, or illegal act. Results or relationships from applying analytical auditing procedures that are not sufficiently explained should be **communicated** to the appropriate levels of management. Internal auditors may recommend appropriate courses of action, depending on the circumstances.*

PA Summary

- Analytical procedures are used to **assess and evaluate information**. The assessment compares information with expectations identified or developed by the auditor.
- Analytical procedures **identify conditions** that may require subsequent procedures, such as (1) unexpected differences; (2) absence of expected differences; (3) potential errors, irregularities, or illegal acts; and (4) other unusual or nonrecurring transactions or events. Thus, they are **planning** tools.
- **Analytical procedures may include** (1) comparison of current and prior period information; (2) comparison with budgets or forecasts; (3) study of relationships of financial and nonfinancial information; (4) study of relationships among elements of information (e.g., interest expense and debt); and (5) comparison with information for other organizational units, with the industry for general economic data.
- Analytical procedures may use monetary amounts, physical quantities, ratios, or percentages.
- Analytical procedures are **used during the engagement** to evaluate information to support engagement results. The extent of their use depends on the (1) significance of the area examined, (2) adequacy of control, (3) availability and reliability of information, (4) precision with which the results of analytical procedures are predictable, (5) availability and comparability of information about the industry, and (6) extent to which other procedures support the results.
- Identification of **unexpected results or relationships** requires additional audit effort. Unexplained results or relationships may indicate an adverse condition.

---

3. **Comparison** of current-period information with similar information for prior periods is a very common analytical auditing procedure.

   a. The comparison may be from year to year, quarter to quarter, the current quarter to the same quarter last year, etc.

   b. Trend analysis is an example of this type of comparison.

   c. Moreover, the comparison is valid only to the extent it allows for known changes affecting the comparability of the organization's information.

4. If a **budget** has been carefully prepared and therefore reflects reasonable expectations about the organization's performance, calculation of **budget variances** is an effective analytical procedure.

   a. Such comparison of current-period results with budgeted amounts is a common cost accounting procedure.

      1) Internal auditors should determine that budgets are reasonable and that variances have been **identified and followed up**.

5. Analysis of the relationships among the elements of accounting information is facilitated by the **double-entry system**.

   a. Some accounts may be **reconciled**. For example, an organization's net operating cash flows for a period may be determined by adjusting net income for changes in receivables, payables, inventories, deferrals, and nonoperating items.

   b. Some other accounts, such as bad debt expense and accounts receivable, are expected to have certain **percentage relationships**.

   c. Turnover analysis is useful for determining lagging collections of receivables (ratio = net sales ÷ average receivables) or slow-moving inventory (ratio = cost of sales ÷ average inventory).

6. Comparisons of client information with **industry information** provide a reference to external benchmarks. Thus, these comparisons may be more useful and reliable than those with internal information.

   a. However, industry averages must be carefully interpreted because of differences between the client's circumstances and those of other firms in the industry.

7. Accounting information may usefully be compared with **operating information**.

   a. For example, inventory, cost of sales, and sales should be consistent with unit production, shipments made, purchases, and the size of the workforce.

8. Information about **economic conditions** (growth in the gross domestic product, interest rate movements, changes in the availability of workers, etc.) should be used to interpret organizational performance information.

   a. Thus, an economic downturn either in the industry or in the general economy may account for a failure to meet expectations.

9. Other **external nonfinancial information** may help to explain financial information.

   a. Demographic trends, such as the aging of the population, domestic political events, and international crises, are among the many external nonfinancial variables that may affect an organization's reporting.

10. Stop and review! You have completed the outline for this subunit. Study multiple-choice questions 12 through 24 beginning on page 57.

1.3 DUE PROFESSIONAL CARE

1. This subunit is relevant to the internal auditors' identification, analysis, evaluation, and recording of information. It includes one General Attribute Standard, one Specific Attribute Standard, three Assurance Implementation Standards, one Consulting Implementation Standard, and five Practice Advisories.

   a. When conducting engagements, internal auditors must research and apply appropriate standards, including the Professional Practices Framework (see *CIA Review* Part I) and other professional, legal, and regulatory standards. This requirement follows from General Attribute Standard 1200.

2. *1200*   ***Proficiency and Due Professional Care*** – *Engagements should be performed with proficiency and due professional care.*

   a. ***PRACTICE ADVISORY 1200-1: PROFICIENCY AND DUE PROFESSIONAL CARE***

      1. *Professional proficiency is the responsibility of the* ***chief audit executive*** *and* ***each internal auditor***. *The chief audit executive should ensure that persons assigned to each engagement collectively possess the necessary knowledge, skills, and other competencies to conduct the engagement properly.*

      2. *Internal auditors should* ***comply with professional standards of conduct***. *The Institute of Internal Auditors' Code of Ethics extends beyond the definition of internal auditing to include two essential components:*

         • ***Principles*** *that are relevant to the profession and practice of internal auditing -- specifically, integrity, objectivity, confidentiality, and competency; and*

         • ***Rules of Conduct*** *that describe behavior norms expected of internal auditors. These rules are an aid to interpreting the Principles into practical applications and are intended to guide the ethical conduct of internal auditors.*

> ## PA Summary
>
> - The CAE and each auditor are responsible for the **collective proficiency** of the IAA and his/her own proficiency, respectively.
> - The CAE should ensure that persons assigned to each engagement collectively possess the necessary **knowledge, skills, and other competencies**.
> - Internal auditors should comply with **The IIA Code of Ethics**.

3. **_1220_**   **_Due Professional Care_** – *Internal auditors should apply the care and skill expected of a reasonably prudent and competent internal auditor. Due professional care does not imply infallibility.*

   a. **_PRACTICE ADVISORY 1220-1: DUE PROFESSIONAL CARE_**

      1. *Due professional care calls for the application of the care and skill expected of a* **reasonably prudent and competent internal auditor in the same or similar circumstances**. *Professional care should, therefore, be appropriate to the complexities of the engagement being performed. In exercising due professional care, internal auditors should be alert to the possibility of intentional wrongdoing, errors and omissions, inefficiency, waste, ineffectiveness, and conflicts of interest. They should also be alert to those conditions and activities where irregularities are most likely to occur. In addition, they should* **identify inadequate controls** *and recommend improvements to promote compliance with acceptable procedures and practices.*

      2. *Due care implies* **reasonable care and competence**, *not infallibility or extra-ordinary performance. Due care requires the auditor to conduct examinations and verifications to a reasonable extent, but does not require detailed reviews of all transactions. Accordingly, internal auditors cannot give absolute assurance that* **noncompliance or irregularities** *do not exist. Nevertheless, the possibility of material irregularities or noncompliance should be considered whenever an internal auditor undertakes an internal auditing assignment.*

> ## PA Summary
>
> - **Due professional care** is the care exercised by a **reasonably prudent and competent auditor in similar circumstances**. The auditor should be alert to intentional wrongdoing, inefficiency, and ineffectiveness. The auditor also must identify controls.
> - The auditor provides reasonable, not absolute, assurance.

4. **_1220.A1_** – *The internal auditor should exercise due professional care by considering the*

   - *Extent of work needed to achieve the engagement's objectives*
   - *Relative complexity, materiality, or significance of matters to which assurance procedures are applied*
   - *Adequacy and effectiveness of risk management, control, and governance processes*
   - *Probability of significant errors, irregularities, or noncompliance*
   - *Cost of assurance in relation to potential benefits*

5. **_1220.A2_** – *The internal auditor should be alert to the significant risks that might affect objectives, operations, or resources. However, assurance procedures alone, even when performed with due professional care, do not guarantee that all significant risks will be identified.*

6. ***1220.C1*** – *The internal auditor should exercise due professional care during a consulting engagement by considering the*

- *Needs and expectations of clients, including the nature, timing, and communication of engagement results*
- *Relative complexity and extent of work needed to achieve the engagement's objectives*
- *Cost of the consulting engagement in relation to potential benefits*

a. **PRACTICE ADVISORY 1000.C1-2: ADDITIONAL CONSIDERATIONS FOR FORMAL CONSULTING ENGAGEMENTS**

The following is the relevant portion of this comprehensive Practice Advisory:

9. *The internal auditor should exercise **due professional care** in conducting a **formal consulting engagement** by understanding the following:*

- *Needs of management officials, including the nature, timing, and communication of engagement results*
- *Possible motivations and reasons of those requesting the service*
- *Extent of work needed to achieve the engagement's objectives*
- *Skills and resources needed to conduct the engagement*
- *Effect on the scope of the audit plan previously approved by the audit committee*
- *Potential impact on future audit assignments and engagements*
- *Potential organizational benefits to be derived from the engagement*

10. *In addition to the due professional care considerations described above, the internal auditor should:*

- *Conduct appropriate meetings and gather necessary information to assess the **nature and extent of the service** to be provided.*
- *Confirm that those receiving the service understand and agree with the relevant guidance contained in the **internal audit charter**, internal audit activity's **policies and procedures**, and other related guidance governing the conduct of consulting engagements. The internal auditor should decline to perform consulting engagements that are prohibited by the terms of the internal audit charter, conflict with the policies and procedures of the internal audit activity, or do **not add value** and promote the best interests of the organization.*
- *Evaluate the consulting engagement for compatibility with the internal audit activity's **overall plan of engagements**. The internal audit activity's risk-based plan of engagements may incorporate and rely on consulting engagements, to the extent deemed appropriate, to provide necessary audit coverage to the organization.*
- ***Document** general terms, understandings, deliverables, and other **key factors** of the formal consulting engagement in a written agreement or plan. It is essential that both the internal auditor and those receiving the consulting engagement **understand and agree** with the reporting and communication requirements.*

PA Summary

- **Due professional care** for a **formal consulting engagement** requires an understanding of the (1) needs of management, (2) reasons for the service, (3) extent of work, (4) resources required, (5) effect on the audit plan, (6) effect on future engagements, and (7) engagement benefits.
- The auditor should assess the **nature and extent of the service**.
- The auditor should confirm that service recipients **agree with related guidance** (e.g., the IAA's charter, policies, and procedures). Engagements should not be performed when they (1) are prohibited by the charter, (2) conflict with policy, or (3) do not add value.
- An engagement should be compatible with the IAA's **overall plan of engagements**. In appropriate circumstances, consulting engagements may provide necessary audit coverage.
- **Key engagement factors** should be **documented** in a **written agreement**.

---

7. Standard 1220 emphasizes that information obtained during the engagement **cannot provide absolute assurance** about the engagement client's activities. The reason is that detailed reviews encompassing all transactions are seldom feasible.

    a. Thus, the process of identifying, analyzing, evaluating, and recording sufficient information entails merely a **reasonable examination**.

8. Due professional care means that the internal auditor's **assertions are substantiated**.

    a. **Inadequate Information**

        1) Diminishes the credibility of the engagement results
        2) Impairs relationships with those to whom the internal auditor reports
        3) Undermines the internal auditor's professional standing

    b. When substantial support is not available for results, the internal auditor must be careful to **disclose** the lack of information.

        1) These circumstances might arise, for example, when critical but unsubstantiated information comes to the internal auditor's attention.

9. The **extent of information gathering** is directly related to the **scope of the service** performed by the internal auditor and the **degree of assurance** to be given. In the exercise of due professional care, the internal auditor must fully disclose these matters, as well as the **criteria** to be applied in making evaluations.

    a. For example, a count of inventory provides quantifiable, objective information as a basis for precise conclusions drawn with a high degree of confidence.

        1) In contrast, a survey of customer service provides more subjective information that permits conclusions with a much lower degree of certainty. In this case, the interested parties should agree on the **evaluative criteria** to be used. Standard 2120.A4 and Practice Advisory 2120.A4-1 address the determination of control criteria.

10. ***2120.A4*** – *Adequate criteria are needed to evaluate the controls. Internal auditors should ascertain the extent to which management has established adequate criteria to determine whether objectives and goals have been accomplished. If adequate, internal auditors should use such criteria in their evaluation. If inadequate, internal auditors should work with management to develop appropriate evaluation criteria.*

    a. ***PRACTICE ADVISORY 2120.A4-1: CONTROL CRITERIA***

        1. *Internal auditors should evaluate the established **operating targets and expectations** and should determine whether those operating standards are acceptable and are being met. When such management targets and criteria are vague, **authoritative interpretations** should be sought. If internal auditors are required to interpret or select operating standards, they should seek **agreement with engagement clients** as to the criteria needed to measure operating performance.*

PA Summary

- Internal auditors should evaluate **operating targets and expectations** and whether they are acceptable and being met. If operating criteria are vague, the IAA seeks **authoritative guidance**. If the IAA must interpret or select criteria, agreement with the client should be sought.

---

11. The professionalism of the information gathering process also depends on the adequacy of **supervision**.

    a. According to **Practice Advisory 2340-1, Engagement Supervision**, "Supervision is a process that begins with planning and continues throughout the examination, evaluation, communicating, and follow-up phases of the engagement."

    b. Among other things, supervision includes determining that (1) the approved **engagement program** is carried out unless changes are both justified and authorized, and (2) **working papers** adequately support the engagement observations, conclusions, and recommendations.

    c. Supervision also extends to performance **appraisals of engagement staff**.

        1) **Appraisal** of each internal auditor's performance is required **at least annually**.

            a) A full explanation of the appraisal process and results should be given to each internal auditor.

        2) The evaluation provides a basis for **counseling** subordinates on their strong and weak attributes, opportunities for advancement, and programs for self-improvement.

        3) The evaluation is a basis for promotions, transfers, and compensation adjustments.

        4) The evaluation is done by the person with responsibility for the particular employee.

        5) **Criteria** for evaluation are weighted and applied to **performance on specific projects**. The criteria include (a) types of skills required (computer, communication, etc.); (b) extent of responsibility; (c) scope and quality of effort; (d) nature of working conditions; (e) knowledge of auditing and of the organization's procedures; (f) auditee relations; (g) improvement since the last appraisal; (h) continuing education; and (i) planning ability.

            a) A performance appraisal of each staff member **after an engagement** is advantageous because the work (and recollections of it) are recent.

            b) **Periodic evaluation** also allows a staff member to improve his/her performance prior to the annual review.

   d.   **Client satisfaction survey.** As part of a **quality assurance process**, internal auditors should gather information from clients (customers of internal auditing services) about the quality of their performance.

       1)   Advantages are future improvement in that performance and better **client-auditor relations** through conflict reduction, greater client participation, and a better understanding of the internal auditing function.

       2)   **Content.** The survey should address matters such as

          a)   Knowledge of the client's objectives and functions
          b)   Quality of services
          c)   Knowledge of auditing principles and methods
          d)   Human relations and communications skills
          e)   Responsiveness to client needs
          f)   Maintenance of client confidentiality
          g)   Training and professional bearing of auditors
          h)   Problem-solving ability and helpfulness
          i)   Productivity, i.e., the value of their observations and findings

12.   Stop and review! You have completed the outline for this subunit. Study multiple-choice questions 25 through 32 beginning on page 62.

1.4 SOURCES OF INFORMATION

1.   Information may be classified based on how it originated and who had access.

2.   **Internal information** originates and remains with the engagement client.

   a.   Payroll records are an example. They are initially generated by the client and then are subsequently processed and retained by the client.

   b.   Lack of involvement of **external parties** reduces the **persuasiveness** of information.

       1)   The **reliability** of information is greater when it comes from sources that are **independent** of the client.

3.   **Internal-external information** originates with the client but is also processed by an external party.

   a.   Examples are canceled checks. These documents are created by the client but then circulate through the banking system.

       1)   A bank's acceptance of a check is some confirmation of its validity.

       2)   Internal-external information is deemed to be more reliable than purely internal information.

4.   **External-internal information** is created by an external party but subsequently processed by the client.

   a.   Such information has greater validity than information initiated by the client, but its value is impaired because of the client's opportunity to alter or destroy it.

       1)   Suppliers' invoices are typical examples of external-internal information. Others include the canceled checks included in a cutoff bank statement received by the auditor directly from the bank.

5.   **External information** is created by an independent party and transmitted directly to the internal auditor. External information is ordinarily regarded as the **most reliable** because it has not been exposed to possible contamination by the client.

   a.   Common examples are confirmations of receivables sent in response to the internal auditor's requests.

6. **Outsourcing services**, such as clerical, accounting, and even internal auditing services, may result in information difficult to classify in this framework.

    a. The outsourcer's employees may supervise employees of the other party. Thus, the records generated may be the joint result of internal and external efforts.

    b. The outsourcing firm should obtain a **right of review**. It should be able to examine information supporting the amounts charged by the other party for the outsourced services.

7. Stop and review! You have completed the outline for this subunit. Study multiple-choice questions 33 through 36 beginning on page 65.

1.5 NATURE OF INFORMATION

1. Information may consist of (a) authoritative documentation, (b) calculations by the internal auditor, (c) internal control, (d) interrelationships among the data, (e) physical existence, (f) subsequent events, (g) subsidiary records, and (h) testimony by the engagement client and third parties.

2. Sawyer, Dittenhofer, and Scheiner, in *Sawyer's Internal Auditing*, 5th edition, pages 324-325, provide the following classification:

    a. **Physical information** consists of the internal auditor's direct observation and inspection of people, property, or activities, e.g., of the counting of inventory.

        1) Photographs, maps, graphs, and charts may provide compelling physical information.

        2) When physical observation is the only information about a significant condition, at least two internal auditors should view it.

    b. **Testimonial information** consists of written or spoken statements of client personnel and others in response to inquiries or interview questions.

        1) Such information may furnish important indications about the direction of engagement work.

        2) Testimonial information may not be conclusive and should be supported by other forms of information when possible.

    c. **Documentary information** exists in some permanent form, such as checks, invoices, shipping records, receiving reports, and purchase orders.

        1) Thus, it is the most common type gathered by internal auditors.
        2) Documentary information may be internal or external.

            a) Examples of external information are replies to confirmation requests, invoices from suppliers, and public information held by a governmental body, such as real estate records.

            b) Examples of internal information include accounting records, receiving reports, purchase orders, depreciation schedules, and maintenance records.

    d. **Analytical information** is drawn from the consideration of the interrelationships among data or, in the case of internal control, the particular policies and procedures of which it is composed.

        1) Analysis produces circumstantial information in the form of inferences or conclusions based on examining the components as a whole for consistencies, inconsistencies, cause-effect relationships, relevant and irrelevant items, etc.

3. Stop and review! You have completed the outline for this subunit. Study multiple-choice questions 37 through 43 beginning on page 66.

1.6 PROCEDURES

1.   Another classification system for engagement information is based on how it is obtained. The broad types of engagement procedures are listed below. However, detailed listings **(work programs)** of specific procedures must be developed for particular situations.

    a.   **Interviewing** is a means of gathering testimonial information.

        1)   It is a vital skill.

           a)   **PA 1210-1** recognizes the importance of interviewing: "Internal auditors should be skilled in dealing with people and in communicating effectively."

        2)   Interviews are conducted with client personnel, other individuals who have contact with the client, and independent third parties.

        3)   Interviewing is especially helpful in obtaining an **understanding of client operations** because of the opportunity to ask questions to clarify preceding answers or to pursue additional information.

           a)   The information obtained from interviews may therefore help the client to understand why unusual conditions have occurred.

        4)   An effective interviewer avoids **biasing the information**.

           a)   Thus, (s)he should avoid **leading questions**.

        5)   The results should be promptly and accurately **recorded** to provide documentation.

           a)   Proper recording avoids the ill effects of memory lapses by both internal auditors and clients.

        6)   Given the inherent unreliability of client testimony, it should be **corroborated** whenever possible.

           a)   However, testimonial information provided by an independent third party may sometimes be sufficient.

    b.   **Recomputing** quantitative data is a means of gathering information that is reliable but limited in value.

        1)   A computation done directly by the internal auditors provides strong and unbiased information regarding accuracy.

        2)   One limitation of recomputation is that it does not provide information about the **reliability of the input**.

           a)   For example, recomputing interest income may be of little use if the underlying receivables are unlikely to be collected.

    c.   **Detail testing** involves **examination of documents** created as part of the activities and transactions being reviewed.

        1)   These documents provide information that is ordinarily superior to testimony that a transaction occurred or that a control procedure was performed.

           a)   **External documents** tend to be more reliable than internal documents.

        2)   Which detail test is chosen depends on its **relevance**.

           a)   The information generated by a detailed test must be "consistent with the objectives for the engagement" **(PA 2310-1)**.

        3)   Two subcategories of detail tests are vouching and tracing.

           a)   **Vouching** involves **verifying recorded amounts** by examining the underlying documents from the final documents to the original documents.

               i)   The engagement objective of working backward is to provide information that recorded amounts reflect valid transactions.

               ii)   Vouching supports the **existence or occurrence assertion**.

           iii)   Vouching is irrelevant to the **completeness assertion**. That some transactions were recorded does not prove that all transactions were recorded.

      b)   **Tracing** involves following transactions forward through the records **from the original documents** to the final summary amounts.

          i)   Thus, the **direction of testing** is the opposite of that for vouching.

          ii)   The objective of tracing is to support the **completeness assertion**.

d.   **Observation** and **inspection** are procedures that involve examination of physical information by the internal auditor.

    1)   Observation and inspection result in information consisting of the internal auditor's **direct experience**. To that extent, it is highly reliable.

      a)   Records may be falsified, so the internal auditor's observation or inspection serves as corroboration.

    2)   The term "observation" is commonly applied to an internal auditor's examination of **activities**, e.g., performance of control procedures.

    3)   The term "inspection" usually refers to the examination of **physical assets**, e.g., machinery.

    4)   Observation and inspection are procedures of **limited usefulness**.

      a)   The **expertise** of the observer or inspector may be insufficient to produce reliable information.

          i)   For example, an internal auditor may not be trained to appraise the worth of items purporting to be works of art, the condition of some agricultural products, or the obsolescence of specific equipment. In these cases, an outside service provider might be consulted.

      b)   Observation and inspection also do not establish whether the engagement client has **title** to what is observed or inspected or whether other parties may have **liens** on such assets.

      c)   Observation and inspection tend to prove **existence and possession** at a given moment in time.

e.   **Scanning** is a search for obvious exceptions in a large quantity of data.

    1)   Scanning is useful and efficient when unusual items are readily definable and the internal auditor is willing to accept a broad range of acceptable values.

      a)   For example, scanning easily detects debit balances in accounts payable or credit balances in cash accounts.

f.   **Statistical sampling** allows the internal auditor to assess quantitatively how closely the sample represents the population at a given level of reliability.

    1)   By **randomly** selecting a sample of appropriate size, the internal auditor can assert, at a specified **level of confidence**, that the **precision interval** constructed using the sample result will contain the true value of the population.

    2)   Statistical techniques permit the internal auditor to control for the **risk (sampling risk)** created when (s)he, for reasons of efficiency, samples a population instead of examining every item.

      a)   These methods do not affect **nonsampling risk**, which may arise from selecting an inappropriate procedure, performing an appropriate procedure improperly, or misevaluating the sample results.

g.   **Verification** is a broad term for the process of determining the truth of previously provided information. It is an intentional effort to establish actual validity. Verification includes **corroboration, comparison, and confirmation**.

    1)   **Corroborative information** is evidence from another source that supplements and confirms other information.

2) **Comparison** (see item 2. in Subunit 1.2).
3) **Confirmation** requests are sent by the internal auditor to parties external to the client. The replies, which are returned directly to the internal auditor, are purely external information.

   a) Confirmation requests are used most commonly to test accounts receivable. However, they are commonly used to confirm cash balances held in financial institutions and liabilities.

   b) A **negative confirmation** requests the recipient to respond only if (s)he disagrees with the information stated.

     i) An **unreturned negative confirmation** request provides some information about existence because it has not been returned with an indication that the addressee is unknown. However, it provides no explicit inference that the intended recipient verified the information.

   c) A **positive confirmation** by the debtor is the most reliable information (other than payment) that the receivable is a valid asset and that it is properly valued.

     i) This information is especially reliable because (a) the customer has no incentive to confirm a nonexisting obligation, and (b) the documentation has not been under the client's control.

     ii) If the internal auditor fails to receive a positive confirmation, alternative procedures, including second and third requests, should be performed.

   d) Confirmations also are sent to **financial institutions** to confirm specified deposits and direct liabilities on loans.

     i) This procedure also requests information about any other deposit and loan accounts that may come to the attention of the institution.

     ii) Accounts payable are sometimes confirmed with vendors, and consigned inventories may be confirmed with consignees.

     iii) The amounts of contingent liabilities are sometimes confirmed with attorneys.

  h. **Analytical procedures** are discussed in Subunit 1.2.

2. Stop and review! You have completed the outline for this subunit. Study multiple-choice questions 44 through 55 beginning on page 68.

1.7 DEGREE OF PERSUASIVENESS

1. The ultimate purpose of information gathering is to provide sufficient support for the internal auditor's **observations, conclusions, and recommendations**.

  a. Although the individual items of information may have drawbacks and therefore different degrees of persuasiveness, the internal auditor's task is to assemble a body of information that provides the requisite support.

  b. During this process, the internal auditor may determine that particular information justifies full reliance, partial reliance, or no reliance.

   1) An internal auditor **fully relies** on information when **no additional corroboration** is needed. Information is corroborative when it supports other information.

a)   For example, the internal auditor may decide that his/her own physical count of inventory provides sufficient, reliable, relevant, and useful information. Another example is the receipt of canceled checks included in a cutoff bank statement received directly from the bank. These items provide external as well as internal documentary information. The information was generated internally but passed through outsiders who confirmed it (honored the checks) before sending it directly to the internal auditor.

2)   Most information merits only **partial reliance** and must be **corroborated**.

a)   For example, **testimonial information** obtained by interviewing client personnel ordinarily should be supplemented by the results of detailed testing and analytical procedures.

b)   Furthermore, information that at some time has passed through the **client's operations** (internal, internal-external, or external-internal information) ordinarily should be reinforced by obtaining assurances about the adequacy and effectiveness of **internal control**.

i)   Thus, the internal auditor should determine that properly designed client controls over the creation, processing, and maintenance of such information are in place and operating effectively. One method of determining this would be to conduct a walk-through of the entire process, collecting all available documentation.

3)   Circumstances may dictate that the internal auditor place little or **no reliance** on certain information. However, such information may be useful in indicating the **direction of the engagement**.

a)   For example, unsupported statements by client management are likely to be significantly discounted because of their tendency toward self-serving bias.

i)   Because the internal auditor's responsibility is to do much more than simply repeat client management's explanations about existing conditions, (s)he must perform other procedures.

ii) Nevertheless, the information furnished by client management may suggest other sources of information.

c.   The following table summarizing the determinants of the persuasiveness of various types of information is from Ratliff, et al., *Internal Auditing: Principles and Techniques*, 2nd edition (1996), page 154:

STRONG	**WEAK**
Objective	Subjective
Documents	Opinions
Knowledgeable or expert opinions	Poorly informed opinions
Direct	Indirect
From systems with good internal control	From systems with poor internal control
Independent of engagement client's operations	Prepared by engagement client
Statistical samples (usually)	Nonstatistical samples (usually)
Corroborated	Uncorroborated
From records prepared on a timely basis	From records prepared after a lapse of time

2.   Stop and review! You have completed the outline for this subunit. Study multiple-choice questions 56 through 61 beginning on page 71.

1.8 RECORDING INFORMATION

1. This subunit concerns the documentation of the work of the internal audit activity by means of engagement records (working papers), whether in traditional form or recorded on electronic media. Issues relating to the functions, content, and preparation of working papers are addressed in one Specific Performance Standard and two Practice Advisories.

2. *2330*   **Recording Information** – *Internal auditors should record relevant information to support the conclusions and engagement results.*

    a. **PRACTICE ADVISORY 2330-1: RECORDING INFORMATION**

        1. *Working papers that document the engagement should be **prepared by the internal auditor** and **reviewed by management** of the internal audit activity. The working papers should record the **information** obtained and the **analyses** made and should support the bases for the **observations** and **recommendations** to be reported. Engagement working papers generally:*

            *   *Provide the **principal support** for the engagement **communications**.*
            *   *Aid in the **planning, performance, and review** of engagements.*
            *   *Document whether the engagement objectives were achieved.*
            *   *Facilitate **third-party reviews**.*
            *   *Provide a basis for evaluating the internal audit activity's **quality program**.*
            *   *Provide support in circumstances such as insurance claims, fraud cases, and lawsuits.*
            *   *Aid in the **professional development** of the internal auditing staff.*
            *   *Demonstrate the internal audit activity's **compliance** with the Standards.*

        2. *The **organization, design, and content** of engagement working papers will depend on the nature of the engagement. Working papers should **document** the following aspects of the engagement process:*

            *   *Planning*
            *   *The examination and evaluation of the adequacy and effectiveness of the system of internal control*
            *   *The engagement procedures performed, the information obtained, and the conclusions reached*
            *   *Review*
            *   *Communicating*
            *   *Follow-up*

        3. *Engagement working papers should be **complete** and include **support for engagement conclusions** reached. Among other things, engagement working papers may include:*

            *   *Planning documents and engagement programs*
            *   *Control questionnaires, flowcharts, checklists, and narratives*
            *   *Notes and memoranda resulting from interviews*
            *   *Organizational data, such as organization charts and job descriptions*
            *   *Copies of important contracts and agreements*
            *   *Information about operating and financial policies*
            *   *Results of control evaluations*
            *   *Letters of confirmation and representation*
            *   *Analysis and tests of transactions, processes, and account balances*
            *   *Results of analytical procedures*
            *   *The engagement's final communications and management's responses*
            *   *Engagement correspondence if it documents engagement conclusions reached*

4. *Engagement working papers may be in the **form** of paper, tapes, disks, diskettes, films, or other media. If engagement working papers are in the form of media other than paper, consideration should be given to generating **backup** copies.*

5. *If internal auditors are **reporting on financial information**, the engagement working papers should document whether the accounting records agree or **reconcile** with such financial information.*

6. *The chief audit executive should establish working paper **policies** for the various types of engagements performed. **Standardized** engagement working papers such as questionnaires and work programs may improve the efficiency of an engagement and facilitate the delegation of engagement work. Some engagement working papers may be categorized as **permanent** or carry-forward engagement files. These files generally contain information of continuing importance.*

7. *The following are typical engagement working paper **preparation techniques**:*

   - *Each engagement working paper should identify the engagement and describe the **contents or purpose** of the working paper.*
   - *Each engagement working paper should be **signed** (or initialed) and **dated** by the internal auditor performing the work.*
   - *Each engagement working paper should contain an **index** or reference number.*
   - *Verification **symbols** (tick marks) should be explained.*
   - ***Sources** of data should be clearly identified.*

PA Summary

- Working papers **document** the engagement, including (1) planning; (2) evaluation of control; (3) procedures performed, information obtained, and conclusions reached; (4) review; (5) communication; and (6) follow-up. They are **prepared** by internal auditors and **reviewed** by IAA management.

- Working papers record **information and analyses** and support **observations**, conclusions, and **recommendations**. They (1) **support communications**; (2) aid in **planning**, **performance, and review**; (3) document whether objectives were achieved; (4) provide a basis for evaluating the **quality program**; (5) support insurance claims, fraud cases, and lawsuits; (6) aid in the staff's **professional development**; and (7) demonstrate **compliance** with the Standards.

- The nature of the engagement determines the **organization, design, and content** of working papers.

- Working papers should be **complete**. They include, for example, (1) planning documents, (2) programs, (3) control materials and evaluations, (4) interview results, (5) important agreements, (6) analyses, (7) policy information, (8) organizational data, (9) confirmations and representations, (10) final communications, and (11) correspondence documenting conclusions.

- If working papers are **not** in paper form, making **backup copies** should be considered.

- The auditors document **reconciliation of financial information**.

- The CAE establishes working paper **policies** for the types of engagements. **Standardized working papers** may improve efficiency, and **permanent files** may be kept.

- Working papers are prepared with appropriate identifying information, verification symbols, and a cross-referencing system. They should be **signed and dated** by preparers.

3.   The following is the section of a comprehensive Practice Advisory that is relevant to recording engagement information:

    a.   ***PRACTICE ADVISORY 1000.C1-2: ADDITIONAL CONSIDERATIONS FOR FORMAL CONSULTING ENGAGEMENTS***

        18.   *Internal auditors should document the work performed to achieve the objectives of a formal consulting engagement and support its results. However,* **documentation requirements applicable to assurance engagements** *do not necessarily apply to consulting engagements.*

4.   **Functions of Working Papers**

    a.   **Effectively and efficiently organized** working papers help to guide the engagement work so that it remains relevant to the engagement objectives.

        1)   Thus, an internal auditor should maintain the focus of the engagement by considering how the work will affect engagement **communications**.

    b.   Working papers **document information** in its numerous forms.

        1)   They record the observations suggested by this information with regard to **exposure to risk**. The information recorded also helps to determine the **extent and significance** of these exposures and possible **corrective action**.

    c.   The information in working papers provides essential background for the internal auditors' **technical discussions** with engagement clients. For example, working papers should fully document the use of statistical sampling techniques. Thus, they should specify such matters as the population sampled, the acceptable levels of sampling risk, how the sample sizes were determined, the sampling approach, and the evaluation of the results. Factors affecting the sample size are the degree of sampling risk (confidence level), the allowance for sampling risk (precision), and the expected error rate.

    d.   **Supervisory review** of the working papers, which is itself documented, aids in the **control** of the engagement.

        1)   **Differences in professional judgment** may arise between the chief audit executive and staff members over significant issues relating to the engagement. The means of resolving these differences may include "documentation and disposition of the differing viewpoints in the engagement working papers" (PA 2340-1).

    e.   Working papers facilitate the **coordination of work** at different locations and the assignment of responsibilities to personnel.

    f.   Review of the internal auditors' working papers is one means by which the **external auditors** may (1) obtain an understanding of the internal audit activity, (2) assess the competence and objectivity of the internal auditors, and (3) determine the effect of the work of the internal auditors on the external audit.

        1)   Coordination with the external auditors is facilitated by access to the working papers.

    g.   The documentation in the working papers helps the internal auditors to prepare for **future engagements** involving the same client.

    h.   Independent reviewers from outside the organization may examine working papers as part of an **external assessment** of the internal audit activity's **quality assurance and improvement program**.

    i.   The law may require that an organization maintain an effective system of **internal accounting control**. Working papers can provide part of the required documentation of compliance.

5. Virtually all internal audit activities now use **computer and telecommunications technology** in the engagement process.

    a. **Generalized software packages** are available that integrate the functions of document preparation, review, recording of review notes, and sharing of files via local area networks, disks, CD-ROM, email, etc.

    b. Auditors use a variety of software to develop materials included in working papers. Programs include **word processing software** to prepare observations, letters, memos, etc.; a **flowcharting package** that permits easy drafting and revision; and **spreadsheet software** for quantitative analyses.

        1) Auditors also can **monitor** the engagement client's data continuously.

        2) **Project management software** can run on a personal computer to create planning documents. It graphically displays optimal job sequences and allocations of time, personnel, and other resources.

    c. The ability to **transfer and share working papers** electronically improves the engagement's efficiency. Hence, documents can be transmitted instantly among remote sites with consequent administrative savings.

        1) **Groupware** provides support for the activities of work groups, e.g., email, electronic meetings, scheduling, and information sharing through linkage of databases. **Lotus Notes** is a leading groupware product.

            a) **Internet browsers** can be used for some groupware functions.

    d. Use of electronic media for the creation, transmission, and storage of working papers raises **security concerns** that do not arise when documents exist only in hard copy. Accordingly, some unique issues are raised by the use of electronic working papers:

        1) Electronic working papers and reviewer comments should be protected from unauthorized access and change.

        2) Information recorded in working papers "scanned in" should have adequate control to ensure its continued integrity.

        3) Working paper retention policies should consider changes made in the original operating system, other software, and hardware to ensure the continued retrievability of electronic working papers throughout the retention cycle.

    e. However, information technology permits **fundamental changes** in the engagement process. New methods of data storage, retrieval, and manipulation may facilitate activities that were not previously feasible, e.g., multiple regression analyses and simulation.

6. Working papers include permanent as well as current files. Among the many types of items recorded in **permanent files** are

    a. Previous engagement communications, responses, and results of follow-up
    b. Engagement communications provided by other organizational subunits
    c. Reviews of the long-term engagement work schedule by senior management
    d. Results of post-engagement reviews
    e. Auditor observations during past engagements that may have future relevance
    f. The chart of accounts with items referenced to engagement projects
    g. Management's operating reports
    h. Applicable engagement work programs and questionnaires
    i. Long-term contracts
    j. Flowcharts of operations
    k. Historical financial information
    l. Project control information
    m. Correspondence about the engagement project
    n. Updated organizational charter, bylaws, minutes, etc.

7. **Preparation Techniques**

a. Working papers should be **consistently and efficiently prepared** to facilitate review. They should be

1) Neat, not crowded, and written on only one side
2) Uniform in size and appearance
3) Economical, avoiding unnecessary copying, listing, or scheduling

a) They should use copies of engagement clients' records if applicable.

4) Arranged in a logical and uniform style

a) The most appropriate arrangement is one that corresponds to the organization of the engagement **work program**. Each section should have statements of purpose and scope followed by observations, conclusions, recommendations, and corrective action.

5) Clear, concise, and complete
6) Restricted to matters that are relevant and significant
7) Written in a simple style

b. Some working papers may be **standardized**. However, some must be customized to meet the requirements of specific engagements.

c. Working papers should have **summaries** throughout to provide the reviewer with a brief statement of information contained in subsequent schedules. Summarization can be accomplished in several ways:

1) The **scope and results** of a procedure may be summarized so that the reviewer can readily understand the

a) Objective of the procedure
b) Relationship between improper transactions and the population sampled
c) Manner in which exceptions were handled
d) Internal auditor's conclusion

2) **Statistical summaries** combine the results recorded in related schedules.
3) **Results summaries** provide significant facts about engagement observations.
4) **Segment summaries** provide narratives about specific parts of an engagement.
5) **Meetings** with engagement clients should be summarized immediately.
6) **Conclusions** may be recorded in the work program as each segment is completed.
7) Summaries of conditions representing **significant risk exposures** are the most important because they will receive the greatest attention. Their nature and materiality should become immediately apparent from the summaries.

d. A good **indexing system** for working papers should be simple and easily expanded.

1) For example, the main sections of the engagement project may be represented by capital letters. Within each main section, worksheets may then be represented by Arabic numerals. If further division is needed, additional numerals may be added, for example, B.2.1.

e. Indexing permits effective **cross-referencing**, which facilitates

1) Supervisory review
2) Performance of subsequent engagements
3) Finding information in the working papers
4) The preparation of the final engagement communication
5) Factual rebuttal of challenges by clearly identifying sources and locations of information

f.   Factors affecting the **structure and content** of working papers include

1)   Scope of the engagement
2)   Intended type and format of the communication
3)   Engagement client statements or activities being reported upon
4)   Nature and condition of controls and records
5)   Internal auditor review and supervision requirement

g.   **Pro forma working papers** are standard forms designed to improve the efficiency of the engagement while ensuring full coverage of all relevant and material matters.

1)   For example, the sheets for the engagement work program might each include separate spaces for engagement objectives and the related procedures.

2)   The formats of standardized working papers depend on the internal auditors' unique needs. They should be flexible enough so as not to be restrictive or to encourage mere performance of the engagement by rote.

8.   Stop and review! You have completed the outline for this subunit. Study multiple-choice questions 62 through 77 beginning on page 73.

1.9 REVIEW OF WORKING PAPERS

1.   This subunit pertains to supervisory review of working papers. It contains one Practice Advisory.

2.   The following are the sections of **PRACTICE ADVISORY 2340-1: *ENGAGEMENT SUPERVISION*** that pertain to supervisory review of working papers:

1.   The chief audit executive is responsible for ensuring that appropriate supervision is provided. Supervision includes determining that engagement working papers adequately **support the engagement observations, conclusions, and recommendations***.*

5.   All engagement working papers should be reviewed to ensure that they properly **support the engagement communications** *and that all* **necessary procedures** *have been performed. Evidence of supervisory review should consist of the reviewer's* **initialing and dating** *each working paper after it is reviewed. Other review techniques that provide evidence of supervisory review include completing an engagement working paper* **review checklist** *or preparing a* **memorandum** *specifying the nature, extent, and results of the review.*

6.   Reviewers may make a written record **(review notes)** *of questions arising from the review process. When* **clearing review notes***, care should be taken to ensure that the working papers provide* **adequate evidence** *that questions raised during the review have been resolved. Acceptable alternatives with respect to* **disposition of review notes** *are as follows:*

•   **Retain the review notes** *as a record of the questions raised by the reviewer and the steps taken in their resolution.*

•   *Discard the review notes after the questions raised have been resolved and the appropriate engagement* **working papers have been amended** *to provide the additional information requested.*

> ### PA Summary
>
> - **Supervision** includes determining that working papers support engagement results.
> - **Review of working papers** should ensure that (1) they support **communications** and (2) necessary **procedures** have been performed. A supervising reviewer initials and dates each working paper. Other review techniques evidencing supervisory review include completing a **review checklist** or preparing a **memorandum**.
> - **Review notes** should not be cleared unless **adequate evidence** exists that issues raised have been resolved. Alternatives for their **disposition** are (1) retention and (2) discarding after the questions raised have been resolved and **working papers amended**.

3. **Supervisory review** should occur as soon as feasible after working papers are completed. A reviewer should determine that

   a. The internal auditors followed the engagement **work program**.
   b. The internal auditors followed the **specific instructions** they received.
   c. The working papers reflect that the work was **performed acceptably**.
   d. The **conclusions** drawn were sound given the information identified.
   e. All planned steps have been taken.
   f. **Clients were consulted** about observations, conclusions, and recommendations; the results of these discussions were recorded; and disputes were resolved.
   g. **Preparation guidelines** for working papers were followed.

4. Stop and review! You have completed the outline for this subunit. Study multiple-choice questions 78 through 83 beginning on page 79.

1.10 CONTROL OF WORKING PAPERS

1. This subunit addresses the issues of control, access, and retention regarding engagement working papers. These matters are covered in two Assurance Implementation Standards, one Consulting Implementation Standard, and four Practice Advisories.

2. *2330.A1 – The chief audit executive should control access to engagement records. The chief audit executive should obtain the approval of senior management and/or legal counsel prior to releasing such records to external parties, as appropriate.*

   a. *PRACTICE ADVISORY 2330.A1-1: CONTROL OF ENGAGEMENT RECORDS*

      1. *Engagement working papers are the **property of the organization**. Engagement working paper files should generally remain under the **control of the internal audit activity** and should be accessible only to authorized personnel.*

      2. *Management and other members of the organization may **request access** to engagement working papers. Such access may be necessary to substantiate or explain engagement observations and recommendations or to use engagement documentation for other business purposes. These requests for access should be subject to the **approval of the chief audit executive**.*

      3. *It is common practice for internal and external auditors to grant access to each other's working papers. Access to working papers by **external auditors** should be subject to the **approval of the chief audit executive**.*

4.   *In some circumstances, **parties outside the organization**, other than external auditors, may request access to working papers and communications. Prior to releasing such documentation, the chief audit executive should obtain the **approval of senior management or legal counsel**, as appropriate.*

PA Summary

- Working papers are **property of the organization**. They should be controlled by the IAA and accessible only to authorized personnel.
- **Requests for access** by members of the organization and external auditors should be approved by the CAE.
- Requests for access by **parties outside the organization** should be approved by senior management or legal counsel.

---

b.   ***PRACTICE ADVISORY 2330.A1-2: LEGAL CONSIDERATIONS IN GRANTING ACCESS TO ENGAGEMENT RECORDS*** (This guidance should be compared with that provided in Study Unit 2 by Practice Advisory 2400-1: Legal Considerations in Communicating Results.)

       <u>Caution</u> – Internal auditors are encouraged to consult legal counsel in all matters involving legal issues. Requirements may vary significantly in different jurisdictions.

       a.   *Internal auditing **engagement records** include reports, supporting documentation, review notes, and correspondence regardless of storage media. Internal auditors with the support of management and governing boards to whom they provide services develop the engagement records. The engagement records are generally produced under the presumption that their **contents** are **confidential** and may contain a **mix of both facts and opinions**. However, those who are not immediately familiar with the organization or its internal audit process may misunderstand these facts and opinions. **Access** to engagement records by **outside parties** has been sought in several different types of proceedings, including criminal prosecutions, civil litigation, tax audits, regulatory reviews, government contract reviews, and reviews by self-regulatory organizations. Virtually all of an organization's records that are not protected by a privilege recognized by the law of the relevant jurisdiction (e.g., an **attorney-client privilege**) are accessible in **criminal proceedings**. In noncriminal proceedings the issue of access is less clear.*

       b.   *Explicit practices in the following documents of the internal audit activity may increase the **control of access to engagement records**. These suggestions are discussed in the paragraphs [below and on the next page]:*

-    *Charter*
-    *Job descriptions*
-    *Internal departmental policies*
-    *Procedures for handling investigations with legal counsel*

       c.   *The **internal audit activity's charter** should address access to and control of organizational records and information regardless of media used to store the records.*

       d.   ***Written job descriptions** should be created for the internal audit activity and should include the complex and varied duties auditors perform. Such descriptions may help internal auditors when addressing requests for engagement records. They will also help internal auditors understand the scope of their work and external parties to comprehend the duties of internal auditors.*

e.   ***Internal departmental policies*** *should be developed in regard to the operation of the internal audit activity. These written practices should cover, among other matters, **what should be included** in engagement records, how long departmental records should be retained, how outside requests for access to departmental records should be handled, and what special practices should be followed in conducting an investigation with legal counsel. These matters are discussed below.*

f.   *A policy relating to the various types of engagements should specify the **content and format of the engagement records** and how internal auditors should handle their **review notes**, i.e., retained as a record of issues raised and subsequently resolved or destroyed so third parties cannot gain access to them. Also, a policy should specify the **length of retention** for engagement records. These time limits will be determined by the needs of the organization as well as **legal requirements**. (It is important to check with legal counsel on this issue.)*

g.   *Departmental policies should explain who in the organization is **responsible** for ensuring the **control and security** of departmental records, **who can be granted access** to engagement records, and how **requests for access** to those records are to be handled. These policies may depend on the practices followed in the industry or legal jurisdiction of the organization. The chief audit executive and others in internal auditing should be alert to **changing practices in the industry** and changing legal precedents. They should anticipate those who might someday seek access to their work products.*

h.   *The **policy granting access to engagement records** should also address the following issues:*

   ● *Process for resolving access issues;*
   ● *Time period for retention of each type of work product;*
   ● *Process for educating and reeducating the internal auditing staff concerning the risks and issues regarding access to their work products; and*
   ● *Requirement for periodically surveying the industry to determine who may want access to the work product in the future.*

i.   *A policy should provide guidance to the internal auditor in determining when an engagement warrants an **investigation**, that is, when it becomes an investigation to be **conducted with an attorney** and what special procedures should be followed in communicating with the legal counsel. The policy should also cover the matter of executing a **proper retention letter** so that any information given to the attorney will be subject to any privilege recognized in the jurisdiction.*

j.   *Internal auditors should also **educate the board and management** about the risks of access to engagement records. The **policies** relating to who may be granted access to engagement records, how those requests are to be handled, and the procedures to be followed when an engagement warrants an investigation should be **reviewed by the audit committee** of the board of directors (or equivalent governing body). The specific policies will vary depending upon the nature of the organization and the access privileges that have been established by law.*

k.   *Careful **preparation of engagement records** is important when disclosure is required. The following steps should be considered:*

- *Only disclose **specific documents requested**. Engagement records with **opinions and recommendations** are generally not released. Documents that reveal attorneys' thought processes or strategies may be privileged and not subject to forced disclosure.*

- *Only release copies, keeping the originals, especially if the documents were prepared in pencil. If the court requests originals, the internal audit activity should keep a copy.*

- ***Label each document as confidential** and place a notation on each document that **secondary distribution is not permitted** without permission.*

PA Summary

- The presumption is that **engagement records** are **confidential**. They may contain **opinions and facts** that may be misunderstood by those unfamiliar with the organization and its audit process.

- Records not subject to a **privilege** are generally accessible to outside parties in **criminal** cases. Access by outsiders in civil cases is unclear.

- The IAA's (1) charter, (2) job descriptions, (3) internal policies, and (4) procedures for investigations should describe practices to improve **access control**.

- The **charter** should address access to and control of records and information regardless of media used.

- **Written job descriptions** should include the duties of auditors. They help internal auditors to address requests for records and to understand the scope of their work. They also help external parties to comprehend the duties of internal auditors.

- **Policies** should address (1) the content and format of records and handling of review notes, (2) their retention period based on legal and organizational requirements, (3) responses to outside requests for access, (4) who may be granted access, (5) special practices for **investigations with legal counsel**, and (6) responsibility for control and security of records.

- Policies may depend on **changing practices** in the industry and changing **legal requirements**.

- The **policy granting access to records** also should address the (1) process for resolving access issues, (2) retention period for each work product, (3) process for educating the staff about access to their work products, and (4) periodic survey to determine who may want access in the future.

- An **investigation** is conducted with **legal counsel**. Thus, the IAA should have policies covering communications with counsel, and execution of a **retention letter**. These policies should be designed to preserve any available **privilege**.

- Auditors should educate the **board and management** about access issues. Policies governing access should be reviewed by the **audit committee**.

- Careful **preparation of engagement records** is important when disclosure is required. Disclosure should be only of **copies of specific items** requested. Records with **opinions and recommendations** are usually not released. Records constituting the attorney's work product may be privileged.

- If a **court** requests original documents, copies should be kept.

- Records should be labeled **confidential** and contain a prohibition against **secondary distribution**.

3.   *2330.A2 – The chief audit executive should develop retention requirements for engagement records. These retention requirements should be consistent with the organization's guidelines and any pertinent regulatory or other requirements.*

   a.   **PRACTICE ADVISORY 2330.A2-1: RETENTION OF RECORDS**

      1.   *Record retention requirements should be designed to include **all engagement records**, regardless of the format in which the records are stored.*

PA Summary

   •   Retention requirements apply to **all engagement records**.

---

4.   *2330.C1 – The chief audit executive should develop policies governing the custody and retention of engagement records, as well as their release to internal and external parties. These policies should be consistent with the organization's guidelines and any pertinent regulatory or other requirements.*

   a.   **PRACTICE ADVISORY 1000.C1-2: ADDITIONAL CONSIDERATIONS FOR FORMAL CONSULTING ENGAGEMENTS**

      The following is the relevant portion of this comprehensive Practice Advisory:

      19.   *Auditors are encouraged to adopt appropriate **record retention policies** and address **related issues**, such as **ownership** of consulting engagement records, in order to protect the organization adequately and avoid potential misunderstandings involving requests for such records. Situations involving legal proceedings, regulatory requirements, tax issues, and accounting matters may call for **special handling** of certain consulting engagement records.*

PA Summary

   •   In **formal consulting engagements**, auditors should adopt appropriate record retention policies and address such related issues as **ownership** of the engagement records. Legal, regulatory, tax, and accounting matters may require **special handling** of the records.

---

5.   Working papers always should be properly **protected**.

   a.   During the field work, they should be in the internal auditor's **physical possession or control** and should be protected against fire, theft, or other disaster. For example, the internal auditor may use the engagement client's safe or other security facilities.

   b.   In the internal audit activity's office, they should be kept in **locked files** and formally signed out when removed from the files.

   c.   **Reviews** by others (government auditors, external auditors, etc.) should occur in the internal audit activity's office.

   d.   If working papers are in **electronic form**, new security issues arise.

      1)   For example, **alterations** may be made without leaving physical traces, and unauthorized remote access may be possible.

      2)   If computer files are protected by **passwords**, a system must be established to ensure that the passwords are protected and that only appropriate personnel have access to them.

3) Inadvertent erasure of computer files may occur through computer malfunction or misuse or as a result of some physical agency. Thus, creating **backups** and **storage off-site** are advisable.

4) Changes made in the original operating system, other software, and hardware should be considered so that **retrievability** of the electronic working papers is ensured during their retention cycle.

6. **Secure files** should be provided for long-term storage of working papers, and itemized records of their location should be maintained.

7. Working papers may be shown to the **client** if audit **objectives** are not compromised.

   a. The **results** of certain procedures may be shared with the client to encourage corrective action.

   b. But **complete disclosure** of working papers may permit client circumvention of the internal auditor's procedures.

   c. Working papers are not shared with engagement clients in surprise engagements, **fraud investigations**, and other special reviews.

   d. **Access** to working papers by management and other members of the organization or by the external auditors should be subject to approval by the chief audit executive.

8. **Retention schedules** should be approved by the organization's counsel to ensure compliance with laws, regulations, or contract requirements.

   a. Working papers should be **destroyed** after they have served their purpose.

   b. Any part of the working papers having continuing value should be brought forward to **current working papers** or to the **permanent file**.

   c. **Review notes** should be retained unless the questions raised have been resolved and the working papers have been amended accordingly.

   d. In some jurisdictions, an accounting firm may be required to prepare and maintain audit working papers and other information related to any audit report for a statutory period. The working papers and other documentation must be in sufficient detail to support the conclusions reached in the report.

9. **Access to working papers** by outside parties may be mandatory in some jurisdictions.

   a. For example, a taxing authority may have a right to obtain working papers.

   b. Other governmental bodies also have been able to gain access to engagement communications and working papers.

   c. In **private litigation**, working papers may be protected from disclosure under a self-evaluative privilege (also called self-critical analysis). However, this privilege is qualified. It tends to be invoked successfully only with regard to subjective internal appraisals, not objective data.

   d. Internal auditors should understand the **access rights** in the organization's industry and develop a **written access policy** that is cleared by legal counsel, management, and the board. For example, this policy may call for (1) segregating objective data from subjective evaluations, (2) limiting the scope of engagements, (3) assigning different internal auditors to particular subjects, or (4) destroying working papers more frequently (a policy option that may itself create legal issues).

10. Stop and review! You have completed the outline for this subunit. Study multiple-choice questions 84 through 88 beginning on page 80.

1.11 STUDY UNIT 1 SUMMARY

1. When performing audit engagements, the auditor considers the type of evidence, its use, its reliability, and the independence and qualifications of the provider.

2. Types of evidence include observations, documentation, representations, and analysis.

3. The auditor considers the time when evidence is available or exists.

4. The auditor should plan to use the best evidence attainable.

5. Information is collected on all matters related to engagement objectives and scope of work.

6. Analytical procedures identify conditions that may require subsequent procedures. Thus, they are planning tools. Identification of unexpected results or relationships requires additional audit effort. Unexplained results or relationships may indicate an adverse condition.

7. Analytical information may include (a) comparisons of current and historical information, (b) comparisons of client and industry information, (c) budget variances, (d) relationships among elements of accounting information, (e) comparisons of accounting and operating information, (f) information about economic conditions, and (g) other nonfinancial information that explains accounting information.

8. The CAE and each auditor are responsible for the collective proficiency of the IAA and his/her own proficiency, respectively. Moreover, internal auditors should comply with conduct standards.

9. Due professional care is the care exercised by a reasonably prudent and competent auditor in similar circumstances. The auditor should be alert to wrongdoing, inefficiency, and ineffectiveness. The auditor also must identify controls. Moreover, the auditor provides reasonable, not absolute, assurance.

10. Due professional care involves considering (a) the extent of work; (b) relative complexity, materiality, or significance of matters to which procedures are applied; (c) adequacy and effectiveness of risk management, control, and governance; (d) probability of significant errors, irregularities, or noncompliance; and (e) cost of assurance relative to benefits.

11. In a formal consulting engagement, an understanding of the engagement must be obtained by an internal auditor who is exercising due professional care. The internal auditor must assess the extent of the service and its compatibility with the IAA's charter, policies and procedures, and plan of engagements.

12. Internal auditors should determine that operating targets and expectations are acceptable and being met. If criteria are vague, internal auditors should seek interpretations. If they must select or interpret criteria, client agreement should be obtained.

13. All phases of the engagement should be supervised. Supervision also extends to appraisals of engagement staff and client satisfaction surveys.

14. Sources of information may be internal, external, or a combination.

15. Information may be physical, testimonial, documentary, or analytical.

16. Information gathering procedures include (a) interviewing, (b) recomputation, (c) detail testing, (d) observation, (e) inspection, (f) scanning, (g) confirmation, and (h) analytical methods.

17. The ultimate purpose of information gathering is to provide sufficient support for the internal auditor's observations, conclusions, and recommendations. Although the individual items of information may have drawbacks and therefore different degrees of persuasiveness, the internal auditor's task is to assemble a body of information that provides the requisite support. During this process, the internal auditor may determine that particular information justifies full reliance, partial reliance, or no reliance.

18. Working papers document the engagement. They are prepared by internal auditors and reviewed by IAA management. Working papers record information and analyses and support observations, conclusions, and recommendations.

19. Documentation standards for assurance and consulting services are not necessarily the same.

20. Effectively and efficiently organized working papers help control engagement work. Working papers also (a) document information, (b) provide background for discussions with clients, (c) facilitate coordination with external auditors, (d) record auditor disagreements, (e) help prepare for future engagements, (f) serve as a basis for quality reviews, and (g) meet legal requirements.

21. Use of electronic media for the creation, transmission, and storage of working papers raises security concerns that do not arise when documents exist only in hard copy. However, information technology permits fundamental changes in the engagement process. New methods of data storage, retrieval, and manipulation may facilitate activities that were not previously feasible, e.g., multiple regression analyses and simulation.

22. Working papers should be consistently and efficiently prepared to facilitate review. Working papers should have summaries throughout to provide the reviewer with a brief statement of information contained in subsequent schedules. A good indexing system for working papers should be simple and easily expanded.

23. Supervision includes determining that working papers support engagement results. Review of working papers should ensure that (a) they support communications and (b) necessary procedures have been performed. The reviewer initials and dates each working paper.

24. Working papers are property of the organization. They should be controlled by the IAA. Requests for access by members of the organization and external auditors should be approved by the CAE. Requests for access by parties outside the organization should be approved by senior management or legal counsel.

25. The presumption is that engagement records are confidential. They may contain opinions and facts that may be misunderstood by those unfamiliar with the organization and its audit process. Records not subject to a legal privilege are accessible to outside parties in criminal cases. Access by outsiders in civil cases is unclear.

QUESTIONS

1.1 Identifying Information

1. The best definition of information identified to achieve an internal auditing engagement's objectives is information that

A. Provides a sound basis for engagement conclusions.

B. Provides an absolute basis for engagement conclusions.

C. Is useful and convincing.

D. Is useful and reliable.

Answer (A) is correct. *(CIA, adapted)*
REQUIRED: The definition of engagement information.
DISCUSSION: Information should be collected on all matters related to the engagement objectives and scope of work. It should be sufficient, reliable, relevant, and useful to provide a sound basis for engagement observations, conclusions, and recommendations (PA 2310-1).
Answer (B) is incorrect because an absolute basis for conclusions is possible only if the internal auditor has perfect knowledge. Answer (C) is incorrect because information must also be sufficient, reliable, and relevant, but each evidentiary item need not be convincing. Answer (D) is incorrect because information must also be relevant and sufficient.

2. Engagement information is usually considered relevant when it is

- A. Derived through valid statistical sampling.
- B. Objective and unbiased.
- C. Factual, adequate, and convincing.
- D. Consistent with the engagement objectives.

Answer (D) is correct.   *(CIA, adapted)*
REQUIRED: The circumstance in which information is usually considered relevant.
DISCUSSION: Information should be sufficient, reliable, relevant, and useful to provide a sound basis for engagement observations, conclusions, and recommendations. Relevant information supports engagement observations, conclusions, and recommendations and is consistent with the objectives for the engagement (PA 2310-1).
Answer (A) is incorrect because whether sampling is appropriate and the results are valid are issues related to the determination of sufficiency and reliability rather than relevance. Answer (B) is incorrect because objectivity and lack of bias do not ensure that information will support observations and recommendations and be consistent with the engagement objectives. Answer (C) is incorrect because sufficient information is factual, adequate, and convincing so that a prudent, informed person would reach the same conclusions as the internal auditor.

3. To determine the sufficiency of information regarding interpretation of a contract, an internal auditor uses

- A. The best obtainable information.
- B. Subjective judgments.
- C. Objective evaluations.
- D. Logical relationships between information and issues.

Answer (C) is correct.   *(CIA, adapted)*
REQUIRED: The way an internal auditor determines the sufficiency of information regarding interpretation of a contract.
DISCUSSION: Information should be sufficient, reliable, relevant, and useful. It is sufficient only if it is so factual, adequate, and convincing that a prudent, informed person would reach the same conclusions as the internal auditor (PA 2310-1). This judgment should be objective. It must be based on a perception of facts and conditions without distortion by personal feelings, prejudices, or interpretations.
Answer (A) is incorrect because the best obtainable information is reliable but not necessarily sufficient. Answer (B) is incorrect because an evaluation of the sufficiency of information requires objective judgments. The "prudent, informed person" language in PA 2310-1 states an objectivity criterion. Answer (D) is incorrect because whether the relationship between the information and the issues is logical is a matter of relevance. Information must be relevant, but relevant information may not be sufficient.

4. Which of the following is an essential factor in evaluating the sufficiency of information? The information must

- A. Be well documented and cross-referenced in the working papers.
- B. Be based on references that are considered competent.
- C. Bear a direct relationship to the observation and include all of the elements of an observation.
- D. Be convincing enough for a prudent person to reach the same decision.

Answer (D) is correct.   *(CIA, adapted)*
REQUIRED: The essential factor in evaluating the sufficiency of information.
DISCUSSION: Sufficient information is factual, adequate, and convincing so that a prudent, informed person would reach the same conclusions as the internal auditor (PA 2310-1).
Answer (A) is incorrect because documentation and cross-referencing are desirable but have no specific relationship to any of the characteristics of information (sufficiency, reliability, relevance, and usefulness). Answer (B) is incorrect because competence is a characteristic of reliable information. Answer (C) is incorrect because relevant information supports engagement observations.

5. An internal auditor is evaluating the advertising function. The organization has engaged a medium-sized local advertising agency to place advertising in magazine publications. As part of the review of the engagement working papers, the internal auditing supervisor is evaluating the information collected. The internal auditor reviewed the language in the advertising for its legality and compliance with fair trade regulations by interviewing the organization's advertising manager, the product marketing director (who may not have been objective), and five of the organization's largest customers (who may not have been knowledgeable). The supervisor can justifiably conclude that the information is

    A. Reliable.

    B. Irrelevant.

    C. Conclusive.

    D. Insufficient.

Answer (D) is correct. *(CIA, adapted)*
    REQUIRED: The conclusion about the information identified.
    DISCUSSION: Information must be sufficient, reliable, relevant, and useful. Sufficient information is factual, adequate, and convincing so that a prudent, informed person would reach the same conclusions as the internal auditor (PA 2310-1). Sufficiency is based on the internal auditor's professional judgment as to the amounts, kinds, and persuasiveness of information required. Testimony from individuals who may be neither objective nor knowledgeable is unlikely to be sufficient.
    Answer (A) is incorrect because the advertising director and the product marketing director are not objective. Answer (B) is incorrect because the information is relevant but not sufficient. Answer (C) is incorrect because the information is not sufficient. Hence, it cannot be conclusive. The inherent limitations of this engagement require that internal auditors rely on information that is merely persuasive rather than convincing beyond all doubt.

6. What characteristic of information is satisfied by an original signed document?

    A. Sufficiency.

    B. Reliability.

    C. Relevance.

    D. Usefulness.

Answer (B) is correct. *(CIA, adapted)*
    REQUIRED: The characteristic of information satisfied by an original signed document.
    DISCUSSION: Reliable information is competent and the best attainable through the use of appropriate procedures. An original document is the prime example of such information.
    Answer (A) is incorrect because sufficient information is factual, adequate, and convincing. The information contained on the document may be none of those things. Answer (C) is incorrect because relevance concerns the relationship of the information to some objective of the engagement. No engagement objective is disclosed in the question. Thus, whether the information on the document is relevant to the investigation cannot be determined. Answer (D) is incorrect because usefulness is achieved if the item helps the organization (the internal auditor, in this case) to accomplish predetermined goals. No such goals are specified.

7. In deciding whether recorded sales are valid, which of the following items of information is most reliable?

    A. A copy of the customer's purchase order.

    B. A memorandum from the director of the shipping department stating that another employee verified the personal delivery of the merchandise to the customer.

    C. Accounts receivable records showing cash collections from the customer.

    D. The shipping document, independent bill of lading, and the invoice for the merchandise.

Answer (D) is correct. *(CIA, adapted)*
    REQUIRED: The most reliable information for deciding whether recorded sales are valid.
    DISCUSSION: Information is reliable if it is competent and the best attainable through the use of appropriate engagement techniques (PA 2310-1). Information is ordinarily more reliable if it is obtained from a source independent of the client. The shipping document and invoice provide direct information that the sale was made, and the bill of lading is externally generated documentation that the merchandise was shipped.
    Answer (A) is incorrect because the customer's purchase order only proves that the item was requested, not sold. Answer (B) is incorrect because this memorandum is an uncorroborated statement. Answer (C) is incorrect because A/R records showing cash collections from the customer are less direct than the shipping document and invoice and provide only circumstantial support regarding the validity of the sale.

Questions 8 through 10 are based on the following information. The chief audit executive is reviewing some of the basic concepts inherent in the performance of an engagement with three internal auditors who are on a rotation assignment. After 6 months in the internal audit activity, they will move back to line positions. Each of them has fairly extensive organizational experience and is on a fast track to a high-level management line position. To develop their analytical decision-making abilities, the CAE pulls some old engagement working papers, holding back the review notes and clearing comments. The CAE asks the team to indicate the informational criteria that are violated.

8.   During the planning stage of an engagement, the internal auditor made an on-site observation of the vehicle maintenance department and included the following statement in a memorandum summary of the results:

> "We noted that several maintenance garages were deteriorating badly. Fencing around the property was in need of repair."

Which of the following informational criteria, if any, is violated?

- A.   Sufficiency.
- B.   Reliability.
- C.   Relevance.
- D.   No criteria are violated.

Answer (D) is correct. *(CIA, adapted)*
REQUIRED: The informational standard(s) violated, if any.
DISCUSSION: The observations made about the vehicle maintenance department contain sufficient information (factual, adequate, and convincing so that a prudent, informed person would reach the same conclusions) that is reliable (competent and the best attainable through the use of appropriate engagement techniques) and relevant (supports engagement observations and recommendations and is consistent with the objectives for the engagement).
Answer (A) is incorrect because the sufficiency criterion has not been violated. Physical observation by the internal auditor is sufficient to determine deterioration and need for repairs. Answer (B) is incorrect because the reliability criterion has not been violated. On-site observation is an appropriate technique to determine deterioration and needed repairs. Answer (C) is incorrect because the relevance criterion has not been violated. The information obtained by the internal auditor supports observations about the physical condition of the department.

9.   The organization's inventories are under the administration of three production managers. The internal auditors perform a standard limited test of finished goods inventory balances every year. During this year's engagement concerning inventories, the internal auditors noted finished goods inventories were abnormally high, sales were consistent with prior years, and returns and allowances appeared normal. The internal auditors performed the usual random sample recount of several finished goods inventory cards without discrepancy and then extended the testing to include 10 raw materials and 10 work-in-process cards, noting no exceptions. The following statement was included in the engagement working papers:

> "Our standard test of finished goods inventories revealed no exceptions to the inventory count. We extended our tests this year to include both raw materials and work-in-process without exception. At the time of our engagement, the supervising inventory managers were not available; however, the division secretary indicated that performance standards were on file. It appears that there is adequate awareness and understanding of the performance standards."

Which of the following informational criteria is **not** violated?

- A.   Sufficiency.
- B.   Reliability.
- C.   Relevance.
- D.   All criteria are violated.

Answer (D) is correct. *(CIA, adapted)*
REQUIRED: The informational standard not violated, if any.
DISCUSSION: The conclusion violates the criteria of sufficiency, reliability, and relevance. The sufficiency criterion is violated because recounting several inventory items is insufficient in light of the abnormally high inventory. The reliability criterion is violated because the performance standard information is not competent. The internal auditors should interview inventory managers to determine their awareness and understanding of the performance standards. The relevance criterion is violated because the information related to raw materials and work-in-process does not pertain to the finished goods inventory.

10. The organization is required to comply with certain specific standards related to environmental issues. One of these standards requires that certain hazardous chemicals be placed in certified containers for shipment to a governmental disposal site. The container must bear an inspection seal signed within the last 90 days by a governmental inspector. Based on the following tests, the internal auditor concluded that the organization was in compliance for the engagement period:

I. Determine from each chemical loading supervisor that compliance requirements are understood.

II. Inspect sealed containers for evidence of leakage.

III. Ask chemical loading personnel about procedures performed.

Which of the following informational criteria, if any, is violated?

    A. Sufficiency.

    B. Reliability.

    C. Relevance.

    D. No criteria are violated.

Answer (A) is correct. *(CIA, adapted)*
REQUIRED: The informational standard(s) violated, if any.
DISCUSSION: Sufficient information is factual, adequate, and convincing so that a prudent, informed person would reach the same conclusions as the internal auditor (PA 2310-1). These tests are insufficient because the internal auditor did not determine that each container had an inspection seal signed within the last 90 days.
Answer (B) is incorrect because the information is reliable. It is competent and the best attainable through the use of appropriate engagement techniques. Answer (C) is incorrect because the information is relevant. It supports engagement observations and recommendations and is consistent with the objectives for the engagement. Answer (D) is incorrect because the sufficiency criterion was violated.

11. An internal auditor has set an engagement objective of determining whether all cash receipts are deposited intact daily. To satisfy this objective, the internal auditor interviewed the controller who gave assurances that all cash receipts are deposited as soon as is reasonably possible. As information that can be used to satisfy the stated engagement objective, the controller's assurances are

    A. Sufficient but not reliable or relevant.

    B. Sufficient, reliable, and relevant.

    C. Not sufficient, reliable, or relevant.

    D. Relevant but not sufficient or reliable.

Answer (D) is correct. *(CIA, adapted)*
REQUIRED: The characteristics of information.
DISCUSSION: Information should be sufficient, reliable, relevant, and useful to provide a sound basis for engagement observations, conclusions, and recommendations. Relevant information supports engagement observations, conclusions, and recommendations and is consistent with the objectives for the engagement. Sufficient information is factual, adequate, and convincing so that a prudent, informed person would reach the same conclusions as the internal auditor. Reliable information is competent and the best attainable through the use of appropriate procedures (PA 2310-1). The controller's assurance is relevant because it pertains to the cash receipts. However, it lacks reliability because it was not obtained from an independent source. Furthermore, the information is not sufficient because, by itself, it does not provide a reasonable basis for a conclusion.

1.2 Analysis and Evaluation

12. Accounts payable schedule verification may include the use of analytical information. Which of the following is analytical information?

    A. Comparing the schedule with the accounts payable ledger or unpaid voucher file.

    B. Comparing the balance on the schedule with the balances of prior years.

    C. Comparing confirmations received from selected creditors with the accounts payable ledger.

    D. Examining vendors' invoices in support of selected items on the schedule.

Answer (B) is correct. *(CIA, adapted)*
REQUIRED: The analytical information.
DISCUSSION: Analytical auditing procedures provide internal auditors with an efficient and effective means of assessing and evaluating information collected in an engagement. The assessment results from comparing information with expectations identified or developed by the internal auditor. Analytical auditing procedures are useful in identifying, among other things, differences that are not expected, the absence of differences when they are expected, potential errors, potential irregularities or illegal acts, or other unusual or nonrecurring transactions or events (PA 2320-1). Thus, they may include comparison of current-period information with budgets, forecasts, or similar information for prior periods.
Answer (A) is incorrect because comparing the schedule with the accounts payable ledger or unpaid voucher file is a test of details. Answer (C) is incorrect because comparing confirmations received from selected creditors with the accounts payable ledger is a test of details. Answer (D) is incorrect because examining vendors' invoices in support of selected items on the schedule is a test of details.

13. Analytical procedures

A. Are considered direct information about the assertion being evaluated.

B. Involve such tests as confirmation of receivables.

C. May provide the best available information for the completeness assertion.

D. Are never sufficient by themselves to support management assertions.

Answer (C) is correct. *(CIA, adapted)*
REQUIRED: The statement that best describes analytical procedures.
DISCUSSION: Analytical procedures usually involve summarizing and comparing data so that trends and other important relationships may be detected. Procedures range from simple comparisons of amounts reported to advanced statistical and modeling techniques. The use of analytical procedures involves judgment and focuses on the overall reasonableness of recorded amounts. Thus, analytical procedures provide information that all transactions and accounts that should be presented are included. In some circumstances, the internal auditor may be able to determine that analytical procedures by themselves provide the desired level of assurance.
Answer (A) is incorrect because, although relevant, analytical information is not direct. It is a means of gathering information without testing particular transactions directly. Answer (B) is incorrect because analytical information involves a study of plausible relationships among data. Confirmation is a substantive test of details. Answer (D) is incorrect because, for assertions of low materiality, analytical information may be considered sufficient.

14. A small city managed its own pension fund. According to the city charter, investments could be made only in bonds, money market funds, or high-quality stocks. The internal auditor has already verified the existence of the pension fund's assets. The fund balance was not very large and was managed by the city treasurer. The internal auditor decided to estimate income from investments of the fund by multiplying the average fund balance by a weighted-average rate based on the current portfolio mix. Upon doing so, the internal auditor found that recorded return was substantially less than was expected. The internal auditor's next procedure should be to

A. Inquire of the treasurer as to the reason that income appears to be less than expected.

B. Prepare a more detailed estimate of income by consulting a dividend and reporting service that lists the interest or dividends paid on specific stocks and bonds.

C. Inform management and the board that fraud is suspected and suggest that legal counsel be called in to complete the investigation.

D. Select a sample of entries to the pension fund income account and trace to the cash journal to determine if cash was received.

Answer (B) is correct. *(CIA, adapted)*
REQUIRED: The next procedure after comparing investment return with the internal auditor's expectations.
DISCUSSION: When analytical procedures have unexpected results, for example, when pension fund assets are suspiciously low, the internal auditor should examine and evaluate those results. This examination and evaluation should include inquiries of management (but not of the treasurer in this case) and other engagement procedures sufficient to explain the difference between the expectations and the results. Unexplained results may be indicative of an error, irregularity, or illegal act (PA 2320-1). Although the substantial difference looks suspicious, the internal auditor should prepare a more detailed estimate before deciding the most appropriate action.
Answer (A) is incorrect because the internal auditor should refine the estimate further before discussing the matter with the treasurer. Even if the internal auditor has confidence in the first estimate, the suspicion of potential fraud should lead the internal auditor to do further work, e.g., tracing the estimated income developed in the first step to the cash receipts book before confronting the treasurer. Answer (C) is incorrect because the internal auditor does not have sufficient information to justify the conclusion that fraud has occurred. Answer (D) is incorrect because this procedure would provide information only about recorded income.

15. An inexperienced internal auditor notified the senior auditor of a significant variance from the engagement client's budget. The senior told the new internal auditor not to worry because the senior had heard that there had been an unauthorized work stoppage that probably accounted for the difference. Which of the following statements is most appropriate?

A. The new internal auditor should have investigated the matter fully and not bothered the senior.

B. The senior used proper judgment in curtailing what could have been a wasteful investigation.

C. The senior should have halted the engagement until the variance was fully explained.

D. The senior should have aided the new internal auditor in formulating a plan for accumulating appropriate information.

Answer (D) is correct. *(CIA, adapted)*
REQUIRED: The senior internal auditor's proper response to a significant budget variance.
DISCUSSION: The variance was not adequately investigated or explained. When analytical procedures identify unexpected results or relationships, the internal auditor should examine and evaluate such results or relationships. The examination and evaluation should include inquiries of management and the application of other engagement procedures until the internal auditor is satisfied that the results or relationships are sufficiently explained. Unexplained results or relationships may be indicative of a significant condition such as a potential error, irregularity, or illegal act. Results or relationships that are not sufficiently explained should be communicated to the appropriate levels of management. The internal auditor may recommend appropriate courses of action, depending on the circumstances (PA 2320-1).
Answer (A) is incorrect because the extent of supervision varies with the proficiency and experience of the internal auditor and the complexity of the engagement (PA 2340-1). An inexperienced internal auditor should refer this matter to the senior. Answer (B) is incorrect because the facts given do not support the conclusion that accumulating additional information would be wasteful. Answer (C) is incorrect because the variance needs explanation, but the engagement should continue.

16. While testing the effectiveness of inventory controls, the internal auditor makes a note in the working papers that most of the cycle count adjustments for the facility involved transactions of the machining department. The machining department also had generated an extraordinary number of cycle count adjustments in comparison with other departments last year. The internal auditor should

A. Interview management and apply other engagement procedures to determine whether transaction controls and procedures within the machining department are adequate.

B. Do no further work because the concern was not identified by the analytical procedures included in the engagement work program.

C. Notify internal auditing management that fraud is suspected.

D. Place a note in the working papers to review this matter in detail during the next engagement.

Answer (A) is correct. *(CIA, adapted)*
REQUIRED: The internal auditor action when tests of controls reveal that most inventory count adjustments involve one department.
DISCUSSION: When analytical procedures identify unexpected results or relationships, the internal auditor should examine and evaluate such results or relationships. The examination and evaluation should include inquiries of management and the application of other engagement procedures until the internal auditor is satisfied that the results or relationships are sufficiently explained. Unexplained results or relationships may be indicative of a significant condition such as a potential error, irregularity, or illegal act (PA 2320-1).
Answer (B) is incorrect because the engagement work program is a guide that does not restrict the auditor from pursuing information unknown at the time that the program was written. Answer (C) is incorrect because the facts do not yet support a conclusion that fraud has occurred. Answer (D) is incorrect because the risk of a material misstatement of inventory should be addressed promptly.

17. An internal auditor decides to perform an inventory turnover analysis for both raw materials inventory and finished goods inventory. The analysis would be potentially useful in

A. Identifying products for which management has not been attuned to changes in market demand.

B. Identifying potential problems in purchasing activities.

C. Identifying obsolete inventory.

D. All of the answers are correct.

Answer (D) is correct. *(CIA, adapted)*
REQUIRED: The reason(s) for performing a turnover analysis.
DISCUSSION: Inventory turnover provides analytical information. It equals cost of sales divided by average inventory. A low turnover ratio implies that inventory is excessive, for example, because the goods are obsolete or because the organization has overestimated demand.

18. Analytical procedures enable the internal auditor to predict the balance or quantity of an item. Information to develop this estimate can be obtained by all of the following **except**

    A. Tracing transactions through the system to determine whether procedures are being applied as prescribed.

    B. Comparing financial data with data for comparable prior periods, anticipated results (e.g., budgets and forecasts), and similar data for the industry in which the entity operates.

    C. Studying the relationships of elements of financial data that would be expected to conform to a predictable pattern based upon the entity's experience.

    D. Studying the relationships of financial data with relevant nonfinancial data.

Answer (A) is correct. *(Publisher, adapted)*
REQUIRED: The procedure not a source of information for analytical procedures.
DISCUSSION: Tracing transactions through the system is a test of controls directed toward the operating effectiveness of internal control, not an analytical procedure.
Answer (B) is incorrect because the basic premise of analytical procedures is that plausible relationships among data may be reasonably expected to exist and continue in the absence of known conditions to the contrary. Well-drafted budgets and forecasts prepared at the beginning of the year should therefore be compared with actual results, and engagement client information should be compared with data for the industry in which the engagement client operates. Answer (C) is incorrect because the internal auditor should expect financial ratios and relationships to exist and to remain relatively stable in the absence of reasons for variation. Answer (D) is incorrect because financial information is related to nonfinancial information; e.g., salary expense should be related to the number of hours worked.

19. A production manager for a moderate-sized manufacturing organization began ordering excessive raw materials and had them delivered to a wholesaler that the manager was running as a side business. The manager falsified receiving documents and approved the invoices for payment. Which of the following engagement procedures is most likely to detect this fraud?

    A. Take a sample of cash disbursements; compare purchase orders, receiving reports, invoices, and check copies.

    B. Take a sample of cash disbursements and confirm the amount purchased, purchase price, and date of shipment with the vendors.

    C. Observe the receiving dock and count materials received; compare the counts with receiving reports completed by receiving personnel.

    D. Perform analytical tests, comparing production, materials purchased, and raw materials inventory levels; investigate differences.

Answer (D) is correct. *(CIA, adapted)*
REQUIRED: The engagement procedure most likely to detect a purchasing fraud.
DISCUSSION: Analytical auditing procedures provide internal auditors with an efficient and effective means of assessing and evaluating information collected in an engagement. The assessment results from comparing information with expectations identified or developed by the internal auditor. Analytical auditing procedures are useful in identifying, among other things, differences that are not expected, the absence of differences when they are expected, potential errors, potential irregularities or illegal acts, or other unusual or nonrecurring transactions or events (PA 2320-1). Hence, the analytical procedures should identify an unexplained increase in materials used.
Answer (A) is incorrect because, given that documents have been falsified, supporting documents exist for each cash disbursement. Answer (B) is incorrect because the vendors will confirm all transactions. Answer (C) is incorrect because, given that the improper orders are shipped to another location, observing receiving dock counts will not detect the fraud.

20. Analytical procedures can best be categorized as

    A. Substantive tests.

    B. Tests of controls.

    C. Qualitative tests.

    D. Budget comparisons.

Answer (A) is correct. *(CIA, adapted)*
REQUIRED: The best classification of analytical procedures.
DISCUSSION: Analytical auditing procedures provide internal auditors with an efficient and effective means of assessing and evaluating information collected in an engagement. The assessment results from comparing information with expectations identified or developed by the internal auditor. Analytical auditing procedures are useful in identifying, among other things, differences that are not expected, the absence of differences when they are expected, potential errors, potential irregularities or illegal acts, or other unusual or nonrecurring transactions or events (PA 2320-1). Thus, analytical procedures are substantive tests.
Answer (B) is incorrect because tests of controls are used to evaluate the design, implementation, and effectiveness of control activities. Answer (C) is incorrect because analytical procedures tend to be quantitative even when nonfinancial information is considered. Answer (D) is incorrect because budget comparisons are only one of many types of analytical procedures.

21. An internal auditor's preliminary analysis of accounts receivable turnover revealed the following rates:

Year 1	Year 2	Year 3
7.3	6.2	4.3

Which of the following is the most likely cause of the decrease in accounts receivable turnover?

A. Increase in the cash discount offered.

B. Liberalization of credit policy.

C. Shortening of due date terms.

D. Increased cash sales.

Answer (B) is correct. *(CIA, adapted)*
REQUIRED: The most likely cause of a decrease in accounts receivable turnover.
DISCUSSION: The accounts receivable turnover ratio equals net credit sales over average accounts receivable. Accounts receivable turnover will decrease if net credit sales decrease or average accounts receivable increase. Liberalization of credit policy will increase receivables.
Answer (A) is incorrect because an increase in cash sales that reduces credit sales as a result of an increased cash discount has an indeterminate effect on the turnover ratio. Both the numerator and the denominator are decreased but not necessarily by the same amount. An increase in cash sales not affecting credit sales has no effect on the ratio. Answer (C) is incorrect because shortening due dates decreases the average accounts receivable outstanding and increases the ratio if other factors are held constant. Answer (D) is incorrect because increased cash sales have an indeterminate effect on the turnover ratio.

22. The internal auditor is evaluating the effectiveness of a sales commission plan adopted 12 months earlier. An engagement procedure likely to provide strong support for the plan's effectiveness is to

A. Calculate the percentage change in monthly sales by product line for the last 3 years.

B. Compare monthly selling costs of this year with those of the 2 preceding years.

C. Regress monthly indices of external economic conditions against sales for the 2 preceding years and compare predictions with reported sales.

D. Compare the ratio of selling costs per dollar of sales each month for the past year with that of other organizations in the industry.

Answer (C) is correct. *(CIA, adapted)*
REQUIRED: The technique to determine the effectiveness of a newly installed sales commission plan.
DISCUSSION: The internal auditor requires information as to whether sales have increased more than could be expected from changes in external economic conditions. Regression analysis is a statistical tool to generate predictions based on projections of current economic conditions. It provides benchmarks whereby current sales may be compared with expected sales to evaluate the effect of the sales commission variable.
Answer (A) is incorrect because simple comparison of month-to-month sales figures does not take into account changes in external economic factors. Answer (B) is incorrect because the effectiveness of the sales commission plan should be measured by the sales generated, not by costs. Additionally, external factors are not taken into account. Answer (D) is incorrect because the effectiveness should be measured by sales generated, not costs.

23. The audit committee has expressed concern that the financial institution has been taking on higher-risk loans in pursuit of short-term profit goals. Which of the following engagement procedures provides the **least** amount of information to address this concern?

A. Perform an analytical review of interest income as a percentage of the investment portfolio in comparison with a group of peer financial institutions.

B. Take a random sample of loans made during the period and compare the riskiness of the loans with that of a random sample of loans made 2 years ago.

C. Perform an analytical review that involves developing a chart to compare interest income plotted over the past 10 years.

D. Develop a multiple-regression time-series analysis of income over the past 5 years including such factors as interest rate in the economy, size of loan portfolio, and dollar amount of new loans each year.

Answer (C) is correct. *(CIA, adapted)*
REQUIRED: The audit procedure least useful in addressing the concern about making riskier loans for short-term purposes.
DISCUSSION: Plotting the changes in interest income over the past 10 years is the least useful procedure. It does not consider other important factors, such as size of the portfolio, changes in interest rates, the development of new financial instruments, the level of inflation, and government regulation.
Answer (A) is incorrect because higher-risk loans should generate higher short-term interest income compared with that earned by comparable institutions. Higher-risk loans have higher yields. Answer (B) is incorrect because a historical comparison of loan risk for the institution addresses the engagement objective. Answer (D) is incorrect because multiple regression explains the change in a dependent variable (interest income) attributable to two or more independent variables. Thus, it allows the internal auditor to estimate how much of the change might be due to a change in the riskiness of the loans.

24. Which result of an analytical procedure suggests the existence of obsolete merchandise?

    A. Decrease in the inventory turnover rate.

    B. Decrease in the ratio of gross profit to sales.

    C. Decrease in the ratio of inventory to accounts payable.

    D. Decrease in the ratio of inventory to accounts receivable.

Answer (A) is correct. *(CIA, adapted)*
    REQUIRED: The analytical procedure that might uncover obsolete merchandise.
    DISCUSSION: Inventory turnover is equal to cost of sales divided by average inventory. If inventory is increasing at a faster rate than sales, the turnover rate decreases and suggests a buildup of unsalable inventory. The ratios of gross profit to sales, inventory to accounts payable, and inventory to accounts receivable do not necessarily change when obsolete merchandise is on hand.

1.3 Due Professional Care

25. Supervision of an internal audit engagement should include

    A. Determining that engagement working papers adequately support the engagement observations.

    B. Assigning staff members to the particular engagement.

    C. Determining the scope of the engagement.

    D. Appraising each internal auditor's performance on at least an annual basis.

Answer (A) is correct. *(CIA, adapted)*
    REQUIRED: The extent of supervision of an engagement.
    DISCUSSION: Supervision includes ensuring that the auditors assigned possess the requisite knowledge, skills, and other competencies to perform the engagement; providing appropriate instructions during the planning of the engagement and approving the engagement program; seeing that the approved engagement work program is carried out unless changes are both justified and authorized; determining that engagement working papers adequately support the engagement observations, conclusions, and recommendations; ensuring that engagement communications are accurate, objective, clear, concise, constructive, and timely; ensuring that engagement objectives are met; and providing opportunities for developing internal auditors' knowledge, skills, and other competencies (PA 2340-1).
    Answer (B) is incorrect because engagement resource allocation is a planning function, not a supervisory function (PA 2230-1). Answer (C) is incorrect because determining the engagement scope is a planning function, not a supervisory function. Answer (D) is incorrect because appraising performance on an annual basis is not a supervisory function of a specific engagement but is part of the management of the human resources of the internal audit activity (PA 2030-1).

26. An internal auditor has some suspicion, but no evidence, of potential misstatement of financial statements. The internal auditor has failed to exercise due professional care if (s)he

    A. Identified potential ways in which a misstatement could occur and ranked the items for investigation.

    B. Informed the engagement manager of the suspicions and asked for advice on how to proceed.

    C. Did not test for possible misstatement because the engagement work program had already been approved by engagement management.

    D. Expanded the engagement work program, without the engagement client's approval, to address the highest ranked ways in which a misstatement may have occurred.

Answer (C) is correct. *(CIA, adapted)*
    REQUIRED: The act in violation of the due professional care standard.
    DISCUSSION: Due professional care requires the exercise of the care and skill expected of a reasonably prudent and competent internal auditor in the same or similar circumstances (PA 1220-1). Because engagement work programs are expected to be modified to reflect changing circumstances, the internal auditor would fail to exercise due professional care if (s)he did not investigate a suspected misstatement solely because the engagement work program had already been approved.
    Answer (A) is incorrect because ranking the ways in which a misstatement could occur is consistent with the due professional care standard. Answer (B) is incorrect because seeking advice is consistent with the due professional care standard. Answer (D) is incorrect because the internal auditor does not need the engagement client's approval to expand the engagement work program.

27. The chief audit executive is responsible for engagement supervision. The most important form of supervision during the fieldwork phase of engagement involves

A. Seeing that the approved engagement work program is carried out unless changes are both justified and authorized.

B. Providing suitable instructions to subordinates at the outset of the engagement and approving the engagement program.

C. Appraising each internal auditor's performance at least annually.

D. Making sure that communications are accurate, objective, clear, concise, constructive, and timely.

Answer (A) is correct. *(CIA, adapted)*
REQUIRED: The most important form of supervision during the fieldwork phase.
DISCUSSION: Supervision includes ensuring that the auditors assigned possess the requisite knowledge, skills, and other competencies to perform the engagement; providing appropriate instructions during the planning of the engagement and approving the engagement program; seeing that the approved engagement work program is carried out unless changes are both justified and authorized; determining that engagement working papers adequately support the engagement observations, conclusions, and recommendations; ensuring that engagement communications are accurate, objective, clear, concise, constructive, and timely; ensuring that engagement objectives are met; and providing opportunities for developing internal auditors' knowledge, skills, and other competencies (PA 2340-1). Execution of the engagement work program requires supervision during fieldwork. The other supervisory tasks are carried out before or after fieldwork.
Answer (B) is incorrect because "at the outset of the engagement" is not during fieldwork. Answer (C) is incorrect because annual performance appraisal is not specific to a particular engagement. Answer (D) is incorrect because engagement communications are prepared at the conclusion of fieldwork.

28. Which of the following statements is true with respect to due professional care?

A. An internal auditor should perform detailed tests of all transactions before communicating results.

B. An item should not be mentioned in an engagement communication unless the internal auditor is absolutely certain of the item.

C. An engagement communication should never be viewed as providing an infallible truth about a subject.

D. An internal auditor has no responsibility to recommend improvements.

Answer (C) is correct. *(CIA, adapted)*
REQUIRED: The true statement about due professional care.
DISCUSSION: Due professional care implies reasonable care and competence, not infallibility or extraordinary performance. Due professional care requires the auditor to conduct examinations and verifications to a reasonable extent, but does not require detailed reviews of all transactions. Accordingly, internal auditors cannot give absolute assurance that noncompliance or irregularities do not exist. Nevertheless, the possibility of material irregularities or noncompliance should be considered whenever an internal auditor undertakes an internal auditing assignment (PA 1220-1).
Answer (A) is incorrect because an internal auditor should conduct reasonable examinations and verifications, but detailed tests of all transactions are not required. Answer (B) is incorrect because absolute assurance need not, and cannot, be given. Answer (D) is incorrect because an internal auditor should recommend improvements to promote compliance with acceptable procedures and practices.

29. The chief audit executive is concerned that a recently disclosed fraud was not uncovered during the last engagement to evaluate cash operations. A review of the working papers indicated that the fraudulent transaction was not included in a properly designed statistical sample of transactions tested. Which of the following applies to this situation?

A. Because cash operations is a high-risk area, 100% testing of transactions should have been performed.

B. The internal auditor acted with due professional care because an appropriate statistical sample of material transactions was tested.

C. Fraud should not have gone undetected in a recently reviewed area.

D. Extraordinary care is necessary in the performance of a cash operations engagement, and the internal auditor should be held responsible for the oversight.

Answer (B) is correct. *(CIA, adapted)*
REQUIRED: The true statement about failure of a properly designed sample to detect fraud.
DISCUSSION: Due professional care implies reasonable care and competence, not infallibility or extraordinary performance. It requires the internal auditor to conduct examinations and verifications to a reasonable extent but does not require detailed reviews of all transactions. Accordingly, internal auditors cannot give absolute assurance that noncompliance or irregularities do not exist. Nevertheless, the possibility of material irregularities or noncompliance should be considered whenever an internal auditor undertakes an internal auditing assignment (PA 1220-1).
Answer (A) is incorrect because a review of all transactions involving cash is neither required nor cost efficient. Answer (C) is incorrect because the internal auditor cannot give absolute assurance of fraud detection. Answer (D) is incorrect because due care implies reasonable care and competence, not infallibility or extraordinary performance.

30. Which of the following items is the internal auditor **not** required to understand to exercise due professional care during a formal consulting engagement?

A. Possible motivations and reasons of those requesting the service.

B. Skills and resources needed to conduct the engagement.

C. Potential impact on the financial statements of the organization.

D. Effect on the scope of the audit plan previously approved by the audit committee.

Answer (C) is correct.   *(Publisher, adapted)*
REQUIRED: The item that the internal auditor is not required to understand to exercise due professional care during a formal consulting engagement.
DISCUSSION: The internal auditor should exercise due professional care in conducting a formal consulting engagement by understanding the following:

- Needs of management officials, including the nature, timing, and communication of engagement results
- Possible motivations and reasons of those requesting the service
- Extent of work needed to achieve the engagement's objectives
- Skills and resources needed to conduct the engagement
- Effect on the scope of the audit plan previously approved by the audit committee
- Potential impact on future audit assignments and engagements
- Potential organizational benefits to be derived from the engagement

The internal auditor is not required to understand the potential impact of the engagement on the financial statements to exercise due professional care during a formal consulting engagement. This is a consideration that should be understood by external auditors.

31. Assurance engagements should be performed with proficiency and due professional care. Accordingly, the Standards require internal auditors to

I. Consider the probability of significant noncompliance

II. Perform assurance procedures with due professional care so that all significant risks are identified

III. Weigh the cost of assurance against the benefits

A. I and II only.

B. I and III only.

C. II and III only.

D. I, II, and III.

Answer (B) is correct.   *(Publisher, adapted)*
REQUIRED: The responsibilities of internal auditors regarding proficiency and due professional care.
DISCUSSION: Standard 1220.A1 states that the exercise of due professional care involves considering the extent of work needed to achieve management's objectives; the relative complexity, materiality, or significance of matters to which assurance procedures are applied; the adequacy and effectiveness of risk management, control, and governance processes; the probability of significant errors, irregularities, or noncompliance; and the cost of assurance in relation to the benefits. Moreover, Standard 1220.A2 states that the internal auditor should be alert to the significant risks that might affect objectives, operations, or resources. However, assurance procedures alone, even when performed with due professional care, do not guarantee that all significant risks will be identified.

32. How often is appraisal of each internal auditor's performance required?

A. At least every 3 years.

B. At least every year.

C. At least every 6 months.

D. At least every 18 years.

Answer (B) is correct.   *(Publisher, adapted)*
REQUIRED: The time period in which each internal auditor's performance is required to be appraised.
DISCUSSION: According to PA 2340-1, supervision extends to employee performance evaluation. Appraisal of each internal auditor's performance is required at least annually. A full explanation of the appraisal process should be given to each internal auditor.

1.4 Sources of Information

33. Ordinarily, what source of information should most affect the internal auditor's conclusions?

    A. External.

    B. Inquiry.

    C. Oral.

    D. Informal.

Answer (A) is correct. *(CIA, adapted)*
    REQUIRED: The source of information that most affects conclusions.
    DISCUSSION: External information is ordinarily more reliable than the other types of information listed because it is generated from sources independent of the engagement client. The internal auditor should select the strongest information available to support engagement observations, conclusions, and recommendations.
    Answer (B) is incorrect because information derived from inquiries is ordinarily less reliable than external information. Answer (C) is incorrect because oral information is ordinarily less reliable than external information. Answer (D) is incorrect because informal information is ordinarily less reliable than external information.

34. An internal auditor's objective is to determine the cause of inventory shortages shown by the physical inventories taken by an independent service organization that used some engagement client personnel. The internal auditor addresses this objective by reviewing the count sheets, inventory printouts, and memos from the last inventory. The source of information and the sufficiency of this information are

    A. Internal and not sufficient.

    B. External and sufficient.

    C. Both external and internal and sufficient.

    D. Both external and internal and not sufficient.

Answer (D) is correct. *(CIA, adapted)*
    REQUIRED: The source of information and the sufficiency of the information listed.
    DISCUSSION: The organization employs an external inventory service and internal personnel for data entry and balancing, so the sources of information are both external and internal. However, the information is not sufficient to determine the cause of the shortages. Sufficient information is factual, adequate, and convincing so that a prudent, informed person would reach the same conclusions as the internal auditor (PA 2310-1, which is in Study Unit 3). The cause attribute of an engagement observation is the reason for the difference between the expected and actual conditions (why the difference exists). The information gathered supports the condition attribute, which is the factual information that the internal auditor found in the course of the examination (what does exist) (PA 2410-1, which is in Study Unit 8). It does not explain why the shortages exist.
    Answer (A) is incorrect because the information is also external. Answer (B) is incorrect because the information is also internal and not sufficient. Answer (C) is incorrect because the information is not sufficient to determine the cause.

35. During an investigation of unexplained inventory shrinkage, an internal auditor is testing inventory additions as recorded in the perpetual inventory records. Because of internal control weaknesses, the information recorded on receiving reports may not be reliable. Under these circumstances, which of the following documents provides the best information about additions to inventory?

    A. Purchase orders.

    B. Purchase requisitions.

    C. Vendors' invoices.

    D. Vendors' statements.

Answer (C) is correct. *(CIA, adapted)*
    REQUIRED: The best information about additions to inventory when receiving reports are unreliable.
    DISCUSSION: The vendors' invoice confirms that the proper amount due has been recorded. Thus, vendors' invoices provide the best source of information about additions to inventory. Vendors' invoices provide an external source of information regarding shipments to the engagement client. These amounts should be equal to quantities added to inventory (after possible adjustment for items returned to the vendor because of damage, etc.).
    Answer (A) is incorrect because the quantity ordered may not equal the quantity shipped by the vendor. Answer (B) is incorrect because the quantity requested in a purchase requisition may not equal the quantity shipped by the vendor as a result of modification by the purchasing department or vendor stockouts. Answer (D) is incorrect because vendors' statements normally list only the invoice number, date, and total. They do not list invoice detail such as quantities shipped.

36. In engagement planning, internal auditors should review all relevant information. Which of the following sources of information would most likely help identify suspected violations of environmental regulations?

A. Discussions with operating executives.

B. Review of trade publications.

C. Review of correspondence the entity has conducted with governmental agencies.

D. Discussions conducted with the external auditors in coordinating engagement efforts.

Answer (C) is correct.   *(CIA, adapted)*
REQUIRED: The source of information that would most likely help identify suspected violations of environmental regulations.
DISCUSSION: Correspondence from regulators is likely to be a valid and relevant source of information about environmental violations. This externally generated documentation and the engagement client's responses thereto may indicate a significant loss exposure for the engagement client.
Answer (A) is incorrect because operating management is a possibly biased source. Answer (B) is incorrect because this source is not sufficiently specific. Answer (D) is incorrect because external auditors do not have ready access to the needed information.

1.5 Nature of Information

37. A letter to the internal auditor in response to an inquiry is an example of which type of information?

A. Physical.

B. Testimonial.

C. Documentary.

D. Analytical.

Answer (B) is correct.   *(CIA, adapted)*
REQUIRED: The kind of information represented by a letter to the internal auditor in response to an inquiry.
DISCUSSION: Information may consist of authoritative documentation, calculations by the internal auditor, internal control, interrelationships among the data, physical existence, subsequent events, subsidiary records, and testimony by the engagement client and third parties. Oral or written statements (e.g., letters to the internal auditor) derived from inquiries or interviews are testimonial information.
Answer (A) is incorrect because physical information results from the verification of the actual existence of something by observation, inspection, or count. Answer (C) is incorrect because documentary information exists in some permanent form, such as checks, invoices, shipping records, receiving reports, and purchase orders. It includes both external information, e.g., bills of lading received by the engagement client from common carriers, and documents originating within the engagement client's organization. Answer (D) is incorrect because analytical information is derived from the study and comparison of relationships among data.

38. The chief audit executive is reviewing the working papers produced by an internal auditor during a fraud investigation. Among the items contained in the working papers is a description of an item of physical information. Which of the following is the most probable source of this item of information?

A. Observing conditions.

B. Interviewing people.

C. Examining records.

D. Computing variances.

Answer (A) is correct.   *(CIA, adapted)*
REQUIRED: The most probable source of physical information.
DISCUSSION: Physical information results from the verification of the actual existence of things, activities, or individuals by observation, inspection, or count. It may take the form of photographs, maps, charts, or other depictions.
Answer (B) is incorrect because interviewing produces testimonial information. Answer (C) is incorrect because the examination of records requires documentary information and produces analytical information. Answer (D) is incorrect because computations and verifications lead to analytical information.

39. An internal auditor takes a photograph of the engagement client's workplace. The photograph is a form of what kind of information?

A. Physical.

B. Testimonial.

C. Documentary.

D. Analytical.

Answer (A) is correct.   *(CIA, adapted)*
REQUIRED: The kind of information represented by a photograph.
DISCUSSION: Physical information results from the verification of the actual existence of things, activities, or individuals by observation, inspection, or count. It may take the form of photographs, maps, charts, or other depictions.
Answer (B) is incorrect because testimonial information consists of oral or written statements derived from inquiries or interviews. Answer (C) is incorrect because documentary information consists of letters, memoranda, invoices, shipping and receiving reports, etc. Answer (D) is incorrect because analytical information is derived from a study and comparison of the relationships among data.

40. Which of the following documents should the internal auditor examine to determine whether only authorized purchases are being accepted by the receiving department?

    A. A bill of lading.

    B. A copy of the purchase order.

    C. An invoice.

    D. Policies and procedures for the receiving function.

Answer (B) is correct. *(CIA, adapted)*
    REQUIRED: The document to examine to determine whether only authorized purchases are being accepted by the receiving department.
    DISCUSSION: In determining whether the accounts accurately reflect the obligations of the firm to vendors, the three items most useful to the auditor are purchase orders, receiving reports, and vendors' invoices. The purchase order provides information as to whether the goods were actually ordered and are a voluntary obligation of the organization. The receiving report confirms that the proper amount was received and the liability recorded in the correct period. The vendor's invoice confirms that the proper amount due has been recorded. An internal auditor will also be interested in the purchase requisitions to determine whether the purchase orders were properly authorized. However, the purchase order, not the requisition, is vital to determining the engagement client's obligation.
    Answer (A) is incorrect because a shipping document (bill of lading) received from the vendor cannot be used to determine whether the purchase was authorized. Answer (C) is incorrect because a billing notice (invoice) received from the vendor cannot be used to determine whether the purchase was authorized. Answer (D) is incorrect because policies and procedures are not transaction documents.

41. Which of the following is an example of documentary information?

    A. A photograph of an engagement client's workplace.

    B. A letter from a former employee alleging a fraud.

    C. A page of the general ledger containing irregularities placed there by the perpetrator of a fraud.

    D. A page of the internal auditor's working papers containing the computations that demonstrate the existence of an error or irregularity.

Answer (C) is correct. *(CIA, adapted)*
    REQUIRED: The example of documentary information.
    DISCUSSION: Documentary information exists in some permanent form, such as checks, invoices, shipping records, receiving reports, and purchase orders. It includes both external information, e.g., shipping documents provided by carriers, and documents originating within the engagement client's organization.
    Answer (A) is incorrect because photographic information is physical. Answer (B) is incorrect because statements received in response to inquiries or interviews are testimonial. Answer (D) is incorrect because the study and comparison of relationships among data results in analytical information.

42. During an engagement to review the personnel function, an internal auditor notes that there are several employee benefit programs and that participation in some of the programs is optional. Which of the following is the best information for assessing the acceptability of various benefit programs to employees?

    A. Discuss satisfaction levels with program participants.

    B. Evaluate program participation ratios and their trends.

    C. Discuss satisfaction levels with the director of personnel.

    D. Evaluate methods used to make employees aware of available program options.

Answer (B) is correct. *(CIA, adapted)*
    REQUIRED: The best information for assessing the acceptability of various benefit programs to employees.
    DISCUSSION: Analytical information obtained by determining employee participation in optional programs is the most persuasive. Actual participation requires an affirmative act that strongly suggests a positive employee evaluation of a program.
    Answer (A) is incorrect because responses from participants do not include testimony by nonparticipants. Answer (C) is incorrect because employee participation ratios are more persuasive than the personnel director's testimony about employee satisfaction. Answer (D) is incorrect because the effectiveness of the means of communicating information about the programs is not relevant to employee satisfaction.

43. In an engagement to review travel expenses, the internal auditor calculates average expenses per day traveled for all sales personnel and then examines detailed receipts for those with high averages. These procedures represent the identification of which types of information?

    A. Documentary and physical.

    B. Analytical and physical.

    C. Documentary and analytical.

    D. Physical and testimonial.

Answer (C) is correct. *(CIA, adapted)*
    REQUIRED: The types of engagement information.
    DISCUSSION: The categories of Information include physical, testimonial, documentary, and analytical. Physical information is obtained by observing people, property, and events. Testimonial information consists of letters or statements in response to inquiries or interviews. Documentary information includes accounting records, outgoing correspondence, receiving reports, etc. Analytical information results from analysis and verification and includes computations and comparisons. The travel expense receipts are documentary information. The calculations of average travel expenses are analytical information. Neither physical information nor testimonial information is involved.

1.6 Procedures

44. Of the following, the information collected by the internal auditor during an engagement is best described as

    A. The records of preliminary planning and surveys, the engagement work program, and the results of fieldwork.

    B. The information documented by the internal auditor and obtained through observing conditions, interviewing people, and examining records.

    C. An intermediate fact, or group of facts, from which the internal auditor can infer the fairness of an assertion being reviewed.

    D. Detailed documentation for systems that do not achieve desired objectives, actions that were taken improperly, and actions that should have been taken but were not.

Answer (B) is correct. *(CIA, adapted)*
    REQUIRED: The best description of audit evidence.
    DISCUSSION: Internal auditors should identify, analyze, evaluate, and record document sufficient information to achieve the engagement's objectives. This process requires performing such procedures as (1) interviewing to obtain testimonial information, (2) observing conditions to obtain physical information, and (3) examining records to obtain documentary information.
    Answer (A) is incorrect because the records of preliminary planning and surveys, the engagement work program, and the results of fieldwork are the working papers. The records of preliminary planning, for example, do not constitute engagement information. Answer (C) is incorrect because an intermediate fact, or group of facts, from which the internal auditor can infer the fairness of an assertion being reviewed is a modified definition of circumstantial evidence. This definition excludes direct evidence. Answer (D) is incorrect because information collected to achieve engagement objectives underlies positive, as well as negative, observations.

45. An internal auditor has set an engagement objective of identifying the existence of personality conflicts that are detrimental to productivity. Which of the following engagement techniques will best meet this objective?

    A. Inspection of documents.

    B. Observation.

    C. Inquiry.

    D. Analytical review.

Answer (C) is correct. *(CIA, adapted)*
    REQUIRED: The engagement technique that meets the engagement objective of identifying the existence of personality conflicts that are detrimental to productivity.
    DISCUSSION: By interviewing selected individuals about the causes of inefficiencies, the internal auditor can expect to obtain input as to the existence and seriousness of personality conflicts that inhibit efficient and effective work.

46. An internal auditor has set an engagement objective of determining whether mail room staff is fully used. Which of the following engagement techniques will best meet this objective?

    A. Inspection of documents.

    B. Observation.

    C. Inquiry.

    D. Analytical review.

Answer (B) is correct. *(CIA, adapted)*
    REQUIRED: The engagement technique to meet the engagement objective of determining whether mail room staff is fully used.
    DISCUSSION: By observing mail room operations at various times on various days of the week, the internal auditor can note whether incoming or outgoing mail backlogs exist and whether mail room staff are busy on mail room activities, idle, or working on other projects.

47. An internal auditor observes that controls over the perpetual inventory system are weak. An appropriate engagement response is to

A. Increase the testing of the inventory controls.

B. Perform turnover ratio tests.

C. Recommend that a physical inventory count be scheduled.

D. Apply gross profit analyses by product lines and compare the results with prior-years' information for reasonableness.

Answer (C) is correct. *(CIA, adapted)*
REQUIRED: The appropriate engagement response when controls over the perpetual inventory system are weak.
DISCUSSION: Observation of a physical inventory is ordinarily the most effective engagement procedure. The internal auditor's direct personal knowledge obtained through observation is more persuasive than information obtained indirectly.
Answer (A) is incorrect because, if the internal auditor's assessed control risk is unreasonably high, testing controls may be inefficient. Answer (B) is incorrect because turnover ratio tests will not provide sufficient information. Answer (D) is incorrect because applying gross profit analyses by product lines and comparing the results with prior-years' information for reasonableness will not provide sufficient information.

48. Which technique is most appropriate for testing the quality of the preliminary survey of payment vouchers described in an internal control questionnaire?

A. Analysis.

B. Evaluation.

C. Verification.

D. Observation.

Answer (C) is correct. *(CIA, adapted)*
REQUIRED: The technique most appropriate for testing the quality of the preliminary survey of payment vouchers described in an internal control questionnaire.
DISCUSSION: Verification is a broad term for the process of determining the truth of previously provided information. It is an intentional effort to establish factual validity. Verification includes corroboration, comparison, and confirmation.
Answer (A) is incorrect because analysis involves examining the interrelationships among data. Answer (B) is incorrect because evaluation involves an estimation of worth and the reaching of conclusions. It would not be appropriate for the yes and no responses of an ICQ. Answer (D) is incorrect because observation is a means of identifying physical information.

49. Which of the substantive fieldwork procedures presented below provides the best information about completeness of recorded revenues?

A. Reconciling the sales journal to the general ledger control account.

B. Vouching charges made to the accounts receivable subsidiary ledger to supporting shipping records.

C. Vouching shipping records to the customer order file.

D. Reconciling shipping records to recorded sales.

Answer (D) is correct. *(CIA, adapted)*
REQUIRED: The procedure that provides the best information about completeness of recorded revenues.
DISCUSSION: The completeness assertion concerns whether all transactions that should be presented are included. To test this assertion with regard to revenues from sales of goods shipped, the internal auditor might trace shipping documents to sales data to determine whether items shipped have been recorded as revenues.
Answer (A) is incorrect because reconciling the sales journal to the general ledger control account would fail to detect unrecorded sales, which would result in no entries to the sales journal or accounts receivable. Answer (B) is incorrect because vouching charges made to the accounts receivable subsidiary ledger to supporting shipping records would fail to detect unrecorded sales, which would result in no entries to the sales journal or accounts receivable. Answer (C) is incorrect because vouching shipping records to the customer order file merely establishes that goods shipped were ordered, not that they were recorded as sales.

50. Confirmations are a highly regarded form of information. Confirmation is most effective in addressing the existence assertion for the

A. Addition of a milling machine to a machine shop.

B. Sale of merchandise during regular course of business.

C. Inventory held on consignment.

D. Granting of a patent for a special process developed by the organization.

Answer (C) is correct. *(CIA, adapted)*
REQUIRED: The circumstance in which confirmation is most effective in addressing the existence assertion.
DISCUSSION: When inventories are held by an outside custodian, such as a consignee, the internal auditor ordinarily obtains direct confirmation in writing from the custodian. Confirmation of consigned goods is most likely to be effective for the existence and rights-and-obligations assertions.
Answer (A) is incorrect because observation and documentation are the most common forms of information for asset additions. Answer (B) is incorrect because account balances but not individual sales transactions are normally confirmed. Answer (D) is incorrect because an examination of the patent document is the best information.

51. One engagement procedure for an engagement to evaluate facilities and equipment is to test the accuracy of recorded depreciation. Which of the following is the best source of information that the equipment in question is in service?

- A. A review of depreciation policies and procedures.

- B. A comparison of depreciation schedules with a listing of insurance appraisals for the same equipment.

- C. A comparison of depreciation schedules with the maintenance and repair logs for the same equipment.

- D. A review of inventory documentation for the equipment.

Answer (C) is correct. *(CIA, adapted)*
REQUIRED: The best source of information that the equipment in question is in service.
DISCUSSION: The maintenance and repair records provide information that equipment exists and is in use. Equipment in service is more likely to require maintenance than retired equipment. However, the best information is the internal auditor's direct observation.
Answer (A) is incorrect because a review of policies and procedures provides no information about the existence assertion for specific assets. Answer (B) is incorrect because a comparison with current insurance records would be inconclusive. Retired equipment could still be insured. Answer (D) is incorrect because retired equipment could still be in the inventory.

52. Which of the following documents provides the most persuasive information concerning the existence and valuation of a receivable?

- A. A credit approval document supported by the customer's audited financial statements.

- B. A copy of a sales invoice to the customer in the engagement client's records.

- C. A positive confirmation received directly from the customer.

- D. A customer's purchase order in the engagement client's records related to the credit sale.

Answer (C) is correct. *(CIA, adapted)*
REQUIRED: The most persuasive information concerning the existence and valuation of a receivable.
DISCUSSION: A positive confirmation by the debtor is the most reliable information other than payment that the receivable is a valid asset and that it is properly valued. This information is especially reliable because the customer has no incentive to confirm a nonexisting obligation and because the documentation has not been under the engagement client's control.
Answer (A) is incorrect because a credit approval document is documentary information in the hands of the engagement client and does not relate directly to the receivable. Answer (B) is incorrect because a copy of a sales invoice to the customer in the engagement client's records is not original and is controlled by the engagement client. Answer (D) is incorrect because, although purchase orders are originated by third parties, the engagement client has an opportunity to alter them.

53. A bank internal auditor wanted to verify the accuracy of the general ledger balance of a depository account. One engagement procedure used in this process was to mail positive confirmations to statistically sampled depositors. However, the number of replies received was not adequate to form a valid conclusion about the account's accuracy. What action should the internal auditor take to accomplish this objective?

- A. Assume that the nonreplies represent tacit agreements by the depositor, document the results, and perform no further work on this engagement procedure.

- B. Expand the original confirmation sample to include additional depositors.

- C. Verify accuracy of the depositors' addresses. Remail confirmation requests a second time with a notation indicating that it is a second request.

- D. Mail negative confirmation requests to all non-replies and document results of testing. If necessary, telephone depositors to inquire about any disagreement with balances confirmed.

Answer (C) is correct. *(CIA, adapted)*
REQUIRED: The action an internal auditor should take when an inadequate number of responses are received in reply to positive confirmation requests.
DISCUSSION: A positive confirmation asks the debtor for a reply. It may ask the respondent to state whether (s)he agrees with the information given or request that the recipient fill in the account balance or provide other information. The latter type of positive confirmation is called a blank form. The negative confirmation asks for a response only when the debtor disagrees. Positive confirmation is therefore useful when an internal auditor wants to obtain documentary information to verify account balances. If the internal auditor fails to receive positive confirmation, alternative procedures including second and third requests should be employed.
Answer (A) is incorrect because the form of the request specifically asks for a reply. Thus, nonreplies provide no assurance, and alternative procedures are necessary.
Answer (B) is incorrect because expanding the sample will result in more responses but will not address the issue of the nonreplies, which are likely to occur at approximately the same rate in the larger sample. Answer (D) is incorrect because negative confirmations require no reply. Hence, they serve no purpose with respect to depositors not responding to the original confirmation requests.

54. Which of the following statements describes an internal control questionnaire?

   A. It provides detailed information regarding the substance of the control system.

   B. It takes less of the engagement client's time to complete than other control evaluation devices.

   C. It requires that the internal auditor be in attendance to properly administer it.

   D. It provides indirect information that might need corroboration.

Answer (D) is correct. *(CIA, adapted)*

REQUIRED: The statement that describes an internal control questionnaire.

DISCUSSION: An internal control questionnaire consists of a series of questions about the controls designed to prevent or detect errors or irregularities. Answers to the questions help the internal auditor to identify specific policies and procedures relevant to specific assertions. They also help in the design of tests of controls to evaluate their effectiveness. The questionnaire provides a framework to assure that specific concerns are not overlooked, but it is not a sufficient means of understanding the entire system. Thus, the evidence obtained is indirect and requires corroboration by means of observation, interviews, flowcharting, examination of documents, etc.

Answer (A) is incorrect because questionnaires usually provide for yes/no responses and therefore provide less detailed information than some other procedures. Answer (B) is incorrect because questionnaires tend to be lengthy, and their completion is time-consuming. Answer (C) is incorrect because an auditor need not be present.

55. During interviews with the inventory management personnel, an internal auditor learned that salespersons often order inventory for stock without receiving the approval of the vice president of sales. Also, detail testing showed that there are no written approvals on purchase orders for replacement parts. The results of detail testing are a good example of

   A. Indirect information.

   B. Circumstantial information.

   C. Corroborative information.

   D. Subjective information.

Answer (C) is correct. *(CIA, adapted)*

REQUIRED: The information obtained from detail testing.

DISCUSSION: Corroborative information is evidence from a different source that supplements and confirms other information. For example, oral testimony that a certain procedure was not performed may be corroborated by the absence of documentation.

Answer (A) is incorrect because detail testing provides direct information that the approvals were not received. Indirect information establishes immediately related facts from which the main fact may be inferred. Answer (B) is incorrect because circumstantial information tends to prove a fact by proving other events or circumstances that afford a basis for a reasonable inference of the occurrence of the fact. Thus, it is also indirect information. Answer (D) is incorrect because subjective information is opinion-oriented and is not dependable for reaching engagement conclusions. No subjective information is present in this situation.

1.7 Degree of Persuasiveness

56. Which of the following types of tests is the most persuasive if an internal auditor wants assurance of the existence of inventory stored in a warehouse?

   A. Examining the shipping documents that support recorded transfers to and from the warehouse.

   B. Obtaining written confirmation from management.

   C. Physically observing the inventory in the warehouse.

   D. Examining warehouse receipts contained in the engagement client's records.

Answer (C) is correct. *(CIA, adapted)*

REQUIRED: The most persuasive type of test if an internal auditor wants assurance of the existence of inventory stored in a warehouse.

DISCUSSION: Direct knowledge obtained through the internal auditor's physical observation is the most reliable information about the existence of the inventory. Reliable information is competent and best attainable through appropriate engagement techniques (PA 2310-1).

Answer (A) is incorrect because shipping documents are not as reliable as personal knowledge. Answer (B) is incorrect because testimonial information is not as reliable as personal knowledge. Answer (D) is incorrect because warehouse receipts are not as reliable as personal knowledge.

57. Documents provide information with differing degrees of persuasiveness. If the engagement objective is to obtain information that payment has actually been made for a specific invoice from a vendor, which of the following documents ordinarily is the most persuasive?

A. An entry in the engagement client's cash disbursements journal supported by a voucher package containing the vendor's invoice.

B. A canceled check, made out to the vendor and referenced to the invoice, included in a cutoff bank statement that the internal auditor received directly from the bank.

C. An accounts payable subsidiary ledger that shows payment of the invoice.

D. A vendor's original invoice stamped "PAID" and referenced to a check number.

Answer (B) is correct. *(CIA, adapted)*
REQUIRED: The most persuasive information that payment has actually been made for a specific invoice from a vendor.
DISCUSSION: A canceled check included in a cutoff bank statement received directly from the bank provides external as well as internal documentary information. The information was generated internally but passed through outsiders who confirmed it (honored the check) before sending it directly to the internal auditor. Such information is very persuasive.
Answer (A) is incorrect because the engagement client either has initiated or had an opportunity to alter the voucher and the invoice. Answer (C) is incorrect because internal information is less persuasive than external information. Answer (D) is incorrect because the invoice is external information of debt but not of payment. The information concerning payment is internal and not persuasive. A reference to a check is not as reliable as the check itself.

58. An internal auditor at a savings and loan association concludes that a secured real estate loan is collectible. Which of the following engagement procedures provides the most persuasive information about the loan's collectibility?

A. Confirming the loan balance with the borrower.

B. Reviewing the loan file for proper authorization by the credit committee.

C. Examining documentation of a recent, independent appraisal of the real estate.

D. Examining the loan application for appropriate borrowers' signatures.

Answer (C) is correct. *(CIA, adapted)*
REQUIRED: The most persuasive information about the loan's collectibility.
DISCUSSION: Real estate appraisals are based on estimated resale value or future cash flows. A recent, independent appraisal provides information about the borrower's ability to repay the loan. Such an appraisal tends to be reasonably reliable because it is timely and derives from an expert source independent of the engagement client.
Answer (A) is incorrect because a confirmation provides information about a loan's existence, not its collectibility. Answer (B) is incorrect because information about the loan's authorization is not relevant to its collectibility. Answer (D) is incorrect because the validity of the loan is not relevant to the borrower's ability to repay the loan.

59. The most persuasive information about the existence of newly acquired computers for the sales department is

A. Inquiry of management.

B. Observation of engagement client's procedures.

C. Physical examination.

D. Documentation prepared externally.

Answer (C) is correct. *(CIA, adapted)*
REQUIRED: The most persuasive information about the existence of newly acquired computers.
DISCUSSION: Information is considered more or less persuasive depending on the engagement client's degree of control. The following is a hierarchy from most persuasive to least persuasive: internal auditor's examination and observation, externally developed information, internally developed information, and oral information from the client. Thus, the most persuasive information about the existence assertion for a new asset is physical examination.
Answer (A) is incorrect because an unsubstantiated response to an inquiry of management is usually considered the least persuasive information. Answer (B) is incorrect because observation of procedures for acquisition would not be as persuasive as examination of the asset. Answer (D) is incorrect because documentation is less relevant to the existence assertion than physical examination.

60. The most persuasive information regarding the asset value of newly acquired computers is

   A. Inquiry of management.

   B. Observation of engagement client's procedures.

   C. Physical examination.

   D. Documentation prepared externally.

Answer (D) is correct. *(CIA, adapted)*
   REQUIRED: The most persuasive information regarding asset value.
   DISCUSSION: Information is considered more or less persuasive depending on how much control the engagement client has over it. The most persuasive information relevant to the valuation assertion is documentation that is prepared externally.
   Answer (A) is incorrect because an unsubstantiated response to an inquiry of management ordinarily yields the least persuasive information. Answer (B) is incorrect because observation of procedures for acquisition would not be as persuasive as documents showing the cost of the asset. Answer (C) is incorrect because physical examination of the asset reveals only limited information as to the asset's value.

61. Which of the following represents the general order of persuasiveness, from most to least, for the types of information listed below:

  I.   Inquiry of management
  II. Observation of engagement client's procedures
  III. Physical examination
  IV. Documentation prepared externally

   A. III, IV, II, I.

   B. IV, I, II, III.

   C. II, IV, I, III.

   D. IV, III, I, II.

Answer (A) is correct. *(CIA, adapted)*
   REQUIRED: The list representing the general order of persuasiveness of information.
   DISCUSSION: The reliability (competence) of information is ordinarily presumed to be greater when it is obtained from independent sources outside the engagement client, internal control is effective, or the information derives from the internal auditor's direct personal knowledge. Information obtained through reliance on the engagement client is less valid and more likely to need corroboration. Hence, the following hierarchy from most persuasive to least persuasive information is consistent with the foregoing presumptions: internal auditor's examination and observation, externally developed information, internally developed information, and oral information from the client.

1.8 Recording Information

62. Which of the following does **not** describe one of the functions of engagement working papers?

   A. Facilitates third-party reviews.

   B. Aids in the planning, performance, and review of engagements.

   C. Provides the principal support for engagement communications.

   D. Aids in the professional development of the operating staff.

Answer (D) is correct. *(CIA, adapted)*
   REQUIRED: The response that does not describe one of the functions of engagement working papers.
   DISCUSSION: Working papers provide the principal support for the engagement communications; aid in planning, performing, and reviewing the engagement; document whether engagement objectives were achieved; facilitate third-party review; provide a basis for evaluating the internal audit activity's quality program; aid in the professional development of the internal auditing (not operating) staff; provide support in the event of fraud, litigation, insurance claims, etc.; and demonstrate compliance with the SPPIA (PA 2330-1).
   Answer (A) is incorrect because the facilitation of third-party reviews is a function of working papers. Answer (B) is incorrect because working papers aid in the planning, performance, and review of engagements. Answer (C) is incorrect because working papers provide the principal support for communications.

63. A working paper is complete when it

   A. Complies with the internal audit activity's format requirements.

   B. Contains all of the attributes of an observation.

   C. Is clear, concise, and accurate.

   D. Satisfies the engagement objective for which it is developed.

Answer (D) is correct. *(CIA, adapted)*
   REQUIRED: The standard for completion of a working paper.
   DISCUSSION: Working papers provide the principal support for engagement communications. They are the documentation of the engagement activities. They record the information obtained and the analyses made and should support the bases for the observations, conclusions, and recommendations to be communicated (PA 2330-1).
   Answer (A) is incorrect because format requirements are superficial and indicate only that mechanical requirements have been met. They do not relate to content. Answer (B) is incorrect because a working paper may relate to only a part of an observation. Answer (C) is incorrect because clarity, conciseness, and accuracy are desirable characteristics of working paper content. These qualities may be present although the working paper is not complete.

64. The primary purpose of an internal auditor's working papers is to

A. Provide documentation of the planning and execution of engagement procedures performed.

B. Serve as a means with which to prepare the financial statements.

C. Document weaknesses in internal control with recommendations to management for improvement.

D. Comply with the Standards.

Answer (A) is correct. *(CIA, adapted)*
REQUIRED: The primary purpose of an internal auditor's working papers.
DISCUSSION: Working papers provide the principal support for the engagement communications; aid in planning, performing, and reviewing the engagement; document whether engagement objectives were achieved; facilitate third-party review; provide a basis for evaluating the internal audit activity's quality program; aid in the professional development of the internal auditing staff; provide support in the event of fraud, litigation, insurance claims, etc.; and demonstrate compliance with the SPPIA (PA 2330-1).
Answer (B) is incorrect because working papers do not provide the means for preparation of the financial statements. Answer (C) is incorrect because documentation of control weaknesses is only one example of working paper content, not the primary purpose for them. Answer (D) is incorrect because the preparation of adequate working papers is a requirement of the Standards but not the primary purpose for their existence.

65. Which of the following is the most important if working papers are to have the characteristics that will ensure that they achieve their primary purposes?

A. Working papers must be of standard format and standard content.

B. Working papers must be properly indexed and cross-referenced to the draft final engagement communication.

C. Working papers must provide sufficient, reliable, and useful information to support the final engagement communication.

D. Working papers must be arranged in logical order following the engagement work program sequence.

Answer (C) is correct. *(CIA, adapted)*
REQUIRED: The most important characteristic of working papers.
DISCUSSION: Working papers that document the engagement should be prepared by the internal auditor and reviewed by management of the internal audit activity. They should record the information obtained and the analyses made and should support the bases for the observations, conclusions, and recommendations to be communicated (PA 2330-1). Information should be sufficient, reliable, relevant, and useful to achieve the engagement's objectives (Standard 2310).
Answer (A) is incorrect because standard content is impossible. Engagements concern different subjects. Answer (B) is incorrect because indexing and cross-referencing are desirable but not as fundamental as providing sufficient, reliable, relevant, and useful information. Answer (D) is incorrect because logical order is desirable but not as fundamental as providing sufficient, reliable, relevant, and useful information.

66. The primary purpose of an engagement working paper prepared in connection with payroll expense is to

A. Record payroll data and analyses to support reported recommendations.

B. Verify the work done by the internal auditor.

C. Record the names of all employees.

D. Provide documentation to support payroll taxes due.

Answer (A) is correct. *(CIA, adapted)*
REQUIRED: The primary purpose of an engagement working paper prepared in connection with payroll expense.
DISCUSSION: Working papers that document the engagement should be prepared by the internal auditor and reviewed by management of the internal audit activity. They should record the information obtained and the analyses made and should support the bases for the observations, conclusions, and recommendations to be communicated (PA 2330-1).
Answer (B) is incorrect because verification of work done is a secondary purpose. Answer (C) is incorrect because a list of employee names is but one part of the information required to support observations, conclusions, and recommendations. Answer (D) is incorrect because payroll expense, not payroll tax, is the subject of this working paper.

67. An internal auditor prepared a working paper that consisted of a list of employee names and identification numbers as well as the following statement:

> By matching random numbers with employee identification numbers, 40 employee personnel files were selected to verify that they contain all documents required by the organization's policy 501. No exceptions were noted.

The internal auditor did not place any tick marks on this working paper. Which one of the following changes will improve the internal auditor's working paper the most?

A. Use of tick marks to show that each file was examined.

B. Removal of the employee names to protect their confidentiality.

C. Justification for the sample size.

D. Listing of the actual documents examined for each employee.

Answer (C) is correct. *(CIA, adapted)*
REQUIRED: The change that will most improve the working paper.
DISCUSSION: The working paper should fully document the use of statistical techniques. Thus, it should specify how the sample size for this attribute sampling application was determined. Factors affecting the sample size are the degree of sampling risk (confidence level), the allowance for sampling risk (precision), and the expected error rate.
Answer (A) is incorrect because tick marks are not necessary. The same procedures were applied to all sample items, and no exceptions were detected. Answer (B) is incorrect because working papers are kept confidential, so removal of employee names is unnecessary. Answer (D) is incorrect because reference to the organization's policy is equivalent to listing the documents examined.

68. Productivity statistics are provided quarterly to the board of directors. An internal auditor checked the ratios and other statistics in the four most recent reports. The internal auditor used scratch paper and copies of the reports to verify the accuracy of computations and compared the data used in the computations with supporting documents. The internal auditor wrote a note for the working papers describing these procedures and then discarded the scratch paper and report copies. The note stated,

> The ratios and other statistics in the quarterly reports to the board were checked for the last 4 quarters and appropriate supporting documents were examined. All amounts appear to be appropriate.

In this situation,

A. Four quarters do not provide a large enough sample on which to base a conclusion,

B. The internal auditor's working papers are not sufficient to facilitate an efficient review of the internal auditor's work.

C. The internal auditor should have included the scratch paper in the working papers.

D. The internal auditor did not consider whether the information in the report to the board was compiled efficiently.

Answer (B) is correct. *(CIA, adapted)*
REQUIRED: The true statement about the internal auditor's verification of quarterly statistics.
DISCUSSION: The internal auditor's working papers do not support the conclusions and engagement results because they do not document the procedures and the information obtained. A reviewer cannot check the internal auditor's work without obtaining additional copies of the quarterly reports and independently recalculating the statistics. The review would be more efficient if the internal auditor had included the graphs in the working papers and had used tick marks with explanations to show which computations were checked and to describe what the internal auditor did to verify the amounts used in the computations.
Answer (A) is incorrect because the problem did not state or imply that sampling was used. Answer (C) is incorrect because scratch papers are usually not suitable for working papers. Unorganized working papers are difficult to review and understand. Answer (D) is incorrect because the problem did not state or imply that an objective of the engagement was to evaluate efficiency.

69. Engagement working papers should include

A. Documentation of the examination and evaluation of the adequacy and effectiveness of the system of internal control.

B. Copies of all source documents examined in the course of the engagement.

C. Copies of all procedures that were reviewed during the engagement.

D. All working papers prepared during a previous engagement performed in the same area.

Answer (A) is correct.   *(CIA, adapted)*
   REQUIRED: The content of working papers.
   DISCUSSION: Working papers document planning; the examination and evaluation of the adequacy and effectiveness of the system of internal control; the procedures performed, the information obtained, and the conclusions reached; review; communicating; and follow-up (PA 2330-1).
   Answer (B) is incorrect because many documents may be examined that prove to be irrelevant to the engagement objectives. These documents need not be included. Answer (C) is incorrect because, in many circumstances, the exact wording of a procedure is not needed to support an observation or recommendation. A reference to the procedure in the working papers may be adequate. Answer (D) is incorrect because some previous working papers may be outdated. However, parts of previous working papers may be included in current working papers subject to updating.

70. Which of the following is an unnecessary feature of a working paper prepared in connection with maintenance costs?

A. The internal auditor has initialed and dated the working paper as of the date completed even though the working paper was prepared over the preceding 4 working days.

B. Total repair expense for the month preceding the engagement is shown.

C. The chief audit executive has initialed the working paper as reviewer although the working paper was prepared by another person.

D. Total acquisition cost of property, plant, and equipment for the preceding month is shown.

Answer (D) is correct.   *(CIA, adapted)*
   REQUIRED: The unnecessary feature of a working paper concerning maintenance costs.
   DISCUSSION: Because total acquisition cost of property, plant, and equipment is irrelevant to maintenance costs, this feature is unnecessary to support the observations, conclusions, and recommendations concerning these costs.
   Answer (A) is incorrect because the date of completion and signature or initials of the internal auditor are important for control of the engagement. Answer (B) is incorrect because the working papers concern maintenance cost, and the amount for the month preceding the engagement is necessary for subsequent period review. Answer (C) is incorrect because working papers that document the engagement should be prepared by the internal auditor and reviewed by management of the internal audit activity.

71. Each individual working paper should, at a minimum, contain

A. An expression of the internal auditor's overall opinion.

B. A tick mark legend.

C. A complete flowchart of the system of internal controls for the area being reviewed.

D. A descriptive heading.

Answer (D) is correct.   *(CIA, adapted)*
   REQUIRED: The minimum content of each working paper.
   DISCUSSION: Each working paper should identify the engagement and describe the contents or purpose of the working paper, for example, in the heading. Also, each working paper should be signed (initialed) and dated by the internal auditor and contain an index or reference number. Furthermore, verification symbols (tick marks) are likely to appear on most working papers and should be explained (PA 2330-1).
   Answer (A) is incorrect because an expression of an opinion in the working papers is premature and an indicator of bias. Answer (B) is incorrect because a tick mark legend should not appear on each working paper. Answer (C) is incorrect because a flowchart of internal controls will likely be included in a working paper at the beginning of a significant engagement segment, but each working paper will not contain a flowchart.

72. The chief audit executive should establish policies for

- A. Indexing and the type of working-paper files maintained.
- B. Defining the hours available for individual engagements.
- C. Defining standardized tick marks and ensuring compliance with them.
- D. Ensuring the written documentation of all conversations held throughout the engagement.

Answer (A) is correct. *(CIA, adapted)*
REQUIRED: The policies to be established by the CAE.
DISCUSSION: The CAE should establish working-paper policies for the types of engagements performed. Among the issues are the use of standardized working papers, the designation of permanent files, indexing, and other related matters. For example, standardized working papers, such as questionnaires and engagement work programs, may improve the efficiency of an engagement and facilitate the delegation of engagement work (PA 2330-1).
Answer (B) is incorrect because the time devoted to an engagement depends on its complexity and other unique circumstances. Answer (C) is incorrect because defining standardized tick marks and ensuring compliance with them is not required. Answer (D) is incorrect because only conversations relevant to the engagement must be documented.

73. Engagement working papers are indexed by means of reference numbers. The primary purpose of indexing is to

- A. Permit cross-referencing and simplify supervisory review.
- B. Support the final engagement communication.
- C. Eliminate the need for follow-up reviews.
- D. Determine that working papers adequately support observations, conclusions, and recommendations.

Answer (A) is correct. *(CIA, adapted)*
REQUIRED: The primary purpose of indexing.
DISCUSSION: Indexing permits cross-referencing, which is important because it simplifies supervisory review either during the engagement or subsequently by creating a trail of related items through the working papers. It thus facilitates preparation of the final engagement communication, later engagements for the same engagement client, and internal and external assessments of the internal audit activity.
Answer (B) is incorrect because the working papers as a whole should support the final engagement communication. Answer (C) is incorrect because follow-up is necessitated by engagement client conditions, not the state of working papers. Answer (D) is incorrect because the purpose of supervisory review of working papers is to determine that working papers adequately support observations, conclusions, and recommendations.

74. When engagement conclusions are challenged, the internal auditor's factual rebuttal is best facilitated by

- A. Summaries in the engagement work program.
- B. Pro forma working papers.
- C. Cross-referencing of the working papers.
- D. Explicit procedures in the engagement work program.

Answer (C) is correct. *(CIA, adapted)*
REQUIRED: The best means of facilitating factual rebuttal when engagement conclusions are challenged.
DISCUSSION: Each working paper should have an index or reference number. Indexing permits cross-referencing, which simplifies supervisory review either during the engagement or subsequently by creating an information trail of related items through the working papers. It thus facilitates preparation of the final engagement communication, later engagements involving the same client, internal and external quality assessments, and factual rebuttal of challenges by clearly identifying sources and locations of facts.

75. Which type of working-paper summary is typically used to consolidate numerical data scattered among several schedules?

- A. Statistical summaries.
- B. Segment summaries.
- C. Results summaries.
- D. Pyramid summaries.

Answer (A) is correct. *(CIA, adapted)*
REQUIRED: The type of working-paper summary used to consolidate numerical data scattered among several schedules.
DISCUSSION: Summarization of facts in the working papers is a means of emphasizing important information, establishing perspective, providing an overview, aiding memory, training staff, facilitating supervisory review, and controlling engagements. By the use of indexing and cross-referencing, summaries may be used to relate different working papers that concern a given point. A statistical summary condenses the related numerical information from engagement work programs.
Answer (B) is incorrect because a segment summary is a narrative with respect to a particular part of the engagement. It should appear at the beginning of each section of the working papers, which should be organized logically according to the different objectives of the engagement. Answer (C) is incorrect because a results summary provides the significant facts about engagement observations. Answer (D) is incorrect because the term "pyramid summaries" is not meaningful in this context.

Questions 76 and 77 are based on the following information.

XYZ
Bank Reconciliation
June 30, Year 1
(Amounts in currency units)

Balance per bank (a)		16,482.97
Deposits in transit (b)		
6/29	2,561.14	
6/30	1,572.28	4,133.42
Subtotal		20,616.39
Outstanding checks (c)		
248	842.11	
952	2,000.00	
968	571.00	
969	459.82	
970	714.25	4,587.18
Subtotal		16,029.21
Bank service charge		12.50
NSF check returned (d)		350.00
Error on check #954		(14.00)
Balance per books (e)	To T/B	16,377.71

Legend:
(a) Confirmed with bank -- see confirmation on W/P A-4.
(b) Verified by tracing to July 15 cut-off statement; traced to cash receipts journal.
(c) Okay.
(d) Examined supporting documentation and traced to final disposition.
(e) Footed total and compared with balance in general ledger.

76. This working paper will be considered deficient if which other relevant engagement working paper is not cross-referenced and included in the cash section of the working-paper file?

A. Petty cash count.

B. Confirmation of cash balance with bank.

C. Copies of deposit slips for deposits in transit.

D. Engagement client representation that the cash balance per books was accurate.

Answer (B) is correct. *(CIA, adapted)*
REQUIRED: The working paper that should be cross-referenced and included in the cash section of the working-paper file.
DISCUSSION: Confirming the cash balance in the bank account as of the end of the period is a standard engagement procedure. It provides direct, externally generated information to support the reported cash amount.
Answer (A) is incorrect because petty cash is not relevant. This working paper concerns cash in the bank. Answer (C) is incorrect because, under ordinary circumstances, copies of deposit slips are not required as long as an adequate explanation of engagement procedures relative to deposits in transit is provided. Answer (D) is incorrect because the engagement client's representation is not relevant when outside confirmation and analysis of cash records supports the cash balance.

77. A deficiency in this working paper is that

A. A standardized cash reconciliation working paper was not used.

B. All verification symbols were not properly explained.

C. Analytical review procedures were not performed.

D. Cross-referencing of working papers was not accomplished.

Answer (B) is correct. *(CIA, adapted)*
REQUIRED: The deficiency in the working paper.
DISCUSSION: Each engagement working paper should contain a heading, which usually consists of the name of the client's organization or function, a title or description of the contents or purpose of the paper, and the date or period covered. Each working paper should be signed (initialed) and dated by the internal auditor and contain an index or reference number. Verification symbols (tick marks) are also likely to appear on most working papers and should be adequately explained in a note (PA 2330-1). In this example, the explanation for tick mark (c) does not detail the procedures used to review outstanding checks.
Answer (A) is incorrect because efficiency can be achieved through standardization; however, not every working paper can be standardized. This working paper may be subject to standardization but is not inadequate in that respect. Answer (C) is incorrect because analytical procedures are usually not as relevant to the examination of cash as to other assets and liabilities. Answer (D) is incorrect because cross-referencing was accomplished.

1.9 Review of Working Papers

78. Engagement working papers should be reviewed to ensure that

A. They are properly cross-referenced to the engagement communications.

B. No issues are open at the conclusion of the fieldwork.

C. They meet or exceed the work standards of the organization's external auditors.

D. They are properly referenced for easy follow-up within the next year.

Answer (B) is correct. *(CIA, adapted)*
REQUIRED: The purpose of reviewing engagement working papers.
DISCUSSION: All engagement working papers should be reviewed to ensure that they properly support the engagement communications and that all necessary engagement procedures have been performed (PA 2340-1). Thus, review is necessary to ensure the completeness of the work.
Answer (A) is incorrect because cross-referencing working papers to the engagement communications is not specifically addressed. Answer (C) is incorrect because whether working papers meet or exceed the work standards of the external auditors is not specifically addressed. Answer (D) is incorrect because proper referencing of working papers for easy follow-up within the next year is not specifically addressed.

79. An internal auditor's working papers should be reviewed by the

A. Management of the engagement client.

B. Management of the internal audit activity.

C. Audit committee of the board.

D. Management of the organization's security division.

Answer (B) is correct. *(CIA, adapted)*
REQUIRED: The proper reviewer of an internal auditor's working papers.
DISCUSSION: Working papers that document the engagement should be prepared by the internal auditor and reviewed by management of the internal audit activity. They should record the information obtained and the analyses made and should support the bases for the observations, conclusions, and recommendations to be communicated (PA 2330-1).
Answer (A) is incorrect because the engagement client should seldom see, much less review, working papers. Answer (C) is incorrect because the audit committee will most likely review summary communications, not working papers. Answer (D) is incorrect because management of the security division might be shown working papers relevant to an investigation but does not have the status of a reviewer.

80. Standardized working papers are often used, chiefly because they allow working papers to be prepared more

A. Efficiently.

B. Professionally.

C. Neatly.

D. Accurately.

Answer (A) is correct. *(CIA, adapted)*
REQUIRED: The reason for standardized working papers.
DISCUSSION: Use of standardized (pro forma) working papers improves engagement efficiency by diminishing the time spent in their preparation. For example, standard forms may be developed for the engagement work program listing, records of the results of interviews, and worksheets.
Answer (B) is incorrect because standard forms do not necessarily result in greater professionalism. Answer (C) is incorrect because standard forms clearly reduce time spent in working-paper preparation but do not necessarily result in greater neatness. Answer (D) is incorrect because standard forms do not necessarily result in greater accuracy.

81. When reviewing engagement working papers, the primary responsibility of an engagement supervisor is to determine that

A. Each worksheet is properly identified with a descriptive heading.

B. Working papers are properly referenced and kept in logical groupings.

C. Standard internal audit activity procedures are adhered to with regard to working paper preparation and technique.

D. Working papers adequately support the engagement observations, conclusions, and recommendations.

Answer (D) is correct. *(CIA, adapted)*
REQUIRED: The primary responsibility of an engagement supervisor when reviewing engagement working papers.
DISCUSSION: Engagement supervision includes reviewing all engagement working papers to ensure that they properly support engagement communications (PA 2340-1). Engagement communications include observations, conclusions, and recommendations. This review is of primary importance because nothing reduces the credibility of an IAA as much as ineptly developed engagement observations that collapse under attack. Descriptive headings, proper referencing, logical grouping, and adherence to procedures appropriate subjects for review, but they are not of primary importance.

82. Which of the following should be identified as a deficiency by an engagement supervisor who is reviewing working papers?

A. A memorandum recorded in the working papers explained why the time budget for a part of the engagement was exceeded.

B. A draft communication concerning an engagement observation recorded in the working papers omitted the criteria used for evaluation.

C. A memorandum recorded in the working papers explained why an engagement work program step was omitted.

D. A letter to the engagement client outlining the scope of the engagement was recorded in the working papers.

Answer (B) is correct. *(CIA, adapted)*
REQUIRED: The deficiency in working papers.
DISCUSSION: Engagement supervision includes reviewing all engagement working papers to ensure that they properly support engagement communications (PA 2340-1). Observations are included in engagement communications. According to PA 2410-1, observations have four attributes: criteria, condition, cause, and effect. Thus, omitting the criteria used in making an evaluation or verification results in a failure to support observations properly.

83. Which of the following actions constitutes a violation of the confidentiality concept regarding working papers? An internal auditor

A. Takes working papers to her hotel room overnight.

B. Shows working papers on occasion to engagement clients.

C. Allows the external auditor to copy working papers.

D. Misplaces working papers occasionally.

Answer (D) is correct. *(CIA, adapted)*
REQUIRED: The action violating the confidentiality concept regarding working papers.
DISCUSSION: Engagement records, such as working papers, are generally produced under the presumption that their contents are confidential and may contain a mix of both facts and opinions. Thus, each document should be labeled as confidential, and a notation should be placed on it prohibiting secondary distribution without permission (PA 2300.A1-2). Moreover, working papers should be protected by limiting access to appropriate personnel. During fieldwork, they should be in the internal auditor's physical possession or control or placed in a secure location. In the internal audit activity's office, they should be kept in locked files and formally signed out when removed. By misplacing working papers occasionally, the internal auditor is violating the confidentiality concept.
Answer (A) is incorrect because continuous physical control of working papers during fieldwork may be appropriate. Answer (B) is incorrect because engagement clients may be shown working papers with the CAE's approval. Answer (C) is incorrect because internal and external auditors commonly grant access to each others' work programs and working papers.

1.10 Control of Working Papers

84. A fire destroyed a large portion of an organization's inventory. Management is filing an insurance claim and needs to use the internal auditors' working papers in preparing the claim. Management

A. May not use the working papers in preparing the claim.

B. May use the working papers in preparing the claim, but such use should be approved by the chief audit executive.

C. Should be precluded from preparing the claim, and this function should be performed by the internal audit activity.

D. May use the working papers in preparing the claim, but such use should be approved by the organization's external auditors.

Answer (B) is correct. *(CIA, adapted)*
REQUIRED: The true statement about working-paper requests.
DISCUSSION: One potential use of engagement working papers is to provide support in circumstances such as insurance claims, fraud cases, and lawsuits (PA 2330-1). Management and other members of the organization may request access to engagement working papers. Such access may be necessary to substantiate or explain engagement observations and recommendations or to use engagement documentation for other business purposes. The CAE should approve these requests (PA 2330.A1-1). Accordingly, the insurance claim is an "other business purpose," and management may use the internal auditors' working papers in preparing the claim.
Answer (A) is incorrect because working papers may be used for "other business purposes." Answer (C) is incorrect because management, not the IAA, should prepare the insurance claim. Answer (D) is incorrect because the approval of external auditors is not needed.

85. Use of electronic working papers

    A. Does not comply with the Standards for supervisory review.

    B. Does not comply with the Standards for documentation criteria.

    C. Does not comply with the Standards for retention requirements.

    D. Raises unique issues, but their use is permitted under the Standards.

Answer (D) is correct. *(Publisher, adapted)*
    REQUIRED: The true statement about electronic working papers.
    DISCUSSION: The Standards apply to engagement records regardless of the form in which they are stored. The Standards encompass the use of traditional hard copy "paper" as well as other forms, such as tape, disk, diskette, films, or other media (PA 2330-1). Some unique issues are raised by the use of electronic working papers:

1. Electronic working papers and reviewer comments should be protected from unauthorized access and change.

2. Information recorded in working papers "scanned in" should have adequate control to ensure its continued integrity.

3. Working paper retention policies should consider changes made in the original operating system, other software, and hardware to ensure the continued retrievability of electronic working papers throughout the retention cycle.

    Answer (A) is incorrect because supervisory review may be facilitated by using electronic media. For example, electronic working papers may be viewed from remote sites. Answer (B) is incorrect because unique control issues exist, but electronic working papers permit more extensive documentation. Answer (C) is incorrect because electronic working papers permit more retentions of information.

86. The internal auditor is most likely to make working papers available to the engagement client when

    A. Fraud is suspected.

    B. The internal auditors have recorded specific damaging comments.

    C. The internal auditor considers the content noncontroversial.

    D. Engagement client comments are needed to evaluate significance and accuracy.

Answer (D) is correct. *(CIA, adapted)*
    REQUIRED: The instance in which the engagement client is most likely to have access to working papers.
    DISCUSSION: When the engagement objectives will not be compromised, the internal auditor may show all or part of the working papers to the engagement client. For instance, the results of certain engagement procedures may be shared with the engagement client to encourage corrective action. Thus, working papers as well as drafts of engagement communications may be reviewed with engagement clients to verify their accuracy, completeness, and significance. But complete disclosure may permit circumvention of the internal auditors' procedures, and working papers should never be shared with engagement clients in fraud investigations.
    Answer (A) is incorrect because working papers are never shown to engagement clients when their involvement in fraud is suspected. Answer (B) is incorrect because the working papers usually should not be shown to engagement clients when internal auditor-client relations might thereby be damaged or the engagement objectives compromised. Answer (C) is incorrect because access to noncontroversial matter may nevertheless permit circumvention of engagement procedures.

87. Working papers should be disposed of when they are of no further use. Retention policies should

    A. Specify a minimum retention period of 3 years.

    B. Be prepared by the audit committee.

    C. Be approved by legal counsel.

    D. Be approved by the external auditor.

Answer (C) is correct. *(CIA, adapted)*
    REQUIRED: The true statement about retention of working papers.
    DISCUSSION: The chief audit executive should develop retention requirements for engagement records. The retention requirements should be consistent with the organization's guidelines and any pertinent regulatory or other requirements (Standard 2330.A2). Thus, approval by the organization's legal counsel is appropriate.
    Answer (A) is incorrect because working papers should not be retained for an arbitrary period. The duration of retention should be a function of usefulness, including legal considerations. Answer (B) is incorrect because the CAE should develop retention policies. Answer (D) is incorrect because retention policies need not be approved by the external auditor.

88. When current-file working papers are no longer of use to the internal audit activity, they should be

A. Destroyed.

B. Placed in the custody of the organizational legal department for safekeeping.

C. Transferred to the permanent file.

D. Transferred to the custody of the engagement client for ease of future records.

Answer (A) is correct.   *(CIA, adapted)*
REQUIRED: The proper disposition of working papers that are no longer useful.
DISCUSSION: Retention schedules should be devised by the chief audit executive and approved by legal counsel to ensure compliance with regulatory or contract requirements. Working papers should be destroyed after they have served their purpose. Any parts having continuing value should be brought forward to current working papers or to the permanent file.
    Answer (B) is incorrect because, if working papers are useful, they should be controlled by the internal auditors. Answer (C) is incorrect because useless working papers should be destroyed. Answer (D) is incorrect because engagement clients should not have custody of confidential papers.

Use Gleim's *CIA Test Prep* for interactive testing with **over 2,000 additional multiple-choice questions**!

STUDY UNIT TWO
COMMUNICATING RESULTS AND
MONITORING PROGRESS

(28 pages of outline)

Communications and the results of monitoring progress are the output of the internal audit activity. These intermediate and final products provide **observations, conclusions, and recommendations** useful to engagement clients. Also, they are a basis for the evaluation of the internal audit activity by senior management and the board and are useful to external parties (auditors, regulatory agencies, and judicial authorities). Thus, communications should be drafted with **due professional care**.

Core Concepts

- Internal auditors should communicate engagement results.
- Communications should include the engagement's objectives and scope as well as applicable conclusions, recommendations, and action plans.
- Final communication of engagement results should, if appropriate, contain the internal auditor's overall opinion or conclusions.
- Communication of the progress and results of consulting engagements will vary in form and content depending on the nature of the engagement and the services requested.
- If a final communication contains a significant error or omission, the chief audit executive should communicate corrected information to all parties who received the original communication.
- When noncompliance with the Standards affects the engagement, the communication of results should disclose the Standard(s) with which compliance was not achieved, the reasons for noncompliance, and its effect.
- Internal auditors should be skilled in dealing with people and in oral and written communications.
- The chief audit executive should communicate results to the appropriate parties. These should include persons who can ensure that the results are given due consideration.
- When releasing results externally, the CAE should assess the risk to the organization, consult with senior management or legal counsel, and restrict use of the results.
- In consulting engagements, the CAE must communicate final results to clients. Significant risk management, control, and governance issues should be communicated to senior management and the board.
- The chief audit executive should establish and maintain a system to monitor the disposition of results communicated to management.
- The follow-up process should ensure that actions have been effectively implemented or that senior management has accepted the risk of inaction.
- The internal audit activity should monitor the disposition of results of consulting engagements to the extent agreed upon with the client.
- When the CAE believes that senior management has accepted a level of residual risk that may be unacceptable to the organization, the CAE should discuss the matter with senior management. If the decision regarding residual risk is not resolved, the CAE and senior management should report the matter to the board for resolution.

2.1 LEGAL CONSIDERATIONS

1. This subunit applies to the legal and regulatory issues that are often addressed in working papers and engagement communications. It consists of one General Performance Standard and one Practice Advisory.

2. **2400   *Communicating Results*** – *Internal auditors should communicate the engagement results.*

    a. ***Caution*** - *Internal auditors are encouraged to consult legal counsel in all matters involving legal issues as requirements may vary significantly in different jurisdictions.*

        PRACTICE ADVISORY 2400-1: *LEGAL CONSIDERATIONS IN COMMUNICATING RESULTS* (This guidance should be compared with that provided in Study Unit 1 by Practice Advisory 2330.A1-2: Legal Considerations in Granting Access to Engagement Records.)

        1. *Internal auditors should exercise caution when including **results** and issuing **opinions** in audit communications and workpapers regarding law and regulatory violations and other **legal issues**. Established **policies and procedures** regarding the handling of these matters and a **close working relationship** with other appropriate areas (legal counsel, compliance, etc.) is strongly encouraged.*

        2. *Internal auditors are required to gather evidence, make analytical judgments, report their results, and ensure corrective action is taken. The internal auditors' requirement for **documenting engagement records may conflict with legal counsel's desire not to leave evidence** that could be used against the organization in a legal proceeding. For example, even if an internal auditor conducts an investigation properly, the facts disclosed may harm the organization counsel's case. **Proper planning and policy making** is essential so that a sudden revelation does not place legal counsel and internal auditor at odds with one another. These policies should include **role definition** and **methods of communication**. The internal auditor and legal counsel should also foster an **ethical and preventive perspective** throughout the organization by sensitizing and educating management about the established policies. Internal auditors should consider the following, especially in connection with engagements that may give rise to disclosing or communicating results to **parties outside the organization**.*

        3. *Some jurisdictions recognize an **attorney-client privilege**. The typical elements of this privilege are*

            *   *a communication;*
            *   *made between privileged persons;*
            *   *in confidence; and*
            *   *for the purpose of seeking, obtaining, or providing legal assistance for the client.*

            *This privilege, which is used primarily to protect communications with attorneys, may also apply to communications with **third parties working with the attorney**.*

4.   *Some jurisdictions have recognized a privilege of **critical self-analysis** that shields self-critical materials, such as the internal auditors' work-product, from being used by an adverse party. In general, the recognition of this privilege is premised on the belief that the confidentiality of the reviews in the instances involved outweighs the valued public interests. As one court explained:*

> *The self-critical analysis privilege has been recognized as a qualified privilege that protects from discovery certain critical self-appraisals. It allows individuals or businesses to candidly assess their compliance with regulatory and legal requirements without creating evidence that may be used against them by their opponents in future litigation. The rationale for the doctrine is that such critical self-evaluation fosters the compelling public interest in observance of the law.*

5.   ***Three requirements** must usually be met for the privilege to apply:*

- *The information subject to the privilege must result from a self-critical analysis undertaken by the party asserting the privilege;*
- *The public must have a strong interest in preserving the free flow of the information contained in the critical analysis; and*
- *The information must be of the type whose flow would be curtailed if discovery were allowed.*

*In some instances, courts also have considered whether the critical analysis preceded or caused the plaintiff's injury. When the analysis comes **after the events giving rise to the claim**, the justification for the privilege is said to be at its strongest.*

6.   *The self-evaluative privilege is less likely to be available when the documents are sought by a **government agency** rather than a private litigant. Presumably, this reluctance results from recognition of the government's relatively stronger interest in enforcing the law. The self-evaluative privilege is particularly relevant to functions and activities that have **established self-regulatory procedures**. Hospitals, securities brokers, and accounting firms are among those that have established such procedures. Most of these procedures are associated with **quality assurance** procedures that have been added to an operating activity such as financial auditing.*

7.   *Some jurisdictions also recognize the **attorney work-product doctrine**. To be protected, documents must be:*

- *some type of work-product (i.e., memo, computer program);*
- *prepared in anticipation of litigation; and*
- *prepared by an agent of the attorney.*

8.   *Documents prepared **before the attorney-client relationship comes into existence** are generally not protected by the work-product doctrine. Delivering documents, prepared before the attorney-client relationship is formed, to the attorney will not protect those documents under the work-product doctrine. In addition, **the doctrine is usually qualified**. The documents may not be protected under the doctrine if a substantial need for the information exists and the information is not otherwise available without undue hardship. For example, in one case, the audit committee of the organization conducted interviews to determine whether any questionable foreign payments were made. Their report was protected under the work-product doctrine except for those portions that contained the results of the interviews with deceased persons.*

PA Summary

- Auditors should be careful about including **results** and expressing **opinions** on **legal issues**. **Policies and procedures** should provide guidance about handling such matters. Thus, a **close relationship** with legal counsel and compliance officials is encouraged.

- Auditors should **document engagement records**. However, this function conflicts with legal counsel's desire not to create evidence that could be used against the organization in a **legal proceeding**. Accordingly, the relationship of legal counsel with the auditors should be governed by **proper planning** and **policy making**. For example, roles should be defined, and methods of communication should be established. Moreover, internal auditors should promote an organizational culture with an **ethical and preventive perspective** on legal and regulatory violations. These matters are especially important when results are disclosed to **outside parties**.

- An **attorney-client privilege** arises when a communication about legal assistance for the client is made between privileged persons in confidence. This privilege also may apply to communications with **third parties working with the attorney**.

- A **privilege of critical self-analysis**, for example, in internal auditors' working papers, may be available in some courts. It allows an organization to assess compliance with legal requirements without creating evidence that may be used against it in future litigation. Such critical self-evaluation fosters the public interest in lawful conduct. This privilege is most likely to be granted when the analysis is made **after the events** resulting in the claim. The privilege also is more likely to be granted when a private party, **not a governmental entity**, is seeking documents.

- Self-evaluative privileges are especially relevant when **established self-regulatory procedures** exist, most of which involve quality assurance.

- Documents, for example, memos or computer programs, are protected by the **attorney work-product doctrine** if they are prepared for litigation by an agent of the attorney. Moreover, the documents must be prepared **after** the attorney-client relationship is created.

- However, the attorney work-product doctrine is **usually qualified**. It does not apply if a substantial need exists, and the information is not otherwise available without undue hardship.

3. Stop and review! You have completed the outline for this subunit. Study multiple-choice question 1 on page 111.

2.2 COMMUNICATION CRITERIA

1. This subunit provides detailed guidance regarding the form and content of engagement communications. It consists of one Specific Performance Standard, two Assurance Implementation Standards, one Consulting Implementation Standard, and two Practice Advisories.

2. ***2410   Criteria for Communicating*** – *Communications should include the engagement's objectives and scope as well as applicable conclusions, recommendations, and action plans.*

a. **_PRACTICE ADVISORY 2410-1: COMMUNICATION CRITERIA_**

1. *Although the format and content of the engagement **final communications** may vary by organization or type of engagement, they should contain, at a minimum, the **purpose, scope, and results** of the engagement.*

2. *Engagement final communications may include background information and summaries. **Background information** may identify the organizational units and activities reviewed and provide relevant explanatory information. It may also include the status of observations, conclusions, and recommendations from prior reports and an indication of whether the report covers a scheduled engagement or is responding to a request. **Summaries**, if included, should be balanced representations of the engagement communication's content.*

3. ***Purpose statements** should describe the engagement objectives and may, if necessary, inform the reader why the engagement was conducted and what it was expected to achieve.*

4. ***Scope statements** should identify the reviewed activities and include, when appropriate, supportive information such as time period reviewed. Related activities not reviewed should be identified if necessary to delineate the boundaries of the engagement. The nature and extent of engagement work performed also should be described.*

5. ***Results** should include observations, conclusions (opinions), recommendations, and action plans.*

6. ***Observations** are pertinent **statements of fact**. [NOTE: They also are known as findings.] Those observations necessary to support or prevent misunderstanding of the internal auditor's conclusions and recommendations should be included in the final engagement communications. Less significant observations or recommendations may be **communicated informally**.*

7. *Engagement observations and recommendations emerge by a process of **comparing what should be with what is**. Whether or not there is a difference, the internal auditor has a foundation on which to build the report. When conditions meet the criteria, acknowledgment in the engagement communications of satisfactory performance may be appropriate. **Observations and recommendations** should be based on the following **attributes**:*

   - ***Criteria:** The standards, measures, or expectations used in making an evaluation and/or verification (what should exist).*
   - ***Condition:** The factual evidence that the internal auditor found in the course of the examination (what does exist).*
   - ***Cause:** The reason for the difference between the expected and actual conditions (why the difference exists).*
   - ***Effect:** The risk or exposure the organization or others encounter because the condition is not consistent with the criteria (the impact of the difference). In determining the degree of risk or exposure, internal auditors should consider the effect their engagement observations and recommendations may have on the organization's operations and financial statements.*
   - *Observations and recommendations may also include engagement **client accomplishments, related issues, and supportive information** if not included elsewhere.*

8.   ***Conclusions (opinions)*** *are the internal auditor's evaluations of the effects of the observations and recommendations on the activities reviewed. They usually put the observations and recommendations in perspective based upon their overall implications. Engagement conclusions, if included in the engagement report, should be* ***clearly identified*** *as such. Conclusions may encompass the entire scope of an engagement or specific aspects. They may cover, but are not limited to, whether* ***operating or program objectives*** *and goals conform with those of the organization, whether the organization's objectives and goals are being met, and whether the* ***activity under review*** *is functioning as intended.*

9.   *Engagement communications should include recommendations for potential improvements, acknowledgments of satisfactory performance, and corrective actions.* ***Recommendations*** *are based on the internal auditor's observations and conclusions. They call for action to correct existing conditions or improve operations. Recommendations may suggest* ***approaches to correcting or enhancing performance*** *as a guide for management in achieving desired results. Recommendations may be* ***general or specific***. *For example, under some circumstances, it may be desirable to recommend a general course of action and specific suggestions for implementation. In other circumstances, it may be appropriate only to suggest further investigation or study.*

10.   *Engagement* ***client accomplishments***, *in terms of improvements since the last engagement or the establishment of a well-controlled operation, may be included in the engagement final communications. This information may be necessary to fairly present the existing conditions and to provide a proper perspective and appropriate balance to the engagement final communications.*

11.   *The engagement* ***client's views*** *about engagement conclusions or recommendations may be included in the engagement communications.*

12.   *As part of the internal auditor's discussions with the engagement client, the internal auditor should* ***try to obtain agreement on the results*** *of the engagement and on a* ***plan of action*** *to improve operations, as needed. If the internal auditor and engagement client disagree about the engagement results, the engagement communications may state* ***both positions and the reasons for the disagreement***. *The engagement client's written comments may be included as an appendix to the engagement report. Alternatively, the engagement client's views may be presented in the body of the report or in a cover letter.*

13.   *Certain information may* ***not be appropriate for disclosure to all report recipients*** *because it is privileged, proprietary, or related to improper or illegal acts. Such information, however, may be disclosed in a separate report. If the conditions being reported involve* ***senior management***, *report distribution should be to the board of the organization.*

14.   ***Interim reports may be written or oral*** *and may be transmitted formally or informally. Interim reports may be used to communicate information that requires* ***immediate attention***, *to communicate a* ***change in engagement scope*** *for the activity under review, or to keep management informed of engagement progress when* ***engagements extend over a long period***. *The use of interim reports does not diminish or eliminate the need for a final report.*

15. *A signed report should be issued after the engagement is completed. Summary reports highlighting engagement results may be appropriate for levels of management above the engagement client. They may be issued separately from or in conjunction with the final report. The term signed means that the authorized internal auditor's name should be manually signed in the report. Alternatively, the signature may appear on a cover letter. The internal auditor authorized to sign the report should be designated by the chief audit executive. If engagement reports are distributed by electronic means, a signed version of the report should be kept on file by the internal audit activity.*

PA Summary

- A **final communication** may vary by organization or type of engagement. However, it should contain at least the **purpose, scope, and results** of the engagement.

- A final communication may include **background information**, such as activities reviewed and the status of observations, conclusions, recommendations from prior reports, and **summaries** of the communication's content.

- **Purpose statements** describe the engagement objectives. **Scope statements** identify the reviewed activities and include the nature and extent of engagement work. **Results** include observations, conclusions (opinions), recommendations, and action plans.

- **Observations** (findings) are relevant **statements of fact**. A final communication should contain those necessary to the conclusions and recommendations. Less significant matters may be **communicated informally**.

- The **attributes** of **observations and recommendations** are (1) **criteria** (standards, measures, expectations, or what should be), (2) **condition** (factual evidence, or what exists), (3) **cause** (why a difference between the actual and expected conditions exists), and (4) **effect** (the risk or exposure resulting from the difference). Observations and recommendations also may include **client accomplishments, related issues, and supportive information**.

- **Conclusions (opinions)** are evaluations of the effects of the observations and recommendations. They should be **clearly identified**. Conclusions may cover whether (1) **operating or program objectives** conform to the organization's, (2) those objectives are being met, and (3) the **activity under review** is functioning as intended.

- **Recommendations** are based on observations and conclusions. They may suggest approaches for correcting or improving performance and be general or specific.

- **Client accomplishments** included in the final communication may be necessary to present fairly the existing conditions and provide a proper perspective and balance. **Client's views** about conclusions or recommendations also may be included.

- The internal auditor tries to reach **agreement with the client** about results and a plan of corrective action. **Disagreements** should be fully disclosed, including both positions and the reasons. The client's written comments may be presented in the report, an appendix, or a cover letter.

- Certain information may need to be **excluded** from a **general-use report** because it is privileged, proprietary, or related to improper acts. Such information may be disclosed in a separate report. If **senior management** is involved, report distribution is to the board.

PA Summary continued on next page

PA Summary continued

- **Interim reports** (oral or written) transmitted formally or informally may communicate (1) information needing immediate attention, (2) a change in the scope of the engagement, or (3) the progress of a long-duration engagement.
- A **signed report** is issued at the end of the engagement. **Summary reports** may be appropriate for levels above the client. The auditor authorized to sign should be designated by the CAE. If reports are distributed electronically, the IAA should keep a signed report on file.

---

3. *2410.A1 – Final communication of engagement results should, where appropriate, contain the internal auditor's overall opinion or conclusions.*

4. *2410.A2 – Internal auditors are encouraged to acknowledge satisfactory performance in engagement communications.*

5. *2410.C1 – Communication of the progress and results of consulting engagements will vary in form and content depending on the nature of the engagement and the services requested.*

   a. *PRACTICE ADVISORY 1000.C1-2: ADDITIONAL CONSIDERATIONS FOR FORMAL CONSULTING ENGAGEMENTS*

      The following is the relevant portion of this comprehensive Practice Advisory:

      15. *Communication of the progress and results of consulting engagements will vary in form and content depending upon the nature of the engagement and the needs of the client. **Reporting requirements** are generally determined by those requesting the consulting service and should meet the objectives as determined and agreed to with management. However, the **format** for communicating the results of the consulting engagement should clearly describe the **nature of the engagement** and any limitations, restrictions, or **other factors** about which users of the information should be made aware.*

PA Summary

- Communications vary with the engagement and client needs. In a formal consulting engagement, **reporting requirements** are usually set by **requesting parties**. However, the **format** should describe the nature of the engagement and **other factors** of which users should be aware.

---

6. **Format of Communications**

   a. **No format is required.** However, the Standards and Practice Advisories prescribe the minimum content and make suggestions for additional inclusions. The format varies with the **type** of communication.

      1) **Formal** communications have carefully structured formats.
      2) **Informal** communications include letters or memoranda to operating management.
      3) **Progress** communications contain brief statements of conditions requiring immediate attention.
      4) **Oral** communications range from formal audiovisual presentations to informal comments.
      5) **Overall** communications state a conclusion (opinion) on the entire operation reviewed.

6) **Deficiency** communications comment only on those matters needing corrective action.

7) **Financial** communications include statements of financial position, results of operations, etc.

8) **Operational** communications discuss the adequacy and effectiveness of risk management and control processes relating to the effectiveness and efficiency of operations and the extent to which results are consistent with objectives.

b. The **format** also depends on the

1) Type of engagement
2) Results
3) Needs of management
4) Nature of the organization and whether it is centralized or decentralized
5) Acceptance by managers of the internal auditors' position in the organization

7. **Observations**

a. **Observations and recommendations** emerge by a process of comparing "what should be" with "what is."

1) Organizational **policies and procedures** delegating authority and assigning responsibilities, textbook illustrations of **generally accepted practices**, and codification of **best practices** in similar organizations are all sound criteria against which to judge current operations.

b. **Favorable observations** should be short and simple; e.g., "Production schedules, levels, and quality were at or ahead of budgeted levels in every case."

c. **Unfavorable observations** need further explanation to justify recommended changes. The following examples were adapted from Sawyer, *The Practice of Modern Internal Auditing*, 2nd edition (1981), pages 444-445:

1) **Summary**

a) Because of inaccurate inventory records, the supply department bought unneeded supplies costing $75,000.

2) **Criteria**

a) Established procedures provide that excess materials returned by the production department shall be entered on the records of the supply department to show the levels of inventory currently on hand and available for issuance.

3) **Condition (facts)**

a) Our tests disclosed that, for a period of 6 months, supplies returned from production had not been entered on the supply department's records.

4) **Cause**

a) We found that the employees responsible for the posting of returned supplies had not been instructed in their duties. In addition, supervisors had not been monitoring the process.

5) **Effect**

a) As a result of the inaccurate inventory records, the organization bought unneeded supplies costing about $75,000.

6) **Recommendation**

    a) We reviewed the conditions with the manager of the supply department, and he agreed to bring the inventory records up to date, issue job instructions to the workers spelling out the need to record returned supplies, and instruct supervisors to monitor the process in the future and to submit written reports on their periodic reviews.

7) **Corrective action taken**

    a) Before we concluded our examination, the manager took all three steps. Our subsequent spot checks showed that the action was effective. We therefore consider this observation closed.

8. **Other Communications**

  a. **Summary reports** highlighting engagement results may be appropriate for levels of management above the client. They may be issued separately from, or in conjunction with, the final engagement communication (PA 2410-1).

  b. **Oral communications** should be used to complement and support written ones.

    1) Oral communications have the following **purposes** (advantages):

      a) **Timeliness**, that is, provision of immediate feedback

        i) Timeliness is important for deficiencies needing immediate engagement client action.

        ii) The internal auditor can provide instant response to engagement client questions, positions, suggestions, etc.

      b) **Improved internal auditor-client relationships**

        i) The internal auditor can become better known to the client and reduce tensions.

        ii) Clients can express their views.

        iii) Oral communications can reduce client resistance to recommendations.

      c) **Additional information** provided to the internal auditor

        i) The internal auditor can assess the strength of client attitudes and convictions.

        ii) Clients can point out internal auditor misunderstandings and errors.

    2) Although oral communications allow for **flexibility**, careful **planning** is necessary, which may include the following steps:

      a) Gain familiarity with the participants.
      b) Determine the objectives.
      c) List the materials, topics, etc., relevant to the objectives.
      d) Arrange the materials in logical order.
      e) Prepare visual aids, handouts, etc.
      f) Practice the presentation.
      g) Anticipate and prepare for questions and arguments from the client.

  c. **Progress (interim) communications** provide a prompt means of documenting a situation requiring immediate action.

    1) They are **preliminary** and should indicate that

      a) Only current information, that is, an incomplete study, is the basis for such communications.

      b) The **final engagement communication** will follow up on the topics covered.

    2) Progress communications prepared by the internal audit staff should be **reviewed** by the chief audit executive or other supervisory personnel.

    3) Progress communications about **deficiency observations** should have the same structure as communications on observations. Deficiencies are described in records of engagement observations and are communicated to management in the form of a single-page executive summary.

    4) Progress communications also may be used to report the status of long, sensitive, or otherwise **special engagements** to the clients and senior management.

9. Stop and review! You have completed the outline for this subunit. Study multiple-choice questions 2 through 29 beginning on page 111.

2.3 QUALITY OF COMMUNICATIONS

1. This subunit addresses the characteristics of information in engagement communications, the treatment of errors and omissions, and noncompliance with the Standards. According to *Sawyer's Internal Auditing* (p. 611), engagement communications are intended to inform, persuade, and get results. They explain the internal auditors' observations, conclusions, and recommendations; attempt to convince the recipients of the engagement communication of their value and validity; and foster beneficial change. Three Specific Performance Standards and three Practice Advisories cover the quality of communications.

2.   **2420**   ***Quality of Communications*** *– Communications should be accurate, objective, clear, concise, constructive, complete, and timely.*

    a. ***PRACTICE ADVISORY 2420-1: QUALITY OF COMMUNICATIONS***

        1. ***Accurate communications*** *are free from errors and distortions and are faithful to the underlying facts. The manner in which the data and evidence are gathered, evaluated, and summarized for presentation should be done with care and precision.*

        2. ***Objective communications*** *are fair, impartial, and unbiased and are the result of a fair-minded and balanced assessment of all relevant facts and circumstances. Observations, conclusions, and recommendations should be derived and expressed without prejudice, partisanship, personal interests, and the undue influence of others.*

        3. ***Clear communications*** *are easily understood and logical. Clarity can be improved by avoiding unnecessary technical language and providing all significant and relevant information.*

        4. ***Concise communications*** *are to the point and avoid unnecessary elaboration, superfluous detail, redundancy, and wordiness. They are created by a persistent practice of revising and editing a presentation. The goal is that each thought will be meaningful but succinct.*

        5. ***Constructive communications*** *are helpful to the engagement client and the organization and lead to improvements where needed. The contents and tone of the presentation should be useful, positive, and well-meaning and contribute to the objectives of the organization.*

        6. ***Complete communications*** *are lacking nothing that is essential to the target audience and include all significant and relevant information and observations to support recommendations and conclusions.*

7.   **Timely communications** *are well-timed, opportune, and expedient for careful consideration by those who may act on the recommendations. The timing of the presentation of engagement results should be set without undue delay and with a degree of urgency so as to enable prompt, effective action.*

PA Summary

- **Accurate** means free from errors and distortions and faithful to the facts. Evidence should be gathered, evaluated, and summarized with care and precision.
- **Objective** communications are fair, impartial, and unbiased. They result from a balanced assessment of all relevant facts and circumstances.
- **Clear** means understandable and logical and avoiding unnecessary technical language and providing all significant and relevant information.
- **Concise** communications are meaningful but succinct. They are the product of persistent editing.
- **Constructive** communications are helpful and lead to needed improvements that contribute to achieving objectives.
- **Complete** means containing all significant, relevant information.
- **Timely** communications enable prompt, effective action. They facilitate careful consideration by those who may act on the recommendations.

---

3.   **2421**   *Errors and Omissions* – *If a final communication contains a significant error or omission, the chief audit executive should communicate corrected information to all parties who received the original communication.*

4.   **2430**   *Engagement Disclosure of Noncompliance with the Standards* – *When noncompliance with the Standards impacts a specific engagement, communication of the results should disclose the:*

- *Standard(s) with which full compliance was not achieved,*
- *Reason(s) for noncompliance, and*
- *Impact of noncompliance on the engagement.*

5.   An internal auditor's obligation regarding professional proficiency in communication is stated in **PA 1210-1: PROFICIENCY**.

3.   *Internal auditors should be skilled in **dealing with people and in communicating effectively**. Internal auditors should understand human relations and maintain satisfactory relationships with engagement clients.*

4.   *Internal auditors should be skilled in **oral and written communications** so that they can clearly and effectively convey such matters as engagement objectives, evaluations, conclusions, and recommendations.*

PA Summary

- Auditors should be skilled in **dealing with people** so as to maintain satisfactory relationships with clients. They should be skilled in oral and written **communications** so as to convey effectively engagement objectives, conclusions, and recommendations.

---

6.   **Style** is a message characteristic that is a major factor in the reader's ability to comprehend the information.

   a.   Simple and clear writing lets nothing impede the transfer of ideas.

   1)   Sentences should be **brief**, but some long ones may be added for variety.

   2)   **Wordiness** should be avoided.

   3)   **Irrelevant** matters should be omitted.

   4)   The writing should flow in **logical succession**.

   5)   The ideas and arguments presented should be **logical**.

   6)   **Consistency** is a virtue. Inconsistent style, sentence structure, or vocabulary is confusing.

   7)   **Ambiguity** is increased by inaccurate choice of vocabulary, by use of pronouns with unclear antecedents, by careless word order, and by dangling modifiers.

   8)   **References** should be well defined. For example, if the introductory matter describes something to be discussed, the subject should be covered.

   b.   The writer should avoid unnecessary **technical jargon** and attempts to impress the reader with scholarly knowledge. The writer should consider the reader's experience and provide just enough information to give an adequate background. Thus, the internal auditor must consider the nature of the audience.

   1)   Terms and concepts with which the reader is likely to be unfamiliar should be carefully defined.

   c.   Writing should be lively, using **action words** to command attention.

   1)   Thus, the communication should use active-voice verbs, although the passive voice may be used occasionally for variety.

   d.   Internal auditors should use objective, fact-based, and neutral language. Emotionally charged words should be avoided. They may provoke a negative reaction from the engagement client.

   e.   Internal auditors must consider not only message characteristics but also **situational factors**. These include, for example, the nature of the audience, prior experience with the audience, and noise (interference) in the communication channel.

7.   All writing needs **editing for content, format, and clerical errors**.

   a.   The reviewer should evaluate

   1)   **Readability.** The communication should report information clearly.

   2)   **Correctness.** Internal auditor statements should be well documented in the detailed sections and in the working papers.

   a)   Formats and the rules of style also should be followed.

   3)   **Appropriateness.** The communication should be tactful and objective. Moreover, the allocation of space to major and minor observations should be balanced.

   b.   All final communications should be carefully **proofread**.

   1)   The **final draft and the previous copy** should be compared by having one person read to another.

   2)   The communication should be **reference-checked**, comparing each factual statement, number, date, and title with source data in the working papers.

   a)   Cross-references should be verified as a separate step.

   b)   Errors in cross-references frequently arise from last-minute changes in page numbers. Thus, they should be one of the last items checked.

   3)   An **overall review** should be undertaken by spreading all the pages out on a desk or table to detect any inconsistencies in format and content.

   4)   Another proofreading should include an examination of each word for **typographical errors**.

c.   The communication often contains matters that are **critical of the client**. Hence, the internal auditor must be careful that nothing might properly be criticized by the client.

8.   The **physical characteristics** of the communication also are significant. They should be tastefully and attractively, but not expensively, presented.

a.   Use of **short paragraphs** and numerous **headings** helps to avoid visual monotony.

b.   A **title** should be as brief as possible subject to the need to be descriptive.

9.   Stop and review! You have completed the outline for this subunit. Study multiple-choice questions 30 through 38 beginning on page 122.

2.4 DISSEMINATING RESULTS

1.   This subunit addresses the communication of engagement results within and outside the organization. A particular concern is the treatment of sensitive information. The pronouncements included are one Specific Performance Standard, two Assurance Implementation Standards, two Consulting Implementation Standards, and two Practice Advisories.

2.   ***2440***   ***Disseminating Results*** – *The chief audit executive should communicate results to the appropriate parties.*

a.   ***PRACTICE ADVISORY 2440-1: RECIPIENTS OF ENGAGEMENT RESULTS***

   1.   *Internal auditors should **discuss conclusions and recommendations with appropriate levels of management** before issuing final engagement communications.*

   2.   *Discussion of conclusions and recommendations is usually accomplished during the course of the engagement or at **post-engagement meetings (exit interviews)**. Another technique is the **review of draft** engagement observations, conclusions, and recommendations by management. These discussions and reviews help ensure that there have been no misunderstandings or misinterpretations of fact by providing the **opportunity for the engagement client to clarify** specific items and to **express views** of the observations, conclusions, and recommendations.*

   3.   *Although the **level of participants** in the discussions and reviews may vary by organization and by the nature of the report, they will generally include those individuals who are **knowledgeable of detailed operations** and those who can **authorize** the implementation of **corrective action**.*

   4.   *The **chief audit executive or a designee** should **review and approve the final engagement communications** before issuance and should decide to whom the report will be **distributed**. The chief audit executive or a designee should approve and may sign all final reports. If specific circumstances warrant, consideration should be given to having the auditor-in-charge, supervisor, or lead auditor sign the report as a representative of the chief audit executive.*

5. *Final engagement communications should be distributed to those members of the organization who are able to ensure that engagement **results are given due consideration**. This means that the report should go to those who are in a position to **take corrective action** or **ensure that corrective action is taken**. The final engagement communications should be distributed to **management of the activity under review**. Higher-level members in the organization may receive only a **summary** communication. Communications may also be distributed to other interested or affected parties such as external auditors and the board.*

PA Summary

- **Conclusions and recommendations** should be discussed with appropriate management during the engagement or at an exit interview. Another technique is review of the **draft report** to provide the client with an opportunity for clarification and an expression of views.

- Participants in discussions and reviews should have **knowledge of operations** and should be able to **authorize** corrective action.

- The **CAE (or designee)** reviews and approves final communications and determines their distribution. In certain circumstances, the auditor-in-charge, supervisor, or lead auditor may **sign** the report as a representative of the CAE.

- Distributees should be persons able to ensure **due consideration of engagement results**, that is, those who can **take corrective action** or **ensure that it is taken**. Final communications should be distributed to **management of the activity under review**. Higher level persons may receive a **summary**. Communications also may be distributed to other interested or affected parties.

---

b. **PRACTICE ADVISORY 2440-2: COMMUNICATIONS OUTSIDE THE ORGANIZATION**

1. *Internal auditors should **review guidance** contained in the engagement agreement or organizational policies and procedures related to **disseminating information outside the organization**. The internal audit activity charter and the audit committee charter may also contain guidance related to disseminating information outside the organization. If such **guidance does not exist**, the internal auditor should facilitate **adoption of appropriate policies** by the organization. Examples of information that could be included in the policies are:*

   - *__Authorization required__ to disseminate information outside the organization.*

   - *__Process for seeking approval__ to disseminate information outside the organization.*

   - *__Guidelines__ for permissible and nonpermissible **types of information** that can be disseminated.*

   - *__Outside persons authorized__ to receive information and the types of information they can receive.*

   - *Related privacy regulations, regulatory requirements, and **legal considerations** for disseminating information outside the organization.*

   - *Nature of assurances, advice, recommendations, opinions, guidance, and other **information that can be included in communications** resulting in dissemination of information outside the organization.*

2.   **Requests** can relate to **information that already exists**, for example, a previously issued internal audit report. Requests can also be received for information that must be created or determined, resulting in **a new internal auditing engagement**. If the request relates to information or a report that already exists, the internal auditor should **review** the information to determine whether it is suitable for dissemination outside the organization.

3.   In certain situations, it may be possible to revise an **existing report or information** to make it **suitable for dissemination** outside the organization. In other situations, it may be possible to generate a new report based on work previously conducted. Appropriate **due professional care** should be exercised when revising, customizing, or creating a new report based on work previously conducted.

4.   When disseminating information outside the organization, the following matters should be considered:

   •   Need for a **written agreement** concerning the information to be disseminated.

   •   **Identification** of information providers, sources, report signers, information recipients, and other **persons related to the report or information** disseminated.

   •   Identification of **objectives, scope, and procedures** to be performed in generating applicable information.

   •   **Nature of report** or other communication, including opinions, inclusion or exclusion of recommendations, disclaimers, limitations, and type of assurance or assertions to be provided.

   •   **Copyright issues** and limitations on further distribution or sharing of the information.

5.   **Engagements** performed to generate internal auditing reports or communications to be disseminated outside the organization should be conducted in accordance with applicable **International Standards for the Professional Practice of Internal Auditing** and include reference to such Standards in the report or other communication.

6.   If, during the conduct of engagements to disseminate information outside the organization, the internal auditor **discovers information deemed to be reportable** to management or the audit committee, the internal auditor should provide suitable communication to appropriate individuals.

PA Summary

•   Auditors should review guidance for **disseminating information outside the organization**. If guidance does not exist, auditors should facilitate adoption of policies. These policies should address (1) authorization requirements, (2) the approval process, (3) guidelines for types of information that may be disseminated, (4) authorized recipients, (5) legal considerations, and (6) the information includible in outside communications.

•   Requests for **existing information** require it to be reviewed to determine its suitability for disclosure. A request for information that must be created or determined results in **a new internal auditing engagement**.

•   **Due professional care** is needed when revising a report or information (or creating a new report) for outside dissemination based on **work previously done**.

> - Outside dissemination **requires considering** (1) the need for a written agreement; (2) identifying persons related to the report or information; (3) identification of objectives, scope, and procedures; (4) nature of the report or other communication; and (5) copyright issues.
> - **Engagements** performed for outside dissemination of results should be in accordance with the **Standards**. If the auditor discovers **reportable information**, it should be suitably communicated.

c. ***PRACTICE ADVISORY 2440-3: COMMUNICATING SENSITIVE INFORMATION WITHIN AND OUTSIDE OF THE CHAIN OF COMMAND***

1. *Internal auditors often come into the possession of **information that is critically sensitive and substantial** to the organization and has **significant potential consequences**. That information may relate to exposures, threats, uncertainties, fraud, waste and mismanagement, illegal activities, abuse of power, misconduct that endangers public health or safety, or other wrongdoings. Those types of matters may adversely affect the organization's reputation, image, competitiveness, success, viability, market values, investments and intangible assets, or earnings. They are likely to increase an organization's **risk exposures**.*

Communicating Sensitive Information to those in the Chain of Command

2. *Once the internal auditor has decided that the new information is substantial and credible, the auditor would normally communicate the information, on a timely basis, to those in **management who can act on it**. In most instances, those communications will resolve the matter from an internal audit perspective, so long as management takes the appropriate action to manage the associated risks. If the communications result in a **conclusion that management, by its inadequate or lack of actions, is exposing the organization to an unacceptable level of risk**, the chief audit executive (CAE) should consider other options to achieve a satisfactory resolution.*

3. *Among those possible actions, the CAE could **discuss concerns** about the risk exposure with **senior management within his or her normal chain of command**. Since the audit or other committee of the governing board would also be expected to be in the CAE's chain of command, the members of the board committee would normally be informed of the CAE's concerns. **If the CAE**, after those discussions with senior management, **is still unsatisfied** and concludes that senior management is exposing the organization to an unacceptable risk and is not taking appropriate action to halt or correct the situation, senior management and the CAE would **present the essential information and their differences of opinion to the members or a committee of the governing board**.*

4. *That simple chain-of-command communication scenario may be accelerated for certain types of sensitive occurrences because of **national laws, regulations, or commonly followed practices**. For instance, in the case of evidence of **fraudulent financial reporting** by an organization, regulations may prescribe that the **audit committee of the board be immediately informed** of the circumstances surrounding the possibility of misleading financial reports, even though senior management and the CAE may be in substantial agreement on what actions need to be taken. Laws and regulations in several countries specify that **members or a committee of the governing board** should be informed of discoveries of violations of criminal, securities, food, drugs, or pollution laws and other illegal acts, such as bribery or other improper payments to government officials or to agents of suppliers or customers.*

Communicating Outside of the Chain of Command

5. In some situations, an internal auditor may face the dilemma of considering whether to communicate the discovered information to persons outside of the normal chain of command or even **outside of the organization**. The act of disclosing adverse information to someone in the organization who is outside of the individual's normal chain of command, or to a governmental agency or other authority that is wholly outside of the organization, is commonly referred to as "**whistle-blowing**."

6. In studies about whistle-blowing, it has been reported that **most whistle-blowers disclose the sensitive information internally**, even if outside of the normal chain of command, particularly if they trust the policies and mechanisms of the organization to investigate an allegation of an illegal or other improper activity and to take appropriate action. However, some persons possessing sensitive information may decide to take the information **outside the organization**, particularly if they fear retribution by their employers or fellow employees, have doubt that the issue will be properly investigated, believe that it will be concealed, or possess evidence about an illegal or improper activity that jeopardizes the health, safety, or well-being of people in the organization or community. The **primary motive** of most whistle-blowers, who are acting on good faith, is to halt the illegal, harmful, or improper behavior.

7. An internal auditor who is facing a similar dilemma and needing to consider all possible options will need to evaluate alternative ways to communicate the risk to some person or group who is outside of his or her normal chain of command. Because of risks and ramifications associated with these approaches, the internal auditor should **proceed with care to evaluate the evidence and the reasonableness of his or her conclusions and to examine the merits and disadvantages of each potential action**. Taking this type of action by an internal auditor may be appropriate if it will result in responsible action by persons in senior management or in governance positions, such as members on the governing board or one of its committees. An internal auditor would likely consider as his or her **last option** that of **communicating outside of the organization's governance structure**. An internal auditor would reserve this type of action for those rare occasions when he or she is convinced that the **risk and its possible consequences are serious** and there is high probability that the organization's existing management and governance mechanisms cannot or will not effectively address the risk.

8. Many member countries in the **OECD** (Organization for Economic Cooperation and Development) have laws or administrative regulations requiring public servants with knowledge of illegal or unethical acts to inform an Inspector General, other public official, or ombudsman. Some **national laws pertaining to whistle-blowing-type actions protect citizens** if they come forward to disclose specific types of improper activities. Among the activities listed in the laws and regulations of those countries are:

   - Criminal offenses and other failures to comply with legal obligations.
   - Acts that are considered miscarriages of justice.
   - Acts that endanger the health, safety, or well-being of individuals.
   - Acts that damage the environment.
   - Activities that conceal or cover up any of the above.

   Other countries offer no guidance or protection. **The internal auditor should be aware of the laws and regulations** of the various localities in which the organization operates and should take actions that are consistent with those legal requirements. The internal auditor should consider obtaining legal advice if he or she is uncertain of the applicable legal requirements.

9. *Many professional associations hold their members to a duty to disclose illegal or unethical activities. The distinguishing mark of a profession is its acceptance of broad responsibilities to the public and its protection of the general welfare. In addition to examining the legal requirements, IIA members and all Certified Internal Auditors should follow the requirements outlined in* **The IIA Code of Ethics** *concerning illegal or unethical acts.*

Internal Auditor's Decision

10. *An internal auditor has a* **professional duty and an ethical responsibility** *to evaluate carefully all the evidence and the reasonableness of his or her conclusions and, then, to decide whether* **further actions may be needed to protect the interests of the organization, its stakeholders, the outside community, or the institutions of society**. *Also, the auditor will need to consider the duty of* **confidentiality, imposed by The IIA Code of Ethics** *to respect the value and ownership of information and avoid disclosing it without appropriate authority, unless there is a legal or professional obligation to do so. In this evaluation process, the auditor should seek the* **advice of legal counsel** *and, if appropriate,* **other experts**. *Those discussions may be helpful in providing a different perspective on the circumstances as well as offering opinions about the potential impact and consequences of various possible actions. The manner in which the internal auditor seeks to resolve this type of complex and sensitive situation may create reprisals and potential liability.*

11. *Ultimately, the internal auditor must make a* **personal decision**. *The decision to communicate outside the normal chain of command should be based on a* **well-informed opinion** *that the wrongdoing is supported by substantial, credible evidence and that a legal or regulatory imperative or a professional or ethical obligation requires further action. The auditor's* **motive** *for acting should be the* **desire to stop** *the* **wrongful, harmful, or improper activity**.

PA Summary

- The auditors may possess **critically sensitive and substantial** new information with significant potential adverse consequences that are likely to increase the organization's **risk exposures**. If the new information is substantial and credible, the auditors normally communicate it on a timely basis to managers who can act on it.

- If management exposes the organization to **unacceptable risk by inaction** on the information, the CAE considers other options.

- If discussions with **senior management in the CAE's chain of command** are unsatisfactory, the essential information and differences of opinion are presented to a committee of the governing board.

- However, national **laws, regulations, or common practices** may require a different response, for example, immediate reporting to a committee of the governing board of certain types of occurrences, e.g., fraudulent financial reporting or illegal acts.

- Auditors may need to consider communicating **outside the chain of command or the organization** (whistle-blowing).

- Most whistle-blowers act internally. However, those who act **outside the organization** typically do not trust its response. The **primary motive** of most whistle-blowers, who are acting on good faith, is to halt the illegal, harmful, or improper behavior.

PA Summary continued on next page

PA Summary continued

- An internal auditor in such circumstances should **carefully evaluate** the evidence, the reasonableness of the conclusions, and the merits of possible actions. The **last option** is communicating outside the governance structure. It should be chosen only when the **risk and the consequences** are serious and will not be effectively addressed internally.

- Many **OECD countries** require **public servants** to report illegal or unethical acts. Some **national laws** protect whistle-blowers. Thus, auditors should be aware of applicable laws and consider obtaining legal advice if uncertain of the applicable legal requirements. Members of The IIA and CIAs also should follow the provisions of The IIA Code of Ethics. An auditor's **professional duty and ethical responsibility** is to evaluate the evidence and the reasonableness of his or her conclusions and decide whether **further actions may be needed** to protect the organization, its stakeholders, the outside community, or the institutions of society. The auditor also needs to consider the duty of confidentiality. The advice of **legal counsel** and other experts may be needed.

- The auditor must make a **personal decision** based on a **well-informed opinion** that the wrongdoing is supported by the evidence and that a legal, professional, or ethical obligation requires action.

3. ***2440.A1*** – *The chief audit executive is responsible for communicating the final results to parties who can ensure that the results are given due consideration.*

4. ***2440.A2*** – *If not otherwise mandated by legal, statutory, or regulatory requirements, prior to releasing results to parties outside the organization, the chief audit executive should:*

- Assess the potential risk to the organization,
- Consult with senior management and/or legal counsel as appropriate, and
- Control dissemination by restricting the use of the results.

5. ***2440.C1*** – *The chief audit executive is responsible for communicating the final results of consulting engagements to clients.*

  a. **PRACTICE ADVISORY 1000.C1-2: ADDITIONAL CONSIDERATIONS FOR FORMAL CONSULTING ENGAGEMENTS**

  The following is the relevant portion of this comprehensive Practice Advisory:

  16. *In some circumstances, the internal auditor may **conclude that the results should be communicated beyond those who received or requested the service**. In such cases, the internal auditor should expand the reporting so that results are communicated to the appropriate parties. When expanding the reporting to other parties, the auditor should conduct the following steps until satisfied with the resolution of the matter:*

  - ***First**, determine what direction is provided in the **agreement** concerning the consulting engagement and related communications.*
  - ***Second**, attempt to convince those receiving or requesting the service to expand **voluntarily** the communication to the appropriate parties.*
  - ***Third**, determine what guidance is provided in the internal audit **charter** or audit activity's **policies and procedures** concerning consulting communications.*
  - ***Fourth**, determine what guidance is provided in the **organization's** code of conduct, code of ethics, and other relative policies, administrative directives, or procedures.*

     •   **Fifth**, *determine what guidance is provided by The IIA's **Standards** and **Code of Ethics**, other standards or codes applicable to the auditor, and any legal or regulatory requirements that relate to the matter under consideration.*

17.   *Internal auditors should **disclose** to management, the audit committee, board, or other governing body of the organization, the **nature, extent, and overall results** of formal consulting engagements along with other reports of internal auditing activities. Internal auditors should keep executive management and the audit committee informed about **how audit resources are being deployed**. Neither detail reports of these consulting engagements nor the specific results and recommendations are required to be communicated. But, an appropriate **description** of these types of engagements and their **significant recommendations** should be communicated and is essential in satisfying the internal auditor's responsibility in complying with Standard 2060, Reporting to the Board and Senior Management.*

PA Summary

- **Results** may need to be communicated **beyond those who received or requested consulting services**. The auditor considers (1) the agreement; (2) whether the receiving or requesting parties will voluntarily expand the communication; (3) the IAA charter, policies, and procedures; (4) the organization's code of ethics and policies; and (5) the Standards and The IIA Code of Ethics.
- The auditor should **disclose** to management and the board the nature, extent, and overall results of a formal consulting engagement along with other IAA reports. Details need not be reported. But appropriate **descriptions** and **significant recommendations** should be communicated.

---

6.   *2440.C2 – During consulting engagements, risk management, control, and governance issues may be identified. Whenever these issues are significant to the organization, they should be communicated to senior management and the board.*

7.   **Reviews and distribution.** Internal auditors should discuss **conclusions and recommendations** with appropriate levels of management before issuing final engagement communications (PA 2440-1). This discussion usually occurs during the engagement or at a post-engagement meeting (an **exit interview** or **closing conference**). Reviews of drafts of communications with clients are a courtesy to them and a form of insurance for the engagement.

    a.   Clients may have discussed all such matters **during the engagement**. They should be given the opportunity to read what will be sent to their superiors. Moreover, seeing the draft report may cause clients to view the results differently.

        1)   Thus, an exit interview improves relations with engagement clients. It involves them in the engagement process (a participative or consultative approach) and ensures that misunderstandings or misinterpretations are avoided. Moreover, the exit interview may increase client support for appropriate management action.

    b.   In **complex operations**, an auditor may easily miss a point or report it incorrectly. Reviewing engagement results in draft form with the client may detect inaccuracies before the final communication is issued.

        1)   Documenting these discussions and reviews can be valuable in preventing or resolving disputes.

    c.   The auditor should carefully consider the following **before the review**:

        1)   The person(s) with whom the draft should be reviewed

        2)   The feasibility of performing some reviews on a group basis

        3)   The timing and order of the reviews

        4)   Sending the draft to the client before the meeting

        5)   The need for face-to-face discussions. Sending copies of the draft to interested parties and receiving their written comments may be sufficient.

    d.   The **auditor should be in charge** of the **post-engagement meeting**.

    e.   The auditor should be prepared for **conflicts and questions**.

        1)   When the auditor has previously experienced difficulty with an individual, that individual's superior may be invited to attend.

        2)   To be able to answer questions promptly, the auditor may wish to **prepare notes**.

        3)   The auditor should be **flexible** on matters not affecting the substance of the matters communicated.

           a)   However, the auditor should **never negotiate the opinion**.

    f.   **Disagreements** should be explained in the engagement communications.

    g.   When the reviews result in **significant changes**, the other people with whom the draft was reviewed should have an opportunity to see, or be told of, the revisions.

    h.   The auditor should maintain **careful records** of the post-engagement meeting, of any objections, and of the manner in which conflicts were resolved.

    i.   When **copies of the draft** are sent to concerned parties for review, the auditor should

        1)   Ask for the timely return of the draft with any comments considered appropriate.

        2)   Set a specific due date for the return of the draft.

        3)   Offer to meet with those who wish to discuss the draft further.

    j.   **Final communications** should be distributed to all those having a direct interest in the engagement. Each communication should contain a **distribution sheet** listing the distributees and indicating with whom it has been reviewed in draft. Distributees include

        1)   The executive to whom the internal audit activity reports

        2)   The person or persons to whom replies will be addressed

        3)   Persons responsible for the activity or activities reviewed

        4)   Persons required to take corrective action

    k.   Information that is **privileged, proprietary, or related to improper or illegal acts** should be disclosed in a separate communication and distributed to the board.

8.   Stop and review! You have completed the outline for this subunit. Study multiple-choice questions 39 through 57 beginning on page 125.

2.5 MONITORING PROGRESS

1. This subunit concerns the final phase of an engagement. Two General Performance Standards, one Assurance Implementation Standard, one Consulting Implementation Standard, and four Practice Advisories address the monitoring of the disposition of engagement results.

2. **2500** *Monitoring Progress* – The chief audit executive should establish and maintain a system to monitor the disposition of results communicated to management.

   a. **PRACTICE ADVISORY 2500-1: MONITORING PROGRESS**

      1. *The chief audit executive should establish* **procedures** *to include the following:*

         - *A time frame within which management's response to the engagement observations and recommendations is required*
         - *An evaluation of* **management's response**
         - *A* **verification** *of the response (if appropriate)*
         - *A* **follow-up** *engagement (if appropriate)*
         - *A* **communications procedure** *that escalates unsatisfactory responses/ actions, including the assumption of risk, to the appropriate levels of management*

      2. *Certain reported observations and recommendations may be so significant as to require* **immediate action** *by management. These conditions should be* **monitored** *by the internal audit activity* **until corrected** *because of the effect they may have on the organization.*

      3. **Techniques used to monitor progress** *effectively include:*

         - *Addressing engagement observations and recommendations to the* **appropriate levels of management** *responsible for taking corrective action.*
         - *Receiving and evaluating management* **responses** *to engagement observations and recommendations* **during the engagement** *or* **within a reasonable time** *period after the engagement results are communicated. Responses are more useful if they include sufficient information for the chief audit executive to evaluate the* **adequacy and timeliness of corrective action**.
         - *Receiving* **periodic updates** *from management in order to evaluate the status of management's efforts to correct previously communicated conditions.*
         - *Receiving and evaluating information from* **other organizational units** *assigned responsibility for procedures of a follow-up or corrective nature.*
         - *Reporting to senior management or the board on the* **status of responses** *to engagement observations and recommendations.*

PA Summary

- The CAE establishes **procedures** to monitor the disposition of reported results. They include (1) a time frame for **management's response**, (2) an evaluation and **verification** of the response (if appropriate), (3) a **follow-up** (if appropriate), and (4) a **communications procedure** for dealing with unsatisfactory responses.
- Observations and recommendations needing **immediate action** should be monitored **until corrected**.
- Observations and recommendations should be addressed to managers **responsible for corrective action**.
- **Management responses** should be received and evaluated during the engagement or within a reasonable time afterward. Responses should be sufficient for the CAE to evaluate the **adequacy and timeliness of corrective action**.
- Management should give **periodic updates**.
- Information should be received and evaluated from **other units** involved in follow-up or correction.
- The **status of responses** should be reported to senior management or the board.

---

3. **2500.A1** – *The chief audit executive should establish a follow-up process to monitor and ensure that management actions have been effectively implemented or that senior management has accepted the risk of not taking action.*

   a. **PRACTICE ADVISORY 2500.A1-1: FOLLOW-UP PROCESS**

      1. Internal auditors should determine that **corrective action was taken** and is achieving the desired results or that senior management or the board has **assumed the risk** of not taking corrective action on reported observations.

      2. **Follow-up** by internal auditors is defined as a process by which they determine the adequacy, effectiveness, and timeliness of actions taken by management on reported engagement observations and recommendations, including those made by **external auditors and others**.

      3. **Responsibility for follow-up** should be defined in the internal audit activity's written **charter**. The **nature, timing, and extent** of follow-up should be determined by the chief audit executive. Factors that should be considered in determining appropriate follow-up procedures are:

         - The significance of the reported observation or recommendation
         - The degree of effort and cost needed to correct the reported condition
         - The impacts that may result should the corrective action fail
         - The complexity of the corrective action
         - The time period involved

      4. In some instances, the chief audit executive may judge that management's oral or written **response shows that action already taken is sufficient** when weighed against the relative importance of the engagement observation or recommendation. On such occasions, follow-up may be performed as part of the next engagement.

      5. Internal auditors should ascertain that **actions taken** on engagement observations and recommendations **remedy** the underlying **conditions**.

6. *The chief audit executive is responsible for* **scheduling follow-up** *activities as part of developing engagement* **work schedules***. Scheduling of follow-up should be based on the* **risk** *and exposure involved, as well as the degree of* **difficulty** *and the significance of* **timing** *in implementing corrective action.*

PA Summary

- Auditors follow up by determining whether (1) effective **corrective action** has been taken or (2) senior management or the board has **assumed the risk** of not taking action.
- **Follow-up** should address the adequacy, effectiveness, and timeliness of actions on reported observations and recommendations, including those by other auditors.
- The **IAA's charter** defines **responsibility for follow-up**. The CAE defines its nature, timing, and extent after considering (1) the significance of what is reported, (2) the effort and cost of correction, (3) the effect of failure of correction, (4) the complexity of correction, and (5) the time involved.
- If **action already taken suffices**, follow-up may be part of the next engagement.
- Auditors should verify that actions **remedy** underlying conditions.
- The CAE includes follow-up as part of the **work schedule**. Scheduling depends on the **risk** involved and the difficulty and timing of corrective action.

---

4. **2500.C1** – *The internal audit activity should monitor the disposition of results of consulting engagements to the extent agreed upon with the client.*

   a. **PRACTICE ADVISORY 1000.C1-2: ADDITIONAL CONSIDERATIONS FOR FORMAL CONSULTING ENGAGEMENTS**

   The following is the portion of this Practice Advisory relevant to Standards 2500.C1:

   20. *The internal audit activity should* **monitor the results of consulting engagements** *to the extent agreed upon with the client. Varying types of monitoring may be appropriate for differing types of consulting engagements. The monitoring effort may depend on various factors, such as management's explicit interest in the engagement or the internal auditor's assessment of the project's risks or value to the organization.*

PA Summary

- The IAA monitors results of consulting as agreed with the client. The type of monitoring may depend on factors such as management's interest in the engagement or the assessment of risk.

---

5. **2600** **Resolution of Management's Acceptance of Risks** – *When the chief audit executive believes that senior management has accepted a level of residual risk that may be unacceptable to the organization, the chief audit executive should discuss the matter with senior management. If the decision regarding residual risk is not resolved, the chief audit executive and senior management should report the matter to the board for resolution.*

a. **<u>*PRACTICE ADVISORY 2600-1: MANAGEMENT'S ACCEPTANCE OF RISKS*</u>**

    1.   *Management is responsible for deciding the **appropriate action** to be taken in response to reported engagement observations and recommendations. The chief audit executive is responsible for **assessing** such management action for the **timely resolution** of the matters reported as engagement observations and recommendations. In deciding the extent of follow-up, internal auditors should consider procedures of a **follow-up** nature **performed by others** in the organization.*

    2.   *As stated in Section 2060 of the Standards, paragraph 3 of Practice Advisory 2060-1, senior management may decide to assume the risk of not correcting the reported condition because of cost or other considerations. The board should be informed of senior management's decision on **all significant engagement observations and recommendations**.*

PA Summary

- Management decides the **action taken** in response to engagement results. The CAE assesses this action for **timely resolution**. The extent of follow-up also is a function of follow-up work **done by others**.
- Senior management **may assume** the risk of noncorrection. The decisions on **all significant engagement observations and recommendations** should be reported to the board.

---

6. **Follow-Up**

    a.   The **internal auditor** should

        1)   Receive all replies by the engagement client to the engagement communications
        2)   Evaluate the adequacy of those replies
        3)   Be convinced that the action taken will cure the defects

    b.   The internal auditor is in the **best position** to carry out this responsibility. (S)he is

        1)   Better acquainted with the **facts** than senior management or other control centers in the organization.
        2)   More **objective** than the operating manager who must take the corrective action.

    c.   The responsibility for determining whether corrective **action is adequate** should be coupled with the **authority** to evaluate the adequacy of replies to engagement communications. The internal auditor should

        1)   Report to management when corrective actions are **not timely or effective**.
        2)   Submit **periodic reports** to management on open engagement observations and recommendations.

    d.   The **adequacy of a response** depends on the circumstances in each case. In general, a satisfactory response

        1)   Addresses itself to the **complete problem**, not just to specific items included in the internal auditor's sample.
        2)   Shows that action also has been taken to **prevent a recurrence** of the deficient condition.

e. In **evaluating the reply**, the internal auditor should be satisfied that the action promised is actually taken. The auditor should

1) Obtain **copies of revised procedures** issued to correct conditions.

2) Make any **field tests** needed to provide assurance that the condition has been corrected.

f. A **formal system** should be designed to **keep engagements open** until adequate corrective action is assured. For example,

1) Provisions should be made for **formal opening and closing** of engagements.

2) The internal auditors should issue a **formal statement of closure**, supported by copies of replies to engagement communications and explanations of the action taken to ensure the adequacy and effectiveness of corrective measures.

a) **Closure reports** are directed to the chief audit executive.

3) Engagements should not be removed from the IAA's **open engagements listing** until all required corrective actions have been taken and evaluated.

7. Stop and review! You have completed the outline for this subunit. Study multiple-choice questions 58 through 64 beginning on page 131.

2.6 STUDY UNIT 2 SUMMARY

1. Auditors should be careful about expressing opinions on legal issues. Policies and procedures should provide guidance about handling such matters. Thus, a close relationship with legal counsel and compliance officials is encouraged.

2. Auditors in certain jurisdictions should understand the attorney-client privilege, the critical self-analysis privilege, and the attorney work-product doctrine.

3. A final communication should contain at least the purpose, scope, and results of the engagement. Observations are relevant statements of fact. A final communication should contain those necessary to the conclusions and recommendations. The attributes of observations and recommendations are (a) criteria (what should be), (b) condition (what is), (c) cause (why a difference exists), and (d) effect (the impact of the difference).

4. Engagement communications may be oral or written, in summary form, and final or interim.

5. Communications should be accurate, objective, clear, concise, constructive, complete, and timely.

6. An error in a final communication is a significant misstatement or omission. Amended reports should be distributed to persons who received the original communication.

7. An auditor should be proficient in oral and written communication and human relations.

8. Conclusions and recommendations should be discussed with appropriate management during the engagement or at an exit interview. Another technique is review of the draft report. The CAE (or designee) reviews and approves final communications and determines their distribution.

9. Auditors should review guidance for disseminating information outside the organization. If guidance does not exist, auditors should facilitate adoption of policies. These policies should address (a) authorization requirements, (b) the approval process, (c) guidelines for types of information that may be disseminated, (d) authorized recipients, (e) legal considerations, and (f) the information includible in outside communications.

10. The auditors may possess critically sensitive and substantial new information with significant potential adverse consequences for the organization. They normally communicate it to managers who can act on it. If discussions with senior management in the CAE's chain of command are unsatisfactory, the essential information and differences of opinion are presented to a committee of the governing board. However, laws, regulations, or common practices may require a different scenario, for example, immediate reporting to a committee of the governing board of certain types of occurrences. Auditors may need to consider communicating outside the chain of command or the organization (whistle-blowing).

11. Results may need to be communicated beyond those who received or requested consulting services. The auditor considers (a) the agreement; (b) whether the receiving or requesting parties will voluntarily expand the communication; (c) the IAA charter, policies, and procedures; (d) the organization's code of ethics and policies; and (e) the Standards and The IIA Code of Ethics.

12. The CAE establishes procedures to monitor the disposition of reported results. Observations and recommendations needing immediate action should be monitored until corrected. Management responses should be received and evaluated within a reasonable time. The status of responses should be reported to senior management or the board.

13. Follow-up should address reported observations and recommendations, including those by other auditors. The IAA's charter defines responsibility for follow-up. The CAE defines its nature, timing, and extent. If action already taken suffices, follow-up may be part of the next engagement. Auditors should verify that actions remedy conditions.

14. Management decides the action taken in response to engagement results. The CAE assesses this action for timely resolution. The extent of follow-up also is a function of follow-up work done by others. Senior management's assumption of the risk of noncorrection should be reported to the board.

QUESTIONS

2.1 Legal Considerations

1. Internal auditors should communicate engagement results promptly but should be careful about communicating matters with legal ramifications. Thus, the roles of the internal audit activity and legal counsel should be defined and policies should be established regarding methods of communication. These measures should address how internal auditors' communications may appropriately be shielded from being used against the organization during legal proceedings. Assuming that the law of a jurisdiction applies to such matters, communications are most likely to be protected when they

A. Consist of documents delivered to an attorney before the attorney-client relationship came into existence.

B. Are created for self-evaluation after the events resulting in a private litigant's claim.

C. Are made to an attorney whether or not in confidence.

D. Are part of the internal auditors' work product and are sought by a government agency.

Answer (B) is correct. *(Publisher, adapted)*
REQUIRED: The communications most likely to be protected from being used against the organization in legal proceedings.
DISCUSSION: Some jurisdictions have recognized a qualified privilege that shields self-critical material, such as the internal auditors' work-product, from discovery. In general, the recognition of this privilege is premised on the belief that the confidentiality of the reviews in the instances involved outweighs the valued public interests. It allows individuals or businesses to assess candidly their compliance with regulatory and legal requirements without creating evidence that may be used against them by their opponents in future legal proceedings. In general, three requirements must usually be met for the privilege to apply: the information subject to the privilege must result from a self-critical analysis undertaken by the party asserting the privilege, the public must have a strong interest in preserving the free flow of the information contained in the critical analysis, and the information must be of the type whose flow would be curtailed if discovery were allowed. Moreover, the justification for the privilege is said to be at its strongest when the analysis follows the events resulting in the plaintiff's claim. The self-evaluative privilege is also more likely to be recognized when documents are sought by a private party rather than by a government agency (PA 2400-1).
Answer (A) is incorrect because documents delivered to an attorney are protected neither by the attorney-client privilege nor by the work-product doctrine if no attorney-client relationship exists. Answer (C) is incorrect because an attorney-client privilege does not exist unless the communication was made in confidence. Answer (D) is incorrect because the work-product doctrine applies to documents only if they are prepared by an agent of the attorney, the self-evaluative privilege is less likely to apply when the documents are sought by a government agency, and the attorney-client privilege applies only to communications in confidence between an attorney and client.

2.2 Communication Criteria

2. Which of the following is not included in the statement of scope in an engagement final communication?

A. Period covered by the engagement.

B. Engagement objectives.

C. Activities not reviewed.

D. Nature and extent of the work performed.

Answer (B) is correct. *(CIA, adapted)*
REQUIRED: The item not included in the statement of scope in an engagement final communication.
DISCUSSION: Scope statements should identify the activities reviewed and include, when appropriate, supportive information such as the time period reviewed. Related activities not reviewed should be identified if necessary to delineate the boundaries of the engagement. The nature and extent of engagement work performed also should be described. A purpose statement describes the engagement objectives (PA 2410-1).
Answer (A) is incorrect because the time period covered is included in the statement of scope. Answer (C) is incorrect because the related activities not reviewed are included in the statement of scope. Answer (D) is incorrect because the nature and extent of the work performed is included in the statement of scope.

3. Which one of the following elements of an assurance engagement is not always required?

- A. A statement that describes the engagement objectives.

- B. A statement that identifies the activities reviewed.

- C. Pertinent statements of fact.

- D. An evaluation of the impact of the observations and recommendations on the activities reviewed.

Answer (D) is correct. *(CIA, adapted)*

REQUIRED: The element of an engagement final communication not always required.

DISCUSSION: A statement of conclusions (opinion) evaluates the impact of engagement observations and recommendations on the activities reviewed (PA 2410-1). A statement of conclusions (opinion) is required only when appropriate (Standard 2410.A1).

Answer (A) is incorrect because statements of the purpose, scope, and results are required. The description of the engagement objectives is in the statement of purpose. Answer (B) is incorrect because statements of the purpose, scope, and results are required. Identification of the activities reviewed is in the statement of scope. Answer (C) is incorrect because statements of the purpose, scope, and results are required. Results include observations, conclusions, recommendations, and action plans. Observations are pertinent statements of fact.

4. A final communication issued by an internal auditor following an assurance engagement should contain an expression of opinion when

- A. The area of the engagement is the financial statements.

- B. The internal auditors' work is to be used by external auditors.

- C. A full-scope engagement has been conducted in an area.

- D. An opinion will improve communications with the readers of the communication.

Answer (D) is correct. *(CIA, adapted)*

REQUIRED: The circumstances in which an engagement final communication issued by an internal auditor should contain an expression of opinion.

DISCUSSION: A statement of conclusions (opinion) evaluates the impact of engagement observations and recommendations on the activities reviewed (PA 2410-1). A statement of conclusions (opinion) is required only when appropriate (Standard 2410.A1). The criterion of appropriateness is improvement in communications.

Answer (A) is incorrect because the area of the engagement is irrelevant to decisions about whether an overall opinion is appropriate. Answer (B) is incorrect because whether the internal auditors' work is to be used by external auditors is irrelevant. The external auditors cannot depend on an overall opinion but must examine details and form their own opinion. Answer (C) is incorrect because an overall opinion is not mandatory.

5. Which of the following best defines an internal auditor's opinion expressed following an assurance engagement?

- A. A summary of the significant engagement observations.

- B. The internal auditor's professional judgment about the situation that was reviewed.

- C. Conclusions that must be included in the final engagement communication.

- D. Recommendations for corrective action.

Answer (B) is correct. *(CIA, adapted)*

REQUIRED: The best definition of an internal auditor's opinion.

DISCUSSION: Conclusions (opinions) are the internal auditor's evaluations of the effects of the observations and recommendations on the activities reviewed. They usually put the observations and recommendations in perspective based upon their overall implications. Engagement conclusions, if included in the final engagement communication, should be clearly identified as such. Conclusions may encompass the entire scope of an engagement or specific aspects. They may cover, but are not limited to, whether operating or program objectives and goals conform with those of the organization, whether the organization's objectives and goals are being met, and whether the activity under review is functioning as intended (PA 2410-1).

Answer (A) is incorrect because the summary of significant observations and recommendations is not an opinion. An opinion is the internal auditor's professional judgment about the situation under review. Answer (C) is incorrect because the Standards do not require the inclusion of opinions. However, the opinion is a desirable component of the final engagement communication. Answer (D) is incorrect because recommendations for corrective action are separate from the opinion. The opinion is the internal auditor's professional judgment.

6. The internal auditor completed work on a segment of the engagement work program. As a result, the internal auditor determined that a modification of the organization's distribution procedures is required. The engagement client agreed and has implemented revised procedures. The internal auditor should

A. Research the problem and recommend in the final engagement communication measures that should be taken.

B. Jointly develop and communicate an appropriate recommendation.

C. Communicate the problem and assume that management will take appropriate action.

D. Indicate in the final engagement communication that the client determined and implemented corrective action.

Answer (D) is correct. *(CIA, adapted)*
REQUIRED: The action an internal auditor should take when an engagement client has implemented changes.
DISCUSSION: Engagement communications may include recommendations for potential improvements and acknowledge satisfactory performance and corrective action. Furthermore, information about engagement client accomplishments may be necessary to represent the existing conditions fairly and to provide a proper perspective and appropriate balance to the final engagement communication (PA 2410-1).

7. A recommendation in a final engagement communication should address what attribute?

A. Cause.

B. Statement of condition.

C. Criteria.

D. Effect.

Answer (A) is correct. *(CIA, adapted)*
REQUIRED: The attribute of a recommendation.
DISCUSSION: Recommendations are based on observations and conclusions. They call for action to correct existing conditions or improve operations. Engagement observations and recommendations should be based on four attributes. Criteria are the standards, measures, or expectations used in making an evaluation or verification (what should exist). Condition is defined as the factual evidence that the internal auditor found in the course of the examination (what does exist). If actual and expected conditions differ, the cause is the reason for the difference between the expected and actual conditions (why the difference exists). The effect is the risk or exposure the organization or others encounter because the condition is not the same as the criteria (the impact of the difference) (PA 2410-1). Thus, a recommendation addresses the cause attribute because it states the necessary corrective action.
Answer (B) is incorrect because the condition attribute simply describes "what is" to serve as a basis for comparison with given criteria. Answer (C) is incorrect because criteria describe "what should be" and are compared with the statement of condition. Answer (D) is incorrect because the effect attribute addresses the importance of an observation.

8. An internal auditor has just completed an engagement and is in the process of preparing the final engagement communication. The observations in the final engagement communication should include

A. Statements of opinion about the cause of an observation.

B. Pertinent factual statements concerning the control weaknesses uncovered during the course of the engagement.

C. Statements of both fact and opinion developed during the course of the engagement.

D. Statements concerning potential future events that may be helpful to the engagement client.

Answer (B) is correct. *(CIA, adapted)*
REQUIRED: The information included in a final engagement communication.
DISCUSSION: Observations are pertinent statements of fact. They should be based on a comparison of what should exist with what does exist. If there is a difference, observations should state the reasons and the resulting effects (PA 2410-1).
Answer (A) is incorrect because observations must be statements of fact rather than statements of opinion. Opinions are the internal auditor's evaluations of the effects of observations and recommendations on the activities reviewed. Answer (C) is incorrect because the observations should include statements of fact, but not statements of opinion. Answer (D) is incorrect because observations concern current, not future, factual conditions or events.

Questions 9 through 13 are based on the following information. The following information is extracted from a draft of an engagement communication prepared upon the completion of an engagement to review the inventory warehousing procedures for a division.

Observations and Recommendations

[#5]
We performed extensive tests of inventory record keeping and quantities on hand. Based on our tests, we have concluded that the division carries a large quantity of excess inventory, particularly in the area of component parts. We expect this is due to the conservatism of local management that does not want to risk shutting down production if the goods are not on hand. However, as noted earlier in this engagement communication, the excess inventory has led to a higher-than-average level of obsolete inventory write-downs at this division. We recommend that production forecasts be established, along with lead times for various products, and used in conjunction with economic order quantity concepts to order and maintain appropriate inventory levels.

[#6]
We noted that receiving reports were not filled out when the receiving department became busy. Instead, the receiving manager would fill out the reports after work and forward them to accounts payable. There is a risk that all items received might not be recorded, or that failing to record them initially might result in some items being diverted to other places. During our tests, we discovered many instances in which accounts payable had to call receiving to obtain a receiving report. We recommend that receiving reports be prepared.

[#7]
Inventory is messy. We recommend that management communicate the importance of orderly inventory management techniques to warehouse personnel to avoid the problems noted earlier about (1) locating inventory when needed for production and (2) incurring unusually large amounts of inventory write-offs because of obsolescence.

[#8]
We appreciate the cooperation of divisional management. We intend to discuss our observations with them and follow up by communicating your reaction to those recommendations included within this engagement communication. Given additional time for analysis, we feel that substantial opportunities are available for significant cost savings, and we are proud to be a part of the process.

---

9. A major deficiency in paragraph #5 related to the completeness of the engagement communication is

   A. There is no indication of the potential cause of the problem.

   B. It does not contain criteria by which the concept of "excessive inventory" is judged.

   C. It does not adequately describe the potential effect of the conditions noted.

   D. The recommendations are not required and are not appropriate given the nature of the problem identified.

Answer (B) is correct. *(CIA, adapted)*
   REQUIRED: The major deficiency in paragraph #5 related to completeness.
   DISCUSSION: An engagement communication presenting observations and recommendations should discuss the criteria, the conditions found, the cause, and the effect. Paragraph #5 is silent on the criteria the internal auditor used in determining that the division had excessive levels of inventory.
   Answer (A) is incorrect because the cause of the problem is attributed to divisional management's conservatism regarding the risk of shutdowns. Answer (C) is incorrect because the engagement communication states that excess inventory has led to write-downs as a result of obsolescence. Answer (D) is incorrect because the recommendations are logically derived from the observations and represent an approach that should be considered by management. Recommendations should be included in engagement communications.

10. A major writing problem in paragraph #5 is

A. The use of potentially emotional words such as "conservatism" of local management.

B. The presentation of observations before recommendations. The engagement communication would have more impact if recommendations are made before the observations are discussed.

C. The specific identification of "component parts" may be offensive to the personnel responsible for those parts and may reflect negatively on them.

D. The reference to other parts of the engagement communication citing excessive inventory write-downs for obsolescence is not appropriate. If there is a problem, it should all be discussed within the context of the specific engagement observation.

Answer (A) is correct. *(CIA, adapted)*
REQUIRED: The major writing problem in paragraph #5.
DISCUSSION: The internal auditor should avoid using emotionally charged words because they might provoke an unexpected, negative reaction from the engagement client. The actions of divisional management could have been described adequately in neutral terms.

Answer (B) is incorrect because the excerpt is from the observations and recommendations section of the engagement communication, not the management executive summary. Thus, it is appropriate to present the observations and their basis before presenting the recommendations. Answer (C) is incorrect because the term "component parts" is not commonly regarded as having a negative connotation. Answer (D) is incorrect because the problem of excessive inventory has been noted in relationship to this observation. As long as the amounts of excessive write-downs have been noted earlier in the communication, it is appropriate to refer to that section for more detail.

11. A major deficiency in paragraph #6 related to the completeness of the engagement communication is

A. The factual support for the observation is not given.

B. The cause of the problem is not defined.

C. The risk is presented in an "over-dramatic" fashion.

D. The recommendation is incomplete.

Answer (D) is correct. *(CIA, adapted)*
REQUIRED: The major deficiency in paragraph #6 related to completeness.
DISCUSSION: The recommendation given is not complete. Receiving reports are being prepared but not on a timely basis or concurrently with the receipt of the goods. The recommendation needs to be more detailed.

Answer (A) is incorrect because the factual support comes from the internal auditors' visual inspection. Answer (B) is incorrect because the cause of the problem (or at least the excuse given) is that concurrent receiving reports are not prepared when the department is busy. Answer (C) is incorrect because the internal auditor describes factually the result that might occur if the control deficiency is not adequately addressed.

12. A major deficiency in paragraph #7 related to the completeness of the engagement communication is

A. No separate section adequately discusses the risks associated with the observation.

B. The recommendation does not follow from the observation. The recommendation could have been reached without any observation.

C. The condition for the observation is not clearly explained.

D. The reference to other parts of the engagement communication citing excessive inventory write-downs for obsolescence is not appropriate. If there is a problem, it should all be discussed within the context of the specific observation.

Answer (C) is correct. *(CIA, adapted)*
REQUIRED: The major deficiency in paragraph #7 related to completeness.
DISCUSSION: The condition is that inventory is "messy." However, "messy" is a word that does not completely, specifically, and factually describe what the internal auditor found during the engagement.

Answer (A) is incorrect because the risks are described in some detail. Answer (B) is incorrect because the recommendation is logically presented. The problem is that the author has mixed a condition and a cause. Answer (D) is incorrect because the problem of excessive inventory has been noted in relationship to this observation. As long as the amounts of excessive write-downs have been noted earlier in the communication, it is appropriate to refer to that section for more detail.

13. A major deficiency in paragraph #8 is

A. The nature of the follow-up action is inappropriate.

B. The observations were not discussed with division management before being presented to upper management.

C. The cost savings mentioned are not supported in the engagement communication.

D. All of the answers are correct.

Answer (D) is correct. *(CIA, adapted)*
REQUIRED: The major deficiency in paragraph #8.
DISCUSSION: The follow-up is insufficient. Following up entails ascertaining that the engagement client has taken appropriate action or that senior management or the board has assumed the risk of not taking corrective action. Moreover, conclusions and recommendations should be discussed at appropriate levels of management before issuing final engagement communications, and interim engagement communications may be transmitted formally or informally. Finally, the statement about opportunities for cost savings is not wholly supported.

Questions 14 through 17 are based on the following information. The following data were gathered during an internal auditor's investigation of the reason for a material increase in bad debts expense. In preparing an engagement communication, each of the items might be classified as criteria, cause, condition, effect, or background information.

1. Very large orders require management's approval of credit.

2. Engagement procedures showed that sales personnel regularly disregard credit guidelines when dealing with established customers.

3. A monthly report of write-offs is prepared but distributed only to the accounting department.

4. Credit reports are used only on new accounts.

5. Accounting department records suggest that uncollectible accounts could increase by 5% for the current year.

6. The bad debts loss increased by $100,000 during the last fiscal year.

7. Even though procedures and criteria were changed to reduce the amount of bad-debt write-offs, the loss of commissions because of written-off accounts has increased for some sales personnel.

8. Credit department policy requires the review of credit references for all new accounts.

9. Current payment records are to be reviewed before extending additional credit to open accounts.

10. To reduce costs, the use of outside credit reports was suspended on several occasions.

11. Because several staff positions in the credit department were eliminated to reduce costs, some new accounts have received only cursory review.

12. According to the new credit manager, strict adherence to established credit policy is not necessary.

---

14. The criteria attribute is best illustrated by items numbered

A. 1, 8, and 9.

B. 2, 10, and 11.

C. 3, 4, and 12.

D. 5, 6, and 7.

Answer (A) is correct. *(CIA, adapted)*
REQUIRED: The items that best illustrate criteria.
DISCUSSION: Engagement observations and recommendations are based on four attributes. One such attribute is criteria, which are the standards, measures, or expectations used in making an evaluation or verification (what should exist) (PA 2410-1). Items 1, 8, and 9 state expectations.
Answer (B) is incorrect because items 2, 10, and 11 best illustrate the condition attribute. Answer (C) is incorrect because items 3, 4, and 12 best illustrate the cause attribute. Answer (D) is incorrect because items 5, 6, and 7 best illustrate the effect attribute.

15. The cause attribute is best illustrated by items numbered

A. 2, 10, and 11.

B. 3, 4, and 12.

C. 5, 6, and 7.

D. 1, 8, and 9.

Answer (B) is correct. *(CIA, adapted)*
REQUIRED: The items that best illustrate cause.
DISCUSSION: Engagement observations and recommendations are based on four attributes. One such attribute is cause, which is the reason for the difference between the expected and actual conditions (why the conditions exist) (PA 2410-1). Items 3, 4, and 12 explain why the deviation from the criteria occurred.
Answer (A) is incorrect because items 2, 10, and 11 best illustrate the condition attribute. Answer (C) is incorrect because items 5, 6, and 7 best illustrate the effect attribute. Answer (D) is incorrect because items 1, 8, and 9 best illustrate the criteria attribute.

16. The condition attribute is best illustrated by items numbered

A. 5, 6, and 7.

B. 1, 8, and 9.

C. 2, 10, and 11.

D. 3, 4, and 12.

Answer (C) is correct. *(CIA, adapted)*
REQUIRED: The items that best illustrate condition.
DISCUSSION: Engagement observations and recommendations are based on four attributes. One such attribute is condition, which is the factual evidence that the internal auditor found in the course of the examination (what does exist)(PA 2410-1). Items 2, 10, and 11 state information gathered by the internal auditor as a result of engagement procedures.
Answer (A) is incorrect because items 5, 6, and 7 best illustrate the effect attribute. Answer (B) is incorrect because items 1, 8, and 9 best illustrate the criteria attribute. Answer (D) is incorrect because items 3, 4, and 12 best illustrate the cause attribute.

17. The effect attribute is best illustrated by items numbered

    A. 3, 4, and 12.

    B. 5, 6, and 7.

    C. 1, 8, and 9.

    D. 2, 10, and 11.

Answer (B) is correct. *(CIA, adapted)*
    REQUIRED: The items that best illustrate effect.
    DISCUSSION: Engagement observations and recommendations are based on four attributes. One such attribute is effect, which is the risk or exposure the organization or others encounter because the condition is not consistent with the criteria (PA 2410-1). Items 5, 6, and 7 describe the impact of the difference.
    Answer (A) is incorrect because items 3, 4, and 12 best illustrate the cause attribute. Answer (C) is incorrect because items 1, 8, and 9 best illustrate the criteria attribute. Answer (D) is incorrect because items 2, 10, and 11 best illustrate the condition attribute.

18. Which of the following is false with respect to the use of interim engagement communications? Interim engagement communications

    A. Are used to communicate information that requires immediate attention.

    B. Are used to communicate a change in engagement scope for the activity under review.

    C. Keep management informed of engagement progress when engagements extend over a long period of time.

    D. Eliminate the need for issuing final engagement communications.

Answer (D) is correct. *(CIA, adapted)*
    REQUIRED: The false statement about interim engagement communications.
    DISCUSSION: Interim engagement communications may be written or oral and may be transmitted formally or informally. They are used to communicate information that requires immediate attention, to communicate a change in engagement scope for the activity under review, or to keep management informed of engagement progress when engagements extend over a long period. The use of interim engagement communications does not diminish or eliminate the need for final engagement communications (PA 2410-1).
    Answer (A) is incorrect because interim engagement communications are used to communicate information that requires immediate attention. Answer (B) is incorrect because interim engagement communications are used to communicate a change in engagement scope for the activity under review. Answer (C) is incorrect because interim engagement communications are used to keep management informed of engagement progress when engagements extend over a long period of time.

19. An internal auditor has completed an engagement to review an organization's activities and is ready to issue a final engagement communication. However, the engagement client disagrees with the internal auditor's conclusions. The internal auditor should

    A. Withhold the issuance of the final engagement communication until agreement on the issues is obtained.

    B. Perform more work, with the engagement client's concurrence, to resolve areas of disagreement. Delay the issuance of the final engagement communication until agreement is reached.

    C. Issue the final engagement communication and indicate that the engagement client has provided a scope limitation that has led to a difference as to the conclusions.

    D. Issue the final engagement communication and state both the internal auditor and engagement client positions and the reasons for the disagreement.

Answer (D) is correct. *(CIA, adapted)*
    REQUIRED: The action to be taken when an engagement client disagrees with an internal auditor's conclusions before the final report is issued.
    DISCUSSION: As part of the internal auditor's discussions with the engagement client, the internal auditor should try to obtain agreement on the results of the engagement and on a plan of action to improve operations, as needed. If the internal auditor and engagement client disagree about the engagement results, the final engagement communication may state both positions and the reasons for the disagreement. The engagement client's written comments may be included as an appendix to the final engagement communication. Alternatively, the engagement client's views may be presented in the body of the final engagement communication or in a cover letter (PA 2410-1).
    Answer (A) is incorrect because, if the engagement is complete, the final engagement communication should be issued in a timely manner. Moreover, agreement with the engagement client is not mandatory. Answer (B) is incorrect because, if the internal auditor is satisfied with the conclusions drawn from the engagement, there is no reason to perform more work. Answer (C) is incorrect because the disagreement on conclusions is not a scope limitation.

20. Final engagement communications should, at a minimum, contain the purpose, scope, and results of the engagement. Engagement observations and recommendations should be based on four attributes: criteria, condition, cause, and effect. The cause can best be described as

   A. Factual evidence that the internal auditor found.

   B. Reason for the difference between the expected and actual conditions.

   C. The risk or exposure because of the condition found.

   D. Resultant evaluations of the effects of the observations and recommendations.

Answer (B) is correct. *(CIA, adapted)*
   REQUIRED: The definition of the cause attribute.
   DISCUSSION: Engagement observations and recommendations should be based on four attributes. Criteria are the standards, measures, or expectations used in making an evaluation or verification (what should exist). Condition is defined as the factual evidence that the internal auditor found in the course of the examination (what does exist). If actual and expected conditions differ, the cause is the reason for the difference between the expected and actual conditions (why the difference exists). The effect is the risk or exposure the organization or others encounter because the condition is not consistent with the criteria (the impact of the difference) (PA 2410-1). Cause provides the answer to the question "Why?" and should be the basis for corrective action.
   Answer (A) is incorrect because factual evidence is the condition attribute. Answer (C) is incorrect because risk or exposure is the effect attribute. Answer (D) is incorrect because evaluations of the effects of the observations and recommendations are the internal auditor's conclusions.

21. An engagement observation is worded as follows:

The capital budget includes funds to purchase 11 new vehicles. Review of usage records showed that 10 vehicles in the fleet of 70 had been driven less than 2,500 miles during the past year. Vehicles have been assigned to different groups whose usage rates have varied greatly. There was no policy requiring rotation of vehicles between high and low usages groups. Lack of criteria for assigning vehicles and a system for monitoring their usage could lead to purchasing unneeded vehicles.

Based on the facts presented, it is appropriate to recommend that management

   A. Establish a minimum of 2,500 miles per quarter as a criterion for assigning vehicles to user groups.

   B. Establish a system to rotate vehicles among users periodically.

   C. Delay the proposed vehicle purchases until the apparent excess capacity is adequately explained or absorbed.

   D. Withhold approval of the capital budget until other projects can be reviewed by internal auditing.

Answer (C) is correct. *(CIA, adapted)*
   REQUIRED: The appropriate recommendation to management based on the facts presented in an engagement observation.
   DISCUSSION: Engagement communications should include recommendations for potential improvements. It may be desirable in some circumstances to recommend a general course of action and specific suggestions for implementation. In other circumstances, it may be appropriate to suggest further study (PA 2410-1). It is not appropriate for internal auditors to establish policies or procedures for the operations they audit.
   Answer (A) is incorrect because recommending specific criteria is not appropriate. Answer (B) is incorrect because establishing a system to rotate vehicles is not an appropriate recommendation; the matter requires further analysis. Answer (D) is incorrect because withholding approval of the capital budget is excessive given the results of the engagement just completed.

22. Engagement observations and recommendations emerge by a process of comparing what should be with what is. In determining "what should be" during an engagement to review an organization's treasury function, which of the following is the least desirable criterion against which to judge current operations?

- A. The operations of the treasury function as documented during the last engagement.

- B. Organizational policies and procedures delegating authority and assigning responsibilities.

- C. Finance textbook illustrations of generally accepted good treasury function practices.

- D. Codification of best practices of the treasury function in relevant industries.

Answer (A) is correct. *(CIA, adapted)*
REQUIRED: The least desirable criterion against which to judge current operations.
DISCUSSION: The criteria attribute of an engagement observation consists of the standards, measures, or expectations used in making an evaluation or verification (PA 2410-1). The least desirable criterion is prior operations. They may or may not have been in compliance with organizational policies and generally accepted practices.
Answer (B) is incorrect because organizational policies and procedures delegating authority and assigning responsibilities is a sound criterion against which to judge current operations. Answer (C) is incorrect because textbook illustrations of generally accepted practices is a sound criterion against which to judge current operations. Answer (D) is incorrect because codification of best practices (benchmarking) in relevant industries is a sound criterion against which to judge current operations.

23. An engagement communication relating to an engagement performed at a bank categorizes observations as "deficiencies" for major problems and "other areas for improvement" for less serious problems. Which of the following excerpts is properly included under "other areas for improvement"?

- A. Many secured loans did not contain hazard insurance coverage for tangible property collateral.

- B. Loan officers also prepare the cashier's checks for disbursement of the loan proceeds.

- C. The bank is incurring unnecessary postage cost by not combining certain special mailings to checking account customers with the monthly mailing of their statements.

- D. At one branch a large amount of cash was placed on a portable table behind the teller lines.

Answer (C) is correct. *(CIA, adapted)*
REQUIRED: The excerpt properly included under "other areas for improvement" in an engagement communication.
DISCUSSION: The attributes of engagement observations include effect, the risk, or exposure because the condition is inconsistent with the criteria. Moreover, the internal auditor must determine the degree of the risk or exposure. That the bank incurs unnecessary postage expense by not combining mailings warrants mentioning but does not constitute a serious risk exposure.
Answer (A) is incorrect because a lack of hazard insurance coverage for collateral is a serious risk exposure for the bank that could have a material effect on its financial statements. Answer (B) is incorrect because loan officers should not be permitted to prepare disbursement checks and grant loans to bank customers. These are duties that must be segregated to prevent possible employee defalcations. Answer (D) is incorrect because failure to limit access to cash violates internal control policies assigning cash to specific individuals for accountability purposes.

24. As a result of an engagement performed at a bank, the internal auditor included the following observation in the final engagement communication:

The late charges were waived on an excessive number of delinquent installment loan payments at the Spring Street Branch. We were informed that late charge waivers are not approved by an officer. Approximately $5,000 per year in revenues are being lost. In order to provide a better control over late charges waived and loss of income, we recommend that a lending officer be responsible for waiving late charges and that this approval be in writing.

Which of the following elements of an observation is not properly addressed?

- A. Criteria or standards.

- B. Condition.

- C. Cause.

- D. Effect.

Answer (A) is correct. *(CIA, adapted)*
REQUIRED: The element of an observation not properly addressed.
DISCUSSION: Observations should include adequate details. In this case, the internal auditor should have specified the percentage of late charges waived that is considered to be excessive. Using subjective terminology when specific data are available does not properly address the criteria or standards element of an observation.
Answer (B) is incorrect because the condition is that excessive late charges are being waived. Answer (C) is incorrect because the cause is that approval by an officer is not required. Answer (D) is incorrect because the effect is the annual loss of $5,000.

25. A governmental agency, constrained by scarce internal audit and human resources, wishes to know the status of its program for licensing automobiles. In particular, management is concerned about the possibility of

- A backlog in new license applications, and
- Poor controls over the collection and processing of application fees.

The results of the preliminary survey and limited testing conducted by the internal audit activity revealed that the licensing process was operating as intended. No major deficiencies were noted. How should the internal audit activity proceed?

A. Perform no further work, issue a formal engagement communication with the survey results, and discuss the results with management.

B. Perform no further work, discuss pertinent issues with management and the executive director, and prepare an engagement work program for future use so that another survey will not be necessary.

C. Complete the engagement as scheduled to ensure that other issues do not exist that were not noted during the survey phase.

D. Send a memorandum communication to the executive director and other concerned parties summarizing the preliminary survey results and indicating that the engagement has been canceled.

Answer (D) is correct. *(CIA, adapted)*
REQUIRED: The action following a preliminary survey and limited testing that revealed a process was operating as intended.
DISCUSSION: According to Sawyer (Sawyer's Internal Auditing, p. 184), when preliminary surveys are effectively conducted, they provide very useful information regarding how well the organization (or surveyed process) is operating. When survey and preliminary testing results indicate "good systems, good controls, good surveillance, and good management . . .," a decision may be made to perform no further engagement procedures. Accordingly, the internal auditor need only communicate this fact, along with summarized survey results, in a memorandum (an informal communication) to the executive director and other concerned parties.
Answer (A) is incorrect because, given that no further work was performed beyond the preliminary survey and limited testing, issuing a formal engagement communication discussing survey results with management would be inappropriate. Answer (B) is incorrect because no engagement work program should be prepared for the future. Because future events may alter existing circumstances, or compliance with policies and procedures may change, an engagement work program written now may be outdated for future use. Also, an engagement communication summarizing survey results should be prepared. Answer (C) is incorrect because an engagement may not be necessary if the survey and limited testing were conducted with due professional care. Given these results, the costs of an engagement may exceed the benefits.

26. As an internal auditor for a multinational chemical producer, you have been assigned to an engagement at a local plant. This plant is similar in age, siting, and construction to two other plants owned by the same organization that have been recently cited for discharge of hazardous wastes. In addition, you are aware that chemicals manufactured at the plant release toxic by-products. Assume that you have evidence that the plant is discharging hazardous wastes. As a certified internal auditor, what is the appropriate communication requirement in this situation?

A. Send a copy of your engagement communication to the appropriate regulatory agency.

B. Ignore the issue because the regulatory inspectors are better qualified to assess the danger.

C. Issue an interim engagement communication to the appropriate levels of management.

D. Note the issue in your working papers but do not report it.

Answer (C) is correct. *(CIA, adapted)*
REQUIRED: The appropriate communication requirement given that the plant is discharging hazardous wastes.
DISCUSSION: The internal auditor informs the appropriate authorities within the organization when (s)he suspects wrongdoing. A certified internal auditor also has an explicit obligation under The IIA *Code of Ethics* to reveal material facts that, if not revealed, could conceal unlawful practices. An interim engagement communication is indicated because the information to be communicated requires immediate attention (PA 2410-1).
Answer (A) is incorrect because internal auditors are not usually responsible for notifying outside authorities of suspected wrongdoing. Answer (B) is incorrect because internal auditors should evaluate risk exposures and controls relating to compliance with laws, regulations, and contracts (Standards 2110.A2 and 2420.A1). Answer (D) is incorrect because the Standards require the reporting of violations of laws, regulations, and contracts.

27. Internal audit activity policy requires that final engagement communications not be issued without a management response. An engagement with significant observations is complete except for management's response. Evaluate the following courses of action and select the best alternative.

A. Issue an interim engagement communication regarding the important issues noted.

B. Modify the policy to allow a specific time period for management's response.

C. Wait for management's response and then issue the engagement communication.

D. Discuss the situation with the external auditors.

Answer (A) is correct. *(CIA, adapted)*
REQUIRED: The best course of action given no management response when the engagement has resulted in significant observations.
DISCUSSION: Interim engagement communications may be used to communicate information that requires immediate attention, to communicate a change in engagement scope for the activity under review, or to keep management informed of engagement progress when engagements extend over a long period. The use of interim engagement communications does not diminish or eliminate the need for a final engagement communication (PA 2410-1). Thus, the significant observations should be presented on an interim basis.
Answer (B) is incorrect because significant observations should be timely communicated. Answer (C) is incorrect because significant observations should be timely communicated. Answer (D) is incorrect because significant observations should be timely communicated to senior management and the board.

28. Engagement field work has identified a number of significant observations. Additional tests from the original engagement work program still have to be performed, but data are not readily available. Evaluate the following and select the best alternative:

A. Do not issue the engagement communication until all testing has been completed.

B. Issue an interim engagement communication to management regarding the negative observations noted.

C. Identify other alternative tests to complete prior to reporting the engagement observations.

D. Perform engagement tests when the final data are available.

Answer (B) is correct. *(CIA, adapted)*
REQUIRED: The best alternative when significant observations are identified and the engagement work program is not complete.
DISCUSSION: Interim engagement communications may be used to communicate information that requires immediate attention, to communicate a change in engagement scope for the activity under review, or to keep management informed of engagement progress when engagements extend over a long period. Such interim engagement communications may be written or oral and may be transmitted formally or informally (PA 2410-1).
Answer (A) is incorrect because significant observations should be communicated promptly to management. Answer (C) is incorrect because significant observations should be communicated to management with mention of other tests to be performed. Answer (D) is incorrect because significant observations should be reported without delay for final testing.

29. An internal auditor has uncovered illegal acts committed by a member of senior management. Such information

A. Should be excluded from the internal auditor's engagement communication and discussed orally with the senior manager.

B. Must be immediately reported to the appropriate government authorities.

C. May be disclosed in a separate communication and distributed to all senior management.

D. May be disclosed in a separate communication and distributed to the board.

Answer (D) is correct. *(CIA, adapted)*
REQUIRED: The appropriate action when an internal auditor discovers illegal acts committed by a member of senior management.
DISCUSSION: Certain information may not be appropriate for disclosure to all communication recipients because it is privileged, proprietary, or related to improper or illegal acts. Such information, however, may be disclosed separately. If the conditions being reported involve senior management, distribution should be to the board of the organization (PA 2410-1).
Answer (A) is incorrect because, although improper or illegal acts may be disclosed in a separate communication, the internal auditor should not discuss such information with individuals who have committed such acts. Answer (B) is incorrect because, in general, internal auditors are responsible to their organization's management rather than outside agencies. In the case of fraud, statutory filings with regulatory agencies may be required. Answer (C) is incorrect because such information should be communicated to individuals to whom senior managers report.

2.3 Quality of Communications

30. The internal audit activity for a chain of retail stores recently concluded an engagement to evaluate sales adjustments in all stores in the Southeast region. The engagement revealed that several stores are costing the organization substantial sums in duplicate credits to customers' charge accounts. The final engagement communication published 8 weeks after the engagement was concluded, incorporated the internal auditors' recommendations to store management that should prevent duplicate credits to customers' accounts. Which of the following standards has been disregarded?

A. The follow-up actions were not adequate.

B. The internal auditors should have implemented appropriate corrective action as soon as the duplicate credits were discovered.

C. Internal auditor recommendations should not be included in the final engagement communication.

D. The final engagement communication was not timely.

Answer (D) is correct. *(CIA, adapted)*
REQUIRED: The standard that was disregarded.
DISCUSSION: Communications should be accurate, objective, clear, concise, constructive, complete, and timely (Standard 2420). Timely communications are issued without undue delay and enable prompt effective action (PA 2420-1). The report, which was not published until 8 weeks after the engagement was concluded, was not issued in a timely fashion, given the significance of the observations and the need for prompt, effective action.
Answer (A) is incorrect because information is not sufficient to evaluate the effectiveness of follow-up. Answer (B) is incorrect because internal auditors may properly make recommendations for potential improvements but should not implement corrective action. Answer (C) is incorrect because internal auditor recommendations are part of the results of the engagement. Final engagement communications should at least include the purpose, scope, and results of the engagement (PA 2410-1).

31. Communication skills are important to internal auditors. The internal auditor should be able to convey effectively all of the following to the engagement client except

A. The engagement objectives for a specific engagement client.

B. The evaluations based on a preliminary survey of an engagement client.

C. The risk assessment used in selecting the area for engagement investigation.

D. Recommendations that are generated in relationship to a specific engagement client.

Answer (C) is correct. *(CIA, adapted)*
REQUIRED: The matter that an internal auditor need not convey to the engagement client.
DISCUSSION: Internal auditors should be skilled in oral and written communications so that they can clearly and effectively convey such matters as engagement objectives, evaluations, conclusions, and recommendations (PA 1210-1). However, the internal auditor's risk assessment is not specifically mentioned in Practice Advisory 1210-1 with respect to communication skills.
Answer (A) is incorrect because the internal auditor should be able to convey effectively engagement objectives. Answer (B) is incorrect because the internal auditor should be able to convey effectively evaluations. Answer (D) is incorrect because the internal auditor should be able to convey effectively recommendations.

32. When a final engagement communication contains a significant error, the Standards require the chief audit executive to

A. Issue a written report to individuals who can ensure that engagement results are given due consideration.

B. Issue a written report to individuals who received the original communication.

C. Communicate corrected information to all individuals who received the original communication.

D. Communicate corrected information to all those who might have relied on the original communication.

Answer (C) is correct. *(Publisher, adapted)*
REQUIRED: The duty of the CAE when a final engagement communication contains a significant error.
DISCUSSION: If a final engagement communication contains a significant error or omission, the CAE should communicate corrected information to all who received the original communication (Standard 2421). Hence, the Standards do not require a written report.

33. Standard 2420, *Quality of Communications*, states seven qualities of good communications. Avoiding unnecessary technical language is best associated with which of the following qualities of communication?

A. Accurate.

B. Concise.

C. Clear.

D. Complete.

Answer (C) is correct. *(Publisher, adapted)*
REQUIRED: The quality best associated with avoiding unnecessary technical language.
DISCUSSION: Communications should be accurate, objective, clear, concise, constructive, complete, and timely (Standard 2420). Clear communications are easily understood and logical. Clarity can be improved by avoiding unnecessary technical language and providing all significant and relevant information (PA 2420-1).
Answer (A) is incorrect because accurate communications avoid errors and distortions. Answer (B) is incorrect because concise communications avoid superfluous detail, redundancy, and wordiness. Answer (D) is incorrect because complete communications lack nothing that is essential to the target audience and include all significant and relevant information and observations to support recommendations and conclusions.

34. Which of the following is not a major purpose of an engagement communication?

A. Inform.

B. Get results.

C. Assign responsibility.

D. Persuade.

Answer (C) is correct. *(CIA, adapted)*
REQUIRED: The item not a major purpose of an engagement communication.
DISCUSSION: According to *Sawyer's Internal Auditing* (p. 611), engagement communications are intended to inform, persuade, and get results. They explain the internal auditors' observations, conclusions, and recommendations, attempt to convince the recipients of the engagement communication of their value and validity, and attempt to foster beneficial change.
Answer (A) is incorrect because informing the board and senior management is a major purpose of an engagement communication. Answer (B) is incorrect because getting results is a major purpose of an engagement communication. Answer (D) is incorrect because persuading the board and senior management that certain conditions exist is a major purpose of an engagement communication.

35. Providing useful and timely information and promoting improvements in operations are goals of internal auditors. To accomplish these goals in their engagement communication, they should

A. Provide senior management with engagement communications that emphasize the operational details of defective conditions.

B. Provide operating management with engagement communications that emphasize general concerns and risks.

C. Provide information in written form before it is discussed with the engagement client.

D. Provide engagement communications that meet the expectations and perceptions of both operational and senior management.

Answer (D) is correct. *(CIA, adapted)*
REQUIRED: The type of engagement communication an internal auditor should issue to provide useful and timely information.
DISCUSSION: An engagement communication should be objective, clear, accurate, concise, constructive, complete, and timely (Standard 2420). Furthermore, to best fulfill their responsibilities for effective communication of the results of their work, internal auditors should provide engagement communications that address the expectations, perceptions, and needs of both operational and senior management. Thus, the engagement communication should contain general concepts that are concerned with matters of significance to the organization as a whole for the benefit of senior management. The engagement communication should also emphasize details of operations for the benefit of operating management.
Answer (A) is incorrect because senior management can best use engagement communications that convey information having organization-wide significance. Answer (B) is incorrect because details of operations are most useful to operating management. Answer (C) is incorrect because information should be discussed with the engagement client before the report is written.

Questions 36 through 38 are based on the following information. An internal auditor has submitted a first draft of an engagement communication to an engagement client in preparation for an exit interview. The following is an excerpt:

The engagement was performed to accomplish several objectives:

- Verify the existence of unused machinery being stored in the warehouse.
- Determine whether machinery had been damaged during storage.
- Review the handling procedures being performed by personnel at the warehouse.
- Determine whether proper accounting procedures are being followed for machinery kept in the warehouse.
- Calculate the current fair value of warehouse inventories.
- Compare the total value of the machinery with accounting records.

It was confirmed that, of the 30 machines selected from purchasing records for the sample, 13 were present on the warehouse floor and another five were on the loading dock ready for conveyance to the production facility. Twelve others had already been sent to the production facility at a previous time. An examination of the accounting procedures used at the warehouse revealed the failure by the warehouse accounting clerk to reconcile inventory records monthly, as required by policy. A sample of 25 machines was examined for possible damage, and all but one was in good condition. It was confirmed by the internal auditors that handling procedures outlined in the warehouse policy manual appear to be adequate, and warehouse personnel apparently were following those procedures, except for the examination of items being received for inventory.

36. When an internal auditor is communicating with engagement clients, both situational factors and message characteristics can damage the communication process. An internal auditor has only limited control over situational factors but has substantial control over message characteristics. Which of the following is a message characteristic that the internal auditor who prepared the engagement communication overlooked?

A. Sequence of message.

B. Nature of the audience.

C. Noise.

D. Prior encounters with the engagement client.

Answer (A) is correct. *(CIA, adapted)*
REQUIRED: The message characteristic the internal auditor overlooked.
DISCUSSION: The internal auditor neglected to organize the information. Because the information being communicated is complicated, the engagement communication's content should be organized in logical succession to facilitate understanding and acceptance. For this reason, standard formats are often used in business communications.
Answer (B) is incorrect because the nature of an audience is a situational factor that is outside the control of the internal auditor. Answer (C) is incorrect because noise is a situational factor that interferes with the effective communication of intended messages. Answer (D) is incorrect because the history of previous encounters is a situational factor that is outside the control of the internal auditor.

37. The objectives of an engagement communication are to inform and to influence. Whether these objectives are met depends on the clarity of the writing. Which of the following principles of communication clarity was violated in the engagement communication?

A. Appropriately organize the communication.

B. Keep most sentences short and simple.

C. Use active voice verbs.

D. All of the answers are correct.

Answer (D) is correct. *(CIA, adapted)*
REQUIRED: The principle(s) of clarity violated in the engagement communication.
DISCUSSION: The communication should be well-organized so that the information is given appropriate attention. Also, effective organization enhances understanding by presenting information in an logical order that clarifies the internal auditor's reasoning. Keeping sentences as short and simple as possible likewise facilitates understanding. Also, active voice verbs are more vivid and concise than passive voice verbs.
Answer (A) is incorrect because an engagement communication should be appropriately organized. Answer (B) is incorrect because an engagement communication should be concise. Answer (C) is incorrect because an engagement communication should use active voice verbs.

38. At a minimum, the following elements should be included in final engagement communications: purpose, scope, and results. Results include observations, conclusions (opinions), recommendations, and action plans (PA 2410-1). Which of the following describes all of the elements missing from the engagement communication?

A. Scope, conclusion, recommendation.

B. Purpose, result, recommendation.

C. Observations, conclusion, recommendation.

D. Purpose, scope, recommendation.

Answer (A) is correct. *(CIA, adapted)*
REQUIRED: The elements missing from the engagement communication.
DISCUSSION: Although a portion of the scope is discussed, the reader cannot determine the significance of the amount of machines selected without knowing the total amount of machines available and the value of the machinery. Also, the conclusion or opinion about the operation is not stated, and the engagement communication makes no recommendations.

2.4 Disseminating Results

39. One purpose of the exit interview is for the internal auditor to

    A. Require corrective action.

    B. Review and verify the appropriateness of the engagement communication based upon client input.

    C. Review the performance of internal auditors assigned to the engagement.

    D. Present the final engagement communication to management.

Answer (B) is correct. *(CIA, adapted)*
REQUIRED: The purpose of the exit interview.
DISCUSSION: The internal auditor should discuss conclusions and recommendations at appropriate levels of management before issuing final engagement communications. Furthermore, discussion of conclusions and recommendations is usually accomplished during the course of the engagement or at postengagement meetings (exit interviews). Another technique is the review of draft engagement conclusions, observations, and recommendations by management of the activity reviewed. These discussions and reviews help ensure that there have been no misunderstandings or misinterpretations of fact by providing the opportunity for the engagement client to clarify specific items and to express views of the observations, conclusions, and recommendations (PA 2440-1).

Answer (A) is incorrect because only management can require corrective action. Answer (C) is incorrect because internal auditor performance is reviewed in private with the individual employee, not at the exit interview. Answer (D) is incorrect because the exit interview is normally based on draft communications. The final engagement communication is subject to modification based on the results of the exit interview.

40. The chief audit executive should disseminate results to the appropriate individuals (Standard 2440). Disseminating information outside the organization

    A. Is prohibited by the Standards.

    B. Requires the elimination of references to the Standards.

    C. Requires that an engagement performed to generate such information be conducted in accordance with the Standards.

    D. Is permissible only if a new engagement is performed.

Answer (C) is correct. *(Publisher, adapted)*
REQUIRED: The true statement about disseminating information outside the organization.
DISCUSSION: Engagements performed to generate internal auditing reports or communications to be disseminated outside the organization should be conducted in accordance with applicable Standards and include reference to such Standards in the report or other communication.

Answer (A) is incorrect because the Standards permit dissemination of information outside the organization. Answer (B) is incorrect because the report or other communication should refer to applicable Standards. Answer (D) is incorrect because, in certain situations, it may be possible to revise an existing report or information to make it suitable for dissemination outside the organization. In other situations, it may be possible to generate a new report based on work previously conducted.

41. Under the laws and regulations of countries in the OECD (Organization for Economic Cooperations and Development), knowledge of certain illegal or unethical acts requires public servants to notify an appropriate official. Which of the following are not such acts?

    A. Acts that affect the environment.

    B. Acts that endanger the health, safety, or well-being of individuals.

    C. Acts that are considered miscarriages of justice.

    D. Criminal offenses and other failures to comply with legal obligations.

Answer (A) is correct. *(Publisher, adapted)*
REQUIRED: The activity not considered illegal or unethical in OECD countries.
DISCUSSION: Among the activities considered illegal or unethical in OECD countries are (1) criminal offenses and other failures to comply with legal obligations; (2) acts that are considered miscarriages of justice; (3) acts that endanger the health, safety, or well-being of individuals; and (4) acts that damage the environment. Also, any activity that conceals or covers up any of the above is considered illegal or unethical. Many activities affect the environment without being illegal or unethical, but those that damage the environment could be either unethical or illegal.

Answer (B) is incorrect because acts that endanger the health, safety, or well-being of individuals could be either illegal or unethical. Answer (C) is incorrect because acts that are considered miscarriages of justice could be either illegal or unethical. Answer (D) is incorrect because criminal offenses and other failures to comply with legal obligations are illegal.

42. The internal audit activity customarily has a dual relationship with management and the audit committee. This means that

A. Management should help the internal audit activity by revising and forwarding engagement communications to the audit committee.

B. The internal audit activity should report directly to the audit committee, without corroborating engagement communications with management.

C. The accuracy of engagement communications should be verified with management, and the internal audit activity should then report to management and the audit committee.

D. Ideally, the internal audit activity works under the audit committee but reports to the chief operating officer on all engagements relating to operations.

Answer (C) is correct.   *(CIA, adapted)*
REQUIRED: The meaning of the IAA's dual relationship with management and the audit committee.
DISCUSSION: When communicating engagement results, internal auditors should discuss conclusions and recommendations at appropriate levels of management, a step that permits verifying the accuracy of engagement communications. Final engagement communications should be distributed to members of the organization who are able to ensure that engagement results are given due consideration, such as the audit committee (PA 2440-1).
Answer (A) is incorrect because the IAA should revise and forward engagement communications to the audit committee. Answer (B) is incorrect because engagement communications should be discussed with the client management. Answer (D) is incorrect because the ideal arrangement is to send all engagement communications to the audit committee.

43. Which of the following actions should not be taken initially when credible evidence exists that the corporation is unnecessarily exposing itself to risk?

A. The chief audit executive may discuss his or her concerns about the risk exposure with senior management within his or her normal chain of command.

B. The chief audit executive may discuss his or her concerns about the risk of exposure with the board of directors.

C. The chief audit executive may discuss his or her concerns with the parties responsible for the risk exposure.

D. The chief audit executive may discuss his or her concerns with someone outside the organization.

Answer (D) is correct.   *(Publisher, adapted)*
REQUIRED: The communication of sensitive information by the chief audit executive.
DISCUSSION: Practice Advisory 2440-3 states that if the internal auditor has credible evidence of exposure to an unnecessary risk, the auditor should normally communicate the information to those in management who can act on it. If the chief audit executive is not satisfied with the result, then other options are available. The chief auditor could discuss his or her concerns with senior management, which often includes members of the board of directors. The chief audit executive should only consider discussion with outside parties if he or she believes that management will not investigate the issue properly and other people may be adversely affected.
Answer (A) is incorrect because discussion with senior management is often one of the first actions taken by the chief audit executive when risks are exposed. Answer (B) is incorrect because the board of directors is normally within the chief audit executive's chain of command, and the chief audit executive is likely to bring up risk exposures to the board of directors. Answer (C) is incorrect because the chief audit executive may believe that the problem can be solved quickly by discussing the issue with those directly responsible for the risk exposure.

44. In which of the following scenarios must the chain of command discussions be accelerated?

A. A manager is not taking adequate steps to protect a patent developed by the corporation.

B. A publicly traded corporation is hiding its liabilities in off-balance-sheet entities.

C. Activities that the corporation engages in may result in environmental damage in the future.

D. Several significant investments held by the corporation are being mismanaged by the corporation.

Answer (B) is correct.   *(Publisher, adapted)*
REQUIRED: The scenario in which the chain of command discussions should be accelerated.
DISCUSSION: Situations involving fraudulent financial reporting by a company with publicly traded securities should be brought to the attention of the audit committee of the board of directors immediately. This action must be taken even if the chief audit executive and management agree on a course of action.
Answer (A) is incorrect because the manager's lack of action affects the corporation's competitiveness and success but would not require the chain of command discussions to be accelerated. Corrective action may be taken before the issue is brought before the board of directors. Answer (C) is incorrect because, although this is an issue that management will have to address in the future, it does not force the acceleration of the chain of command discussions. Answer (D) is incorrect because mismanagement of funds may be corrected at lower levels in the corporation. Although the misallocation of resources may result in losses, it does not require the acceleration of the chain of command discussions.

45. Which of the following is not an example of "whistle-blowing?"

    A. Informing the chief executive officer about a manager who engages in fraudulent related party transactions.

    B. Telling the manager of a different department about illegal elimination of toxic wastes by the corporation.

    C. Exposing an unsafe working environment to OSHA.

    D. Writing a letter to a newspaper about illegal hiring practices of the corporation.

Answer (A) is correct. *(Publisher, adapted)*
    REQUIRED: The scenario that is not whistle-blowing.
    DISCUSSION: Some situations may cause the internal auditor to consider whether to discuss sensitive information with people outside the normal chain of command or people outside of the corporation. Whistle-blowing is defined as the act of disclosing adverse information to someone in the organization who is outside of the individual's normal chain of command, or to a governmental agency or other authority that is wholly outside of the organization (Practice Advisory 2440-3).
    Answer (B) is incorrect because whistle-blowing includes telling anyone outside of the chain of command even if they are still within the organization. Answer (C) is incorrect because disclosure of adverse information to a governmental agency is considered whistle-blowing. Answer (D) is incorrect because the disclosure of adverse information to an party outside the organization is considered whistle-blowing.

46. For which situation should the internal auditor consider communicating sensitive information outside the organization's governance structure?

    A. The internal auditor believes the corporation does not have the resources to address the problem efficiently.

    B. Action by management may take longer than the internal auditor believes is necessary to correct the problem.

    C. The internal auditor believes that the problem will not be properly investigated by management.

    D. An outside agency may be able to help the corporation correct the problem faster than the corporation could on its own.

Answer (C) is correct. *(Publisher, adapted)*
    REQUIRED: The situation in which sensitive information should be discussed outside the organization's governance structure.
    DISCUSSION: In most cases of whistleblowing, whistleblowers will disclose sensitive information internally, even if not within the normal chain of command, if they trust the policies and mechanisms of the organization to investigate the problem. If the whistleblower doubts the problem will be properly investigated by the corporation, (s)he may consider disclosing the problem to an outside party.
    Answer (A) is incorrect because management and the board of directors may still take corrective action and seek outside assistance if they believe it is necessary. Revealing sensitive information prematurely would put the corporation at an unnecessary risk. Answer (B) is incorrect because management is taking appropriate action and the internal auditor should work with management and the board of directors to correct problems before involving an outside party. Answer (D) is incorrect because management and the board of directors have the responsibility to decide how to handle the problem. If management or the board of directors believes that an outside party should be consulted, management and the board of directors may make that decision.

47. Which of the following should not be one of the primary reasons why an internal auditor may communicate sensitive information outside the normal chain of command?

    A. The desire to stop the wrongful, harmful, or improper activity.

    B. Legal advice indicates that the internal auditor should disclose the sensitive information to an outside party.

    C. A professional obligation requires disclosure of the activity to an outside party.

    D. The internal auditor does not agree with how the board or directors or management may correct the problem.

Answer (D) is correct. *(Publisher, adapted)*
    REQUIRED: The item not a primary reason an internal auditor should disclose sensitive information to an outside party.
    DISCUSSION: The choice to disclose sensitive information is a personal choice. The decision to communicate outside the normal chain of command should be based on a well-informed opinion that the wrongdoing is supported by credible evidence and that a legal or professional obligation requires further action. The internal auditor's motive for outside disclosure should be the desire to stop the wrongful, harmful, or improper activity.
    Answer (A) is incorrect because the primary motive of outside disclosure to get management or the board of directors to stop the activity they are engaged in. Answer (B) is incorrect because the internal auditor will often consult legal counsel before deciding what course of action to take with regard to the activity. Answer (C) is incorrect because a professional obligation often forces the internal auditor to disclose to outside parties. The IIA Code of Ethics requires IIA members and certified internal auditors to adhere to the disclosure requirements of illegal or unethical acts.

48. An engagement performed at an organization's payroll department has revealed various control weaknesses. These weaknesses along with recommendations for corrective actions were addressed in the final engagement communication. This communication should be most useful to the organization's

    A. Treasurer.

    B. Audit committee of the board of directors.

    C. Payroll manager.

    D. President.

Answer (C) is correct. *(CIA, adapted)*
    REQUIRED: The person most likely to benefit from the receipt of a payroll department engagement communication.
    DISCUSSION: Final engagement communications should be distributed to those members of the organization who are able to ensure that engagement results are given due consideration. This means that the engagement communication should go to those who are in a position to take corrective action or to ensure that corrective action is taken. The final engagement communication should be distributed to the management of the activity under review (PA 2440-1). A communication on control weaknesses in the payroll function should be most useful to the payroll manager because (s)he is in a position to take corrective action.
    Answer (A) is incorrect because the treasurer is not responsible for the payroll department. Answer (B) is incorrect because the audit committee is not in operational control of the department. Answer (D) is incorrect because the president is not in operational control of the department.

49. Which of the following combinations of participants is most appropriate to attend an exit interview?

    A. The responsible internal auditor and representatives from management who are knowledgeable about detailed operations and who can authorize implementation of corrective action.

    B. The chief audit executive and the executive in charge of the activity or function reviewed.

    C. Staff internal auditors who conducted the field work and operating personnel in charge of the daily performance of the activity or function reviewed.

    D. Staff auditors who conducted the field work and the executive in charge of the activity or function reviewed.

Answer (A) is correct. *(CIA, adapted)*
    REQUIRED: The combination of participants most appropriate to attend an exit interview.
    DISCUSSION: The internal auditor should discuss conclusions and recommendations at appropriate levels of management before issuing final engagement communications. Although the level of participants in the discussions and reviews may vary, they will usually include those individuals who are knowledgeable about detailed operations and who have the authority to implement corrective action (PA 2440-1).
    Answer (B) is incorrect because the CAE and the executive in charge of the activity reviewed may not be knowledgeable about the details. Answer (C) is incorrect because staff auditors and operating personnel might not have the necessary perspectives or authority. Answer (D) is incorrect because the staff auditors might lack the proper perspective and authority.

50. The chief audit executive or a designee is required to decide to whom the final engagement communication will be distributed. Observations concerning significant internal control weakness are included in an engagement communication on the accounts payable system of an organization whose securities are publicly traded. Which of the following is the most likely reason that the CAE has chosen to send copies of this engagement communication to the board and the external auditor?

    A. The board and external auditor are normally sent copies of all internal audit engagement communications as a courtesy.

    B. The board and external auditor will need to take corrective action based on the observations.

    C. The activities of the board and external auditor may be affected because of the potential for misstated financial statements.

    D. A regulatory agency's guidelines require such distribution.

Answer (C) is correct. *(CIA, adapted)*
    REQUIRED: The most likely reason for distributing copies of an engagement communication containing observations about significant control weaknesses in the accounts payable system.
    DISCUSSION: Engagement communications should be distributed to those members of the organization who are able to ensure that engagement results are given due consideration. Communications may also be distributed to other interested or affected parties such as external auditors and the board (PA 2440-1). The potential for misstated financial statements created by the internal control weaknesses should be of interest to the board and the external auditor.
    Answer (A) is incorrect because normal distribution is to management of the activity under review and others in a position to take corrective action or ensure that corrective action is taken. Answer (B) is incorrect because operating management is responsible for taking corrective action. Answer (D) is incorrect because such a requirement is unlikely.

51. Which of the following is not an objective of the exit interview for an engagement performed by the internal auditors?

   A. To resolve conflicts.

   B. To discuss the observations, conclusions, and recommendations.

   C. To identify concerns for future engagements.

   D. To identify management's actions and responses to the observations, conclusions, and recommendations.

Answer (C) is correct. *(CIA, adapted)*
   REQUIRED: The item that is not an objective of the exit interview.
   DISCUSSION: The internal auditor should discuss conclusions and recommendations at appropriate levels of management before issuing final engagement communications. Furthermore, discussion of conclusions and recommendations is usually accomplished during the course of the engagement or at post-engagement meetings (exit interviews). Another technique is the review of draft engagement observations, conclusions, and recommendations by management of the activity evaluated. These discussions and reviews help ensure that there have been no misunderstandings or misinterpretations of fact by providing the opportunity for the engagement client to clarify specific items and to express views of the observations, conclusions, and recommendations (PA 2440-1). Identifying concerns for future engagements is not a primary objective of the exit interview.
   Answer (A) is incorrect because resolving conflicts is an objective of the exit interview. Answer (B) is incorrect because reaching an agreement on the facts is an objective of the exit interview. Answer (D) is incorrect because determining management's action plan and responses is an objective of the exit interview.

52. Several levels of management are interested in the results of an engagement performed in the marketing department. What is the best method of communicating the results of the engagement?

   A. Write detailed communications for each level of management.

   B. Write a communication to the marketing management and give summary communications to other management levels.

   C. Discuss results with marketing management and issue a summary communication to senior management.

   D. Discuss results with all levels of management.

Answer (B) is correct. *(CIA, adapted)*
   REQUIRED: The best method of communicating the results of an engagement.
   DISCUSSION: Final engagement communications should be distributed to those members of the organization who are able to ensure that engagement results are given due consideration. This means that the engagement communication should go to those who are in a position to take corrective action or to ensure that corrective action is taken. The final engagement communication should be distributed to management of the activity under review. Higher-level members in the organization may receive only a summary. Communications may also be distributed to other interested or affected parties such as external auditors and the board (PA 2440-1).
   Answer (A) is incorrect because each level of management does not need a detailed communication. Answer (C) is incorrect because a formal, detailed written communication should be addressed to marketing management if that is the level of management able to act on the engagement results. Answer (D) is incorrect because observations, conclusions, and recommendations should be discussed with the appropriate levels of management, but an engagement communication should still be issued.

53. Exit interviews serve to ensure the accuracy of the information used by an internal auditor. A secondary purpose of an exit interview is to

   A. Get immediate action on a recommendation.

   B. Improve relations with the engagement clients.

   C. Agree to the appropriate distribution of the final engagement communication.

   D. Brief senior management on the results of the engagement.

Answer (B) is correct. *(CIA, adapted)*
   REQUIRED: The secondary purpose of an exit interview.
   DISCUSSION: The internal auditor should discuss conclusions and recommendations at appropriate levels of management before issuing final engagement communications. Discussion with the engagement client not only provides a quality control review but is also a courtesy that enhances the internal auditor-client relationship. In addition, the exit interview is an important aspect of the participative approach to internal auditing because it involves the client in the engagement process as well as in any recommended changes arising from the engagement. People are more likely to accept changes if they have participated in the decisions and in the methods used to implement changes. Moreover, the participative approach tends to engender feelings of mutual liking and trust that contribute to amicable relationships, which produce a more favorable environment for the engagement effort.
   Answer (A) is incorrect because an interim engagement communication would have been used to obtain immediate action on a recommendation. Answer (C) is incorrect because the distribution of communications is not a secondary purpose of an exit interview. Answer (D) is incorrect because senior management ordinarily should be given a summary of the results.

54. A purpose of the internal auditors' exit interview with appropriate levels of management is to

- A. Inform members of the board of engagement results.
- B. Present the final engagement communication to the chief executive officer.
- C. Obtain information to evaluate internal control.
- D. Generate commitment for appropriate managerial action.

Answer (D) is correct.   *(CIA, adapted)*
   REQUIRED: The purpose of the exit interview.
   DISCUSSION: The internal auditor should discuss conclusions and recommendations at appropriate levels of management before issuing final engagement communications. Discussion with the engagement client not only provides a quality control review but is also a courtesy that enhances the internal auditor-client relationship. In addition, the exit interview is an important aspect of the participative approach to internal auditing because it involves the client in the engagement process as well as in any recommended changes arising from the engagement. People are more likely to accept changes if they have participated in the decisions and in the methods used to implement changes. Moreover, the participative approach tends to engender feelings of mutual liking and trust that contribute to amicable relationships, which produce a more favorable environment for the engagement effort.
   Answer (A) is incorrect because the board would ordinarily receive a summary communication. Answer (B) is incorrect because the final engagement communication is generated after the exit interview. Answer (C) is incorrect because the consideration of controls occurs at an early stage of the engagement.

55. Internal auditors should discuss conclusions and recommendations at appropriate levels of management before issuing final engagement communications. Which of the following is the primary reason that an exit interview should be documented by the internal auditor?

- A. The information may be needed if a dispute arises.
- B. The Standards require that exit interviews be documented.
- C. The information may be needed to revise future engagement work programs.
- D. Closing conference documentation becomes a basis for future engagements.

Answer (A) is correct.   *(CIA, adapted)*
   REQUIRED: The primary reason an exit interview should be documented.
   DISCUSSION: The internal auditor should discuss conclusions and recommendations at appropriate levels of management before issuing final engagement communications. Furthermore, discussion of observations, conclusions, and recommendations is usually accomplished during the course of the engagement or at post-engagement meetings (exit interviews). Another technique is the review of draft engagement observations, conclusions, and recommendations by management of the activity reviewed. These discussions and reviews help ensure that there have been no misunderstandings or misinterpretations of fact by providing the opportunity for the engagement client to clarify specific items and to express views of the observations, conclusions, and recommendations (PA 2440-1). Documenting these discussions and reviews can be valuable in preventing or resolving disputes.
   Answer (B) is incorrect because documentation of exit interviews is not specifically required by the Standards. Answer (C) is incorrect because notes taken during the exit interview may lead to a revised engagement work program, but that result is not the primary purpose of the practice. Answer (D) is incorrect because planning future engagements is not the primary purpose of documenting an exit interview.

56. The internal audit activity has recently completed an engagement to evaluate the organization's accounts payable function. The chief audit executive decided to issue a summary in conjunction with the final engagement communication. Who is most likely to receive the summary only?

- A. Accounts payable manager.
- B. External auditor.
- C. Controller.
- D. Audit committee of the board.

Answer (D) is correct.   *(CIA, adapted)*
   REQUIRED: The most likely recipient(s) of the summary engagement communication.
   DISCUSSION: Final engagement communications should be distributed to those members of the organization who are able to ensure that engagement results are given due consideration. This means that the communication should go to those who are in a position to take corrective action or to ensure that corrective action is taken. The final engagement communication should be distributed to management of the activity under review. Higher-level members in the organization may receive only a summary communication (PA 2440-1). Summary communications may be appropriate for levels of management above the engagement client (PA 2410-1).
   Answer (A) is incorrect because the accounts payable manager is best served by receiving a copy of the full final engagement communication. Answer (B) is incorrect because the external auditor needs the details in the full engagement communication. Answer (C) is incorrect because the controller is responsible for the accounting function and is more likely to receive the full engagement communication than the audit committee.

57. In a well-developed management environment, the internal audit activity would:

A. Report the results of an audit engagement to line management as well as to senior management.

B. Conduct initial audits of new computer systems after they have begun operating.

C. Interface primarily with senior management, minimizing interactions with line managers who are the subjects of internal audit work.

D. Focus primarily on asset management and report results to the audit committee.

Answer (A) is correct. *(CIA, adapted)*
REQUIRED: The action of the internal audit activity in a well-developed management environment.
DISCUSSION: In a well-developed management system, the internal auditing function is used to provide a more direct benefit to line operations by providing feedback to operating management as well as to senior management. Moreover, final engagement communications should be distributed to those members of the organization who are able to ensure that engagement results are given due consideration. This means that the report should go to those who are in a position to take corrective action or ensure that corrective action is taken. The final engagement communications should be distributed to management of the activity under review (PA 2440-1).
Answer (B) is incorrect because emphasis should be placed on the audits of proposed products and systems. These early examinations could be used to determine the feasibility or desirability of changes before these changes are implemented. Answer (C) is incorrect because the role of the internal auditor involves interfacing with management at the operating level as well as at the senior level. Answer (D) is incorrect because asset management is not a primary focus of the internal audit activity.

2.5 Monitoring Progress

58. Follow-up activity may be required to ensure that corrective action has taken place for certain observations made in an assurance engagement. The internal audit activity's responsibility to perform follow-up activities as required should be defined in the

A. Internal audit activity's written charter or the agreement with the client.

B. Mission statement of the audit committee.

C. Engagement memo issued prior to each engagement.

D. Purpose statement within applicable engagement communications.

Answer (A) is correct. *(CIA, adapted)*
REQUIRED: The authoritative source defining the IAA's responsibility to perform follow-up activities.
DISCUSSION: Follow-up is a process by which internal auditors determine the adequacy, effectiveness, and timeliness of actions taken by management on reported engagement observations and recommendations including those made by external auditors and others. Responsibility for follow-up in an assurance engagement should be defined in the IAA's written charter (PA 2500.A1-1). In a consulting engagement, the extent of monitoring of the disposition of results depends upon the agreement with the client.
Answer (B) is incorrect because follow-up is not specified in the content of the audit committee's mission statement. Answer (C) is incorrect because the engagement memo may contain a statement about responsibility for follow-up, but it should be based on the wording and authority of the IAA's charter. Answer (D) is incorrect because follow-up authority and responsibility may be cited in applicable engagement communications, but the definition should be stated first in the IAA's charter.

59. Internal auditors realize that at times corrective action is not taken even when agreed to by the appropriate parties. Thus, in an assurance engagement, internal auditors should

A. Decide the extent of necessary follow-up work.

B. Allow management to decide when to follow up because follow-up is management's ultimate responsibility.

C. Decide to conduct follow-up work only if management requests the internal auditor's assistance.

D. Write a follow-up engagement communication with all observations and recommendations and their significance to the operations.

Answer (A) is correct. *(CIA, adapted)*
REQUIRED: The auditor's responsibility to follow up.
DISCUSSION: The nature, timing, and extent of follow-up in an assurance engagement should be determined by the chief audit executive (PA 2500.A1-1).
Answer (B) is incorrect because determining the timing of follow-up is not management's responsibility; it is the responsibility of the CAE. Answer (C) is incorrect because determining the nature and extent of follow-up is the CAE's responsibility. Management's responsibility is to decide the appropriate action to be taken in response to reported engagement observations and recommendations. Answer (D) is incorrect because the internal auditors must decide the extent of follow-up before submitting a follow-up engagement communication.

60. Assume that the internal auditors' observations are so serious that, in their view, they require immediate action by management. Which of the following statements regarding the internal auditors' responsibility with respect to communicating results and follow-up are true?

I.   The conditions should be actively monitored by the internal auditors until corrected.

II. The initial observations should be communicated to senior management and the audit committee even if the engagement is not complete.

III. The internal auditors should test the actions implemented by management to determine if they remedy the problem.

A. I only.

B. II only.

C. II and III only.

D. I, II, and III.

Answer (D) is correct. *(CIA, adapted)*
REQUIRED: The true statement(s) regarding the internal auditors' responsibility for communicating results and following up observations requiring immediate action.
DISCUSSION: Certain reported observations and recommendations may be so significant as to require immediate action by management. These conditions should be monitored by the IAA until corrected because of the effect they may have on the organization. The CAE should establish procedures to determine a time frame within which management's response to the observations is required, to evaluate the response, to verify the response, to conduct a follow-up engagement, and to transmit unsatisfactory responses or actions to the appropriate management levels (PA 2500-1).

61. The preliminary survey discloses that corrective action was never taken on a prior reported assurance engagement observation. Subsequent field work confirms that the condition still exists. Which of the following courses of action should the internal auditors pursue?

A. Take no action. To do otherwise would be an exercise of operational control.

B. Discuss the issue with the chief audit executive. The problem requires an ad hoc solution.

C. Discuss the issue with the person(s) responsible for the problem. (S)he or they should know how to solve the problem.

D. Order the person(s) responsible to correct the problem. (S)he or they have had long enough to do so.

Answer (C) is correct. *(CIA, adapted)*
REQUIRED: The internal auditors' course of action indicated when a prior engagement observation did not result in corrective action.
DISCUSSION: Internal auditors should follow up to ascertain that appropriate action is taken on reported observations and recommendations. Internal auditors should determine that corrective action was taken and is achieving the desired results, or that senior management or the board has assumed the risk of not taking corrective action on reported observations (PA 2500.A1-1). Also, discussion of conclusions and recommendations should occur at appropriate levels of management before issuing final engagement communications (PA 2440-1). Client management is at "an appropriate" level. Obtaining client cooperation (or at least understanding) is a vital part of the solution of any problem.
Answer (A) is incorrect because the condition observed may place the organization at risk until the situation changes or the condition is corrected. Answer (B) is incorrect because conditions that have not been corrected are not unique and do not require ad hoc solutions. Answer (D) is incorrect because the internal auditors have no line authority over the client. To exercise such authority impairs objectivity.

62. Upon reviewing the final communication of engagement results, senior management decided to assume the risk of not implementing corrective action on certain engagement observations. Evaluate the following and select the best alternative for the chief audit executive:

A. Notify regulatory authorities of management's decision.

B. Perform additional engagement procedures to further identify the policy violations.

C. Conduct a follow-up engagement to determine whether corrective action was taken.

D. Discuss the matter with senior management and possibly the board if the residual risk accepted is excessive.

Answer (D) is correct. *(CIA, adapted)*
REQUIRED: The best choice when management agrees to assume the risk of not implementing corrective action.
DISCUSSION: According to Standard 2600, "When the chief audit executive believes that senior management has accepted a level of residual risk that may be unacceptable to the organization, the chief audit executive should discuss the matter with senior management. If the decision regarding residual risk is not resolved, the chief audit executive and senior management should report the matter to the board for resolution."
Answer (A) is incorrect because regulatory authorities do not need to be notified. Management has decided to assume responsibility, and no regulatory violations were mentioned. Answer (B) is incorrect because additional procedures are not required unless the CAE believes that the residual risk assumed is too great. Answer (C) is incorrect because a follow-up engagement is not required unless the CAE believes that the residual risk assumed is too great.

63. Why should organizations require assurance engagement clients to reply promptly and outline the corrective action that has been implemented on reported observations?

A. To remove items from the pending list as soon as possible.

B. To effect savings or to institute compliance as early as possible.

C. To indicate concurrence with the engagement observations.

D. To ensure that the engagement work schedule is kept up to date.

Answer (B) is correct. *(CIA, adapted)*
REQUIRED: The reason clients should promptly reply and outline the corrective action that has been implemented on reported observations.
DISCUSSION: Communications should be timely to enable prompt corrective action, and they should be distributed to those in a position to take corrective action or to ensure that corrective action is taken (PA 2420-1 and PA 2440-1). Moreover, internal auditors should follow up to ascertain that appropriate action is taken on reported engagement observations and recommendations. The internal auditors should determine that corrective action being taken has the desired results or that senior management or the board has assumed the risk of not taking corrective action (PA 2500.A1-1). Consequently, it follows that the objectives of engagements and the timely reporting of observations and recommendations would be defeated if engagement clients do not promptly implement and report on corrective action.
Answer (A) is incorrect because removing items from the pending list concerns a mechanical and immaterial aspect of the communication process. Answer (C) is incorrect because the client may not concur with the observations and recommendations. This dispute may or may not be considered in closing the engagement. Answer (D) is incorrect because ensuring that the engagement work schedule is kept up to date is an administrative function of the IAA.

64. An organization's internal auditors have conducted a series of assurance engagements. The resulting recommendations have been readily accepted by engagement clients because of the potential cost savings. Given the acceptance of the cost savings engagements and the scarcity of internal auditing resources, the manager in charge of these engagements also decided that follow-up action was not needed. The manager reasoned that cost savings should be sufficient to motivate the client to implement the engagement recommendations. Thus, follow-up was not scheduled as a regular part of the engagement plan. Was the manager's decision appropriate?

A. Yes. Follow-up is not customary.

B. No. The internal auditors should determine whether the client has appropriately implemented all of the engagement recommendations.

C. No. Scarcity of resources is not a sufficient reason to omit follow-up.

D. Yes. Given sufficient evidence of motivation by the client, follow-up is not needed.

Answer (C) is correct. *(CIA, adapted)*
REQUIRED: The propriety of the manager's decision to omit follow-up from the engagement plan.
DISCUSSION: The CAE should establish and maintain a system to monitor the disposition of results communicated to management (Standard 2500). Accordingly, follow-up is required. Cost (lack of resources) is a factor in determining the nature, timing, and extent of follow-up, not in determining whether to follow up.

Use Gleim's *CIA Test Prep* for interactive testing with **over 2,000 additional multiple-choice questions!**

STUDY UNIT THREE
SPECIFIC ENGAGEMENTS I

(34 pages of outline)

Internal auditors provide many services. This study unit is the first of two describing some of the specific assurance and consulting engagements that internal auditors may perform.

According to Sawyer, Dittenhofer, and Scheiner, in *Sawyer's Internal Auditing* (Altamonte Springs, FL: The Institute of Internal Auditors, 5th ed., 2003, page 30), internal auditing services may be classified in three categories:

Financial. *The analysis of the economic activity of an entity as measured and reported by accounting methods.*

Compliance. *The review of both financial and operating controls and transactions to see how well they conform with established laws, standards, regulations, and procedures.*

Operational. *The comprehensive review of the varied functions within an enterprise to appraise the efficiency and economy of operations and the effectiveness with which those functions achieve their objectives.*

The IIA publication, *Tone at the Top* (March 2006), describes these categories as follows:

Financial auditing *looks at the past to determine whether financial information was properly recorded and adequately supported. It also assesses whether the financial statements about past performance are fair, accurate, and reliable.*

Compliance auditing *looks at the past, but also examines the present, asking such questions as:*

- *Have we adhered to laws and regulations?*
- *Are we currently complying with legal and regulatory requirements?*
- *What are our organization's corporate standards of business conduct?*
- *Do all members of our staff and management team consistently comply with internal policies and procedures?*

Operational auditing *focuses on the here and now, with a clear perspective on the possibilities for the future. It is closely aligned with the organization's mission, vision, and objectives. It also evaluates the effectiveness (ensuring the right things are done), efficiency (ensuring things are done the right way), and economy (ensuring cost-effectiveness) of operations. This mindset includes such areas as product quality, customer service, revenue maximization, expense minimization, fraud prevention, asset safeguarding, corporate social responsibility and citizenship, streamlined workflows, safety, and planning for the future. With an eye on the horizon, it concentrates on what's working and what's not, and the many opportunities for improvement tomorrow and beyond.*

The three categories correspond to the three **objectives of internal control** defined in the Committee of Sponsoring Organizations (COSO) control framework. The five **components of control** represent what is needed to achieve those objectives.

The services described also may be performed by **external auditors**, for example, in outsourcing or cosourcing engagements. Nevertheless, the traditional focus of external auditors is on the fair presentation of general purpose financial information. By contrast, the traditional focus of internal auditors is on supporting management and governance authorities in performing their functions.

Core Concepts

- Internal audit services may be classified as financial, compliance, and operational.
- Financial audits may follow the cycle approach to internal accounting control. They also may apply an audit risk model and an assertions model.
- In a financial audit, an auditor must make judgments about materiality and audit risk. Audit risk is composed of inherent risk, control risk, and detection risk.
- Audit procedures are performed to achieve audit objectives. Substantive tests are (1) tests of details or (2) analytical procedures.
- A financial audit should provide reasonable assurance about whether the statements are free of material misstatement caused by error or fraud.
- Based on the results of the risk assessment, the IAA should evaluate the adequacy and effectiveness of controls encompassing the organization's governance, operations, and information systems. This should include:
  - Reliability and integrity of financial and operational information.
  - Effectiveness and efficiency of operations.
  - Safeguarding of assets.
  - Compliance with laws, regulations, and contracts.
- The nature of consulting services should be defined in the audit charter.
- Internal auditors may provide consulting services relating to operations for which they had previous responsibilities.
- If internal auditors have potential impairments to independence or objectivity relating to proposed consulting services, disclosure should be made to the client prior to accepting the engagement.
- The CAE should decline the consulting engagement or obtain competent advice and assistance if the internal audit staff lacks the knowledge, skills, or other competencies needed to perform all or part of the engagement.
- The internal auditor should exercise due professional care during a consulting engagement.
- Consulting engagement objectives should be consistent with the overall values and goals of the organization.
- The CAE should consider accepting proposed consulting engagements based on potential to improve management of risks and the organization's operations and to add value. Accepted engagements should be included in the audit plan.
- During consulting engagements, internal auditors should address risks and controls consistent with the objectives and be alert to other significant risks and control weaknesses.
- Internal auditors should incorporate knowledge of risks and controls gained from consulting engagements into the process of identifying and evaluating significant risk exposures.
- Internal auditors should establish an understanding with consulting engagement clients about objectives, scope, respective responsibilities, and other expectations. For significant engagements, this understanding should be documented.
- Consulting engagement objectives should address risks, controls, and governance processes to the extent agreed with the client.
- In consulting engagements, internal auditors should ensure that the scope is sufficient to address the agreed-upon objectives. If internal auditors develop reservations about the scope, they should be discussed with the client to determine whether to continue.
- Work programs for consulting engagements may vary in form and content, depending upon the nature of the engagement.
- Communication of the progress and results of consulting engagements will vary in form and content, depending upon the nature of the engagement and the needs of the client.
- The CAE is responsible for communicating the final results of consulting engagements to clients.
- During consulting engagements, risk management, control, and governance issues may be identified. Whenever these issues are significant, they should be communicated to senior management and the board.

- The CAE should develop policies governing the custody and retention of engagement records and their release to internal and external parties. These policies should be consistent with the organization's guidelines and any pertinent regulatory or other requirements.
- The IAA should monitor the disposition of results of consulting engagements to the extent agreed upon with the client.
- Control self-assessment (CSA) is a method of evaluating the control system using traditional audit concepts, risk analysis, and self-assessment by involved parties.

3.1 FINANCIAL ENGAGEMENTS

1. An audit of financial information may follow the **cycle approach to internal accounting control**. A cycle is a grouping of **transactions**. The following is one model:

   a. **Revenues and Cash Collections**

      1) Processing customer orders
      2) Customer acceptance and granting credit
      3) Shipping goods
      4) Recording sales and receivables
      5) Billing customers
      6) Receiving, processing, and recording cash receipts
      7) Providing for, and writing off, bad debts
      8) Receiving, processing, and recording sales returns
      9) Providing for adjustments, allowances, warranties, and other credits

   b. **Acquisitions and Expenditures**

      1) Processing purchase requests
      2) Issuing purchase orders
      3) Receiving goods and services
      4) Processing vendor invoices, receiving reports, and purchase orders
      5) Disbursing cash
      6) Accounting for receipts, liabilities, cash expenditures, and accrued expenses

   c. **Production or Conversion**

      1) Inventory planning
      2) Receipt and storage of goods
      3) Production or conversion of goods or provision of services
      4) Accounting for costs, deferred costs, and property
      5) Storage of produced or converted goods
      6) Shipment

   d. **Financial Capital and Payment**

      1) Issuing long-term debt and stock
      2) Paying interest and dividends
      3) Repurchase of equity and debt securities and payment at maturity
      4) Maintaining detailed records for payment of interest, dividends, and taxes
      5) Purchases and sales of investments
      6) Recording receipts of interest and dividends
      7) Recording stock options and treasury stock
      8) Accounting for investing and financing transactions

   e. **Personnel and Payroll**

      1) Hiring employees
      2) Authorizing payroll rates, deductions, etc.
      3) Timekeeping
      4) Payroll preparation and payment
      5) Filing payroll tax returns and paying the taxes

     f.   **External Financial Reporting**

         1)   Preparation of financial statements
         2)   Disclosure of related information
         3)   Controls over financial reporting
         4)   Selection of accounting principles
         5)   Unusual or nonrecurring items
         6)   Contingencies

2.   An **audit risk** model and an **assertions** model may be used to develop an approach to a financial statement audit. This approach is consistent with cycle auditing.

    a.   The auditor must make judgments about **materiality** and audit risk in determining the **nature, timing, and extent of procedures** to apply and in evaluating the results.

    b.   **Audit risk** is the risk that an auditor may unknowingly fail to modify the opinion on materially misstated financial statements.

    c.   Audit risk has three **components** that may be assessed in quantitative terms, such as percentages, or in nonquantitative terms that range, for example, from a minimum to a maximum. These components are considered at the account balance or class-of-transactions level, i.e., with respect to particular assertions.

         1)   **Inherent risk** is the susceptibility of an assertion to material misstatement in the absence of related controls. It cannot be changed by the auditor.

         2)   **Control risk** is the risk that internal control will not prevent or detect on a timely basis a material misstatement that could occur in an assertion.

         3)   **Detection risk** is the risk that the auditor will not detect a material misstatement that exists in an assertion. It is a function of the effectiveness of an audit procedure and its application by the auditor. It can be changed by the auditor.

    d.   The concept of **materiality** recognizes that some matters, but not all, are important for fair presentation of the financial statements. The auditor's responsibility does not extend to immaterial matters.

         1)   Materiality is a matter of **professional judgment** influenced by the needs of reasonable people who will rely on the financial statements. An item is material if its misstatement or omission might affect the judgment of a reasonable person who relies on the financial statements.

         2)   Materiality judgments are made in light of surrounding circumstances and involve **qualitative and quantitative** considerations. Thus, qualitative factors may cause misstatements of relatively small amounts to be material.

         3)   Audit risk and materiality have an **inverse relationship**. Thus, the risk of a large misstatement may be low, but the risk of a small misstatement may be high.

         4)   The auditor ordinarily considers materiality based on the smallest aggregate level of material misstatements in the financial statements.

    e.   Audit risk and materiality are considered in **planning** the audit, **designing audit procedures**, and **evaluating** whether the financial statements are presented fairly, in all material respects.

    f.   A decrease in the acceptable level of audit risk or in the amounts considered material will result in the auditor's modifying the audit program to obtain greater assurance from substantive testing. The auditor may select **more effective** procedures, apply procedures **nearer to year-end**, or **increase the extent** of particular tests.

    g.   Because an audit is a cumulative process, information obtained during the audit may lead to **revision of auditor judgments** about audit risk and materiality.

    h.   When **evaluating audit findings**, the auditor considers the individual and total effects of misstatements not corrected by the entity. This consideration addresses qualitative and quantitative factors. Moreover, the consideration should include **likely misstatement**, not merely known misstatement.

1) The auditor should document the nature and effect of **total misstatements** in addition to the conclusion about whether they cause the financial statements to be materially misstated.

i. Most audit work in a financial statement audit may be viewed as obtaining and evaluating evidence about **assertions**. They are **representations** by management embodied in financial statement components. They can be explicit or implicit. The following are possible categories of assertions:

1) **Transactions and Events for a Period**

   a) **Occurrence.** Recorded items relate to the entity and have occurred.
   b) **Completeness.** Items that should be recorded were recorded.
   c) **Accuracy.** Data related to recorded items were recorded properly.
   d) **Cutoff.** Items were recorded in the proper period.
   e) **Classification.** Items were recorded in the proper accounts.

2) **Balances at Period-End**

   a) **Existence.** The items exist.
   b) **Rights and obligations.** The rights to assets are held or controlled, and the liabilities are obligations.
   c) **Completeness.** Items that should be recorded were recorded.
   d) **Valuation and allocation.** Amounts are proper, and resulting adjustments are proper.

3) **Presentation and Disclosure**

   a) The (1) occurrence, (2) rights and obligations, (3) completeness, (4) accuracy, (5) classification, and (6) valuation assertions also apply to disclosures.
   b) **Understandability.** Items are clearly expressed.

j. **Development of audit objectives.** The auditor develops specific audit objectives considering the specific circumstances of the entity, including the nature of its economic activity and the accounting practices unique to its industry.

1) Audit objectives and procedures do not necessarily have a one-to-one relationship. Some procedures may relate to more than one objective.

   a) A combination of procedures may be needed to achieve one objective.

k. **Selecting substantive tests.** Substantive tests consist of tests of the details of transactions and balances **(tests of details)** and **analytical procedures**. After developing the audit objectives, the auditor should select appropriate substantive tests. For this purpose, the auditor evaluates (1) the risk of material misstatement of the financial statements, including the assessed levels of inherent and control risk, and (2) the expected effectiveness and efficiency of such tests.

1) The auditor should consider the

   a) Nature and materiality of the items being tested
   b) Kinds and reliability of available evidence
   c) Nature of the audit objective to be achieved

2) For example, a substantive test related to the **existence assertion** involves selecting items included in a financial statement amount and then searching for relevant evidence (proof of the financial event). The **direction of testing**, from the records to the evidence, is critical in meeting the objective.

   a) A substantive test related to the **completeness assertion** involves selecting evidence indicating that an item should be included in an amount (proof of the financial event) and then investigating whether it is included in the account balance.

b)   The direction of testing for **existence and completeness assertions** is illustrated below.

```
┌─────────────────────────┐   ◄─── Test of Existence ───   ┌─────────────────────────┐
│ Proof of Financial Event│                                 │   Recorded Balance      │
│ (e.g., Physical Assets) │   ─── Test of Completeness ──►  │ (e.g., Records of Assets)│
└─────────────────────────┘                                 └─────────────────────────┘
```

l.   **Influence of data processing methods.** The **audit objectives** do not change based on the method of processing information (manually or electronically).

1)   Methods of applying **audit procedures** to gather evidence, however, may be influenced by the data processing method. The more computerized an accounting system, the more the auditor must use **computer-assisted audit techniques (CAATs)** to obtain evidence.

m.   **Procedures** should be **adequate** to achieve the audit objectives.

n.   **Evidence** should be **sufficient** to form conclusions about the validity of assertions.

o.   **Fraud risk.** The auditor should plan and perform the audit to obtain **reasonable assurance** about whether the financial statements are free of material misstatement, whether caused by error or fraud.

1)   **Management** is responsible for programs and controls that prevent, deter, and detect fraud.

2)   **Management and governance bodies** (e.g., the board and audit committee) must set the proper tone and maintain a culture of honesty.

3)   The **three conditions** ordinarily present when fraud exists include

a)   **Pressures or incentives** to commit fraud,

b)   **Opportunity**, and

c)   The capacity to **rationalize** misconduct.

4)   The types of fraud relevant to the financial statement auditor include misstatements arising from

a)   **Fraudulent financial reporting.** These are intentional misstatements or omissions to deceive users, such as altering accounting records or documents, misrepresenting or omitting significant information, and misapplying accounting principles.

b)   **Misappropriation of assets.** These result from theft, embezzlement, or an action that causes payment for items not received.

5)   The information obtained may be considered in terms of the three conditions, but an **identifiable risk** may exist when not all conditions have been observed, especially rationalization. The extent of a condition may by itself create a fraud risk, e.g., pressure to reach an earnings goal.

a)   Fraud risks vary with the entity's size, complexity, ownership, etc.

b)   Fraud risks may relate to specific assertions or the set of statements.

c)   High **inherent risk** of an assertion about an account balance or transaction class may exist when it is susceptible to management manipulation.

d)   Identifying fraud risks involves considering the type of risk and its significance, likelihood, and pervasiveness.

e)   The auditor must address the risk of **management override** of controls in all audits because of its unpredictability.

f)   The auditor ordinarily should assume the existence of fraud risk relating to **improper revenue recognition**.

6)   **Fraud** is fully covered in Study Unit 10.

3.   This section addresses the internal auditor's role in responding to requirements for organizations to improve their governance and financial reporting processes. The IIA has issued a Practice Advisory relevant to conducting financial audit engagements. It interprets the following Assurance Implementation Standard:

> *2120.A1 – Based on the results of the risk assessment, the internal audit activity should evaluate the adequacy and effectiveness of controls encompassing the organization's governance, operations, and information systems. This should include:*
>
> - *Reliability and integrity of financial and operational information.*
> - *Effectiveness and efficiency of operations.*
> - *Safeguarding of assets.*
> - *Compliance with laws, regulations, and contracts.*

a.   **PRACTICE ADVISORY 2120.A1-4: AUDITING THE FINANCIAL REPORTING PROCESS**

1.   *The published reports of **corporate governance failures** in the United States and other countries underscore the need for change to achieve greater **accountability and transparency** by all organizations' profit making, nonprofit, and governmental. Senior management, boards of directors, internal auditors, and external auditors are the cornerstones of the foundation on which effective organizational governance is built. The internal audit activity plays a key role in support of good organizational governance. It is uniquely positioned to assist in improving an organization's operations by evaluating and improving the effectiveness of risk management, control, and governance processes. Recent initiatives have put the spotlight on the need for **senior management** to be more **accountable** for the information contained in an organization's financial reports. Senior management and the audit committee of many organizations are requesting additional services from the internal audit activity to **improve the governance and financial reporting processes**. These requests include evaluations of the organization's internal controls over financial reporting and the reliability and integrity of its financial reports.*

Reporting on Internal Control

2.   *An organization's audit or other board committee and internal auditing activity have **interlocking goals**. The core role of the chief audit executive (CAE) is to ensure that the audit committee receives the support and assurance services it needs and requests. One of the primary objectives of the audit committee is **oversight** of the organization's **financial reporting processes** to ensure their reliability and fairness. The committee and senior management typically request that the internal audit activity perform sufficient audit work and gather other available information during the year to **form an opinion on the adequacy and effectiveness of the internal control processes**. The CAE normally communicates that overall evaluation, on a timely basis, to the committee. The committee will evaluate the coverage and adequacy of the CAE's report and may incorporate its conclusion in the committee's report to the governing board.*

3.   Internal audit activity's **work plans and specific assurance engagements** begin with a careful **identification of the exposures** facing the organization. Thus, internal audit's work plan is based on the risks and the **assessment of the risk management and control processes** maintained by management to mitigate those risks. Among the events and transactions included in the identification of risks are:

- New businesses, including mergers and acquisitions
- New products and systems
- Joint ventures and partnerships
- Restructuring
- Management estimates, budgets, and forecasts
- Environmental matters
- Regulatory compliance

A Framework for Internal Control

4.   The assessment of a system of internal control of an organization should employ a broad definition of control. The IIA believes that the most effective internal control guidance available today is the report **Internal Control - Integrated Framework**, published in 1992 and 1994 by the Committee of Sponsoring Organizations (COSO) of the Treadway Commission. While use of the **COSO model** is widely accepted, it may be appropriate to use some **other recognized and credible model**. Sometimes, regulatory or legal requirements will specify the use of a particular model or control design for an organization or industry within a country.

5.   Several **conclusions** in the Internal Control - Integrated Framework report are relevant to this discussion.

- Internal control is **defined broadly**. It is not limited to accounting controls and is not narrowly restricted to financial reporting.
- While accounting and financial reports are important issues, there are **other important aspects of the business**, such as resource protection; operational efficiency and effectiveness; and compliance with rules, regulations, and organization policies. These factors also have an impact on financial reporting.
- Internal control is **management's responsibility**. The participation of all persons within an organization is required if it is to be effective.
- The control framework is tied to the **business objectives** and is **flexible** enough to be adaptable.

Reporting on the Effectiveness of Internal Control

6.   The CAE should provide to the audit committee internal audit's **assessment of the effectiveness of the organization's system of controls**, including its judgment on the **adequacy of the control model or design**. A governing board must rely on management to maintain an adequate and effective internal control system. It will reinforce that reliance with **independent oversight**. The board or its audit (or other designated) committee should ask the following questions, and the CAE may be expected to assist in answering them.

(a) **Is there a strong ethical environment and culture?**

- Do **board members and senior executives** set examples of high integrity?
- Are **performance and incentive targets** realistic, or do they create excessive pressure for short-term results?

- Is the organization's **code of conduct** reinforced with training and top-down communication? Does the message reach the **employees** in the field?
- Are the organization's **communication channels** open? Do all levels of management get the information they need?
- Is there **zero tolerance for fraudulent financial reporting** at any level?

(b) **How does the organization identify and manage risks?**

- Is there a **risk management process**, and is it effective?
- Is risk managed throughout the organization?
- Are **major risks** candidly discussed with the board?

(c) **Is the control system effective?**

- **Are the organization's controls over the financial reporting process comprehensive**, including preparation of financial statements, related notes, and the other required and discretionary disclosures that are an integral part of the financial reports?
- Do senior and line management demonstrate that they **accept control responsibility**?
- Is there an increasing frequency of "surprises" occurring at the senior management, board, or public levels from the organization's reported financial results or in the accompanying financial disclosures?
- Is **communication and reporting** good throughout the organization?
- Are controls seen as enhancing the **achievement of objectives** or a "necessary evil"?
- Are **qualified people** hired promptly, and do they receive adequate training?
- Are **problems** fixed quickly and completely?

(d) **Is monitoring strong?**

- Is the **board** independent of management, free of conflicts of interest, well informed, and inquisitive?
- Does **internal audit** have the support of senior management and the audit committee?
- Do the **internal and external auditors** have and use open lines of communication and private access to all members of senior management and the audit committee?
- Is **line management** monitoring the control process?
- Is there a program to monitor outsourced processes?

7. **Internal controls cannot ensure success.** Bad decisions, poor managers, or environmental factors can negate controls. Also, dishonest management may **override controls** and ignore or stifle communications from subordinates. An active and independent governing board should be coupled with open and truthful communications from all components of management. Also, it should be assisted by capable financial, legal, and internal audit functions. In these circumstances, the board is capable of identifying problems and providing effective oversight.

Roles for the Internal Auditor

8.   **Adequate resources** *should be committed to helping senior management, the audit committee, and the external auditor with their responsibilities in the upcoming year's financial reporting regimen. Otherwise, the CAE needs to review internal audit's risk assessment and audit plans for the year. The* **financial reporting process** *encompasses the steps to create the information and prepare financial statements, related notes, and other accompanying disclosures in the organization's financial reports.*

9.   **The CAE's allocation of the internal audit's resources to the financial reporting, governance, and control processes should be consistent with the organization's risk assessment.** *The CAE should perform procedures that provide a* **level of assurance** *to senior management and the audit committee that controls surrounding the processes supporting the development of financial reports are* **adequately designed and effectively executed.** *The controls should be adequate to ensure the prevention and detection of significant errors, irregularities, incorrect assumptions and estimates, and other events that could result in inaccurate or misleading financial statements, related notes, or other disclosures.*

10.   *The following are lists of suggested topics that the CAE may consider in supporting the organization's* **governance process and the oversight responsibilities** *of the governing board and its audit committee (or other designated committee). The purpose is to ensure the reliability and integrity of financial reports.*

      (a) **Financial Reporting**

      - *Providing information relevant to the* **appointment** *of the independent accountants.*

      - **Coordinating** *audit plans, coverage, and scheduling with the* **external auditors.**

      - *Sharing* **audit results** *to the external auditors.*

      - **Communicating pertinent observations** *to the external auditors and audit committee about accounting policies and policy decisions (including accounting decisions for discretionary items and off-balance sheet transactions), specific components of the financial reporting process, and unusual or complex financial transactions and events (e.g., related-party transactions, mergers and acquisitions, joint ventures, and partnership transactions).*

      - *Participating in the financial reports and disclosures* **review process** *with the audit committee, external auditors, and senior management. Evaluating the* **quality of financial reports,** *including those filed with regulatory agencies.*

      - **Assessing the adequacy and effectiveness of the organization's internal controls,** *specifically those controls over the financial reporting process. This assessment should consider the organization's susceptibility to fraud and the effectiveness of programs and controls to mitigate or eliminate those exposures.*

- **Monitoring management's compliance with the organization's code of conduct** and ensuring that ethical policies and other procedures promoting ethical behavior are being followed. An important factor in establishing an effective ethical culture in the organization is that members of senior management set a good example of ethical behavior and provide open and truthful communications to employees, the board, and outside stakeholders.

(b) Corporate Governance

- Reviewing **corporate policies** relating to compliance with laws and regulations, ethics, conflict of interests, and the timely and thorough investigation of misconduct and fraud allegations.
- Reviewing pending **litigation or regulatory proceedings** bearing on organizational risk and governance.
- Providing information on **employee conflicts of interest, misconduct, fraud**, and other outcomes of the organization's ethical procedures and reporting mechanisms.

(c) Corporate Control

- Reviewing the **reliability and integrity** of the organization's operating and financial information compiled and reported by the organization.
- Performing an analysis of the **controls over critical accounting policies** and comparing them with preferred practices (e.g., transactions in which questions are raised about revenue recognition or off-balance sheet accounting treatment should be reviewed for compliance with appropriate generally accepted accounting standards).
- Evaluating the reasonableness of **estimates and assumptions** used in preparing **operating and financial reports**.
- Ensuring that **estimates and assumptions** included in **disclosures or comments** are in line with underlying organizational information and practices and with similar items reported by other companies, if appropriate.
- Evaluating the process of preparing, reviewing, approving, and posting **journal entries**.
- Evaluating the adequacy of controls in the **accounting function**.

PA Summary

- **Corporate governance failures** underscore the need for greater **accountability and transparency** by all organizations. Senior management, boards, and auditors are the basis for effective governance. Many organizations are requesting additional services from the IAA to **improve the governance and financial reporting processes**, including evaluations of controls over financial reporting and the reliability and integrity of financial reports.

- The core role of the CAE is to ensure that the audit committee receives the **support and assurance services** it needs and requests. One of the primary objectives is **oversight** of **financial reporting** to ensure reliability and fairness. The IAA typically performs sufficient work and gathers other information to **form an opinion on the adequacy and effectiveness of control**. The CAE communicates that evaluation to the committee, which evaluates the report and may incorporate its conclusion in its report to the governing board.

- The IAA's work plans and specific assurance engagements begin with identification of risk exposures and its work plan is based on the risks and the assessment of the RMC processes that mitigate those risks. Among the matters considered are (1) new businesses, products, and systems; (2) joint ventures and partnerships; (3) restructuring; (4) estimates, budgets, and forecasts; (5) environmental issues; and (6) compliance.

- The most effective control guidance is the **Internal Control – Integrated Framework**, by the Committee of Sponsoring Organizations (COSO). But another **recognized and credible model** may be used unless the law requires otherwise. Control is **defined broadly**. It is not limited to accounting control and financial reporting. **Other aspects of the business** are important, such as resource protection, efficiency and effectiveness, and compliance. These factors also affect financial reporting. Control is **management's responsibility** and requires everyone's participation. The framework is tied to **business objectives** and should be **adaptable**.

- The IAA's report on control assesses effectiveness but also includes a judgment on the **adequacy of the control model or design**. The board relies on management to maintain effective control but reinforces that reliance with **independent oversight**. The board should ask, and the CAE assist in answering, questions about (1) the ethical environment and culture, (2) how risks are identified and managed, (3) the effectiveness of control, and (4) the strength of monitoring.

- **Internal controls cannot ensure success** because bad decisions, poor or dishonest managers, or environmental factors can negate controls. The CAE must review the risk assessment and audit plans for the year if **adequate resources** have not been committed to the financial reporting regimen. The **financial reporting process** involves creating information and preparing statements, notes, and disclosures in financial reports. **IAA resources** should be allocated to financial reporting, governance, and control processes in accordance with the risk **assessment**.

- Audit procedures should provide **assurance** that controls over financial reporting are adequately designed and effectively executed. Controls should ensure the prevention and detection of significant errors, irregularities, incorrect assumptions and estimates, and other events that could misstate financial statements, note, or disclosures.

- The CAE considers many factors related to financial reporting, corporate governance, and corporate control when supporting the governance process. The purpose is to ensure the reliability of financial reports.

4.   Stop and review! You have completed the outline for this subunit. Study multiple-choice questions 1 through 25 beginning on page 169.

3.2 CONSULTING ENGAGEMENTS

1.   **Consulting services** are "advisory and related client service activities, the nature and scope of which are agreed upon with the client and which are intended to add value and improve an organization's governance, risk management, and control processes without the internal auditor assuming management responsibility. Examples include counsel, advice, facilitation, and training" **(Glossary)**. The IIA has issued 20 Consulting Implementation Standards and three Practice Advisories relevant to consulting engagements.

2.   *1000.C1 – The nature of consulting services should be defined in the audit charter.*

   a.   ***PRACTICE ADVISORY 1000.C1-1: PRINCIPLES GUIDING THE PERFORMANCE OF CONSULTING ACTIVITIES OF INTERNAL AUDITORS***

      1.   ***Value Proposition*** *– The value proposition of the internal audit activity is realized within every organization that employs internal auditors in a manner that suits the culture and resources of that organization. That value proposition is captured in the* **definition of internal auditing** *and includes assurance and consulting activities designed to add value to the organization by bringing a systematic, disciplined approach to the areas of governance, risk, and control.*

      2.   ***Consistency with Internal Audit Definition*** *– A disciplined, systematic evaluation methodology is incorporated in each internal audit activity. The list of services can generally be incorporated into the broad categories of assurance and consulting. However, the services may also include* **evolving forms of value-adding services** *that are consistent with the broad definition of internal auditing.*

      3.   ***Audit Activities Beyond Assurance and Consulting*** *– There are multiple internal auditing services. Assurance and consulting are not mutually exclusive and do not preclude other internal auditing services, such as investigations and nonauditing roles. Many audit services will have both an assurance and consultative (advising) role.*

      4.   ***Interrelationship between Assurance and Consulting*** *– Internal audit consulting enriches value-adding internal auditing. While consulting is often the direct result of assurance services, it should also be recognized that assurance could also be generated from consulting engagements.*

      5.   ***Empower Consulting Through the Internal Audit Charter*** *– Internal auditors have traditionally performed many types of consulting services, including the analysis of controls built into developing systems, analysis of security products, serving on task forces to analyze operations and make recommendations, and so forth. The board (or audit committee) should empower the internal audit activity to perform additional services if they do* **not represent a conflict of interest** *or detract from its obligations to the committee. That empowerment should be reflected in the internal audit charter.*

6. __Objectivity__ – *Consulting services may enhance the auditor's* **understanding of business processes or issues** *related to an assurance engagement and do not necessarily impair the auditor's or the internal audit activity's objectivity. Internal auditing is not a management decision-making function. Decisions to adopt or implement recommendations made as a result of an internal auditing advisory service should be made by management. Therefore, internal auditing objectivity should not be impaired by the decisions made by management.*

7. __Internal Audit Foundation for Consulting Services__ – *Much of consulting is a natural* **extension of assurance** *and investigative services and may represent informal or formal advice, analysis, or assessments. The internal audit activity is* **uniquely positioned** *to perform this type of consulting work based on (a) its adherence to the highest standards of objectivity and (b) its breadth of knowledge about organizational processes, risk, and strategies.*

8. __Communication of Fundamental Information__ – *A primary internal auditing value is to provide* **assurance** *to senior management and audit committee directors. Consulting engagements cannot be rendered in a manner that masks information that in the judgment of the chief audit executive (CAE) should be presented to senior executives and board members. All consulting is to be understood in that context.*

9. __Principles of Consulting Understood by the Organization__ – *Organizations must have ground rules for the performance of consulting services that are understood by all members of an organization, and these rules should be codified in the audit charter approved by the audit committee and promulgated in the organization.*

10. __Formal Consulting Engagements__ – *Management often engages* **outside consultants** *for formal consulting engagements that last a significant period of time. However, an organization may find that the internal audit activity is uniquely qualified for some formal consulting tasks. If an internal audit activity undertakes to perform a formal consulting engagement, the internal audit group should bring a* **systematic, disciplined approach** *to the conduct of the engagement.*

11. __CAE Responsibilities__ – *Consulting services permit the CAE to enter into dialogue with management to address specific managerial issues. In this dialogue, the breadth of the engagement and time frames are made responsive to management needs. However, the CAE retains the prerogative of* **setting the audit techniques** *and the* **right of reporting** *to senior executives and audit committee members when the nature and materiality of results pose significant risks to the organization.*

12. __Criteria for Resolving Conflicts or Evolving Issues__ – *An internal auditor is first and foremost an internal auditor. Thus, in the performance of all services, the internal auditor is guided by The IIA Code of Ethics and the Attribute and Performance Standards of the International Standards for the Professional Practice of Internal Auditing. The resolution of any unforeseen conflicts or activities should be consistent with the Code of Ethics and Standards.*

PA Summary

- The **value proposition** of the IAA is realized in a way suiting the organization's culture and resources. It is reflected in the **definition of internal auditing**. It extends to assurance, consulting, and other evolving forms of value-adding services, including nonaudit roles, investigations, and activities that combine assurance and consulting. Moreover, consulting may result from assurance or vice versa.

- The IAA performs consulting, e.g., analysis of controls in systems development. The board and charter should therefore empower consulting that is not a conflict of interest. Consulting may enhance understanding of business processes and does not necessarily impair objectivity because management makes decisions about adoption of IAA recommendations.

- Consulting is often an **extension of assurance**. It may consist of formal (informal) advice, analysis, or assessments. The IAA is uniquely positioned to do such work because of its objectivity and breadth of knowledge.

- A primary IAA value is to **provide assurance** to senior management and the audit committee. Consulting must not conceal information that should be reported as part of that function.

- The **organization's rules for consulting** should be understood by all its members. They should be codified in the charter.

- Instead of hiring outsiders for **formal consulting** tasks, the organization may find that the IAA is uniquely qualified for some of these engagements. In **formal consulting**, the IAA should adopt a systematic, disciplined approach.

- The breadth and time frame of an engagement are based on **managerial needs**. But the **CAE** should set audit techniques and be able to report to senior managers and the board when results indicate significant risk.

- Internal auditors should follow the **Code of Ethics** and the **Standards** when performing all services, even those involving unforeseen conflicts and activities.

b. ***PRACTICE ADVISORY 1000.C1-2: ADDITIONAL CONSIDERATIONS FOR FORMAL CONSULTING ENGAGEMENTS***

The following is the portion of this comprehensive Practice Advisory relevant to Standard 1000.C1:

Definition of Consulting Services

1. The **Glossary** in the **Standards** defines "consulting services" as follows: *"Advisory and related client service activities, the nature and scope of which are agreed with the client and which are intended to add value and improve an organization's governance, risk management, and control processes without the internal auditor assuming management responsibility. Examples include counsel, advice, facilitation, and training."*

2. *The chief audit executive should determine the methodology to use for **classifying engagements** within the organization. In some circumstances, it may be appropriate to conduct a "blended" engagement that incorporates elements of both consulting and assurance activities into one consolidated approach. In other cases, it may be appropriate to distinguish between the assurance and consulting components of the engagement.*

3.   *Internal auditors may conduct consulting services as part of their **normal or***
      ***routine activities** as well as in response to **requests by management**. Each*
      organization should consider the type of consulting activities to be offered and
      determine if specific policies or procedures should be developed for each type
      of activity. Possible categories could include:

    ● **Formal consulting** *engagements – planned and subject to written*
      agreement.

    ● **Informal consulting** *engagements – routine activities, such as*
      participation on standing committees, limited-life projects, ad-hoc
      meetings, and routine information exchange.

    ● **Special consulting** *engagements – participation on a merger and*
      acquisition team or system conversion team.

    ● **Emergency consulting** *engagements – participation on a team*
      established for recovery or maintenance of operations after a disaster or
      other extraordinary business event or a team assembled to supply
      temporary help to meet a special request or unusual deadline.

4.   *Auditors generally should not agree to conduct a consulting engagement simply*
      to circumvent, or to allow others to circumvent, requirements that would
      *normally apply to an **assurance engagement** if the service in question is more*
      appropriately conducted as an assurance engagement. This does not preclude
      adjusting methodologies if services once conducted as assurance engagements
      are deemed more suitable to being performed as a consulting engagement.

PA Summary

● The **Glossary** in the Standards defines "consulting services." The CAE determines
  the methods for classifying engagements. Blended rather than separate
  assurance and consulting engagements may be appropriate.

● Consulting may be done as a routine IAA function or in response to requests by
  management.

● Consulting engagements may be formal, informal, special, and emergency.
  Formal engagements are planned and subject to written agreement. **Informal
  engagements** are routine, such as ad-hoc meetings and routine information
  exchange. An example of a **special engagement** is participation on a system
  conversion team. **Emergency engagements** involve participation on a team
  established (1) for recovery operations after an extraordinary business event or
  (2) to supply temporary help to meet a special request or unusual deadline.

● Consulting should **not** be done to **avoid the requirements** of an assurance
  engagement. But adjusting methods is appropriate if services once conducted as
  assurance engagements are more suitably performed as consulting engagements.

c. ***PRACTICE ADVISORY 1000.C1-3: ADDITIONAL CONSIDERATIONS FOR CONSULTING ENGAGEMENTS IN GOVERNMENT ORGANIZATIONAL SETTINGS***

1. This Practice Advisory provides guidance for government audit organizations conducting work in compliance with IIA Standards, but whose local governance rules, audit standards, policies, or legislation more strictly limit **non-assurance (consulting) services**. The **parameters** within which an organization plans to provide non-assurance (consulting) services should be included in the internal audit **charter**. They should be supported by the policies and procedures of the internal audit activity. The guidance in this PA may assist organizations in developing relevant language and policies to manage the provision of non-assurance (consulting) services.

2. ***Core Elements of the Role of Auditors.*** Through their assurance (audit) engagements, auditors help to ensure that management is accountable for meeting organizational objectives and complying with internal and external requirements for how operations and activities are carried out. Although these engagements can include an "assistance" dimension through the inclusion of **recommendations for improvement**, the auditor does not bear ultimate responsibility for making or authorizing the improvement. Should an auditor **take responsibility for implementing or authorizing** operational improvements, whether recommended in the course of an audit (assurance) engagement, or as a separate non-audit (consulting) engagement, the auditor is very likely **jeopardizing** the **independence and objectivity** that are essential to the role of audit.

   Even when assisting an organization through non-audit (consulting) activities, auditors should keep their activities within boundaries that define the **core elements of the audit function**. These core elements include:

   - Auditors should be **independent**. They should avoid relationships and situations that compromise their **objectivity**.
   - Auditors should **not audit their own work**.
   - Auditors should not perform **management functions** or make management decisions.[1]

   The elements are "core" because they support the fundamental value proposition of audit, namely, the principle that an objective third party is **attesting to** (or providing assurance to) the **credibility of management's assertions**. Accordingly, to protect their ability to provide assurance, auditors must minimize potential threats to auditor independence that can arise when the same audit function is also providing non-audit (consulting) services.

   In addition to the core elements above, other threats to auditor independence have been identified, including the conduct of non-audit (consulting) work that

   - Creates a mutuality of interest; or
   - Places auditors in the role of advocate for the company.[2]

---

[1] This principle has been articulated by numerous standard-setting bodies, including guidance published by IAASB/IFAC in its Code of Professional Ethics and the U.S. Government Accountability Office in its Generally Accepted Government Auditing Standards.

[2] This risk is raised in the January 2003 Smith Report on Audit Committees and Combined Code Guidance, appointed by the Financial Reporting Council, and is addressed in guidance published by ICAEW (Institute of Chartered Accountants in England and Wales), among others.

3. **Governing Rules.** *Specific jurisdictional rules that set restrictions on the work of auditors outside the audit (assurance) role may apply only to auditors conducting the external (financial statement or statutory) audit, or they may apply to auditors performing all types of audits. Moreover, the rules may have been established in the audit function's enabling legislation, imposed by oversight or regulatory bodies, or included in codes of ethics or auditing standards required for audits of specific organizations or jurisdictions.[3] It is the Chief Audit Executive's responsibility to ensure that the audit function's* **charter** *and its* **policies and procedures** *comply with relevant governing rules.*

    Moreover, even where the audit function is not subject to governing rules that restrict non-audit (consulting) services, CAEs will nevertheless need to ensure that the **quality assurance system** *is designed to manage or minimize threats to auditor independence or objectivity. Otherwise, non-audit (consulting) assignments could have the long-term effect of compromising the audit function's ability to carry out its audit (assurance) role. In addition, an audit function's engagement in non-audit (consulting) work that compromises its independence could prevent other auditors from relying on the audit function's work.*

4. **Activities that Compromise Objectivity or Independence.** *Auditors' ability to engage in non-audit (consulting) work without compromising their independence depends to some extent on where they "draw the line" between assisting or consulting in the sense of advising, versus assisting by doing work that is the responsibility of management. For example, providing advice on appropriate controls during system design with the clear understanding that management has responsibility for accepting or rejecting the advice would have a limited impact on the auditor's objectivity toward that system in the future. By contrast, if the auditor led the system design team, decided which controls to select, or oversaw the implementation of the recommended controls, the auditor's future ability to objectively evaluate that system would be significantly impaired. However, other non-audit assignments may not be as clear-cut. Accordingly, audit functions need to develop procedures for* **reviewing potential non-audit (consulting) assignments** *and determining whether they present a* **threat to independence or objectivity.** *The review used to determine the effect on future independence and objectivity should be documented. This* **documentation** *should be provided to external quality control reviewers during the QAR engagement.*

---

[3] *Examples of specific restrictions include U.K.'s Government Internal Audit Standard 2.4.2, which states: "Objectivity is presumed to be impaired when individual auditors review any activity in which they have previously had executive responsibility, or in which they have provided consultancy advice." This standard is supplemented by Good Practice Guidance on Consultancy, which states: "In this role it is important that the internal auditor offers advice to management and does not undertake the task on behalf of, or as a substitute for, management. Acceptance by management of the advice offered by the internal auditor does not transfer or reduce management's accountability for their own areas of responsibility." (3.5.3)*

5. ***Processes for Minimizing Threats to Objectivity or Independence.*** *The audit function should **implement controls** that assist in reducing the potential for non-audit (consulting) projects to compromise objectivity of individual auditors, or the independence of the audit function as a whole. Techniques may include:*

    a. *Charter language defining non-audit (consulting) service parameters.*

    b. *Policies and procedures limiting type, nature, or level of participation in non-audit (consulting) projects.*

    c. *Use of a screening process for non-audit (consulting) projects, with limits on accepting engagements that might threaten objectivity.*

    d. *Segregation of non-audit (consulting) units from units conducting audits (assurance engagements) within the same audit function.*

    e. *Rotation of auditors on engagements.*

    f. *Employing outside providers for carrying out non-audit (consulting) engagements, or for conducting assurance engagements in activities where the audit function's prior involvement in non-audit (consulting) work has been determined to impair objectivity/independence.*

    g. *Disclosure in audit reports where objectivity was impaired by participation in a prior non-audit (consulting) project.*

*Attachment A provides examples of relevant language for some of these types of control techniques. It is **omitted** because of space considerations.*

PA Summary

- A **government IAA's** provision of consulting services may be limited by local law, audit standards, etc. The parameters of these services should be defined in its **charter** and supported by its **policies and procedures**.

- **Assurance services** help ensure management's **accountability**. These services include an assistance dimension when auditors recommend operational improvements. But auditors jeopardize their **independence and objectivity** by being responsible for implementing or authorizing improvements, even those arising from consulting.

- When consulting, auditors should stay within the bounds of the **core elements** of the audit function. These give credibility to the auditors' attestation to management assertions. Core elements support the principle that an **objective third party** is providing assurance about the assertions. The core elements that protect auditors' ability to give assurance are (1) independence, (2) objectivity, (3) not auditing one's own work, and (4) not performing functions or making decisions that are managerial.

- Other **threats to auditor independence** include consulting work that (1) creates a mutuality of interest or (2) positions auditors as advocates for the organization.

- **Governing rules** may restrict the IAA's consulting services. These rules may apply to external auditors or all auditors. They may be based on law, regulation, a code of ethics, or audit standards. The CAE should ensure that the IAA's charter, policies, and procedures **comply** with the governing rules.

- Even if restrictive governing rules do not apply, the **quality assurance system** should minimize **threats to auditor independence or objectivity** posed by consulting. Otherwise, the IAA's assurance role and the ability of other auditors to rely on its work may be compromised. **Avoiding these threats** depends in part on distinguishing between (1) merely advising and (2) assuming management responsibilities.

PA Summary continued on next page

PA Summary continued

- The IAA should have **documented** procedures for review of threats to independence and objectivity. The documentation should be available to external quality control reviewers.
- The IAA should implement **controls** to reduce the potential threats to auditor independence or objectivity posed by consulting. These controls may include
    - Charter language defining consulting service parameters
    - Policies and procedures limiting type, nature, or level of participation in consulting
    - Screening consulting projects, with limits on engagements threatening objectivity
    - Segregation of consulting units from assurance units in the audit function
    - Rotation of auditors
    - Employing outside providers for (1) consulting or (2) assurance engagements involving activities subject to prior consulting work that impaired objectivity or independence
    - Disclosure in audit reports when objectivity was impaired by participation in a prior consulting project

---

3.   **1130.C1** – *Internal auditors may provide consulting services relating to operations for which they had previous responsibilities.*

4.   **1130.C2** – *If internal auditors have potential impairments to independence or objectivity relating to proposed consulting services, disclosure should be made to the engagement client prior to accepting the engagement.*

   a.   The following is the portion of Practice Advisory 1000.C1-2 relevant to Standards 1130.C1 and 1130.C2:

   Independence and Objectivity in Consulting Engagements

   5.   *Internal auditors are sometimes requested to provide consulting services relating to* **operations for which they had previous responsibilities or had conducted assurance services**. *Prior to offering consulting services, the Chief Audit Executive should confirm that* **the board** *understands and approves the concept of providing consulting services. Once approved, the internal audit* **charter** *should be amended to include authority and responsibilities for consulting activities, and the internal audit activity should develop appropriate* **policies** *and* **procedures** *for conducting such engagements.*

   6.   *Internal auditors should maintain their* **objectivity** *when drawing conclusions and offering advice to management. If* **impairments to independence or objectivity** *exist prior to commencement of the consulting engagement, or subsequently develop during the engagement,* **disclosure** *should be made immediately to management.*

   7.   *Independence and objectivity may be impaired if* **assurance services** *are provided* **within one year after a formal consulting engagement**. *Steps can be taken to minimize the effects of impairment by assigning different auditors to perform each of the services, establishing independent management and supervision, defining separate accountability for the results of the projects, and disclosing the presumed impairment.* **Management should be responsible** *for accepting and implementing recommendations.*

8. *Care should be taken, particularly involving consulting engagements that are ongoing or continuous in nature, so that internal auditors do not inappropriately or unintentionally **assume management responsibilities** that were not intended in the original objectives and scope of the engagement.*

PA Summary

- The **board** should approve, and the **charter** should provide authority for, consulting services relating to operations for which internal auditors had (1) previous responsibility or (2) performed assurance services. The IAA should have **policies and procedures** for these services.

- **Objectivity** should be maintained, and **impairment** of objectivity or **independence** should be **disclosed**. Impairment may occur if an **assurance service** is performed within a year. Steps should be taken to minimize the effects of impairment, and **management** should be responsible for implementing recommendations.

- Internal auditors should not **inappropriately assume management responsibilities**.

---

5. ***1210.C1** – The chief audit executive should decline the consulting engagement or obtain competent advice and assistance if the internal audit staff lacks the knowledge, skills, or other competencies needed to perform all or part of the engagement.*

6. ***1220.C1** – The internal auditor should exercise due professional care during a consulting engagement by considering the:*

   - *Needs and expectations of engagement clients, including the nature, timing, and communication of engagement results.*
   - *Relative complexity and extent of work needed to achieve the engagement's objectives.*
   - *Cost of the consulting engagement in relation to potential benefits.*

7. ***2130.C1** – Consulting engagement objectives should be consistent with the overall values and goals of the organization.*

   a. The following is the portion of Practice Advisory 1000.C1-2 relevant to the Standards above:

   ### Due Professional Care in Consulting Engagements

   9. *The internal auditor should exercise **due professional care** in conducting a **formal consulting engagement** by understanding the following:*

      - *Needs of management officials, including the nature, timing, and communication of engagement results.*
      - *Possible motivations and reasons of those requesting the service.*
      - *Extent of work needed to achieve the engagement's objectives.*
      - *Skills and resources needed to conduct the engagement.*
      - *Effect on the scope of the audit plan previously approved by the audit committee.*
      - *Potential impact on future audit assignments and engagements.*
      - *Potential organizational benefits to be derived from the engagement.*

10. In addition to the independence and objectivity evaluation and due professional care considerations, the internal auditor should:

- Conduct appropriate meetings and gather necessary information to assess the **nature and extent of the service** to be provided.

- Confirm that those receiving the service understand and agree with the relevant guidance contained in the **internal audit charter**, internal audit activity's **policies and procedures**, and other related guidance governing the conduct of consulting engagements. The internal auditor should decline to perform consulting engagements that are prohibited by the terms of the internal audit charter, conflict with the policies and procedures of the internal audit activity, or do not add value and promote the best interests of the organization.

- Evaluate the consulting engagement for compatibility with the internal audit activity's **overall plan of engagements**. The internal audit activity's risk-based plan of engagements may incorporate and rely on consulting engagements, to the extent deemed appropriate, to provide necessary audit coverage to the organization.

- **Document** general terms, understandings, deliverables, and other **key factors** of the formal consulting engagement in a written agreement or plan. It is essential that both the internal auditor and those receiving the consulting engagement understand and agree with the reporting and communication requirements.

PA Summary

- **Due professional care** for a **formal consulting engagement** requires an understanding of the (1) needs of management, (2) reasons for the service, (3) extent of work, (4) resources required, (5) effect on the audit plan, (6) effect on future engagements, and (7) engagement benefits.

- The auditor should assess the **nature and extent of the service**.

- The auditor should confirm that service recipients **agree with related guidance** (e.g., the IAA's charter, policies, and procedures). Engagements should not be performed when they (1) are prohibited by the charter, (2) conflict with policy, or (3) do not add value.

- An engagement should be compatible with the IAA's **overall plan of engagements**. In appropriate circumstances, consulting engagements may provide necessary audit coverage.

- **Key engagement factors** should be **documented** in a **written agreement**.

---

8. **2010.C1** – The chief audit executive should consider accepting proposed consulting engagements based on the engagement's potential to improve management of risks, add value, and improve the organization's operations. Those engagements that have been accepted should be included in the plan.

9. **2110.C1** – During consulting engagements, internal auditors should address risk consistent with the engagement's objectives and should be alert to the existence of other significant risks.

10. **2110.C2** – Internal auditors should incorporate knowledge of risks gained from consulting engagements into the process of identifying and evaluating significant risk exposures of the organization.

11. *2120.C1* – During consulting engagements, internal auditors should address controls consistent with the engagement's objectives and should be alert to the existence of any significant control weaknesses.

12. *2120.C2* – Internal auditors should incorporate knowledge of controls gained from consulting engagements into the process of identifying and evaluating significant risk exposures of the organization.

13. *2201.C1* – Internal auditors should establish an understanding with consulting engagement clients about objectives, scope, respective responsibilities, and other client expectations. For significant engagements, this understanding should be documented.

14. *2210.C1* – Consulting engagement objectives should address risks, controls, and governance processes to the extent agreed upon with the client.

15. *2220.C1* – In performing consulting engagements, internal auditors should ensure that the scope of the engagement is sufficient to address the agreed-upon objectives. If internal auditors develop reservations about the scope during the engagement, these reservations should be discussed with the client to determine whether to continue with the engagement.

16. *2240.C1* – Work programs for consulting engagements may vary in form and content depending upon the nature of the engagement.

    a. The following is the portion of Practice Advisory 1000.C1-2 relevant to the Standards above:

Scope of Work in Consulting Engagements

    11. Internal auditors should reach an **understanding** about the **objectives and scope** of the consulting engagement with those receiving the service. Any reservations about the value, benefit, or possible negative implications of the consulting engagement should be communicated to those receiving the service. Internal auditors should design the scope of work to ensure that **professionalism, integrity, credibility, and reputation** of the internal audit activity will be maintained.

    12. In planning **formal consulting engagements**, internal auditors should design objectives to meet the appropriate needs of management **officials receiving these services**. In the case of **special requests** by management, internal auditors may consider the following actions if they believe that the **objectives** that should be pursued go **beyond those requested** by management:

        • Persuade management to include the additional objectives in the consulting engagement; or

        • Document the fact that the objectives were not pursued and disclose that observation in the final communication of consulting engagement results; and

        • Include the objectives in a separate and subsequent assurance engagement.

    13. **Work programs** for formal consulting engagements should document the objectives and scope of the engagement, as well as the methodology to be used in satisfying the objectives. The **form and content** of the program may vary depending on the nature of the engagement. In establishing the **scope of the engagement**, internal auditors may expand or limit the scope to satisfy management's request. However, the internal auditor should be satisfied that the projected scope of work will be **adequate to meet the objectives** of the engagement. The objectives, scope, and terms of the engagement should be **periodically reassessed** and adjusted during the course of the work.

14. *Internal auditors should be observant of the **effectiveness of risk management and control processes** during formal consulting engagements. Substantial risk exposures or material control weaknesses should be brought to the attention of management. In some situations the auditor's concerns should also be communicated to executive management, the audit committee, or the board of directors. Auditors should (a) determine the **significance** of exposures or weaknesses and the **actions** taken or contemplated to mitigate or correct these exposures or weaknesses and (b) ascertain the **expectations** of executive management, the audit committee, and board in having these matters reported.*

PA Summary

- Internal auditors should have an understanding about the **objectives and scope** of the consulting engagement. They also should communicate reservations about the engagement to the recipients of the service and maintain their professionalism.

- The objectives of **formal engagements** should meet the needs of the recipients of services. For **special request** engagements, internal auditors may consider the following actions if they believe that the **objectives** should go **beyond those requested**:

    1) Persuade management to include the additional objectives or
    2) Document and disclose in the final communication of results that those objectives were not pursued and include them in a later assurance engagement.

- **Work programs** should document objectives and methods. The **form and content** of the program may vary. The scope depends on management's request, but it should be adequate to meet the objectives. Moreover, the objectives, scope, and terms of the engagement should be **periodically reassessed**.

- **Substantial risk exposures** or **material control weaknesses** should be reported to management. In some cases, reporting to higher levels also is indicated. Auditors should determine (1) the **significance** of these matters, (2) **actions** taken or considered, and (3) **expectations** of higher authorities about reporting.

---

17. ***2410.C1*** – *Communication of the progress and results of consulting engagements will vary in form and content depending upon the nature of the engagement and the needs of the client.*

18. ***2440.C1*** – *The chief audit executive is responsible for communicating the final results of consulting engagements to clients.*

19. ***2440.C2*** – *During consulting engagements, risk management, control, and governance issues may be identified. Whenever these issues are significant to the organization, they should be communicated to senior management and the board.*

    a. The following is the portion of Practice Advisory 1000.C1-2 relevant to the Standards above:

Communicating the Results of Consulting Engagements

15.   *Communication of the **progress and results** of consulting engagements will vary in form and content depending upon the nature of the engagement and the needs of the client. **Reporting requirements** are generally determined by those requesting the consulting service and should meet the objectives as determined and agreed to with management. However, the **format** for communicating the results of the consulting engagement should clearly describe the **nature of the engagement and any** limitations, restrictions, or **other factors** about which users of the information should be made aware.*

16.   *In some circumstances, the internal auditor may **conclude that the results should be communicated beyond those who received or requested the service**. In such cases, the internal auditor should expand the reporting so that results are communicated to the appropriate parties. When expanding the reporting to other parties, the auditor should take the following steps until satisfied with the resolution of the matter:*

- * **First**, determine what direction is provided in the **agreement** concerning the consulting engagement and related communications.*

- * **Second**, attempt to convince those receiving or requesting the service to expand **voluntarily** the communication to the appropriate parties.*

- * **Third**, determine what guidance is provided in the internal audit **charter** or audit activity's **policies and procedures** concerning consulting communications.*

- * **Fourth**, determine what guidance is provided in the **organization's** code of conduct, code of ethics, and other relative policies, administrative directives, or procedures.*

- * **Fifth**, determine what guidance is provided by The IIA's **Standards** and **Code of Ethics**, other standards or codes applicable to the auditor, and any legal or regulatory requirements that relate to the matter under consideration.*

17.   *Internal auditors should **disclose** to management, the audit committee, board, or other governing body of the organization the **nature, extent, and overall results** of formal consulting engagements along with other reports of internal auditing activities. Internal auditors should keep executive management and the audit committee informed about **how audit resources are being deployed**. Neither detail reports of these consulting engagements nor the specific results and recommendations are required to be communicated. But, an appropriate **description** of these types of engagements and their **significant recommendations** should be communicated and is essential in satisfying the internal auditor's responsibility in complying with **Standard 2060, Reporting to the Board and Senior Management**.*

PA Summary

- Communications vary with the engagement and client needs. In a formal consulting engagement, **reporting requirements** are usually set by **requesting parties**. However, the **format** should describe the nature of the engagement and **other factors** of which users should be aware.

- **Results** may need to be communicated **beyond those who received or requested consulting services**. The auditor considers (1) the agreement; (2) whether the receiving or requesting parties will voluntarily expand the communication; (3) the IAA charter, policies, and procedures; (4) the organization's code of ethics and policies; and (5) the Standards and The IIA Code of Ethics.

- The auditor should **disclose** to management and the board the nature, extent, and overall results of a formal consulting engagement along with other IAA reports. Details need not be reported. But appropriate **descriptions** and **significant recommendations** should be communicated.

---

20.   ***2330.C1*** – *The chief audit executive should develop policies governing the custody and retention of engagement records, as well as their release to internal and external parties. These policies should be consistent with the organization's guidelines and any pertinent regulatory or other requirements.*

    a.   The following is the portion of Practice Advisory 1000.C1-2 relevant to Standard 2330.C1:

Documentation Requirements for Consulting Engagements

    18.   Internal auditors should **document the work** performed to achieve the objectives of a formal consulting engagement and support its results. However, documentation **requirements applicable to assurance engagements do not necessarily apply** to consulting engagements.

    19.   Auditors are encouraged to adopt appropriate **record retention policies** and address **related issues**, such as **ownership** of consulting engagement records, in order to protect the organization adequately and to avoid potential misunderstandings involving requests for these records. Situations involving legal proceedings, regulatory requirements, tax issues, and accounting matters may call for **special handling of certain consulting engagement records**.

PA Summary

- **Documentation** requirements for **assurance engagements** do not necessarily apply to **consulting engagements**.

- In **formal** consulting engagements, auditors should adopt appropriate **record retention policies** and address such **related issues** as ownership of the engagement records. Legal, regulatory, tax, and accounting matters may require **special treatment** in the records.

21. **2500.C1** – *The internal audit activity should monitor the disposition of results of consulting engagements to the extent agreed upon with the client.*

   a. The following is the portion of Practice Advisory 1000.C1-2 relevant to Standard 2500.C1:

   20. *The internal audit activity should* **monitor the results of consulting engagements** *to the extent agreed upon with the client. Varying types of monitoring may be appropriate for differing types of consulting engagements. The monitoring effort may depend on various factors, such as management's explicit interest in the engagement or the internal auditor's assessment of the project's risks or value to the organization.*

PA Summary

- The IAA monitors results of consulting as agreed with the client.

---

22. Stop and review! You have completed the outline for this subunit. Study multiple-choice questions 26 through 37 beginning on page 176.

3.3 CONTROL SELF-ASSESSMENT (CSA)

1. CSA is a method for examining and evaluating the organization's system of control. It combines traditional **internal auditing concepts, risk analysis**, and **self-assessment**.

2. According to a publication of The IIA's Research Foundation, *Control Self-Assessment: Experience, Current Thinking, and Best Practices* (1996, pp. 1-2), CSA involves:

   a. **Front-end planning** and **preliminary audit work.**

   b. The gathering of a group of people into a same time/same place **meeting**, typically involving a facilitation seating arrangement (U-shaped table) and a meeting **facilitator**. The participants are **"process owners"** -- management and staff who are involved with the particular issues under examination, who know them best, and who are critical to the implementation of appropriate process controls.

   c. A **structured agenda**, which the facilitator uses to lead the group through an examination of the process's risks and controls. Frequently the agenda will be based on a well-defined **framework or model** so that participants can be sure to address all necessary issues. A model may focus on controls, risks, or on a specific issues framework developed for that project.

   d. **Optionally**, the presence of a **scribe** to take an **online transcription** of the session and of **electronic voting technology** to enable participants to voice their perceptions of the issues anonymously.

   e. **Reporting** and the development of **action plans**.

3. Accordingly, CSA **typically employs a workshop-facilitation approach** to self-assessment that is structured, documented, and repetitive. Thus, it should be contrasted with an approach that merely surveys employees regarding risks and controls.

4. CSA's **basic philosophy** is that control is the responsibility of everyone in the organization. The people who work within the process, i.e., employees and managers, are asked for their assessments of risks and controls in their process.

5. The IIA offers a CSA Qualification that may be earned by completing selected seminars on CSA and related topics.

6.   Beginning in 1999, The IIA offered its first specialty certification, the **Certification in Control Self-Assessment (CCSA).** Candidates must pass a computerized examination (paper-and-pencil format outside of North America) and meet educational and experience requirements. The CSA certification will satisfy the experience requirement. The examination tests CSA fundamentals, process, and integration, as well as such related topics as risk, controls, and business objectives.

7.   A CIA candidate should understand the objectives of CSA, its advantages to an organization, its long-term objectives, and the controls best evaluated by the program.

8.   This section describes self-assessment methods and the role of internal auditors in the process. The IIA has issued a Practice Advisory on this subject. It interprets the following Assurance Implementation Standard:

> *2120.A1 – Based on the results of the risk assessment, the internal audit activity should evaluate the adequacy and effectiveness of controls encompassing the organization's governance, operations, and information systems. This should include:*

> - *Reliability and integrity of financial and operational information.*
> - *Effectiveness and efficiency of operations.*
> - *Safeguarding of assets.*
> - *Compliance with laws, regulations, and contracts.*

a.   **PRACTICE ADVISORY 2120.A1-2: USING CONTROL SELF-ASSESSMENT FOR ASSESSING THE ADEQUACY OF CONTROL PROCESSES**

1.   **Senior management** *is charged with overseeing the establishment, administration, and evaluation of the processes of risk management and control.* **Operating managers'** *responsibilities include assessment of the risks and controls in their units. Internal and external* **auditors** *provide varying degrees of assurance about the state of effectiveness of the risk management and control processes of the organization. Both managers and auditors have an interest in using techniques and tools that* **sharpen the focus and expand the efforts to assess risk management and control** *processes that are in place and to identify ways to improve their effectiveness.*

2.   *A methodology encompassing* **self-assessment surveys and facilitated-workshops** *called CSA is a useful and efficient approach for managers and internal auditors to collaborate in assessing and evaluating control procedures. In its purest form, CSA* **integrates business objectives and risks with control processes.** *Control self-assessment is also referred to as "control/risk self-assessment" or "CRSA." Although CSA practitioners use a number of differing techniques and formats, most implemented programs* **share some key features and goals.** *An organization that uses self-assessment will have a* **formal, documented process** *that allows management and work teams, who are directly involved in a business unit, function, or process, to participate in a structured manner for the* **purpose** *of:*

> - *Identifying risks and exposures.*
> - *Assessing the control processes that mitigate or manage those risks.*
> - *Developing action plans to reduce risks to acceptable levels.*
> - *Determining the likelihood of achieving the business objectives.*

3. **The outcomes** *that may be derived from self-assessment methodologies are:*

    - *People in the business units become* **trained** *and experienced in* **assessing risks** *and* **associating control processes** *with managing those risks and improving the chances of achieving business objectives.*

    - **Informal, "soft" controls** *are more easily identified and evaluated.*

    - *People are motivated to take* **"ownership"** *of the control processes in their units, and corrective actions taken by the work teams are often more effective and timely.*

    - *The entire objectives-risks-controls infrastructure of an organization is subject to greater* **monitoring and continuous improvement.**

    - **Internal auditors** *become involved in and knowledgeable about the self-assessment process by serving as facilitators, scribes, and reporters for the work teams and as trainers in risk and control concepts supporting the CSA program.*

    - *The internal audit activity acquires* **more information** *about the control processes within the organization and can leverage that additional information in allocating its scarce resources. The result is greater effort devoted to investigating and performing tests of business units or functions that have significant control weaknesses or high residual risks.*

    - **Management's responsibility** *for the risk management and control processes of the organization is reinforced, and managers will be less tempted to abdicate those activities to specialists, such as auditors.*

    - *The primary role of the internal audit activity will continue to include the* **validation of the evaluation process** *by performing tests and the expression of its professional judgment about the adequacy and effectiveness of the whole risk management and control system.*

4. *The wide* **variety of approaches** *used for CSA processes in organizations reflects the differences in industry, geography, structure, organizational culture, degree of employee empowerment, dominant management style, and the manner of formulating strategies and policies. That observation suggests that the success of a particular type of CSA program in one organization may not be replicated in another. The* **CSA process should be customized** *to fit the unique characteristics of each organization. Also, it suggests that a CSA approach needs to be* **dynamic and change** *with the continual development of the organization.*

5. *The* **three primary forms of CSA** *programs are facilitated team workshops, surveys, and management-produced analysis. Organizations often combine more than one approach.*

6. **Facilitated team workshops** *gather information from work teams representing different levels in the business unit or function. The format of the workshop may be based on objectives, risks, controls, or processes.*

    - **Objective-based format** *focuses on the best way to accomplish a business objective. The workshop begins by* **identifying the controls presently in place** *to support the objective and, then, determining the residual risks remaining. The aim of the workshop is to decide whether the control procedures are working effectively and are resulting in residual risks within an acceptable level.*

- **Risk-based format** focuses on **listing the risks** to achieving an objective. The workshop begins by listing all possible barriers, obstacles, threats, and exposures that might prevent achieving an objective and, then, examining the control procedures to determine if they are sufficient to manage the key risks. The aim of the workshop is to determine significant residual risks. This format takes the work team through the **entire objective-risks-controls** formula.

- **Control-based format** focuses on how well the **controls in place are working**. This format is different from the two above because **the facilitator identifies the key risks and controls** before the beginning of the workshop. During the workshop, the work team assesses how well the controls mitigate risks and promote the achievement of objectives. The aim of the workshop is to produce an analysis of the gap between how controls are working and how well management expects those controls to work.

- **Process-based format** focuses on selected activities that are elements of a chain of processes. The processes are usually a series of related activities that go from some beginning point to an end, such as the various steps in purchasing, product development, or revenue generation. This type of workshop usually covers the identification of the **objectives of the whole process and the various intermediate steps.** The aim of the workshop is to evaluate, update, validate, improve, and even streamline the whole process and its component activities. This workshop format may have a greater breadth of analysis than a control-based approach by covering multiple objectives within the process and by supporting concurrent management efforts, such as reengineering, quality improvement, and continuous improvement initiatives.

7. The **survey form of CSA** uses a questionnaire that tends to ask mostly simple "Yes/No" or "Have/Have Not" questions that are carefully written to be understood by the target recipients. Surveys are often used if the desired respondents are too numerous or widely dispersed to participate in a workshop. They are also preferred if the culture in the organization may hinder open, candid discussions in workshop settings or if management desires to minimize the time spent and costs incurred in gathering the information.

8. The form of self-assessment called **"management-produced analyses"** covers most other approaches by management groups to produce information about selected business processes, risk management activities, and control procedures. The analysis is often intended to reach an informed and timely judgment about **specific characteristics of control** procedures and is commonly **prepared by a team in staff or support role**. The internal auditor may synthesize this analysis with other information to enhance the understanding about controls and to share the knowledge with managers in business or functional units as part of the organization's CSA program.

9. All self-assessment programs assume that managers and members of the work teams possess an **understanding of risk and control concepts** and use those concepts in communications. For training sessions, to facilitate the orderly flow of workshop discussions and as a check on the completeness of the overall process, **organizations often use a control framework**, such as the **COSO** (Committee of Sponsoring Organizations) and **CoCo** (Canadian Criteria of Control Board) models.

10. In the typical CSA **facilitated workshop**, a report will be largely created during the deliberations. A group consensus will be recorded for the various segments of the discussions, and the group will review the **proposed final report** before the end of the final session. Some programs will use anonymous voting techniques to ensure the free flow of information and viewpoints during the workshops and to aid in negotiating differences between viewpoints and interest groups.

11. **Internal audit's investment in some CSA programs** is fairly significant. It may sponsor, design, implement and, in effect, own the process; conduct the training; supply the facilitators, scribes, and reporters; and orchestrate the participation of management and work teams. **In other CSA programs, internal audit's involvement is minimal**, serving as interested party and consultant for the whole process and as ultimate verifier of the evaluations produced by the teams. In most programs, internal audit's investment in the organization's CSA efforts is somewhere between the two extremes described above. As the level of internal audit's involvement in the CSA program and individual workshop deliberations increases, the **chief audit executive should monitor the objectivity of the internal audit staff**, take steps to **manage that objectivity** (if necessary), and **augment internal audit testing** to ensure that bias or partiality do not affect the final judgments of the staff. **Standard 1120** states: "Internal auditors should have an impartial, unbiased attitude and avoid conflicts of interest."

12. A CSA program **augments the traditional role of the internal audit activity** by assisting management in fulfilling its responsibilities to establish and maintain risk management and control processes and by evaluating the adequacy of that system. Through a CSA program, the internal audit activity and the business units and functions **collaborate to produce better information** about how well the **control processes are working** and how significant the **residual risks** are.

13. Although providing staff support for the CSA program as facilitator and specialist, the internal audit activity often finds that it **may reduce the effort spent in gathering information about control procedures and eliminate some testing**. A CSA program should increase the coverage of assessments of control processes across the organization, improve the quality of corrective actions made by the process owners, and focus internal audit's work on **reviewing high-risk processes and unusual situations**. It can focus on validating the evaluation conclusions produced by the CSA process, synthesizing the information gathered from the components of the organization, and expressing its overall judgment about the effectiveness of controls to senior management and the audit committee.

PA Summary

- **Senior management** oversees the processes of risk management and control **(RMC)**. **Operating managers** assess risks and controls in their units. **Auditors** provide assurance about the effectiveness of RMC processes. All want to (1) sharpen the focus of, and expand efforts to assess, RMC processes and (2) improve their effectiveness,

- **Control self-assessment (CSA)** is a collaboration between managers and auditors to **evaluate control**. CSA **integrates business objectives and risks with control processes**. Programs vary but share key features. A **formal, documented** process allows those directly involved to participate in (1) identifying risks and exposures, (2) assessing relevant controls, (3) developing plans, and (4) estimating the probability of achieving objectives.

- **Outcomes** of CSA may include (1) **training** in assessment of the objectives-risks-controls infrastructure, (2) recognition of **soft** controls, (3) willingness to take **ownership** of control, (4) greater monitoring and continuous improvements, (5) greater **internal auditor** knowledge of CSA, (6) **more information** about control and better **allocation of resources** to audits of control, (7) reinforcement of **management's responsibility** for control, and (8) continuation of the IAA's primary role in validation of the evaluation process by testing and expressing judgment on the adequacy and effectiveness of the RMC process.

- The **variety of approaches** used for CSA reflects the differences among organizations. Accordingly, the CSA process should be customized to fit the organization. CSA also should change as the organization develops.

- The **facilitated team workshop** form of CSA may be based on (1) objectives, (2) risks, (3) controls, or (4) processes. A **final report** should reflect the group consensus.

- **Objective-based format** focuses on the best way to accomplish an objective. It **identifies relevant controls** and determines the **residual risks**. The aim is to decide whether controls are effective and result in acceptable residual risks.

- **Risk-based format** focuses on **listing the risks** of achieving an objective and examining the controls to determine whether they suffice to manage the key risks. The aim is to determine significant residual risks.

- **Control-based format** differs because **the facilitator identifies the key risks and controls** before the workshop begins. The work team assesses how well the controls mitigate risks and promote the achievement of objectives. The aim is to analyze the gap between actual and expected performance of controls.

- **Process-based format** focuses on selected activities in a chain of processes. The processes are a series of related activities from a beginning to an end, such as the steps in purchasing. This workshop format identifies the **objectives of the whole process and the intermediate steps**. The aim is to improve the whole process and its activities. This format may have greater breadth than a control-based approach. It covers multiple objectives within the process and supports such efforts as reengineering, quality improvement, and continuous improvement.

- The **survey** form of CSA uses a simple questionnaire. Surveys are often used when a workshop is impracticable, the culture may hinder open discussion, or the time spent and costs incurred must be minimized.

- The **management analysis** form of CSA often addresses specific aspects of control and is prepared by support staff. The internal auditor may combine this and other information to better understand controls and to share knowledge with managers.

> - CSA programs assume an understanding of risk and control concepts. Thus, CSA often uses of a **control framework**, e.g., COSO or CoCo, that facilitates training and discussion and serves as a check on the completeness of the process.
> - **Internal audit's involvement** in CSA may range from ownership of the process to service as a consultant. As involvement in the CSA program and workshop deliberations increases, the CAE **should monitor the objectivity of the internal audit staff**, **manage that objectivity** (if necessary), and **augment testing** to ensure that bias does not affect final judgments.
> - The IAA and business units collaborate in CSA to produce **better information** about the effectiveness of controls and the significance of residual risks.
> - A CSA program may **reduce the audit effort** devoted to control. It should increase the coverage of control assessments, improve the quality of corrective action, and focus audit work on **reviewing high-risk processes and unusual situations**.

9. Stop and review! You have completed the outline for this subunit. Study multiple-choice questions 38 through 50 beginning on page 180.

3.4 STUDY UNIT 3 SUMMARY

1. Internal auditing services may be classified in three categories:

   a. Financial. "The analysis of the economic activity of an entity as measured and reported by accounting methods."

   b. Compliance. "The review of both financial and operating controls and transactions to see how well they conform with established laws, standards, regulations, and procedures."

   c. Operational. "The comprehensive review of the varied functions within an enterprise to appraise the efficiency and economy of operations and the effectiveness with which those functions achieve their objectives."

2. An audit of financial information may follow the cycle approach to internal accounting control. A cycle is a grouping of transactions. The following is one model: (a) revenues and cash collections, (b) acquisitions and expenditures, (c) production or conversion, (d) financial capital and payment, (e) personnel and payroll, and (f) external financial reporting.

3. Audit risk is the risk that an auditor may unknowingly fail to modify the opinion on materially misstated financial statements. It has three components:

   a. Inherent risk is the susceptibility of an assertion to material misstatement in the absence of related controls. It cannot be changed by the auditor.

   b. Control risk is the risk that internal control will not prevent or detect on a timely basis a material misstatement that could occur in an assertion.

   c. Detection risk is the risk that the auditor will not detect a material misstatement that exists in an assertion. It is a function of the effectiveness of an audit procedure and its application by the auditor. It can be changed by the auditor.

4. The concept of materiality recognizes that some matters, but not all, are important for fair presentation of the financial statements.

5. The auditor develops specific audit objectives considering the specific circumstances of the entity, including the nature of its economic activity and the accounting practices unique to its industry.

6. The three conditions ordinarily present when fraud exists include (a) pressures or incentives to commit fraud, (b) opportunity, and (c) the capacity to rationalize misconduct.

7. Legal and regulatory actions require senior management to be more accountable for financial reports. Thus, internal auditors must perform additional services to improve governance and financial reporting. The CAE's core role is to ensure that the audit committee receives needed support and assurance services. A prime objective of the audit committee is to oversee financial reporting. Thus, the IAA is usually requested to form an opinion on the adequacy and effectiveness of internal control over financial reporting and the reliability of financial reports.

8. The value proposition of the IAA is reflected in the definition of internal auditing. It extends to consulting and other value-adding services, including activities that combine assurance and consulting. The charter should empower consulting that is not a conflict of interest. Consulting may enhance understanding of business processes and does not necessarily impair objectivity.

9. Blended assurance and consulting engagements may be appropriate. Consulting may be done as a routine IAA function or in response to requests by management. The categories of consulting engagements are formal, informal, special, and emergency.

10. The parameters within which a government IAA will provide consulting services should be defined in its charter and supported by its policies and procedures. Auditors may recommend operational improvements. Auditors jeopardize their independence and objectivity by being responsible for implementing or authorizing improvements, even those arising from consulting. The core elements of the audit function support attestation to management assertions. The following are core elements: (a) independence, (b) objectivity, (c) not auditing one's own work, and (d) not performing functions or making decisions that are managerial.

11. The board should approve, and the charter should provide authority for, consulting services relating to operations for which internal auditors had (a) previous responsibility or (b) performed assurance services. The IAA should have policies and procedures for these services.

12. In a formal consulting engagement, an understanding of the engagement must be obtained. The internal auditor must assess the extent of the service and its compatibility with the IAA's charter, policies and procedures, and plan of engagements.

13. Internal auditors should have an understanding about the objectives and scope of services and maintain their professionalism. The objectives of formal engagements should meet the needs of the recipients of services. For special request engagements, internal auditors may consider additional objectives.

14. In a formal consulting engagement, reporting requirements are usually set by requesting parties. However, the format should describe the nature of the engagement and other factors of which users should be aware.

15. Results may need to be communicated beyond those who received or requested consulting services. The auditor considers (a) the agreement; (b) whether the receiving or requesting parties will voluntarily expand the communication; (c) the IAA charter, policies, and procedures; (d) the organization's code of ethics and policies; and (e) the Standards and The IIA Code of Ethics.

16. The IAA monitors results of consulting as agreed with the client.

17. CSA is a collaboration between managers and internal auditors to evaluate control. Programs vary but share key features. A formal, documented process allows those directly involved to participate in (a) identifying risks and exposures, (b) assessing relevant controls, (c) developing plans, and (d) estimating the probability of achieving objectives.

QUESTIONS

3.1 Financial Engagements

1. The chief executive officer wants to know whether the purchasing function is properly meeting its charge to "purchase the right materials at the right time in the right quantities." Which of the following types of engagements addresses this request?

- A. A financial engagement relating to the purchasing department.

- B. An operational engagement relating to the purchasing function.

- C. A compliance engagement relating to the purchasing function.

- D. A full-scope engagement relating to the manufacturing operation.

Answer (B) is correct. *(CIA, adapted)*
REQUIRED: The type of engagement that determines whether the purchasing function is effective and efficient.
DISCUSSION: According to *Sawyer's Internal Auditing* (The IIA 1996, p. 4), an operational engagement involves a "comprehensive review of the varied functions within an enterprise to appraise the efficiency and economy of operations and the effectiveness with which those functions achieve their objectives."
Answer (A) is incorrect because a financial engagement involves the analysis of the economic activity of an entity as measured and reported by accounting methods. Answer (C) is incorrect because a compliance engagement is a review of both financial and operating controls and transactions to determine conformity with established standards. It tests adherence to management's policies, procedures, and plans designed to ensure certain actions. Answer (D) is incorrect because a full-scale engagement relating to the manufacturing operation has financial, compliance, and operational aspects. It exceeds the chief executive officer's request.

2. The primary difference between operational engagements and financial engagements is that in the former the internal auditors

- A. Are not concerned with whether the client entity is generating information in compliance with financial accounting standards.

- B. Are seeking to help management use resources in the most effective manner possible.

- C. Start with the financial statements of the client entity and works backward to the basic processes involved in producing them.

- D. Can use analytical skills and tools that are not necessary in financial engagements.

Answer (B) is correct. *(CIA, adapted)*
REQUIRED: The main distinction between operational and financial engagements.
DISCUSSION: Financial engagements are primarily concerned with forming an opinion on the fairness of the financial statements. Operational engagements evaluate accomplishment of established objectives and goals for operations or programs and economical and efficient use of resources.
Answer (A) is incorrect because the reliability and integrity of financial information are important in operational engagements. Information systems provide data for decision making, control, and compliance with external requirements. Answer (C) is incorrect because a financial engagement entails using financial statements as a starting point. Answer (D) is incorrect because analytical skills are necessary in all types of engagements.

3. During an operational engagement, the internal auditors compare the current staffing of a department with established industry standards to

- A. Identify bogus employees on the department's payroll.

- B. Assess the current performance of the department and make appropriate recommendations for improvement.

- C. Evaluate the adequacy of the established internal controls for the department.

- D. Determine whether the department has complied with all laws and regulations governing its personnel.

Answer (B) is correct. *(CIA, adapted)*
REQUIRED: The purpose of comparing the current staffing of a department with established industry standards.
DISCUSSION: According to *Sawyer's Internal Auditing* (The IIA 1996, p. 4), an operational engagement involves a "comprehensive review of the varied functions within an enterprise to appraise the efficiency and economy of operations and the effectiveness with which those functions achieve their objectives."
Answer (A) is incorrect because the internal auditors would not be concerned with payroll processing during this type of testing and evaluation. Answer (C) is incorrect because comparison of staffing levels with industry standards will not test the adequacy of internal controls. Answer (D) is incorrect because the internal auditors would be more concerned with legal requirements during a compliance engagement.

4. An operational engagement relating to the production function includes a procedure to compare actual costs with standard costs. The purpose of this engagement procedure is to

    A. Determine the accuracy of the system used to record actual costs.

    B. Measure the effectiveness of the standard cost system.

    C. Assess the reasonableness of standard costs.

    D. Assist management in its evaluation of effectiveness and efficiency.

Answer (D) is correct. *(CIA, adapted)*
    REQUIRED: The purpose in an operational engagement relating to the production function of comparing actual and standard costs.
    DISCUSSION: According to *Sawyer's Internal Auditing* (The IIA 1996, p. 4), an operational engagement involves a "comprehensive review of the varied functions within an enterprise to appraise the efficiency and economy of operations and the effectiveness with which those functions achieve their objectives." A comparison of actual and standard costs addresses efficiency and economy issues.
    Answer (A) is incorrect because the comparison will not determine the accuracy of actual costs. Answer (B) is incorrect because the comparison will not determine the effectiveness of the system. Answer (C) is incorrect because the comparison will not determine the reasonableness of standard costs.

5. A determination of cost savings is most likely to be an objective of a(n)

    A. Program-results engagement.

    B. Financial engagement.

    C. Compliance engagement.

    D. Operational engagement.

Answer (D) is correct. *(CIA, adapted)*
    REQUIRED: The form of engagement in which a determination of cost savings is an objective.
    DISCUSSION: According to *Sawyer's Internal Auditing* (The IIA 1996, p. 4), an operational engagement involves a "comprehensive review of the varied functions within an enterprise to appraise the efficiency and economy of operations and the effectiveness with which those functions achieve their objectives."
    Answer (A) is incorrect because a program-results engagement addresses accomplishment of program objectives. Answer (B) is incorrect because a financial engagement concerns the safeguarding of assets and the reliability and integrity of information. Answer (C) is incorrect because a compliance engagement relates to compliance with legal, regulatory, procedural, and other requirements.

6. Most audit work in a financial statement audit consists of obtaining and evaluating evidence about

    A. Internal controls.

    B. Assertions.

    C. Fraud.

    D. Material errors.

Answer (B) is correct. *(Publisher, adapted)*
    REQUIRED: The purpose of most work in a financial statement audit.
    DISCUSSION: Most audit work in a financial statement audit is ultimately directed toward obtaining and evaluating evidence about assertions. The measure of the validity of this evidence lies in the auditor's judgment. The assertions are representations by management that are embodied in financial statement components and can be either explicit or implicit. The five assertions are: completeness, rights and obligations, valuation or allocation, existence or occurrence, and statement presentation and disclosure.
    Answer (A) is incorrect because the assessment of control risk is done to determine the nature, timing, and extent of substantive procedures performed to gather evidence about the assertions. Answer (C) is incorrect because an auditor identifies and assesses risks that may result in a material misstatement due to fraud. Thus, fraud-related procedures ultimately are directed toward possible misstatement of financial statement assertions. Answer (D) is incorrect because an auditor performs procedures to obtain reasonable assurance about whether the assertions in the financial statements are materially misstated as a result of error or fraud.

7. The existence of audit risk is recognized by the statement in the auditor's standard report that the

A. Auditor is responsible for expressing an opinion on the financial statements, which are the responsibility of management.

B. Financial statements are presented fairly, in all material respects, in conformity with GAAP.

C. Audit includes examining, on a test basis, evidence supporting the amounts and disclosures in the financial statements.

D. Auditor obtains reasonable assurance about whether the financial statements are free of material misstatement.

Answer (D) is correct. *(CPA, adapted)*
   REQUIRED: The wording in the standard report that recognizes the existence of audit risk.
   DISCUSSION: Audit risk is the risk that an auditor may unknowingly fail to modify the opinion on materially misstated financial statements. The exercise of due professional care allows the auditor to provide only reasonable, not absolute, assurance that the financial statements are free of material misstatement, whether caused by error or fraud.
   Answer (A) is incorrect because the introductory paragraph of the standard audit report states the degree of the auditor's responsibility. Answer (B) is incorrect because this language indicates the auditor's belief that the statements as a whole are not materially misstated. Answer (C) is incorrect because the scope paragraph of the audit report recognizes that examining all items under audit is not feasible.

8. The risk that an auditor's procedures will lead to the conclusion that a material misstatement does not exist in an account balance when, in fact, such misstatement does exist is

A. Audit risk.

B. Inherent risk.

C. Control risk.

D. Detection risk.

Answer (D) is correct. *(CPA, adapted)*
   REQUIRED: The risk that audit procedures will fail to detect a material misstatement.
   DISCUSSION: Detection risk is the risk that the auditor will not detect a material misstatement that exists in an assertion. It is affected by the auditor's procedures and can be changed at his/her discretion.
   Answer (A) is incorrect because audit risk includes inherent risk and control risk, which are not affected by the auditor's procedures. Answer (B) is incorrect because inherent risk is the susceptibility of an assertion to material misstatement in the absence of related controls. Answer (C) is incorrect because control risk is the risk that a material misstatement will not be prevented or detected by internal control.

9. Inherent risk and control risk differ from detection risk in that they

A. Arise from the misapplication of auditing procedures.

B. May be assessed in either quantitative or nonquantitative terms.

C. Exist independently of the financial statement audit.

D. Can be changed at the auditor's discretion.

Answer (C) is correct. *(CPA, adapted)*
   REQUIRED: The way in which inherent risk and control risk differ from detection risk.
   DISCUSSION: Inherent risk is the susceptibility of an assertion to a material misstatement in the absence of related controls. Control risk is the risk that internal control will not prevent or detect a material misstatement. Inherent and control risks exist independently of the audit and cannot be changed by the auditor. Detection risk is the risk that the auditor will not detect a material misstatement that exists in an assertion. It can be changed at the auditor's discretion by altering the nature, timing, or extent of the audit procedures.
   Answer (A) is incorrect because the misapplication of auditing procedures may affect detection risk but is independent of inherent and control risk. Answer (B) is incorrect because all three risks may be assessed either quantitatively or nonquantitatively. Answer (D) is incorrect because inherent risk and control risk must be assessed and cannot be changed at the auditor's discretion.

10. The acceptable level of detection risk is inversely related to the

A. Assurance provided by substantive tests.

B. Risk of misapplying auditing procedures.

C. Preliminary judgment about materiality levels.

D. Risk of failing to discover material misstatements.

Answer (A) is correct. *(CPA, adapted)*
   REQUIRED: The relationship between detection risk and the assurance provided by substantive tests.
   DISCUSSION: An auditor considers internal control to assess control risk. (S)he also assesses inherent risk. The greater (lower) the assessed levels of control risk and inherent risk, the lower (greater) the acceptable level of detection risk. Hence, the relationship between substantive testing and detection risk is inverse.
   Answer (B) is incorrect because the risk of misapplying auditing procedures is related to the auditor's training and experience. Answer (C) is incorrect because preliminary judgments about materiality are used by the auditor to determine the acceptable level of audit risk. Detection risk is just one component of audit risk. Answer (D) is incorrect because the acceptable level of detection risk is an inverse function of the assessments of control risk and inherent risk.

11. As the acceptable level of detection risk decreases, an auditor may

A. Reduce substantive testing by relying on the assessments of inherent risk and control risk.

B. Postpone the planned timing of substantive tests from interim dates to the year-end.

C. Eliminate the assessed level of inherent risk from consideration as a planning factor.

D. Lower the assessed level of control risk from the maximum level to below the maximum.

Answer (B) is correct. *(CPA, adapted)*
REQUIRED: The action of the auditor as the acceptable level of detection risk decreases.
DISCUSSION: A decrease in the acceptable level of detection risk or in the amount considered material will result in the auditor's modifying the audit program to obtain greater assurance from substantive testing by (1) selecting a more effective audit procedure, (2) applying procedures nearer to year-end, or (3) increasing the extent of particular tests.
Answer (A) is incorrect because substantive testing would be increased. Answer (C) is incorrect because the auditor should always consider the assessed level of inherent risk in the planning phase of an audit. Answer (D) is incorrect because control risk is assessed prior to determining the acceptable level of detection risk.

12. Which of the following audit risk components may be assessed in nonquantitative terms?

	Control Risk	Detection Risk	Inherent Risk
A.	Yes	Yes	Yes
B.	No	Yes	Yes
C.	Yes	Yes	No
D.	Yes	No	Yes

Answer (A) is correct. *(CPA, adapted)*
REQUIRED: The audit risk components that may be assessed in nonquantitative terms.
DISCUSSION: The components of audit risk may be assessed in quantitative terms, such as percentages, or in nonquantitative terms that range, for example, from a minimum to a maximum.

13. Holding other planning considerations equal, a decrease in the amount of misstatements in a class of transactions that an auditor could tolerate most likely would cause the auditor to

A. Apply the planned substantive tests prior to the balance sheet date.

B. Perform the planned auditing procedures closer to the balance sheet date.

C. Increase the assessed level of control risk for relevant financial statement assertions.

D. Decrease the extent of auditing procedures to be applied to the class of transactions.

Answer (B) is correct. *(CPA, adapted)*
REQUIRED: The effect of reducing tolerable misstatement.
DISCUSSION: A decrease in the acceptable level of detection risk or in the amount considered material will result in the auditor's modifying the audit program to obtain greater assurance from substantive testing by (1) selecting a more effective audit procedure, (2) applying procedures nearer to year-end, or (3) increasing the extent of particular tests. Tolerable misstatement should not exceed the auditor's preliminary judgments about materiality, so its decrease is a reduction in materiality that requires greater assurance from substantive testing.
Answer (A) is incorrect because applying tests at interim dates reduces the assurance provided. Answer (C) is incorrect because control risk is assessed based on consideration of the client's controls. Answer (D) is incorrect because decreasing their effectiveness reduces the assurance provided.

14. Which of the following would an auditor most likely use in determining the auditor's preliminary judgment about materiality?

A. The anticipated sample size of the planned substantive tests.

B. The entity's annualized interim financial statements.

C. The results of the internal control questionnaire.

D. The contents of the management representation letter.

Answer (B) is correct. *(CPA, adapted)*
REQUIRED: The factor most likely used in determining the preliminary judgment about materiality.
DISCUSSION: Preliminary judgment about materiality might be based on annualized interim financial statements or prior-period financial statements providing that recognition is given for major changes in the entity's circumstances and relevant changes in the economy or the entity's industry.
Answer (A) is incorrect because the auditor's preliminary judgment about materiality is used to determine the sample sizes for substantive tests. Sample sizes are calculated during evidence collection. Answer (C) is incorrect because results of the internal control questionnaire are considered during the assessment of control risk. Answer (D) is incorrect because the contents of the management representation letter are determined near the end of the audit.

15. Which of the following is a false statement about materiality?

A. The concept of materiality recognizes that some matters are important for fair presentation of financial statements in conformity with GAAP, while other matters are not important.

B. An auditor considers materiality for planning purposes in terms of the largest aggregate level of misstatements that could be material to any one of the financial statements.

C. Materiality judgments are made in light of surrounding circumstances and necessarily involve both quantitative and qualitative judgments.

D. An auditor's consideration of materiality is influenced by the auditor's perception of the needs of a reasonable person who will rely on the financial statements.

Answer (B) is correct. *(CPA, adapted)*
REQUIRED: The false statement about materiality.
DISCUSSION: The auditor ordinarily considers materiality based on the smallest aggregate level of material misstatements in the financial statements.
Answer (A) is incorrect because the auditor's responsibility does not extend to immaterial matters. Answer (C) is incorrect because qualitative factors may cause misstatements of relatively small amounts to be material. Answer (D) is incorrect because an item is material if its misstatement or omission might affect the judgment of a reasonable person who relies on the financial statements.

16. Which of the following is a false statement about audit objectives?

A. There should be a one-to-one relationship between audit objectives and procedures.

B. Audit objectives should be developed in light of management assertions about the financial statement components.

C. Selection of tests to meet audit objectives should depend upon the understanding of internal control.

D. The auditor should resolve any substantial doubt about any of management's material financial statement assertions.

Answer (A) is correct. *(Publisher, adapted)*
REQUIRED: The false statement about audit objectives.
DISCUSSION: There is not necessarily a one-to-one relationship between audit objectives and procedures. Some procedures may relate to more than one objective, while multiple procedures may be needed to achieve a single objective.
Answer (B) is incorrect because assertions made by management should be considered when the auditor develops objectives. Answer (C) is incorrect because the understanding of internal control and the assessed control risk affect the nature, timing, and extent of substantive tests. Answer (D) is incorrect because the auditor must refrain from forming an opinion until (s)he has gathered sufficient competent evidence to remove any substantial doubt about a material assertion by management. Otherwise, (s)he must qualify the opinion or disclaim an opinion.

17. Management makes certain assertions that are embodied in financial statement components. For example, two such categories of assertions are completeness and valuation or allocation. Which of the following is not a broad category of management assertions?

A. Transactions and events for a period.

B. Presentation and disclosure.

C. Balances at period-end.

D. Errors or fraud.

Answer (D) is correct. *(Publisher, adapted)*
REQUIRED: The category of assertions not explicitly listed.
DISCUSSION: Management implicitly represents that the financial statements are free from material misstatements. But this representation is not explicitly noted as a category of management assertions. Management assertions in the financial statements can be classified using the following categories: (1) transactions and events for a period (occurrence, completeness, accuracy, cutoff, and classification), (2) balances at period-end (existence, rights and obligations, completeness, and valuation and allocation), and (3) presentation and disclosure (most of the preceding assertions plus understandability).
Answer (A) is incorrect because transactions and events for a period is a category listed. Answer (B) is incorrect because presentation and disclosure is a category listed. Answer (C) is incorrect because balances at period-end is a category listed.

18. The objective of tests of details of transactions performed as substantive tests is to

A. Comply with generally accepted auditing standards.

B. Attain assurance about the reliability of the accounting system.

C. Detect material misstatements in the financial statements.

D. Evaluate whether management's policies and procedures operated effectively.

Answer (C) is correct. *(CPA, adapted)*
REQUIRED: The objective of tests of details.
DISCUSSION: Substantive tests are (1) tests of the details of transactions and balances and (2) analytical procedures. They are performed to detect material misstatements in the financial statement assertions.
Answer (A) is incorrect because the auditor may use a variety of techniques and is not required to use tests of the details of transactions to comply with GAAS. Answer (B) is incorrect because tests of controls are applied to test the reliability of the accounting system and other elements of internal control. Answer (D) is incorrect because tests of controls are used to determine whether policies or procedures operated effectively.

19. In testing the existence assertion for an asset, an auditor ordinarily works from the

A. Financial statements to the potentially unrecorded items.

B. Potentially unrecorded items to the financial statements.

C. Accounting records to the supporting evidence.

D. Supporting evidence to the accounting records.

Answer (C) is correct. *(CPA, adapted)*
REQUIRED: The usual procedure testing the existence assertion for an asset.
DISCUSSION: The existence assertion concerns whether assets or liabilities of the entity exist at a given time. The direction of testing is ordinarily from the accounting records to the supporting evidence, including direct observation of the inventory. Unrecorded items relate to the completeness assertion. The auditor should select evidence indicating that an item should be included in an amount and then investigate.

20. An auditor observes the mailing of monthly statements to a client's customers and reviews evidence of follow-up on errors reported by the customers. This test of controls most likely is performed to support management's financial statement assertion(s) of

	Presentation and Disclosure	Existence
A.	Yes	Yes
B.	Yes	No
C.	No	Yes
D.	No	No

Answer (C) is correct. *(CPA, adapted)*
REQUIRED: The financial statement assertion(s) related to observing the client's follow-up on errors reported on monthly statements.
DISCUSSION: The existence assertion relates to whether the related balance exists at the balance sheet date. Observation of the mailing of monthly statements as well as observing the correction of reported errors provides evidence that controls may be effective in ensuring that there are actual client customers.

21. In determining whether transactions have been recorded, the direction of the audit testing should be from the

A. General ledger balances.

B. Adjusted trial balance.

C. Original source documents.

D. General journal entries.

Answer (C) is correct. *(CPA, adapted)*
REQUIRED: The direction of testing to determine whether transactions have been recorded.
DISCUSSION: Determining whether transactions have been recorded is a test of the completeness assertion. Thus, beginning with the original source documents and tracing the transactions to the appropriate records would determine whether they were recorded.

22. Identification of an appropriate population to sample is dependent upon audit objectives. A population of entries in an asset repairs expense file is an appropriate population if the audit objective is to determine whether

A. Expenditures for fixed assets have been improperly expensed.

B. Noncapital repair expenditures have been properly charged to expense.

C. Noncapital repair expenditures have been recorded in the proper period.

D. Expenditures for fixed assets have been recorded in the proper period.

Answer (A) is correct. *(CIA, adapted)*
REQUIRED: The audit objective that justifies sampling from a repairs expense file.
DISCUSSION: An auditor should vouch significant debits in the repairs expense file to supporting documentation to determine whether capitalizable expenditures have been expensed. Expenditures that extend the life of a fixed asset or significantly improve its functioning should be capitalized.
Answer (B) is incorrect because ascertaining that all noncapital expenditures have been expensed would require testing of expense accounts and selected asset accounts in addition to the repairs expense account. Answer (C) is incorrect because ascertaining that noncapital repair expenditures have been recorded in the proper time period requires sampling from more than one accounting period. Answer (D) is incorrect because ascertaining that capitalizable fixed assets expenditures were recorded in the proper accounting period involves sampling from the fixed asset file.

23. Which of the following statements reflects an auditor's responsibility for detecting errors and fraud?

A. An auditor is responsible for detecting employee errors and simple fraud, but not for discovering fraudulent acts involving employee collusion or management override.

B. An auditor should plan the audit to detect errors and fraud that are caused by departures from GAAP.

C. An auditor is not responsible for detecting errors and fraud unless the application of GAAS would result in such detection.

D. An auditor should design the audit to provide reasonable assurance of detecting errors and fraud that are material to the financial statements.

Answer (D) is correct. *(CPA, adapted)*
REQUIRED: The statement reflecting the auditor's responsibility for detecting errors and fraud.
DISCUSSION: The auditor must plan and perform the audit so that the financial statements do not contain material misstatements, whether caused by error or fraud. Thus, the consideration of fraud should be logically integrated into the overall audit process in a manner consistent with other pronouncements, e.g., those on planning and supervision, audit risk and materiality, and internal control.

24. Which of the following circumstances most likely would cause an auditor to consider whether material misstatements exist in an entity's financial statements?

A. Management places little emphasis on meeting earnings projections of external parties.

B. The board of directors oversees the financial reporting process and internal control.

C. Reportable conditions previously communicated to management are not corrected.

D. Transactions selected for testing are not supported by proper documentation.

Answer (D) is correct. *(CPA, adapted)*
REQUIRED: The circumstance most likely to cause an auditor to consider whether material misstatements due to fraud exist.
DISCUSSION: Fraud risk factors relate to misstatements arising from (1) fraudulent financial reporting and (2) misappropriation of assets. Each of these categories may be further classified according to the three conditions that ordinarily exist when fraud occurs: (1) incentives/pressures, (2) opportunities, and (3) attitudes/rationalizations. For example, an opportunity for misappropriation of assets may arise because of inadequate control over assets reflected by a lack of timely and appropriate documentation of transactions, such as credit memos for returns of goods.
Answer (A) is incorrect because a risk factor exists when excessive pressure is placed on management to reach expectations of external parties. Answer (B) is incorrect because the board's involvement reduces the likelihood of material misstatements due to fraud. Answer (C) is incorrect because management may properly evaluate the costs and benefits of corrections in deciding whether to correct reportable conditions.

25. Which of the following characteristics most likely will heighten an auditor's concern about the risk of material misstatements due to fraud in an entity's financial statements?

A. The entity's industry is experiencing declining customer demand.

B. Employees who handle cash receipts are not bonded.

C. Bank reconciliations usually include in-transit deposits.

D. Equipment is often sold at a loss before being fully depreciated.

Answer (A) is correct.   *(CPA, adapted)*
REQUIRED: The characteristic most likely to increase the auditor's concern about material misstatements due to fraud.
DISCUSSION: Certain risk factors are related to misstatements arising from fraudulent reporting. These factors may be grouped in three categories: (1) incentives/pressures, (2) opportunities, and (3) attitudes/rationalizations. One set of risk factors in the incentives/pressures category concerns threats to financial stability or profitability by economic, industry, or entity operating conditions, such as significant declines in customer demand.
Answer (B) is incorrect because failure to bond employees is a potential control weakness, but it may be compensated for. Answer (C) is incorrect because in-transit deposits are items requiring reconciliation. Answer (D) is incorrect because equipment is often disposed of prior to being fully depreciated.

3.2 Consulting Engagements

26. Internal auditors may provide consulting services that add value and improve an organization's operations. The performance of these services

A. Impairs internal auditors' objectivity with respect to an assurance service involving the same engagement client.

B. Precludes generation of assurance from a consulting engagement.

C. Should be consistent with the internal audit activity's empowerment reflected in the charter.

D. Imposes no responsibility to communicate information other than to the engagement client.

Answer (C) is correct.   *(Publisher, adapted)*
REQUIRED: The internal auditors' responsibility regarding consulting services.
DISCUSSION: According to Standard 1000.C1, the nature of consulting services should be defined in the charter. Internal auditors have traditionally performed many types of consulting services, including the analysis of controls built into developing systems, analysis of security products, serving on task forces to analyze operations and make recommendations, and so forth. The board (or audit committee) should empower the internal audit activity to perform additional services if they do not represent a conflict of interest or detract from its obligations to the committee. That empowerment should be reflected in the internal audit charter (PA 1000.C1-1).
Answer (A) is incorrect because consulting services do not necessarily impair objectivity. Decisions to implement recommendations made as a result of a consulting service should be made by management. Thus, decision-making by management does not impair the internal auditors' objectivity. Answer (B) is incorrect because assurance and consulting services are not mutually exclusive. One type of service may be generated from the other. Answer (D) is incorrect because a primary internal auditing value is to provide assurance to senior management and audit committee directors. Consulting engagements cannot be rendered in a manner that masks information that in the judgment of the chief audit executive (CAE) should be presented to senior executives and board members (PA 1000.C1-1).

27. Consulting services

A. May enhance the auditor's understanding of business processes or issues related to an assurance engagement but will always impair the auditor's or the internal audit activity's independence.

B. To be performed by the internal audit activity should be authorized by management if they do not represent a conflict of interest.

C. Should not be performed by the internal audit activity because they impair objectivity.

D. Are a natural extension of assurance and investigative services and may represent informal or formal advice, analysis, or assessments.

Answer (D) is correct.   *(Publisher, adapted)*
REQUIRED: The true statement about consulting services.
DISCUSSION: According to PA 1000.C1-1, "Much of consulting is a natural extension of assurance and investigative services and may represent informal or formal advice, analysis, or assessments. The internal audit activity is uniquely positioned to perform this type of consulting work based on (a) its adherence to the highest standards of objectivity and (b) its breadth of knowledge about organizational processes, risk, and strategies."
Answer (A) is incorrect because consulting services may enhance the auditor's understanding of business processes or issues related to an assurance engagement and do not necessarily impair the internal audit activity's objectivity and independence. Answer (B) is incorrect because the board or audit committee should empower the internal audit activity to perform additional services if they do not represent a conflict of interest or detract from its obligations to the committee. Answer (C) is incorrect because an organization may find that the internal audit activity is uniquely qualified for some formal consulting tasks.

28. Advisory and related client service activities, the nature and scope of which are agreed upon with the client, are best described as

    A. Internal audit services.

    B. Assurance services.

    C. Consulting services.

    D. External assurance services.

Answer (C) is correct. *(Publisher, adapted)*
    REQUIRED: The term for advisory and related client service activities, the nature and scope of which are agreed upon with the client.
    DISCUSSION: The IIA defines consulting services as "advisory and related client service activities, the nature and scope of which are agreed upon with the client and which are intended to add value and improve an organization's governance, risk management, and control processes while not assuming management responsibility. Examples include counsel, advice, facilitation, and training."

29. Which of the following statements is false?

    A. A disciplined, systematic evaluation methodology is incorporated in each internal audit activity. The list of services can generally be incorporated into two broad categories of assurance and consulting.

    B. Assurance and consulting are mutually exclusive and do preclude other auditing services such as investigations and nonauditing roles.

    C. Many audit services will have both an assurance and consultative role.

    D. Internal audit consulting enriches value-adding internal auditing.

Answer (B) is correct. *(Publisher, adapted)*
    REQUIRED: The false statement regarding consulting and assurance services.
    DISCUSSION: PA 1000.C1-1 lists twelve principles that should guide the performance of consulting activities of internal auditors. It states, "Assurance and consulting are not mutually exclusive and do not preclude other auditing services such as investigations and nonauditing roles."

30. Who is responsible for determining the methodology to use for classifying engagements within the organization?

    A. The chief audit executive.

    B. Management.

    C. The board.

    D. The audit committee.

Answer (A) is correct. *(Publisher, adapted)*
    REQUIRED: The person/group that is responsible for determining the methodology to use for classifying engagements within the organization.
    DISCUSSION: According to PA 1000.C1-2, the chief audit executive should determine the methodology to use for classifying engagements within the organization. In some circumstances, it may be appropriate to conduct a "blended" engagement that incorporates elements of both consulting and assurance activities into one consolidated approach. In other cases, it may be appropriate to distinguish between the assurance and consulting components of the engagement.

31. Before internal auditors begin to offer consulting services to an organization, a number of things need to happen within the organization. What is the order in which the following items should be performed?

  I. The internal audit charter should be amended to include authority and responsibilities for consulting activities.

  II. The CAE should confirm that the board understands and approves the concept of providing consulting services.

  III. The internal audit activity should develop appropriate policies and procedures for conducting such engagements.

    A. I, II, III.

    B. II, III, I.

    C. II, I, III.

    D. III, II, I.

Answer (C) is correct. *(Publisher, adapted)*
    REQUIRED: The order in which the specified items should be performed before internal auditors offer consulting services.
    DISCUSSION: PA 1000.C1-2 states, internal auditors are sometimes requested to provide consulting services relating to operations for which they had previous responsibilities or had conducted assurance services. Prior to offering consulting services, the chief audit executive should confirm that the board understands and approves the concept of providing consulting services. Once approved, the internal audit charter should be amended to include authority and responsibilities for consulting activities, and the internal audit activity should develop appropriate policies and procedures for conducting such engagements.

32. An internal auditor performed a formal consulting engagement for XYZ Corporation on June 1, Year 1. When is the earliest time the auditor can perform assurance services for XYZ Corporation and be considered independent and objective?

    A. January 1, Year 2.

    B. June 1, Year 2.

    C. July 1, Year 1.

    D. June 2, Year 1.

Answer (B) is correct. *(Publisher, adapted)*
    REQUIRED: The earliest date the internal auditor can perform assurance services and be considered independent and objective.
    DISCUSSION: According to PA 1000.C1-2, "Independence and objectivity may be impaired if assurance services are provided within one year after a formal consulting engagement. Steps can be taken to minimize the effects of impairment by assigning different auditors to perform each of the services, establishing independent management and supervision, defining separate accountability for the results of the projects, and disclosing the presumed impairment."

33. Internal auditors should design the scope of work in a consulting engagement to ensure that all of the following will be maintained except

    A. Independence.

    B. Integrity.

    C. Credibility.

    D. Professionalism.

Answer (A) is correct. *(Publisher, adapted)*
    REQUIRED: The attribute of the IAA that need not be maintained in a consulting engagement.
    DISCUSSION: Internal auditors should reach an understanding of the objectives and scope of the consulting engagement with those receiving the service. Any reservations about the value, benefit, or possible negative implications of the consulting engagement should be communicated to those receiving the service. Internal auditors should design the scope of work to ensure that professionalism, integrity, credibility, and reputation of the internal audit activity will be maintained (PA 1000.C1-2). During a consulting engagement, the internal auditor is acting as an advocate for management, and independence is not required.

34. The internal auditor for ABC Corporation has received a special request from management. The internal auditor believes that the objectives that should be pursued go beyond those requested by management. What should the internal auditor do?

    A. Refuse to accept the engagement unless he can persuade management to include the additional objectives in the consulting engagement.

    B. Include the objectives that he feels are necessary in the current consulting engagement and inform management in the final communication of the engagement results.

    C. Document the fact that the objectives were not pursued and disclose that observation to the audit committee in a formal report.

    D. Try to persuade management to include the additional objectives in the consulting engagement.

Answer (D) is correct. *(Publisher, adapted)*
    REQUIRED: The action an internal auditor should consider if he believes that the objectives of a consulting engagement that should be pursued are beyond those requested by management.
    DISCUSSION: In planning formal consulting engagements, internal auditors should design objectives to meet the appropriate needs of management officials receiving these services. In the case of special requests by management, internal auditors may consider the following actions if they believe that the objectives that should be pursued go beyond those requested by management: (1) persuade management to include the additional objectives in the consulting engagement; or (2) document the fact that the objectives were not pursued, disclose that observation in the final communication of consulting engagement results, and include the objectives in a separate and subsequent assurance engagement (PA 1000.C1-2).
    Answer (A) is incorrect because the internal auditor has no reason not to accept the consulting engagement. Answer (B) is incorrect because the internal auditor should not perform any services that go beyond the scope or objectives of the services understood and agreed upon with management. Answer (C) is incorrect because the internal auditor is only reporting to those receiving the services during a consulting engagement, i.e., management.

35. Substantial risk exposures or material control weaknesses discovered during a formal consulting engagement should be brought to the attention of management. In some situations, the internal auditor's concerns also should be communicated to

    A. Executive management.

    B. Audit committee.

    C. Board of directors.

    D. All of the answers are correct.

Answer (D) is correct. *(Publisher, adapted)*
    REQUIRED: The group(s) to whom the internal auditor may communicate his/her concerns about substantial risk exposures or material control weaknesses discovered during a formal consulting engagement.
    DISCUSSION: Internal auditors should be observant of the effectiveness of risk management and control processes during formal consulting engagements. Substantial risk exposures or material control weaknesses should be brought to the attention of management. In some situations the auditor's concerns should also be communicated to executive management, the audit committee, and/or the board of directors. (PA 1000.C1-2)

36. An internal auditor concludes that the results of a consulting engagement should be communicated beyond those who received or requested the services. The auditor should follow a series of steps until satisfied with the resolution. In what order should the auditor perform the following steps?

I. Attempt to convince those receiving or requesting the service to expand voluntarily the communication to the appropriate parties.

II. Determine what guidance is provided in the organization's code of conduct, code of ethics, and other relative policies, administrative directives, or procedures.

III. Determine what direction is provided in the agreement concerning the consulting engagement and related communications.

    A. II, I, III.

    B. I, II, III.

    C. III, I, II.

    D. I, III, II.

Answer (C) is correct. *(Publisher, adapted)*
REQUIRED: The order that the internal auditor should follow to expand the reporting of a consulting engagement to other parties.
DISCUSSION: When expanding the reporting to other parties, the auditor should take the following steps until satisfied with the resolution of the matter:

- First, determine what direction is provided in the agreement concerning the consulting engagement and related communications.
- Second, attempt to convince those receiving or requesting the service to expand voluntarily the communication to the appropriate parties.
- Third, determine what guidance is provided in the internal audit charter or audit activity's policies and procedures concerning consulting communications.
- Fourth, determine what guidance is provided in the organization's code of conduct, code of ethics, and other relative policies, administrative directives, or procedures.
- Fifth, determine what guidance is provided by The IIA's Standards and Code of Ethics, other standards or codes applicable to the auditor, and any legal or regulatory requirements that relate to the matter under consideration. (PA 1000.C1-2)

37. Which statement about consulting engagements is true?

    A. Documentation requirements applicable to assurance engagements apply to consulting engagements.

    B. The internal audit activity should monitor every aspect of a consulting engagement to ensure it is being conducted to the extent agreed upon with the client.

    C. Internal auditors should keep executive management and the audit committee informed about how audit resources are being deployed.

    D. Work programs for formal consulting engagements should address policies and issues related to ownership of consulting engagement records to protect the organization and avoid any potential misunderstandings.

Answer (C) is correct. *(Publisher, adapted)*
REQUIRED: The true statement about consulting engagements.
DISCUSSION: Internal auditors should disclose to management, the audit committee, board, or other governing body of the organization the nature, extent, and overall results of formal consulting engagements along with other reports of internal auditing activities. Internal auditors should keep executive management and the audit committee informed about how audit resources are being deployed. Neither detail reports of these consulting engagements nor the specific results and recommendations are required to be communicated.
(PA 1000.C1-2)
Answer (A) is incorrect because documentation requirements applicable to assurance engagements do not necessarily apply to consulting engagements. Answer (B) is incorrect because the internal audit activity should only monitor the results of consulting engagements to the extent agreed upon with the client. Answer (D) is incorrect because work programs for formal consulting engagements should document the objectives and scope of the engagement as well as the methodology to be used in satisfying the objectives.

3.3 Control Self-Assessment (CSA)

38. Which group is charged with overseeing the establishment, administration, and evaluation of the processes of risk management and control?

- A. Operating managers.
- B. Internal auditors.
- C. External auditors.
- D. Senior management.

Answer (D) is correct. *(Publisher, adapted)*
REQUIRED: The group charged with overseeing the establishment, administration, and evaluation of the processes of risk management and control.
DISCUSSION: Senior management is charged with overseeing the establishment, administration, and evaluation of the processes of risk management and control. Operating managers' responsibilities include assessment of the risks and controls in their units. Internal and external auditors provide varying degrees of assurance about the state of effectiveness of the risk management and control processes of the organization. (PA 2120.A1-2)
Answer (A) is incorrect because operating managers' responsibilities include assessment of the risk management and control. Answer (B) is incorrect because internal auditors provide varying degrees of assurance about the state of effectiveness of the risk management and control processes of the organization. Answer (C) is incorrect because external auditors provide varying degrees of assurance about the state of effectiveness of the risk management and control processes of the organization.

39. Control self-assessment is a process that involves employees in assessing the adequacy of controls and identifying opportunities for improvement within an organization. Which of the following are reasons to involve employees in this process?

- I. Employees become more motivated to do their jobs right.
- II. Employees are objective about their jobs.
- III. Employees can provide an independent assessment of internal controls.
- IV. Managers want feedback from their employees.

- A. I and II.
- B. III and IV.
- C. I and IV.
- D. II and IV.

Answer (C) is correct. *(CIA, adapted)*
REQUIRED: The reasons to involve employees in control self-assessment.
DISCUSSION: Control self-assessment is consistent with total quality management's continuous improvement of quality in every aspect of organizational activities. For total quality management to be effective, all members of the organization must participate. Employees should be empowered, that is, adequately trained, provided with necessary information and tools, involved in important decisions, and fairly compensated. Participation by employees has a positive effect on motivation because it tends to increase commitment to the job and results in greater personal satisfaction. Moreover, full employee participation requires two-way communication and therefore encourages feedback from employees.
Answer (A) is incorrect because employees often lack the perspective required to be objective about their jobs or performance. Answer (B) is incorrect because, although employees can be involved in assessing internal controls, their assessments are not independent. Answer (D) is incorrect because employees often lack the perspective required to be objective about their jobs or performance.

40. Which outcome can be derived from self-assessment methodologies?

- A. Formal, "hard" controls are more easily identified and evaluated.
- B. Management will become involved in and knowledgeable about the self-assessment process by serving as facilitators, scribes, and reporters for the work teams.
- C. Auditor's responsibility for the risk management and control processes of the organization will be reinforced.
- D. People are motivated to take "ownership" of the control processes in their units and corrective actions taken by work teams are often more effective and timely.

Answer (D) is correct. *(Publisher, adapted)*
REQUIRED: The outcome that can be derived from self-assessment methodologies.
DISCUSSION: According to PA 2120.A1-2, one of the possible outcomes that may be derived from self-assessment methodologies is that people are motivated to take "ownership" of the control processes in their units and corrective actions taken by work teams are often more effective and timely.
Answer (A) is incorrect because informal, "soft" controls are more easily identified and evaluated. Answer (B) is incorrect because internal auditors will become involved in and knowledgeable about the self-assessment process by serving as facilitators, scribes, and reporters for the work teams and as trainers of risk and control concepts supporting the CSA program. Answer (C) is incorrect because management's responsibility for the risk management and control processes of the organization is reinforced, and managers will be less tempted to abdicate those activities to specialists, such as auditors.

41. Of the three primary forms of CSA programs, which one is designed to gather information from work teams representing different levels in the business unit or function?

    A. Auditor-produced analysis.

    B. Facilitated team workshops.

    C. Surveys.

    D. Management-produced analysis.

Answer (B) is correct. *(Publisher, adapted)*
    REQUIRED: The form of CSA program designed to gather information from work teams representing different levels in the business unit of function.
    DISCUSSION: The three primary forms of CSA programs are facilitated team workshops, surveys, and management-produced analysis. Facilitated team workshops gather information from work teams representing different levels in the business unit or function. The format of the workshop may be based on objectives, risks, controls, or processes.

42. Which type of team workshop format begins by listing all possible barriers, obstacles, threats, and exposures that might prevent achieving an objective?

    A. Objective-based format.

    B. Control-based format.

    C. Process-based format.

    D. Risk-based format.

Answer (D) is correct. *(Publisher, adapted)*
    REQUIRED: The team workshop format that begins by listing all possible barriers, obstacles, threats, and exposures that might prevent achieving an objective.
    DISCUSSION: The risk based format focuses on listing the risks to achieving an objective. The workshop begins by listing all possible barriers, obstacles, threats, and exposures that might prevent achieving an objective and, then, examining the control procedures to determine if they are sufficient to manage the key risks. The aim of the workshop is to determine significant residual risks. This format takes the work team through the entire objective-risks-controls formula.

43. The element(s) of control self-assessment (CSA) based on a facilitated team workshop approach include

  I. Treating participating employees as process owners.

  II. Taking surveys of employees regarding risks and controls.

  III. Interviewing employees separately in the field.

    A. I only.

    B. II only.

    C. II and III.

    D. I, II, and III.

Answer (A) is correct. *(Publisher, adapted)*
    REQUIRED: The element(s) of CSA.
    DISCUSSION: According to The IIA, an element of CSA is "The gathering of a group of people into a same time/same place meeting, typically involving a facilitation seating arrangement (U-shaped table) and a meeting facilitator. The participants are 'process owners' -- management and staff who are involved with the particular issues under examination, who know them best, and who are critical to the implementation of appropriate process controls."

44. Which of the following statements about control self-assessment (CSA) is false?

    A. CSA is usually an informal and undocumented process.

    B. In its purest form, CSA integrates business objectives and risks with control processes.

    C. CSA is also known as control/risk self-assessment or CRSA.

    D. Most implemented CSA programs share some key features and goals.

Answer (A) is correct. *(Publisher, adapted)*
    REQUIRED: The false statement regarding CSA.
    DISCUSSION: A methodology encompassing self-assessment surveys and facilitated-workshops called CSA is a useful and efficient approach for managers and internal auditors to collaborate in assessing and evaluating control procedures. In its purest form, CSA integrates business objectives and risks with control processes. Control self-assessment is also referred to as "control/risk self-assessment" or "CRSA." Although CSA practitioners use a number of differing techniques and formats, most implemented programs share some key features and goals. The process is a formal and documented way of allowing participation by those who are directly involved in the business unit, function, or process (PA 2120.A1-2).

45. In which format of facilitated team workshop does the facilitator identify the key risks and controls before the beginning of the workshop?

A. Control-based format.

B. Objective-based format.

C. Risk-based format.

D. Process-based format.

Answer (A) is correct. *(Publisher, adapted)*
REQUIRED: The format in which the facilitator identifies key risks and controls prior to the workshop.
DISCUSSION: Control-based format focuses on how well the controls in place are working. This format is different from the two above because the facilitator identifies the key risks and controls before the beginning of the workshop. During the workshop, the work team assesses how well the controls mitigate risks and promote the achievement of objectives. The aim of the workshop is to produce an analysis of the gap between how controls are working and how well management expects those controls to work.

46. The aim of which format of facilitated team workshop is to decide whether control procedures are working effectively and resulting in residual risks within an acceptable level?

A. Control-based format.

B. Objective-based format.

C. Process-based format.

D. Risk-based format.

Answer (B) is correct. *(Publisher, adapted)*
REQUIRED: The format of facilitated team workshop that aims to decide whether control procedures are working effectively and resulting in residual risks within an acceptable level.
DISCUSSION: Objective-based format focuses on the best way to accomplish a business objective. The workshop begins by identifying the controls presently in place to support the objective and, then, determining the residual risks remaining. The aim of the workshop is to decide whether the control procedures are working effectively and are resulting in residual risks within an acceptable level.
Answer (A) is incorrect because the aim of a control-based format is to produce an analysis of the gap between how controls are working and how well management expects those controls to work. Answer (C) is incorrect because the aim of a process-based format is to evaluate, update, validate, improve, and even streamline the whole process and its component activities. Answer (D) is incorrect because the aim of a risk-based format is to determine significant residual risks.

47. Which of the three primary forms of CSA programs should be used if management wants to minimize the time spent and costs incurred in gathering the information?

A. Management-produced analysis.

B. Facilitated team workshop.

C. Auditor-produced analysis.

D. Survey.

Answer (D) is correct. *(Publisher, adapted)*
REQUIRED: The form of CSA that minimizes the time spent or costs of gathering information.
DISCUSSION: The survey form of CSA uses a questionnaire that tends to ask mostly simple "Yes/No" or "Have/Have Not" questions that are carefully written to be understood by the target recipients. They are preferred if the culture in the organization may hinder open, candid discussions in workshop settings or if management desires to minimize the time spent and costs incurred in gathering the information. (PA 2120.A1-2)
Answer (A) is incorrect because this form of CSA program is not designed to minimize time spent and costs incurred in gathering the information. Answer (B) is incorrect because this form of CSA program is not designed to minimize time spent and costs incurred in gathering the information. Answer (C) is incorrect because this is not one of the three primary forms of CSA programs.

48. Which one of the three primary types of CSA programs allows for internal auditor involvement to synthesize this analysis with other information to enhance the understanding about controls and to share the knowledge?

- A. Facilitated team workshop.
- B. Management-produced analysis.
- C. Survey.
- D. Auditor-produced analysis.

Answer (B) is correct. *(Publisher, adapted)*
REQUIRED: The form of CSA program that allows for internal auditor involvement to synthesize this analysis with other information to enhance the understanding about controls and to share the knowledge.
DISCUSSION: The form of self-assessment called "management-produced analysis" covers most approaches by management groups to produce information about selected business processes, risk management activities, and control procedures. The internal auditor may synthesize this analysis with other information to enhance the understanding about controls and to share the knowledge with managers in business or functional units as part of the organization's CSA program. (PA 2120.A1-2)
Answer (A) is incorrect because facilitated team workshops gather information from work teams representing different levels in the business unit or function. Answer (C) is incorrect because the survey form of CSA uses a questionnaire that tends to ask mostly simple "Yes/No" or "Have/Have Not" questions that are carefully written to be understood by the target recipients. Answer (D) is incorrect because auditor-produced analysis is not one of the three primary forms of CSA programs.

49. Which forms of control self-assessment assume that managers and members of work teams possess an understanding of risk and control concepts and use those concepts in communications?

- A. The management-produced analysis forms.
- B. The management-produced analysis and facilitated team workshop forms.
- C. The management-produced analysis and survey forms.
- D. All self-assessment programs.

Answer (D) is correct. *(Publisher, adapted)*
REQUIRED: The forms of CSA based on the assumption that managers and members of work teams possess an understanding of risk and control concepts and use them in communications.
DISCUSSION: All self-assessment programs assume that managers and members of the work teams possess an understanding of risks and controls concepts and using those concepts in communications. For training sessions, to facilitate the orderly flow of workshop discussions and as a check on the completeness of the overall process, organizations often use a control framework, such as the COSO (Committee of Sponsoring Organizations) and CoCo (Canadian Criteria of Control Board) models.

50. In most programs, the internal audit's investment in the organization's CSA efforts is how large?

I. Internal audit sponsors, designs, implements, and in effect owns the process; conducts the training; supplies the facilitators, scribes, and reporters; and orchestrates the participation of management and work teams.

II. Internal audit serves as an interested party and consultant to the whole process and as ultimate verifier of evaluations produced by the teams.

- A. I only.
- B. II only.
- C. Usually somewhere between I and II.
- D. Never more than II, and sometimes less.

Answer (C) is correct. *(Publisher, adapted)*
REQUIRED: The most common investment in an organization's CSA efforts by internal audit.
DISCUSSION: Internal audit's investment in some CSA programs is fairly significant. It may sponsor, design, implement and, in effect, own the process; conduct the training; supply the facilitators, scribes, and reporters; and orchestrate the participation of management and work teams. In other CSA programs, internal audit's involvement is minimal, serving as interested party and consultant of the whole process and as ultimate verifier of the evaluations produced by the teams. In most programs, internal audit's investment in the organization's CSA efforts is somewhere between the two extremes described above. (PA 2120.A1-2)

Use Gleim's *CIA Test Prep* for interactive testing with **over 2,000 additional multiple-choice questions!**

STUDY UNIT FOUR
SPECIFIC ENGAGEMENTS II

(32 pages of outline)

This study unit is the second of two describing the wide variety of engagements internal auditors may perform.

Core Concepts

- The Glossary provides the following definition of compliance:

    Conformity and adherence to policies, plans, procedures, laws, regulations, contracts, or other requirements.

- The internal audit activity evaluates and contributes to the improvement of risk management, control, and governance processes using a systematic and disciplined approach.

- Compliance programs help to prevent unintentional violations, detect illegality, and deter intentional violations. Internal auditors evaluate these programs.

- The entity-wide risk management assessment includes Environmental Health and Safety risks.

- An organization subject to environmental laws and regulations having a significant effect on its operations should establish an environmental management system. One feature of this system is environmental auditing, which includes reviewing the adequacy and effectiveness of the controls over hazardous waste. It also extends to review of the reasonableness of contingent liabilities accrued for environmental remediation.

- The organization should have a comprehensive plan to cope with business interruptions.

- In a due diligence engagement, internal auditors gather information for the use of management in deciding whether to enter into a major transaction.

- TQM is a comprehensive approach to quality. It treats the pursuit of quality as a basic organizational function that is as important as production or marketing.

- Benchmarking is one of the primary tools used in TQM. It is a means of helping organizations with productivity management and business process review. It is therefore a source of consulting engagements for internal auditors.

- Effective management control requires performance measurement and feedback. This process affects allocation of resources to organizational subunits. It also affects decisions about managers' compensation, advancement, and future assignments.

- Information security is an expansion of the assurance services performed by auditors. The creation of organization-wide computer networks with potentially thousands of points of access by outside parties has caused risks to proliferate. Thus, fragmented risk management and control processes may be inadequate.

- The IAA should have competent auditing resources for evaluating internal and external risks to information security.

- Privacy controls are legally required in most countries. Privacy definitions vary: (1) personal privacy, (2) privacy of space, (3) privacy of communications, and (4) privacy of information.

4.1 COMPLIANCE AUDITING

1. Internal auditors should **assess compliance in specific areas** as part of their role in organizational governance. They also should conduct follow-up and report on management's response to regulatory body reviews. Such engagements tend to be more objective and require less judgment than many others. They determine whether actual operations comply with specific standards, i.e., specific policies, procedures, laws, etc. Given the expanding scope of governmental regulation, these duties have assumed increased importance. This subunit contains one General Performance Standard and two Practice Advisories. The first PA addresses the broad subject of compliance with legal requirements. The second PA addresses the specific area of compliance with environmental laws and regulations.

2. The **Glossary** provides the following definition of **compliance**:

    Conformity and adherence to policies, plans, procedures, laws, regulations, contracts, or other requirements.

3. ***2100***   *<u>Nature of Work</u> – The internal audit activity evaluates and contributes to the improvement of risk management, control, and governance processes using a systematic and disciplined approach.*

    a. <u>**PRACTICE ADVISORY 2100-5: LEGAL CONSIDERATIONS IN EVALUATING REGULATORY COMPLIANCE PROGRAMS**</u>

        <u>**Caution**</u> *– Internal auditors are encouraged to **consult legal counsel** in all matters involving legal issues as requirements may vary significantly in different jurisdictions.*

        1) **Compliance programs** *assist organizations in preventing inadvertent employee violations, detecting illegal activities, and discouraging intentional employee violations. They can also help prove insurance claims, determine director and officer liability, create or enhance corporate identity, and decide the appropriateness of punitive damages. Internal auditors should **evaluate an organization's regulatory compliance programs** in light of the following suggested steps for effective compliance programs.*

        2) *The organization should **establish compliance standards and procedures** to be followed by its employees and other agents who are reasonably capable of reducing the prospect of criminal conduct.*

            *   *The organization should develop a **written business code of conduct** that clearly identifies prohibited activities. This code should be written in language that all employees can understand, avoiding legalese.*

            *   *A good code provides **guidance to employees on relevant issues**. Checklists, a question and answer section, and reference to additional sources for further information all help make the code user-friendly.*

            *   *The organization should create an **organizational chart** identifying board members, senior officers, senior compliance officer, and department personnel who are responsible for implementing compliance programs.*

            *   *Codes of conduct that are viewed as legalistic and "one-sided" by employees may increase the risk that employees will engage in unethical or illegal behavior, but codes that are viewed as **straightforward and fair** tend to decrease the risk that employees will engage in such activity.*

            *   *Companies using reward systems that attach financial **incentives** to apparently **unethical or illegal behavior** can expect a poor compliance environment.*

            *   *Companies with international operations should institute a compliance program on a **global basis**, not just for selected geographic locations. Such programs should reflect appropriate local conditions, laws, and regulations.*

3. ***Specific*** *individual(s) within **high-level personnel** of the organization should be assigned **overall responsibility** to oversee regulatory compliance with standards and procedures.*

   - *High-level personnel of the organization means individuals who have **substantial control** of the organization or who have a **substantial role in the making of policy** within the organization.*

   - *High-level personnel of the organization includes: a director; an executive officer; an individual in charge of a major business or functional unit of the organization, such as sales, administration, or finance; and an individual with a substantial ownership interest.*

   - *To be fully effective, the **CEO and other senior management** must have **significant involvement** in the program.*

   - *In some organizations, assigning chief compliance responsibilities to the company's **general counsel** may convince employees that management is not committed to the program, that the program is important to the legal department only and not the firm as a whole. In other organizations, the opposite may be true.*

   - *In a large company with several business units, compliance responsibilities should be assigned to high-level personnel in **each unit**.*

   - *It is not enough for the company to create the position of chief compliance officer and to select the rest of the compliance unit. The company should also ensure that those personnel are **appropriately empowered and supplied** with the resources necessary for carrying out their mission. Compliance personnel should have adequate access to senior management. The chief compliance officer should report directly to the CEO.*

4. *The organization should use **due care** not to delegate substantial discretionary authority to individuals the organization knows, or should know through the exercise of **due diligence**, have a **propensity to engage in illegal activities**.*

   - *Companies should **screen applicants** for employment at all levels for evidence of past wrongdoing, especially wrongdoing within the company's industry.*

   - *Employment **applications** should inquire as to past criminal convictions. Professionals should be asked about any history of discipline by licensing boards.*

     NOTE: Disciplinary actions of licensing boards generally are a matter of public record. They can be checked on the Internet.

   - *Care should be taken to ensure that the company does not infringe upon employees' and applicants' **privacy rights under applicable laws**. Many jurisdictions have laws limiting the amount of information a company can obtain in performing background checks on employees.*

5. *The organization should take steps to **communicate effectively its standards and procedures** to all employees and other agents, e.g., by requiring participation in training programs or by disseminating publications that explain in a practical manner what is required.*

   - *The effectiveness of a compliance program will depend upon the ways in which it is communicated to employees. Generally, an **interactive format** works better than a lecture. Programs communicated in person tend to work better than programs communicated entirely through video or game formats. Programs that are **periodically repeated** work better than one-time presentations.*

- The best programs include **employee training** that allows employees to practice new techniques and use new information. Such activities are particularly appropriate with regard to management training but are effective with regard to employees at all levels.

- The **language** used by an organization's code of conduct and employee manual should be **easy to understand**. Alternative methods of communicating the code and the employee manual to employees lacking more formal education must be found and implemented.

- Compliance tips, statements, and warnings should be disseminated to employees through a **variety of available media**: newsletters, posters, email, questionnaires, and presentations.

- Organizations should present the program on **multiple occasions** to different sets of employees, targeting the information presented to the areas important to each functional group of employees. The **information should be tailored** to that group's job requirements. For example, environmental compliance information should be directed to those departments, such as manufacturing or real property management, that have an increased likelihood of violating or detecting violations of such laws and regulations. On the other hand, providing such training to a department with no such responsibilities could be detrimental, inspiring employee apathy or a belief that the program was not well constructed.

- **New employees** should receive **basic compliance training** as part of their orientation. Later, they can be incorporated into ongoing compliance efforts in their departments.

- **Agents** of the organization should be asked to attend a presentation specifically geared toward them. It is important that an organization inform its agents of the **organization's core values**, and that the actions of its agents that are attributable to the company will be **monitored** in connection with the compliance program. The organization should be prepared to cease doing business with agents who fail to adhere to the organization's compliance standards.

- Organizations should **require employees to periodically certify** that they have read, understood, and complied with the company's code of conduct. This information should be related annually to senior management and the board of directors.

- All **ethics-related documents** – codes of conduct, human resources policies/manuals, etc. – should be **readily available** to all employees. Continuous access availability, such as through the organization's **intranet**, is strongly encouraged.

6. The organization should take reasonable steps to achieve compliance with its standards, e.g., by (a) using **monitoring and auditing systems** reasonably designed to detect criminal conduct by its employees and other agents and (b) having in place and publicizing a **reporting system**. Employees and other agents should be able to use this system to report criminal conduct by others within the organization without fear of retribution.

- The organization should devote an amount of resources to the **internal audit plan** that is appropriate given the size of the company and the difficulty of the audit task. The audit plan should concentrate on the organization's **activities in each of its businesses**.

- *The audit plan should also include a **review of the organization's compliance program and its procedures**, including reviews to determine whether written materials are effective, communications have been received by employees, detected violations have been appropriately handled, discipline has been even-handed, whistle-blowers have not been retaliated against, and the compliance unit has fulfilled its responsibilities. The auditors should review the compliance program to determine whether it can be improved and should solicit employee input in that regard.*

- *Each program should have a **"hotline" or other reporting system** under which employees can report activity that they believe to be unethical, illegal, or against the company's code of conduct. Employees must be free to report such behavior without fear of reprisal.*

- *An **attorney** monitoring the hotline is better able to protect information that may be shielded from disclosure in a particular jurisdiction, for example, by the attorney-client privilege or the attorney work-product doctrine. However, one study observed that employees have little confidence in hotlines answered by the legal department or by an outside service. The same study showed that employees have even less confidence in write-in reports or an off-site ombudsperson, but have the most confidence in **hotlines answered by an in-house representative and backed by a nonretaliation policy**.*

- *Use of an on-site ombudsperson is more effective if the **ombudsperson reports directly** to the chief compliance officer or the board of directors, if the ombudsperson can **keep the names of whistle-blowers secret**, if the ombudsperson provides **guidance** to whistle-blowers, and if the ombudsperson undertakes **follow-up** review to ensure that retaliation has not occurred. Additionally, some jurisdictions now recognize a **limited ombudsperson privilege** under which the ombudsperson is protected from disclosing confidential communications made by whistle-blowers to the ombudsperson.*

- *An effective tool for uncovering unethical or illegal activity is the **ethics questionnaire**. Each employee of the organization should receive a questionnaire, which asks whether the employee is aware of kickbacks, bribes, or other wrongdoing. To **protect a privilege**, the questionnaire should be sent by organization counsel; contain a statement that the questionnaire is protected by privilege; require the employee to complete, sign, and return the questionnaire without making a copy; and contain a statement that the organization retains the right to disclose information provided to the company to government agencies or in litigation. Note that a privilege will be lost if the questionnaire is disclosed to outside parties.*

7. *The standards should be **consistently enforced** through appropriate disciplinary mechanisms, including, as appropriate, discipline of individuals responsible for the failure to detect an offense. **Adequate discipline** of individuals responsible for an offense is a necessary component of enforcement; however, the form of discipline that will be appropriate will be case specific.*

- *The compliance program should contain a disciplinary system under which those who violate the organization's code of conduct receive **punishment appropriate to the offense**, such as warning, loss of pay, suspension, transfer, or termination. If an employee is found to have committed some illegal act, the organization might have to terminate that employee, in keeping with the organization's obligation to use "due care not to delegate substantial discretionary authority to individuals whom the organization knew, or should have known through the exercise of due diligence, had a propensity to engage in illegal activities" (see paragraph 4).*

- *Discipline under the program must be **fair**. The program has slight chance of succeeding if unethical or illegal activity goes unpunished, especially if tied to the activities of senior management or big producers. Ignored wrongdoing by such persons will encourage such behavior in the rest of the workforce.*

- *Termination or other **discipline of employees may be limited** by whistle-blower laws, exceptions to the employee-at-will doctrine, employee or union contracts, and employer responsibilities with regard to discrimination, wrongful discharge, and employer bad faith laws/doctrines.*

- *The program should provide for the **discipline of managers and other responsible persons** who knew or should have known of misconduct and did not report it. Failure of the program to do so may cause a court to find that the program is not effective.*

8. *Organizations should be scrupulous and thorough in **documenting employee discipline**. The organization should be able to prove that it made its best efforts to collect information with regard to any incident and took appropriate action based upon the information available.*

9. *After an offense has been detected, the organization should take all reasonable steps to **respond appropriately** to the offense and to **prevent further similar offenses** -- including any necessary modifications to its program to prevent and detect violations of law.*

   - *The organization should respond appropriately to each offense detected by the compliance program. Appropriate responses include **disciplinary action** taken with regard to those who engaged in misconduct.*

   - *In some circumstances, an appropriate response could require **self-reporting** the violation to the government, **cooperation** with governmental investigations, and the **acceptance of responsibility** for the violation. Note that, similar to the existence of an effective compliance program, making these responses could result in a court lowering the amount of the organization's fine.*

   - ***Failure to detect or prevent a serious violation** could indicate that the compliance program needs a major overhaul. At a minimum, after any violation is detected, compliance personnel should examine the program to determine whether changes need to be made.*

   - *One change that may be required in light of a violation could be the **replacement or shuffling of compliance personnel**. In fact, the organization may need to discipline or replace any manager who fails to detect or prevent misconduct in the areas under the manager's supervision, especially if the violation is one that the manager should have detected.*

PA Summary

- **Compliance programs** help to prevent unintentional violations, detect illegality, deter intentional violations, prove insurance claims, determine liability, enhance corporate identity, and decide the appropriateness of punitive damages. Internal auditors **evaluate** these programs.

- **Compliance standards and procedures** should be established, including a **clearly written, straightforward, and fair business code of conduct** that provides **guidance to employees on relevant issues** and is user-friendly. Also, an **organizational chart** should identify personnel responsible for compliance programs. Moreover, **financial incentives** should not reward misconduct, and international organizations should have a compliance program on a **global basis** that reflects local conditions and laws.

- **Specific high-level personnel** who are properly empowered and supplied with necessary resources should have overall responsibility for the compliance program. Senior management also should be involved. High-level personnel have **substantial control** of the entity or a **substantial role** in making policy. Furthermore, compliance personnel should have adequate access to senior management, and the chief compliance officer should report directly to the CEO.

- **Due care** should be used not to delegate authority to those with a tendency to **illegality**. **Applications** should inquire about criminal convictions or discipline by licensing boards, and applicants should be **screened** in a lawful manner that does not infringe upon **privacy rights**.

- Standards and procedures, including readily available **ethics-related documents**, should be **communicated effectively**, preferably in an interactive format and on multiple occasions. Training programs and publications are typical methods. The best training allows employees to practice new techniques and use new information. Compliance information should be conveyed through a **variety of available media**. Moreover, the program should be presented to different sets of employees, **targeting the information** to the areas important to each functional group and its job requirements. **New employees** should receive **basic compliance training** as part of their orientation, and **agents** of the entity should be given a presentation specifically for them. Agents should understand the entity's **core values** and that their actions will be **monitored**. Organizations also should **require employees to certify periodically** that they have read, understood, and complied with the code of conduct. This information should be relayed annually to senior management and the board.

- **Monitoring and auditing systems** for detecting illegality and employee "hotline" **reporting systems** should be used. For example, the **internal audit plan** should be given appropriate resources and apply to all of the entity's businesses. Also, it should include a **review of the compliance program**. The review considers effectiveness of written materials, employee receipt of communications; handling of **violations**, fairness of discipline, observance of any protections afforded to informants, and fulfillment of compliance unit responsibilities.

- **Attorney-client and attorney work-product privileges** protect certain information disclosed to (or produced by) an attorney from being used by an adverse party in a legal proceeding. An **attorney** monitoring the hotline is best able to protect the privileges. However, employees may have little confidence in such hotlines or in write-in reports or an off-site ombudsperson. But they may have confidence in **hotlines answered by an in-house representative and backed by a nonretaliation policy**.

PA Summary continued on next page

PA Summary continued

- An **on-site ombudsperson** is more effective if (s)he (1) **reports directly** to the chief compliance officer or the board, (2) can **keep the names of informants secret**, (3) provides **guidance** to informants, and (4) undertakes **follow-up** to ensure that retaliation has not occurred.

- An **ethics questionnaire** should be sent to each employee asking whether the employee is aware of kickbacks, bribes, or other wrongdoing.

- Compliance standards should be **consistently enforced** by adequate, fair, case-specific discipline. **Punishment should be appropriate to the offense**, such as a warning, loss of pay, suspension, transfer, or termination. Furthermore, the program should provide for the **discipline of managers and other responsible persons** who knew or should have known of misconduct and did not report it. Failure to do so may cause a court to find that the program is not effective.

- Employee discipline should be thoroughly **documented** so that the entity will be able to prove that it made its best effort to collect information and took appropriate action.

- After detection, the response should be appropriate and designed to **prevent other similar offenses**. In some circumstances, an appropriate response could require **self-reporting** the violation to the government, **cooperation** with investigations, and the **acceptance of responsibility**. But an effective compliance program and appropriate responses could result in more lenient punishment.

- **Failure to detect or prevent a serious violation** could indicate that the compliance program needs a major overhaul. One change that may be required could be the **replacement or transfer of compliance personnel**.

b. **PRACTICE ADVISORY 2100-7: THE INTERNAL AUDITOR'S ROLE IN IDENTIFYING AND REPORTING ENVIRONMENTAL RISKS**

   Potential Risks

   1. *The Chief Audit Executive (CAE) should include the **environmental, health, and safety (EH&S) risks** in any entity-wide risk management assessment and assess the activities in a balanced manner relative to other types of risk associated with an entity's operations. Among the **risk exposures that should be evaluated** are: organizational reporting structures; likelihood of causing environmental harm, fines, and penalties; expenditures mandated by governmental agencies; history of injuries and deaths; record of losses of customers, and episodes of negative publicity and loss of public image and reputation.*

   2. *If the CAE finds that the management of the EH&S risks largely depends on an **environmental audit function, the CAE needs to consider the implications** of that organizational structure and its effects on operations and the reporting mechanisms. If the CAE finds that the exposures are not adequately managed and residual risks exist, that conclusion would normally result in changes to the internal audit activity's plan of engagements and further investigations.*

   3. *The majority of environmental audit functions report to their organization's environmental component or general counsel, not to the CAE. The **typical organizational models for environmental auditing** fall into one of the following scenarios:*

      - *The CAE and environmental audit chief are in separate functional units with little contact with each other.*
      - *The CAE and environmental audit chief are in separate functional units and coordinate their activities.*
      - *The CAE has responsibility for auditing environmental issues.*

4. According to an IIA flash **report on environmental auditing issues**:

    - *About one-half of the environmental auditors seldom meet with a committee of the governing board and only 40 percent have some contact with the CAE.*

    - *Seventy percent of the organizations reported that environmental issues are not regularly included on the agenda of the governing board.*

    - *About 40 percent of the organizations reported that they had paid fines or penalties for environmental violations in the past three years. Two-thirds of the respondents described their environmental risks as material.*

5. The Environmental, Health and Safety Auditing Roundtable (new name is The Auditing Roundtable) commissioned Richard L. Ratliff of Utah State University and a group of researchers to perform a study of environmental, health, and safety auditing. The **researchers' findings** related to the **risk and independence** issues are as follows:

    - *The EH&S audit function is somewhat **isolated from other organizational auditing activities**. It is organized separately from internal auditing, only tangentially related to external audits of financial statements, and **reports to an EH&S executive**, rather than to the governing board or to senior management. This structure suggests that management believes EH&S auditing to be a technical field that is best placed within the EH&S function of the organization.*

    - *With that organizational placement, EH&S auditors could be **unable to maintain their independence**, which is considered one of the principal requirements of an effective audit function. EH&S audit managers typically report administratively to the executives who are responsible for the physical facilities being audited. Thus, poor EH&S performance would reflect badly on the **facilities management team**, who would therefore try to exercise their authority and influence over what is reported in audit findings, how audits are conducted, or what is included in the audit plan. This potential subordination of the auditors' professional judgment, even when only apparent, violates auditor **independence and objectivity**.*

    - *It is also common for **written audit reports** to be distributed no higher in the organization than to **senior environmental executives**. Those executives may have a potential conflict of interest, and they may curtail further distribution of EH&S audit findings to senior management and the governing board.*

    - *Audit information is often classified as either (a) subject to the attorney-client privilege or attorney work-product doctrine (if available in the relevant jurisdiction); (b) secret and confidential; or (c) if not confidential, then closely held. This results in severely restricted access to EH&S audit information.*

Suggestions for the Chief Audit Executive

6. The CAE should foster a **close working relationship with the chief environmental officer** and **coordinate activities** with the plan for environmental auditing. When the environmental audit function reports to someone other than the CAE, the CAE should offer to **review the audit plan and the performance of engagements**. Periodically, the CAE should schedule a **quality assurance review** of the environmental audit function if it is organizationally independent of the internal audit activity. That review should determine if the environmental risks are being adequately addressed. An **EH&S audit program** could be either (a) compliance-focused (i.e., verifying compliance with laws, regulations, and the entity's own EH&S policies, procedures, and performance objectives) or (b) management systems-focused (i.e., providing assessments of management systems intended to ensure compliance with legal and internal requirements and the mitigation of risks), or (c) a combination of both approaches.

7.   The CAE should **evaluate whether the environmental auditors**, who are not part of the CAE's organization, are in **compliance** with recognized professional **auditing standards** and a recognized **code of ethics**. The Board of Environmental, Health, & Safety Auditor Certifications (BEAC), as well as The IIA, publish practice standards and ethical codes.

8.   The CAE should **evaluate the organizational placement and independence of the environmental audit function** to ensure that significant matters resulting from serious risks to the enterprise are reported up the chain of command to the audit or other committee of the governing board. The CAE also should **facilitate** the **reporting** of significant **EH&S risk and control issues** to the audit (or other board) committee.

NOTE: The IAA has an established place in the organization and normally has a broad scope of work permitting ready assimilation of the new function. Moreover, the CAE should be responsible to an individual in the organization with sufficient authority to promote independence and to ensure broad audit coverage, adequate consideration of engagement communications, and appropriate action on engagement recommendations. The CAE also should have direct communication with the board. Thus, it is an advantage to conduct environmental audits under the direction of the IAA because it has the appropriate organizational status.

PA Summary

- The entity-wide risk management assessment includes **environmental, health, and safety (EH&S) risks**. Risk exposures to be evaluated are (1) faulty reporting structures; (2) likelihood of causing environmental harm, fines, and penalties; (3) expenditures mandated by regulators; (4) history of injuries and deaths; (5) loss of customers; and (6) negative publicity and loss of public reputation.

- The **typical organization model for environmental auditing** is one of the following: (1) the CAE and environmental audit chief are in separate functions and have little contact, (2) they are in separate functions and coordinate their activities, or (3) the CAE has responsibility for auditing environmental issues.

- Given an **environmental audit function**, the CAE considers the **implications** for organizational structure, operations, reporting, and the audit plan.

- Researchers' findings related to **risk and independence** for the EH&S audit function include the following:

  1)   It is **isolated from other organizational auditing activities** and usually **reports to an EH&S executive**, not the board or senior management.

  2)   Thus, EH&S auditors could be **unable to maintain their independence**. EH&S audit managers typically report administratively to executives responsible for the facilities audited. Poor EH&S performance would reflect badly on the **facilities management team**, who might influence audit findings, how audits are conducted, or the audit plan.

  3)   **Written audit reports** are commonly distributed no higher than to **senior environmental executives**. Those executives may have a conflict of interest and curtail further distribution of findings.

  4)   Access to EH&S audit information is restricted when classified as (a) subject to the attorney-client privilege or the attorney-work-product privilege (where such privileges are recognized); (b) secret and confidential; or (c) if not confidential, then closely held.

> - The CAE should have a **close relationship** with the chief environmental officer and **coordinate activities**. The CAE may offer to **review** the environmental audit function's **plan and performance**. The CAE also should schedule a **quality assurance** review of the function and evaluate its organizational placement and **independence** and compliance with **standards**.
>
>   1) An **EH&S audit program** could be (a) compliance-focused, (b) management-systems-focused, or (c) a combination of both approaches.
>   2) The CAE should **facilitate** the **reporting** of significant **EH&S risk and control issues** to the audit (or other board) committee.

4. An organization subject to environmental laws and regulations having a significant effect on its operations should establish an **environmental management system**.

   a. One feature of this system is **environmental auditing**, which includes reviewing the adequacy and effectiveness of the controls over hazardous waste. It also extends to review of the reasonableness of **contingent liabilities** accrued for environmental remediation.

   b. According to a research report prepared for **The IIA Research Foundation**,

   An environmental management system is an organization's structure of responsibilities and policies, practices, procedures, processes, and resources for protecting the environment and managing environmental issues.

   Environmental auditing is an integral part of an environmental management system whereby management determines whether the organization's environmental control systems are adequate to ensure compliance with regulatory requirements and internal policies.

   c. The report describes seven **types of environmental audits**.

   1) **Compliance audits** are the most common form for industries. Their extent depends on the degree of risk of noncompliance. They are detailed, site-specific audits of current operations, past practices, and planned future operations. Compliance audits usually entail a review of all environmental media the site may contaminate, including air, water, land, and wastewater. Moreover, they have quantitative and qualitative aspects and should be repeated periodically. Compliance audits range in intensity from preliminary assessments to detailed tests, installation of groundwater monitoring wells, and laboratory analyses.

   2) Environmental issues may arise from practices that were legal when they were undertaken. **Environmental management systems audits** determine whether systems are in place and operating properly to manage future environmental risks.

   3) **Transactional audits** also are called acquisition and divestiture audits, property transfer site assessments, property transfer evaluations, and due diligence audits. They assess the environmental risks and liabilities of land or facilities prior to a property transaction. Current landowners may be responsible for contamination whether or not they caused it.

      a) Transactional audits require **due diligence** (a reasonable level of research) from the auditor, but what constitutes due diligence for each phase of a transactional audit and the definitions of the phases are questions for debate. These phases are often characterized as follows:

         i) Phase I -- qualitative site assessments involving a review of records and site reconnaissance

   ii) Phase II -- sampling for potential contamination

   iii) Phase III -- confirming the rate and extent of contaminant migration and the cost of remediation

  b) A transactional audit addresses all media exposures and all hazardous substances, e.g., radon, asbestos, PCBs, operating materials, and wastes.

4) **Treatment, storage, and disposal facility audits.** The law may require that hazardous materials be tracked from cradle to grave by means of a document (a manifest). All owners in the chain of title may be liable. For example, if a company contracts with a transporter to dispose of hazardous waste in a licensed landfill, and the landfill owner contaminates the environment, all the entities and their officers may be financially liable for cleanup.

  a) TSDF audits are conducted on facilities the entity owns, leases, or manages, or on externally owned facilities where the entity's waste is treated, stored, or disposed. Thus, when an outside vendor is used for these purposes, the audit should consist of such procedures as (1) reviewing the vendor's documentation on hazardous material, (2) reviewing the financial solvency of the vendors, (3) reviewing the vendor's emergency response planning, (4) determining that the vendor is approved by the governmental entity that is responsible for environmental protection, (5) obtaining the vendor's permit number, and (6) inspecting the vendor's facilities.

5) A **pollution prevention audit** determines how waste can be minimized and pollution can be eliminated at the source. The following is a pollution prevention hierarchy useful in such an audit:

  a) Recovery as a usable product
  b) Elimination at the source
  c) Recycling and reuse
  d) Energy conservation
  e) Treatment
  f) Disposal
  g) Release

6) **Environmental liability accrual audits.** Recognizing, quantifying, and reporting liability accruals may require redefinition of such parameters as "probable," "measurable," and "estimable." When an environmental issue becomes a liability is also unclear.

  a) The internal auditors may be responsible for assessing the reasonableness of cost estimates for environmental remediation. Due diligence may require assistance from independent experts, such as qualified consulting engineers.

7) **Product audits** determine whether products are environmentally friendly and whether product and chemical restrictions are being met. This process may result in the development of fully recyclable products, changes in the use and recovery of packaging materials, and the phaseout of some chemicals.

5. Stop and review! You have completed the outline for this subunit. Study multiple-choice questions 1 through 30 beginning on page 217.

4.2 BUSINESS CONTINUITY

1.   The IIA has issued a Practice Advisory on the auditing of the organization's preparedness for business disruption **(contingency planning)**. It interprets Specific Performance Standard 2110.

2.   ***2110***   ***Risk Management*** *– The internal audit activity should assist the organization by identifying and evaluating significant exposures to risk and contributing to the improvement of risk management and control systems.*

    a.   **PRACTICE ADVISORY 2110-2: THE INTERNAL AUDITOR'S ROLE IN THE BUSINESS CONTINUITY PROCESS**

        1.   **Business interruption** *can result from natural occurrences and accidental or deliberate criminal acts. Those interruptions can have significant financial and operational ramifications. Auditors should evaluate the organization's readiness to deal with business interruptions. A* **comprehensive plan** *would provide for emergency response procedures, alternative communication systems and site facilities, information systems backup, disaster recovery, business impact assessments and resumption plans, procedures for restoring utility services, and maintenance procedures for ensuring the readiness of the organization in the event of an emergency or disaster.*

        2.   *Internal auditing activity should assess the organization's* **business continuity planning** *process on a regular basis to ensure that senior management is aware of the state of disaster preparedness.*

        3.   *Many organizations do not expect to experience an interruption or lengthy delay of normal business processes and operations due to a disaster or other unforeseen event. Many business experts say that it is not* **if** *a disaster will occur, but* **when** *it will occur. Over time, an organization will experience an event that will result in the loss of information, access to properties (tangible or intangible), or the services of personnel. Exposure to those types of risks and the planning for business continuity is an integral part of an organization's risk management process. Advance planning is necessary to minimize the loss and ensure continuity of an organization's* **critical business functions**. *It may enable the organization to maintain an* **acceptable level of service** *to its stakeholders.*

        4.   *A crucial element of business recovery is the existence of a comprehensive and current* **disaster recovery plan**. *Internal auditors can play a role in the organization's planning for disaster recovery. Internal audit activity can (a) assist with the risk analysis, (b) evaluate the design and comprehensiveness of the plan after it has been drawn up, and (c) perform periodic assurance engagements to verify that the plan is kept up to date.*

        Planning

        5.   *Organizations rely upon internal auditors for analysis of operations and assessment of risk management and control processes. Internal auditors acquire an understanding of the overall business operations and the individual functions and how they interrelate with one another. This positions the internal audit activity as a valuable resource in* **evaluating the disaster recovery plan during its formulation** *process.*

        6.   *The internal audit activity can help with an assessment of an organization's* **internal and external environment**. *Internal factors that may be considered include the turnover of management and changes in information systems, controls, and major projects and programs. External factors may include changes in outside regulatory and business environment and changes in markets and competitive conditions, international financial and economic conditions, and technologies. Internal auditors can help* **identify risks** *involving critical business activities and* **prioritize functions** *for recovery purposes.*

Evaluation

7.   *Internal auditors can make a contribution as objective participants when they* **review** *the proposed business continuity and disaster recovery plan for* **design, completeness, and overall adequacy**. *The auditor can examine the plan to determine that it reflects the operations that have been included and evaluated in the risk assessment process and contains sufficient internal control concerns and prescriptions. The internal auditor's comprehensive knowledge of the organization's business operations and applications enables it to assist during the* **development phase** *of the business continuity plan by evaluating its organization, comprehensiveness, and recommended actions to manage risks and maintain effective controls during a recovery period.*

Periodic Assurance Engagements

8.   *Internal auditors should periodically audit the organization's business continuity and disaster recovery plans. The audit objective is to verify that the* **plans are adequate** *to ensure the timely resumption of operations and processes after adverse circumstances and that they reflect the* **current business operating environment**.

9.   *Business continuity and disaster recovery plans can become outdated very quickly. Coping with and responding to changes is an inevitable part of the task of management. Turnover of managers and executives and changes in system configurations, interfaces, and software can have a major impact on these plans. The internal audit activity should examine the recovery plan to determine whether (a) it is structured to* **incorporate important changes** *that could take place over time and (b) the revised plan will be* **communicated to the appropriate people** *inside and outside the organization.*

10.   **During the audit**, *internal auditors should consider:*

- *Are all plans up to date? Do procedures exist for updating the plans?*
- *Are all critical business functions and systems covered by the plans? If not, are the reasons for omissions documented?*
- *Are the plans based on the risks and potential consequences of business interruptions?*
- *Are the plans fully documented and in accordance with organizational policies and procedures? Have functional responsibilities been assigned?*
- *Is the organization capable of and prepared to implement the plans?*
- *Are the plans tested and revised based on the results?*
- *Are the plans stored properly and safely? Is the location of and access to the plans known to management?*
- *Are the locations of alternate facilities (backup sites) known to employees?*
- *Do the plans call for coordination with local emergency services?*

Internal Audit's Role After a Disaster

11.   *There is an important role for the internal auditors to play immediately after a disaster occurs. An organization is more vulnerable after a disaster has occurred, and it is trying to recover. During that* **recovery period**, *internal auditors should* **monitor** *the* **effectiveness** *of the recovery and control of operations. The internal audit activity should identify areas where internal controls and mitigating actions should be improved and* **recommend improvements** *to the entity's business continuity plan. The internal audit can also provide support during the recovery activities.*

12. *After the disaster, usually within several months, internal auditors can assist in **identifying the lessons learned** from the disaster and the recovery operations. Those observations and recommendations may enhance activities to recover resources and update the next version of the business continuity plan.*

13. *In the final analysis, it is **senior management** who will determine the degree of the **internal auditor's involvement** in the business continuity and disaster recovery processes, considering their knowledge, skills, independence, and objectivity.*

PA Summary

- **Business interruption** can have significant financial and operational effects. The organization should have a **comprehensive disaster recovery plan** to cope with business interruptions. It should provide for emergency response, alternative communications and site facilities, systems backup, disaster recovery, impact assessments, resumption plans, restoration of utility service and readiness procedures.

- **Auditors** should regularly assess continuity planning.

- Interruptions and losses are inevitable. Thus, **planning** is integral to the RMP so that losses may be minimized, continuity of **critical business functions** ensured, and an **acceptable level of service** maintained.

- Internal auditors analyze operations, assess the RMP and controls, and understand how functions interrelate. Thus, the IAA can help assess an organization's **internal and external environment**, **identify risks** involving critical business activities, and **prioritize functions** for recovery purposes.

- Internal auditors **review** the proposed plan for **design, completeness, and overall adequacy**. The plan should reflect the operations included and evaluated in the risk assessment and contain sufficient control.

- Internal auditors should perform **periodic assurance engagements** to verify that the **plan is adequate** and reflects the **current business operating environment**. The IAA should examine the plan to determine whether (1) it is structured to **incorporate important changes**, and (2) the revised plan will be **communicated to the appropriate people** inside and outside the organization.

- **During the audit**, internal auditors should consider whether the plan

  1) Is kept up to date.
  2) Covers all critical business functions and systems and documents the reasons for omissions.
  3) Is based on risks and consequences.
  4) Is fully documented in accordance with policies and procedures and assigns functional responsibilities.
  5) Can be implemented.
  6) Is tested and revised based on results.
  7) Is stored properly and safely.
  8) States locations of backup sites that are known to employees.
  9) Calls for coordination with emergency services.

- During the **recovery period**, internal auditors **monitor the effectiveness** of recovery and control of operations and **identify improvements**. Afterward, they may identify **lessons learned**.

- **Senior management** determines **auditor involvement** in the continuity and recovery processes.

3. Stop and review! You have completed the outline for this subunit. Study multiple-choice questions 31 and 32 on page 228.

4.3 DUE DILIGENCE

1. The term **due diligence** is applied to a service in which internal auditors and others (external auditors, tax experts, finance professionals, attorneys, etc.) determine the **business justification** for a major transaction (business combination, joint venture, divestiture, etc.) and whether that justification is valid.

    a. Internal auditors might, for example, review operations (purchasing, shipping and receiving, inventory management, etc.), internal control over information systems, the compatibility of the organizational cultures, and finance and accounting issues.

    b. The due diligence process establishes whether the expected **benefits of the transaction** (wider markets, more skilled employees, access to intellectual property, operating synergies, etc.) are likely to be realized. It also may facilitate the realization of those benefits by improving the effectiveness and efficiency of the **implementation of the transaction**.

    c. One of the keys to the effectiveness and efficiency of the engagement is **coordination** among the groups involved. For example, the same software should be used for preparation of electronic working papers to facilitate sharing of information.

    d. The **final report** should be factual, not subjective, with supporting information indexed and backed up on computer disks.

        1) The report should contain an **executive summary** with key points highlighted.

        2) The **cycle approach** used by the acquiring entity to organize its business is a desirable means of structuring the report.

2. The term due diligence may be used for other engagements, for example, certain environmental audits.

3. Stop and review! You have completed the outline for this subunit. Study multiple-choice questions 33 and 34 on page 229.

4.4 QUALITY

1. The **total quality management (TQM)** approach can increase revenues and decrease costs significantly. Thus, the internal audit activity's services rendered with respect to the quality function have the potential to add substantial value. Indeed, the improvement of operations is part of the definition of internal auditing.

    a. Quality is best viewed from **multiple perspectives**: attributes of the product (performance, serviceability, durability, etc.), customer satisfaction, conformity with manufacturing specifications, and value (relation of quality and price).

    b. TQM is a **comprehensive approach** to quality. It treats the pursuit of quality as a basic organizational function that is as important as production or marketing.

        1) **Definition.** TQM is the **continuous pursuit of quality** in every aspect of organizational activities through

            a) A philosophy of doing it right the first time,
            b) Employee training and empowerment,
            c) Promotion of teamwork,
            d) Improvement of processes, and
            e) Attention to satisfaction of customers, both internal and external.

    c. TQM emphasizes the **supplier's relationship with the customer**, identifies customer needs, and recognizes that everyone in a process is at some time a customer or supplier of someone else, either within or outside the organization.

        1) Thus, TQM begins with external customer requirements, identifies internal customer-supplier relationships and requirements, and establishes requirements for external suppliers.

    d. The **management of quality** is not limited to quality management staff, engineers, production personnel, etc.

        1) Given the **organization-wide scope** of TQM and of the internal audit activity, the role of the internal auditors is to evaluate the entire quality function. In particular, the internal audit activity should be well-qualified to **perform risk assessments** and promote continuous improvement of **controls**. The personnel involved in the technical improvements of processes may be unqualified with regard to risk management and control issues.

            a) The internal audit activity should perform procedures to provide **assurance** that the **basic objectives** of TQM are reached: customer satisfaction, continuous improvement, and promotion of teamwork.

            b) TQM concepts also are applicable to the **operations of the internal audit activity** itself. For example, periodic internal assessments of those operations may "include benchmarking of the internal audit activity's practices and performance metrics against relevant best practices of the internal audit profession" (PA 1311-1).

    e. The **costs of quality** must be assessed in terms of relative costs and benefits. Thus, an organization should attempt to minimize its total cost of quality. Moreover, nonquantitative factors must also be considered. For example, an emphasis on quality improves competitiveness, enhances employee expertise, and generates goodwill.

        1) **Conformance costs** include costs of prevention and costs of appraisal, which are financial measures of internal performance.

            a) **Prevention** attempts to avoid defective output. These costs include preventive maintenance, employee training, review of equipment design, and evaluation of suppliers. Prevention is less costly than detection and correction of defective output.

            b) **Appraisal** embraces such activities as statistical quality control programs, inspection, and testing.

                i) A traditional quality-control process in manufacturing consists of mass inspection of goods only at the end of a production process. A major deficiency of the traditional control process is that it does not focus on reviewing the entire production process for efficiency and effectiveness. Preventing defects and increasing efficiency by improving the production process raises quality standards and decreases costs.

        2) **Nonconformance costs** include costs of internal failure (a financial measure of internal performance) and external failure costs (a financial measure of customer satisfaction).

            a) **Internal failure** costs occur when defective products are detected before shipment. Examples are scrap, rework, tooling changes, and downtime.

            b) The costs of **external failure**, e.g., warranty costs, product liability costs, and loss of customer goodwill, arise when problems occur after shipment.

            c) **Environmental costs** are also external failure costs, e.g., fines for nonadherence to environmental law and loss of customer goodwill.

3) **Quality cost indices** may be calculated to measure the cost of maintaining a given level of quality, for example, total quality costs divided by direct labor costs.

4) Examples of **nonfinancial measures of internal performance** are manufacturing cycle efficiency (value-added production time ÷ manufacturing cycle time), ratio of good output to total output, defects per product line, the half-life method (time required to reduce the defect ratio by 50%), and new product development time.

5) Examples of **nonfinancial measures of customer satisfaction** are percentage of defective goods shipped, customer complaints, customer response time, on-time deliveries, survey data, and market share.

f. Well-known management expert W. Edwards Deming formulated the following 14 points as a basis for improving quality:

1) Constant purpose (better use of all resources)
2) New philosophy
3) Give up on quality by inspection
4) Avoid the constant search for lowest-cost suppliers
5) Seek continuous improvement
6) Train everyone
7) Provide real leadership
8) Drive fear of expressing ideas and asking questions out of the workplace
9) Promote teamwork
10) Avoid slogans and targets
11) Get rid of numerical quotas
12) Remove barriers that stifle pride in workmanship
13) Education and self-improvement are key
14) The transformation is everyone's job

g. **Organizational structure.** TQM advocates replacement of the traditional hierarchical structure with **teams** of people from different specialties. Quality circles, cross-functional teams, virtual teams, self-directed teams, and problem-solving teams are examples. This change follows from TQM's emphasis on empowering employees and teamwork.

1) Employees should have proper training, necessary information, and the best tools; be fully engaged in the decision process, including sharing ideas and removing obstacles to process improvement; and receive fair compensation.

a) If such **empowered employees** are assembled in teams of individuals with the required skills, TQM theorists believe they will be more effective than people performing their tasks separately in a rigid structure.

2. **Benchmarking** is one of the primary tools used in TQM. It is a means of helping organizations with productivity management and **business process review**. It is therefore a source of **consulting engagements** for internal auditors.

a. Benchmarking is a continuous evaluation of the **practices of the best organizations** in their class and the adaptation of processes to reflect the best of these practices. It involves (1) analysis and measurement of key outputs against those of the best organizations and (2) identifying the underlying key actions and causes that contribute to the performance difference.

1) **Best practices** are recognized by authorities in the field and by customers for generating outstanding results. They are generally innovative technically or in their management of human resources.

2) Benchmarking is an ongoing process that entails **quantitative and qualitative measurement** of the difference between the organization's **performance** of an activity and the performance by the benchmark organization.

b.   The following are kinds of benchmarking:

1)   **Competitive benchmarking** studies an organization in the same industry.

2)   **Process (function) benchmarking** studies operations of organizations with similar processes regardless of industry. Thus, the benchmark need not be a competitor or even a similar entity.

a)   This method may introduce new ideas that provide a significant competitive advantage.

3)   **Strategic benchmarking** is a search for successful competitive strategies.

4)   **Internal benchmarking** is the application of best practices in one part of the organization to its other parts.

c.   The first phase in the benchmarking process is to select and **prioritize benchmarking projects**.

1)   An organization must understand its critical success factors and business environment to **identify key business processes and drivers** and to develop parameters defining what processes to benchmark. The **criteria** for selecting what to benchmark relate to the reasons for the existence of a process and its importance to the entity's mission, values, and strategy. These reasons are based in large part on **satisfaction of end users or customer needs**.

d.   The next phase is to **organize benchmarking teams**. A team organization is appropriate because it permits a fair division of labor, participation by those responsible for implementing changes, and inclusion of a variety of functional expertise and work experience.

1)   **Team members** should have (a) knowledge of the function to be benchmarked, (b) respected positions in the organization, (c) good communication skills, (d) teaming skills, (e) motivation to innovate and to support cross-functional problem solving, and (f) project management skills.

2)   The benchmarking team must thoroughly investigate and document the organization's **internal processes**. The organization should be seen as a series of processes, not as a fixed structure.

a)   A **process** is a network of related and independent activities joined by their outputs. One way to understand a process is to trace the path a request for a product or service takes through the organization.

b)   The team must develop a **family of measures** that are true indicators of process performance. The team also must develop a **process taxonomy**, a set of process elements, measures, and phrases that describes the process to be benchmarked.

c)   The development of **key indicators for performance measurement** in a benchmarking context is an extension of the basic **evaluative function** of internal auditors. Internal auditors evaluate governance, risk management, and control processes. Evaluation requires **adequate criteria** to have been established by management. In the absence of these criteria, internal auditors must work with management to develop "appropriate evaluation criteria" (**Performance Standard 2120.A4**).

e.   **Researching and identifying best-in-class performance** is often the most difficult phase. The critical steps are

1)   Setting up databases,

2)   Choosing information-gathering methods (internal sources, external public domain sources, and original research),

3)   Formatting questionnaires (lists of questions prepared in advance), and

4)   Selecting benchmarking partners.

f.   **Data analysis** involves identifying performance gaps, understanding the reasons they exist, and prioritizing the key activities that will facilitate the **behavioral and process changes** needed to implement recommendations.

1)   Sophisticated statistical and other methods may be needed when the study involves many variables, testing of assumptions, or presentation of quantified results.

g.   **Leadership** is most important in the **implementation phase** because the team must be able to justify its recommendations. Moreover, the process improvement teams must manage the implementation of approved changes.

3.   Internal auditors may conduct a **performance audit** to provide assurance about the organization's **key performance indicators**. They also may conduct a **consulting engagement** to design such a performance measurement system.

a.   Effective **management control** requires **performance measurement** and feedback. This process affects allocation of resources to organizational subunits. It also affects decisions about managers' compensation, advancement, and future assignments.

1)   Furthermore, evaluating their performance serves to motivate managers to **optimize the measures** in the performance evaluation model. However, that model may be inconsistent with the organization's model for managerial decision making.

a)   To achieve consistency, the models should be **synchronized**. For example, if senior management wishes to maximize results over the long term, subordinates should be evaluated over the long term.

b)   Unfortunately, information systems seldom provide information on the outcomes of individual decisions, and senior managers may be unaware of desirable options not chosen. Moreover, performance feedback usually applies to specific responsibility centers for specific periods. The result is that use of the same criteria for **decision making** and **managerial evaluation** may be difficult.

b.   The trend in performance measurement is the **balanced scorecard** approach to managing the implementation of the firm's strategy. It is an accounting report that connects the firm's **critical success factors (CSFs)** determined in a strategic analysis to measurements of its performance. CSFs are **financial and nonfinancial measures** of the elements of firm performance vital to competitive advantage.

1)   A firm identifies its CSFs by means of a **SWOT analysis** that addresses internal factors (strengths and weaknesses) and external factors (opportunities and threats).

a)   The firm's greatest strengths are its **core competencies**. These are the basis for its competitive advantages and strategy.

b)   **Strengths and weaknesses** are internal resources or a lack of them, for example, technologically advanced products, a broad product mix, capable management, leadership in R&D, modern production facilities, and a strong marketing organization.

c)   **Opportunities and threats** arise from such externalities as government regulation, advances in technology, and demographic changes. They may be reflected in such competitive conditions as

i)   Raising or lowering of **barriers to entry** into the firm's industry

ii)   Changes in the **intensity of rivalry** within the industry, for example, because of overcapacity or high exit barriers

iii)   The relative availability of **substitutes** for the firm's products or services

          iv)   Bargaining power of **customers**, which tends to be greater when switching costs are low and products are not highly differentiated

          v)   Bargaining power of **suppliers**, which tends to be higher when suppliers are few

    d)   The SWOT analysis and identification of CSFs helps the firm to determine its **competitive strategy**.

    e)   The SWOT analysis tends to highlight the basic factors of cost, quality, and the speed of product development and delivery.

2)   Once the firm has identified its CSFs, it must establish **specific measures for each CSF** that are both relevant to the success of the firm and reliably stated. Thus, the balanced scorecard varies with the strategy adopted by the firm, for example, product differentiation or cost leadership either in a broad market or a narrowly focused market (a focus strategy). These measures provide a basis for implementing the firm's competitive strategy.

3)   By providing measures that are nonfinancial as well as financial, long-term as well as short-term, and internal as well as external, the balanced scorecard deemphasizes short-term financial results and focuses attention on CSFs.

4)   The **development and implementation** of a comprehensive balanced scorecard requires active participation by senior management. This involvement will assure the cooperation of lower-level managers in the identification of objectives, appropriate measures, targeted results, and methods of achieving the results.

    a)   The scorecard should contain measures at the **detail level** to permit everyone to understand how his/her efforts affect the firm's results.

    b)   The scorecard and the strategy it represents must be **communicated** to all managers and used as a basis for **compensation** decisions.

    c)   The scorecard should include **lagging indicators** (such as output and financial measures). It also should include **leading indicators** (such as many types of nonfinancial measures), but only if they are predictors of ultimate financial performance.

    d)   The scorecard should permit a determination of whether certain **objectives** are being achieved at the expense of others. For example, reduced spending on customer service may improve short-term financial results at a significant cost suggested by a decline in customer satisfaction measures.

5)   The following are **problems in implementation** of the balanced scorecard approach:

    a)   Using too many measures, with a consequent loss of focus on CSFs

    b)   Failing to evaluate personnel on nonfinancial as well as financial measures

    c)   Including measures that will not have long-term financial benefits

    d)   Not understanding that subjective measures (such as customer satisfaction) are imprecise

    e)   Trying to achieve improvements in all areas at all times

    f)   Lack of awareness that the connection between nonfinancial measures and ultimate financial success may not continue to be true

6)   A typical balanced scorecard includes measures in four categories:

a)   **Financial.** The **CSFs** may be sales, fair value of the firm's stock, profits, and liquidity. **Measures** may include sales, projected sales, accuracy of sales projections, new product sales, stock prices, operating earnings, earnings trend, revenue growth, gross margin percentage, cost reductions, economic value added, return on investment (or any of its variants), net present value, cash flow coverage and trends, turnover (assets, receivables, and inventory), and interest coverage.

b)   **Customer.** The **CSFs** may be customer satisfaction, customer retention rate, dealer and distributor relationships, marketing and selling performance, prompt delivery, and quality. **Measures** may include returns, complaints, survey results, coverage and strength of distribution channels, market research results, training of marketing people, sales trends, market share and its trend, on-time delivery rate, service response time and effectiveness, and warranty expense.

c)   **Internal business processes.** The **CSFs** may be quality, productivity (an input-output relationship), flexibility of response to changing conditions, operating readiness, and safety. **Measures** may include rate of defects, amounts of scrap and rework, returns, survey results, field service reports, warranty costs, vendor defect rate, cycle (lead) time, labor and machine efficiency, setup time, scheduling effectiveness, downtime, capacity usage, maintenance, and accidents and their results.

d)   **Learning, growth, and innovation.** The **CSFs** may be development of new products, promptness of their introduction, human resource development, morale, and competence of the work force. **Measures** may include new products marketed, amount of design changes, patents and copyrights registered, R&D personnel qualifications, actual versus planned shipping dates, hours of training, skill set levels attained, personnel turnover, personnel complaints and survey results, financial and operating results, technological capabilities, organizational learning, and industry leadership.

4.   One approach to **business process review** is **reengineering** (also called **business process reengineering**). It involves process innovation and core process redesign. Instead of improving existing procedures, it finds new ways of doing things.

a.   The emphasis is on simplification and **elimination of nonvalue-adding activities**. Thus, reengineering is not continuous improvement, it is not simply downsizing or modifying an existing system, and it should be reserved for the most important processes.

1)   An organization may need to **adapt quickly** and radically to change. Thus, reengineering is usually a cross-departmental process of innovation requiring substantial investment in information technology and retraining. Successful reengineering may bring dramatic improvements in customer service and the speed with which new products are introduced.

2)   Reengineering may be contrasted with **automation**, or the computerization of existing manual methods; **rationalization**, or the streamlining of procedures to make automation more efficient; and a **paradigm shift**, or a complete change in the very nature of the business.

b.   One well-known tool useful in reengineering is **work measurement**, a process that involves analysis of activities. The nature and extent of a task, the procedures needed for its execution, and the efficiency with which it is carried out are determined by work measurement.

   1)   This technique is appropriate when management takes an **engineered-cost** approach to control. Such an approach is indicated when the workload is divisible into control-factor units, for example, accounting entries made, lines of text word processed, or number of packages shipped. The cost of a **control-factor unit** is treated as a variable cost for budgeting purposes.

   2)   One method used for work measurement is **micromotion study**, which requires videotaping the performance of a job, e.g., assembly-line activities.

   3)   Another method is **work sampling**, making many random observations of an activity to determine what steps it normally requires.

c.   Reengineering and TQM techniques eliminate many traditional **controls**. They exploit modern technology to improve productivity and decrease the number of clerical workers. Thus, the emphasis is on developing controls that are automated and self-correcting and require minimal human intervention.

   1)   The emphasis shifts to monitoring **internal control** so management can determine when an operation may be out of control and corrective action is needed.

      a)   Most reengineering and TQM techniques also assume that humans will be motivated to work actively in improving operations when they are full participants in the process.

   2)   **Monitoring** assesses the quality of internal control over time. Management considers whether internal control is properly designed and operating as intended and modifies it to reflect changing conditions. Monitoring may be in the form of separate, periodic evaluations or of ongoing monitoring.

      a)   Ongoing monitoring occurs as part of routine operations. It includes management and supervisory review, comparisons, reconciliations, and other actions by personnel as part of their regular activities.

d.   **Internal auditors** may perform the functions of determining whether the reengineering process has senior management's support, recommending areas for consideration, and developing audit plans for the new system. However, they should not become directly involved in the implementation of the process. This involvement would impair their independence and objectivity.

5.   Stop and review! You have completed the outline for this subunit. Study multiple-choice questions 35 through 55 beginning on page 229.

4.5 INFORMATION SECURITY AND PRIVACY

1. Information security is an expansion of the **assurance services** performed by auditors. The creation of organization-wide computer networks with potentially thousands of points of access by outside parties has caused risks to proliferate. Thus, fragmented risk management and control processes may be inadequate.

    a. The **role of the internal audit activity** in these circumstances is to assess risks, monitor the implementation of corrective action, and evaluate controls.

    b. The internal audit activity also may function in a **consulting** capacity by identifying security issues and by working with users of information systems and with systems security personnel to devise and implement controls.

    c. The internal audit activity should work closely with the audit committee, board, etc., to assist in the performance of the **governance function** with respect to information security.

2. This subunit covers the related topics of security and privacy in two Practice Advisories that interpret the General Performance Standard on the nature of work and one Practice Advisory that interprets the General Performance Standard on performing the engagement.

    NOTE: **Physical security**, such as safeguards against environmental risks and unauthorized access to computer terminals, remains an internal auditing concern even though software controls now provide most protection for information.

3. *2100*   *Nature of Work* – *The internal audit activity evaluates and contributes to the improvement of risk management, control, and governance processes using a systematic and disciplined approach.*

    a. *PRACTICE ADVISORY 2100-2: INFORMATION SECURITY*

        1. *Internal auditors should determine that management and the board, the audit committee, or other governing body has a clear understanding that information security is a **management responsibility**. This responsibility includes **all critical information** of the organization, regardless of the media in which the information is stored.*

        2. *The chief audit executive should determine that the internal audit activity possesses, or has access to, **competent auditing resources** to evaluate information security and **associated risk exposures**. This includes both **internal and external** risk exposures, including exposures relating to the organization's relationships with outside entities.*

        3. *Internal auditors should determine that the board, audit committee, or other governing body has sought assurance from management that information security **breaches and conditions that might represent a threat** to the organization will promptly be made known to those performing the internal auditing activity.*

        4. *Internal auditors should assess the effectiveness of **preventive, detective, and mitigative measures** against **past attacks**, as deemed appropriate, and **future attempts** or incidents deemed likely to occur. Internal auditors should confirm that the board, audit committee, or other **governing body** has been **appropriately informed** of threats, incidents, vulnerabilities exploited, and corrective measures.*

        5. *Internal auditors should **periodically assess** the organization's information security practices and **recommend**, as appropriate, enhancements to or implementation of new controls and safeguards. Following an assessment, an **assurance report** should be provided to the board, audit committee, or other appropriate governing body. Such assessments can either be conducted as **separate stand-alone engagements** or as **multiple engagements** integrated into other audits or engagements conducted as part of the approved audit plan.*

PA Summary

- Information security is a **management responsibility** for all critical information regardless of its form.
- The IAA should have **competent auditing resources** for evaluating internal and external risks to information security.
- Internal auditors should determine that the governing body has sought assurance from management that the IAA will be promptly notified about security **breaches and conditions that might represent a threat**.
- Internal auditors assess the effectiveness of **preventive, detective, and mitigative measures** against past and future attacks. The governing body should be appropriately informed.
- Internal auditors also should **periodically assess** security practices, **recommend** new or improved controls, and provide an **assurance report**. Such assessments can be made as **separate engagements** or as **multiple engagements** integrated with other elements of the audit plan.

b. Another aspect of internal auditing's role regarding information security is to evaluate compliance with laws and regulations concerning **privacy**. Thus, internal auditors determine the existence and content of requirements relating to privacy (after consulting with legal counsel). They also determine that systems are designed in accordance with those requirements, compliance is achieved, and compliance is documented.

c. ***PRACTICE ADVISORY 2100-8: THE INTERNAL AUDITOR'S ROLE IN EVALUATING AN ORGANIZATION'S PRIVACY FRAMEWORK***

1. *Concerns relating to the protection of personal privacy are becoming more apparent, focused, and global as advancements in **information technology and communications** continually introduce new risks and threats to privacy. **Privacy controls are legal requirements** for doing business in most of the world.*

2. ***Privacy definitions vary widely** depending upon country, culture, political environment, and legal framework. Privacy can encompass **personal** privacy (physical and psychological); privacy of **space** (freedom from surveillance); privacy of **communication** (freedom from monitoring); and privacy of **information** (collection, use, and disclosure of personal information by others). **Personal information** generally refers to information that can be associated with a specific individual or that has identifying characteristics that might be combined with other information to do so. It can include any factual or subjective information, recorded or not, in any form or medium. Personal information might include, for example:*

    - *Name, address, identification numbers, income, or blood type;*
    - *Evaluations, comments, social status, or disciplinary actions; and*
    - *Employee files, credit records, loan records.*

3. *Privacy is a **risk management issue**. Failure to protect privacy and personal information with the appropriate controls can have **significant consequences** for an organization. For example, it can damage the reputation of individuals and the organization, lead to legal liability issues, and contribute to consumer and employee mistrust.*

4. *There are a variety of laws and regulations developing worldwide relating to the protection of personal information. As well, there are generally accepted policies and practices that can be applied to the privacy issue.*

5.   It is clear that good privacy practices contribute to **good governance** and accountability. The **governing body** (e.g., the board of directors, head of an agency, or legislative body) **is ultimately accountable** for ensuring that the principal risks of the organization have been identified and the appropriate systems have been implemented to mitigate those risks. This includes establishing the necessary **privacy framework** for the organization and monitoring its implementation.

6.   The internal auditor can contribute to ensuring good governance and accountability by playing a role in helping an organization meet its privacy objectives. The internal auditor is uniquely positioned to **evaluate the privacy framework** in their organization and **identify the significant risks** along with the appropriate **recommendations** for their mitigation.

7.   In the evaluation of the privacy framework, the internal auditor should consider the following:

   •   The various **laws, regulations, and policies** relating to privacy in their respective jurisdictions (including any jurisdiction where the organization conducts business);

   •   Liaison with **in-house legal counsel** to determine the exact nature of such laws, regulations, and other standards and practices applicable to the organization and the country/countries in which it does business;

   •   Liaison with **information technology specialists** to ensure information security and data protection controls are in place and regularly reviewed and assessed for appropriateness;

   •   The level or maturity of the organization's **privacy practices**. Depending upon the level, the **internal auditor may have differing roles**. The auditor may **facilitate** the development and implementation of the **privacy program**, conduct a **privacy risk assessment** to determine the needs and risk exposures of the organization, or may review and provide **assurance** on the effectiveness of the privacy policies, practices, and controls across the organization. If the internal auditor assumes a portion of the responsibility for developing and implementing a privacy program, the auditor's **independence** may be impaired.

8.   Typically, the internal auditor could be expected to **identify** the types and appropriateness of **information gathered** by their organization that is deemed personal or private, the **collection methodology** used, and whether the organization's use of the information so collected is in accordance with its **intended use** and the **laws** in the areas where the information is gathered, held, and used.

9.   Given the **highly technical and legal nature of the topic**, the internal auditor should ensure that the appropriate in-depth **knowledge and capacity** to conduct any such evaluation of the privacy framework is available, using third-party experts if necessary.

PA Summary

- Privacy controls are **legally required** in most countries because advances in **IT and communications** continually create new threats.
- **Privacy definitions** vary: (1) **personal** privacy (physical and psychological), (2) privacy of **space** (freedom from surveillance), (3) privacy of **communication** (freedom from monitoring), and (4) privacy of **information** (collection, use, and disclosure of personal information by others).

     1)   **Personal information** is any information that can be associated with a specific individual or that might be combined with other information to do so.
- Privacy is a **risk management issue**. Failing to protect privacy and personal information has significant legal and business consequences for an organization.
- Good privacy practices contribute to **good governance** and accountability. The **governing body** of an organization is **ultimately accountable** for managing privacy risk, e.g., by establishing and monitoring a **privacy framework**.
- The internal auditor **evaluates the privacy framework**, identifies significant risks, and makes recommendations. The internal auditor also considers (1) laws, regulations, and practices in relevant jurisdictions; (2) the advice of legal counsel; and (3) the security efforts of IT specialists.
- Depending on the level or maturity of the organization's **privacy practices**, the role of the internal auditor may be to (1) facilitate the privacy program, (2) do a privacy risk assessment, or (3) perform an assurance service. However, assumption of responsibility may impair **independence**.
- The internal auditor identifies (1) personal **information gathered**, (2) **collection methods**, and (3) whether use of the information is in accordance with its **intended use** and **applicable law**.
- Given the difficulty of the technical and legal issues, the internal auditor should have or obtain the **knowledge and capacity** to evaluate the privacy framework, using outside service providers if needed.

---

4.   **Privacy engagements** address the **security** of personal information, especially information stored in computerized systems. An example is health-care information in the files of insurers and providers.

   a.   The organization should **comply** with governmental statutory and regulatory mandates. Internal auditors should consult the organization's **legal counsel** and then communicate the requirements to those responsible for designing and implementing the required safeguards.

      1)   Internal auditors should determine that the requirements are incorporated into the information system and that compliance is achieved in its operation.

   b.   Personal information should be protected from both unauthorized intrusion and misuse by those who have authorized access.

   c.   Privacy should be balanced with the need to allow appropriate and prompt availability of personal information to legitimate users.

   d.   The organization should **document** compliance with privacy and other legal requirements.

   e.   **Benefits** of the security arrangements should exceed the **costs**. For example, **encryption** techniques are an expensive way to address threats to the security of private information. Other methods, such as access controls, may be more appropriate relative to the assessed risk.

f.   The internal auditors have an ethical obligation to maintain the **confidentiality** of private information.

1)   "Internal auditors shall be prudent in the use and protection of information acquired in the course of their duties" **(Rule of Conduct 3.1)**.

2)   "Internal auditors shall not use information for any personal gain or in any manner that would be contrary to the law or detrimental to the legitimate and ethical objectives of the organization" **(Rule of Conduct 3.2)**.

5.   **2300**   **Performing the Engagement** – *Internal auditors should identify, analyze, evaluate, and record sufficient information to achieve the engagement's objectives.*

a.   **PRACTICE ADVISORY 2300-1: THE INTERNAL AUDITOR'S USE OF PERSONAL INFORMATION IN CONDUCTING AUDITS**

1.   *Concerns relating to the protection of* **personal privacy and information** *are becoming more apparent, focused, and global as advancements in information technology and communications continually introduce new risks and threats to privacy.* **Privacy controls** *are legal requirements for doing business in most of the world.*

2.   *Personal information generally refers to information that can be associated with a* **specific individual** *or that has identifying characteristics that might be combined with other information to do so. It can include any factual or subjective information, recorded or not, in any form or media. Personal information might include, for example:*

*   *Name, address, identification numbers, income, or blood type;*
*   *Evaluations, comments, social status, or disciplinary actions; and*
*   *Employee files, credit records, loan records.*

3.   *For the most part,* **laws** *require organizations to* **identify the purposes** *for which personal information is collected, at or before the time the information is collected; and that personal information not be used or disclosed for purposes other than those for which it was collected, except with the consent of the individual or as required by law.*

4.   *It is important that the internal auditor* **understands and complies with all laws** *regarding the use of personal information in their jurisdiction and those jurisdictions where their organization conducts business.*

5.   *The internal auditor must understand that it may be* **inappropriate**, *and in some cases illegal, to access, retrieve, review, manipulate, or use personal information in conducting* **certain internal audit engagements**.

6.   *The internal auditor should* **investigate issues** *before initiating audit effort and seek advice from in-house legal counsel if there are any questions or concerns in this respect.*

PA Summary

- Threats to **personal privacy and information** have increased because of IT and communications advances. Thus, laws require **privacy controls**.
- Personal information identifies a **specific individual**. Examples are identification numbers, income, blood type, evaluations, disciplinary actions, employee files, credit records, and loan records.
- The law usually requires organizations to **identify the purposes** for which personal information is collected, at or before the time it is collected. Its use or disclosure for other purposes is generally prohibited, except with consent or as required by law.
- The internal auditor must **understand and comply with all laws** regarding the use of personal information.
- Access to or use of personal information may be inappropriate or illegal in **certain engagements**.
- The internal auditor should **investigate issues** before initiating audit effort and seek advice from counsel if issues arise regarding use of personal information.

---

6. Stop and review! You have completed the outline for this subunit. Study multiple-choice questions 56 through 59 beginning on page 235.

4.6 OTHER ENGAGEMENTS

1. **Process (functional) engagements** are operational audit engagements that follow a process crossing organizational lines, service units, and geographical locations.

   a. The focus is on **operations** and how **effectively and efficiently** the organizational units affected will cooperate.

   b. These engagements tend to be challenging because of their scope and the need to deal with organizational units that may have **conflicting objectives**.

   c. **Typical processes or functions** are

      1) Purchasing and receiving
      2) Distribution of services, materials, and supplies to users in the organization
      3) Modification of products
      4) Safety practices
      5) Scrap handling and disposal
      6) Development of budgets
      7) Marketing
      8) Management of depreciable assets

2. A **program-results engagement** is intended to obtain information about the costs, outputs, benefits, and effects of a program. It attempts to measure the accomplishment and relative success of the undertaking.

   a. Because benefits often cannot be quantified in financial terms, a special concern is the ability to measure **effectiveness**. Thus, clear definitions of **objectives and standards** should be provided at the outset of the program.

   b. A **program** is a funded activity not part of the normal, continuing operations of the organization, such as an expansion or a new information system.

3. Engagements involving **third parties** may be necessary when vital **controls** affecting transactions exist outside the organization.

    a. One example is the **outsourcing** of the entity's information processing function to a **service organization**.

    b. Another example is **electronic data interchange (EDI)**. In this case, the internal auditors must be concerned with the controls maintained by **trading partners** as well as by an organization (a **trusted third-party network** or TTP) that provides the EDI service.

    c. See Study Unit 7 for the related Practice Advisories.

4. **Contract engagements.** Internal auditors often perform engagements to monitor and evaluate significant **construction contracts** and **operating contracts** that involve the provision of services. The usual types of arrangements for such contracts are lump-sum (fixed-price), cost-plus, and unit-price.

    a. **Lump-sum contracts.** The internal auditor may have little to evaluate when the work is performed in accordance with the contract. However, reviewing such an agreement may call for consideration of

        1) Progress payments.
        2) Incentives (e.g., for early completion).
        3) An escalator clause (e.g., one causing the entire price to be due in the event of some breach of the contract).
        4) Adjustments for labor costs (e.g., premiums paid to obtain necessary labor).
        5) Change orders.

    b. **Cost-plus contracts** are ways to cope with uncertainties about costs by setting a price equal to cost plus a fixed amount or cost plus a fixed percentage of cost. A problem is that the contractor may have little incentive for **economy and efficiency**, a reason for careful review by the internal auditors. These contracts may have provisions for

        1) Setting cost ceilings, with any savings shared by the parties.
        2) Incentives for early completion.

    c. **Unit-price contracts** are often used when a convenient measure of work is available, such as acres of land cleared, cubic yards of earth moved, or square footage patrolled by a security service.

        1) The key issue is accurate measurement of the work performed.

    d. To protect the organization, internal auditors should be involved **throughout the contracting process**, not merely the performance phase. They should review the terms of the contract and

        1) Procedures for bidding (e.g., competitive bidding).
        2) Procedures for cost estimation and control.
        3) Budgets and financial forecasts.
        4) The contractor's information and control systems.
        5) The contractor's financial position.
        6) Funding and tax matters.
        7) Progress of the project and costs incurred.

5. Internal auditors may perform consulting engagements to provide **internal control training** to the employees of the organization.

    a. Such training may involve instruction about the organization's objectives, standards, policies, procedures, performance measurements, and feedback methods.

    b. In addition to providing courses for client personnel, the internal audit activity may offer internships to some **new managers**. Among other things, these managers will gain experience in **assessing controls**.

    c.   As part of their coordination with **external auditors**, the internal auditors may provide opportunities for joint training in control issues and other matters.

    d.   **Internal auditors** also should undergo internal control training, for example, with regard to control frameworks, specific controls and control objectives, standards, technological developments, and new professional literature.

    e.   A result of **control self-assessment** is training for people in business units. Participants "become trained and experienced in assessing risks and associating control processes with managing those risks and improving the chances of achieving business objectives" (PA 2100.A1-2).

    f.   The **ethical culture of an organization** is linked to the governance process and is the most important **soft control**.

        1)   Internal auditors have many roles in supporting the ethical culture, including those of ethics counselor and ethics expert.

6.   Stop and review! You have completed the outline for this subunit. Study multiple-choice questions 60 and 61 on page 236.

4.7 STUDY UNIT 4 SUMMARY

1.   Internal auditors should assess compliance in specific areas as part of their role in organizational governance. They also should conduct follow-up and report on management's response to regulatory body reviews.

2.   Compliance standards and procedures should be established, e.g., a straightforward and fair code of conduct and incentives that do not reward misconduct. Authority should not be delegated to those with a tendency to illegality. Applicants should be screened in a lawful manner. Monitoring and auditing systems for detecting illegality and employee "hotline" reporting systems should be used. For example, the internal audit plan should be given appropriate resources and apply to all of the entity's businesses. Also, it should include a review of the compliance program.

3.   The CAE should have a close relationship with the chief environmental officer and coordinate activities. The CAE may offer to review the environmental audit function's plan and performance. The CAE should schedule a quality assurance review of that function and evaluate its compliance with standards. The CAE evaluates the independence of the environmental audit functions. The CAE facilitates reporting of EH&S issues to the board.

4.   According to a research report prepared for The IIA Research Foundation,

> *An environmental management system is an organization's structure of responsibilities and policies, practices, procedures, processes, and resources for protecting the environment and managing environmental issues.*

> *Environmental auditing is an integral part of an environmental management system whereby management determines whether the organization's environmental control systems are adequate to ensure compliance with regulatory requirements and internal policies.*

5.   Auditors should assess continuity planning. Interruptions are inevitable. Thus, planning is integral to the risk management process so that loss may be minimized, continuity ensured, and service maintained. Internal auditors assist with risk analysis, evaluate the disaster plan, and perform assurance services to verify that it is updated. During the recovery period, internal auditors monitor the effectiveness of recovery and control of operations and identify improvements. Afterward, they may identify lessons learned.

6.   The term due diligence is applied to a service in which internal auditors and others determine the business justification for a major transaction and whether that justification is valid. The term "due diligence" may be used for other engagements, for example, certain environmental audits.

7.   The total quality management (TQM) approach can increase revenues and decrease costs significantly. Thus, the internal audit activity's services rendered with respect to the quality function have the potential to add substantial value. Indeed, the improvement of operations is part of the definition of internal auditing. Benchmarking is a continuous evaluation of the practices of the best organizations in their class and the adaptation of processes to reflect the best of these practices. It involves (a) analysis and measurement of key outputs against those of the best organizations and (b) identifying the underlying key actions and causes that contribute to the performance difference.

8.   Internal auditors may conduct a performance audit to provide assurance about the organization's key performance indicators. They also may conduct a consulting engagement to design such a performance measurement system. The trend in performance measurement is the balanced scorecard approach to managing the implementation of the firm's strategy. It is an accounting report that connects the firm's critical success factors (CSFs) determined in a strategic analysis to measurements of its performance.

9.   One approach to business process review is reengineering (also called business process reengineering). It involves process innovation and core process redesign. Instead of improving existing procedures, it finds new ways of doing things.

10.   Information security is a management responsibility for all critical information. Internal auditors assess the effectiveness of measures against past and future attacks. The governing body should be appropriately informed. Internal auditors also should periodically assess security practices, recommend new or improved controls, and provide an assurance report.

11.   The internal auditor evaluates the privacy framework, identifies risks, and makes recommendations. The internal auditor also considers (a) laws, regulations, and practices; (b) the advice of legal counsel; and (c) the security efforts of IT specialists. The role of the internal auditor may be to facilitate the privacy program, do a privacy risk assessment, or perform an assurance service. However, assumption of responsibility may impair independence. The internal auditor identifies (a) personal information gathered, (b) collection methods, (c) intended uses, and (d) applicable laws.

12.   The auditor must comply with all laws regarding use of personal information. Access to or use of personal information may be inappropriate or illegal in certain engagements.

13.   Internal auditors also may perform engagements to audit (a) processes (functions), (b) program results, (c) third-party controls, and (d) certain contracts. The provision of internal control training is a typical consulting engagement.

QUESTIONS

4.1 Compliance Auditing

1. Compliance programs assist organizations by doing which of the following?

I.   Evaluating business continuity.
II. Determining director and officer liability.
III. Evaluating disaster recovery plans.

    A. I only.

    B. II only.

    C. I and II only.

    D. I, II, and III.

Answer (B) is correct. *(Publisher, adapted)*
    REQUIRED: The way(s) in which compliance programs help organizations.
    DISCUSSION: Compliance programs assist organizations in preventing inadvertent employee violations, detecting illegal activities, and discouraging intentional employee violations. They can also help prove insurance claims, determine director and officer liability, create or enhance corporate identity, and decide the appropriateness of punitive damages. Evaluating the business continuity and evaluating the disaster recovery plans are both major components of auditing e-commerce activities.

2. Internal auditing engagements vary in their degree of objectivity. Of the following, which is likely to be the most objective?

    A. Compliance engagement relating to an organization's overtime policy.

    B. Operational engagement relating to the personnel function's hiring and firing procedures.

    C. Performance engagement relating to the marketing department.

    D. Financial control engagement relating to payroll procedures.

Answer (A) is correct. *(CIA, adapted)*
    REQUIRED: The most objective type of engagement.
    DISCUSSION: A compliance engagement relating to overtime policy is likely to be the most objective. It determines whether actual operations conform to specific management policies and procedures, which are likely to be well defined and documented. For example, determining whether overtime was properly paid requires less judgment than whether a control is properly designed.
    Answer (B) is incorrect because an operational engagement relating to hiring and firing procedures involves substantial subjectivity. Personnel decisions are difficult to quantify. Answer (C) is incorrect because evaluating the creative activities of the marketing department is highly subjective. Answer (D) is incorrect because assessment of financial control over payroll procedures is somewhat subjective. Control may be achieved in various ways.

3. An organization should establish compliance standards and procedures and should develop a written business code of conduct to be followed by its employees. Which of the following is true concerning business codes of conduct and the compliance standards?

    A. Compliance standards should be straightforward and reasonably capable of reducing the prospect of criminal conduct.

    B. The compliance standards should be codified in the charter of the audit committee.

    C. Companies with international operations should institute various compliance programs, based on selective geographic locations, that reflect appropriate local regulations.

    D. In order to prevent future legal liability, the code should consist of legal terms and definitions.

Answer (A) is correct. *(Publisher, adapted)*
    REQUIRED: The true statement regarding the code of conduct and compliance standards.
    DISCUSSION: The code of conduct should clearly identify prohibited activities, making compliance standards reasonably capable of reducing the prospect of criminal conduct (i.e., discouraging intentional employee violations). In addition, codes that are straightforward and fair tend to decrease the risk that employees will engage in unethical or illegal behavior (Practice Advisory 2100-5).
    Answer (B) is incorrect because, according to The IIA, the charter of the audit committee should include: (1) reviewing the effectiveness of the system for monitoring compliance with laws and regulations and the results of management's investigation and follow-up (including disciplinary action) of any instances of noncompliance; (2) reviewing the findings of any examinations by regulatory agencies, and any auditor observations; (3) reviewing the process for communicating the code of conduct to company personnel, and for monitoring compliance therewith; and (4) obtaining regular updates from management and company legal counsel regarding compliance matters. Answer (C) is incorrect because companies with international operations should institute a compliance program on a global basis, not just for selective geographic locations. Such programs should reflect appropriate local conditions, laws, and regulations (Practice Advisory 2100-5). Answer (D) is incorrect because the code should be written in a language that all employees can understand, avoiding legalese (Practice Advisory 2100-5).

Questions 4 through 6 are based on the following information. A certified internal auditor is the chief audit executive for a large city and is planning the engagement work schedule for the next year. The city has a number of different funds, some that are restricted in use by government grants and some that require compliance reports to the government. One of the programs for which the city has received a grant is job retraining and placement. The grant specifies certain conditions a participant in the program must meet to be eligible for the funding.

4. The internal auditors randomly select participants in the job retraining program for the past year to verify that they had met all the eligibility requirements. This type of engagement is concerned with

    A. Compliance.

    B. Operational effectiveness.

    C. Economy and efficiency.

    D. Program results.

Answer (A) is correct. *(CIA, adapted)*
    REQUIRED: The type of engagement performed.
    DISCUSSION: The scope of work of internal auditing includes assurance services that involve evaluating the risk exposures and controls relating to the organization's governance, operations, and information systems. This evaluation extends to risk exposures and controls regarding compliance with laws, regulations, and contracts. Selection of participants in the job retraining program to verify satisfaction of eligibility requirements is a compliance procedure.
    Answer (B) is incorrect because an operational effectiveness engagement consists of a comprehensive review of the overall job retraining program. Answer (C) is incorrect because an economy and efficiency engagement considers the cost of the program compared with objectives achieved. Answer (D) is incorrect because a program-results engagement attempts to measure accomplishments and relative success of the program.

5. The chief audit executive plans an engagement to verify that the job retraining program complies with applicable grant provisions. One of the provisions is that the city adopt a budget for the program and subsequently follow procedures to ensure that the budget is adhered to and that only allowable costs are charged to the program. In performing an engagement concerning compliance with this provision, the internal auditors should perform all of the following procedures except

    A. Determine that the budget was reviewed and approved by supervisory personnel within the city.

    B. Determine that the budget was reviewed and approved by supervisory personnel within the granting agency.

    C. Select a sample of expenditures to determine that the expenditures are (1) properly classified as to type, (2) appropriate to the program, and (3) designed to meet the program's objectives.

    D. Compare actual results with budgeted results and determine the reason for deviations. Determine if such deviations have been approved by appropriate officials.

Answer (B) is correct. *(CIA, adapted)*
    REQUIRED: The procedure not performed in a compliance engagement.
    DISCUSSION: The activities of the granting agency are not relevant to a compliance engagement relating to the city's use of the grant funds. The internal auditors are only responsible for determining whether the city is in compliance with the requirements of the grant.
    Answer (A) is incorrect because the internal auditors should determine that the city has complied with the requirement to adopt a budget. Answer (C) is incorrect because checking a sample of expenditures might reveal expenditures charged to the wrong account to bypass budgeting control. Answer (D) is incorrect because the internal auditors should verify that the city has complied with the requirement to adhere to the budget.

6. The internal auditors must determine the applicable laws and regulations. Which of the following procedures would be the least effective in learning about the applicable laws and regulations?

    A. Make inquiries of the city's chief financial officer, legal counsel, or grant administrators.

    B. Review prior-year working papers and inquire of officials as to changes.

    C. Review applicable grant agreements.

    D. Discuss the matter with the audit committee and make inquiries as to the nature of the requirements and the audit committee's objectives for the engagement.

Answer (D) is correct. *(CIA, adapted)*
    REQUIRED: The least effective procedure for learning about applicable laws and regulations.
    DISCUSSION: Discussing the matter with the audit committee would not be helpful. The members are not likely to know the applicable laws and regulations. The audit committee's oversight activities do not provide specific expertise needed to help the internal auditors understand the applicable laws and regulations.
    Answer (A) is incorrect because making inquiries of the city's chief financial officer, legal counsel, or grant administrators is an effective way to learn about the applicable laws and regulations. Answer (B) is incorrect because reviewing prior-year working papers is an effective way to learn about the applicable laws and regulations. Answer (C) is incorrect because reviewing applicable grant agreements is an effective way to learn about the applicable laws and regulations.

7. Which of the following is least likely to exemplify a good compliance environment?

    A. An international company that institutes a global compliance program that reflects local conditions, laws, and regulations.

    B. A company that creates an organizational chart, identifying personnel who are responsible for implementing compliance programs.

    C. A company whose code of conduct provides guidance to employees on relevant issues.

    D. A company that rewards employees for charging travel hours in order to take advantage of the tax benefits.

Answer (D) is correct. *(Publisher, adapted)*
REQUIRED: The entity with the poorest compliance environment.
DISCUSSION: Companies using reward systems that attach financial incentives to apparently unethical or illegal behavior can expect a poor compliance environment. For instance, a company rewarding its employees for charging travel hours makes itself vulnerable to fraud. Employees may start charging false travel hours to receive additional rewards. Thus, the tax benefit that the company is trying to take advantage of by offering such an incentive may be negated by fraudulent employee practices. A good compliance environment is created when an organization does the following:

- Develops a written, straightforward business code of conduct that clearly identifies prohibited activities, provides guidance to employees on relevant issues, and decreases the risk that employees will engage in unethical or illegal behavior (Practice Advisory 2100-5).

- Creates an organizational chart identifying board members, senior officers, senior compliance officer, and department personnel who are responsible for implementing compliance programs (Practice Advisory 2100-5).

- Institutes a compliance program on a global basis, not just for selective geographic locations, which reflects appropriate local conditions, laws, and regulations (Practice Advisory 2100-5).

8. Environmental compliance information and training is most applicable and should be provided to which of the following departments?

    A. Sales.

    B. Human resources.

    C. Manufacturing.

    D. Information technology.

Answer (C) is correct. *(Publisher, adapted)*
REQUIRED: The department to which environmental compliance information and training most applies.
DISCUSSION: When presenting compliance information and training, different sets of employees should be targeted based on areas important to each functional group, and the information should be tailored to that group's job requirements (Practice Advisory 2100-5). Environmental compliance, in this case, is not in reference to the market or information technology environment, but the physical environment. Thus, information regarding environmental compliance is most applicable to the manufacturing department, since this department has an increased likelihood of violating or detecting violations of such laws and regulations.

9. The chief compliance officer of an organization should report to the

    A. Chief executive officer.

    B. Chief general counsel.

    C. Chief operating officer.

    D. Chief audit executive.

Answer (A) is correct. *(Publisher, adapted)*
REQUIRED: The supervisor to whom the chief compliance officer reports.
DISCUSSION: It is not enough for a company to create the position of chief compliance officer and to select the rest of the compliance unit. The company should also ensure that these personnel are appropriately empowered and supplied with the resources necessary for carrying out their mission. Furthermore, compliance personnel should have adequate access to senior management. A reporting structure in which the chief compliance officer reports directly to the chief executive officer (CEO) is indicative of this access (Practice Advisory 2100-5).
Answer (B) is incorrect because the chief general counsel in many organizations is assigned chief compliance responsibilities. In many companies, however, such a structure may convince employees that management is not committed to the program and that the program is important only to the legal department. Anyone assigned chief compliance responsibilities should report to the CEO. Answer (C) is incorrect because the chief compliance officer should report to the CEO, not the COO. Answer (D) is incorrect because the chief compliance officer should report to the CEO, not the chief audit executive.

10. An organization should use due care not to delegate substantial discretionary authority to individuals the organization knows have a propensity to engage in illegal activities. Which of the following are steps an organization can take to ensure that such individuals are detected?

I.   Screening of applicants for employment at all levels for evidence of past wrongdoing, especially past criminal convictions within the company's industry.

II. Asking professionals about any history of discipline in front of licensing boards.

III. Performing background checks on employees' or applicants' credit reports to ensure that they are financially sound and are unlikely to commit theft or fraud.

    A.   I only.

    B.   III only.

    C.   I and II only.

    D.   I, II, and III.

Answer (C) is correct.   *(Publisher, adapted)*
   REQUIRED: The due diligence steps an organization can take when hiring individuals.
   DISCUSSION: As part of the exercise of due diligence, an organization can take a number of steps to protect itself against individuals who have a propensity to engage in illegal activities. For instance, a company can screen applicants for employment at all levels for evidence of past wrongdoing, especially wrongdoing within the company's industry. Furthermore, it may inquire as to past criminal convictions, and professionals may be asked about any history of discipline in front of licensing boards. Care should be taken, however, to ensure that the company does not infringe upon employees' and applicants' privacy rights under applicable laws, since many jurisdictions have laws limiting the amount of information a company may obtain in performing background checks on employees (Practice Advisory 2100-5).

11. An ombudsperson is most effective when the individual

I.   Is located on-site.

II. Reports to the chief compliance officer or the board of directors.

III. Is located off-site.

IV. Reports to no one, thus ensuring a whistle-blower's secrecy.

    A.   II only.

    B.   I and II only.

    C.   I and IV only.

    D.   III and IV only.

Answer (B) is correct.   *(Publisher, adapted)*
   REQUIRED: The characteristic(s) of an effective ombudsperson.
   DISCUSSION: Use of an ombudsperson is more effective if the ombudsperson is located on-site, reports directly to the chief compliance officer or the board of directors, keeps the names of whistle-blowers secret, provides guidance to whistle-blowers, and undertakes follow-up review to ensure that retaliation has not occurred. An ombudsperson must report to someone at a high level in the organization who is empowered to initiate a change in organization policies based on the ombudsperson's findings; thus, reporting to no one is not an option. In addition, an ombudsperson's location on-site promotes employee confidence in the ombudsperson.

12. Employees have the most confidence in a hotline monitored by which of the following?

    A.   An expert from the legal department, backed by a non-retaliation policy.

    B.   An in-house representative, backed by a retaliation policy.

    C.   An on-site ombudsperson, backed by a non-retaliation policy.

    D.   An off-site attorney who can better protect attorney-client privilege.

Answer (C) is correct.   *(Publisher, adapted)*
   REQUIRED: The hotline monitor that employees have the most confidence in.
   DISCUSSION: Although an attorney monitoring the hotline is better able to protect attorney-client and work-product privileges, one study observed that employees have little confidence in hotlines answered by the legal department or by an outside service. The same study showed that employees have even less confidence in write-in reports or an off-site ombudsperson, but have the most confidence in hotlines answered by an in-house representative (or an on-site ombudsperson) and backed by a non-retaliation policy.
   Answer (A) is incorrect because employees have little confidence in hotlines answered by the legal department. Answer (B) is incorrect because a retaliation policy would dissuade whistle-blowers from coming forth due to concern of possible backlash. Answer (D) is incorrect because employees have little confidence in hotlines monitored by the legal department or by an outside service. Thus, they would have even less confidence in an outside attorney.

13. An internal audit plan should include a review of the organization's compliance program and its procedures, including reviews to determine all but which of the following?

- A. The effectiveness of written materials.
- B. The receipt of communications by employees.
- C. The appropriate handling of detected violations.
- D. The performance of full background checks on employees and new hires.

Answer (D) is correct. *(Publisher, adapted)*
REQUIRED: The review that is not included in an internal audit plan, with regard to the organization's compliance program.
DISCUSSION: The audit plan should include a review of the organization's compliance program and its procedures, including reviews to determine whether written materials are effective, communications have been received by employees, detected violations have been appropriately handled, discipline has been even-handed, whistle-blowers have not been retaliated against, and the compliance unit has fulfilled its responsibilities. The auditors should review the compliance program to determine whether it can be improved and should solicit employee input. Moreover, companies should screen applicants for employment at all levels and should inquire as to past criminal convictions, taking care not to infringe upon employees' and applicants' privacy rights. However, a review of the performance of full background checks is not included in an audit plan as part of the review of an organization's compliance program.

14. Which of the following is an effective tool for uncovering unethical or illegal activity in an organization?

- A. The screening of applicants.
- B. The ethics interview.
- C. The background check.
- D. The ethics questionnaire.

Answer (D) is correct. *(Publisher, adapted)*
REQUIRED: The tool used to uncover unethical or illegal activity.
DISCUSSION: An effective tool for uncovering unethical or illegal activity is the ethics questionnaire. Each employee of the organization should receive a questionnaire that asks whether the employee is aware of kickbacks, bribes, or other wrongdoing. To protect privilege, the questionnaire should (1) be sent by organization counsel; (2) contain a statement that the questionnaire is protected by privilege; (3) require the employee to complete, sign, and return the questionnaire without making a copy; and (4) contain a statement that the organization retains the right to disclose information provided to the company to government agencies or in litigation. The questionnaire's instructions should also note that privilege will be lost if the questionnaire is disclosed to outside parties.
Answer (A) is incorrect because screening applicants for employment is a way to detect past criminal activity and wrongdoing. Thus, it is of no use in uncovering unethical or illegal activity currently ongoing in an organization. Answer (B) is incorrect because an ethics interview may cause discomfort to an employee, and an employee may not believe that the interview is protected by privilege or as confidential as an ethics questionnaire. Answer (C) is incorrect because the background check is a way to detect past wrongdoing, not ongoing or current unethical or illegal activities.

15. Which of the following are forms of punishment for those who violate an organization's code of conduct?

I. A warning.
II. Loss of pay.
III. Suspension.
IV. Termination.

- A. I and II only.
- B. I, III, and IV only.
- C. I, II, and III only.
- D. I, II, III, and IV.

Answer (D) is correct. *(Publisher, adapted)*
REQUIRED: The forms of punishment for a violation of an organization's code of conduct
DISCUSSION: Those who violate the organization's code of conduct should receive punishment appropriate to the offense, such as warning, loss of pay, suspension, transfer, or termination. Nevertheless, if an employee is found to have committed some illegal act, the organization might have to terminate that employee, in keeping with the organization's obligation to use "due care not to delegate substantial discretionary authority to individuals whom the organization knew, or should have known through the exercise of due diligence, had a propensity to engage in illegal activities."

16. Termination or other discipline of employees may be limited by all of the following except

    A. Whistle-blower laws.

    B. Employer responsibilities with regard to employer good faith doctrines.

    C. Union contracts.

    D. Exceptions to the employee-at-will doctrine.

Answer (B) is correct. *(Publisher, adapted)*
    REQUIRED: The item that does not limit the termination or other discipline of employees.
    DISCUSSION: Termination or other discipline of employees may be limited by whistle-blower laws, exceptions to the employee-at-will doctrine, employee or union contracts, and employer responsibilities with regard to discrimination, wrongful discharge, and employer bad faith laws/doctrines.

17. An organization with an effective regulatory compliance program displays which of the following characteristics?

    A. It punishes unethical or illegal activity based on seniority.

    B. It disciplines those who knew of the misconduct and did not report it, and holds harmless those who should have known, but did not know.

    C. After an offense is detected, the organization takes the necessary steps – short of modifying its entire program – to prevent further similar offenses.

    D. It is scrupulous in documenting employee discipline.

Answer (D) is correct. *(Publisher, adapted)*
    REQUIRED: The characteristics of an organization with an effective regulatory compliance program.
    DISCUSSION: Organizations should be scrupulous and thorough in documenting employee discipline. The organization should be able to prove that it made its best efforts to collect information with regard to any incident and took appropriate action based upon the information available.
    Answer (A) is incorrect because discipline under the program must be fair. The program has slight chance of succeeding if unethical or illegal activity goes unpunished, especially if tied to the activities of senior management or big producers. Ignored wrongdoing by such persons will encourage wrongful behavior in the rest of the workforce. Answer (B) is incorrect because the program should provide for the discipline of managers and other responsible persons who knew or should have known of misconduct and did not report it. Answer (C) is incorrect because, after an offense has been detected, the organization should take all reasonable steps to respond appropriately to the offense and to prevent further similar offenses, including any necessary modifications to its program to prevent and detect violations of law.

18. Which of the following is true regarding appropriate responses to an offense detected by an organization's compliance program?

    I. Disciplinary action taken against those engaged in misconduct is an appropriate response.

    II. Self-reporting the violation to the government is an appropriate response.

    III. Acceptance of responsibility for the violation is an appropriate response.

    IV. An appropriate response can lower the amount of an organization's court fines.

    A. I and II only.

    B. I and III only.

    C. I, II, and III only.

    D. I, II, III, and IV.

Answer (D) is correct. *(Publisher, adapted)*
    REQUIRED: The true statement(s) regarding appropriate responses to an offense detected by an organization's compliance program.
    DISCUSSION: An organization should respond appropriately to each offense detected by the compliance program. Appropriate responses include disciplinary action taken with regard to those who engaged in misconduct. In some circumstances, an appropriate response could require self-reporting the violation to the government, cooperation with governmental investigations, and the acceptance of responsibility for the violation. Similar to the existence of an effective compliance program, making these responses could result in a court lowering the amount of the organization's fine.

19. A manufacturing organization uses hazardous materials in production of its products. An audit of these hazardous materials may include

I. Recommending an environmental management system as a part of policies and procedures.

II. Verifying the existence of "cradle to grave" (creation to destruction) tracking records for these materials.

III. Using consultants to avoid self-incrimination of the firm in the event illegalities were detected in an environmental audit.

IV. Evaluating the cost provided for in an environmental liability accrual account.

    A. II only.

    B. I and II only.

    C. I, II, and IV only.

    D. III and IV only.

Answer (C) is correct. *(CIA, adapted)*
    REQUIRED: The test(s) performed in an audit of hazardous materials.
    DISCUSSION: An organization subject to environmental laws and regulations having a significant effect on its operations should establish an environmental management system. One feature of this system is environmental auditing, which includes reviewing the adequacy and effectiveness of the controls over hazardous waste. Environmental auditing is in large measure a response to laws that impose management requirements on generators, transporters, and owners of waste as well as on operators of treatment, storage, and disposal facilities. For example, some laws provide for cradle-to-grave control of hazardous waste. Environmental auditing also extends to review of the reasonableness of contingent liabilities accrued for environmental remediation.
    Answer (A) is incorrect because a hazardous materials audit may include verifying tracking records. Answer (B) is incorrect because a hazardous materials audit may include recommending an environmental management system and verifying tracking records. Answer (D) is incorrect because use of consultants is not necessary to avoid self-incrimination. Internal auditors who discover violations of environmental laws are not required to report to external parties.

20. An organization is considering purchasing a commercial property. Because of the location of the property and the known recent history of activities on the property, management has asked the internal audit activity, in cooperation with legal counsel, to provide a preliminary identification of any environmental liability. The strongest reason supporting management's decision to request such an investigation is

    A. The potential for future liability may outweigh any advantages achieved by obtaining the property.

    B. Management will be able to pay a lower price for the property if environmental contamination can be identified.

    C. The current owner would be required by law to clean up all identified contamination before the sale is closed.

    D. Regulatory agencies require a purchaser to identify and disclose all actual and potential instances of contamination.

Answer (A) is correct. *(CIA, adapted)*
    REQUIRED: The strongest reason for management to request the internal audit activity to investigate a land purchase for any environmental liability.
    DISCUSSION: The internal auditors should conduct a transactional audit prior to the acquisition of property. A current landowner may be held responsible for environmental contamination by previous owners. Thus, a buyer (or lender) can attempt to identify and quantify a problem, determine its extent, and estimate the potential liability and cost of cleanup. This information can then be reflected in the terms of the transaction.
    Answer (B) is incorrect because, although the price of contaminated property may be lower, management may want to avoid the potential liability altogether by not purchasing the property. Answer (C) is incorrect because the current owner may agree to clean up the site but may be under no legal obligation to do so. Answer (D) is incorrect because purchasers are not required to disclose any instances of contamination, whether actual or potential.

21. Internal auditors are increasingly called on to perform audits related to an organization's environmental stewardship. Which of the following does not describe the objectives of a type of environmental audit?

    A. Determine whether environmental management systems are in place and operating properly to manage future environmental risks.

    B. Determine whether environmental issues are considered as part of economic decisions.

    C. Determine whether the organization's current actions are in compliance with existing laws.

    D. Determine whether the organization is focusing efforts on ensuring that its products are environmentally friendly, and confirm that product and chemical restrictions are met.

Answer (B) is correct. *(CIA, adapted)*
    REQUIRED: The item that does not describe the objectives of an environmental audit.
    DISCUSSION: Determining whether environmental issues are considered as part of economic decisions is an audit procedure. It does not describe the objectives of an environmental audit.
    Answer (A) is incorrect because an environmental management system audit determines whether environmental management systems are in place and operating properly to manage future environmental risks. Answer (C) is incorrect because a compliance audit determines whether the organization's current actions are in compliance with existing laws. Answer (D) is incorrect because a product audit determines whether the organization focuses efforts on ensuring that its products are environmentally friendly and confirms that product and chemical restrictions are met.

22. An internal auditor has been requested to perform a review of an organization's process for developing accruals for its liability to clean up toxic waste sites. The audit should determine whether

A. The organization monitors governmental investigations to identify locations where it may be potentially responsible for a waste site clean-up.

B. The organization has identified the situations in which it is potentially responsible for cleaning up a waste site.

C. Clean-up costs are reasonably estimated.

D. All of the answers are correct.

Answer (D) is correct. *(CIA, adapted)*
REQUIRED: The objectives of an audit of environmental liabilities.
DISCUSSION: The internal auditor must perform an environmental liability accrual audit. Such accruals are necessary because all owners of hazardous materials in the chain of title are liable. Hence, a contingent liability may exist not only when an organization is a current owner of a toxic waste site but also when it is a former owner. The organization should therefore engage in sufficient fact finding to identify potential liabilities and estimate their amounts.

23. In any entity-wide risk management assessment, the CAE should include risks associated with which kind of the following activities?

A. Environmental.

B. Health.

C. Safety.

D. All of the answers are correct.

Answer (D) is correct. *(Publisher, adapted)*
REQUIRED: The risks associated with which kind of activities that should be included in any entity-wide risk management assessment by the CAE.
DISCUSSION: Chief Audit Executive (CAE) should include the environmental, health, and safety (EH&S) risks in any entity-wide risk management assessment and assess the activities in a balanced manner relative to other types of risk associated with an entity's operations. Among the risk exposures that should be evaluated are organizational reporting structures; likelihood of causing environmental harm, fines, and penalties; expenditures mandated by Environmental Protection Agency (EPA) or other governmental agencies; history of injuries and deaths; record of losses of customers, and episodes of negative publicity and loss of public image and reputation.
Answer (A) is incorrect because any entity-wide risk management assessment should include environmental risks. Answer (B) is incorrect because any entity-wide risk management assessment should include health risks. Answer (C) is incorrect because any entity-wide risk management assessment should include safety risks.

24. The Environmental, Health, and Safety Auditing Roundtable (EH&S; new name is The Auditing Roundtable) commissioned Richard L. Ratliff of Utah State University and a group of researchers to perform a study of environmental, health, and safety auditing. The study found that the EH&S audit function is a

A. Technical field that is best placed within the internal audit function.

B. Subjective field that is best placed within the internal audit function.

C. Technical field that is best placed within the EH&S function.

D. Subjective field that is best placed within the EH&S function.

Answer (C) is correct. *(Publisher, adapted)*
REQUIRED: The findings of The Auditing Roundtable study on what management believes is the proper place in the organizational structure for the EH&S audit function.
DISCUSSION: The researchers found that the EH&S audit function is somewhat isolated from other organizational auditing activities. It is organized separately from internal auditing and is only tangentially related to external audits of financial statements. It reports to an EH&S executive, not to the governing board or to senior management. This structure suggests that management believes EH&S auditing to be a technical field that is best placed within the EH&S function of the organization.
Answer (A) is incorrect because the study's findings suggest that management believes EH&S auditing is best placed within the EH&S function, not the internal audit function. Answer (B) is incorrect because the study's findings suggest that management believes EH&S auditing is a technical field, not a subjective field and because it is best placed within the EH&S function, not the internal audit function. Answer (D) is incorrect because the study's findings suggest that management believes EH&S auditing is a technical field, not a subjective field.

25. Which of the following suggestions for the CAE related to EH&S auditing is false?

A. The CAE should foster a close working relationship with the chief environmental officer and coordinate activities with the plan for environmental auditing.

B. At least once every three years, the CAE should schedule a quality assurance review of the environmental audit function if it is organizationally independent of the internal audit function.

C. The CAE should evaluate the organizational placement and independence of the environmental audit function to ensure that significant matters resulting from serious risks to the enterprise are reported up the chain of command.

D. The CAE should evaluate whether the environmental auditors, who are not part of the CAE's organization, are in compliance with recognized professional auditing standards and a recognized code of ethics.

Answer (B) is correct. *(Publisher, adapted)*
REQUIRED: The CAE suggestion that is falsely stated.
DISCUSSION: According to PA 2100-7, the CAE should foster a close working relationship with the chief environmental officer and coordinate activities with the plan for environmental auditing. In those instances where the environmental audit function reports to someone other than the CAE, the CAE should offer to review the audit plan and the performance of engagements. Periodically, the CAE should schedule a quality assurance review of the environmental audit function if it is organizationally independent of the internal audit activity. That review should determine if the environmental risks are being adequately addressed. The CAE should evaluate whether the environmental auditors, who are not part of the CAE's organization, are in compliance with recognized professional auditing standards and a recognized code of ethics. The CAE should evaluate the organizational placement and independence of the environmental audit function to ensure that significant matters resulting from serious risks to the enterprise are reported up the chain of command to the audit or other committee of the governing board.

26. All of the following would be part of a factory's control system to prevent release of wastewater that does not meet discharge standards except:

A. Performing chemical analysis of the water, prior to discharge, for components specified in the permit.

B. Specifying (by policy, training, and advisory signs) which substances may be disposed of via sinks and floor drains within the factory.

C. Periodically flushing sinks and floor drains with a large volume of clean water to ensure pollutants are sufficiently diluted.

D. Establishing a preventive maintenance program for the factory's pretreatment system.

Answer (C) is correct. *(CIA, adapted)*
REQUIRED: The procedure not a part of a factory's control system to prevent release of wastewater not meeting discharge standards.
DISCUSSION: Periodic dilution may not always prevent the release of pollutants that exceed the discharge limits. In the pollution prevention hierarchy used in pollution prevention audits, release without treatment is the least desirable option.
Answer (A) is incorrect because performing chemical analysis of the water, prior to discharge, for components specified in the permit is part of a factory's control system. Answer (B) is incorrect because specifying (by policy, training, and advisory signs) which substances may be disposed of via sinks and floor drains within the factory is part of a factory's control system. Answer (D) is incorrect because establishing a preventive maintenance program for the factory's pretreatment system is part of a factory's control system.

Questions 27 through 30 are based on the following information. An organization has two manufacturing facilities. Each facility has two manufacturing processes and a separate packaging process. The processes are similar at both facilities. Raw materials used include aluminum, materials to make plastic, various chemicals, and solvents. Pollution occurs at several operational stages, including raw materials handling and storage, process chemical use, finished goods handling, and disposal. Waste products produced during the manufacturing processes include several that are considered hazardous. The nonhazardous waste is transported to the local landfill. An outside waste vendor is used for the treatment, storage, and disposal of all hazardous waste.

Management is aware of the need for compliance with environmental laws. The organization recently developed an environmental policy including a statement that each employee is responsible for compliance with environmental laws.

27. Management is evaluating the need for an environmental audit program. Which one of the following should not be included as an overall program objective?

A. Conduct site assessments at both facilities.

B. Verify organizational compliance with all environmental laws.

C. Evaluate waste minimization opportunities.

D. Ensure management systems are adequate to minimize future environmental risks.

Answer (A) is correct. *(CIA, adapted)*
REQUIRED: The item not an overall objective of an environmental audit program.
DISCUSSION: An environmental audit program determines whether the organization's internal controls relevant to compliance with environmental policies, plans, procedures, laws, and regulations are adequate and effective. A specific procedure intended to achieve these objectives is a site assessment. This step would be performed during a specific environmental audit, such as a compliance or transactional audit. According to The IIA's publication on environmental auditing, there are seven types of environmental audits: compliance audits; environmental management system audits; transactional audits; treatment, storage, and disposal facility audits; pollution prevention audits; environmental liability accrual audits; and product audits.
Answer (B) is incorrect because an objective in a compliance audit is to verify company compliance with all environmental laws. Answer (C) is incorrect because an objective in a pollution prevention audit is to evaluate waste minimization opportunities. Answer (D) is incorrect because an objective in an environmental management system audit is to ensure management systems are adequate to minimize future environmental risks.

28. In many countries, the organization generating hazardous waste is responsible for the waste from "cradle to grave" (creation to destruction). A potential risk to the organization is the use of an outside vendor to process hazardous waste. Which of the following steps should be performed during a review of the waste vendor?

A. Review the vendor's documentation on hazardous material.

B. Review the financial solvency of the vendor.

C. Review the vendor's emergency response planning.

D. All of these steps should be performed during a review of the waste vendor.

Answer (D) is correct. *(CIA, adapted)*
REQUIRED: The procedure(s) performed during a review of an outside hazardous waste processor.
DISCUSSION: In addition to the procedures listed, the internal auditor should determine that the vendor is approved by the governmental entity that is responsible for environmental protection and should obtain the vendor's permit number. The internal auditor also should conduct an inspection of the vendor's facilities.

29. An advantage of conducting environmental audits under the direction of the internal audit activity is that

    A. Independence and authority are already in place.

    B. Technical expertise is more readily available.

    C. The financial aspects are de-emphasized.

    D. Internal auditing work products are confidential.

Answer (A) is correct. *(CIA, adapted)*
    REQUIRED: The advantage of conducting environmental audits under the direction of the IAA.
    DISCUSSION: The CAE should evaluate the organizational placement and independence of the environmental audit function to ensure that significant matters resulting from serious risks to the enterprise are reported up the chain of command to the audit or other committee of the governing board. The CAE also should facilitate the reporting of significant EH&S risk and control issues to the audit (or other board) committee (PA 2100-7). Thus, an advantage of conducting environmental audits under the direction of the IAA is that it has the appropriate organizational status. The IAA has an established place in the organization and normally has a broad scope of work permitting ready assimilation of the new function. Moreover, the CAE should be responsible to an individual in the organization with sufficient authority to promote independence and to ensure broad audit coverage, adequate consideration of engagement communications, and appropriate action on engagement recommendations.
    Answer (B) is incorrect because environmental audits are highly complex and require technical expertise. This complexity is an advantage of employing an environmental auditing group directed by a technically oriented department. Internal auditors normally do not have the technical expertise necessary to assume primary responsibility. Answer (C) is incorrect because an IAA is preferable when financial issues are important. Answer (D) is incorrect because engagement results should be disseminated to appropriate individuals (Standard 2440).

30. Management is exploring different ways of reducing or preventing pollution in manufacturing operations. The objective of a pollution prevention audit is to identify opportunities to minimize waste and eliminate pollution at the source. In what order should the following opportunities to reduce waste be considered?

    I. Recycling and reuse
    II. Elimination at the source
    III. Energy conservation
    IV. Recovery as a usable product
    V. Treatment

    A. V, II, IV, I, and III.

    B. IV, II, I, III, and V.

    C. I, III, IV, II, and V.

    D. III, IV, II, V, and I.

Answer (B) is correct. *(CIA, adapted)*
    REQUIRED: The order in which opportunities to reduce waste should be considered.
    DISCUSSION: A pollution prevention audit is a type of environmental audit that emphasizes source reduction and other strategies to minimize waste. Avoiding emissions may be cheaper and more efficient than exercising control after creation of pollutants. The first step in the pollution prevention hierarchy is to determine whether production processes yield materials that can be sold as separate products. The second step is source reduction, for example, by reengineering processes. The third step is recycling and reuse. Step four is conservation of energy. Steps five and six are treatment and disposal. Finally, the step with the lowest priority is release of pollutants into the environment.

4.2 Business Continuity

31. With respect to business interruptions, what is the most crucial element of business recovery?

    A. Information systems backup.

    B. Alternative communication systems and site facilities.

    C. Business impact assessments and resumption plans.

    D. Disaster recovery plan.

Answer (D) is correct. *(Publisher, adapted)*
    REQUIRED: The most crucial element of business recovery after business interruptions.
    DISCUSSION: A crucial element of business recovery is the existence of a comprehensive and current disaster recovery plan. A comprehensive plan would provide for emergency response procedures, alternative communication systems and site facilities, information systems backup, disaster recovery, business impact assessments and resumption plans, procedures for restoring utility services, and maintenance procedures for ensuring the readiness of the organization in the event of an emergency or disaster.
    Answer (A) is incorrect because information systems backup should be included in the disaster recovery plan, which is the most crucial element of business recovery. Answer (B) is incorrect because alternative communication systems and site facilities should be included in the disaster recovery plan, which is the most crucial element of business recovery. Answer (C) is incorrect because business impact assessments and resumption plans should be included in the disaster recovery plan, which is the most crucial element of business recovery.

32. The audit objective when auditing an organization's business continuity and disaster recovery plan is to

I. Verify that the plan is adequate to ensure the timely resumption of operations and processes after adverse circumstances.

II. Verify it is structured to incorporate important changes that could take place over time.

III. Verify that it reflects the current business operating environment.

    A. I and II.

    B. I and III.

    C. II and III.

    D. I, II, and III.

Answer (D) is correct. *(Publisher, adapted)*
    REQUIRED: The audit objective when auditing an organization's business continuity and disaster recovery plans.
    DISCUSSION: According to PA 2110-2, internal auditors should periodically audit the organization's business continuity and disaster recovery plan. The audit objective is to verify that the plan is adequate to ensure the timely resumption of operations and processes after adverse circumstances, and that it reflects the current business operating environment. Furthermore, the internal audit activity should examine the recovery plan to determine whether (1) it is structured to incorporate important changes that could take place over time, and (2) the revised plan will be communicated to the appropriate people inside and outside the organization.
    Answer (A) is incorrect because the audit objective when auditing an organization's disaster recovery and business continuity plan includes verifying that the plan is adequate to ensure the timely resumption of operations and processes after adverse circumstances. Answer (B) is incorrect because the audit objective when auditing an organization's disaster recovery and business continuity plan includes verifying that it is structured to incorporate important changes that could take place over time. Answer (C) is incorrect because the audit objective when auditing an organization's disaster recovery and business continuity plan includes verifying that the plan is adequate to ensure the timely resumption of operations and processes after adverse circumstances.

4.3 Due Diligence

33. Internal auditors are often called upon to either perform or assist the external auditor in performing a due diligence review. A due diligence review may be

A. A review of interim financial statements as directed by an underwriting firm.

B. An operational audit of a division of an organization to determine if divisional management is complying with laws and regulations.

C. A review of operations as requested by the audit committee to determine whether the operations comply with audit committee and organizational policies.

D. A review of financial statements and related disclosures in conjunction with a potential acquisition.

Answer (D) is correct. *(CIA, adapted)*
REQUIRED: The nature of a due diligence review.
DISCUSSION: A due diligence engagement is a service to determine the business justification for a major transaction, such as a business combination, and whether that justification is valid. Thus, the internal auditors and others may be part of a team that reviews the acquiree's operations, controls, financing, or disclosures of financial information.
Answer (A) is incorrect because, although the reviews may be used by the underwriter, they are not directed by the underwriter. Answer (B) is incorrect because the due diligence review is not an internal operational audit. Answer (C) is incorrect because the due diligence review is not an internal review for compliance with organizational policies.

34. An organization is considering purchasing a small toxic waste disposal business. The internal auditors are part of the team doing a due diligence review for the acquisition. The scope of the internal auditors' work will most likely not include

A. An evaluation of the merit of lawsuits currently filed against the acquiree.

B. A review of the acquiree's procedures for acceptance of waste material and comparison with legal requirements.

C. Analysis of the acquiree's compliance with, and disclosure of, loan covenants.

D. Assessment of the efficiency of the operations of the acquiree.

Answer (A) is correct. *(CIA, adapted)*
REQUIRED: The procedure not included in a due diligence review for an acquisition.
DISCUSSION: An evaluation of the merit of lawsuits requires legal expertise. At most, internal auditors are required to have an appreciation of the fundamentals of commercial law, that is, an ability to recognize the existence of problems or potential problems and to determine the further research to be undertaken or the assistance to be obtained (PA 1210.1). Hence, the internal auditors' responsibility is limited to using outside service providers to evaluate the merits of the lawsuits.
Answer (B) is incorrect because compliance with laws, regulations, and contracts is within the scope of internal auditing. Answer (C) is incorrect because compliance with laws, regulations, and contracts is within the scope of internal auditing. Answer (D) is incorrect because internal auditors evaluate controls, including those over effectiveness and efficiency of operations.

4.4 Quality

35. A traditional quality control process in manufacturing consists of mass inspection of goods only at the end of a production process. A major deficiency of the traditional control process is that

A. It is expensive to do the inspections at the end of the process.

B. It is not possible to rework defective items.

C. It is not 100% effective.

D. It does not focus on improving the entire production process.

Answer (D) is correct. *(CIA, adapted)*
REQUIRED: The major deficiency of a traditional quality control process.
DISCUSSION: The process used to produce the goods is not thoroughly reviewed and evaluated for efficiency and effectiveness. Preventing defects and increasing efficiency by improving the production process raises quality standards and decreases costs.
Answer (A) is incorrect because other quality control processes can also be expensive. Answer (B) is incorrect because reworking defective items may be possible although costly. Answer (C) is incorrect because no quality control system will be 100% effective.

Questions 36 and 37 are based on the following information. The management and employees of a large household goods moving company decided to adopt total quality management (TQM) and continuous improvement (CI). They believed that, if their company became nationally known as adhering to TQM and CI, one result would be an increase in the company's profits and market share.

36. The primary reason for adopting TQM was to achieve

A. Greater customer satisfaction.

B. Reduced delivery time.

C. Reduced delivery charges.

D. Greater employee participation.

Answer (A) is correct. *(CIA, adapted)*
REQUIRED: The primary reason for adopting TQM.
DISCUSSION: TQM is an integrated system that anticipates, meets, and exceeds customers' needs, wants, and expectations.
Answer (B) is incorrect because reduced delivery time is one of many potential activities that need improvement. Answer (C) is incorrect because reduced delivery charges is one of many potential activities that need improvement. Answer (D) is incorrect because increased employee participation is necessary to achieve TQM, but it is not the primary purpose for establishing the program.

37. Quality is achieved more economically if the company focuses on

A. Appraisal costs.

B. Prevention costs.

C. Internal failure costs.

D. External failure costs.

Answer (B) is correct. *(CIA, adapted)*
REQUIRED: The necessary focus for achieving quality more economically.
DISCUSSION: Prevention attempts to avoid defective output. Prevention costs include preventive maintenance, employee training, review of equipment design, and evaluation of suppliers. Prevention is less costly than detection and correction of defective output.

38. Under a total quality management (TQM) approach

A. Measurement occurs throughout the process, and errors are caught and corrected at the source.

B. Quality control is performed by highly trained inspectors at the end of the production process.

C. Upper management assumes the primary responsibility for the quality of the products and services.

D. A large number of suppliers are used in order to obtain the lowest possible prices.

Answer (A) is correct. *(CIA, adapted)*
REQUIRED: The true statement about total quality management.
DISCUSSION: Total quality management emphasizes quality as a basic organizational function. TQM is the continuous pursuit of quality in every aspect of organizational activities. One of the basic tenets of TQM is doing it right the first time. Thus, errors should be caught and corrected at the source.
Answer (B) is incorrect because total quality management emphasizes discovering errors throughout the process, not inspection of finished goods. Answer (C) is incorrect because all members of the organization assume responsibility for quality of the products and services. Answer (D) is incorrect because the total quality management philosophy recommends limiting the number of suppliers to create a strong relationship.

39. Which of the following is a characteristic of total quality management (TQM)?

A. Management by objectives.

B. On-the-job training by other workers.

C. Quality by final inspection.

D. Education and self-improvement.

Answer (D) is correct. *(CIA, adapted)*
REQUIRED: The characteristic of TQM.
DISCUSSION: Education and self-improvement are essential. Knowledge is opportunity. Hence, continuous improvement should be everyone's primary career objective.
Answer (A) is incorrect because one of the 14 points recommends elimination of numerical quotas. MBO causes aggressive pursuit of numerical quotas. Answer (B) is incorrect because informal learning from coworkers serves to entrench bad work habits. One of the 14 points stresses proper training of everyone. Answer (C) is incorrect because another of the 14 points states that quality by final inspection is unnecessary if quality is built in from the start.

40. In which of the following organizational structures does total quality management (TQM) work best?

A. Hierarchal.

B. Teams of people from the same specialty.

C. Teams of people from different specialties.

D. Specialists working individually.

Answer (C) is correct.   *(CIA, adapted)*
REQUIRED: The structure in which TQM works best.
DISCUSSION: TQM advocates replacement of the traditional hierarchal structure with teams of people from different specialties. This change follows from TQM's emphasis on empowering employees and teamwork. Employees should have proper training, necessary information, and the best tools; be fully engaged in the decision process; and receive fair compensation. If such empowered employees are assembled in teams of individuals with the required skills, TQM theorists believe they will be more effective than people performing their tasks separately in a rigid structure.
Answer (A) is incorrect because hierarchal organization stifles TQM. Answer (B) is incorrect because TQM works best with teams of people from different specialties. Answer (D) is incorrect because teamwork is essential for TQM.

41. Which of the following quality costs are nonconformance costs?

A. Systems development costs.

B. Costs of inspecting in-process items.

C. Environmental costs.

D. Costs of quality circles.

Answer (C) is correct.   *(Publisher, adapted)*
REQUIRED: The nonconformance costs.
DISCUSSION: Nonconformance costs include internal and external failure costs. External failure costs include environmental costs, e.g., fines for violations of environmental laws and loss of customer goodwill.
Answer (A) is incorrect because systems development costs are prevention (conformance) costs. Answer (B) is incorrect because costs of inspecting in-process items are appraisal (conformance) costs. Answer (D) is incorrect because costs of quality circles are prevention (conformance) costs.

42. Quality costing is similar in service and manufacturing organizations. Nevertheless, the differences between these organizations have certain implications for quality management. Thus,

A. Direct labor costs are usually a higher percentage of total costs in manufacturing organizations.

B. External failure costs are relatively greater in service organizations.

C. Quality improvements resulting in more efficient use of labor time are more likely to be accepted by employees in service organizations.

D. Poor service is less likely to result in loss of customers than a faulty product.

Answer (B) is correct.   *(Publisher, adapted)*
REQUIRED: The true statement distinguishing quality considerations in service and manufacturing organizations.
DISCUSSION: External failure costs arise when problems occur after delivery. They occur because products or services are nonconforming or otherwise do not satisfy customers. External failure costs in service enterprises are even more important than in manufacturing environments. Faulty goods sometimes may be reworked or replaced to a customer's satisfaction, but poor service tends to result in a loss of customers.
Answer (A) is incorrect because direct labor costs are usually a higher percentage of total costs in service organizations. Answer (C) is incorrect because service activities are usually more labor intensive than in modern manufacturing environments. Thus, more efficient labor usage is more likely to be viewed as a threat to employee job security in service organizations. Answer (D) is incorrect because the badwill resulting from poor service may be even more likely than a defective product to result in loss of customers.

43. Which of the following criteria would be most useful to a sales department manager in evaluating the performance of the manager's customer-service group?

A. The customer is always right.

B. Customer complaints should be processed promptly.

C. Employees should maintain a positive attitude when dealing with customers.

D. All customer inquiries should be answered within 7 days of receipt.

Answer (D) is correct.   *(CIA, adapted)*
REQUIRED: The criterion most useful for evaluating a customer-service group.
DISCUSSION: A criterion that requires all customer inquiries to be answered within 7 days of receipt permits accurate measurement of performance. The quantitative and specific nature of the appraisal using this standard avoids the vagueness, subjectivity, and personal bias that may afflict other forms of personnel evaluations.
Answer (A) is incorrect because customer orientation is difficult to quantify. Answer (B) is incorrect because the standard specified is vague. Answer (C) is incorrect because no measure of a positive attitude has been specified for the employee.

44. Using the balanced scorecard approach, an organization evaluates managerial performance based on

    A. A single ultimate measure of operating results, such as residual income.

    B. Multiple financial and nonfinancial measures.

    C. Multiple nonfinancial measures only.

    D. Multiple financial measures only.

Answer (B) is correct. *(Publisher, adapted)*
    REQUIRED: The nature of the balanced scorecard approach.
    DISCUSSION: The trend in managerial performance evaluation is the balanced scorecard approach. Multiple measures of performance permit a determination as to whether a manager is achieving certain objectives at the expense of others that may be equally or more important. These measures may be financial or nonfinancial and usually include items in four categories: (1) financial; (2) customer; (3) internal business processes; and (4) learning, growth, and innovation.
    Answer (A) is incorrect because the balanced scorecard approach uses multiple measures. Answer (C) is incorrect because the balanced scorecard approach includes financial measures. Answer (D) is incorrect because the balanced scorecard approach includes nonfinancial measures.

45. Focusing on customers, promoting innovation, learning new philosophies, driving out fear, and providing extensive training are all elements of a major change in organizations. These elements are aimed primarily at

    A. Copying leading organizations to better compete with them.

    B. Focusing on the total quality of products and services.

    C. Being efficient and effective at the same time, in order to indirectly affect profits.

    D. Managing costs of products and services better, in order to become the low-cost provider.

Answer (B) is correct. *(CIA, adapted)*
    REQUIRED: The purpose of focusing on customers, promoting innovation, learning new philosophies, driving out fear, and providing extensive training.
    DISCUSSION: TQM is a comprehensive approach to quality. It treats the pursuit of quality as a basic organizational function that is as important as production or marketing. TQM is the continuous pursuit of quality in every aspect of organizational activities through a philosophy of doing it right the first time, employee training and empowerment, promotion of teamwork, improvement of processes, and attention to satisfaction of customers, both internal and external. TQM emphasizes the supplier's relationship with the customer, identifies customer needs, and recognizes that everyone in a process is at some time a customer or supplier of someone else, either within or without the organization.
    Answer (A) is incorrect because competitive benchmarking is just one tool for implementing TQM. Answer (C) is incorrect because TQM's primary focus is not profitability. Answer (D) is incorrect because TQM's primary focus is not cost reduction.

46. Total quality management in a manufacturing environment is best exemplified by

    A. Identifying and reworking production defects before sale.

    B. Designing the product to minimize defects.

    C. Performing inspections to isolate defects as early as possible.

    D. Making machine adjustments periodically to reduce defects.

Answer (B) is correct. *(CIA, adapted)*
    REQUIRED: The activity characteristic of TQM.
    DISCUSSION: Total quality management emphasizes quality as a basic organizational function. TQM is the continuous pursuit of quality in every aspect of organizational activities. One of the basic tenets of TQM is doing it right the first time. Thus, errors should be caught and corrected at the source, and quality should be built in (designed in) from the start.

47. One of the main reasons that implementation of a total quality management program works better through the use of teams is

    A. Teams are more efficient and help an organization reduce its staffing.

    B. Employee motivation is always higher for team members than for individual contributors.

    C. Teams are a natural vehicle for sharing ideas, which leads to process improvement.

    D. The use of teams eliminates the need for supervision, thereby allowing a company to reduce staffing.

Answer (C) is correct. *(CIA, adapted)*
    REQUIRED: The reason that implementation of a TQM program works better through the use of teams.
    DISCUSSION: TQM promotes teamwork by modifying or eliminating traditional (and rigid) vertical hierarchies and instead forming flexible groups of specialists. Quality circles, cross-functional teams, and self-managed teams are typical formats. Teams are an excellent vehicle for encouraging the sharing of ideas and removing process improvement obstacles.
    Answer (A) is incorrect because teams are often inefficient and costly. Answer (B) is incorrect because high motivation does not directly affect the process improvement that is the key to quality improvement. Answer (D) is incorrect because the use of teams with less supervision and reduced staffing may be by-products of TQM, but they are not ultimate objectives.

48. Which of the following is a key to successful total quality management?

    A. Training quality inspectors.

    B. Focusing intensely on the customer.

    C. Creating appropriate hierarchies to increase efficiency.

    D. Establishing a well-defined quality standard, then focusing on meeting it.

Answer (B) is correct. *(CIA, adapted)*
    REQUIRED: The key to successful total quality management.
    DISCUSSION: TQM emphasizes satisfaction of customers, both internal and external. TQM considers the supplier's relationship with the customer, identifies customer needs, and recognizes that everyone in a process is at some time a customer or supplier of someone else, either within or without the organization. Thus, TQM begins with external customer requirements, identifies internal customer-supplier relationships and requirements, and establishes requirements for external suppliers.
    Answer (A) is incorrect because total quality management (TQM) de-emphasizes specialized quality inspectors. Answer (C) is incorrect because centralization often needs to be reduced to implement a TQM process. Answer (D) is incorrect because TQM involves continuous improvement; once a standard is reached, continuous improvement requires its constant reevaluation.

49. One of the main reasons total quality management (TQM) can be used as a strategic weapon is that

    A. The cumulative improvement from a company's TQM efforts cannot readily be copied by competitors.

    B. Introducing new products can lure customers away from competitors.

    C. Reduced costs associated with better quality can support higher shareholder dividends.

    D. TQM provides a comprehensive planning process for a business.

Answer (A) is correct. *(CIA, adapted)*
    REQUIRED: The reason TQM can be used as a strategic weapon.
    DISCUSSION: TQM is a comprehensive approach to quality. It treats the pursuit of quality as a basic organizational function that is as important as production or marketing. Because TQM affects every aspect of the organization's activities, it permeates the organizational culture. Thus, the cumulative effect of TQM's continuous improvement process can attract and hold customers and cannot be duplicated by competitors.
    Answer (B) is incorrect because new products can be quickly copied by competitors and therefore do not provide a sustained competitive advantage. Answer (C) is incorrect because TQM does not focus solely on cost reduction. Answer (D) is incorrect because TQM is only one tool of strategic management.

50. Managerial performance may be measured in many ways. For example, an internal nonfinancial measure is

    A. Market share.

    B. Delivery performance.

    C. Customer satisfaction.

    D. Manufacturing lead time.

Answer (D) is correct. *(Publisher, adapted)*
    REQUIRED: The internal nonfinancial measure.
    DISCUSSION: Feedback regarding managerial performance may take the form of financial and nonfinancial measures that may be internally or externally generated. Moreover, different measures have a long-term or short-term emphasis. Examples of internal nonfinancial measures are product quality, new product development time, and manufacturing lead time (cycle time).
    Answer (A) is incorrect because market share is an external nonfinancial measure. Answer (B) is incorrect because delivery performance is an external nonfinancial measure. Answer (C) is incorrect because customer satisfaction is an external nonfinancial measure.

51. An organization's managerial decision-making model for capital budgeting is based on the net present value of discounted cash flows. The same organization's managerial performance evaluation model is based on annual divisional return on investment. Which of the following is true?

    A. Divisional managers are likely to maximize the measures in the decision-making model.

    B. Divisional managers are likely to maximize the measures in the performance evaluation model.

    C. The manager has an incentive to accept a project with a positive net present value that initially has a negative effect on net income.

    D. The use of models with different criteria promotes goal congruence.

Answer (B) is correct. *(Publisher, adapted)*
    REQUIRED: The true statement about use of different models for decision making and managerial evaluation.
    DISCUSSION: Effective management control requires performance measurement and feedback. This process affects allocation of resources to organizational subunits. It also affects decisions about managers' compensation, advancement, and future assignments. Furthermore, evaluating their performance serves to motivate managers to optimize the measures in the performance evaluation model. However, that model may be inconsistent with the organization's model for managerial decision making.
    Answer (A) is incorrect because self-interest provides an incentive to maximize the measures used in performance evaluation. Answer (C) is incorrect because a manager evaluated on the basis of annual ROI has an interest in maximizing short-term net income, not long-term NPV. Answer (D) is incorrect because the models should be synchronized so that the goals of the organization and the manager are congruent.

52. On a balanced scorecard, which of the following is not a customer measure?

A. Market share.

B. Economic value added.

C. Service response time.

D. Warranty expense.

Answer (B) is correct. *(Publisher, adapted)*
REQUIRED: The item that is not a customer measure on a balanced scorecard.
DISCUSSION: Customer measures include market share and its trend, service response time, delivery performance, warranty returns, expense, complaints, and survey results. Economic value added, or EVA, is a financial measure.
Answer (A) is incorrect because market share and its trend is a customer measure. Answer (C) is incorrect because service response time is a customer measure. Answer (D) is incorrect because warranty expense is a customer measure.

53. Reengineering is the thorough analysis, fundamental rethinking, and complete redesign of essential business processes. The intended result is a dramatic improvement in service, quality, speed, and cost. An internal auditor's involvement in reengineering should include all of the following except

A. Determining whether the process has senior management's support.

B. Recommending areas for consideration.

C. Developing audit plans for the new system.

D. Directing the implementation of the redesigned process.

Answer (D) is correct. *(CIA, adapted)*
REQUIRED: The item not included in an internal auditor's involvement in reengineering.
DISCUSSION: Internal auditors should not become directly involved in the implementation of the redesign process. This involvement would impair their independence and objectivity. Staff assignments of internal auditors should be rotated periodically whenever it is practicable to do so.

54. Monitoring is an important component of internal control. Which of the following items would not be an example of monitoring?

A. Management regularly compares divisional performance with budgets for the division.

B. Data processing management regularly generates exception reports for unusual transactions or volumes of transactions and follows up with investigation as to causes.

C. Data processing management regularly reconciles batch control totals for items processed with batch controls for items submitted.

D. Management has asked internal auditing to perform regular audits of the controls over cash processing.

Answer (C) is correct. *(CIA, adapted)*
REQUIRED: The item not an example of monitoring.
DISCUSSION: Monitoring assesses the quality of internal control over time. Management considers whether internal control is properly designed and operating as intended and modifies it to reflect changing conditions. Monitoring may be in the form of separate, periodic evaluations or of ongoing monitoring. Ongoing monitoring occurs as part of routine operations. It includes management and supervisory review, comparisons, reconciliations, and other actions by personnel as part of their regular activities. However, reconciling batch control totals is a processing control.
Answer (A) is incorrect because budgetary comparison is a typical example of a monitoring control. Answer (B) is incorrect because investigation of exceptions is a monitoring control used by lower-level management to determine when their operations may be out of control. Answer (D) is incorrect because internal auditing is a form of monitoring. It serves to evaluate management's other controls.

55. An example of an internal nonfinancial benchmark is

A. The labor rate of comparably skilled employees at a major competitor's plant.

B. The average actual cost per pound of a specific product at the company's most efficient plant.

C. A $50,000 limit on the cost of employee training programs at each of the company's plants.

D. The percentage of customer orders delivered on time at the company's most efficient plant.

Answer (D) is correct. *(CIA, adapted)*
REQUIRED: The internal nonfinancial benchmark.
DISCUSSION: Benchmarking is a continuous evaluation of the practices of the best organizations in their class and the adaptation of processes to reflect the best of these practices. It entails analysis and measurement of key outputs against those of the best organizations. This procedure also involves identifying the underlying key actions and causes that contribute to the performance difference. The percentage of orders delivered on time at the company's most efficient plant is an example of an internal nonfinancial benchmark.
Answer (A) is incorrect because the labor rate of comparably skilled employees at a major competitor's plant is a subsequent phase. Answer (B) is incorrect because the average actual cost per pound of a specific product at the company's most efficient plant is a subsequent phase. Answer (C) is incorrect because a $50,000 limit on the cost of employee training programs at each of the company's plants is a subsequent phase.

4.5 Information Security and Privacy

56. Which of the following statements is false with respect to information security?

A. Internal auditors should determine that management and the board, audit committee, or other governing body have a clear understanding that information security is the responsibility of the internal audit activity.

B. The chief audit executive should determine that the internal audit activity possesses, or has access to, competent auditing resources to evaluate information security and associated risk exposures.

C. Internal auditors should periodically assess the organization's information security practices and recommend, as appropriate, enhancements to, or implementation of, new controls and safeguards.

D. Internal auditors should assess the effectiveness of preventive, detective, and mitigative measures against past attacks, as deemed appropriate, and future attempts or incidents deemed likely to occur.

Answer (A) is correct. *(Publisher, adapted)*
REQUIRED: The false statement about information security.
DISCUSSION: According to PA 2100-2, internal auditors should determine that management and the board, audit committee, or other governing body have a clear understanding that information security is a management responsibility. This responsibility includes all critical information of the organization regardless of media in which the information is stored.

57. The internal auditors' ultimate responsibility for information security includes

A. Identifying technical aspects, risks, processes, and transactions to be examined.

B. Determining the scope and degree of testing to achieve engagement objectives.

C. Periodically assessing information security practices.

D. Documenting engagement procedures.

Answer (C) is correct. *(Publisher, adapted)*
REQUIRED: The internal auditors' ultimate responsibility for information security.
DISCUSSION: "Internal auditors should periodically assess the organization's information security practices and recommend, as appropriate, enhancements to, or implementation of, new controls and safeguards. Following an assessment, an assurance report should be provided to the board, audit committee, or other appropriate governing body. Such assessments can either be conducted as separate stand-alone engagements or as multiple engagements integrated into other audits or engagements conducted as part of the approved audit plan" (PA 2100-2).
Answer (A) is incorrect because an engagement work program is part of the planning process, which includes identifying technical aspects, risks, processes, and transactions to be examined. Answer (B) is incorrect because an engagement work program is part of the planning process, which includes determining the scope and degree of testing to achieve engagement objectives. Answer (D) is incorrect because an engagement work program is part of the planning process, which includes documenting engagement procedures.

58. Which of the following is not a role of the internal audit activity in performing assurance services?

A. Assessing information systems security risks.

B. Working with information system users and system security personnel to implement controls.

C. Monitoring the implementation of corrective action.

D. Evaluating security controls.

Answer (B) is correct. *(Publisher, adapted)*
REQUIRED: The answer choice that is not a role of the internal audit activity in performing assurance services.
DISCUSSION: The role of the internal audit activity with respect to assurance services is to assess information systems security risks, monitor the implementation of corrective action, and evaluate security controls. The internal audit activity may also function in a consulting capacity by identifying security issues and by working with users of information systems and with systems security personnel to devise and implement controls.
Answer (A) is incorrect because assessing information systems security risks is part of the role the internal audit activity with respect to assurance services. Answer (C) is incorrect because monitoring the implementation of corrective action is part of the role the internal audit activity with respect to assurance services. Answer (D) is incorrect because evaluating security controls is part of the role the internal audit activity with respect to assurance services.

59. Which of the following is not an issue that internal auditors should address when performing a privacy engagement?

A. Compliance with governmental statutory and regulatory mandates.

B. Documentation of compliance with privacy and other legal requirements.

C. Whether the benefits of the security arrangements exceed the costs.

D. The moral imperative for management to provide accurate private information.

Answer (D) is correct. *(Publisher, adapted)*
REQUIRED: The issue that need not be addressed in a privacy engagement.
DISCUSSION: Six issues should be addressed: (1) compliance with governmental mandates, (2) protection of personal information from both unauthorized intrusion and misuse by those who have authorized access, (3) balancing of privacy with the need to allow appropriate and prompt availability of personal information to legitimate users, (4) documentation of compliance with privacy and other legal requirements, (5) whether the benefits of security arrangements exceed the costs, and (6) the ethical imperative for the internal auditors to maintain the confidentiality of private information. There is no moral imperative for management to provide accurate private information.

4.6 Other Engagements

60. Which type of engagement focuses on operations and how effectively and efficiently the organizational units affected will cooperate?

A. Program-results engagement.

B. Process engagement.

C. Privacy engagement.

D. Compliance engagement.

Answer (B) is correct. *(Publisher, adapted)*
REQUIRED: The engagement that focuses cooperation of operating subunits.
DISCUSSION: Process engagements tend to be challenging because of their scope and the need to deal with subunits that may have conflicting objectives.
Answer (A) is incorrect because a program-results engagement obtains information about the costs, outputs, benefits, and effects of a program. Answer (C) is incorrect because privacy engagements address the security of personal information. Answer (D) is incorrect because compliance engagements address compliance with all laws and regulations.

61. Which type of engagement attempts to measure the accomplishment and relative success of the undertaking?

A. Program-results engagement.

B. Privacy engagement.

C. Process engagement.

D. Compliance engagement.

Answer (A) is correct. *(Publisher, adapted)*
REQUIRED: The engagement to measure the accomplishment and relative success of the undertaking.
DISCUSSION: A program-results engagement obtains information about the costs, outputs, benefits, and effects of a program. It attempts to measure the accomplishment and relative success of the undertaking. Because benefits often cannot be quantified in financial terms, a special concern is the ability to measure effectiveness. A program is a funded activity not part of the normal, continuing operations of the organization.
Answer (B) is incorrect because a privacy engagement addresses the security of personal information. Answer (C) is incorrect because a process engagement addresses how effectively and efficiently operating units cooperate. Answer (D) is incorrect because a compliance engagement addresses compliance with related laws and regulations.

Use Gleim's *CIA Test Prep* for interactive testing with **over 2,000 additional multiple-choice questions!**

STUDY UNIT FIVE
INFORMATION TECHNOLOGY I

(40 pages of outline)

This study unit addresses the nature and modes of computer processing, the elements of the IT function, and basic control concepts. It continues with a treatment of computer hardware and operating systems. The concluding subunits concern various aspects of system security, including planning for business continuity in the event of an interruption of computer processing.

Part II of the exam should have 5 to 7 IT questions. On Part II, The IIA tests IT at the awareness level. However, the same IT topics are tested at the proficiency level on Part III. Thus, a candidate sitting only for Part II need only be comfortable with the terms and concepts in Study Units 5 and 6 of Part II. But a candidate who intends to take Parts II and III should understand that Study Units 5 and 6 in Part II and Study Units 8, 9, and 10 in Part III significantly overlap. In this scenario, studying Parts II and III simultaneously is efficient.

Core Concepts

- Characteristics such as the uniform processing of transactions and the loss of segregation of functions distinguish computer-based from manual systems.

- All information processing must be properly controlled. Controls over information systems can be classified as general controls and application controls.

- The earliest forms of computer processing were highly centralized. Increasingly, processing is becoming decentralized.

- With distributed processing, an organization determines which parts of an application are better performed locally and which parts are better performed at some other, possibly centralized, site.

- A computer's hardware includes a central processing unit (CPU), data entry devices such as keyboards and scanners, output devices such as monitors and printers, and storage devices such as hard drives.

- When an organization develops a new system, the life-cycle approach allows for enhanced management and control of the process.

- System security encompasses data integrity, access controls, application controls, systems development standards, change controls, controls over end-user computing, and Internet security.

- A computer center should have a reconstruction and recovery plan that will allow it to regenerate important programs and database files.

5.1 INTRODUCTION TO IT

1.   **Characteristics.** The use of computers in business information systems has fundamental effects on the nature of business transacted, the procedures followed, the risks incurred, and the methods of mitigating those risks. These effects flow from the characteristics that distinguish computer-based from manual processing.

   a.   **Transaction trails.** A complete trail useful for audit and other purposes might exist for only a short time or only in computer-readable form. The nature of the trail is often dependent on the transaction processing mode, for example, whether transactions are batched prior to processing or whether they are processed immediately as they happen.

   b.   **Uniform processing of transactions.** Computer processing uniformly subjects like transactions to the same processing instructions and thus virtually eliminates clerical error, but programming errors (or other similar systematic errors in either the hardware or software) will result in all like transactions being processed incorrectly when they are processed under the same conditions.

   c.   **Segregation of functions.** Many controls once performed by separate individuals may be concentrated in computer systems. Hence, an individual who has access to the computer may perform incompatible functions. As a result, other controls may be necessary to achieve the control objectives ordinarily accomplished by segregation of functions.

   d.   **Potential for errors and fraud.** The potential for individuals, including those performing control procedures, to gain unauthorized access to data, to alter data without visible evidence, or to gain access (direct or indirect) to assets may be greater in computer systems. Decreased human involvement in handling transactions can reduce the potential for observing errors and fraud. Errors or fraud in the design or changing of application programs can remain undetected for a long time.

   e.   **Potential for increased management supervision.** Computer systems offer management many analytical tools for review and supervision of operations. These additional controls may enhance internal control. For example, traditional comparisons of actual and budgeted operating ratios and reconciliations of accounts are often available for review on a more timely basis. Furthermore, some programmed applications provide statistics regarding computer operations that may be used to monitor actual processing.

   f.   **Initiation or subsequent execution of transactions by computer.** Certain transactions may be automatically initiated or certain procedures required to execute a transaction may be automatically performed by a computer system. The authorization of these transactions or procedures may not be documented in the same way as those in a manual system, and management's authorization may be implicit in its acceptance of the design of the system.

   g.   **Dependence of controls in other areas on controls over computer processing.** Computer processing may produce reports and other output that are used in performing manual control procedures. The effectiveness of these controls can be dependent on the effectiveness of controls over the completeness and accuracy of computer processing. For example, the effectiveness of a manual review of a computer-produced exception listing is dependent on the controls over the production of the listing.

2. **Classification of controls.** The broad categories are outlined as follows:

    a. **General controls** apply to all computer activities. They often include controls over the development, modification, and maintenance of computer programs and controls over the use of and changes to data maintained on computer files. General controls encompass

        1) The plan of organization and operation of the computer activity

            a) **Organizational controls** address the proper segregation of duties and responsibilities within the computer processing environment.

            b) **Operating controls** ensure efficient and effective operation within the computer department.

                i) These controls also ensure that proper procedures are followed in case of data loss because of error or disaster.

                ii) Typical operating controls include the proper labeling of all files both internally (machine-readable file header and trailer labels) and externally, halt and error procedures, duplicate files, and reconstruction procedures for files.

        2) The procedures for documenting, reviewing, testing, and approving systems or programs and changes in them

            a) **Program development and documentation controls** are concerned with the proper planning, development, writing, and testing of computer application programs.

                i) These activities require proper documentation, including flowcharts, listings, and run manuals for programs already written.

                ii) Controls over proper authorization of any changes in existing programs are also necessary.

        3) Controls built into the equipment by the manufacturer (**hardware controls**)

            a) Hardware controls ensure the proper internal handling of data as they are moved and stored. They include parity checks, echo checks, read-after-write checks, and any other procedure built into the equipment to ensure data integrity.

        4) Controls over access to equipment and data files

            a) **Access controls** provide assurance that only authorized individuals use the system and that usage is for authorized purposes. Such controls include physical safeguards of equipment, proper library security, and passwords.

        5) Other data and procedural controls affecting overall computer operations

    b. **Application controls** relate to specific tasks performed by the system. They should provide reasonable assurance that the recording, processing, and reporting of data are properly performed. Application controls relate to individual computerized accounting applications, for example, programmed edit controls for verifying customers' account numbers and credit limits.

        1) **Input controls** provide reasonable assurance that data received for processing have been properly authorized, converted into machine-sensible form, and identified. They also provide reasonable assurance that data (including data transmitted over communication lines) have not been lost, suppressed, added, duplicated, or otherwise improperly changed. Moreover, input controls relate to rejection, correction, and resubmission of data that were initially incorrect.

2) **Processing controls** provide reasonable assurance that processing has been performed as intended for the particular application. All transactions should be processed as authorized, no authorized transactions should be omitted, and no unauthorized transactions should be added.

3) **Output controls** provide assurance that the processing result (such as account listings or displays, reports, files, invoices, or disbursement checks) is accurate and that only authorized personnel receive the output.

3. **Functional areas of IT operations.** Controls should ensure the efficiency and effectiveness of IT operations. They include proper segregation of the duties within the IT environment. Thus, the responsibilities of systems analysts, programmers, operators, file librarians, the control group, and others should be assigned to different individuals, and proper supervision should be provided.

a. **Segregation of duties.** This general control is vital because a traditional segregation of responsibilities for authorization, recording, and access to assets may not be feasible in an IT environment.

1) For example, a computer may print checks, record disbursements, and generate information for reconciling the account balance, which are activities customarily segregated in a manual system.

a) If the same person provides the input and receives the output for this process, a significant control weakness exists. Accordingly, certain tasks should not be combined.

4. **Responsibilities of IT Personnel**

a. **Systems analysts** are specifically qualified to analyze and design computer information systems. They survey the existing system, analyze the organization's information requirements, and design new systems to meet those needs. The design specifications will guide the preparation of specific programs by computer programmers.

1) Systems analysts should not have access to computer equipment, production programs, data files, and input-output controls.

b. The **database administrator (DBA)** is the individual who has overall responsibility for developing and maintaining the database and for establishing controls to protect its integrity.

1) Thus, only the DBA should be able to update **data dictionaries**.

2) In small systems, the DBA may perform some functions of a **database management system (DBMS)** (see Subunit 6.2). In larger applications, the DBA uses a DBMS as a primary tool.

c. **Programmers** design, write, test, and document the specific programs according to specifications developed by the analysts.

1) Programmers as well as analysts may be able to modify programs, data files, and controls. Thus, they should have no access to computer equipment and files or to copies of programs used in production.

d. The **webmaster** is responsible for the content of the organization's website. (S)he works closely with programmers and network technicians to ensure that the appropriate content is displayed and that the site is reliably available to users.

e. **Operators** are responsible for the day-to-day functioning of the computer center, whether the organization runs a mainframe, servers, or anything in between.

    1) Operators load data, mount storage devices, and operate the equipment. Operators should not be assigned programming duties or responsibility for systems design. Accordingly, they also should have no opportunity to make changes in programs and systems as they operate the equipment.

        a) Ideally, computer operators should not have programming knowledge or access to documentation not strictly necessary for their work.

f. **Help desks** are usually a responsibility of computer operations because of the operational nature of their functions. Help desk personnel log reported problems, resolve minor problems, and forward more difficult problems to the appropriate information systems resources, such as a **technical support unit** or **vendor assistance**.

g. **Network technicians** maintain the bridges, hubs, routers, switches, cabling, and other devices that interconnect the organization's computers. They are also responsible for maintaining the organization's connection to other networks such as the Internet.

h. **End users** need access to applications data and functions only.

5. **Data center operations** may occur in a centralized data processing facility that is responsible for the storage, management, and dissemination of data and information. A data center may be either an internal department or a separate organization that specializes in providing data services to others. A data center may operate in several possible modes.

a. **Batch mode.** Batch processing is the accumulation and grouping of transactions for processing on a delayed basis. The batch approach is suitable for applications that can be processed at intervals and involve large volumes of similar items, e.g., payroll, sales, inventory, and billing.

    1) **Service bureaus** perform batch processing for subscribers. This off-site mode of processing requires a user to prepare input and then transmit it to the bureau, with attendant increase in security problems. Employing a service bureau is one means of **outsourcing.**

    2) Hiring a **facilities management organization** is another. A facilities management organization operates and manages an internal data processing activity. It may manage hardware, software, system development, system maintenance, and staffing. The facilities manager may own all of the hardware and software and employ all the personnel.

b. **Online mode.** An online processing system is in direct communication with the computer, giving it the capability to handle transactions as they are entered. An online system permits both immediate posting (updating) and inquiry of master files as transactions occur.

    1) **Real-time processing** involves processing an input record and receiving the output soon enough to affect a current decision-making process. In a real-time system, the user interacts with the system to control an ongoing activity.

    2) The term "online," often used with "real time," indicates that the decision maker is in direct communication with the computer. **Online, real-time systems** usually permit access to the main computer from multiple remote terminals.

c. Many applications use **combined batch and online** modes.

    1) In such systems, users continuously enter transactions in online mode throughout the workday, collecting them in batches. The computer can then take advantage of the efficiencies of batch mode overnight when there are fewer users logged on to the system.

d.   A **timesharing** system allows many users to have access through remote terminals to a CPU (see item 4. in Subunit 5.2) owned by a vendor of computing services. The CPU services them alternately. Timesharing differs from multiprogramming because the CPU devotes a fixed time to each user's program.

e.   **Totally centralized systems.** All data processing and systems development are done at one data processing center.

1)   All processing is done by one large computer.

2)   Remote users are serviced via data communications channels between themselves and the center.

3)   Terminals at the remote sites are usually dumb terminals (providing communications only, with no stand-alone processing capabilities).

4)   Requests for development of new systems are submitted for the consideration of the centralized systems development group.

5)   The centralized staff is large.

6)   Advantages of total centralization arise primarily from (a) possible economies of scale and (b) the strengthening of control through segregation of duties.

f.   **Totally decentralized systems.** Data processing functions are independently developed at each remote site. Each site has its own smaller computer and its own staff.

1)   In a completely decentralized system, each computer stands alone, independent of any centralized or other computer.

2)   The primary advantages of a decentralized system are that

a)   The individual units' personnel identify more closely with the system.

b)   Development projects are more easily accepted and meet local needs better.

g.   **Downsizing** consists of moving organization-wide applications to mid-range or networked computers. The purpose is to reduce costs by using less expensive systems that are more versatile than larger, more expensive systems.

1)   Factors to consider when downsizing include the following:

a)   Downsized applications are less reliable than their mainframe predecessors because they usually are newer and thus have not been tested extensively.

b)   Downsized technology is less reliable and lacks the monitoring and control features that permit recovery from minor processing interruptions.

c)   Security is better on larger mainframe systems.

d)   Downsized applications increase complexity because data becomes fragmented across multiple systems.

e)   Applications with very large databases still require very large computers (i.e., mainframes) in order to make data accessible.

f)   Mainframes allow for easier and cheaper data entry.

h.   **Distributed Data Processing**

1)   In a distributed data processing system, the organization's processing needs are examined in their totality.

2)   Information is analyzed to determine which parts of the application are better performed locally and which parts are better performed at some other, possibly centralized, site.

a)   For example, an organization may prefer to use workstations rather than a mainframe for ad hoc queries to avoid the expense and the possible degradation of response time on the host computer.

b)   An advantage of distributed processing is **fail-soft protection**, that is, the ability to continue processing at all sites except a nonfunctioning one.

3)   The key distinction between decentralized and distributed systems is the interconnection among the nodes (sites) in the network.

4)   EXAMPLE: In processing a sales order, order entry may be handled by an intelligent terminal. Upon the completion of the sales order, the terminal will transmit it to a computer in a local warehouse. This computer will determine whether the item is available by interrogating an inventory file at the organization's manufacturing plant. If the item is available, the paperwork is produced locally at the warehouse, and the clerk at the terminal is notified. If it is not available, the plant's computer determines the probable delay before the item is available. This information is transmitted via the local warehouse computer to the terminal. If this delay is acceptable to the customer, the production paperwork is performed at the plant. Thus, the actual processing of the order entry is shared by the intelligent terminal, the warehouse computer, and the manufacturing plant computer.

5)   The increased **interdependence among processing sites** allows greater flexibility in systems design and the possibility of an optimal distribution of processing tasks. The process of deciding on the best distribution of processing capabilities (hardware), safeguards (controls), information (files and databases), and personnel is complex.

6)   **Cooperative processing** is a system in which computers in a distributed processing network can share the use of application programs belonging to another end user. The system assigns different machines the functions they perform best in executing a transaction-based application program. In other words, separate sections of an application may reside on different computers. In contrast, traditional distributed processing performed a task on one computer, with other computers used for communications.

a)   For example, a personal computer may be more cost effective for entering and validating data for the application. It is better suited for frequent screen updating and graphical user interfaces. A mainframe might handle file input and output.

7)   Updating data in a distributed system may require special protocols. Thus, a **two-phase commit disk-writing protocol** is used. If data is to be updated in two places, databases in both locations are cleared for updating before either one performs (commits) the update. In the first phase, both locations agree to the update. In the second phase, both perform the update.

8)   The development of distributed systems may be hindered because of the existence of legacy systems, which are applications developed with older technology that are an integral part of the entity's computer processing and are difficult to modify or replace. Conversely, less software has been developed for the newer distributed processing technology.

9)   **Response times** in distributed networks will depend on the volume of data traffic; i.e., the greater the data traffic, such as transactions, security checking and other network functions, and backups, the longer the response time.

10) **Backing up** software and data files also is a significant issue in distributed and cooperative systems. Because the systems are controlled by users, not a central information processing department, user management must be responsible for adequate backup.

6. **Computer auditing.** One Specific Attribute Standard and one Practice Advisory address this topic.

> **1220**   *Due Professional Care* – Internal auditors should apply the care and skill expected of a reasonably prudent and competent internal auditor. Due professional care does not imply infallibility.

a. **PRACTICE ADVISORY 1220-2: COMPUTER ASSISTED AUDIT TECHNIQUES (CAATs)**

NOTE: The content outline uses the term "information technology (IT)." However, certain Practice Advisories use the synonym "information systems (IS)."

1. *NEED FOR GUIDANCE*

Computer Assisted Audit Techniques (CAATs) are important tools for the auditor in performing audits. CAATs include many types of tools and techniques, such as generalized audit software, utility software, test data, application software tracing and mapping, and audit expert systems. CAATs may be used in performing various **audit procedures,** including:

- Tests of details of transactions and balances
- Analytical review procedures
- Compliance tests of IS general controls
- Compliance tests of IS application controls
- Penetration testing (efforts to evade security measures to probe for weaknesses)

CAATs may produce a large proportion of the **audit evidence** developed on audits and, as a result, the auditor should carefully **plan** for and exhibit **due professional care** in the use of CAATs.

2. *PLANNING*

Decision Factors for Using CAATs

When planning the audit, the auditor should consider an appropriate combination of **manual techniques and CAATs**. In determining whether to use CAATs, the factors to be considered include:

- Computer knowledge, expertise, and experience of the auditor
- Availability of suitable CAATs and IS facilities
- Efficiency and effectiveness of using CAATs over manual techniques
- Time constraints
- Integrity of the information system and IT environment
- Level of audit risk

CAATs Planning Steps

The major steps to be undertaken by the auditor in preparing for the application of the selected CAATs are

- Set the **audit objectives** of the CAATs
- Determine the **accessibility and availability** of the organization's IS facilities, programs/systems, and data
- Define the **procedures** to be undertaken (e.g., statistical sampling, recalculation, confirmation, etc.)
- Define **output** requirements
- Determine **resource** requirements, e.g., personnel, CAATs, processing environment (organization's IS facilities or audit IS facilities)
- Obtain **access** to the organizations IS facilities, programs/system, and data, including file definitions

- *Document **CAATs** to be used, including objectives, high-level flowcharts, and run instructions*

Arrangements with the Auditee

*Data files, such as detailed transaction files, are often only retained for a short period of time; therefore, the auditor should make arrangements for the **retention of the data** covering the appropriate audit time frame. **Access** to the organization's IS facilities, programs/systems, and data should be arranged for well in advance of the needed time period in order to minimize the effect on the organization's production environment. The auditor should assess the effect that **changes to the production programs/systems** may have on the use of the CAATs. In doing so, the auditor should consider the effect of these changes on the integrity and usefulness of the CAATs, as well as the integrity of the programs/systems and data used by the auditor.*

Testing the CAATs

*The auditor should **obtain reasonable assurance** of the **integrity, reliability, usefulness, and security** of the CAATs through appropriate planning, design, testing, processing, and review of documentation. This should be done before reliance is placed upon the CAATs. The nature, timing, and extent of testing is dependent on the commercial availability and stability of the CAATs.*

Security of Data and CAATs

*When CAATs are used to **extract information** for data analysis, the auditor should verify the integrity of the information system and IT environment from which the data are extracted. CAATs can be used to extract sensitive program/ system information and production data that should be kept confidential. The auditor should safeguard the program/system information and production data with an appropriate level of **confidentiality and security**. In doing so, the auditor should consider the level of confidentiality and security required by the organization owning the data and **any relevant legislation**. The auditor should use and document the results of appropriate procedures to provide for the ongoing integrity, reliability, usefulness, and security of the CAATs. For example, this should include a review of program maintenance and program **change controls** over **embedded audit software** to determine that only authorized changes were made to the CAATs. When the CAATs reside in an environment not under the control of the auditor, an **appropriate level of control** should be in effect to identify changes to the CAATs. When the CAATs are changed, the auditor should obtain assurance of their integrity, reliability, usefulness, and security through **appropriate planning, design, testing, processing, and review of documentation** before reliance is placed on the CAATs.*

3. **PERFORMANCE OF AUDIT WORK**

Gathering Audit Evidence

The use of CAATs should be controlled by the auditor to provide reasonable assurance that the audit objectives and the detailed specifications of the CAATs have been met. The auditor should:

- *Perform a reconciliation of control totals if appropriate*
- *Review output for reasonableness*
- *Perform a review of the logic, parameters, or other characteristics of the CAATs*
- *Review the organization's general IS controls that may contribute to the integrity of the CAATs (e.g., program change controls and access to system, program, and/or data files)*

Generalized Audit Software

When using generalized audit software to access the production data, the auditor should take appropriate steps to protect the **integrity** of the organization's data. With **embedded audit software**, the auditor should be involved in **system design**, and the techniques will have to be developed and maintained within the organization's application programs/systems.

Utility Software

When using utility software, the auditor should confirm that no **unplanned interventions** have taken place during processing, and the utility software has been obtained from the appropriate **system library**. The auditor also should take appropriate steps to protect the **integrity** of the organization's system and files. These utilities can easily damage the system and its files.

Test Data

When using test data, the auditor should be aware that test data only point out the potential for erroneous processing; this technique does **not evaluate actual production data**. The auditor also should be aware that test data analysis can be extremely **complex and time consuming**, depending on the number of transactions processed, the number of programs tested, and the complexity of the programs/systems. Before using test data, the auditor should verify that the test data will **not permanently affect the live system.**

Application Software Tracing and Mapping

When using application software tracing and mapping, the auditor should confirm that the **source code** being evaluated generated the **object program currently used in production**. The auditor should be aware that application software tracing and mapping only points out the potential for erroneous processing; it does not evaluate actual production data.

Audit Expert Systems

When using audit expert systems, the auditor should be thoroughly knowledgeable of the operations of the system to confirm that the **decision paths** followed are appropriate to the given audit environment/situation.

4. **CAATs DOCUMENTATION**

Work Papers

The step-by-step CAATs process should be sufficiently documented to provide adequate audit evidence. Specifically, the audit work papers should contain **sufficient documentation** to describe the CAATs' application, including the details set out in the following sections.

Planning

Documentation should include:

- CAATs objectives
- CAATs to be used
- Controls to be exercised
- Staffing and timing

Execution

Documentation should include:

- *CAATs preparation and testing procedures and controls*
- *Details of the tests performed by the CAATs*
- *Details of inputs (e.g., data used, file layouts), processing (e.g., CAATs high-level flowcharts, logic) and outputs (e.g., log files, reports)*
- *Listing of relevant parameters or source code*

Audit Evidence

Documentation should include:

- *Output produced*
- *Description of the audit analysis work performed on the output*
- *Audit findings*
- *Audit conclusions*
- *Audit recommendations*

5. ### REPORTING

Description of CAATs

*The objectives, scope, and methodology section of the report should contain a **clear description of the CAATs used**. This description should not be overly detailed, but it should provide a good **overview** for the reader. The description of the CAATs used should also be included in the body of the report, where the **specific finding** relating to the use of the CAATs is discussed. If the description of the CAATs used is applicable to several findings, or is too detailed, it should be discussed briefly in the objectives, scope, and methodology section of the report and the reader referred to an appendix with a more detailed description.*

Appendix - Glossary

Application Software Tracing and Mapping: *Specialized tools that can be used to analyze the flow of data through the processing logic of the application software and document the logic, paths, control conditions, and processing sequences. Both the command language or job control statements and programming language can be analyzed. This technique includes program/ system mapping, tracing, snapshots, parallel simulations, and code comparisons.*

Audit Expert Systems: *Expert or decision support systems that can be used to assist auditors in the decision-making process by automating the knowledge of experts in the field. This technique includes automated risk analysis, system software, and control objectives software packages.*

Computer Assisted Audit Techniques (CAATs): *Any automated audit techniques, such as generalized audit software, utility software, test data, application software tracing and mapping, and audit expert systems.*

Generalized Audit Software: *A computer program or series of programs designed to perform certain automated functions. These functions include reading computer files, selecting data, manipulating data, sorting data, summarizing data, performing calculations, selecting samples, and printing reports or letters in a format specified by the auditor. This technique includes software acquired or written for audit purposes and software embedded in production systems.*

Test Data: Simulated transactions that can be used to test processing logic, computations, and controls actually programmed in computer applications. Individual programs or an entire system can be tested. This technique includes Integrated Test Facilities (ITFs) and Base Case System Evaluations (BCSEs).

Utility Software: Computer programs provided by a computer hardware manufacturer or software vendor and used in running the system. This technique can be used to examine processing activity, test programs, review system activities and operational procedures, evaluate data file activity, and analyze job accounting data.

PA Summary

- **CAATs** may be used to obtain **audit evidence** through tests of details and controls, analytical review, and penetration testing efforts to evade security measures.
- The auditor should **plan** the use of CAATs and apply them with **due professional care**.
- When planning the audit, the auditor should consider an appropriate combination of **manual techniques and CAATs**. When deciding whether to use CAATs, the auditor considers such factors as (1) their availability, (2) the relative advantages of manual procedures, (3) his/her own expertise, (4) availability of IS facilities, (5) time limits, (6) the degree of audit risk, and (7) integrity of the information system and IT environment.
- **Planning** involves (1) setting audit objectives, (2) resolving accessibility and availability issues, (3) defining procedures, (4) determining output and resource requirements, and (5) documenting the CAATs to be used.
- The auditor should arrange for **retention of data** covering the audit time frame and access to (1) facilities, (2) programs, (3) systems, and (4) data in advance of the needed time period to minimize the effect on the production environment. The auditor also assesses the effects of changes in production programs and systems.
- The auditor should obtain **reasonable assurance** of the (1) integrity, (2) reliability, (3) usefulness, and (4) security of CAATs before relying on them. The auditor should document **procedures** to provide this assurance, for example, a review of program maintenance and **change controls** over **embedded audit software** to determine that only authorized changes were made. When CAATs are not controlled by the auditor, **appropriate control** should be in effect. When CAATs are changed, the auditor should obtain assurance through **appropriate planning, design, testing, processing, and review of documentation**.
- The auditor should verify the integrity of the IS and IT environment from which sensitive information is extracted using CAATs. Furthermore, the auditor should safeguard the program/system information and production data obtained with appropriate **confidentiality and security**. For this purpose, the auditor considers the requirements of the auditee and relevant legislation.
- The use of CAATs should be controlled by the auditor. Thus, the auditor (1) reviews output, (2) reconciles control totals, (3) reviews characteristics of the CAATs, and (4) reviews the relevant general IS controls.
- An issue in the use of **generalized audit software** is data integrity. For embedded audit software, another issue is system design.
- Use of **utility software** raises issues regarding **unplanned intervention** during processing, whether the software is from the appropriate **system library**, and the **integrity** of systems and files.

- The **test data** approach does **not evaluate actual production data**. It is also complex and time consuming and may contaminate the live system.
- An auditor using application software **tracing and mapping** verifies that the **source code** evaluated generated the production program. But tracing and mapping does not evaluate actual production data.
- An auditor using an **expert system** confirms that decision paths are appropriate.
- **Working papers** should sufficiently document the application of CAATs. **Planning** documentation extends to (1) CAATs objectives, (2) CAATs used, (3) controls, (4) staffing, and (5) timing. Documentation of **execution** includes (1) preparation and testing procedures and controls; (2) details of the tests; (3) details on input, processing, and output; and (4) listing of relevant parameters or source code. Documentation of **audit evidence** includes (1) output; (2) analysis of the output; and (3) audit findings, conclusions, and recommendations.
- The objectives, scope, and methodology section of the report should **clearly describe** the CAATs used. If the description is not too detailed and does not apply to several findings, it is included with the discussion in the body of the report of a **specific finding** related to use of CAATs.

7. **Types of Software Technology Used by Internal Auditors**

   a. Auditors increasingly rely on software tools to accomplish virtually all auditing activities. They ordinarily use two major types of software:

      1) Software that generates the paperwork for the audit, such as word processing, spreadsheet, and electronic working paper software

         a) Internal auditors' use of word processing and spreadsheet software is usually limited to basic office tasks and is therefore not covered in this study unit.

      2) Software used to analyze financial information

   b. **Computer-assisted audit techniques (CAATs)** may be used during every phase of the audit process, from planning to reporting. CAATs may be systems-based or transaction-based, or provide automated methods for extracting and analyzing data.

      1) The following are the most common types of CAATs:

         a) **Generalized audit software** performs automated functions. It is useful for both tests of controls and substantive tests.

         b) **Utility software** performs routine processing tasks, such as sorting and merging.

         c) **Application software tracing and mapping** can follow an audit trail of information generated by the computer system as it processes transactions.

         d) **Expert systems software** automates the knowledge and logic of experts in a certain field to help an auditor with decision making and risk analysis.

2) The leading CAAT software packages are currently Audit Command Language (ACL®) and Interactive Data Extraction and Analysis (IDEA™) software. These software packages, designed specifically for use in auditing, perform 11 major functions.

a) Aging. An auditor can test the aging of accounts receivable.

b) Duplicate identification. Duplicate data can be organized by data field and subsequently identified.

c) Exportation. Data can be transferred to other software.

d) Extraction. Data can be extracted for exception analysis.

e) Gap identification. Gaps in information can be automatically noted.

f) Joining and merging. Two separate data files may be joined or merged to combine and match information.

g) Sampling. Samples of the data can be prepared and analyzed.

h) Sorting. Information can be sorted by any data field.

i) Stratification. Large amounts of data can be organized by specific factors, thereby facilitating analysis.

j) Summarization. Data can be organized to identify patterns.

k) Total fields. Totals for numeric fields can be quickly and accurately calculated.

c. Using the **integrated test facility (ITF)** method, the auditor creates a dummy record within the client's actual system (e.g., a fictitious employee in the personnel and payroll file). Dummy and actual transactions are processed (e.g., time records for the dummy employee and for actual employees). The auditor can test the edit checks by altering the dummy transactions and evaluating error listings.

1) The primary advantage of this method is that it tests the actual program in operation.

2) The primary disadvantages are that the method requires considerable coordination, and the dummy transactions must be purged prior to internal and external reporting. Thus, the method is not used extensively by external auditors.

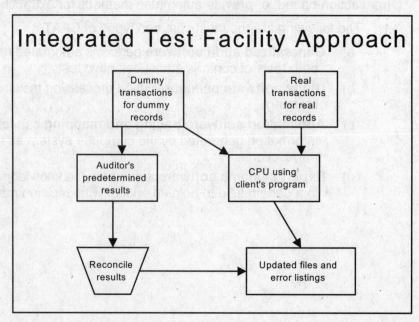

d. An **embedded audit module** is an integral part of an application system that is designed to identify and report actual transactions and other information that meet criteria having audit significance.

1) An advantage is that it permits continuous monitoring of online, real-time systems.

2) A disadvantage is that **audit hooks** must be programmed into the operating system and applications programs to permit insertion of audit modules.

e. **Other Forms of Electronic Media Used by Internal Auditors**

1) **The Internet**, including the World Wide Web, is a series of networks throughout the world that facilitates information transfer among computers. Thus, it is a useful audit tool for gathering and disseminating audit-related information.

a) The Internet carries an abundance of information useful to auditors.

i) **Search engines** for the World Wide Web allow anyone to perform keyword searches.

ii) An auditor can research topics involving the auditee's operations.

iii) An auditor can verify information on the Internet as well as perform fraud investigations.

iv) The Internet can be used to stay informed about emerging technologies.

b) The majority of Internet usage by internal auditors, however, is for electronic communication. **Email** permits transfer, receipt, and storage of messages within or between computer systems. It can be used to

i) Contact specialists
ii) Communicate with remote members of the audit team
iii) Distribute audit working papers and reports
iv) Correspond with management and other departments
v) Transmit files

2) An **intranet** is a network that operates like the Internet but is limited to a specific organization. Uses include

a) Electronic communication among employees
b) Access to the organization's databases
c) Posting of daily news and reports
d) Development of sites to provide information on each department

3) **Image processing** is a method used to convert paper documents into electronic images. **Scanning devices** are used to perform image processing.

a) Image processing can help internal auditors to convert audit documentation into an electronic format.

b) These documents can subsequently be stored, sorted, and extracted along with other electronic information.

8. Stop and review! You have completed the outline for this subunit. Study multiple-choice questions 1 through 17 beginning on page 277.

5.2 OPERATING SYSTEMS AND COMPUTER DEVICES

1. Systems software, which is ordinarily purchased from vendors, performs the fundamental tasks needed to manage computer resources (the CPU, communications devices, and peripherals).

   a. An **operating system** is essential software that acts as an interface between application software and the hardware. It manages access to the computer's resources by concurrent applications and, in a network system, concurrent users.

      1) OS/360, MVS, OS/390, Z/OS, and VM are various operating systems for IBM **mainframes**.

      2) Powerful **workstations**, like those from Sun Microsystems, often run proprietary operating systems such as Solaris.

      3) **Server** operating systems include Unix and Microsoft Windows 2000. Inherent networking capabilities are an important part of server operating systems.

      4) DOS and Windows are Microsoft operating systems for **desktop computers**.

2. The **operating system** mediates between the application programs and the computer hardware.

   a. To communicate with the user, the operating system of a PC may include a **graphical user interface (GUI)**. It employs graphical icons to represent activities, programs, and files. The computer mouse is used to select icons. A GUI simplifies computer usage compared with older systems that require the typing of text-based commands on a keyboard.

      1) **Windows** is a GUI shell initially developed by Microsoft to run in conjunction with the DOS operating system.

      2) Windowing is the characteristic that allows a computer to display more than one program on the screen at the same time. Each program has its own section of the screen, but only one program can interact with the user at a given time.

   b. An operating system also manages job scheduling and accounts for computer usage, controls input and output, assigns storage locations in main memory, and protects data in the event of a system malfunction.

   c. Furthermore, an operating system may permit a single configuration of hardware to function in several different modes.

      1) **Batch processing** entails periodic processing of accumulated groups of transactions. It is typical of older systems or of those in which extremely large numbers of transactions must be processed. Contrast with **online processing**, which involves immediate and direct entry of transactions.

      2) **Multiprogramming.** The operating system processes a program until an input or output operation is required. Because input or output can be handled by peripheral hardware, the CPU can begin executing another program's instructions while input or output is in progress and thereby increase its throughput. Several programs are being processed concurrently, but only one is actually being executed in the CPU. **Throughput** is the quantity of work processed in a given period. It is used as a measuring tool to evaluate processors.

      3) **Multitasking** is multiprogramming on a single-user operating system. For example, a PC user might be able to display a spreadsheet program and a word processing program on the screen at the same time.

      4) **Multiprocessing.** The operating system in conjunction with multiple CPUs executes instructions from more than one program simultaneously.

5) **Virtual storage.** The operating system automatically separates user programs into small fixed-length pages or variable-length segments, allowing the user to have access to a memory virtually equivalent to the total of primary and secondary memories.

6) **Paging.** A page is part of a program. Paging is a memory-swapping technique. The major portion of a program or set of data may be kept in secondary memory while the remainder is held in primary memory. This swapping means that the "virtual" capacity of primary memory is greatly expanded.

d. **Internal audit program for an operating system.** The controls are difficult to audit because of the high degree of technical expertise required. The auditor should determine whether

1) Change controls are implemented. Changes should be documented and approved by an independent authority, such as a computer operations manager. Also, changes should be made when the processing risk is lowest.

2) Operating system upgrades are installed promptly.

3) Utility programs are available only on a need-to-use basis. Such use should be recorded.

4) Duties are segregated appropriately. Systems and applications programming should not be done by the same people.

5) Systems programmers are well trained. Provision for backup should be made if they need to be replaced.

6) Employee and terminal data in operating system tables is regularly updated.

7) No redundant software has been acquired. The entity should not be incurring maintenance costs for unused software.

8) Thorough studies of systems software requests are made prior to purchase to determine compatibility.

9) Errors are systematically tracked, summarized, and corrected.

3. **Hardware** is the configuration of electronic, magnetic, and mechanical devices that perform input, processing, output, storage, control, communications, and data preparation functions in a computer system.

a. Fourth-generation hardware uses **very large-scale integrated circuits (VLSIC)** based on silicon chips that contain millions of transistors per chip. This kind of integrated circuit is a **semiconductor**. Thus, memory, logic, and control features can be combined on a chip, or **microprocessor**. This technology has resulted in huge increases in memory size and processing speeds, a rapid decline in computing costs, and the widespread use of microprocessors in everyday products.

1) Chip speed depends on **word length**, **cycle speed** (measured in megahertz or millions of cycles per second), and **data bus width** (also measured in bits).

2) **Reduced instruction set computing (RISC)** is another means of increasing chip speed. It reduces the number of instructions hardwired into a chip.

4.   All computers have at least one **central processing unit (CPU)** that works in conjunction with peripheral devices.

   a.   The CPU is the main element of a computer system. The major function of the CPU is to fetch stored instructions and data, decode the instructions, and carry out the instructions in the **arithmetic-logic unit (ALU)**. The principal components of the CPU are the ALU (one or more) and the control unit.

      1)   The **control unit** directs and coordinates the entire computer system.

      2)   **Primary storage** is closely connected to the CPU in the central processor. It consists of electronic components that store letters, numbers, and special characters used in processing. The purposes of primary storage are to hold the operating system, part or all of a program being executed, and data used by the program.

         a)   Internal primary storage includes **register memory**, used for ultra high speed and very brief storage of small amounts of data and instructions immediately before use; **cache memory**, used for high-speed storage of frequently used data and programs; and **random-access memory (RAM)**, used to store large quantities of data. Data may be read from or written on RAM. A power interruption causes erasure of RAM.

         b)   **Read-only memory (ROM)** is permanent storage used to hold the basic low-level programs and data. ROM can be read from but not written to; ROM chips are obtained from the manufacturer with programs already stored in them. A power interruption does not erase data written on ROM or on magnetic secondary storage devices. However, a power interruption may corrupt the data.

            i)   **Programmable ROM** (PROM) can be programmed once.

            ii) **Erasable programmable ROM** (EPROM) can be erased using a special process and then reprogrammed.

   b.   Computer systems are typically classified by **computing power**, dictated by CPU speed, memory capacity, and hardware architecture (and thus cost).

      1)   **Personal computers (microcomputers)** range in price and performance from low-end personal computers to powerful desktop models. **Workstations** are also desktop machines, but they are often classified separately from personal computers because of their enhanced mathematical and graphical abilities. In addition, workstations have the capacity to execute more complicated tasks simultaneously than a personal computer. Thus, they tend to be used by scientists and engineers, for example, for simulations and computer-aided design, and in the financial services industry.

         a)   Because of the large number of personal computers in use and aggressive pricing strategies, current personal computer prices have become very attractive. Moreover, personal computers have crossed into the minicomputer arena by providing comparable power and multi-user capabilities previously unavailable until recent technological improvements.

         b)   By adding a modem and communications software, the personal computer can also serve as an interface with other computers. Accordingly, many of the same control and security concerns that apply to larger computers also apply to a personal computer environment.

         c)   **Notebook, laptop, and palmtop computers** are the smallest forms of personal computers.

    2) **Mainframes** are large, general-purpose computers characterized by large memory sizes and very rapid processing speeds. They often provide data communications, support many terminal users, are capable of handling large databases, and can execute many millions of instructions per second (MIPS).

    3) **Supercomputers** are ultra powerful machines designed for scientific, military, and business applications involving very large numbers of variables. They can process up to hundreds of billions of instructions per second by using **parallel processing** technology.

    4) A **server** may be any of the foregoing types of computers. It is specially configured to support a network by permitting users to share files, databases, software, and peripherals.

    5) A **network computer** is a personal computer that does not store programs and data but rather downloads them via the Internet or a company's own network.

5. **Peripheral devices** include items of equipment, other than the CPU, that provide for input, storage, output, outside communication, or additional facilities. They function much more slowly than the CPU, and a system is said to be input-output bound when the speed of peripheral devices determines the speed of task completion.

    a. **Data Entry Devices**

        1) A **data entry terminal** with a **keyboard** is online equipment that is a common input device. The terminal includes a monitor that allows display of user input and computer output.

        2) A **magnetic ink character reader (MICR)** is used in the banking industry to read the magnetic ink on checks.

        3) An **optical character reader (OCR)** does not need special ink and can read bar codes and alphanumeric characters.

            a) A **turnaround document** is computer output prepared in such a way that it can eventually be used as a source document for an input transaction. For example, an optical character recognition document might be used as a sales invoice to be mailed to a customer and returned with the payment. Thus, no new document would have to be prepared to record the payment.

        4) An alternative to keyboard and text-based input is the use of a **computer mouse**. Its point and click function controls a cursor on the video display screen. The user pushes a button on the mouse to choose the command indicated by the cursor.

        5) **Touch screen** technology provides another limited alternative to keyboard input. Commands or data can be entered by touching the sensitized surface of a monitor.

        6) **Digital scanners** convert documents and pictures into digital form.

        7) **Voice recognition** input devices are still another alternative to keyboard input. These systems compare the speaker's voice patterns with prerecorded patterns. Advanced systems now have large vocabularies and shorter training periods. They allow for dictation and are therefore not limited to simple commands.

        8) New forms of mobile data acquisition methods are available.

            a) **Palmtop computers** are miniature notebook computers with keyboard input.

            b) **Pen-based input** is possible with devices that have a flat screen on which the user can print directly with a special stylus.

            c) Other special devices may be used to gather inventory data, read meters, inspect goods, etc. Moreover, manufacturers may use infrared, ultraviolet, and other devices to automate the acquisition of production data.

9) **Sensors** collect information directly for transmittal to a computer.

10) **Point-of-sale terminals** and **automated teller machines** are other input devices.

b. **Output Devices**

1) A **monitor** or **video display terminal** (a cathode ray tube or CRT) can be used to display output and is the most common output device.

2) **Printers** are also common devices used solely for output. Printers may print one character, one line, or one page at a time at varying speeds and with varying quality. Some newer printers have limited processing ability.

3) A **plotter** is an output device that draws graphs on paper.

4) A **voice output device** converts digital data into speech using prerecorded sounds.

c. **Secondary Storage Devices**

1) **Floppy disk drives** serve as low-capacity backup devices for PCs. The most common floppy disk is 3 1/2" with a capacity up to 2.8 MB.

2) **Hard disk drives** provide a permanent location for data and system files. A vast array of internal and external drives exist, providing gigabytes of flexible storage options. Popular external drives are available with removable cartridges. This trend has created a practically endless amount of storage space. One possibility is a **redundant array of inexpensive disks (RAID)** (also called a redundant array of inexpensive drives or redundant array of independent disks). It is a grouping of numerous hard disk drives, a control chip, and software that allows for data delivery along multiple paths. RAID is used in fault-tolerant systems because, if one drive fails, the other disks can compensate for the loss. It can also improve access time since data can be read simultaneously from multiple disks.

3) **Magnetic tape drives** are based on older (and cheaper) technology but are still used for system backup and data transfer. Tape density is from 1,600 to 6,250 bytes per inch. However, tape cartridges with much higher densities are now replacing reels in large computers. Small cartridges are used in PCs.

a) **DAT (digital audiotape)** is primarily used as a backup in imaging systems and as a master for CD-ROM.

4) **CD-ROM (compact disk/read-only memory) drives.** CD-ROMs are laser-optical disks that are almost identical to CD-audio disks. They provide capacities of over 660 MB.

a) **WORM (write once/read many)** optical disks allow the user to write once without the possibility of erasure. However, erasable optical disks are also available.

b) **Digital video (versatile) disks (DVDs)** have greater storage capacity than CD-ROMs. They can store up to 5 gigabytes of video, audio, graphics, and text data.

5) A multitude of storage devices exists. Capacity, reliability, convenience, and speed are limited only by the amount a user is willing to spend.

d. **Other Peripheral Equipment**

1) **Controllers** are hardware units designed to operate (control) specific input or output units, e.g., terminals and printers. These devices eliminate the need for the CPU to operate such devices. The term "buffers and channels" is also sometimes used to describe devices that link the CPU with input/output devices and storage units.

2) A **console** consists of a video display terminal (VDT), a keyboard, and a printer. It is used for communication between the operator or maintenance engineer and the computer.

    a) It permits the computer to exchange instructions with the operator, logs jobs, and provides a printout of activity that can be reviewed by auditors and the control group.

3) A **node** is a hardware device in a network that can act as a message buffer (hold part of the message until the rest is received), switch messages, and serve as an error control. A node can be a computer, controller, or multiplexor.

6. Stop and review! You have completed the outline for this subunit. Study multiple-choice questions 18 through 28 beginning on page 282.

5.3 DEVELOPMENT OF SYSTEMS AND APPLICATIONS

1. **Systems Development**

    a. The **life-cycle approach** is the traditional methodology applied to the development of large, highly structured application systems.

        1) A major advantage of the life-cycle approach is enhanced management and control of the development process. The systems development cycle may be divided into three steps: (1) definition, (2) development, and (3) installation and operation.

            a) **Definition.** The following phases are involved:

                i) A **proposal** for a new or modified application should be prepared indicating the need for the application, the support for it within the organization, and scheduling considerations (timing of the project, employee availability, etc.).

                ii) **Feasibility studies** should be conducted to determine whether the system is technically, economically, and operationally feasible.

                iii) **Information requirements** must be ascertained, including the inquiries to be made by users, reports generated, database needs, and operating characteristics.

                iv) The **general (conceptual) design** contains the users' description of the application, required inputs and outputs, the functions to be carried out, an overview of the processing flow (relationship of the most important programs, files, inputs, and outputs), an overview of controls, and outlines of documentation.

            b) **Development**

                i) **Physical System Design**

- This phase involves work by specialists to develop specifications for
  - Work flow and programs (but not coding)
  - Controls and points where they should be implemented
  - Hardware
  - Security measures, including backup
  - Data communications
  - Quality assurance testing for the balance of the development process

- One approach to design of the physical system is **top-down design**, which is the practice of defining a system by its general purpose and then progressively refining the level of detail in the form of a hierarchy.

  - The top-down method begins with analysis of broad organizational goals, objectives, and policies as the bases for the design process. This step requires an understanding of the entity's environment and significant activities.

  - The next step is to determine the decisions to be made by managers and the information required to make those decisions. The necessary reports, databases, inputs, processing methods, and equipment specifications can then be defined.

  - A weakness of the top-down approach is that it tends to concentrate on managers' information needs at the expense of the design of efficient transaction processing at the operational level.

- An alternative is the **bottom-up** approach, which begins at the operational level, designs each functional unit, and then ties these units together at each management level of the organization.

  - This approach builds on existing capabilities and allows for evolutionary growth of organizational functions.

- **Structured design** of the physical system is a modular approach. Each module (subsystem) is functionally defined, and the degree of interdependence among the modules is minimized. This process simplifies development and enhances adaptability of the components of the system but requires careful definition of modules and the linkages (interfaces) between them.

- **HIPO** (Hierarchy-Input-Process-Output) is a documentation technique developed by IBM that relies on stylized charts depicting increasingly more detailed levels of the system.

ii) **Physical database design** depends on the existing system.

- New files or a new database may have to be designed.
- Modifying an existing database may be feasible.
- If the existing database provides for the new application, modification may not be necessary.

iii) **Procedure development** includes writing technical manuals, forms, and other materials for all persons who will use, maintain, or otherwise work with the system.

- A **printer layout chart** is a gridded spacing chart that is an aid to designing documents and reports generated as hardcopy paper output by a printer.

iv) **Flowcharting** is an essential aid in the development process. A flowchart is a pictorial representation of the definition, analysis, or solution of a problem in which symbols are used to depict operations, data flow, equipment, etc. Flowcharts may be created for a system, program, or document.

v) Other means of documenting the decision logic reflected in systems are matrices (presentations of pairs of conditions and resulting actions), decision tables, decision trees, and pseudocode.

vi) **Data flow diagrams** are employed in **structured systems analysis**. They use just four basic symbols. Data flow diagrams show how data flow to, from, and within the system and the processes that manipulate the data. A data flow diagram can be used to depict lower-level details as well as higher-level processes. A system can be divided into subsystems, and each subsystem can be further subdivided at levels of increasing detail. Thus, any process can be expanded as many times as necessary to show the required level of detail.

- **Action diagrams** are process logic notations that combine graphics and text to support the definition of technical rules.
- **Program structure charts** are graphical depictions of the hierarchy of modules or instructions in a program.
- **Conceptual data modules** are independent definitions of the data requirements that are explained in terms of entities and relationships.

vii) **Program development** entails coding programs in accordance with the specifications in the physical design phase and then testing the results.

- **Structured programming** divides the system's set of programs into discrete modules by functional specifications. The objective is to create modules that are independent logical units, each of which has one entry and one exit point. Data sharing among modules should also be minimized. This method reduces the complexity created when instructions jump back and forth among different sections of the program.
- Structured analysis relies on diagrams, not narrative. See the discussion of data flow diagrams above.
- Each module can be coded by a separate team to
  - Facilitate security because no one group knows the complete set of programs
  - Expedite the development process because several programming teams can work simultaneously
  - Facilitate maintenance because a change or patch need only be module-specific, a less complicated procedure than fitting a patch to a complex, multifunction program
- **Computer-aided software engineering (CASE)** applies the computer to software design and development. It provides the capacity to maintain on the computer all of the system documentation, e.g., data flow diagrams, data dictionaries, and pseudocode (structured English); to develop executable input and output screens; and to generate program code in at least skeletal form. Thus, CASE facilitates the creation, organization, and maintenance of documentation and permits some automation of the coding process.

- **Object-oriented programming** combines data and the related procedures into an object. Thus, an object's data can be operated on only within the object. If the procedures (called methods) for manipulating the data in an object are changed, no other parts of the program are affected. The idea of limiting code that operates on an object to its own source code unit is called encapsulation.

  - The basic concepts of object-oriented programming are class and inheritance. Programs are written by describing the creation and interaction of objects. One class of objects can inherit the characteristics of a more general class. Thus, a basic advantage of object-oriented programming is reusability of the code.

  - However, the methods unique to a subclass may override an inherited method. When override occurs, the object responds to the same message but executes its method, not the inherited method. Accordingly, the advantage of having objects that inherit properties is that program code can be written once for the class instead of having to be rewritten for each instance of similar objects in the class.

- **Visual programming** creates programs by choosing objects from a library and arranging them in a desired sequence rather than by writing code. It is an offshoot of object-oriented programming. The process of creating software in this way is sometimes referred to as rapid application development.

c) **Installation and Operation**

i) Training and educating system users is important not only for proper use of the system but also to offset the resistance of users whose jobs may have been substantially changed.

ii) Acceptance testing by users of inputs, outputs, programs, and procedures is necessary to determine that the new system meets their needs.

iii) Systems conversion is the final testing and switchover. If a direct cutover (immediate full implementation of and switch to the new system) is not indicated, other options include the following:

- **Parallel operation** is the operation of the old and new systems simultaneously until satisfaction is obtained that the new system is operating as expected.

- **Pilot operation** (modular or phase-in conversion) is the conversion to the new or modified system by module or segment, e.g., one division, department, function, or branch of the company at a time. One disadvantage is the extension of the conversion time.

iv) Systems follow-up or post-audit evaluation is a subsequent review of the efficiency and effectiveness of the system after it has operated for a substantial time (e.g., 1 year).

b. **Prototyping** is an approach that involves creating a working model of the system requested, demonstrating it for the user, obtaining feedback, and making changes to the underlying code.

    1) This process repeats through several iterations until the user is satisfied with the system's functionality.

    2) Formerly, this approach was derided as being wasteful of resources and tending to produce unstable systems, but with vastly increased processing power and high-productivity development tools, prototyping can, in some cases, be an efficient means of systems development.

c. **Application authentication** is a means of taking a user's identity from the operating system on which the user is working and passing it to an authentication server for verification. This can be designed into an application from its inception.

d. Systems development should be overseen by an **information systems steering committee** consisting of senior managers who represent the functional areas of the organization, such as information systems, accounting, and marketing.

    1) It provides overall guidance for information systems activities to ensure that goals are consistent with those of the organization. Thus, the steering committee establishes priorities for implementing applications and either performs or approves high-level planning.

2. **Documentation** supports and explains data processing applications, including systems development. It is helpful to operators and other users, control personnel, new employees, and auditors as well as to programmers and analysts who are maintaining the old or developing a new system. The auditor considers documentation to be an important internal control activity. Documentation should be secured in a library, and access should be carefully controlled. It should be subject to uniform standards regarding flowcharting techniques, coding methods, and modification procedures (including proper authorization).

a. **System documentation** includes narrative descriptions, flowcharts, the system definition used for development, input and output forms, file and record layouts, controls, program change authorizations, and backup procedures.

b. **Program documentation** contains descriptions, program flowcharts and decision tables, program listings or source code, test data, input and output forms, detailed file and record layouts (describing the data structure, e.g., field lengths and types), change requests, operator instructions, and controls.

c. **Operating documentation** (computer run manual) provides information about setup, necessary files and devices, input procedures, console messages and responsive operator actions, run times, recovery procedures, disposal of output, and control.

d. **Procedural documentation** includes the system's master plan and operations to be performed, documentation standards, procedures for labeling and handling files, and standards for systems analysis, programming, operations, security, and data definition.

e. **User documentation** describes the system and procedures for data entry, error checking and correction, and formats and uses of reports.

3. **Systems and Program Acquisition and Development Controls**

   a. **Standards** for systems design and programming should be established. These standards represent user needs and system requirements determined during the systems analysis.

      1) Higher-level logical units of the system can be described using **pseudocode**, a structured, informal version of English. Pseudocode can depict the overall design of the software without getting into the details of the particular programming language to be used.

   b. Studies of the economic, operational, and technical **feasibility** of new applications will necessarily entail evaluations of existing as well as proposed systems.

   c. Changes in the computer system should be subject to strict controls **(change controls)**.

   d. Proposed programs should be tested with incorrect or incomplete data as well as typical data to determine if controls have been properly implemented in the program.

      1) **Test data** should test all branches of the program, including the program's edit capabilities. The edit function includes sequence checks, valid field tests, reasonableness checks, and other tests of the input data.

      2) Expected results should be calculated and compared with actual performance. These results should include both accurate output and error messages.

   e. To avoid **legal liability**, controls should also be implemented to prevent use of unlicensed software not in the public domain. A **software licensing agreement** permits a user to employ either a specified or an unlimited number of copies of a software product at given locations, at particular machines, or throughout the company. The agreement may restrict reproduction or resale, and it may provide for subsequent customer support and product improvements.

4. **Change Control**

   a. Changes in the computer system should be subject to strict controls. For example, a written request for an application program change should be made by a user department and authorized by a designated manager or committee.

      1) The program should then be redesigned using a **working copy**, not the version currently in use. Also, the systems documentation must be revised.

      2) Changes in the program will be tested by the user, the internal auditor, and a systems employee who was not involved in designing the change.

      3) **Approval** of the documented change and the results of testing should be given by a systems manager. The change and test results may then be accepted by the user.

      4) Unauthorized program changes can be detected by **code comparison**. The version in use should be periodically compared with a copy controlled by the auditors. Software can be used to perform this procedure.

         a) Versions of critical application programs should be stored in **object code**. Most users lack the technical skill to modify object code.

5. **End-User Computing (EUC)**

   a. End-user computing involves user-created or user-acquired systems that are maintained and operated outside of traditional information systems controls.

     1) **Environmental control risks** that are more likely in an EUC environment include copyright violations that occur when unauthorized copies of software are made or when software is installed on multiple computers.

     2) **Access** to application programs and related data by unauthorized persons is another concern because of lack of physical access controls, application-level controls, and other controls found in mainframe or networked environments.

     3) Moreover, an EUC environment may be characterized by inadequate **backup, recovery, and contingency planning** that may result in an inability to re-create the system or its data.

     4) **Program development, documentation, and maintenance** may also suffer from the lack of centralized control found in larger systems.

       a) The risk of allowing end users to develop their own **applications** is decentralization of control. End-user-developed applications may not be subject to an independent outside review by systems analysts and are not created in the context of a formal development methodology. These applications may lack appropriate standards, controls, and quality assurance procedures.

       b) Moreover, when end users create their own applications and files, **private information systems** may proliferate in which data are largely uncontrolled. Systems may contain the same information, but end-user applications may update and define the data in different ways. Thus, determining the location of data and ensuring data consistency become more difficult.

       c) The auditors should determine that the EUC applications contain **controls** that allow users to rely on the information produced. Identification of applications is more difficult than in a traditional centralized computing environment because few people know about and use them. The auditor's first concern is to discover their existence and their intended functions. One approach is to take an organization-wide inventory of major EUC applications. An alternative is to review major EUC applications in concert with the function or department that is the major user.

         i) The next step is **risk assessment**. The EUC applications that represent high-risk exposures are chosen for audit, for example, because they support critical decisions or are used to control cash or physical assets.

         ii) The third step is to review the controls included in the applications chosen in the second phase.

     5) In a personal computer setting, the user is often the programmer and operator. Thus, the protections afforded by segregation of duties are eliminated.

     6) The **audit trail** is diminished because of the lack of history files, incomplete printed output, etc.

     7) In general, available security features for stand-alone machines are limited compared with those in a network configuration.

b. **Application software** includes the programs that perform the tasks required by end users, e.g., standard accounting operations.

1) Applications may be developed internally or purchased from vendors.

a) Vendor-produced software is in either **source code** (not machine language) or **object code** (machine language), but vendors prefer to sell the latter.

b) Application software production is a vital aspect of system development, and control over its maintenance (changes to meet new user needs) after implementation is likewise crucial.

2) A **spreadsheet** is one type of application software that is especially helpful to accountants, auditors, and business people. It displays an on-screen financial model in which the data are presented in a grid of columns and rows. An example is a financial statement spreadsheet.

a) An electronic spreadsheet permits the creation of a template containing the model of the mathematical relationships among the variables as defined by the user. It specifies the inputs, the computational algorithms, and the format of the output. The effects of changes in assumptions can be seen instantly because a change in one value results in an immediate recomputation of related values.

b) Thus, in designing a spreadsheet model, the first step is to define the problem. This step is followed by an identification of relevant inputs and outputs, and the development of assumptions and decision criteria. Finally, formulas must be documented.

c) Excel and Lotus 1-2-3 are common spreadsheet programs.

3) Software is **copyrightable**, but a substantial amount is in the public domain. Networks of computer users may share such software.

a) **Shareware** is software made available for a fee (usually with an initial free trial period) by the owners to users through a distributor (or websites or electronic bulletin board services).

b) **Software piracy** is a problem for vendors. The best way to detect an illegal copy of application software is to compare the serial number on the screen with the vendor's serial number.

i) Use of unlicensed software increases the risk of introducing computer viruses into the organization. Such software is less likely to have been carefully tested.

ii) To avoid legal liability, controls also should be implemented to prevent use of unlicensed software that is not in the public domain. A **software licensing agreement** permits a user to employ either a specified or an unlimited number of copies of a software product at given locations, at particular machines, or throughout the organization. The agreement may restrict reproduction or resale, and it may provide subsequent customer support and product improvements.

iii) Software piracy can expose an organization's people to both **civil** (up to $150,000 for each program copied) and **criminal** (up to $250,000, five years in jail, or both) penalties. The **Business Software Alliance (BSA)** is a worldwide trade group that coordinates software vendors' efforts to prosecute the illegal duplication of software.

    c)   Diskless workstations increase security by preventing the copying of software to a floppy disk from a workstation. This control not only protects the company's interests in its data and proprietary programs but also guards against theft of licensed third-party software.

    d)   To shorten the installation time for revised software in a network, an organization may implement **electronic software distribution (ESD)**, which is the computer-to-computer installation of software on workstations. Instead of weeks, software distribution can be accomplished in hours or days and can be controlled centrally. Another advantage of ESD is that it permits the tracking of PC program licenses.

4)   **Integrated packages** include two or more applications, e.g., spreadsheets, word processing, database management, graphics, and email. The advantage is that the package does not require redundant data entry and maintenance. However, the individual applications in an integrated package tend not to be as powerful as the stand-alone versions. A **software suite** differs from an integrated package because the applications have all the features of the stand-alone versions.

5)   A **browser** is software that permits a computer to retrieve and recognize HTML (see item 4. in Subunit 6.1) files. Web browsers allow the user to display the textual and graphical information that makes up much of the World Wide Web. It can also provide audio and video presentations and the ability to use email, bulletin boards, discussion groups, etc.

6)   **Email (electronic mail)** permits transfer, receipt, and storage of messages within or between computer systems. The "mail" consists of electronically transmitted messages. A user's "mailbox" is the storage area allocated for messages. The advantages of email are high-speed transmission, reduction of message preparation costs, and the possibility of sending or reading messages at a convenient time. Moreover, email can be read wherever the recipient may be, provided (s)he has access to a terminal. Email can also be sent to remote offices via modem.

    a)   A typical system permits a user to answer messages, compose or delete messages, edit, file, forward messages to other users, move items among files, read, retrieve from files, scan contents of files, send messages, and print.

7)   **Voice mail** converts spoken messages from analog to digital form, transmits them over a network, and stores them on a disk. Messages are then converted back to analog form when the recipient desires to hear them. Afterward, they may be saved, forwarded, or deleted.

8)   Conducting an electronic meeting among several parties at remote sites is **teleconferencing**. It can be accomplished by telephone or email group communication software. **Videoconferencing** permits the conferees to see each other on video screens. These practices have grown in recent years as companies have attempted to cut their travel costs.

9)   A **fax machine** can scan a document, convert its text and graphics to digital form, and then transmit the result over telephone lines. The recipient's fax machine can then create a facsimile of the transmitted document.

10)   An electronic **bulletin board system (BBS)** is a database that allows computer users to read or post messages.

c. **Basic Architectures for Desktop Computing** (Types of End-User Computing Environments)

1) **Client-server model.** A client-server system divides processing of an application between a client machine on a network and a server. This division depends on which tasks each is best suited to perform.

    a) However, **user interaction** is ordinarily restricted to the client part of the application. This portion normally consists of the user interface, data entry, queries, and receipt of reports.

    b) The **server** customarily manages peripheral hardware and controls access to shared databases. Thus, a client-server application must be designed as separate software components that run on different machines but appear to be one application.

    c) **Security** for client-server systems may be more difficult than in a mainframe-based system because of the numerous access points. They also use distributed processing methods that result in heightened risk of unauthorized access to data and processing. New methods of accessing data and processing, such as remote procedure calls, are also available.

2) **Dummy terminal model.** In this architecture, desktop machines that lack stand-alone processing power have access to remote computers in a network. To run an application, programs are downloaded to the terminal. These machines are relatively inexpensive because they have no disk drives.

3) The **application server model** involves a three-tiered or distributed network application. The middle (application) tier translates data between the database (back-end) server and the user's (front-end) server. The application server also performs business logic functions, transaction management, and load balancing.

    a) **Business logic functions** interpret transactions and determine how they will be processed, e.g., applicable discounts, shipping methods, etc. Mainly performed by the application server in contrast to the presentation logic performed by the user's front end server.

    b) **Transaction management** keeps track of all of the steps in transaction processing to ensure completion, editing, and/or deletion.

    c) **Load balancing** is a process to distribute data and data processing among available servers, e.g., evenly to all servers or to the next available server.

6. Stop and review! You have completed the outline for this subunit. Study multiple-choice questions 29 through 43 beginning on page 285.

5.4 SYSTEM SECURITY

1. **Data Integrity**

    a. The difficulty of maintaining the integrity of the data is the most significant limitation of computer-based audit tools.

    b. Electronic evidence is difficult to authenticate and easy to fabricate.

    c. Internal auditors must be careful not to treat computer printouts as traditional paper evidence. The data security factors pertaining to electronic evidence must be considered.

    d. The degree of reliance on electronic evidence by the auditor depends on the effectiveness of the controls over the system from which such evidence is taken.

e. The most important control is to install an **organization-wide network security policy**. This policy should promote the following objectives:

1) **Availability.** The intended and authorized users should be able to access data to meet organizational goals.

2) **Security, privacy, and confidentiality.** The secrecy of information that could adversely affect the organization if revealed to the public or competitors should be ensured.

3) **Integrity.** Unauthorized or accidental modification of data should be prevented.

2. **Access Control**

a. **Access control software** protects files, programs, data dictionaries, processing, etc., from unauthorized access; restricts use of certain devices (e.g., terminals); and may provide an audit trail of both successful and unsuccessful access attempts. For example, a **firewall** separates internal from external networks.

1) Many controls once performed by separate individuals may be concentrated in computer systems. Hence, an individual who has access to the computer may perform **incompatible functions**. As a result, other control procedures may be necessary to achieve the control objectives ordinarily accomplished by segregation of functions. Examples of these controls follow.

b. **Physical security controls** limit physical access and protect against environmental risks and natural catastrophes such as fire and flood.

1) **Keypad devices** allow entry of a password or code to gain entry to a physical location or computer system.

2) **Card reader controls** are based on reading information from a magnetic strip on a credit, debit, or other access card. Controls can then be applied to information about the cardholder contained on the magnetic strip.

c. **Logical security controls** are needed because of the use of communications networks and connections to external systems. User identification and authentication, restriction of access, and the generation of audit trails are required in this environment. Thus, access controls have been developed to prevent improper use or manipulation of data files and programs. They ensure that only those persons with a bona fide purpose and authorization have access to computer systems.

1) **Passwords and ID numbers.** The use of passwords and identification numbers is an effective control in an online system to prevent unauthorized access to computer files. Lists of authorized persons are maintained in the computer. The entry of passwords or identification numbers; a prearranged set of personal questions; and the use of badges, magnetic cards, or optically scanned cards may be combined to avoid unauthorized access.

a) A **security card** may be used with a personal computer so that users must sign on with an ID and a password. The card controls the machine's operating system and records access data (date, time, duration, etc.).

b) Proper **user authentication** by means of a password requires password-generating procedures to ensure that valid passwords are known only by the proper individuals. Thus, a password should not be displayed when entered at a keyboard.

c) Password security may also be compromised in other ways. For example, **log-on procedures** may be cumbersome and tedious. Thus, users often store log-on sequences on their personal computers and invoke them when they want to use mainframe facilities. A risk of this practice is that anyone with access to the personal computers could log on to the mainframe.

d) To be more effective, passwords should consist of random letters, symbols, and numbers. They should not contain words or phrases.

2) **File attributes** can be assigned to control access to and the use of files. Examples are read/write, read only, archive, and hidden.

3) A **device authorization table** restricts file access to those physical devices that should logically need access. For example, because it is illogical for anyone to access the accounts receivable file from a manufacturing terminal, the device authorization table will deny access even when a valid password is used.

    a) Such tests are often called **compatibility tests** because they ascertain whether a code number is compatible with the use to be made of the information. Thus, a user may be authorized to enter only certain kinds of data, have access only to certain information, have access but not updating authority, or use the system only at certain times. The lists or tables of authorized users or devices are sometimes called **access control matrices**.

4) A **system access log** records all attempts to use the system. The date and time, codes used, mode of access, data involved, and operator interventions are recorded.

5) **Encryption** involves using a fixed algorithm to manipulate plaintext. The information is sent in its manipulated form and the receiver translates the information back into plaintext. Although data may be accessed by tapping into the transmission line, the encryption key is necessary to understand the data being sent.

    a) For example, a web server (a computer that delivers web pages to the Internet) should be secure. It should support a security protocol that encrypts messages to protect transactions from third party detection or tampering.

    b) See item 6. on page 273.

6) A **callback** feature requires the remote user to call the computer, give identification, hang up, and wait for the computer to call the user's authorized number. This control ensures acceptance of data transmissions only from authorized modems. However, call forwarding may thwart this control.

7) **Controlled disposal of documents.** One method of enforcing access restrictions is to destroy data when they are no longer in use. Thus, paper documents may be shredded and magnetic media may be erased.

8) **Biometric technologies.** These are automated methods of establishing an individual's identity using physiological or behavioral traits. These characteristics include fingerprints, retina patterns, hand geometry, signature dynamics, speech, and keystroke dynamics.

9) **Automatic log-off** (disconnection) of inactive data terminals may prevent the viewing of sensitive data on an unattended data terminal.

10) **Utility software restrictions.** Utility software may have privileged access and therefore be able to bypass normal security measures. Performance monitors, tape and disk management systems, job schedulers, online editors, and report management systems are examples of utility software. Management can limit the use of privileged software to security personnel and establish audit trails to document its use. The purpose is to gain assurance that its uses are necessary and authorized.

11) **Security personnel.** An organization may need to hire security specialists. For example, developing an information security policy for the organization, commenting on security controls in new applications, and monitoring and investigating unsuccessful access attempts are appropriate duties of the information security officer.

3. **Application Controls**

   a. Crucial to the development of programs for particular applications is the inclusion of application controls (input, processing, and output controls). **Input controls** provide reasonable assurance that data received for processing have been properly authorized, converted into machine-sensible form, and identified and that data (including data transmitted over communication lines) have not been lost, suppressed, added, duplicated, or otherwise improperly changed. Input controls also relate to rejection, correction, and resubmission of data that were initially incorrect.

     1) **Edit checks**, such as those discussed below and on the next page, are programmed into the software.

       a) **Error listing.** Editing (validation) of data should produce a cumulative automated error listing that includes not only errors found in the current processing run but also uncorrected errors from earlier runs. Each error should be identified and described, and the date and time of detection should be given. Sometimes, the erroneous transactions may need to be recorded in a suspense file. This process is the basis for developing appropriate reports.

       b) **Field checks** are tests of the characters in a field to verify that they are of an appropriate type for that field. For example, the field for a Social Security number should not contain alphabetic characters.

       c) **Financial totals** summarize dollar amounts in an information field in a group of records.

       d) A **hash total** is a control total without a defined meaning, such as the total of employee numbers or invoice numbers, that is used to verify the completeness of data. Thus, the hash total for the employee listing by the personnel department could be compared with the total generated during the payroll run.

       e) **Limit and range checks** are based on known limits for given information. For example, hours worked per week will not equal 200.

       f) **Preformatting.** To avoid data entry errors in online systems, a screen prompting approach may be used that is the equivalent of the preprinted forms routinely employed as source documents. The dialogue approach, for example, presents a series of questions to the operator. The preformatted screen approach involves the display of a set of boxes for entry of specified data items. The format may even be in the form of a copy of a transaction document.

       g) **Reasonableness (relationship) tests** check the logical correctness of relationships among the values of data items on an input and the corresponding master file record. For example, it may be known that employee John Smith works only in departments A, C, or D; thus, a reasonableness test could be performed to determine that the payroll record contains one of the likely department numbers. In some texts, the term "reasonableness test" is defined to encompass limit checks.

       h) **Record count** is a control total of the number of records processed during the operation of a program.

       i) **Self-checking digits** may be used to detect incorrect identification numbers. The digit is generated by applying an algorithm to the ID number. During the input process, the check digit is recomputed by applying the same algorithm to the code actually entered.

j) **Sequence checks** determine that records are in proper order. For example, a payroll input file is likely to be sorted into Social Security number order. A sequence check can then be performed to verify record order.

k) **Sign checks** ensure that data in a field have the appropriate arithmetic sign. For example, hours worked in a payroll record should always be a positive number.

l) **Validity checks** are tests of identification numbers or transaction codes for validity by comparison with items already known to be correct or authorized. For example, Social Security numbers on payroll input records can be compared with Social Security numbers authorized by the personnel department.

2) **Key verification** entails rekeying input and comparing the results.

3) A **redundancy check** requires sending additional data items to serve as a check on the other transmitted data; for example, part of a customer name could be matched against the name associated with the transmitted customer number.

4) An **echo check** is an input control over transmission along communications lines. Data are sent back to the user's terminal for comparison with the transmitted data.

5) **Completeness checks** of transmission of data determine whether all necessary information has been sent. The software notifies the sender if something is omitted.

   a) A complementary transmission control numbers and dates each message sent from a given terminal. This procedure allows verification of the completeness of the sequence and establishment of control totals for each terminal.

b. **Processing controls** provide reasonable assurance that processing has been performed as intended for the particular application, i.e., that all transactions are processed as authorized, that no authorized transactions are omitted, and that no unauthorized transactions are added.

1) Some input controls are also processing controls, e.g., limit, reasonableness, and sign tests.

2) Other tests of the logic of processing are posting, cross-footing, and zero-balance checks.

   a) Comparing the contents of a record before and after updating is a **posting** check.

   b) **Cross-footing** compares an amount to the sum of its components.

   c) A **zero-balance check** adds the positive and negative amounts posted. The result should be zero.

3) **Run-to-run control totals** (e.g., record counts or certain critical amounts) should be generated and checked at designated points during processing.

   a) **Proof account activity listing.** In an online system, the change in a file for the day can be compared with source information.

4) **Internal header and trailer labels** ensure that incorrect files are not processed.

   a) A matching test should make certain an updating transaction is matched with the appropriate master file.

5) Programs used in processing should be tested, for example, by reprocessing actual data with a known result or by employing test data.

6) **End-of-file procedures** should be available to avoid errors such as prematurely closing the transaction file when the end of the current master file is reached. The transaction file may contain new records to be added to the master file.

7) **Concurrency controls** manage situations in which two or more programs attempt to use a file or database at the same time.

8) An **audit trail** should be created through the use of input-output control logs, error listings, transaction logs, and transaction listings.

9) **Key integrity checks** prevent the updating process from creating inaccuracies in keys. Keys are attributes of records that permit them to be sorted. A **primary key** is the data item(s) that is the principal identifier, e.g., the vendor number. A **secondary key** is an alternative used for either sorting or special processing, e.g., the payment date on the vendor's invoice.

c.   **Output controls** provide assurance that the processing result (such as account listings or displays, reports, magnetic files, invoices, or disbursement checks) is accurate and that only authorized personnel receive the output.

1) The **data control group** supervises output control.

a)   The daily **proof account activity listings** (changes in master files) should be sent to users for review.

b)   **Error listings** should be received directly from the system by the control group, which should make any necessary inquiries and send the errors to users for correction and resubmission.

c)   The **console log** should be reviewed for unusual interruptions, interventions, or other activity.

d)   Output should be distributed in accordance with distribution registers that list authorized users.

e)   **End-of-job markers** on the last page of printed output permits verification that the entire report has been received.

f)   **Spooler controls** prevent access to spooled output, i.e., to the results of processing that are temporarily stored in an intermediate file rather than immediately printed.

2) An important detective control is **user review** of output. Users should be able to determine when output is incomplete or not reasonable, particularly when the user prepared the input. Thus, users as well as computer personnel have a quality assurance function.

4.   **Internet Security**

a.   Connection to the Internet presents security issues. Thus, the organization-wide network security policy should at the very least include

1) A user account management system

2) Installation of an Internet firewall

3) Methods, such as encryption, to ensure that only the intended user receives the information and that the information is complete and accurate

b.   **User account management** involves installing a system to ensure that

1) New accounts are added correctly and assigned only to authorized users.

2) Old and unused accounts are removed promptly.

3) Passwords are changed periodically, and employees are educated on how to choose a password that cannot be easily guessed (e.g., a password of at least six diverse characters that do not form a word should be chosen).

c. A **firewall** separates an internal network from an external network (e.g., the Internet) and prevents passage of specific types of traffic. It identifies names, Internet Protocol (IP) addresses, applications, etc., and compares them with programmed access rules.

1) A firewall may have any of the following features:

a) A **packet filtering system** examines each incoming network packet and drops (does not pass on) unauthorized packets.

b) A **proxy server** maintains copies of web pages to be accessed by specified users. Outsiders are directed there, and more important information is not available from this access point.

c) An **application gateway** limits traffic to specific applications.

d) A **circuit-level gateway** connects an internal device, e.g., a network printer, with an outside TCP/IP port. It can identify a valid TCP session.

e) **Stateful inspection** stores information about the state of a transmission and uses it as background for evaluating messages from similar sources.

2) Firewall systems ordinarily produce **reports** on organization-wide Internet use, unusual usage patterns, and system penetration attempts. These reports are very helpful to the internal auditor as a method of continuous monitoring, or logging, of the system.

a) Firewalls do not provide adequate protection against **computer viruses**. Thus, an organization should include one or more of the antivirus measures discussed in Study Unit 6 in its network security policy.

d. Data traveling across the network can be encoded so that it is indecipherable to anyone except the intended recipient.

e. **Other Controls**

1) **Authentication** measures verify the identity of the user, thus ensuring that only the intended and authorized users gain access to the system.

a) Most firewall systems provide authentication procedures.

b) Access controls are the most common authentication procedures.

2) **Checksums** help ensure the integrity of data by checking whether the file has been changed. The system computes a value for a file and then proceeds to check whether this value equals the last known value for this file. If the numbers are the same, the file has likely remained unchanged.

5. **Data Storage**

a. Storing all related data on one storage device creates security problems.

1) If hardware or software malfunctions occur, or unauthorized access is achieved, the results could be disastrous.

2) Greater emphasis on security is required to provide backup and restrict access to the database.

a) For example, the system may employ **dual logging**, that is, use of two transaction logs written simultaneously on separate storage media. It may also use a snapshot technique to capture data values before and after transaction processing. The files that store these values can be used to reconstruct the database in the event of data loss or corruption.

3) The responsibility for creating, maintaining, securing, and restricting access to the database belongs to the **Database Administrator (DBA)**.

4) A **database management system (DBMS)** includes security features. Thus, a specified user's access may be limited to certain data fields or logical views depending on the individual's assigned duties.

6. **Encryption**

   a. Encryption technology converts data into a code. A program codes data prior to transmission. Another program decodes it after transmission. Unauthorized users may still be able to access the data, but, without the encryption key, they will be unable to decode the information.

   b. Encryption software uses a fixed algorithm to manipulate **plaintext** and an encryption key to introduce variation. The information is sent in its manipulated form **(cyphertext)**, and the receiver translates the information back into plaintext. Although data may be accessed by tapping into the transmission line, the encryption key is necessary to understand the data being sent. The machine instructions necessary to code and decode data can constitute a 20-to-30% increase in system overhead.

   c. Encryption technology may be either hardware- or software-based. Two major types of encryption software exist.

      1) **Public-key**, or asymmetric, encryption requires two keys: The public key for coding messages is widely known, but the private key for decoding messages is kept secret by the recipient. Accordingly, the parties who wish to transmit coded messages must use algorithmically related **pairs** of public and private keys. The sender searches a directory for the recipient's public key, uses it to encode the message, and transmits the message to the recipient. The recipient uses the public key and the related private (secret) key to decode the message.

         a) One advantage of public-key encryption is that the message is encoded using one key and decoded using another. In contrast, private-key encryption requires both parties to know and use the secret key.

         b) A second advantage is that neither party knows the other's private key. The related public-key and private-key pair is issued by a **certificate authority** (a third-party fiduciary, e.g., VeriSign or Thawte). However, the private key is issued only to one party.

            i) Thus, **key management** in a public-key system is more secure than in a secret-key system because the parties do not have to agree on, transmit, and handle the one secret key.

         c) **RSA**, named for its developers (Rivest, Shamir, and Adelman), is the most commonly used public-key method.

         d) A public-key system is used to create **digital signatures (fingerprints)**.

            i) A digital signature is a means of **authentication** of an electronic document, for example, of the validity of a purchase order, acceptance of a contract, or financial information.

               • The sender uses its private key to encode all or part of the message, and the recipient uses the sender's public key to decode it. Hence, if that key decodes the message, the sender must have written it.

               • One variation is to send the message in both plaintext and cyphertext. If the decoded version matches the plaintext version, no alteration has occurred.

    ii)   A **digital certificate** is another means of authentication used in e-business. The certificate authority issues a coded electronic certificate that contains the holder's name, a copy of its public key, a serial number, and an expiration date. The certificate verifies the holder's identity.

- The recipient of a coded message uses the certificate authority's public key (available on the Internet) to decode the certificate included in the message. The recipient then determines that the certificate was issued by the certificate authority. Moreover, the recipient can use the sender's public key and identification data to send a coded response.

  - Such methods might be used for transactions between sellers and buyers using credit cards.

- A certificate also may be used to provide assurance to customers that a website is genuine.

- The **public key infrastructure** permits secure monetary and information exchange over the Internet. Thus, it facilitates e-business.

- Protocols commonly used for coding and decoding functions on the Internet are **SSL** (Secure Sockets Layer) and **S-HTTP** (Secure Hypertext Transport Protocol).

- **Digital time stamping services** verify the time (and possibly the place) of a transaction. For example, a document may be sent to a service, which applies its digital stamp and then forwards the document.

    2)   **Private-key**, or symmetric, encryption requires only a single (secret) key for each pair of parties that want to send each other coded messages.

        a)   **Data Encryption Standard (DES)**, a shared private-key method developed by the U.S. government, is the most prevalent secret-key method. It is based on numbers with 56 binary digits.

        b)   The **Advanced Encryption Standard (AES)** is a recently adopted cryptographic algorithm for use by U.S. government organizations to protect sensitive information. The AES will be widely used on a voluntary basis by organizations, institutions, and individuals as well as by the U.S. government.

7.   Stop and review! You have completed the outline for this subunit. Study multiple-choice questions 44 through 55 beginning on page 290.

5.5 CONTINGENCY PLANNING

1.   **Backup and recovery policies and procedures.** A computer center should have a reconstruction and recovery plan that will allow it to regenerate important programs and database files. The center should create backup (duplicate) copies of data files, databases, programs, and documentation; store backup copies offsite; and plan for auxiliary processing on alternate systems or at another site.

2.   The organization must undertake contingency planning and risk analysis. During an early stage of contingency planning for information systems, management must determine how various processing disruptions may affect the entity. **Risk analysis** identifies and prioritizes critical applications, evaluates their organizational impact, determines recovery time frames and minimum hardware platform requirements, assesses insurance coverage, identifies exposures and their implications, and develops recovery plans.

3.   It is important in any information processing environment not to lose or otherwise destroy data. Not only is the loss of data a problem, but the organization may also require continuous processing without disruptions. For these reasons, it is imperative that any system have adequate backup and recovery procedures in the event of system failure, power loss, or other potential corruption of data. The procedures implemented will normally be a function of the specific computer environment, type of processing, or storage mode.

   a.   **Batch processing.** Magnetic tape and magnetic disks are used.

      1)   **Checkpoint procedures** involve capturing all the values of data and program indicators at specified points and storing these values in another file. If processing is interrupted, it can be resumed at the last checkpoint rather than at the beginning of the run.

   b.   **Online processing.** Magnetic disks are used for online processing.

      1)   **Rollback and recovery** procedures involve the dumping of the master file's contents and associated data structures onto a backup file. In the event of a faulty run, the dump is used together with the transaction log or file to reconstruct the file.

   c.   **Database management systems** use magnetic disks for online processing.

      1)   **Database systems** require a more elaborate backup procedure. Normally, recovery and restart procedures must provide for continued operations during reconstruction of lost information.

      2)   **Dual logging** involves the use of two transaction logs written simultaneously on two separate storage media.

      3)   **Before-image/after-image** captures the data values before and after transaction processing and stores them in files. These files can be used to re-create the database in the event of data loss or corruption.

   d.   **Fully protected systems** have generator or battery backup to prevent data destruction and downtime from electrical power disturbances. Loss of electrical power or voltage fluctuations need not disturb the vulnerable contents of main memory if a noninterruptible system is in place.

   e.   **Fault-tolerant computer systems** have additional hardware and software as well as a backup power supply. A fault-tolerant computer has additional chips and disk storage.

   f.   **Protection from malicious software and attacks.** An example of malicious software is a computer virus, a software program that infects another program or a system's primary storage (main memory) by altering its logic. Infection often results in the destruction of data. Once infected, a software program can spread the virus to other software programs. Obtaining software through a shareware network or by downloading from an electronic bulletin board is a typical cause of infection. Propagation of viruses through email attachments is also common.

      1)   To protect against viruses, three types of controls should be implemented.

         a)   **Preventive controls** include establishing a formal security policy, using only clean and certified copies of software, not using shareware software, checking new software with antivirus software, restricting access, and educating users.

         b)   **Detective controls** include making file size and date/time stamp comparisons.

         c)   **Corrective controls** include ensuring that clean backup is maintained and having a documented plan for recovery from a virus.

      2)   For more on malicious software and a full discussion of attacks on computer systems, see the next study unit.

      g.   **Hot-site and cold-site backup facilities.** A hot site is a service bureau. It is a fully operational processing facility that is immediately available. A cold site is a shell facility where the user can quickly install computer equipment.

          1)   A hot site with updated software and data that can begin operations in minutes is a **flying-start site**.

4.   Stop and review! You have completed the outline for this subunit. Study multiple-choice questions 56 through 59 beginning on page 293.

5.6 STUDY UNIT 5 SUMMARY

1.   Characteristics such as the uniform processing of transactions and the loss of segregation of functions distinguish computer-based from manual systems.

2.   Controls over information technology can be classified as general controls (those over all of an organization's processing) and application controls (those over a particular system within the organization).

3.   Key functions within IT include systems analyst, database administrator, programmer, webmaster, and operator.

4.   Batch processing is the accumulation and grouping of transactions for processing on a delayed basis. An online processing system is in direct communication with the computer, giving it the capability to handle transactions as they are entered.

5.   With distributed processing, an organization determines which parts of an application are better performed locally and which parts are better performed at some other, possibly centralized, site.

6.   A computer's operating system mediates between the application programs and the computer hardware.

7.   A computer's hardware includes a central processing unit (CPU), data entry devices such as keyboards and scanners, output devices such as monitors and printers, and storage devices such as hard drives.

8.   When an organization develops a new system, the life-cycle approach allows for enhanced management and control of the process.

9.   The systems development life cycle can be divided into the following steps: system feasibility, logical system design, physical system design, physical database design, program development, system testing, installation, training, and maintenance.

10.   Documentation supports and explains data processing applications, including systems development.

11.   Changes in the computer system should be subject to strict controls.

12.   End-user computing involves user-created or user-acquired systems that are maintained and operated outside of traditional information systems controls.

13.   System security encompasses data integrity, access controls, application controls, systems development standards, change controls, controls over end-user computing, and Internet security.

14.   A computer center should have a reconstruction and recovery plan that will allow it to regenerate important programs and database files.

QUESTIONS

5.1 Introduction to IT

1. Which of the following statements accurately describes the impact that automation has on the controls normally present in a manual system?

A. Transaction trails are more extensive in a computer-based system than in a manual system because there is always a one-for-one correspondence between data entry and output.

B. Responsibility for custody of information assets is more concentrated in user departments in a computer-based system than it is in a manual system.

C. Controls must be more explicit in a computer-based system because many processing points that present opportunities for human judgment in a manual system are eliminated.

D. The quality of documentation becomes less critical in a computer-based system than it is in a manual system because data records are stored in machine-readable files.

Answer (C) is correct. *(CIA, adapted)*
REQUIRED: The impact that automation has on the controls normally present in a manual system.
DISCUSSION: Using a computer does not change the basic concepts and objectives of control. However, the use of computers may modify the control techniques used. The processing of transactions may be combined with control activities previously performed separately, or control function may be combined within the information system activity.
Answer (A) is incorrect because the "paper trail" is less extensive in an information system. Combining processing and controls within the system reduces documentary evidence. Answer (B) is incorrect because information assets are more likely to be under the control of the information system function. Answer (D) is incorrect because documentation is more important in an information system. Information is more likely to be stored in machine-readable form than in hard copy.

2. The practice of maintaining a test program library separate from the production program library is an example of

A. An organizational control.

B. Physical security.

C. An input control.

D. A concurrency control.

Answer (A) is correct. *(CIA, adapted)*
REQUIRED: The type of control represented by separating the test and production program libraries.
DISCUSSION: This separation is an organizational control. Organizational controls concern the proper segregation of duties and responsibilities within the information systems department. Although proper segregation is desirable, functions that would be considered incompatible if performed by a single individual in a manual activity are often performed through the use of an information systems program or series of programs. Thus, compensating controls may be necessary, such as library controls, effective supervisions, and rotation of personnel. Segregating test programs makes concealment of unauthorized changes in production programs more difficult.
Answer (B) is incorrect because physical security (e.g., climate control and restrictions on physical access) is another aspect of organizational control. Answer (C) is incorrect because input controls validate the completeness, accuracy, and appropriateness of input. Answer (D) is incorrect because concurrency controls manage situations in which two or more programs attempt to use a file or database at the same time.

3. In traditional information systems, computer operators are generally responsible for backing up software and data files on a regular basis. In distributed or cooperative systems, ensuring that adequate backups are taken is the responsibility of

A. User management.

B. Systems programmers.

C. Data entry clerks.

D. Tape librarians.

Answer (A) is correct. *(CIA, adapted)*
REQUIRED: The persons responsible for ensuring that adequate backups are taken in distributed or cooperative systems.
DISCUSSION: In distributed or cooperative systems, the responsibility for ensuring that adequate backups are taken is the responsibility of user management. The systems are under the control of users, not a central information processing department.
Answer (B) is incorrect because distributed environments have no systems programmers comparable to those at central sites for traditional systems. Answer (C) is incorrect because distributed environments may not have data entry clerks. Users typically perform their own data entry. Answer (D) is incorrect because, in distributed environments, there are no tape librarians.

4. Which of the following would not be appropriate to consider in the physical design of a data center?

    A. Evaluation of potential risks from railroad lines and highways.

    B. Use of biometric access systems.

    C. Design of authorization tables for operating system access.

    D. Inclusion of an uninterruptible power supply system and surge protection.

Answer (C) is correct. *(CIA, adapted)*
REQUIRED: The inappropriate consideration in the physical design of a data center.
DISCUSSION: Authorization tables for operating system access address logical controls, not physical controls.
Answer (A) is incorrect because external risks should be evaluated to determine the center's location. Answer (B) is incorrect because biometric access systems control physical access to the data center. These devices identify such unique physical qualities as fingerprints, voice patterns, and retinal patterns. Answer (D) is incorrect because power supply systems and surge protection are included in data center design. Thus, two separate power lines, line conditioning equipment, and backup power are typical elements in the design.

5. What type of information system uses communications capabilities to make needed data and computing capability available to end users at separate locations?

    A. Distributed processing system.

    B. Time-sharing system.

    C. Online processing system.

    D. Personal computing system.

Answer (A) is correct. *(CIA, adapted)*
REQUIRED: The system that uses communications capabilities to make needed data available for end users at separate locations.
DISCUSSION: The advent of less expensive and smaller computers has permitted the development of a different alternative to centralization or decentralization. In a distributed data processing system, the organization's processing needs are examined in their totality. The decision is not whether an application should be done centrally or locally but, rather, which parts of the application are better performed by smaller local computers and which parts are better performed at some other, possibly centralized, site. In essence, the best distribution of processing tasks within application areas is sought. The key distinction between decentralized and distributed systems is the interconnection among the nodes (sites) in the network.
Answer (B) is incorrect because time-sharing systems are terminal-oriented systems that are connected to a central processing site. Answer (C) is incorrect because an online processing system operates under direct control of the CPU. Answer (D) is incorrect because a personal computing system is a microcomputer resource dedicated to a single user, usually in a stand-alone configuration.

6. The purpose of input controls is to ensure the

    A. Authorization of access to data files.

    B. Authorization of access to program files.

    C. Completeness, accuracy, and validity of updating.

    D. Completeness, accuracy, and validity of input.

Answer (D) is correct. *(CIA, adapted)*
REQUIRED: The purpose of input controls.
DISCUSSION: Input controls provide reasonable assurance that data received for computer processing have been properly authorized and are in a form suitable for processing, i.e., complete, accurate, and valid. Input controls also relate to rejection, correction, and resubmission of data that were initially incorrect.
Answer (A) is incorrect because access controls authorize access to data files. Answer (B) is incorrect because access controls authorize access to program files. Answer (C) is incorrect because processing controls ensure the completeness, accuracy, and validity of updating.

7. Payroll master file updates are sent from a remote terminal to a mainframe program on a real-time system. A control that works to ensure accuracy of the transmission is a(n)

    A. Echo check.

    B. Protection ring.

    C. Hash total.

    D. Integrated test facility.

Answer (A) is correct. *(CIA, adapted)*
REQUIRED: The control that works to ensure accuracy of the transmission.
DISCUSSION: An echo check is a hardware control that provides for a peripheral device to return (echo) a signal sent by the CPU. For example, the CPU sends a signal to the printer, and the printer, just prior to printing, sends a signal back to the CPU verifying that the proper print position has been activated.
Answer (B) is incorrect because a protection ring prevents accidental writing on a tape file. A real-time system would not use tape files. Answer (C) is incorrect because hash totals are used to control data sent to a batch system, not a real-time system. Answer (D) is incorrect because integrated test facilities are useful in testing real-time systems but cannot be used to ensure completeness of data transmissions.

8. Detecting errors in random access memory is a function of

    A. Memory protection.

    B. Parity checking.

    C. Validity checking.

    D. Range checking.

Answer (B) is correct. *(CIA, adapted)*
    REQUIRED: The control that detects errors in random access memory.
    DISCUSSION: A parity check adds the bits in a character or message and checks the sum to determine if it is odd or even, depending on whether the computer has odd or even parity. This check verifies that all data have been transferred without loss. For example, if the computer has even parity, a bit will be added to a binary coded character or message that contains an odd number of bits. No bit is added if a character or message in binary form has an even number of bits.
    Answer (A) is incorrect because memory protection prohibits programs from accessing memory outside their designated ranges. Answer (C) is incorrect because for hardware, validity checking verifies that a machine-level instruction is a valid instruction; for applications, validity checking verifies that transaction data are complete, authorized, and reasonable. Answer (D) is incorrect because range checking verifies that input data values are within pre-determined ranges.

9. A catalog company has been experiencing an increasing incidence of problems in which the wrong products have been shipped to the customer. Most of the customer orders come in over the telephone, and an operator enters the data into the order system immediately. Which of the following control procedures, if properly implemented, would address the problem?

    I.   Have the computer automatically assign a sequential order number to each customer order.

    II. Implement a self-checking digit algorithm for each product number and request entries by product number.

    III. Request entries by product number, have the computer program identify the product and price, and require the operator to orally verify the product description with the customer.

    A. II only.

    B. I, II, and III.

    C. II and III only.

    D. I and II only.

Answer (C) is correct. *(CIA, adapted)*
    REQUIRED: The procedure(s) to prevent incorrect shipments.
    DISCUSSION: A self-checking digit detects incorrect codes. The digit is generated by applying an algorithm to the code. During input, the digit is recomputed by applying the algorithm to the code actually entered. Oral verification also addresses the problem of incorrectly identifying the product number. Assigning a sequential number to the customer's order helps build an audit trail but does not address the product identification issue.

10. Which one of the following input controls or edit checks would catch certain types of errors within the payment amount field of a transaction?

    A. Record count.

    B. Echo check.

    C. Check digit.

    D. Limit check.

Answer (D) is correct. *(CIA, adapted)*
    REQUIRED: The input control or edit check that detects errors within the payment amount field of a transaction.
    DISCUSSION: A limit, reasonableness, or range test determines whether an amount is within a predetermined limit for given information. It can only detect certain errors (i.e., those that exceed the acceptable limit).
    Answer (A) is incorrect because a record count determines the number of documents entered into a process. Answer (B) is incorrect because an echo check tests the reliability of computer hardware. For example, the CPU sends a signal to a printer that is echoed just prior to printing. The signal verifies that the proper print position has been activated. Answer (C) is incorrect because a self-checking number is generated by applying an algorithm to an identification number.

11. The key verification process associated with keying records for input to a computer system is

A. Effectively used to detect the erroneous recording of data on source documents.

B. Inexpensive and therefore widely used.

C. Used to detect errors introduced by the keying process.

D. Ordinarily used with a computer program written to check the data.

Answer (C) is correct. *(CIA, adapted)*
REQUIRED: The purpose of key verification.
DISCUSSION: Key verification is a procedure to determine if the keying process was performed properly. Information from source documents is rekeyed on a special keyboard by another operator and compared with that previously recorded.
Answer (A) is incorrect because key verification does not detect errors in the source documents. Answer (B) is incorrect because, although widely used, key verification effectively doubles the work and is expensive. Answer (D) is incorrect because key verification is a manual process.

12. Output controls ensure that the results of computer processing are accurate, complete, and properly distributed. Which of the following is not a typical output control?

A. Reviewing the computer processing logs to determine that all of the correct computer jobs executed properly.

B. Matching input data with information on master files and placing unmatched items in a suspense file.

C. Periodically reconciling output reports to make sure that totals, formats, and critical details are correct and agree with input.

D. Maintaining formal procedures and documentation specifying authorized recipients of output reports, checks, or other critical documents.

Answer (B) is correct. *(CIA, adapted)*
REQUIRED: The procedure not a typical output control.
DISCUSSION: Output controls often include comparing output totals with input and processing totals; reviewing computer logs; auditing output reports to ensure that totals, formats, and details are accurate and reconcilable; and specifying authorized recipients by formal means. The data control group also performs important output control functions. Matching the input data with information held on master or suspense files is a processing control, not an output control. It ensures that data are complete and accurate during updating.
Answer (A) is incorrect because reviewing the computer processing logs is an output control. Answer (C) is incorrect because periodically reconciling output reports is an output control. Answer (D) is incorrect because maintaining formal procedures and documentation specifying authorized recipients is an output control.

13. Which of the following represents a limitation on the use of generalized audit software (GAS)?

A. It requires lengthy detailed instructions in order to accomplish specific tasks.

B. It has limited application without significant modification.

C. It requires significant programming knowledge to be used effectively.

D. It can only be used on hardware with compatible operating systems.

Answer (D) is correct. *(CIA, adapted)*
REQUIRED: The disadvantage of using GAS.
DISCUSSION: Diversity of programming languages, computers, systems designs, and differing data structures makes generalized audit software impossible to apply in certain situations.
Answer (A) is incorrect because the use of GAS is normally more efficient. Less time is required to write instructions to accomplish a function than to manually select and examine items. Answer (B) is incorrect because the program is generalized, i.e., designed to be used on a variety of systems without significant modifications. Answer (C) is incorrect because an advantage is that GAS requires minimal knowledge of computer technology.

14. When an auditor performs tests on a computerized inventory file containing over 20,000 line items, that auditor can maintain independence and perform most efficiently by

A. Asking the console operator to print every item that cost more than $100.

B. Using a generalized audit software package.

C. Obtaining a printout of the entire file and then selecting each nth item.

D. Using the systems department's programmer to write an extraction program.

Answer (B) is correct. *(CIA, adapted)*
REQUIRED: The method to maintain independence and perform efficiently in testing an inventory file.
DISCUSSION: Independence can be preserved when the auditor acquires general audit software (GAS) from an external source rather than relying on auditee-developed audit software. Also, efficiency is enhanced to the extent GAS can be used (as compared to manual auditing or writing special audit programs).
Answer (A) is incorrect because independence is jeopardized when an operator is involved in the process. Answer (C) is incorrect because printing out the entire file is both unnecessary and inefficient. Answer (D) is incorrect because overreliance on an auditee's programmer impairs independence.

15. Computer technology makes it possible to perform paperless audits. For example, in an audit of computer-processed customer accounts receivable balances, an auditor might use a personal computer to access the accounts receivable files directly and copy selected customer records into the computer for audit analysis. Which of the following is an advantage of this type of paperless audit of accounts receivable balances?

A. It reduces the amount of substantive testing required.

B. It allows immediate processing of audit data on a spreadsheet working paper.

C. It increases the amount of technical skill required of the auditor.

D. It allows direct confirmation of customer account balances.

Answer (B) is correct. *(CIA, adapted)*
REQUIRED: The advantage of a paperless audit of accounts receivable balances.
DISCUSSION: Electronic spreadsheets are software packages that display multicolumn worksheets, which may be used as automated audit working papers. A major advantage of this type of auditing is the ability to process data immediately using personal computer software without first having to enter the data manually into the computer.
Answer (A) is incorrect because audit technology has no direct effect on the amount of substantive testing required. Answer (C) is incorrect because the need for increased expertise is not an advantage. Answer (D) is incorrect because processing computer files does not in itself provide confirmation of customer account balances, although software may assist in preparing confirmation requests.

16. Which of the following strategies will a CPA most likely consider in auditing an entity that processes most of its financial data only in electronic form, such as a paperless system?

A. Continuous monitoring and analysis of transaction processing with an embedded audit module.

B. Increased reliance on internal control activities that emphasize the segregation of duties.

C. Verification of encrypted digital certificates used to monitor the authorization of transactions.

D. Extensive testing of firewall boundaries that restrict the recording of outside network traffic.

Answer (A) is correct. *(CPA, adapted)*
REQUIRED: The audit strategy for an electronic environment.
DISCUSSION: An audit module embedded in the client's software routinely selects and abstracts certain transactions. They may be tagged and traced through the information system. An alternative is recording in an audit log, that is, in a file accessible only by the auditor.
Answer (B) is incorrect because the same level of segregation of duties as in a manual system is not feasible in highly sophisticated computer systems. Answer (C) is incorrect because encrypted digital signatures help ensure the authenticity of the sender of information, but verifying them is a less pervasive and significant procedure than continuous monitoring of transactions. Answer (D) is incorrect because firewalls exclude unauthorized activity from entering a system; however, such activity would be independent of the internal processing of financial information.

17. Which of the following concepts distinguishes the retention of computerized audit documentation from the traditional hard copy form?

A. Analyses, conclusions, and recommendations are filed on electronic media and are therefore subject to computer system controls and security procedures.

B. Evidential support for all findings is copied and provided to local management during the closing conference and to each person receiving the final report.

C. Computerized data files can be used in computer audit procedures.

D. Audit programs can be standardized to eliminate the need for a preliminary survey at each location.

Answer (A) is correct. *(CIA, adapted)*
REQUIRED: The distinction between computerized audit documentation and the traditional hard copy.
DISCUSSION: The only difference between the computerized audit documentation and hard copy form is how the working papers are stored. Electronic audit documentation is saved either on disks or hard drive, whereas hard copy is stored in a file cabinet. Unlike computerized audit documentation, hard copies are not subject to computer controls and security procedures.
Answer (B) is incorrect because evidential support would be retained and provided on the basis of the nature of the finding and not the media used for storing audit documentation. Answer (C) is incorrect because this capability is not an exclusive function of computerized audit documentation. Answer (D) is incorrect because, though the nature of the preliminary survey may change in some cases, the requirement for this phase of the audit is not eliminated by computerized audit documentation.

5.2 Operating Systems and Computer Devices

18. Regardless of the language in which an application program is written, its execution by a computer requires that primary memory contain

    A. A utility program.

    B. An operating system.

    C. Compiler.

    D. Assembly.

Answer (B) is correct. *(D. Payne)*
REQUIRED: The item necessary to execute an application program.
DISCUSSION: An operating system (e.g., UNIX or Windows) is required in all computerized systems to oversee the elements of the CPU and the interaction of the hardware components.
Answer (A) is incorrect because utility programs are application programs that are usually attached to larger programs. They perform various activities, such as sorting data, merging files, converting data from one medium to another, and printing. Answer (C) is incorrect because a compiler converts (compiles) a program written in a source language, such as FORTRAN, into machine language. Answer (D) is incorrect because an assembler translates an assembly language program into machine language. Assembly language uses mnemonic codes for each machine language instruction.

19. What type of computer processing system is characterized by data that are assembled from more than one location and records that are updated immediately?

    A. Personal computer systems.

    B. Data compression systems.

    C. Batch processing systems.

    D. Online, real-time systems.

Answer (D) is correct. *(CPA, adapted)*
REQUIRED: The system allowing data entry from multiple locations and immediate updating.
DISCUSSION: Real-time processing involves processing an input record and receiving the output soon enough to affect a current decision-making process. In a real-time system, the user interacts with the system to control an ongoing activity. Online indicates that the decision maker is in direct communication with the computer. Online, real-time systems usually permit access to the main computer from multiple remote terminals.
Answer (A) is incorrect because access from multiple locations is more typical of larger computer systems than of personal computer systems. Answer (B) is incorrect because data compression systems encode data to take up less storage space. Answer (C) is incorrect because batching of transactions requires assembly of data at one place and a delay in updating.

20. Misstatements in a batch computer system caused by incorrect programs or data may not be detected immediately because

    A. Errors in some transactions may cause rejection of other transactions in the batch.

    B. The identification of errors in input data typically is not part of the program.

    C. There are time delays in processing transactions in a batch system.

    D. The processing of transactions in a batch system is not uniform.

Answer (C) is correct. *(CPA, adapted)*
REQUIRED: The reason errors may not be detected immediately in a batch computer system.
DISCUSSION: Transactions in a batch computer system are grouped together, or batched, prior to processing. Batches may be processed either daily, weekly, or even monthly. Thus, considerable time may elapse between the initiation of the transaction and the discovery of an error.
Answer (A) is incorrect because the transactions within the batch are typically not contingent upon one another. Answer (B) is incorrect because edit checks can be incorporated into batch processing environments. However, the edit checks are used to test the transactions in batches. Answer (D) is incorrect because a batch of transactions is typically processed uniformly.

21. Which of the following statements most likely represents a disadvantage for an entity that keeps data files on a server rather than on a manual system?

    A. Attention is focused on the accuracy of the programming process rather than errors in individual transactions.

    B. It is usually easier for unauthorized persons to access and alter the files.

    C. Random error associated with processing similar transactions in different ways is usually greater.

    D. It is usually more difficult to compare recorded accountability with the physical count of assets.

Answer (B) is correct. *(CPA, adapted)*
REQUIRED: The disadvantage of server-based data files.
DISCUSSION: In a manual system, one individual is usually assigned responsibility for maintaining and safeguarding the records. However, in a server environment, the data files may be subject to change by others without documentation or an indication of who made the changes.
Answer (A) is incorrect because the focus on programming is an advantage of using a server. A software program allows transactions to be processed uniformly. Answer (C) is incorrect because it describes a disadvantage of a manual system. Answer (D) is incorrect because the method of maintaining the files is independent of the ability to compare this information in the file with the physical count of assets.

22. Computers containing more than one central processing unit (CPU) are increasingly common. This feature enables a computer to execute multiple instructions from multiple programs simultaneously. This process is

A. Time sharing.

B. Multitasking.

C. Multiprocessing.

D. Batch processing.

Answer (C) is correct. *(Publisher, adapted)*
REQUIRED: The term for executing multiple programs with multiple CPUs.
DISCUSSION: Multiprocessing greatly increases system efficiency by executing multiple programs on the same computer at the same time. In systems with only one CPU, although multiple programs may be active simultaneously, program instructions can only be executed for one of these programs at a time.
Answer (A) is incorrect because, in time sharing, the CPU spends a fixed amount of time on each program. Answer (B) is incorrect because multitasking is multiprogramming on a single-user operating system. It is the process of having multiple programs active at a given time, although the CPU is executing instructions from only one program at a time. Answer (D) is incorrect because batch processing entails execution of a list of instructions from beginning to end without interruption.

23. Which of the following statements about desktop computers, servers, and mainframe computers is true?

A. Desktop computers usually cost more than servers but less than mainframes.

B. Because of the increased use of desktop computers, there will be little need for mainframes in the near future.

C. Servers must be programmed directly in machine language while mainframes use higher-level language.

D. The cost per transaction to process on each type of computer has decreased in recent years.

Answer (D) is correct. *(Publisher, adapted)*
REQUIRED: The true statement concerning desktop computers, servers, and mainframe computers.
DISCUSSION: Advances in technology have resulted in less expensive computers and increased computing power. The cost to process transactions on all kinds of computers has therefore decreased.
Answer (A) is incorrect because desktop computers may cost less than $1,000. Relative to desktop computers, servers are more costly, more powerful, have more memory, and are able to interface with more peripheral equipment. Mainframes are large computers with many peripheral devices and large memories. There is virtually no upper limit on the cost of a mainframe. Answer (B) is incorrect because, although desktop computers have become extremely popular, e.g., for word processing, databases, other business-related activities, and Internet use, large mainframes are still necessary for simulations and processing not possible on other smaller computers. Servers fill the gap between desktop and mainframe computers, particularly for use in networks. Answer (C) is incorrect because all three computers ordinarily may be programmed in higher-level languages.

24. In the accounting department of a large organization, the most likely use of a CD-ROM would be to

A. Create permanent audit trails of EDI transactions.

B. Store images of documents received in the department.

C. Record the front and back of checks returned from the bank.

D. Provide a way to look up accounting standards and guidelines.

Answer (D) is correct. *(CIA, adapted)*
REQUIRED: The most likely use of a CD-ROM in an accounting department.
DISCUSSION: CD-ROM (compact disk, read-only memory) is a fixed optical medium appropriate for storage of very large quantities of unchanging information. Researching standards is the best use of CD-ROM technology for an accounting department because the data are static enough for periodic updates to remain sufficiently current. CD-ROMs commonly use indexing and searching facilities that make reference works usable. However, the use of CD-ROMs will decline as the prices of erasable optical disks become more attractive.
Answer (A) is incorrect because creating permanent audit trails of EDI transaction sequences is likely to be accomplished with write once, read many times (WORM) devices. Answer (B) is incorrect because maintaining images of documents with graphical components is likely to be done with redundant arrays of inexpensive disks (RAID). This technology is a magnetic medium that provides a primary storage method for imaging systems. Answer (C) is incorrect because recording the front and back of checks in banking applications is likely to be done with a microform such as microfilm.

25. Internal auditors often encounter different personal computer platforms in separate operating divisions or geographic locations. Which of the following statements is true?

I. Most data and programs from one personal computer platform are transferable to another environment only through translation and emulation programs.

II. Neither data nor programs are transferable when the hardware is not identical.

III. Neither data nor programs are transferable when the operating systems are not identical.

IV. Most data and many programs are transferable among environments through shareware programs.

    A. I only.

    B. I and IV only.

    C. III only.

    D. II and III only.

Answer (A) is correct. *(CIA, adapted)*
    REQUIRED: The true statement(s) about personal computer platforms.
    DISCUSSION: An emulator is a hardware device that permits one system to imitate another, that is, to use the same data and programs and obtain the same results as the other system. A translator is a program that translates from one programming language into another.
    Answer (B) is incorrect because shareware does not transfer data. Shareware is a program that can be freely copied and tested before purchase. If the party obtaining the shareware continues to use it, there is an obligation to send payment to the author. Shareware typically is found on bulletin boards and online information systems. Answer (C) is incorrect because there are facilities to transfer data and programs between disparate operating systems. Answer (D) is incorrect because there are facilities to transfer data and programs between some environments.

26. Response time on a local area network (LAN) was so slow that programmers working on applications kept their code on their own workstations rather than on the server. As a result, daily backups of the server did not contain the current source code. The best approach to detect deteriorating response time is

    A. Parallel testing.

    B. Integrated test facility.

    C. Performance monitoring.

    D. Program code comparison software.

Answer (C) is correct. *(CIA, adapted)*
    REQUIRED: The best approach to detect deteriorating response time.
    DISCUSSION: Performance monitoring is the systematic measurement and evaluation of operating results such as transaction rates, response times, and incidence of error conditions. Performance monitoring will reveal trends in capacity usage so that capacity can be upgraded before response deteriorates to the point that users behave in unintended or undesirable ways.
    Answer (A) is incorrect because parallel testing is an approach to implementing a new system. Answer (B) is incorrect because an ITF is an audit tool that uses a fictitious entity against which data transactions are processed. Answer (D) is incorrect because program code comparison software is used to detect unauthorized changes in programs.

27. A manufacturer is considering using bar-code identification for recording information on parts used by the manufacturer. A reason to use bar codes rather than other means of identification is to ensure that

    A. The movement of all parts is recorded.

    B. The movement of parts is easily and quickly recorded.

    C. Vendors use the same part numbers.

    D. Vendors use the same identification methods.

Answer (B) is correct. *(CIA, adapted)*
    REQUIRED: The reason to use bar codes.
    DISCUSSION: Bar-code scanning is a form of optical character recognition. Bar codes are a series of bars of different widths that represent critical information about the item. They can be read and the information can be instantly recorded using a scanner. Thus, bar coding records the movement of parts with minimal labor costs.
    Answer (A) is incorrect because any identification method may fail to record the movement of some parts. Answer (C) is incorrect because each vendor has its own part-numbering scheme. Answer (D) is incorrect because each vendor has its own identification method, although vendors in the same industry often cooperate to minimize the number of bar-code systems they use.

28. A manufacturer of complex electronic equipment such as oscilloscopes and microscopes has been shipping its products with thick paper manuals but wants to reduce the cost of producing and shipping this documentation. Of the following, the best medium for the manufacturer to use to accomplish this result is

  A. Write once/read many (WORM).

  B. Digital audiotape (DAT).

  C. Compact disk/read-only memory (CD-ROM).

  D. Computer output to microfilm (COM).

Answer (C) is correct. *(CIA, adapted)*
REQUIRED: The best way to reduce the cost of producing and shipping documentation.
DISCUSSION: CD-ROM is cheaper to produce and ship than the existing paper, yet it permits large volumes of text and images to be reproduced. Users of the electronic equipment are likely to have access to CD-ROM readers on PCs for using such documentation.
Answer (A) is incorrect because WORM is an optical storage technique often used as an archival medium. Answer (B) is incorrect because DAT is primarily used as a backup medium in imaging systems and as a master for CD-ROM. Answer (D) is incorrect because COM is used for frequent access to archived documents, such as canceled checks in banking applications.

5.3 Development of Systems and Applications

29. The process of monitoring, evaluating, and modifying a system as needed is referred to as systems

  A. Analysis.

  B. Feasibility study.

  C. Maintenance.

  D. Implementation.

Answer (C) is correct. *(CMA, adapted)*
REQUIRED: The term for the process of monitoring, evaluating, and modifying a system.
DISCUSSION: Systems maintenance must be undertaken by systems analysts and applications programmers continually throughout the life of a system. Maintenance is the redesign of the system and programs to meet new needs or to correct design flaws. These changes should be part of a regular program of preventive maintenance.
Answer (A) is incorrect because systems analysis is the process of determining user problems and needs, surveying the organization's present system, and analyzing the facts. Answer (B) is incorrect because a feasibility study determines whether a proposed system is technically, operationally, and economically feasible. Answer (D) is incorrect because implementation involves training and educating users, testing, conversion, and follow-up.

30. Effective internal control for application development should provide for which of the following?

I. A project steering committee to initiate and oversee the system

II. A technical systems programmer to evaluate systems software

III. Feasibility studies to evaluate existing systems

IV. The establishment of standards for systems design and programming

  A. I and III only.

  B. I, II, and IV only.

  C. I, III, and IV only.

  D. II, III, and IV only.

Answer (C) is correct. *(CISA, adapted)*
REQUIRED: The components of effective internal control for application development.
DISCUSSION: Effective systems development requires participation by top management. This can be achieved through a steering committee composed of higher-level representatives of system users. The committee approves or recommends projects and reviews their progress. Studies of the economic, operational, and technical feasibility of new applications necessarily entail evaluations of existing systems. Another necessary control is the establishment of standards for system design and programming. Standards represent user and system requirements determined during systems analysis.
Answer (A) is incorrect because standards must be established. Answer (B) is incorrect because a technical systems programmer has a role in the development and modification of the operating system but not necessarily in applications development. The technical support in this area would be provided by systems analysts rather than programmers. Answer (D) is incorrect because a technical systems programmer has a role in the development and modification of the operating system but not necessarily in applications development.

31. Which of the following should be emphasized before designing any system elements in a top-down approach to new systems development?

A. Types of processing systems being used by competitors.

B. Computer equipment to be used by the system.

C. Information needs of managers for planning and control.

D. Controls in place over the current system.

Answer (C) is correct.   *(CIA, adapted)*
REQUIRED: The matter to be emphasized before designing a new system.
DISCUSSION: The top-down method begins with analysis of broad organizational goals, objectives, and policies as a basis for the design process. This step requires an understanding of the entity's environment and significant activities. The next step is to determine the decisions made by managers and the information required to make them. The necessary reports, databases, inputs, processing methods, and equipment specifications can then be defined. The weakness of the top-down approach is that it tends to concentrate on managers' information needs at the expense of the design of efficient transaction processing at the operational level.
Answer (A) is incorrect because the needs of the organization should be the overriding factor in systems development. Answer (B) is incorrect because the equipment selection should be a function of the processing needs, not vice versa. Answer (D) is incorrect because functional controls should be designed for the new system.

32. A benefit of using computer-aided software engineering (CASE) technology is that it can ensure that

A. No obsolete data fields occur in files.

B. Users become committed to new systems.

C. All programs are optimized for efficiency.

D. Data integrity rules are applied consistently.

Answer (D) is correct.   *(CIA, adapted)*
REQUIRED: The benefit of CASE.
DISCUSSION: CASE is an automated technology (at least in part) for developing and maintaining software and managing projects. A benefit of using CASE technology is that it can ensure that data integrity rules, including those for validation and access, are applied consistently across all files.
Answer (A) is incorrect because obsolete data fields must be recognized by developers or users. Once recognized, obsolete data fields can be treated consistently in CASE procedures. Answer (B) is incorrect because using CASE will not ensure user commitment to new systems if they are poorly designed or otherwise do not meet users' needs. Answer (C) is incorrect because, although it has the potential to accelerate system development, CASE cannot ensure that all programs are optimized for efficiency. In fact, some CASE-developed modules may need to be optimized by hand to achieve acceptable performance.

33. CASE (computer-aided software engineering) is the use of the computer to aid in the development of computer-based information systems. Which of the following could not be automatically generated with CASE tools and techniques?

A. Information requirements determination.

B. Program logic design.

C. Computer program code.

D. Program documentation.

Answer (A) is correct.   *(CIA, adapted)*
REQUIRED: The item not automatically generated by CASE.
DISCUSSION: CASE applies the computer to software design and development. It maintains on the computer a library of standard program modules and all of the system documentation, e.g., data flow diagrams, data dictionaries, and pseudocode (structured English); permits development of executable input and output screens; and generates program code in at least skeletal form. Thus, CASE facilitates the creation, organization, and maintenance of documentation and permits some automation of the coding process. However, information requirements must be determined prior to using CASE.

34. Object technology has become important in companies' strategic use of information systems because of its potential to

A. Permit quicker and more reliable development of systems.

B. Maintain programs written in procedural languages.

C. Minimize data integrity violations in hierarchical databases.

D. Streamline the traditional "waterfall" systems development methodology.

Answer (A) is correct.   *(CIA, adapted)*
REQUIRED: The reason object technology is likely to become more important in companies' strategic use of information systems.
DISCUSSION: An object-oriented approach is intended to produce reusable code. Because code segments can be reused in other programs, the time and cost of writing software should be reduced.
Answer (B) is incorrect because object technology has the potential to support faster maintenance of programs written in object-oriented, but not procedural, languages. Answer (C) is incorrect because object technology is being applied to relational, but not hierarchical, databases. Answer (D) is incorrect because object technology is typically implemented in a prototyping environment.

35. User acceptance testing is more important in an object-oriented development process than in a traditional environment because of the implications of the

A. Absence of traditional design documents.

B. Lack of a tracking system for changes.

C. Potential for continuous monitoring.

D. Inheritance of properties in hierarchies.

Answer (D) is correct. *(CIA, adapted)*
REQUIRED: The reason user acceptance testing is more important in an object-oriented development process.
DISCUSSION: In object-oriented development, all objects in a class inherit the properties of higher classes in the hierarchy. Thus, changes in one object may affect many other objects, and the extent and effects of errors significantly increase. Testing one object provides no assurance that the objects are properly coordinated. Accordingly, user acceptance testing to verify correct functioning of the whole system becomes more important.
Answer (A) is incorrect because, instead of traditional design documents, items such as the business model, narratives of process functions, iterative development screens, computer processes and reports, and product descriptions guides are produced in object-oriented development. Answer (B) is incorrect because, in general, object-oriented development systems include tracking systems for changes made in objects and hierarchies. Answer (C) is incorrect because object-oriented systems are usually developed in client-server environments, so the potential exists for continuous monitoring of system use. However, continuous monitoring typically occurs during system operation, not during development.

36. A systems development approach used to quickly produce a model of user interfaces, user interactions with the system, and process logic is called

A. Neural networking.

B. Prototyping.

C. Reengineering.

D. Application generation.

Answer (B) is correct. *(CIA, adapted)*
REQUIRED: The approach used to produce a model of user interfaces, user interactions with the system, and process logic.
DISCUSSION: Prototyping produces the first model(s) of a new system. This technique usually employs a software tool for quick development of a model of the user interface (such as by report or screen), interaction of users with the system (for example, a menu-screen approach or data entry), and processing logic (the executable module). Prototyping stimulates user participation because the model allows quick exploration of concepts and development of solutions with quick results.
Answer (A) is incorrect because neural networking involves hardware or software that imitates the processing activities of the human brain. Answer (C) is incorrect because reengineering salvages reusable components of existing systems and restructures them to develop new systems or to improve the old systems. Answer (D) is incorrect because an application generator is software that can be used to develop an application simply by describing its requirements to the computer rather than by writing a procedural program.

37. An MIS manager has only enough resources to install either a new payroll system or a new data security system, but not both. Which of the following actions is most appropriate?

A. Giving priority to the security system.

B. Leaving the decision to the MIS manager.

C. Increasing MIS staff output in order for both systems to be installed.

D. Having the information systems steering committee set the priority.

Answer (D) is correct. *(CISA, adapted)*
REQUIRED: The appropriate action given inadequate resources.
DISCUSSION: The needs assessment and cost-benefit analysis should be conducted by those responsible for making the decision. In this case, the information systems steering committee is the appropriate decision maker.
Answer (A) is incorrect because not enough information is given to conclude that priority should be given to the security system. Answer (B) is incorrect because the MIS manager should not be the only decision maker. Answer (C) is incorrect because the question indicates that development of both systems is not possible.

38. Which of the following is the most appropriate activity for an internal auditor to perform during a review of systems development activity?

A. Serve on the MIS steering committee that determines what new systems are to be developed.

B. Review the methodology used to monitor and control the system development function.

C. Recommend specific automated procedures to be incorporated into new systems that will provide reasonable assurance that all data submitted to an application are converted to machine-readable form.

D. Recommend specific operational procedures that will ensure that all data submitted for processing are converted to machine-readable form.

Answer (B) is correct. *(CIA, adapted)*
REQUIRED: The procedure to perform during a review of systems development activity.
DISCUSSION: Auditor objectivity is not impaired when (s)he recommends standards of control for systems or reviews procedures before implementation. However, drafting procedures for systems and designing, installing, and operating systems are not audit functions. Thus, reviewing the methodology used by an organization is an appropriate activity that enables the internal auditor to determine whether (s)he can rely on the systems development activity to design and implement appropriate automated controls within applications.
Answer (A) is incorrect because service on a management decision-making committee is an operating responsibility and would impair audit objectivity. Answer (C) is incorrect because making recommendations for automated procedures is an operating responsibility. Answer (D) is incorrect because recommending operational procedures is an operating responsibility.

39. Traditional information systems development procedures that ensure proper consideration of controls may not be followed by users developing end-user computing (EUC) applications. Which of the following is a prevalent risk in the development of EUC applications?

A. Management decision making may be impaired due to diminished responsiveness to management's requests for computerized information.

B. Management may be less capable of reacting quickly to competitive pressures due to increased application development time.

C. Management may place the same degree of reliance on reports produced by EUC applications as it does on reports produced under traditional systems development procedures.

D. Management may incur increased application development and maintenance costs for EUC systems, compared with traditional (mainframe) systems.

Answer (C) is correct. *(CIA, adapted)*
REQUIRED: The risk in development of EUC applications.
DISCUSSION: End-user developed applications may not be subject to an independent outside review by systems analysts and are not created in the context of a formal development methodology. These applications may lack appropriate standards, controls, quality assurance procedures, and documentation. A risk of end-user applications is that management may rely on them as much as traditional applications.
Answer (A) is incorrect because EUC systems typically increase flexibility and responsiveness to management's information requests. Such systems are more easily modified. Answer (B) is incorrect because EUC systems typically reduce application development cycle time. Answer (D) is incorrect because EUC systems typically result in reduced application development and maintenance costs.

40. Traditional information systems development and operational procedures typically involve four functional areas. The systems analysis function focuses on identifying and designing systems to satisfy organizational requirements. The programming function is responsible for the design, coding, testing, and debugging of computer programs necessary to implement the systems designed by the analysis function. The computer operations function is responsible for data preparation, program/job execution, and system maintenance. The user function provides the input and receives the output of the system. Which of these four functions is often poorly implemented or improperly omitted in the development of a new end-user computing (EUC) application?

A. Systems analysis function.

B. Programming function.

C. Computer operations function.

D. User function.

Answer (A) is correct. *(CIA, adapted)*
REQUIRED: The function often omitted in development of a new EUC application.
DISCUSSION: Systems analysis is one step that is not absolutely required in the development of a system. The desire to produce a system quickly may result in this step being eliminated or poorly implemented. A system is often produced and then analyzed to see if it will satisfy the needs of the organization. In an EUC application, the systems analysis is often incomplete or omitted.
Answer (B) is incorrect because, without programming, there would be no system. Answer (C) is incorrect because, without computer operations, the system would not be able to do anything. Answer (D) is incorrect because, without users, there would be no need for the system.

41. Responsibility for the control of end-user computing exists at the organizational, departmental, and individual user level. Which of the following should be a direct responsibility of the individual users?

    A. Acquisition of hardware and software.

    B. Taking equipment inventories.

    C. Strategic planning of end-user computing.

    D. Physical security of equipment.

Answer (D) is correct. *(CIA, adapted)*
    REQUIRED: The direct responsibility of an individual user.
    DISCUSSION: End-user computing involves user-created or user-acquired systems that are maintained and operated outside of traditional information systems controls. In this environment, an individual user is ordinarily responsible for the physical security of the equipment (s)he uses.
    Answer (A) is incorrect because the acquisition of hardware and software is an organizational- and departmental-level responsibility. Answer (B) is incorrect because taking equipment inventories is an organizational-level responsibility. Answer (C) is incorrect because strategic planning is an organizational- and departmental-level responsibility.

42. Auditors often make use of computer programs that perform routine processing functions, such as sorting and merging. These programs are made available by computer companies and others and are specifically referred to as

    A. Compiler programs.

    B. Supervisory programs.

    C. Utility programs.

    D. User programs.

Answer (C) is correct. *(CPA, adapted)*
    REQUIRED: The term for programs used to perform routine functions.
    DISCUSSION: Utility programs are provided by manufacturers of equipment to perform routine processing tasks required by both clients and auditors, such as extracting data, sorting, merging, and copying. Utility programs are pretested, are independent of the client's own programming efforts, and furnish useful information without the trouble of writing special programs for the engagement.
    Answer (A) is incorrect because compiler programs convert source programs written in a higher-level language into computer-readable object programs, i.e., into machine language. Answer (B) is incorrect because supervisory programs, also termed operating systems, are master programs responsible for controlling operations within a computer system. Answer (D) is incorrect because user programs are those prepared for a particular application.

43. An internal auditor is reviewing the computer logic diagram.

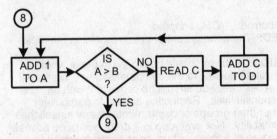

This diagram represents which of the following?

    A. Program loop.

    B. Data validity check.

    C. Balance test.

    D. Limit test.

Answer (A) is correct. *(CIA, adapted)*
    REQUIRED: The operation described by the computer logic diagram.
    DISCUSSION: Variable A will be increased by 1 and C will be added to D repetitively until A exceeds B. The diagram illustrates a program loop, a technique for performing repeated iterations of an instruction a specified number of times.
    Answer (B) is incorrect because a data validity check compares the bits of each transmitted character with the valid combinations of bits. Answer (C) is incorrect because a balance test compares a gross amount with its components. Answer (D) is incorrect because a limit test ascertains whether a number falls within a predetermined range of reasonable values.

5.4 System Security

44. Which of the following issues would be of most concern to an auditor relating to an organization's Internet security policy?

A. Auditor documentation.

B. System efficiency.

C. Data integrity.

D. Rejected and suspense item controls.

Answer (C) is correct.   *(Publisher, adapted)*
REQUIRED: The item of most concern to the auditor relating to Internet security.
DISCUSSION: Controls are intended to ensure the integrity, confidentiality, and availability of information. An auditor relies on the integrity of the system's data and programs in making critical decisions throughout the audit process.
Answer (A) is incorrect because auditor documentation is not as crucial as data integrity. Answer (B) is incorrect because efficiency does not affect the basis for critical auditor decisions using information provided by the system. Answer (D) is incorrect because rejected and suspense item controls represent a portion of the techniques used to ensure data integrity.

45. Management's enthusiasm for computer security seems to vary with changes in the environment, particularly the occurrence of other computer disasters. Which of the following concepts should be addressed when making a comprehensive recommendation regarding the costs and benefits of computer security?

I.   Potential loss if security is not implemented

II. Probability of occurrences

III. Cost and effectiveness of the implementation and operation of computer security

A. I only.

B. I and II only.

C. III only.

D. I, II, and III.

Answer (D) is correct.   *(CIA, adapted)*
REQUIRED: The concept(s) that should be addressed in an analysis of cost-benefit considerations.
DISCUSSION: Potential loss is the amount of dollar damages associated with a security problem or loss of assets. Potential loss times the probability of occurrence is an estimate (expected value) of the exposure associated with lack of security. It represents a potential benefit associated with the implementation of security measures. To perform a cost-benefit analysis, the costs should be considered. Thus, all three items need to be addressed.

46. As organizations become more computer integrated, management is becoming increasingly concerned with the quality of access controls to the computer system. Which of the following provides the most accountability?

	Option I	Option II	Option III	Option IV
Restrict access by:	Individuals	Groups	Individuals	Departments
Identify computer data at:	Field level	Workstation	Workstation	Individual record level
Restrict access:	Need to know	Right to know	Normal processing by employee type	Items identified as processed by department
Identify users by:	Password	Password	Key access to workstation, or password on workstation	Departmental password
Limit ability to:	Delete, add, or modify data	Add or delete files	Add, delete, or modify data stored at workstation	Add, delete, or modify data normally processed by department

A. Option I.

B. Option II.

C. Option III.

D. Option IV.

Answer (A) is correct.   *(CIA, adapted)*
REQUIRED: The access control option providing the most accountability.
DISCUSSION: Access should be limited to those whose activities necessitate access to the computer system. Moreover, the degree of access allowed should be consistent with an individual's responsibilities. Restricting access to particular individuals rather than groups or departments clearly establishes specific accountability. Not everyone in a group will need access or the same degree of access. Thus, passwords assigned to individuals should be required for identification of users by the system. Furthermore, data should be restricted at the field level, not the workstation level. It may be possible to limit access to a workstation, but most workstations are connected to larger mainframe or network databases. Thus, the security at the workstation level only would be insufficient.

47. An equipment manufacturer maintains dial-up ports into its order-entry system for the convenience of its customers worldwide so they may order parts as they need them. The manufacturer promises 48-hour delivery anywhere in the world for 95% of these parts orders. Because of the cost and sensitive nature of certain electronic parts, the manufacturer needs to maintain secure access to its order-entry system. The best technique for monitoring the security of access is

    A. Integrated test facility for the order-entry system.

    B. Tracing of transactions through the order-entry system.

    C. Transaction selection of order-entry transactions.

    D. Logging of unsuccessful access attempts.

Answer (D) is correct. *(CIA, adapted)*
    REQUIRED: The best technique for monitoring the security of access.
    DISCUSSION: An access log should be used to record all attempts to use the system. The date and time, codes used, mode of access, and data involved are recorded. The system should monitor unsuccessful attempts because repeated attempts could suggest that someone is trying random or patterned character sequences in order to identify a password.
    Answer (A) is incorrect because use of an integrated test facility (ITF) is a technique by which an auditor selects transactions and processing functions and applies the transactions to a fictitious entity during a normal processing cycle along with regular transactions. This technique cannot determine whether the data themselves are legitimate. Answer (B) is incorrect because tracing follows the path of a transaction during processing but is inadequate to determine whether a transaction is legitimate. Answer (C) is incorrect because transaction selection uses an independent computer program to monitor and select transactions for internal audit review. Like tracing, it fails to determine whether a transaction is legitimate. It would be an appropriate technique to apply to transactions suspected to be illegitimate.

48. Data access security related to applications may be enforced through all the following except

    A. User identification and authentication functions incorporated in the application.

    B. Utility software functions.

    C. User identification and authentication functions in access control software.

    D. Security functions provided by a database management system.

Answer (B) is correct. *(CIA, adapted)*
    REQUIRED: The functions through which data access security cannot be enforced.
    DISCUSSION: Utility programs perform routine functions (e.g., sorting and copying), are available to all users and are promptly available for many different applications. Utility programs are one of the more serious weaknesses in data access security because some can bypass normal access controls.
    Answer (A) is incorrect because, although there is a migration of control of this type away from applications to other software, the large bulk of these controls still reside in application software. Answer (C) is incorrect because access control software has as one of its primary objectives improving data access security for all data on the system. Answer (D) is incorrect because most database management systems provide for improved data access security while they are running.

49. Most organizations are concerned about the potential compromise of passwords. Which of the following procedures would be the most effective in controlling against a perpetrator obtaining someone else's password?

    A. Allow only the users to change their passwords and encourage them to change passwords frequently.

    B. Implement a computer program that tests to see that the password is not easily guessed.

    C. Implement the use of "see-through" authentication techniques whereby the user uses a card to generate a password and verifies both the key and the generated password to the system.

    D. Limit password authorization to time of day and location.

Answer (C) is correct. *(CIA, adapted)*
    REQUIRED: The most effective procedure for protecting passwords.
    DISCUSSION: See-through authentication techniques, such as the one described, require the user to have two of the three important elements to authenticate oneself to the system, i.e., a possession (the card used to generate the password), knowledge (the new password), or a personal characteristic (e.g., fingerprints).
    Answer (A) is incorrect because users often choose passwords that are easily guessed. Answer (B) is incorrect because a program to test passwords is useful but less effective than see-through authentication. Answer (D) is incorrect because limiting access to times and locations is helpful in certain environments but not when the system allows dial-up access.

50. Passwords for personal computer software programs are designed to prevent

    A. Inaccurate processing of data.

    B. Unauthorized access to the computer.

    C. Incomplete updating of data files.

    D. Unauthorized use of the software.

Answer (D) is correct. *(CIA, adapted)*
    REQUIRED: The function of passwords.
    DISCUSSION: The use of passwords is an effective control in an online system to prevent unauthorized access to computer files. Lists of authorized users are maintained in the computer. The entry of passwords or ID numbers; a prearranged act of personal questions; and use of badges, magnetic cards, or optically scanned cards may be combined to avoid unauthorized access.
    Answer (A) is incorrect because passwords concern authorization, not accuracy of data. Answer (B) is incorrect because passwords do not prevent physical access to the computer. Answer (C) is incorrect because passwords concern authorization, not completeness of data.

51. The primary objective of security software is to

    A. Control access to information system resources.

    B. Restrict access to prevent installation of unauthorized utility software.

    C. Detect the presence of viruses.

    D. Monitor the separation of duties within applications.

Answer (A) is correct. *(CIA, adapted)*
    REQUIRED: The primary objective of security software.
    DISCUSSION: The objective of security software is to control access to information system resources, such as program libraries, data files, and proprietary software. Security software identifies and authenticates users, controls access to information, and records and investigates security related events and data.
    Answer (B) is incorrect because security software will control the use of utilities, not their installation. Answer (C) is incorrect because antivirus software detects the presence of viruses. Answer (D) is incorrect because security software may be a tool to establish, but does not monitor, separation of duties.

52. A controller became aware that a competitor appeared to have access to the company's pricing information. The internal auditor determined that the leak of information was occurring during the electronic transmission of data from branch offices to the head office. Which of the following controls would be most effective in preventing the leak of information?

    A. Asynchronous transmission.

    B. Encryption.

    C. Use of fiber-optic transmission lines.

    D. Use of passwords.

Answer (B) is correct. *(CIA, adapted)*
    REQUIRED: The most effective control over electronic transmission of data.
    DISCUSSION: Encryption software uses a fixed algorithm to manipulate plain text and an encryption key (a set of random data bits used as a starting point for application of the algorithm) to introduce variation. Although data may be accessed by tapping into the transmission line, the encryption key is necessary to understand the data being sent.
    Answer (A) is incorrect because asynchronous transmission is a method of data transmission, not a means of safeguarding data. It is used for slow, irregular transmissions, such as from a keyboard terminal. Each character is marked by a start and stop code. Answer (C) is incorrect because, although fiber-optic transmission lines are difficult to tap, their use will not prevent theft of unencrypted data by someone who has access to them. Answer (D) is incorrect because use of passwords will control access at the sending location and the head-office computer. However, passwords will not prevent someone from tapping the transmission line.

53. The use of message encryption software

    A. Guarantees the secrecy of data.

    B. Requires manual distribution of keys.

    C. Increases system overhead.

    D. Reduces the need for periodic password changes.

Answer (C) is correct. *(CIA, adapted)*
    REQUIRED: The effect of message encryption software.
    DISCUSSION: Encryption software uses a fixed algorithm to manipulate plain text and an encryption key (a set of random data bits used as a starting point for application of the algorithm) to introduce variation. The machine instructions necessary to encrypt and decrypt data constitute system overhead. As a result, processing speed may be slowed.
    Answer (A) is incorrect because no encryption approach absolutely guarantees the secrecy of data. Answer (B) is incorrect because keys may also be distributed electronically via secure key transporters. Answer (D) is incorrect because periodic password changes are needed. Passwords are the typical means of validating users' access to unencrypted data.

54. All administrative and professional staff in a corporate legal department prepare documents on terminals connected to a host LAN file server. The best control over unauthorized access to sensitive documents in the system is

    A. Required entry of passwords for access to the system.

    B. Physical security for all disks containing document files.

    C. Periodic server backup and storage in a secure area.

    D. Required entry of passwords for access to individual documents.

Answer (D) is correct. *(CIA, adapted)*
REQUIRED: The best control over unauthorized access to sensitive documents in a local area network.
DISCUSSION: Different passwords may be required to access the system, to read certain files, and to perform certain other functions. Required entry of passwords for access to individual documents is the best single control over unauthorized access to sensitive documents.
Answer (A) is incorrect because password security for access to the system permits all departmental employees access to all documents in the system. Answer (B) is incorrect because this system uses no floppy disks. Answer (C) is incorrect because periodic server backup and storage in a secure area is a good security/backup procedure, but it would not prevent access to sensitive documents online.

55. An auditor has just completed a physical security audit of a data center. Because the center engages in top-secret defense contract work, the auditor has chosen to recommend biometric authentication for workers entering the building. The recommendation might include devices that verify all of the following except

    A. Fingerprints.

    B. Retina patterns.

    C. Speech patterns.

    D. Password patterns.

Answer (D) is correct. *(CIA, adapted)*
REQUIRED: The method that does not provide biometric authentication.
DISCUSSION: Biometric technologies are automated methods of establishing an individual's identity using physiological or behavioral traits. These characteristics include fingerprints, retina patterns, hand geometry, signature dynamics, speech, and keystroke dynamics.

5.5 Contingency Planning

56. Contingency plans for information systems should include appropriate backup agreements. Which of the following arrangements would be considered too vendor-dependent when vital operations require almost immediate availability of computer resources?

    A. A "hot site" arrangement.

    B. A "cold site" arrangement.

    C. A "cold and hot site" combination arrangement.

    D. Using excess capacity at another data center within the organization.

Answer (B) is correct. *(CIA, adapted)*
REQUIRED: The contingency plan that is too vendor-dependent.
DISCUSSION: Organizations should maintain contingency plans for operations in the case of a disaster. These plans usually include off-site storage of important backup data and an arrangement for the continuation of operations at another location. A "cold site" has all needed assets in place except the needed computer equipment and is vendor-dependent for timely delivery of equipment.
Answer (A) is incorrect because a "hot site" has all needed assets in place and is not vendor-dependent. Answer (C) is incorrect because a "cold and hot site" combination allows the "hot site" to be used until the "cold site" is prepared and is thus not too vendor-dependent. Answer (D) is incorrect because excess capacity would ensure that needed assets are available and would not be vendor-dependent.

57. Each day, after all processing is finished, a bank performs a backup of its online deposit files and retains it for 7 days. Copies of each day's transaction files are not retained. This approach is

    A. Valid, in that having a week's worth of backups permits recovery even if one backup is unreadable.

    B. Risky, in that restoring from the most recent backup file would omit subsequent transactions.

    C. Valid, in that it minimizes the complexity of backup/recovery procedures if the online file has to be restored.

    D. Risky, in that no checkpoint/restart information is kept with the backup files.

Answer (B) is correct. *(CIA, adapted)*
    REQUIRED: The true statement about retention of backup files but not each day's transaction files.
    DISCUSSION: At appropriate intervals, the disk files should be copied on magnetic tape so that restart procedures can begin at those points if data are lost or destroyed. However, not retaining each day's transaction files is risky because information processed since the last backup file was created will be lost.
    Answer (A) is incorrect because the practice of not retaining daily transaction data is unsound in that the bank loses a day's transactions for each backup that is unreadable. Answer (C) is incorrect because the practice of not retaining daily transaction data certainly minimizes complexity but at the expense of losing transaction data if the online file must be restored from the backup. Answer (D) is incorrect because checkpoint/restart information is not needed. The backups are created after all processing is finished for the day.

58. A company updates its accounts receivable master file weekly and retains the master files and corresponding update transactions for the most recent 2-week period. The purpose of this practice is to

    A. Verify run-to-run control totals for receivables.

    B. Match internal labels to avoid writing on the wrong volume.

    C. Permit reconstruction of the master file if needed.

    D. Validate groups of update transactions for each version.

Answer (C) is correct. *(CIA, adapted)*
    REQUIRED: The purpose of periodic retention of master files and transaction data.
    DISCUSSION: The grandfather-father-son approach normally employs magnetic tapes to furnish backup in a batch processing system. The procedure involves creation and retention of three generations of master files so that lost or destroyed data may be regenerated from the remaining master files and transaction data. In this case, a master file (the grandfather) and the first week's transactions are used to generate a second master file (the father). This file and the second week's transactions are the basis for the current master file (the son). Online systems employ rollback and recovery procedures; i.e., the master file is periodically dumped onto a storage medium. Reconstruction is then possible using the backup copy and the transactions log.
    Answer (A) is incorrect because comparison of batch totals is a control over the completeness of processing, not a recovery procedure. Answer (B) is incorrect because internal labels may avoid destruction of data but do not aid in recovery. Answer (D) is incorrect because validation may avoid destruction of data but does not aid in recovery.

59. Good planning will help an organization restore computer operations after a processing outage. Good recovery planning should ensure that

    A. Backup/restart procedures have been built into job streams and programs.

    B. Change control procedures cannot be bypassed by operating personnel.

    C. Planned changes in equipment capacities are compatible with projected workloads.

    D. Service level agreements with owners of applications are documented.

Answer (A) is correct. *(CIA, adapted)*
    REQUIRED: The condition ensured by good recovery planning.
    DISCUSSION: The disaster plan should embrace data center recovery, critical application recovery, and network recovery. It should be updated and current with regard to recent test results and new applications, equipment, and network configurations. The plan should also ensure that backup facilities are still able to process critical applications and that end-user responsibility is established. Another essential component of a disaster recovery plan is that backup/restart procedures have been anticipated and provided for in the application systems.
    Answer (B) is incorrect because whether change control procedures can be bypassed is not usually a consideration in disaster recovery planning. Answer (C) is incorrect because planned rather than actual changes in equipment capacities are not relevant in disaster recovery planning. Answer (D) is incorrect because ensuring that service level agreements with owners of critical applications are adequate is not a function of disaster recovery planning.

Use Gleim's **CIA Test Prep** for interactive testing with **over 2,000 additional multiple-choice questions**!

STUDY UNIT SIX
INFORMATION TECHNOLOGY II

(31 pages of outline)

This study unit begins with a consideration of communications, with a primary emphasis on computer networks, including the Internet. It then addresses how an information system permits efficient storage, access to, and updating of data through the development of databases. The evolution of computer networks and databases is vital to the rapid growth of e-business. Electronic data interchange (EDI) and its offshoot, electronic funds transfer (EFT) are likewise major elements in the e-business explosion. The next subunit considers the development of systems that connect all of an enterprise's applications. The study unit concludes with coverage of the severe threats posed by viruses and other malicious software and by other means used to assault the computer systems of businesses.

No Standards or Practice Advisories are included in this study unit.

Core Concepts

- The movement of data among CPUs and remote devices requires special hardware and software and telecommunications technology.

- Computers are linked in networks, which can be classified by geographical extent (e.g., LAN, WAN), services offered (e.g., public-switched, VAN), or topology (e.g., bus, ring, start).

- The Internet is a network of networks all over the world. It facilitates inexpensive communication and information transfer among computers.

- A database is a series of related files combined to eliminate redundancy of data items. The relational database has been the most cost-effective architecture.

- Electronic data interchange (EDI) is the leading method of carrying on e-commerce. It involves the communication of data in standardized format directly from a computer in one entity to a computer in another entity.

- Enterprise resource planning (ERP) is intended to integrate enterprise-wide information systems by creating one database linked to all of an organization's applications.

- Malicious software may exploit a known hole or weakness in an application or operating system program to evade security measures. Examples include Trojan horses, viruses, and worms.

6.1 DATA COMMUNICATIONS AND NETWORKS

1.   The movement of data among CPUs and remote devices requires special hardware and software and telecommunications technology.

   a.   To connect computers and remote terminals, the following devices may be used:

   1)   **Front-end processors** perform message switching, move data to primary storage, translate coded data, and otherwise relieve the host computer of certain communications control functions.

   a)   They are located between the computer and the modem in the network.
   b)   Nonprogrammable units are known as communications controllers.

   2)   **Multiplexers** are switching devices that route or channel the flow of data. They intermix the two-way flow of data so that data may flow over one line. A multiplexer channel permits sending more than one message on a communication line **(interleaving)**. Thus, several terminals may be able to share a communication line to a CPU.

   a)   A **concentrator** is a programmable device that collects messages until it has enough to be transmitted in a burst of signals to the host computer.

   3)   A **modem (modulator-demodulator)** is a hardware device to convert digital signals from terminals and the CPU into analog signals for transmission across data (usually telephone) lines. The receiving modem converts the analog signal back to digital form for use by the receiving terminal or CPU.

   a)   If **digital transmission** facilities are available, however, a modem is not required. Instead, the user employs a digital interface or **data service unit (DSU)** as a connection with the digital transmission service.

   i)   Digital transmission is less prone to error because it is less sensitive to electrical interference.

   b)   One way in which modems may differ is in their **bit rates**, not to be confused with **baud rates**. The bit rate, usually measured in bits per second, is a measurement of the transmission speed. The baud rate is the number of signal changes or cycles per period of time and cannot exceed the bandwidth of the communication channel.

   i)   At high speeds, more than one bit may be transmitted by a signal change. Hence, the bit rate may be greater than the baud rate.

   ii)   A telecommunications medium's transmission capacity depends on its frequency, i.e., the number of signal changes or cycles per second that can be sent through the medium as measured in **hertz**. The **bandwidth** is the range of frequencies from highest to lowest that a given telecommunications channel can accommodate. As the bandwidth increases, the capacity of the medium also increases.

   4)   **Communications channels** differ from the data channels connecting the CPU and peripheral equipment. These communications media for transmitting data are classified according to their capacity:

   a)   **Narrowband (baseband)**, e.g., telegraph lines
   b)   **Voiceband**, e.g., telephone lines
   c)   **Broadband**, which provides multiple paths and therefore permits simultaneous transmission of different kinds of data.

   i)   Examples are fiber-optic cable, microwave circuits, and satellite channels.

   d)   **Baseband network**, a type of LAN used solely for data communications

5) The following are other hardware items used to connect computers in a network:

   a) A **hub** is a central connecting device in a network that joins communications lines in a star configuration.

      i) **Passive hubs** are connecting units that add nothing to the data passing through them.

      ii) **Active hubs**, also sometimes called **multiport repeaters**, regenerate the data bits to maintain a strong signal.

      iii) **Intelligent hubs** provide added functionality, such as network management, bridging, routing, and switching.

   b) A **switch** is another connecting device. Each port on a switch can give full bandwidth to a single server, client, or hub.

   c) **Bridges** connect two or more LAN segments together. The segments can be of similar or dissimilar types. Bridges improve network performance by keeping traffic contained within smaller segments.

   d) **Routers** are devices that route data packets from one local area network (LAN) or wide area network (WAN) to another. Routers read the network address in each transmitted frame and make a decision on how to send it based on the most expedient route. They also perform the central switching function on the **Internet**.

b. **Transmission media** include the following:

   1) **Twisted copper wire** is used for analog communication by telephone. It is a slow medium for data transmission, but new software and hardware have improved its capacity.

   2) **Coaxial cable** is used for cable television, high-speed modems, and LANs. It consists of thickly insulated copper wire that is faster and more interference free than twisted wire.

   3) **Fiber-optic cable** uses light impulses that travel through clear flexible tubing half the size of a human hair. Fiber-optic cables are not subject to electrical interference and are highly reliable. They provide for extremely flexible and fast data transmission. The signal remains strong across long distances; i.e., it does not tend to weaken (attenuate). Fiber-optic cables have been proven to be more tamper resistant than the other media listed. Optical transmissions cannot be wiretapped. It is also more expensive.

   4) **Wireless** transmission media use the **electromagnetic spectrum**. For example, **microwave systems** use high-frequency radio signals transmitted through the atmosphere. Satellites may serve as relay points. They may be the conventional high, stationary orbit variety or the cheaper low-orbit satellites that require less powerful ground transmitters.

      a) **Pagers** have long been used to alert the recipient of a message, but newer systems permit transmission of brief **text messages**.

      b) A **cell phone** uses radio waves to transmit voice and data through antennas in a succession of cells or defined geographic areas. Two-way digital data transmission via cell phone is made possible by the transmission standard **CDPD (Cellular Digital Packet Data)**.

      c) Networks **(mobile data networks)** have been established expressly for two-way data transmission between handheld computers.

      d) **Personal communications services (PCS)** is a cellular technology based on lower-power, higher-frequency radio waves. Cells must be smaller and more numerous, but the phones should be smaller and less expensive and be able to operate where other such devices cannot.

e) A **personal digital assistant (PDA)** is a handheld computer with pen-based input. It may have wireless telecommunication capabilities, for example, email, fax, and document data transmission.

c. **Transmission modes** may be asynchronous or synchronous.

1) **Asynchronous** or **start-stop transmission** is used for slow, irregular transmissions, such as from a keyboard terminal. Each character is marked by a start and stop bit.

2) **Synchronous transmission** is used when rapid, continuous transmission is desired. It transfers blocks of characters without start and stop bits but requires that the sending and receiving modems be synchronized.

d. The following are the types of **transmission circuits**:

1) **Simplex** transmission is in one direction only, such as for display purposes (e.g., a public address system).

2) **Half-duplex** transmission is in both directions but not at the same time. It is appropriate when processing is online but a response is not required (e.g., a walkie-talkie).

3) **Duplex** transmission is in both directions at once, which is a necessity for real-time processing (e.g., a telephone).

e. **Teleprocessing** is computer processing via remote terminals. Communications software for teleprocessing is necessarily complex because of the multiple tasks to be performed when many terminals are in simultaneous use. The CPU, the front-end processor, and the concentrator all may have communications software.

1) This software performs the following **functions**:

a) Receives input, locates the appropriate program, loads it into memory, transmits the input to the program, and passes the output to the user

b) Identifies and corrects errors and provides for security. Encryption is a typical security measure. A program codes data prior to transmission. Another program decodes it after transmission.

c) Maintains a log of activity and a database or file of updated records

d) Manages buffers (special storage areas) that hold input before processing

e) Manages the sequencing and proper routing of messages

2) A **protocol** is a set of rules for message transmission among the devices in the network. Each device should adhere to the same protocol.

3) **Snapshot** copies of files are created at time intervals so that the files will be available on the mainframe. A risk of snapshot files is that they could be obsolete by the time they are downloaded.

2. **Types of networks.** A network consists of multiple connected computers at multiple locations. Computers that are electronically linked permit an organization to assemble and share transaction and other information among different physical locations.

a. **Private networks** are dedicated facilities, e.g., satellites, microwave transmitters, or telephone lines, leased from a common carrier. Hence, no dial-up access is required, and security is enhanced. A **PBX (private branch exchange)** is a special computer at an organization's facility used to store, hold, transfer, and redial telephone calls. It can carry both voice and data and can switch digital data among computers and office equipment, e.g., printers, copiers, and fax machines. A PBX uses telephone lines, so its data transmission capacity is limited.

b. **Public-switched networks** use public telephone lines. This arrangement may be the most economical, but data transmission may be of lower quality, no connection may be available, and security measures may be ineffective.

c. **Value-added networks (VANs)** are private networks that transmit the data of subscribing entities. To compete with the Internet, these third-party networks add value by providing error detection and correction services, electronic mailbox facilities for EDI purposes, EDI translation, and security for email and data transmissions.

1) **Packet switching** is one way in which a VAN adds value by improving the efficiency of transmissions. Packet switching divides a file into small packages that are sent independently by available communication channels through a network and then reassembled at the receiving end.

   a) **Frame relay** is faster and less expensive but, unlike packet switching, does not involve error correction. Frames are similar to packets. They are best used for data rather than voice or video communication.

   b) **Asynchronous transfer mode (ATM)** is a technology that avoids the need for separate networks. It switches audio, video, graphics, and data among users at whatever speed the network can operate and regardless of whether the computers are from different vendors. It also eliminates protocol conversion by dividing information into cells, each containing 53 bytes.

   c) **Internet Protocol (IP)** is the packet-switching protocol upon which the Internet is built. Other protocols, such as TCP/IP, are built on top of IP to allow computers to connect to each other across many network nodes.

d. A **local area network (LAN)** is a local distributed computer system, e.g., within a single office. Computers, communication devices, and other equipment are linked by cable. Special software facilitates efficient data communication among the hardware devices. The channel technology may be baseband or broadband. Baseband allows one path for transmission of video, voice, text, or graphics, and only one data type may be transmitted. **Broadband** provides multiple paths.

1) The LAN's hardware consists of several microcomputers either attached to a host computer, linked as part of several LANs that may or may not communicate with a host computer, or connected together but not connected to a host computer.

   a) A **peer-to-peer network** operates without a mainframe or server.

2) A LAN also may use **wireless spread spectrum broadcasting** rather than a direct cable link. However, a wireless LAN is likely to have slower response times.

3) A **network interface card** links personal computers and printers in a LAN that is connected by coaxial cable, twisted pair, or optical fiber. The card creates an address for each message, determines the data transmission rate and the size of message units, and specifies how the components are connected (the topology).

4) A **server** is a computer in the LAN that functions as a librarian. It stores programs and files for users and determines who obtains access to what. It also contains the **network operating system**.

5) A **gateway** is a means of connecting otherwise incompatible networks, nodes, or devices. It converts one set of communication protocols to another.

6) **Ethernet** is a set of LAN standards that allows networking products from different vendors to communicate with each other. It is the most widely used LAN technology.

7) A **baseband network** is used solely for data communications.

e. **Wide area networks (WAN)** provide data communication and file sharing among remote offices. A WAN may combine switched and dedicated lines, microwave transmission, and satellite communication. Common carriers determine rates and connections between lines, but content and management (routing of messages, editing, protocols, etc.) are the responsibility of the customer.

f. **Virtual private networks (VPN)**

1) Businesses have traditionally relied on private **leased lines** to link offices so that workers could share information over a WAN. However, while providing a high degree of privacy, leased lines are expensive to set up and maintain. For many organizations, a leased line may be impractical, providing more bandwidth than is needed at too high a price.

2) VPNs emerged as a relatively inexpensive way to solve this problem. Rather than maintain a point-to-point leased line, an organization connects each office or LAN to a local **Internet service provider** and routes data through the Internet using shared, low-cost public bandwidth as the communications backbone.

3) However, the major concern in using a public network for electronic data exchange is **security**. Unprotected data sent across the Internet are susceptible to being viewed, copied, or modified by unauthorized parties. The success of VPNs will depend on the development of secure encryption products that protect data while in transit across the Internet.

g. Given the worldwide proliferation of computer networks, **connectivity** has become a major issue. The desire for greater connectivity favors open systems.

1) **Open systems** are those for which suppliers provide components whose interfaces are defined by public standards. For example, the U.S. government specifies that its suppliers adhere to the **UNIX operating system** and the telecommunications protocols developed for the Internet. In contrast, a closed system's components are built to proprietary standards so that the equipment made by other suppliers could not interface with the existing system. Accordingly, converting to open systems increases the number of vendors from which substitutable components can be acquired, which increases price competition for equipment.

2) Although uniform standards for telecommunications, networking, operating systems, and user interfaces have not yet emerged, some standards have been created by governments, industry associations, and international organizations.

a) **Open Systems Interconnect (OSI)** has been developed by the International Organization for Standardization. It is a seven-layer reference model that allows different types of computers and networks to communicate.

b) **Integrated Services Digital Network (ISDN)** provides international standards for voice, video, and data communications over telephone lines.

3. **Voice Communications**

a. **Voice communications channels** differ from the data channels connecting the CPU and peripheral equipment. They are the communications media for transmitting voice data and are classified according to their capacity.

1) An example of a voiceband channel is a telephone line.

2) **Internet telephony** is any transmission of two-way voice communication that uses the Internet for all or part of its path. This can be performed with traditional telephone devices; desktop computers equipped with a sound card, microphone, and speakers; or terminals dedicated to this function.

b. **Voice recognition** input devices are still another alternative to keyboard input. These systems compare the speaker's voice patterns with prerecorded patterns. Advanced systems now have large vocabularies and shorter training periods. They allow for dictation and are not limited to simple commands.

c. A **voice output device** converts digital data into speech using prerecorded sounds.

d. **Pagers** have long been used to alert the recipient of a message, but newer systems now permit transmission of brief text messages.

e. A **cell phone** uses radio waves to transmit voice and data through antennas in a succession of cells or defined geographic areas.

f. **Personal communications services (PCS)** is a cellular technology based on lower-power, higher-frequency radio waves. Cells must be smaller and more numerous, but the phones should be smaller and less expensive and be able to operate where other such devices cannot.

4. **The Internet and Related Networks**

a. The **Internet** is a **network of networks** all over the world.

1) The Internet is descended from the original ARPANet, a product of the Defense Department's Advanced Research Projects Agency (ARPA), introduced in 1969.

a) The idea was to have a network that could not be brought down during an enemy attack by bombing a single central location. ARPANet connected computers at universities, corporations, and government. In view of the growing success of the Internet, ARPANet was retired in 1990.

2) The Internet facilitates inexpensive communication and information transfer among computers, with gateways allowing mainframe computers to interface with personal computers.

a) Very high-speed **Internet backbones** carry signals around the world and meet at **network access points**.

3) Most Internet users obtain connections through **Internet service providers (ISPs)** that in turn connect either directly to a backbone or to a larger ISP with a connection to a backbone.

a) The topology of the backbone and its interconnections may once have resembled a spine with ribs connected along its length but is now almost certainly more like a fishing net wrapped around the world with many circular paths.

4) The three main parts of the Internet are the **servers** that hold information, **clients** that view the information, and the **transmission control protocol/ Internet protocol (TCP/IP)** suite of protocols that connect the two.

5) The Internet was initially restricted to email and text-only documents.

a) In the 1980s, English computer scientist Tim Berners-Lee conceived the idea of allowing users to click on a word or phrase (a **hyperlink**) on their screens and having another document automatically be displayed.

b) Berners-Lee created a simple coding mechanism called **hypertext markup language (HTML)** to perform this function. He also created a set of rules called **hypertext transfer protocol (HTTP)** to allow hyperlinking across the Internet rather than on just a single computer. He then created a piece of software, called a **browser**, that allowed users to read HTML from any brand of computer. The result was the **World Wide Web** (often simply called The Web).

        i)   As the use of HTML and its successor languages spread, it became possible to display rich graphics and streaming audio and video in addition to text.

        ii)   **Extensible markup language (XML)** was developed by an international consortium and released in 1998 as an open standard usable with many programs and platforms.

- XML codes all information in such a way that a user can determine not only **how it should be presented** but also **what it is**, i.e., all computerized data may be tagged with identifiers.
- Unlike HTML, XML uses **codes that are extensible, not fixed**. Thus, if an industry can agree on a set of codes, software for that industry can be written that incorporates those codes.

6)   With the explosive growth of the World Wide Web in the 1990s, whole **new distribution channels** opened up for businesses. Consumers can browse a vendor's catalog using the rich graphics of the web, initiate an order, and remit payment, all from the comfort of their homes.

    a)   An organization's **presence** on the Web is constituted in its **website**. The website consists of a **home page**, the first screen encountered by users, and subsidiary **web pages** (screens constructed using HTML or a similar language).

    b)   Every page on the World Wide Web has a unique address, recognizable by any web-enabled device, called a **universal resource locator (URL)**. However, just because the address is recognizable does not mean it is accessible to every user -- security is a major feature of any organization's website.

7)   An **intranet** permits sharing of information throughout an organization by applying Internet connectivity standards and web software (e.g., browsers) to the organization's internal network.

    a)   An intranet addresses the connectivity problems of an organization with many types of computers. It is ordinarily restricted to those within the organization and to outsiders after appropriate identification.

    b)   An **extranet** consists of the linked intranets of two or more organizations, for example, of a supplier and its customers. It typically uses the public Internet as its transmission medium but requires a password for access.

5. Applications

a.   **Electronic mail** permits transfer, receipt, and storage of messages within or between computer systems. The "mail" consists of electronically transmitted messages. A user's "mailbox" is the storage area allocated for messages. The advantages of electronic mail are high-speed transmission, reduction of message preparation costs, and the possibility of sending or reading messages at a convenient time.

    1)   A typical system permits a user to answer messages, compose or delete messages, edit, file, forward messages to other users, move items among files, read, retrieve from files, scan contents of files, send messages, and print.

b.   **Voice mail** converts spoken messages from analog to digital form, transmits them over a network, and stores them on a disk. Messages are then converted back to analog form when the recipient desires to hear them. Afterward, they may be saved, forwarded, or deleted.

    c.   Conducting an electronic meeting among several parties at remote sites is **teleconferencing**. It can be accomplished by telephone or electronic mail group communication software.

       1)   **Videoconferencing** permits the conferees to see each other on video screens.

       2)   These practices have grown in recent years as companies have attempted to cut their travel costs.

    d.   A **fax machine** can scan a document, convert its text and graphics to digital form, and then transmit the result over telephone lines. The recipient's fax machine can then create a facsimile of the transmitted document.

    e.   An **electronic bulletin board** is a database into which computer users may dial to read or post messages.

    f.   **Electronic commerce** is discussed in more detail in Study Unit 7.

6.   **Network Configurations (Topologies)**

    a.   **Point-to-point** networks provide a separate, direct link between each remote terminal and the CPU.

    b.   **Multidrop** (or **bus**) networks provide links for each terminal to a single communications line connected to the CPU. However, only one terminal may send or receive messages at one time. A superior but more costly alternative is to use a line-sharing device (a multiplexor or a concentrator) to connect the group of terminals to the CPU.

       1)   **Ethernet** is an example of a network technology that is based on a bus topology.

    c.   **Ring networks** have no central computer. Each computer can communicate with every other computer, but their connection forms a closed loop in which data pass from one device to another, always in one direction.

       1)   In a **token ring network**, a packet of data (the token) passes along the network. Each computer reads it and either accepts data from it, loads data onto the token, or allows it to pass without change.

       2)   Once strongly promoted by **IBM**, the token ring topology has drastically declined in usage with improvements in the speed and cost of Ethernet technology.

    d.   **Completely connected networks** have direct links among all computer locations.

    e.   **Star networks** permit each remote computer a direct link to the central location but not to other remote computers.

7.   **Basic Architectures for Desktop Computing**

    a.   **Client-server model.** A client-server system divides processing of an **application** between a **client machine** on a network and a server. This division depends on which tasks each is best suited to perform.

       1)   **User interaction** is ordinarily restricted to the client part of the application. This portion normally consists of the user interface, data entry, queries, and receipt of reports. Moreover, many applications, e.g., word processing and spreadsheet software, reside on the client computer.

       2)   The **server** customarily manages peripheral hardware and controls access to shared **databases**. Thus, a client-server application must be designed as separate software components that run on different machines but appear to be one application.

3) **Security** for client-server systems may be more difficult than in a highly centralized mainframe-based system because of the numerous access points. They also use **distributed processing** methods that result in heightened risk of unauthorized access to data and processing. New methods of accessing data and processing are also available. For example, **remote procedure calls (RPC)** in a distributed system allow a program on one computer to call on a subroutine on another computer.

4) A variety of servers are encountered on the Internet, including those that allow the transmission and receipt of electronic mail **(mail servers)**; retrieval of files from other computers **(file servers)**; and access to documents, files, and programs on the web **(web server)**.

   a) A **commerce server** is a type of web server with business-related features, such as the **Secure Electronic Transaction (SET)** protocol for encrypting all transmissions between the client and the commerce server, **digital certificates** for identification of the client and server, and methods for permitting the client to run programs on the server.

5) The client-server model has the advantages of a **robot**. Unlike a human being, a server does not require compensation and is able to work 24 hours of every day. It also can cope with many (possibly thousands) of clients at a time who can access the server over the Internet from anywhere at any time with no time-related charges.

b. **Terminal.** This is a specific kind of client-server architecture. A user can directly run applications and access data on a server from a client computer known as a terminal.

   1) A **dumb terminal** allows only text display and input. A client computer may run a terminal application to connect to a remote computer over a network, or a device such as a **video display terminal (VDT)** may be connected via a serial cable to a timesharing computer.

   2) A **smart terminal** allows display of graphics and use of a windowing environment on the server. A smart terminal also may download applications from the server to execute on the client. Examples of smart terminals include X-Terminal for UNIX and Remote Desktop and Terminal Services Client for Windows.

8. Stop and review! You have completed the outline for this subunit. Study multiple-choice questions 1 through 10 beginning on page 326.

6.2 DATABASES

1. A **database** is a series of related files combined to eliminate redundancy of data items.

   a. A single integrated system allows for improved data accessibility.

   b. When systems within the organization are not integrated, they not only may contain different data but also may define and update data in inconsistent ways. Thus, determining the location of data and ensuring their consistency are more difficult.

   c. EXAMPLE: The various files related to human resources in the conventional record systems of most organizations include payroll, work history, and permanent personnel data.

   1) An employee's name must appear in each of these files when they are stored and processed separately. The result is redundancy. When data are combined in a database, each data item is usually stored only once.

d. The data are stored physically on **direct-access storage devices** (e.g., magnetic disks). They are also stored for efficient access.

    1) The most frequently accessed items are placed in the physical locations permitting the fastest access.

    2) When these items were stored in separate files under older file-oriented systems, the physical locations were usually similar to the logical structure of the data. Items that logically belonged together were stored in physical proximity to one another.

    3) A **logical data model** is a user view. It is the way a user describes the data and defines their interrelationships based on the user's needs, without regard to how the data are physically stored.

2. To understand the vast improvement in performance brought about by database technology, it is helpful to review the development of file structures.

a. The early mainframe computers used **flat files**, meaning that all the records, and all the data elements within each record, followed one behind the other. Much early mainframe storage was on magnetic tape, which naturally stored data in this fashion.

b. EXAMPLE: Here are two records excerpted from a tape file:

Record	Customer	Street	City	Order_Nbr	Part_Nbr_1	Qty_1	Price_1	Ext_1	Part_Nbr_2	Qty_2	Price_2	Ext_2
116385	Zeno's Paradox Hardware	10515 Prince Avenue	Athens, GA	19742133	A316	3	$0.35	$1.05	G457	12	$1.15	$13.80

———————— (Many intervening records) ————————

Record	Customer	Street	City	Order_Nbr	Part_Nbr_1	Qty_1	Price_1	Ext_1
122406	Zeno's Paradox Hardware	10515 Prince Avenue	Athens, GA	19742259	A316	4	$0.35	$1.40

c. Two inefficiencies are apparent at once in this method of accessing data:

    1) The customer's address has to be stored with every order the customer places, taking up much unnecessary storage.

    2) All intervening records must be read and skipped over in order to find both records pertaining to this customer.

3. Database technology overcame these two difficulties. There are three main ways of organizing a database.

a. A **tree** or **hierarchical structure** arranges data in a one-to-many relationship in which each record has one antecedent but may have an unlimited number of subsequent records.

    1) EXAMPLE: One customer, many orders; one order, many parts.

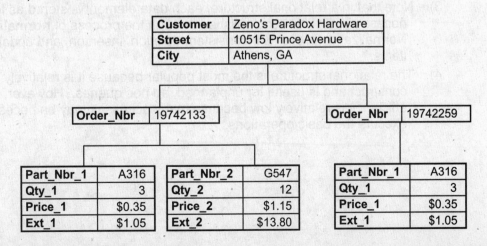

2)   Because the records are not stored one after the other, a tree database structure stores a **pointer** with each record. The pointer is the storage address of the next record.

3)   The tree structure cuts down on data redundancy, but retains the necessity of searching every record to fulfill a query. Thus, like the flat file, adding new records is awkward and ad hoc queries are inefficient.

b.   The **network structure** connects every record in the database with every other record.

1)   This was an attempt to make queries more efficient. However, the huge number of cross-references inherent in this structure makes maintenance far too complex.

c.   A **relational structure** organizes data in a conceptual arrangement.

1)   An individual data item is called a **field, column, or attribute** (e.g., name, date, amount).

a)   Related fields are brought together in a **record, row, or tuple** (e.g., for a single sales transaction).

b)   Multiple records make up a **file, table, or relation** (e.g., sales).

c)   Tables can be **joined** or **linked** based on common fields rather than on high-overhead pointers or linked lists as in other database structures.

2)   EXAMPLE:

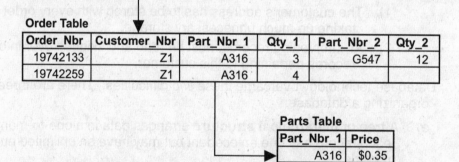

Customer Table

Customer_Nbr	Customer	Street	City
X1	Xylophones To Go	3846 MN Lamar Blvd	Oxford, MS
Y1	Yellow Dog Software	1012 E Tennessee St	Tallahassee, FL
Z1	Zeno's Paradox Hardware	10515 Prince Avenue	Athens, GA

Order Table

Order_Nbr	Customer_Nbr	Part_Nbr_1	Qty_1	Part_Nbr_2	Qty_2
19742133	Z1	A316	3	G547	12
19742259	Z1	A316	4		

Parts Table

Part_Nbr_1	Price
A316	$0.35
G547	$1.15

3)   Note that in a relational structure, each data element is stored as few times as necessary. This is accomplished through the process of **normalization**. Normalization prevents inconsistent deletion, insertion, and updating of data items.

4)   The relational structure is the most popular because it is relatively easy to construct and is useful for unplanned, ad hoc queries. However, its processing efficiency is relatively low because many accesses may be necessary to execute the basic operations.

5) The three **basic operations** in the relational model are selecting, joining, and projecting.

   a) **Selecting** creates a subset of records that meet certain criteria.

   b) **Joining** is the combining of relational tables based on a common field or combination of fields.

   c) **Projecting** results in the requested subset of columns from the table. This operation creates a new table containing only the required information.

6) **Cardinality** expresses the bounds (a minimum and a maximum) of the association between related entities. For example, a college class must have a minimum of 3 students and can have a maximum of 59. The student-class relationship has a cardinality limit expressed as (3, 59).

d. The data in a database are subject to the constraint of **referential integrity**. This means that if data are collected about something, e.g., a payment voucher, all reference conditions regarding it must be met; thus, for a voucher to exist, a vendor must also exist.

e. A **distributed database** is stored in two or more physical sites using either replication or partitioning.

   1) The **replication** or **snapshot** technique makes duplicates to be stored at multiple locations.

      a) Changes are periodically copied and sent to each location. If a database is small, storing multiple copies may be cheaper than retrieving records from a central site.

   2) **Fragmentation** or **partitioning** stores specific records where they are most needed.

      a) For example, a financial institution may store a particular customer's data at the branch where (s)he usually transacts his/her business. If the customer executes a transaction at another branch, the pertinent data are retrieved via communications lines.

      b) One variation is the **central index**. A query to this index obtains the location in a remote database where the complete record is to be found.

      c) Still another variation is the **ask-the-network distributed database**. In this system, no central index exists. Instead, the remote databases are polled to locate the desired record.

   3) Updating data in a distributed system may require special protocols.

      a) Thus, a **two-phase commit** disk-writing protocol is used. If data are to be updated in two places, databases in both locations are cleared for updating before either one performs (commits) the update.

      b) In the first phase, both locations agree to the update. In the second phase, both perform the update.

f. A **deadly embrace** (deadlock) occurs when each of two transactions has a lock on a single data resource.

   1) When deadly embraces occur, the DBMS must have an algorithm for undoing the effects of one of the transactions and releasing the data resources it controls so that the other transaction can run to completion. Then, the other transaction is restarted and permitted to run to completion.

   2) If deadly embraces are not resolved, response time worsens or the system eventually fails.

4. A **database management system (DBMS)** is an integrated set of computer programs that create the database, maintain the elements, safeguard the data from loss or destruction, and make the data available to applications programs and inquiries.

    a. The DBMS allows programmers and designers to work independently of the physical and logical structure of the database.

        1) Before the development of DBMSs, programmers and systems designers needed to consider the logical and physical structure of the database with the creation of every new application. This was extremely time consuming and therefore expensive.

    b. The **schema** is a description of the overall logical structure of the database using **data-definition language**, which is the connection between the logical and physical structures of the database.

        1) A **subschema** describes a particular user's (application's) view of a part of the database using data definition language.

    c. A fundamental characteristic of databases is that applications are independent of the database structure; when writing programs or designing applications to use the database, only the name of the desired item is necessary.

    d. A data item is identified using the **data manipulation language**, after which the DBMS locates and retrieves the desired item(s).

        1) The data manipulation language is used to add, delete, retrieve, or modify data or relationships.

    e. The physical structure of the database can be completely altered without having to change any of the programs using the data items. Thus, different users may define different views of the data (subschemas).

5. **Other Database Definitions**

    a. The **database administrator (DBA)** is the individual who has overall responsibility for developing and maintaining the database and for establishing controls to protect its integrity.

        1) Thus, only the DBA should be able to update data dictionaries. In small systems, the DBA may perform some functions of a DBMS. In larger applications, the DBA uses a DBMS as a primary tool.

    b. The **data dictionary** is a file, either computer or manual, that describes both the physical and logical characteristics of every data element in a database.

        1) The data dictionary includes, for example, the name of the data element (e.g., employee name, part number), the amount of disk space required to store the data element (in bytes), and what kind of data is allowed in the data element (e.g., alphabetic, numeric)

            a) The data dictionary also provides a mapping from the data element to every application where it is updated and vice versa.

        2) Thus, the data dictionary contains, the size, format, usage, meaning and ownership of every data element as well as what persons, programs, reports, and functions use the data element.

        3) In an advanced data dictionary, a change in a data element automatically changes related programs.

    c. The **database mapping facility** is software that is used to evaluate and document the structure of the database.

    d. The **data control language** specifies the privileges and security rules governing database users.

    e. **Data command interpreter languages** are symbolic character strings used to control the current state of DBMS operations.

6. Storing all related data on one storage device creates **security problems**.

   a. Should hardware or software malfunctions occur, or unauthorized access be achieved, the results could be disastrous.

   b. Greater emphasis on security is required to provide backup and restrict access to the database.

      1) For example, the system may employ **dual logging**, that is, use of two transaction logs written simultaneously on separate storage media.

      2) It may also use a snapshot technique to capture data values before and after transaction processing.

      3) The files that store these values can be used to reconstruct the database in the event of data loss or corruption.

   c. The responsibility for creating, maintaining, securing, and restricting access to the database belongs to the database administrator.

   d. A DBMS includes security features. Thus, a specified user's access may be limited to certain data fields or logical views depending on the individual's assigned duties.

7. Databases and the associated DBMS permit efficient storage and retrieval of data for formal system applications.

   a. They also permit increased ad hoc accessing of data (e.g., to answer inquiries for data not contained in formal system outputs) as well as updating of files by transaction processing.

   b. These increased capabilities, however, result in increased cost because they require

      1) The use of sophisticated hardware (direct-access devices)
      2) Sophisticated software (the DBMS)
      3) Highly trained technical personnel (database administrator, staff)
      4) Increased security controls

8. An **object-oriented database** is a response to the need to store not only numbers and characters but also graphics and multimedia applications.

   a. Translating these data into tables and rows is difficult. However, in an object-oriented database, they can be stored, along with the procedures acting on them, within an object.

9. In a **hypermedia database**, blocks of data are organized into nodes that are linked in a pattern determined by the user so that an information search need not be restricted to the predefined organizational scheme. A node may contain text, graphics, audio, video, or programs.

   a. Hybrid systems containing object-oriented and relational database capabilities have also been developed.

10. Advanced database systems provide for **online analytical processing (OLAP)**, also called multidimensional data analysis, which is the ability to analyze large amounts of data from numerous perspectives.

    a. OLAP is an integral part of the data warehouse concept.

11. A **data warehouse** contains not only current operating data but also historical information from throughout the organization. Thus, data from all operational systems is integrated, consolidated, and standardized into an organization-wide database into which data is copied periodically. This data is maintained on one platform and can be read but not changed. Graphics and query software and analytical tools assist users. Accordingly, **data mining** is facilitated by a data warehouse.

12. Stop and review! You have completed the outline for this subunit. Study multiple-choice questions 11 through 28 beginning on page 329.

6.3 E-COMMERCE, EDI, AND EFT

1. **E-commerce (EC)** is the purchase and sale of goods and services by electronic means. **E-business** is a more comprehensive term defined as all methods of conducting business electronically.

   a. EC may occur via online transactions on public networks, electronic data interchange (EDI), and email.

2. **Security issues** for EC include

   a. The correct identification of the transacting parties **(authentication)**

   b. Determination of who may rightfully make decisions, such as entering into contracts or setting prices **(authorization)**

   c. Methods for protecting the confidentiality and integrity of information, providing evidence of the transmission and receipt of documents, and guarding against repudiation by the sender or recipient

   d. The trustworthiness of listed **prices** and the confidentiality of **discounts**

   e. The confidentiality and integrity of orders, payments, delivery addresses, and confirmations

   f. The proper extent of **verification** of payment data

   g. The best **method of payment** to avoid wrongdoing or disagreements

   h. Lost or duplicated transactions

   i. Determining who bears the risk of fraud

3. **Responses to security issues** include

   a. Encryption and the associated authentication methods

   b. Adherence to legal requirements, such as privacy statutes

   c. Documenting trading agreements, especially the terms of trade and methods of authorization and authentication

   d. Agreements for end-to-end security and availability with providers of information services and VANs

   e. Disclosure by public trading systems of their terms of business

   f. The capacity of the host computer to avoid downtime and repel attacks

4. **Electronic Data Interchange (EDI)** is the communication of electronic documents directly from a computer in one entity to a computer in another entity, for example, to order goods from a supplier or to transfer funds. EDI was the first step in the evolution of e-business.

   a. EDI was developed to enhance JIT (just-in-time) inventory management.

   b. **Advantages of EDI** include reduction of clerical errors, speed of transactions, and elimination of repetitive clerical tasks. EDI also eliminates document preparation, processing, and mailing costs.

   c. **Risks of EDI** include

      1) Security of information

         a) End-to-end data encryption is a security procedure that protects data during transmission.

      2) Loss of data

   d. An extension of EDI is computer-stored records, which can be less expensive than traditional physical file storage.

5. **EDI Terms and Components**

    a. **Standards** concern procedures to convert written documents into a standard electronic document-messaging format to facilitate EDI.

        1) In the U.S., the American National Standards Institute's Accredited Standards Committee X.12 provides standards.

        2) Many international entities use **UN/EDIFACT** (United Nations EDI for Administration, Commerce, and Transport).

    b. **Conventions** are the procedures for arranging data elements in specified formats for various accounting transactions, e.g., invoices, materials releases, and advance shipment notices.

    c. A **data dictionary** prescribes the meaning of data elements, including specification of each transaction structure.

    d. **Transmission protocols** are rules to determine how each electronic envelope is structured and processed by the communications devices.

        1) Normally, a group of transactions is combined in an electronic envelope and transmitted into a communications network.

        2) Rules are required for transmission and the separation of envelopes.

    e. Because EDI formats and elements vary, a large entity may gain a competitive advantage by forcing trading partners to adopt its standards. Other entities will need to negotiate EDI standards.

6. **Methods of Communication among Computers** (Telephone lines and modems are typically used.)

    a. **Point-to-point** is the most traditional EDI connection. Both parties have fixed computer connections, and the computers are used solely for EDI. The direct connection that is created forces all the computers to be compatible with each other. A point-to-point arrangement is very similar to networks within one entity.

    b. **Value-added networks** (VANs) are private mailbox-type services in which the sender's and receiver's computers are never directly connected to each other. Instead, both parties to the EDI arrangement subscribe to a third-party VAN provider. Because of the third-party buffer, the VAN users are not required to conform to the same standards, conventions, and protocols. Also, VANs can store messages (in a mailbox), so the parties can batch outgoing and incoming messages.

        1) Encryption, preferably by physically secure hardware rather than software, is a critical control.

    c. The **Internet** is a means of conducting business directly with a trading partner. It can be used in a more open environment in which one firm transmits documents to another. This approach is based on less formal agreements between the trading partners than in EDI and requires the sending firm to format the documents into the format of the receiving firm.

7. **Electronic funds transfer (EFT)** is a service provided by financial institutions worldwide that is based on electronic data interchange (EDI) technology. EFT transaction costs are lower than for manual systems because documents and human intervention are eliminated from the transaction process.

    a. A typical application of EFT is the direct deposit of payroll checks in employees' accounts or the automatic withdrawal of payments for cable and telephone bills, mortgages, etc.

8.   **Implications for Internal Auditors**

a.   EDI eliminates the paper documents, both internal and external, that are the traditional basis for many procedures performed in substantive testing and in tests of controls.

1)   An organization that has **reengineered** its procedures and processes to take full advantage of EDI may have eliminated even the electronic equivalents of paper documents. For example, the buyer's **point-of-sale (POS) system** may directly transmit information to the seller, which delivers on a JIT basis. Purchase orders, invoices, and receiving reports are eliminated and replaced with

a)   A long-term contract establishing quantities, prices, and delivery schedules;

b)   Production schedules;

c)   Advance ship notices;

d)   Evaluated receipts settlements (periodic payment authorizations transmitted to the trading partner with no need for matching purchase orders, invoices, and receiving reports); and

e)   Payments by EFT.

2)   Internal auditors must seek new forms of evidence to support assertions about EDI transactions, whether the evidence exists at the client organization, the trading partner, or a third party, such as a VAN. Examples of such evidence are

a)   The authorized paper purchase contract,

b)   An electronic completed production schedule image, and

c)   Internal and external evidence of evaluated receipts settlements sent to the trading partner.

3)   Internal auditors must evaluate digital signatures and reviews when testing controls.

4)   Internal auditors may need to consider other subsystems when testing a particular subsystem. For example, production cycle evidence may be needed to test the expenditure cycle.

9.   **Extensible markup language (XML)** was developed by an international consortium and released in 1998 as an open standard usable with many programs and platforms. XML is a variation of HTML (hypertext markup language), which uses fixed codes (tags) to describe how webpages and other hypermedia documents should be presented. XML codes all information in such a way that a user can also determine what it is. Thus, all computerized data may be tagged with identifiers. Also, unlike HTML, XML uses tags that are extensible, not fixed. Accordingly, if an industry can agree on a set of codes, software for that industry can be written that incorporates those codes. For example, XML allows the user to label the Uniform Product Code (UPC), price, color, size, etc., of goods so that other systems will know exactly what the tag references mean. In contrast, HTML tags would only describe how items are placed on a page and provide links to other pages and objects.

a.   Standard setters and other entities are attempting to find ways to incorporate XML with EDI.

b.   **Extensible business reporting language (XBRL)** for Financial Statements is the specification developed by an AICPA-led consortium for commercial and industrial entities that report in accordance with U.S. GAAP. It is a variation of XML that is expected to decrease the costs of generating financial reports, reformulating information for different uses, and sharing business information using electronic media.

10. **EDI controls** will vary with the organization's objectives and applications.

    a. Authorized users with independent access may include

        1) The people initiating transactions
        2) The people authorizing transactions
        3) Other authorizing parties
        4) Senders for exceptional transactions

    b. **Message authentication** may be accomplished using smart cards and other hardware and software techniques. Protection of message integrity by authentication is especially important for such EDI applications as EFT and ordering.

    c. Messages also must be protected from interception or tampering while in transit. Controls include

        1) Encryption
        2) Numerical **sequencing** to identify missing or false messages
        3) **Nonrepudiation** methods

            a) **Digital certificates** are used to prove origination and delivery so that parties cannot disclaim responsibility for sending or receiving a message.

            b) EC sellers and buyers routinely provide acknowledgments and confirmations, respectively, in a website dialogue to avoid later disputes.

            c) In an EDI application, control over nonrepudiation is achieved by sequencing, encryption, and authentication.

11. **Secure Electronic Transaction (SET)** is a trademarked protocol that provides a common security standard, especially with regard to Internet card (credit, debit, or chip) purchases. It is supported by Visa and Mastercard through an organization called **SETCo**.

    a. SET encrypts the details of payment transactions at all times so as to ensure privacy and data integrity. It also ensures that the identities of sellers and buyers are authenticated using digital signatures (DSs) and certificates (DCs).

    b. SET is based on a hierarchy of **certificate authorities (CAs)** that parallels financial relationships outside cyberspace.

        1) SETCo issues DCs to **payment brands**.
        2) A SET DC allows a payment brand to become a CA and issue DCs to its **member-banks**.
        3) A SET DC then allows a member bank to become a CA and issue DCs to **merchants** and **cardholders**.

            a) Thus, a merchant obtains the backing of a payment brand when it receives a DC authenticating its identity from its "acquirer" bank.

            b) The cardholder's DC is equivalent to a plastic card used in a physical transaction. It is kept in a SET-enabled **electronic wallet** stored on the holder's computer or on the card issuer's server.

                i) The wallet also contains such other data as the customer's payment brand account number and the expiration date.

                ii) The customer obtains the wallet from an authorized financial institution.

            c) The payment transaction data in the wallet are **encrypted** until decoded by the seller-merchant's acquirer bank. The information must be decoded so that the customer's bank can authorize the transaction. The information is recorded for purposes of notice of approval to the customer and seller.

        d)   In the SET system, the interface between the seller-merchant and its acquirer bank is the **payment gateway**. It serves to authorize payment for multiple types of cards. The gateway

            i)   Decodes the SET messages

            ii)   Authenticates all parties involved

            iii) Reformats the message so that it is compatible with the merchant's point-of-sale system

       4)   All CAs must confirm the identities of those seeking DCs so as to ensure their authenticity.

12.   Email is a quick, informal, but often insecure method of business communication.

    a.   **Email risks** that need to be controlled include

       1)   Unauthorized access or modification

       2)   Unreliability or denial of service

       3)   Inaccurate addressing or misdirection

       4)   The effects of change to more rapid communication and of transmitting messages person to person

       5)   Legal issues, such as nonrepudiation

       6)   Remote user access to email

       7)   External access to employee lists

    b.   The organization should have an **acceptable use policy** that

       1)   Limits Internet access to authorized persons

       2)   Provides for removal of unused accounts and those of departed employees

       3)   Prescribes what email accounts contractors may use

       4)   Requires a disclaimer on every email indicating that the message is the sender's, not the organization's

       5)   Describes what may be disclosed in email

       6)   Reserves the organization's right to inspect email

       7)   Explicitly permits or prohibits private use

       8)   Requires attachments to be screened by antivirus software before being opened

       9)   Provides for educating users about the dangers of malicious software, indicators of email attacks, and measures for coping with suspicious items

13.   A **publicly available system**, for example, a web server, publishes information that must be protected. If the integrity of this information is compromised, the reputation of the organization may be damaged.

    a.   The organization should implement formal policies and procedures for creating such a system.

       1)   These policies and procedures should be consistent with legal requirements where the system is located or business is conducted, for example, legislation protecting the privacy of the collection, storage, and use of personal information.

       2)   Information entry should be timely, complete, and accurate.

       3)   Access does not inadvertently allow entry to other networks.

       4)   Responsibility and accountability for (ownership of) a website should be determined so that all changes are made by the owner (a function or person).

       5)   The acceptable use policy should create an environment in which employees know their rights and responsibilities, and the organization's brand name (reputation) is safeguarded.

14. Stop and review! You have completed the outline for this subunit. Study multiple-choice questions 29 through 40 beginning on page 333.

6.4 ENTERPRISE-WIDE RESOURCE PLANNING

1. **Enterprise resource planning (ERP)** is the latest phase in the development of computerized systems for managing organizational resources. ERP is intended to **integrate** enterprise-wide information systems by creating **one database** linked to all of an organization's applications.

    a. ERP connects all functional subsystems (human resources, the financial accounting system, production, marketing, distribution, purchasing, receiving, order processing, shipping, etc.) and also connects the organization with its suppliers and customers.

        1) Thus, ERP facilitates demand analysis and materials requirements planning.

        2) By decreasing lead times, it improves just-in-time inventory management.

        3) Even more importantly, ERP's coordination of all operating activities permits flexible responses to shifts in supply and demand.

    b. The disadvantages of ERP are its extent and complexity, which make customization of the software difficult and costly.

    c. The leading comprehensive product in the field is **SAP R/3**. Other ERP products are marketed by Oracle, PeopleSoft, and J. D. Edwards.

    d. Because ERP software is costly and complex, it is usually installed only by the largest enterprises. However, mid-size organizations are increasingly likely to buy ERP software.

    e. Many of the benefits of ERP result from the accompanying **business process reengineering**.

        1) Using ERP software that reflects the **best practices** forces the linked subunits in the organization not only to redesign and improve their processes but also to conform to one standard.

        2) An organization may wish to undertake a reengineering project before choosing ERP software. The project should indicate what best practices already exist in the organization's processes. This approach may be preferable for a unique enterprise in a highly differentiated industry.

            a) Carrying out a reengineering project before installing an ERP system defines what process changes are needed and which vendor software should be used.

            b) If the organization is not especially unique, vendor software probably is already based on industry best practices. In these circumstances, a preliminary reengineering project may not be needed. Thus, the organization should simply conform its processes to the software.

        3) The processes reflected in the ERP software may differ from the organization's. In this case, the better policy is usually to change the organization's processes. **Customizing** the ERP software is expensive and difficult, and it may result in bugs and awkwardness in adopting upgrades.

            a) Implementing an ERP system is likely to encounter significant resistance because of its comprehensiveness. Most employees will have to change ingrained habits and learn to use new technology. Hence, successful implementation requires effective **change management**.

2. **Materials requirements planning (MRP)** was an early attempt to create an integrated computer-based information system. It was designed to plan and control materials used in a production setting.

    a. MRP was a push system. It assumed that the demand for materials is typically dependent upon some other factor, which can be programmed. Thus, the timing of deliveries is vital to avoid production delays.

    b. For example, an auto manufacturer need only tell the system how many autos of each type are to be manufactured. The MRP system then generates a complete list of every part and component needed. MRP, in effect creates schedules of when items on inventory will be needed in the production departments.

        1) If parts are not in stock, the system will automatically generate a purchase order on the proper date (considering lead times) so that deliveries will arrive on time. Hence, effective application of MRP necessitates the generation of accurate data about costs and amounts of inventory, set-up costs, and costs of downtime.

3. **Manufacturing resource planning (MRP II)** continued the evolution begun with MRP. It is a closed-loop manufacturing system that integrates all facets of a manufacturing business, including production, sales, inventories, schedules, and cash flows. The same system is used for the accounting, finance, and directing functions, which use the same transactions and numbers.

    a. MRP II includes forecasting and planning capacities for generating cash and other budgets.

    b. MRP II uses an MPS (master production schedule), a statement of the anticipated manufacturing schedule for selected items for selected periods. (MRP also used the MPS. Thus, MRP is a component of an MRP II system).

4. The **traditional ERP system** is one in which subsystems share data and coordinate their activities.

    a. Thus, if marketing receives an order, it can quickly verify that inventory is sufficient to notify shipping to process the order.

        1) Otherwise, production is notified to manufacture more of the product, with a consequent automatic adjustment of output schedules.

        2) If materials are inadequate for this purpose, the system will issue a purchase order.

        3) If more labor is needed, human resources will be instructed to reassign or hire employees.

        4) The foregoing business processes (and others) should interact seamlessly in an ERP system. Moreover, the current generation of ERP software also provides the capability for smooth (and instant) interaction with the business processes of external parties.

    b. The subsystems in a traditional ERP system are internal to the organization. Hence, they are often called **back-office** functions. The information produced is principally (but not exclusively) intended for internal use by the organization's managers.

5. The current generation of ERP software **(ERP II)** has added **front-office** functions. These connect the organization with customers, suppliers, shareholders or other owners, creditors, and strategic allies (e.g., the members of a trading community or other business association). Accordingly, an ERP II system has the following interfaces with its back-office functions:

    a. **Supply-chain management** applications for an organization focus on relationships extending from its suppliers to its final customers. Issues addressed include distribution channels, warehousing and other logistical matters, routing of shipments, and sales forecasting.

        1) In turn, one organization's supply chain is part of a **linked chain** of multiple organizations. This chain stretches from the producers of raw materials, to processors of those materials, to entities that make intermediate goods, to assemblers of final products, to wholesalers, to retailers, and lastly to ultimate consumers.

        2) Supply chain management involves a **two-way exchange of information**. For example, a customer may be able to track the progress of its order, and the supplier may be able to monitor the customer's inventory. Thus, the customer has better information about order availability, and the supplier knows when the customer's inventory needs replenishment.

        3) An **advanced planning and scheduling system** may be an element of a supply chain management application for a manufacturer. It controls the flow of materials and components within the chain. Schedules are created given projected costs, lead times, and inventories.

    b. **Customer relationship management** applications extend to customer service, finance-related matters, sales, and database creation and maintenance.

        1) Integrated data is helpful in better understanding customer needs, such as product preference or location of retail outlets. Thus, the organization may be able to optimize its sales forecasts, product line, and inventory levels.

            a) **Business intelligence** software is used to analyze customer data.

    c. **Partner relationship management** applications connect the organization not only with such partners as customers and suppliers but also with owners, creditors, and strategic allies (for example, other members of a joint venture).

        1) **Collaborative business partnerships** may arise between competitors or arise between different types of organizations, such as a manufacturer partnering with an environmental group. Special software may be helpful to the partners in sharing information, developing a common strategy, and measuring performance.

6. The following are the main elements of the **architecture** of an ERP:

    a. Current ERP systems have a **client-server configuration** with, possibly, scores or hundreds of client (user) computers.

        1) So-called **thin clients** have little processing ability, but **fat clients** may have substantial processing power.

        2) The system may have multiple servers to run applications and contain databases.

        3) The network architecture may be in the form of a **local area network** or **wide-area network**, or users may connect with the server(s) via the **Internet**.

        4) An ERP system may use almost any of the available **operating systems** and **database management systems**.

    b.   An advantage of an ERP system is the elimination of data redundancy through the use of a **central database**. In principle, information about an item of data is stored once, and all functions have access to it.

        1) Thus, when the item (such as a price) is updated, the change is effectively made for all functions. The result is reliability **(data integrity)**.

            a) If an organization has separate systems for its different functions, the item would have to be updated whenever it was stored. Failure of even one function to update the item would cause loss of data integrity. For example, considerable inefficiency may arise when different organizational subunits (IT, production, marketing, accounting, etc.) have different data about prices and inventory availability.

    c.   An organization may not have the resources, desire, or need for an ERP system with the greatest degree of integration (e.g., SAP R/3).

        1) An alternative to a comprehensive system is a **best-of-breed approach**. Thus, an organization might install a traditional ERP system from one vendor and add e-commerce and other extended applications from separate niche vendors.

            a) An organization that adopts this approach needs to use **middleware**, that is, software that permits different applications to communicate and exchange data. This type of middleware is called an **extended application interface**.

    d.   An ERP system that extends to customers, suppliers, and others uses **Internet portals**. In this case, a portal is a website through which authorized external users may gain access to the organization's ERP.

        1) Portals provide links to related websites and services (e.g., newsletters, email, and e-commerce capabilities).

7.   **Implementation of ERP** may take years and cost millions. Moreover, a poor implementation may cause the project to fail regardless of the quality of the software.

    a.   However, more rapid and less costly implementation may be possible if no customization is done.

    b.   The initial step is to do **strategic planning** and to organize a **project team** that is representative of affected employee groups.

    c.   The second step is to **choose ERP software** and a **consulting firm**.

        1) One possibility is to choose the software before the consultants because the first decision may affect the second.

        2) Another option is to hire consultants to help with the selection of the software.

            a) The organization may then hire other consultants to help with implementation.

    d.   The third and longest step is **preimplementation**.

        1) The length of the **process design** phase is a function of the extent of

            a) Reengineering
            b) Customization of the software

        2) **Data conversion** may be delayed because of disagreements about the means of defining every data field, for example, whether codes should have independent meaning.

        3) The ERP system and its interfaces must be **tested**.

     e.   **Implementation** ("going live") is not the final step. **Follow-up** is necessary to monitor the activities of the numerous employees who have had to change their routines. For example, a mistake caused by reverting to the old method of entering a sales order may have pervasive consequences in a new integrated system: a credit check, rescheduling of production, and ordering of materials.

     f.   **Training** should be provided during implementation not only regarding technical matters but also to help employees understand the reasons for process changes. For example, the employees who enter sales orders should know what the effects will be throughout the system.

         1)   Other **change management** techniques include effective communication to allay employee fears and the creation of user-friendly documents and interfaces.

8.   The **costs** of an ERP system include

     a.   Losses from an unsuccessful implementation, e.g., sales declines

     b.   Purchasing hardware, software, and services

     c.   Data conversion from legacy systems to the new integrated system (but conversion software may help)

     d.   Training

     e.   Design of interfaces and customization

     f.   Software maintenance and upgrades

     g.   Salaries of employees working on the implementation

9.   The **benefits** of an ERP system may be hard to quantify. They include

     a.   Lower inventory costs

     b.   Better management of liquid assets

     c.   Reduced labor costs and greater productivity

     d.   Enhanced decision making

     e.   Elimination of data redundancy and protection of data integrity

     f.   Avoidance of the costs of other means of addressing needed IT changes

     g.   Increased customer satisfaction

     h.   More rapid and flexible responses to changed circumstances

     i.   More effective supply chain management

     j.   Integration of global operations

10. Stop and review! You have completed the outline for this subunit. Study multiple-choice questions 41 through 47 beginning on page 337.

6.5 MALICIOUS SOFTWARE AND ATTACKS

1.   The business assurance objective in the SAC model that is most concerned with malicious software (malware) is **protectability**. Thus, IT assets should be protected from "unauthorized access, use, or harm."

   a.   Control, e.g., over access and change management, should be in place to achieve the objective of protectability.

   b.   Moreover, **security awareness** by all concerned should be heightened. Consequently, the business assurance objective of **accountability** is also pertinent. The roles, actions, and responsibilities for security should be defined.

2.   Malware may exploit a known hole or weakness in an application or operating system program to evade security measures. Such a vulnerability may have been caused by a programming error. It may also have been intentionally (but not maliciously) created to permit a programmer simple access (a back door) for correcting the code.

   a.   Having bypassed security controls, the intruder can do immediate damage to the system or install malware.

      1)   A **Trojan horse** is an apparently innocent program (e.g., a spreadsheet) that includes a hidden function that may do damage when activated.

         a)   For example, it may contain a **virus**, that is, program code that copies itself from file to file. The virus may destroy data or programs. A common way of spreading a virus is by email attachments and downloads.

         b)   A **worm** copies itself not from file to file but from computer to computer, often very rapidly. Repeated replication overloads a system by depleting memory or disk space.

      2)   A **logic bomb** is much like a Trojan horse except it activates only upon some occurrence, e.g., on a certain date.

         a)   A maliciously created **back door** can be used for subsequent high level access to data, computers, and networks.

      3)   Malware may create a **denial of service** by overwhelming a system or website with more traffic than it can handle.

         a)   In other cases, malware infection may have few or no effects noticeable by users.

3.   **Controls** to prevent or detect infection by malware are particularly significant for file servers in large networks. The following are broad control objectives:

   a.   A policy should require use only of authorized software.

   b.   A policy should require adherence to licensing agreements.

   c.   A policy should create accountability for the persons authorized to maintain software.

   d.   A policy should require safeguards when data or programs are obtained by means of external media.

   e.   Antivirus software should continuously monitor the system for viruses (or worms) and eradicate them. It should also be immediately upgraded as soon as information about new threats becomes available.

   f.   Software and data for critical systems should be regularly reviewed.

   g.   Investigation of unauthorized files or amendments should be routine.

   h.   Email attachments and downloads (and files on unauthorized media or from networks that are not secure) should be checked.

   i.   Procedures should be established and responsibility assigned for coping with malware.

1) Procedures should reflect an understanding that another organization that has transmitted malware-infected material may have done so unwittingly and may need assistance. If such events occur repeatedly, however, termination of agreements or contracts may be indicated.

2) Procedures and policies should be documented, and employees must understand the reasons for them.

j. Business continuity plans should be drafted, e.g., data and software backup.

k. Information about malware should be verified, and appropriate alerts given.

l. Responsible personnel should be aware of the possibility of hoaxes, false messages intending to create fear of a malware attack. For example, a spurious email message may be received instructing users to delete supposedly compromised files.

m. Qualified personnel should be relied upon to distinguish **hoaxes** from malware.

4. The following are **specific controls**:

a. All computer media (incoming or outgoing) may be scanned by **sheep dip** (dedicated) computers.

b. Nonscreened media should not be allowed on the organization's computers.

c. Scanning may be done of standalone computers or those on networks as another line of defense if media control fails.

d. Software may reside in memory to scan for malware communicated through a network.

e. Email gateways may have software to scan attachments.

f. Network servers may have software to detect and erase or store malware.

g. Scanning software on a standalone device should be upgraded when it is networked.

5. Use of external rather than internal expertise for coping with malware problems may be more costly and time consuming but less risky.

a. **External service providers** should be subject to the terms of a contract, and access and other controls should be in place.

6. Off-site computers and media of employees should be subject to malware controls, such as screening.

7. Response to threats via **covert channels** and **Trojan horse** programs include the following:

a. Purchases should be of evaluated products from trusted suppliers.

b. Purchases should be in source code so that it is verifiable. This code should be inspected and tested prior to use.

c. Access to, and changes in, code should be restricted after it is put in use.

d. The availability of security patches for bugs in programs should be monitored constantly, especially regarding such items as network operating systems, email servers, routers, and firewalls. Patches should be tested and installed promptly.

e. Trusted employees should be assigned to key systems.

f. Known Trojan horses can be detected by scanning.

g. Reviewing data outflows, for example, through the firewall, may detect suspicious activity meriting investigation.

8. **Hosts** are the most common targets in a network because they furnish services to other requesting hosts.

a. Protective measures include promptly installing the most recent patches, fixes, and updates.

1) How they affect other elements of the system should be considered.

2) Updates should be tested before installation.

9. **Password Attacks**

    a.   A number of methods may be used.

        1)   A **brute-force attack** uses password cracking software to try large numbers of letter and number combinations to access a network.

            a)   A simple variation is the use of password cracking software that tries all the words in a dictionary.

        2)   Passwords (and user accounts) also may be discovered by Trojan horses, IP spoofing, and packet sniffers.

            a)   **Spoofing** is identity misrepresentation in cyberspace, for example, by using a false website to obtain information about visitors.

            b)   **Sniffing** is the use of software to eavesdrop on information sent by a user to the host computer of a website.

    b.   Once an attacker has access, (s)he may do anything the rightful user could have done.

        1)   If that user has privileged access, the attacker may create a back door to facilitate future entry despite password and status changes.

        2)   The attacker also may be able to leverage the initial access to obtain greater privileges than the rightful user.

    c.   If a user has the same password for multiple hosts, cracking that password for one compromises all.

    d.   Expensive methods of thwarting password attacks are one-time password and cryptographic authentication.

    e.   Optimal passwords are randomly generated 8-character or longer combinations of numbers, uppercase and lowercase letters, and special symbols.

        1)   A disadvantage is that users often write down passwords that are hard to remember. However, software has been developed that encrypts passwords to be kept on a handheld computer. Thus, the user only needs to know one password.

10. A **man-in-the-middle attack** takes advantage of networking packet sniffing and routing and transport protocols.

    a.   These attacks may be used to

        1)   Steal data
        2)   Obtain access to the network during a rightful user's active session
        3)   Analyze the traffic on the network to learn about its operations and users
        4)   Insert new data or modify the data being transmitted
        5)   Deny service

    b.   Cryptography is the effective response to man-in-the-middle attacks. The encrypted data will be useless to the attacker unless it can be decrypted.

11. A **denial-of-service attack** is an attempt to overload a system (e.g., a network or Web server) with false messages so that it cannot function (a system crash).

    a.   A distributed attack comes from multiple sources, for example, the machines of innocent parties infected by Trojan horses. When activated, these programs send messages to the target and leave the connection open.

    b.   The attack may establish as many network connections as possible to exclude other users, overload primary memory, or corrupt file systems.

c. **Responses**

    1) Firewalls should not permit use of **Internet relay chat** channels or other TCP/IP ports unless for business purposes. Thus, the organization should determine what relay kits have been installed, e.g., by employees connected to virtual private networks via cable or DSL.

        a) These methods, intrusion detection, systems, and penetration testing may prevent a system from being used to make a denial-of-service attack.

    2) The best protection by the target is the Internet service provider (ISP). The ISP can establish rate limits on transmissions to the target's website.

        a) Thus, only a defined amount of message packets with certain characteristics are allowed to reach the site.

12. **Intrusion Detection Systems (IDS)**

  a. If an organization's computer system has external connections, an IDS is needed to respond to security breaches.

    1) The IDS complements the computer system's firewalls. It responds to attacks on

        a) The **network infrastructure** (protected by the network IDS component)

            i) Routers
            ii) Switches
            iii) Bandwidth

        b) **Servers** (protected by the host IDS component)

            i) Operating systems
            ii) Applications

    2) An IDS responds to an attack by

        a) Taking action itself
        b) Alerting the management system

  b. A **host IDS** provides maximum protection only when the software is installed on each computer. It may operate in the following ways:

    1) The aggressive response is to monitor every call on the operating system and application as it occurs.

    2) A less effective method of preventing attacks is analysis of access log files.

    3) A host IDS may also identify questionable processes and verify the security of system files.

  c. A **network IDS** works by using sensors to examine packets traveling on the network. Each sensor monitors only the segment of the network to which it is attached. A packet is examined if it matches a **signature**.

    1) **String signatures** (certain strings of text) are potential signs of an attack.

    2) **Port signatures** alert the IDS that a point subject to frequent intrusion attempts may be under attack.

        a) A **port** in this sense (as opposed to the physical serial and parallel ports on a personal computer) is a logical connection to the system.

            i) A **port number** included in the message header stipulates how the message will be handled. Because many port numbers are widely known, an attacker may be able to send messages to determine whether ports are open and therefore vulnerable.

    3) A **header signature** is a suspicious combination in a packet header.

    d.   The preferable IDS combines host IDS and network IDS components.

        1)   A host IDS has greater potential for preventing a specific attack, but the network IDS provides a necessary overall perspective. Thus, a host IDS should be in place for each host, with a network IDS for the whole system.

    e.   **Knowledge-based detection** is based on information about the system's weaknesses and searches for intrusions that take advantage of them.

        1)   This type of IDS depends on frequent and costly updating of information about intrusion methods. It is also specialized with respect to those methods and operating system methods.

            a)   Problems are compounded when different versions of the operating system (or different operating systems) are in place.

    f.   **Behavior-based detection** presumes that an attack will cause an observable anomaly. Actual and normal system behavior (a model of expected operations) are compared. A discrepancy results in an alert.

        1)   This approach is more complete than the knowledge-based approach because every attack should be detected. However, the level of accuracy is lower. False alarms may be generated, so the model must be updated whenever operational changes are made.

        2)   The advantages of behavior-based detection are that

            a)   Knowledge of specific new intrusion techniques is not necessary.
            b)   It is less specific to particular operating systems.

    g.   **Responses to detection of an intrusion** normally include an automatic component. Continuous monitoring and response by individuals may not be feasible or sufficiently rapid.

        1)   An **automatically acting IDS** provides continuous security. It responds without the presence of humans. Responses may include

            a)   Disconnecting the entire network from outside access
            b)   Locking access to all or part of the system
            c)   Slowing the system's activity to reduce injury
            d)   Validating the external user
            e)   Sending console, email, pager, or phone messages to appropriate personnel

        2)   **Alarmed systems resources** are dummy files or accounts, for example, a default administrator account with a default password set. They are traps for an intruder.

            a)   Access to a dummy resource results in automatic action or notice to appropriate employees.
            b)   The advantage of this method is that it is uncomplicated and cheap.
            c)   The disadvantage is that authorized persons may inadvertently cause an alarm.

13.   Stop and review! You have completed the outline for this subunit. Study multiple-choice questions 48 through 59 beginning on page 339.

6.6 STUDY UNIT 6 SUMMARY

1. The development of the local area network (LAN) allowed for huge productivity gains by allowing workers to share information without the need for the high expense and specialized staff of a mainframe.

2. In a client/server network, the devices play specialized roles. This configuration allows for each function in the network to be performed by the most appropriate hardware platform.

3. A client is any device that uses the resources of another object, whether that other object be another device or a software program.

4. A server is a device or program that provides services for other devices and programs.

5. Public switched networks, value-added networks, and virtual private networks are possible configurations for wide area networks (WAN), i.e., networks used by organizations that span more than a single building.

6. The Internet is a network of networks all over the world.

7. The Internet facilitates inexpensive communication and information transfer among computers, with gateways allowing mainframe computers to interface with personal computers.

8. An intranet permits sharing of information throughout an organization by applying Internet connectivity standards and web software (e.g., browsers) to the organization's internal network.

9. A database is a series of related files combined to eliminate redundancy of data items.

10. Early solutions such as flat files and network databases were awkward to maintain and required high machine overhead.

11. The relational database has been the most cost-effective architecture. Relational databases employ normalization techniques to ensure that data items are stored with as little redundancy as possible. Also, relational databases have very powerful search features.

12. A database management system is an integrated set of computer programs that centralize and greatly ease the tasks of administering the database.

13. A database administrator is the individual with overall responsibility for developing and maintaining the database and for establishing controls to protect its integrity.

14. E-business is an umbrella term referring to all methods of conducting business electronically.

15. E-commerce is a narrower term referring to financial transactions with outside parties, e.g., the purchase and sale of goods and services.

16. Electronic data interchange (EDI) is the leading method of carrying on e-commerce. It involves the communication of data in standardized format directly from a computer in one entity to a computer in another entity.

17. EDI services are often provided by third-party communications vendors through services known as value-added networks (VANs).

18. Enterprise resource planning (ERP) is intended to integrate enterprise-wide information systems by creating one database linked to all of an organization's applications.

19. Malicious software may exploit a known hole or weakness in an application or operating system program to evade security measures. Examples include Trojan horses, viruses, and worms.

20. Password attacks include brute-force, spoofing, and sniffing.

21. If an organization's computer system has external connections, an intrusion detection system is needed to respond to security breaches.

QUESTIONS

6.1 Data Communications and Networks

1. When two devices in a data communications system are communicating, there must be agreement as to how both data and control information are to be packaged and interpreted. Which of the following terms is commonly used to describe this type of agreement?

- A. Asynchronous communication.
- B. Synchronous communication.
- C. Communication channel.
- D. Communication protocol.

Answer (D) is correct. *(CIA, adapted)*
REQUIRED: The agreement as to how both data and control information are to be packaged and interpreted.
DISCUSSION: A protocol is a set of formal rules or conventions governing communication between a sending and a receiving device. It prescribes the manner by which data are transmitted between these communications devices. In essence, a protocol is the envelope within which each message is transmitted throughout a data communications network.
Answer (A) is incorrect because asynchronous communication is a mode of transmission. Communication is in disjointed segments, typically character by character, preceded by a start code and ended by a stop code. Answer (B) is incorrect because synchronous communication is a mode of transmission in which a continuous stream of blocks of characters result in faster communications. Answer (C) is incorrect because a communication channel is a transmission link between devices in a network. The term is also used for a small processor that controls input-output devices.

2. Advantages of using fiber-optic cable are that

I.   The signal is attenuated.
II. Data are transmitted rapidly.
III. It is small and flexible.
IV. It is unaffected by electrical interference.

- A. I and III only.
- B. I and IV only.
- C. I, II, and III only.
- D. II, III, and IV only.

Answer (D) is correct. *(CISA, adapted)*
REQUIRED: The advantages of fiber optics.
DISCUSSION: A fiber-optic cable uses light impulses that travel through clear flexible tubing half the size of a human hair. Fiber-optic cables are not subject to electrical interference and are highly reliable. They provide for extremely flexible and fast data transmission. The signal remains strong across long distances; i.e., it does not tend to weaken (attenuate).

3. A real estate brokerage firm is moving into a building that is already equipped with extensive telephone wiring. The firm is considering the installation of a digital private branch exchange (PBX) to connect computers and other office devices such as copying machines, printers, and facsimile machines. A limitation of using a PBX-based system for this network is that

- A. The firm would be dependent on others for system maintenance.
- B. The system cannot easily handle large volumes of data.
- C. Coaxial cabling would have to be installed throughout the building.
- D. Relocating devices in the office would be difficult and expensive.

Answer (B) is correct. *(CIA, adapted)*
REQUIRED: The limitation of a PBX system.
DISCUSSION: A PBX has the advantage of using existing telephone lines and therefore not needing special wiring. Moreover, equipment can be moved without necessitating rewiring. However, because PBX-based systems use telephone wiring (most often copper wire), they cannot easily handle large volumes of data.
Answer (A) is incorrect because the company would be responsible for all maintenance of the equipment, although it could contract for service. Answer (C) is incorrect because PBXs use telephone wiring. LANs typically require their own coaxial cabling. Answer (D) is incorrect because PBX-based systems do not require rewiring when devices are moved.

4. Large organizations often have their own telecommunications networks for transmitting and receiving voice, data, and images. Very small organizations, however, are unlikely to be able to make the investment required for their own networks and are more likely to use

A. Public switched lines.

B. Fast-packet switches.

C. Standard electronic mail systems.

D. A WAN.

Answer (A) is correct. *(CIA, adapted)*
REQUIRED: The telecommunications networks likely to be used by small organizations.
DISCUSSION: Companies can use public switched lines (phone lines) on a per-transmission basis. This option is the most cost-effective way for low-volume users to conduct telecommunications.
Answer (B) is incorrect because fast-packet switches receive transmissions from various devices, break the data into packets, and route them over a network to their destination. They are typically installed by telecommunication utility companies and other large companies that have their own networks. Answer (C) is incorrect because electronic mail systems do not allow for voice transmissions. Answer (D) is incorrect because large organizations would use a wide area network.

5. A local area network (LAN) is best described as a(n)

A. Computer system that connects computers of all sizes, workstations, terminals, and other devices within a limited proximity.

B. System to allow computer users to meet and share ideas and information.

C. Electronic library containing millions of items of data that can be reviewed, retrieved, and analyzed.

D. Method to offer specialized software, hardware, and data-handling techniques that improve effectiveness and reduce costs.

Answer (A) is correct. *(CMA, adapted)*
REQUIRED: The best description of a local area network (LAN).
DISCUSSION: A LAN is a local distributed computer system, often housed within a single building. Computers, communication devices, and other equipment are linked by cable. Special software facilitates efficient data communication among the hardware devices.
Answer (B) is incorrect because a LAN is more than a system to allow computer users to share information; it is an interconnection of a computer system. Answer (C) is incorrect because a LAN is not a library. Answer (D) is incorrect because a LAN does not require specialized hardware.

6. Using a telecommunications provider affects in-house networks. To prepare for changes resulting from enhanced external network services, management should

A. Optimize in-house networks to avoid bottlenecks that would limit the benefits offered by the telecommunications provider.

B. Plan for rapid implementation of new capabilities in anticipation of ready acceptance of the new technology.

C. Downsize the company's disaster recovery plan to recognize the increasing role of the telecommunications provider.

D. Enhance the in-house network management to minimize dependence on the telecommunications provider for network management.

Answer (A) is correct. *(CIA, adapted)*
REQUIRED: The appropriate action to prepare for changes resulting from enhanced external network services.
DISCUSSION: To prepare the company for changes resulting from the enhanced external network services, management should take appropriate action. A number of bottlenecks may limit the benefits that can be derived from the external network. For example, conversion from analog to digital technology is necessary to achieve rapid improvements in bandwidth and speed and to improve access to telecommunications services. Furthermore, applications, systems software, and communications protocols must be able to process information in a format and in a manner acceptable to end users. Communications security also has heightened importance as greater amounts of data are transmitted from remote sites.
Answer (B) is incorrect because resistance to change, inflexible organizational structures, and skepticism about the technology should be expected and must be successfully managed if the company is to reap the benefits. Answer (C) is incorrect because a company's disaster recovery plan should be enhanced to ensure the reliability of the network. Answer (D) is incorrect because network management may now be primarily a function, yet it will become more of a partnership arrangement with the communications carrier.

7. Which of the following statements about voice communications is true?

A. Modern voice recognition input devices have large vocabularies and short training periods.

B. A voice output device converts speech into digital data.

C. Cell phones and PCS services use the same frequency radio waves.

D. Pagers can alert users to the receipt of messages but cannot transmit text.

Answer (A) is correct. *(Publisher, adapted)*
REQUIRED: The true statement about voice communications.
DISCUSSION: Voice recognition input devices provide an alternative to keyboard input. These systems compare the speaker's voice patterns with prerecorded patterns. Advanced systems now have large vocabularies and shorter training periods. They allow for dictation and are not limited to simple commands.
Answer (B) is incorrect because a voice output device converts digital data into speech using prerecorded sounds. Answer (C) is incorrect because PCS services use lower-power, higher-frequency radio waves than cell phones. Answer (D) is incorrect because newer pager systems permit transmission of text messages.

8. The Internet consists of a series of networks that include

A. Gateways to allow personal computers to connect to mainframe computers.

B. Bridges to direct messages through the optimum data path.

C. Repeaters to physically connect separate local area networks (LANs).

D. Routers to strengthen data signals between distant computers.

Answer (A) is correct. *(CIA, adapted)*
REQUIRED: The composition of the Internet.
DISCUSSION: The Internet facilitates information transfer between computers. Gateways are hardware or software products that allow translation between two different protocol families. For example, a gateway can be used to exchange messages between different email systems.
Answer (B) is incorrect because routers are used to determine the best path for data. Answer (C) is incorrect because bridges connect LANs. Answer (D) is incorrect because repeaters strengthen signals.

9. Which of the following is true concerning HTML?

A. The acronym stands for HyperText Material Listing.

B. The language is among the most difficult to learn.

C. The language is independent of hardware and software.

D. HTML is the only language that can be used for Internet documents.

Answer (C) is correct. *(Publisher, adapted)*
REQUIRED: The true statement concerning HTML.
DISCUSSION: HTML is the most popular language for authoring Web pages. It is hardware and software independent, which means that it can be read by several different applications and on many different kinds of computer operating systems. HTML uses tags to mark information for proper display on Web pages.
Answer (A) is incorrect because HTML is the acronym for HyperText Markup Language. Answer (B) is incorrect because the language is relatively easy to learn. Almost anyone can learn and use HTML, not just computer programmers. Answer (D) is incorrect because a number of other languages can be used for Internet transmissions, including JAVA and XML.

10. In distributed data processing, a ring network

A. Has all computers linked to a host computer, and each linked computer routes all data through the host computer.

B. Links all communication channels to form a loop, and each link passes communications through its neighbor to the appropriate location.

C. Attaches all channel messages along one common line with communication to the appropriate location via direct access.

D. Organizes itself along hierarchical lines of communication usually to a central host computer.

Answer (B) is correct. *(CMA, adapted)*
REQUIRED: The true statement about a ring network in a distributed data processing system.
DISCUSSION: In a distributed system, an organization's processing needs are examined in their totality. The decision is not whether an application should be done centrally or locally, but rather which parts are better performed by small local computers as intelligent terminals, and which parts are better performed at some other, possibly centralized, site. The key distinction between decentralized and distributed systems is the interconnection among the nodes in the network. A ring network links all communication channels to form a loop and each link passes communications through its neighbor to the appropriate location.
Answer (A) is incorrect because a star network routes all data through the host computer. Answer (C) is incorrect because a bus network attaches all channel messages along one common line with communication to the appropriate location via direct access. Answer (D) is incorrect because a tree configuration is organized along hierarchical lines to a host computer.

6.2 Databases

11. Of the following, the greatest advantage of a database (server) architecture is

    A. Data redundancy can be reduced.

    B. Conversion to a database system is inexpensive and can be accomplished quickly.

    C. Multiple occurrences of data items are useful for consistency checking.

    D. Backup and recovery procedures are minimized.

Answer (A) is correct. *(CIA, adapted)*
    REQUIRED: The greatest advantage of a database architecture.
    DISCUSSION: Data organized in files and used by the organization's various applications programs are collectively known as a database. In a database system, storage structures are created that render the applications programs independent of the physical or logical arrangement of the data. Each data item has a standard definition, name, and format, and related items are linked by a system of pointers. The programs therefore need only to specify data items by name, not by location. A database management system handles retrieval and storage. Because separate files for different applications programs are unnecessary, data redundancy can be substantially reduced.
    Answer (B) is incorrect because conversion to a database is often costly and time consuming. Answer (C) is incorrect because a traditional flat-file system, not a database, has multiple occurrences of data items. Answer (D) is incorrect because given the absence of data redundancy and the quick propagation of data errors throughout applications, backup and recovery procedures are just as critical in a database as in a flat-file system.

12. An internal auditor encounters a batch-processed payroll in which each record contains the same type of data elements, in the same order, with each data element needing the same number of storage spaces. Which file structure would most appropriately be used to support this set of records?

    A. Single flat file structure.

    B. Hierarchical structure.

    C. Network structure.

    D. Relational structure.

Answer (A) is correct. *(CIA, adapted)*
    REQUIRED: The file structure in which each record has the same type and order of data elements and the same storage requirements.
    DISCUSSION: In a single flat file structure, all attributes and field lengths in a record are identical to those in the other records. The structure is typically a table or spreadsheet with records for rows and attributes for columns.
    Answer (B) is incorrect because a hierarchical or tree structure is used to express relationships in which one attribute or item is related to many others in layers of subordinate records. Answer (C) is incorrect because a network structure expresses complex relationships in which many attributes are related to many others. Answer (D) is incorrect because a relational structure is not unlike the flat structure but is far more sophisticated. It gives the system the ability to handle many data relationships that were not anticipated by the designers. It uses a series of tables in which each table defines a relationship.

13. In an inventory system on a database management system (DBMS), one stored record contains part number, part name, part color, and part weight. These individual items are called

    A. Fields.

    B. Stored files.

    C. Bytes.

    D. Occurrences.

Answer (A) is correct. *(CIA, adapted)*
    REQUIRED: The term for the data elements in a record.
    DISCUSSION: A record is a collection of related data items (fields). A field (data item) is a group of characters representing one unit of information.
    Answer (B) is incorrect because a file is a group or set of related records ordered to facilitate processing. Answer (C) is incorrect because a byte is a group of bits (binary digits). It represents one character. Answer (D) is incorrect because occurrences is not a meaningful term in this context.

14. An inventory clerk, using a computer terminal, views the following on screen: part number, part description, quantity on-hand, quantity on-order, order quantity and reorder point for a particular inventory item. Collectively, these data make up a

    A. Field.

    B. File.

    C. Database.

    D. Record.

Answer (D) is correct. *(CIA, adapted)*
    REQUIRED: The term for the collection of data described.
    DISCUSSION: A record is a collection of related data items (fields). A field (data item) is a group of characters representing one unit of information. The part number, part description, etc., are represented by fields.
    Answer (A) is incorrect because field refers to a single data item. Answer (B) is incorrect because file refers to multiple records. Answer (C) is incorrect because database refers to multiple files.

15. An entity has the following invoices in a batch:

Invoice Number	Product	Quantity	Unit Price
201	F10	150	$ 5.00
202	G15	200	$10.00
203	H20	250	$25.00
204	K35	300	$30.00

Which of the following numbers represents the record count?

A. 1

B. 4

C. 810

D. 900

Answer (B) is correct. *(CPA, adapted)*
REQUIRED: The record count.
DISCUSSION: Input controls in batch computer systems are used to determine that no data are lost or added to the batch. Depending on the sophistication of a particular system, control may be accomplished by using record counts, batch totals, or hash totals. A record count establishes the number of source documents and reconciles it to the number of output records. The total number of invoices processed is an example of a record count. In this case, the record count is 4.
Answer (A) is incorrect because 1 is the number of batches. Answer (C) is incorrect because 810 is a hash total of the invoice numbers. Answer (D) is incorrect because 900 is the total quantity of items.

16. Which of the following is the elementary unit of data storage used to represent individual attributes of an entity?

A. Database.

B. Data field.

C. File.

D. Record.

Answer (B) is correct. *(CIA, adapted)*
REQUIRED: The elementary unit of data storage that is used to represent individual attributes of an entity.
DISCUSSION: A data item (or field) is a group of characters. It is used to represent individual attributes of an entity, such as an employee's address. A field is an item in a record.
Answer (A) is incorrect because a database is an organized collection of files. Answer (C) is incorrect because a file is a collection of records. Answer (D) is incorrect because a record is a collection of data items.

17. A file-oriented approach to data storage requires a primary record key for each file. Which of the following is a primary record key?

A. The vendor number in an accounts payable master file.

B. The vendor number in a closed purchase order transaction file.

C. The vendor number in an open purchase order master file.

D. All of the answers are correct.

Answer (A) is correct. *(CIA, adapted)*
REQUIRED: The item(s) used as a primary record key.
DISCUSSION: The primary record key uniquely identifies each record in a file. Because there is only one record for each vendor in an accounts payable master file, the vendor number would be the appropriate key.
Answer (B) is incorrect because purchase order files can have multiple purchase orders made out to the same vendor. The primary key in purchase order files would be the purchase order number because it is the only unique identifier for the record. Answer (C) is incorrect because purchase order files can have multiple purchase orders made out to the same vendor. The primary key in purchase order files would be the purchase order number because it is the only unique identifier for the record. Answer (D) is incorrect because not all of the answer choices are correct.

18. A business is designing its storage for accounts receivable information. What data file concepts should be used to provide the ability to answer customer inquiries as they are received?

A. Sequential storage and chains.

B. Sequential storage and indexes.

C. Record keys, indexes, and pointers.

D. Inverted file structure, indexes, and internal labels.

Answer (C) is correct. *(CIA, adapted)*
REQUIRED: The data file concepts needed to answer customer inquiries as they are received.
DISCUSSION: A record key is an attribute that uniquely identifies or distinguishes each record from the others. An index is a table listing storage locations for attributes, often including those other than the unique record key attribute. A pointer is a data item that indicates the physical address of the next logically related record.
Answer (A) is incorrect because the ability to respond immediately to customers requires direct access. Answer (B) is incorrect because the ability to respond immediately to customers requires direct access. Answer (D) is incorrect because internal labels are used to indicate various things to the computer, such as the contents of various types of data storage media, the beginning of each file (with identification information), and the end of each file. However, they do not provide information for locating specific records in a file. An inverted file structure (inverted list) is an index based on a secondary key, for example, years of experience rather than an employee number (the primary key).

19. Auditors making database queries often need to combine several tables to get the information they want. One approach to combining tables is known as

- A. Extraction.
- B. Joining.
- C. Sorting.
- D. Summarization.

Answer (B) is correct. *(CIA, adapted)*
REQUIRED: The approach to combining tables when making database queries.
DISCUSSION: In CAAT software packages, joining is the combining of data files based on a common data element. For example, if rows in a table containing information about specified parts have been selected, the result can be joined with a table that contains information about suppliers. The join operation may combine the two tables using the supplier number (assuming both tables contained this element) to provide information about the suppliers of particular parts.
Answer (A) is incorrect because extraction selects data containing specified criteria from a data file; it does not combine tables. Answer (C) is incorrect because sorting allows the auditor to organize data by any data field, not combine tables. Answer (D) is incorrect because summarization reports on the information contained in several tables but does not combine the tables.

20. Users making database queries often need to combine several tables to get the information they want. One approach to combining tables is

- A. Joining.
- B. Merging.
- C. Projecting.
- D. Pointing.

Answer (A) is correct. *(CIA, adapted)*
REQUIRED: The approach to combining tables when making database queries.
DISCUSSION: Joining is the combining of two or more relational tables based on a common data element. For example, if a supplier table contains information about suppliers and a parts table contains information about parts, the two tables can be joined using the supplier number (assuming both tables contain this attribute) to give information about the supplier of particular parts.
Answer (B) is incorrect because the three basic operations in a relational database are selecting, joining, and projecting. Answer (C) is incorrect because projecting is the basic operation in a relational database that results in a subset consisting of columns (fields) in a table. This operation creates a new table containing only the required information. Answer (D) is incorrect because a pointer is a data element attached to a record that gives the address of another record.

21. All of the following are methods for distributing a relational database across multiple servers except

- A. Snapshot (making a copy of the database for distribution).
- B. Replication (creating and maintaining replica copies at multiple locations).
- C. Normalization (separating the database into logical tables for easier user processing).
- D. Fragmentation (separating the database into parts and distributing where they are needed).

Answer (C) is correct. *(CIA, adapted)*
REQUIRED: The item not a method for distributing a relational database across multiple servers.
DISCUSSION: A distributed database is stored in two or more physical sites. The two basic methods of distributing a database are partitioning and replication. However, normalization is a process of database design, not distribution. Normalization is the term for determining how groups of data items in a relational structure are arranged in records in a database. This process relies on "normal forms," that is, conceptual definitions of data records and specified design rules. Normalization is intended to prevent inconsistent updating of data items. It is a process of breaking down a complex data structure by creating smaller, more efficient relations, thereby minimizing or eliminating the repeating groups in each relation.
Answer (A) is incorrect because the snapshot technique makes duplicates to be stored at multiple locations. Answer (B) is incorrect because the replication technique makes duplicates to be stored at multiple locations. Changes are periodically copied and sent to each location. If a database is small, storing multiple copies may be cheaper than retrieving records from a central site. Answer (D) is incorrect because fragmentation or partitioning stores specific records where they are most needed. For example, a financial institution may store a particular customer's data at the branch where (s)he usually transacts his/her business. If the customer executes a transaction at another branch, the pertinent data is retrieved via communications lines.

22. When required to read customer data, the operating system finds the primary key value in a file whose records contain key values and their corresponding physical addresses. In this situation, the most likely file organization for customer data is

    A. A direct-access file.

    B. An indexed sequential file.

    C. A sequential file.

    D. A text file.

Answer (B) is correct. *(CIA, adapted)*
    REQUIRED: The organization of a file whose records contain key values and corresponding physical addresses.
    DISCUSSION: If records are stored sequentially on a direct-access storage device, the records can be accessed directly using the indexed-sequential-access method. An index of key fields is maintained that lists the physical location of the record corresponding to each key field.
    Answer (A) is incorrect because a direct-access file has no index file. Answer (C) is incorrect because a sequential file has no index file. Answer (D) is incorrect because a text file would probably not be used in this situation.

23. In a database system, locking of data helps preserve data integrity by permitting transactions to have control of all the data needed to complete the transactions. However, implementing a locking procedure could lead to

    A. Inconsistent processing.

    B. Rollback failures.

    C. Unrecoverable transactions.

    D. Deadly embraces (retrieval contention).

Answer (D) is correct. *(CIA, adapted)*
    REQUIRED: The potential problem of a locking procedure.
    DISCUSSION: In a distributed processing system, the data and resources a transaction may update or use should be held in their current status until the transaction is complete. A deadly embrace occurs when two transactions need the same resource at the same time. If the system does not have a method to cope with the problem efficiently, response time worsens or the system eventually fails. The system should have an algorithm for undoing the effects of one transaction and releasing the resources it controls so that the other transaction can run to completion.
    Answer (A) is incorrect because inconsistent processing occurs when a transaction has different effects depending on when it is processed. Data locking ensures consistent processing. Answer (B) is incorrect because rollback failure is the inability of the software to undo the effects of a transaction that could not be run to completion. A rollback failure is not caused by data locking. However, data locking may lead to situations in which rollback is required. Answer (C) is incorrect because unrecoverable transactions are not a typical symptom of locking procedures.

24. One advantage of a database management system (DBMS) is

    A. That each organizational unit takes responsibility and control for its own data.

    B. The cost of the data processing department decreases as users are now responsible for establishing their own data handing techniques.

    C. A decreased vulnerability as the database management system has numerous security controls to prevent disasters.

    D. The independence of the data from the application programs, which allows the programs to be developed for the user's specific needs without concern for data capture problems.

Answer (D) is correct. *(CMA, adapted)*
    REQUIRED: The advantage of a DBMS.
    DISCUSSION: A fundamental characteristic of databases is that applications are independent of the database structure; when writing programs or designing applications to use the database, only the name of the desired item is necessary. Programs can be developed for the user's specific needs without concern for data capture problems. Reference can be made to the items using the data manipulation language, after which the DBMS takes care of locating and retrieving the desired items. The physical or logical structure of the database can be completely altered without having to change any of the programs using the data items; only the schema requires alteration.
    Answer (A) is incorrect because each organizational unit develops programs to make use of elements of a broad database. Answer (B) is incorrect because data handling techniques are still the responsibility of the data processing department; it is the use of the data that is departmentalized. Answer (C) is incorrect because the DBMS is no safer than any other database system.

25. Which of the following is a false statement about a database management system application environment?

    A. Data are used concurrently by multiple users.

    B. Data are shared by passing files between programs or systems.

    C. The physical structure of the data is independent of user needs.

    D. Data definition is independent of any one program.

Answer (B) is correct. *(CISA, adapted)*
    REQUIRED: The false statement about data in a DBMS environment.
    DISCUSSION: In this kind of system, applications use the same database. There is no need to pass files between applications.
    Answer (A) is incorrect because the advantage of a DBMS is that data can be used concurrently by multiple users. Answer (C) is incorrect because, when a DBMS is used, the physical structure of the data is independent of user needs. Answer (D) is incorrect because, when a DBMS is used, the data are defined independently of the needs of any one program.

26. Which of the following should not be the responsibility of a database administrator?

   A. Design the content and organization of the database.

   B. Develop applications to access the database.

   C. Protect the database and its software.

   D. Monitor and improve the efficiency of the database.

Answer (B) is correct. *(CIA, adapted)*
   REQUIRED: The item not the responsibility of a database administrator.
   DISCUSSION: The database administrator (DBA) is the person who has overall responsibility for developing and maintaining the database. One primary responsibility is for designing the content of the database. Another responsibility of the DBA is to protect and control the database. A third responsibility is to monitor and improve the efficiency of the database. The responsibility of developing applications to access the database belongs to systems analysts and programmers.
   Answer (A) is incorrect because designing the content and organization of the database is a responsibility of the database administrator. Answer (C) is incorrect because protecting the database and its software is a responsibility of the database administrator. Answer (D) is incorrect because monitoring and improving the efficiency of the database is a responsibility of the database administrator.

27. The responsibilities of a data administrator (DA) include monitoring

   A. The database industry.

   B. The performance of the database.

   C. Database security.

   D. Backup of the system.

Answer (A) is correct. *(Publisher, adapted)*
   REQUIRED: The responsibilities of a data administrator.
   DISCUSSION: The DA handles administrative issues that arise regarding the database. The DA acts as an advocate by suggesting new applications and standards. One of the DA's responsibilities is to monitor the database industry for new developments. In contrast, the database administrator (DBA) deals with the technical aspects of the database.

28. To trace data through several application programs, an auditor needs to know what programs use the data, which files contain the data, and which printed reports display the data. If data exist only in a database system, the auditor could probably find all of this information in a

   A. Data dictionary.

   B. Database schema.

   C. Data encryptor.

   D. Decision table.

Answer (A) is correct. *(CIA, adapted)*
   REQUIRED: The information source in a database needed to trace data through several application programs.
   DISCUSSION: The data dictionary is a file (possibly manual but usually computerized) in which the records relate to specified data items. It contains definitions of data items, the list of programs used to process them, and the reports in which data are found. Only certain persons or entities are permitted to retrieve data or to modify data items. Accordingly, these access limitations are also found in the data dictionary.
   Answer (B) is incorrect because the schema describes the structure of the database. Answer (C) is incorrect because an encryptor encodes data. Answer (D) is incorrect because a decision table is a type of logic diagram that presents in matrix form the decision points and related actions reflected in a computer program.

6.3 E-Commerce, EDI, and EFT

29. All of the following are potential security issues for e-commerce except

   A. Correct identification of transacting parties.

   B. Proliferation of computer viruses.

   C. Determining who may rightfully make transaction decisions.

   D. Verification of payment data.

Answer (B) is correct. *(Publisher, adapted)*
   REQUIRED: The process that is not a potential security issue for e-commerce.
   DISCUSSION: E-commerce is the purchase and sale of goods and services by electronic means. E-commerce may occur via online transactions on public networks, electronic data interchange (EDI), and email. Security issues for e-commerce include the correct identification of transacting parties (authentication), determining who may rightfully make decisions (authorization), and verification of payment data. While proliferation of computer viruses is a general security issue with regard to information systems, it is not a specific risk associated with e-commerce.
   Answer (A) is incorrect because authentication is a security issue related to e-commerce. Answer (C) is incorrect because authorization is a security issue related to e-commerce. Answer (D) is incorrect because verification of payment data is a security issue related to e-commerce.

30. Companies now can use electronic transfers to conduct regular business transactions. Which of the following terms best describes a system in which an agreement is made between two or more parties to electronically transfer purchase orders, sales orders, invoices, and/or other financial documents?

- A. Electronic mail (email).
- B. Electronic funds transfer (EFT).
- C. Electronic data interchange (EDI).
- D. Electronic data processing (EDP).

Answer (C) is correct. *(CIA, adapted)*
REQUIRED: The term best describing electronic transfer of documents.
DISCUSSION: Electronic data interchange is the electronic transfer of documents between businesses. EDI was developed to enhance just-in-time (JIT) inventory management. Advantages include speed, reduction of clerical errors, and elimination of repetitive clerical tasks and their costs.
Answer (A) is incorrect because email can send text or document files, but the term encompasses a wide range of transfers. EDI specifically applies to the system described in the question. Answer (B) is incorrect because electronic funds transfer (EFT) refers to the transfer of money. Answer (D) is incorrect because electronic data processing (EDP) is a generic term for computerized processing of transaction data within organizations.

Questions 31 and 32 are based on the following information. A multinational company has an agreement with a value-added network (VAN) that provides the encoding and communications transfer for the company's electronic data interchange (EDI) and electronic funds transfer (EFT) transactions. Before transfer of data to the VAN, the company performs online preprocessing of the transactions. The internal auditor is responsible for assessing preprocessing controls. In addition, the agreement between the company and the VAN states that the internal auditor is allowed to examine and report on the controls in place at the VAN on an annual basis. The contract specifies that access to the VAN can occur on a surprise basis during the second or third quarter of the company's fiscal year. This period was chosen so it would not interfere with processing during the VAN's peak transaction periods. This provision was not reviewed with internal auditing. The annual audit plan approved by the board of directors specifies that a full audit would be done during the current year.

---

31. Which one of the following would not be included as a reason for the company to use EFT with the EDI system?

- A. To take advantage of the time lag associated with negotiable instruments.
- B. To allow the company to negotiate discounts with EDI vendors based upon prompt payment.
- C. To improve its cash management program.
- D. To reduce input time and input errors.

Answer (A) is correct. *(CIA, adapted)*
REQUIRED: The item not a reason for using EFT.
DISCUSSION: The float period is the time lag between transmittal of a regular check (a negotiable instrument) and its clearance through regular banking channels. Float is eliminated by EFT.
Answer (B) is incorrect because payment schedules may be based on the time required to process invoices, prepare checks, and transmit checks. Using EFT, payment is instantaneous, and payment schedules can be based on other criteria, e.g., discounts for prompt payment. Answer (C) is incorrect because EFT allows for more effective control of payments and transfers among accounts. Answer (D) is incorrect because integration of EDI and EFT eliminates manual input of transaction data, a process that introduces errors into the accounting system.

---

32. Which one of the following is least likely to be recommended by the auditor when an EDI-EFT system is being designed?

- A. The identity of the individual approving an electronic document should be stored as a data field.
- B. Disaster recovery plans should be established.
- C. Data security procedures should be written to prevent changes to data by unauthorized individuals.
- D. Remote access to electronic data should be denied.

Answer (D) is correct. *(CIA, adapted)*
REQUIRED: The least likely audit recommendation when an EDI-EFT system is being designed.
DISCUSSION: One of the benefits of an EDI-EFT system is that it can provide remote access at any time from any place if telecommunications links are available. However, appropriate controls should prevent unauthorized access.
Answer (A) is incorrect because approval information is needed to provide an audit trail. Answer (B) is incorrect because disaster recovery plans are needed to ensure that the company can continue to function if the system crashes. Answer (C) is incorrect because individuals should not be able to update data without proper identification and authentication.

33. Which of the following is usually a benefit of transmitting transactions in an electronic data interchange (EDI) environment?

    A. A compressed business cycle with lower year-end receivables balances.

    B. A reduced need to test computer controls related to sales and collections transactions.

    C. An increased opportunity to apply statistical sampling techniques to account balances.

    D. No need to rely on third-party service providers to ensure security.

Answer (A) is correct. *(CPA, adapted)*
    REQUIRED: The benefit of EDI.
    DISCUSSION: EDI transactions are typically transmitted and processed in real time. Thus, EDI compresses the business cycle by eliminating delays. The time required to receive and process an order, ship goods, and receive payment is greatly reduced compared with that of a typical manual system. Accordingly, more rapid receipt of payment minimizes receivables and improves cash flow.
    Answer (B) is incorrect because use of a sophisticated processing system would increase the need to test computer controls. Answer (C) is incorrect because computer technology allows all transactions to be tested rather than just a sample. Answer (D) is incorrect because EDI often uses a VAN (value-added network) as a third-party service provider, and reliance on controls provided by the VAN may be critical.

34. The emergence of electronic data interchange (EDI) as standard operating practice increases the risk of

    A. Unauthorized third-party access to systems.

    B. Systematic programming errors.

    C. Inadequate knowledge bases.

    D. Unsuccessful system use.

Answer (A) is correct. *(CIA, adapted)*
    REQUIRED: The risk increased by the emergence of EDI as standard operating practice.
    DISCUSSION: EDI is the communication of electronic documents directly from a computer in one entity to a computer in another entity. EDI for business documents between unrelated parties has the potential to increase the risk of unauthorized third-party access to systems because more outsiders will have access to internal systems.
    Answer (B) is incorrect because systematic programming errors are the result of misspecification of requirements or lack of correspondence between specifications and programs. Answer (C) is incorrect because inadequate knowledge bases are a function of lack of care in building them. Answer (D) is incorrect because a benefit of EDI is to improve the efficiency and effectiveness of system use.

35. Which of the following risks is not greater in an electronic funds transfer (EFT) environment than in a manual system using paper transactions?

    A. Unauthorized access and activity.

    B. Duplicate transaction processing.

    C. Higher cost per transaction.

    D. Inadequate backup and recovery capabilities.

Answer (C) is correct. *(CIA, adapted)*
    REQUIRED: The risk not greater in an EFT environment than in a manual system using paper transactions.
    DISCUSSION: EFT is a service provided by financial institutions worldwide that is based on EDI technology. EFT transaction costs are lower than for manual systems because documents and human intervention are eliminated from the transactions process.
    Answer (A) is incorrect because unauthorized access and activity is a risk specific to EFT. Answer (B) is incorrect because inaccurate transaction processing (including duplication) is a risk specific to EFT. Answer (D) is incorrect because inadequate backup and recovery capabilities is a risk specific to EFT.

36. Which of the following are essential elements of the audit trail in an electronic data interchange (EDI) system?

    A. Network and sender/recipient acknowledgments.

    B. Message directories and header segments.

    C. Contingency and disaster recovery plans.

    D. Trading partner security and mailbox codes.

Answer (A) is correct. *(CPA, adapted)*
    REQUIRED: The essential element in an EDI audit trail.
    DISCUSSION: An audit trail allows for the tracing of a transaction from initiation to conclusion. Network and sender/recipient acknowledgments relate to the transaction flow and provide for the tracking of transactions.
    Answer (B) is incorrect because message directories and header segments provide information controlling the message, such as originating and destination stations, message type and priority level, which are part of the message and not the audit trail. Answer (C) is incorrect because, although contingency and disaster recovery plans are important controls, they do not relate to the audit trail. Answer (D) is incorrect because, although maintaining control over security and mailbox codes is an important control, it does not relate to the audit trail.

37. Which of the following is a false statement about XBRL?

   A. XBRL is freely licensed.

   B. XBRL facilitates the automatic exchange of information.

   C. XBRL is used primarily in the U.S.

   D. XBRL is designed to work with a variety of software applications.

Answer (C) is correct.   *(Publisher, adapted)*
   REQUIRED: The false statement about XBRL.
   DISCUSSION: XBRL stands for eXtensible Business Reporting Language. It is being developed for business and accounting applications. It is an XML-based application used to create, exchange, and analyze financial reporting information and is being developed for worldwide use.
   Answer (A) is incorrect because the AICPA-led consortium that developed XBRL has promoted the application as a freely licensed product. Answer (B) is incorrect because XBRL will facilitate the exchange of information. Answer (D) is incorrect because XBRL will allow exchange of data across many platforms and will soon be integrated into accounting software applications and products.

38. Which of the following statements is true concerning internal control in an electronic data interchange (EDI) system?

   A. Preventive controls generally are more important than detective controls in EDI systems.

   B. Control objectives for EDI systems generally are different from the objectives for other information systems.

   C. Internal controls in EDI systems rarely permit control risk to be assessed at below the maximum.

   D. Internal controls related to the segregation of duties generally are the most important controls in EDI systems.

Answer (A) is correct.   *(CPA, adapted)*
   REQUIRED: The true statement about EDI controls.
   DISCUSSION: In general, preventive controls are more important than detective controls because the benefits typically outweigh the costs. In electronic processing, once a transaction is accepted, there is often little opportunity to apply detective controls. Thus, it is important to prevent errors or frauds before they happen.
   Answer (B) is incorrect because the basic control objectives are the same regardless of the nature of the processing: to ensure the integrity of the information and to safeguard the assets. Answer (C) is incorrect because, to gather sufficient evidence in a sophisticated computer system, it is often necessary to rely on the controls. Control risk may be assessed at below the maximum if relevant controls are identified and tested and if the resulting evidential matter provides the degree of assurance necessary to support the assessed level of control risk. Answer (D) is incorrect because the level of segregation of duties achieved in a manual system is usually not feasible in a computer system.

39. A control that a company can use to detect forged EDI messages is to

   A. Acknowledge all messages initiated externally with confirming messages.

   B. Permit only authorized employees to have access to transmission facilities.

   C. Delay action on orders until a second order is received for the same goods.

   D. Write all incoming messages to a write-once/read-many device for archiving.

Answer (A) is correct.   *(CIA, adapted)*
   REQUIRED: The control to detect forged EDI messages.
   DISCUSSION: If the company acknowledges messages initiated externally, the alleged sender will have the opportunity to recognize that it had not sent the message and will then be able to notify the company of the potential forgery. Then corrective action can be taken by the company.
   Answer (B) is incorrect because permitting only authorized employees to have access to transmission facilities controls for unauthorized access to the facilities but would not detect forged EDI messages. Answer (C) is incorrect because delaying action on orders until a second order is received for the same goods defeats the purpose of using EDI, namely, rapid communication followed by rapid response. Answer (D) is incorrect because writing all incoming messages to a write-once/read-many device is a good practice, but it will not detect forgeries.

40. Which of the following statements about SET (Secured Electronic Transaction) is false?

    A. SET is a trademarked protocol that provides individualized security standards.

    B. SET is based on a hierarchy of certificate authorities.

    C. SET authenticates users with digital certificates and digital signatures.

    D. SET is supported through an organization called SETCo.

Answer (A) is correct. *(Publisher, adapted)*
    REQUIRED: The false statement about SET.
    DISCUSSION: SET (Secured Electronic Transaction) is a trademarked protocol that provides a common security standards, especially with regard to Internet card purchases. It is supported by Visa and MasterCard through an organization called SETCo. SET encrypts the details of payment transactions at all times so as to ensure privacy and data integrity. It also ensures that the identities of buyers and sellers are authenticated using digital signatures and digital certificates. SET is based on a hierarchy of certificate authorities that parallels financial relationships outside cyberspace.
    Answer (B) is incorrect because SET is based in a hierarchy of certificate authorities that parallels financial relationships outside cyberspace. Answer (C) is incorrect because SET authenticates sellers and buyers using digital signatures and certificates. Answer (D) is incorrect because SET is supported by Visa and MasterCard through an organization called SETCo.

6.4 Enterprise-Wide Resource Planning

41. An enterprise resource planning (ERP) system integrates the organization's computerized subsystems and may also provide links to external parties. An advantage of ERP is that

    A. The reengineering needed for its implementation should improve business processes.

    B. Customizing the software to suit the unique needs of the organization will facilitate upgrades.

    C. It can be installed by organizations of all sizes.

    D. The comprehensiveness of the system reduces resistance to change.

Answer (A) is correct. *(Publisher, adapted)*
    REQUIRED: The advantage of ERP.
    DISCUSSION: The benefits of ERP may significantly derive from the business process reengineering that is needed for its implementation. Using ERP software that reflects the best practices forces the linked subunits in the organization not only to redesign and improve their processes but also to conform to one standard.
    Answer (B) is incorrect because the disadvantages of ERP are its extent and complexity, which make customization of the software difficult and costly. Answer (C) is incorrect because ERP software is costly and complex. It is usually installed only by the largest enterprises. Answer (D) is incorrect because implementing an ERP system is likely to encounter significant resistance because of its comprehensiveness.

42. A manufacturing resource planning (MRP II) system

    A. Performs the same back-office functions for a manufacturer as an ERP system.

    B. Uses a master production schedule.

    C. Lacks the forecasting and budgeting capabilities typical of an ERP system.

    D. Performs the same front-office functions for a manufacturer as an ERP system.

Answer (B) is correct. *(Publisher, adapted)*
    REQUIRED: The true statement about MRP II.
    DISCUSSION: Manufacturing resource planning (MRP II) continued the evolution begun with MRP. It is a closed-loop manufacturing system that integrates all facets of manufacturing, including production, sales, inventories, schedules, and cash flows. The same system is used for accounting and finance functions, which use the same transactions and numbers. MRP II uses an MPS (master production schedule), a statement of the anticipated manufacturing schedule for selected items for selected periods. (MRP also used the MPS. Thus, MRP is a component of an MRP II system.)
    Answer (A) is incorrect because an MRP II system does not integrate all the subsystems internal to the organization (back-office functions), such as human resources and customer service. Answer (C) is incorrect because MRP II includes forecasting and planning capacities for generating cash and other budgets. Answer (D) is incorrect because MRP, MRP II, and traditional ERP do not provide for front-office functions, that is, connections with customers, suppliers, owners, creditors, and strategic allies.

43. In a traditional ERP system, the receipt of a customer order may result in

I. Customer tracking of the order's progress

II. Automatic replenishment of inventory by a supplier

III. Hiring or reassigning of employees

IV. Automatic adjustment of output schedules

    A. I, II, and IV only.

    B. I and III only.

    C. III and IV only.

    D. I, II, III, and IV.

Answer (C) is correct. *(Publisher, adapted)*
REQUIRED: The possible effects of receipt of a customer order by a traditional ERP system.
DISCUSSION: The traditional ERP system is one in which subsystems share data and coordinate their activities. Thus, if marketing receives an order, it can quickly verify that inventory is sufficient to notify shipping to process the order. Otherwise, production is notified to manufacture more of the product, with a consequent automatic adjustment of output schedules. If materials are inadequate for this purpose, the system will issue a purchase order. If more labor is needed, human resources will be instructed to reassign or hire employees. However, the subsystems in a traditional ERP system are internal to the organization. Hence, they are often called back-office functions. The information produced is principally (but not exclusively) intended for internal use by the organization's managers.
    The current generation of ERP software (ERP II) has added front-office functions. Consequently, ERP II but not traditional ERP is capable of customer tracking of the order's progress and automatic replenishment of inventory by a supplier.

44. What are the possible characteristics of a client-server configuration in a current ERP system?

I. Thin clients, local area network, single server

II. Fat clients, wide area network, multiple servers

III. Fat clients, connection via Internet, and single server

    A. I, II, and III.

    B. II and III only.

    C. II only.

    D. I only.

Answer (A) is correct. *(Publisher, adapted)*
REQUIRED: The elements of a client-server configuration in a current ERP system.
DISCUSSION: Current ERP systems have a client-server configuration with, possibly, scores or hundreds of client (user) computers. Clients may be thin or fat. So-called thin clients have little processing ability, but fat clients may have substantial processing power. The system may have multiple servers to run applications and contain databases. The network architecture may be in the form of a local area network (LAN) or wide-area network (WAN), or users may connect with the server(s) via the Internet. An ERP system may use almost any of the available operating systems and database management systems.
    Answer (B) is incorrect because an ERP system also may have thin clients connected via a LAN. Answer (C) is incorrect because an ERP system also may have thin clients connected via a LAN or the Internet with one server. Answer (D) is incorrect because an ERP system also may have fat clients connected via a WAN or the Internet to multiple servers.

45. A principal advantage of an ERP system is

    A. Program-data dependence.

    B. Data redundancy.

    C. Separate data updating for different functions.

    D. Centralization of data.

Answer (D) is correct. *(Publisher, adapted)*
REQUIRED: The principal advantage of an ERP system
DISCUSSION: An advantage of an ERP system is the elimination of data redundancy through the use of a central database. In principle, information about an item of data is stored once, and all functions have access to it. Thus, when the item (such as a price) is updated, the change is effectively made for all functions. The result is reliability (data integrity).
    Answer (A) is incorrect because an ERP system uses a central database and a database management system. A fundamental characteristic of a database is that applications are independent of the physical structure of the database. Writing programs or designing applications to use the database requires only the names of desired data items, not their locations.
Answer (B) is incorrect because an ERP system eliminates data redundancy. Answer (C) is incorrect because an ERP system is characterized by one-time data updating for all organizational functions.

46. The current generation of ERP software (ERP II) has added front-office functions like

    A. Inventory control.

    B. Human resources.

    C. Purchasing.

    D. Customer service.

Answer (D) is correct. *(Publisher, adapted)*
    REQUIRED: The front-office function addressed by ERP II.
    DISCUSSION: The current generation of ERP software (ERP II) has added front-office functions. Customer relationship management applications in ERP II extend to customer service, finance-related matters, sales, and database creation and maintenance. Integrated data are helpful in better understanding customer needs, such as product preference or location of retail outlets. Thus, the organization may be able to optimize its sales forecasts, product line, and inventory levels.
    Answer (A) is incorrect because inventory control is a back-office function. Answer (B) is incorrect because human resources is a back-office function. Answer (C) is incorrect because purchasing is a back-office function.

47. The current generation of ERP software (ERP II) may include an advanced planning and scheduling system that

    A. Determines the location of retail outlets.

    B. Connects the organization with other members of a joint venture.

    C. Controls the flow of a manufacturer's materials and components through the supply chain.

    D. Permits tracking of orders by customers.

Answer (C) is correct. *(Publisher, adapted)*
    REQUIRED: The function of an advanced planning and scheduling system.
    DISCUSSION: An advanced planning and scheduling system may be an element of a supply chain management application for a manufacturer. It controls the flow of materials and components within the chain. Schedules are created given projected costs, lead times, and inventories.
    Answer (A) is incorrect because customer relationship management applications in ERP II extend to customer service, finance-related matters, sales, and database creation and maintenance. Integrated data are helpful in better understanding customer needs, such as product preference or location of retail outlets. Answer (B) is incorrect because partner relationship management applications connect the organization not only with such partners as customers and suppliers but also with owners, creditors, and strategic allies (for example, other members of a joint venture). Answer (D) is incorrect because an advanced planning scheduling system is used by a manufacturer to control flows through the supply chain. Other software permits customers to obtain information about order availability.

6.5 Malicious Software and Attacks

48. Which of the following is a computer program that appears to be legitimate but performs some illicit activity when it is run?

    A. Hoax virus.

    B. Web crawler.

    C. Trojan horse.

    D. Killer application.

Answer (C) is correct. *(CPA, adapted)*
    REQUIRED: The apparently legitimate computer program that performs an illicit activity.
    DISCUSSION: A Trojan horse is a computer program that appears friendly, for example, a game, but that actually contains an application destructive to the computer system.
    Answer (A) is incorrect because a hoax virus is a false notice about the existence of a computer virus. It is usually disseminated through use of distribution lists and is sent by email or via an internal network. Answer (B) is incorrect because a web crawler (a spider or bot) is a computer program created to access and read information on websites. The results are included as entries in the index of a search engine. Answer (D) is incorrect because a killer application is one that is so useful that it may justify widespread adoption of a new technology.

49. The best preventive measure against a computer virus is to

A. Compare software in use with authorized versions of the software.

B. Execute virus exterminator programs periodically on the system.

C. Allow only authorized software from known sources to be used on the system.

D. Prepare and test a plan for recovering from the incidence of a virus.

Answer (C) is correct.   *(CIA, adapted)*
   REQUIRED: The best preventive measure against a computer virus.
   DISCUSSION: Preventive controls are designed to prevent errors before they occur. Detective and corrective controls attempt to identify and correct errors. Preventive controls are usually more cost beneficial than detective or corrective controls. Allowing only authorized software from known sources to be used on the system is a preventive measure. The authorized software from known sources is expected to be free of viruses.
   Answer (A) is incorrect because comparing software with authorized versions is a detective control used to determine whether only authorized versions of the software are being used on the system. Answer (B) is incorrect because executing virus exterminator programs is a corrective control against a computer virus. Answer (D) is incorrect because preparing and testing a plan for virus recovery is a corrective control against a computer virus.

50. Managers at a consumer products company purchased personal computer software from only recognized vendors, and prohibited employees from installing nonauthorized software on their personal computers. To minimize the likelihood of computer viruses infecting any of its systems, the company should also

A. Restore infected systems with authorized versions.

B. Recompile infected programs from source code backups.

C. Institute program change control procedures.

D. Test all new software on a stand-alone personal computer.

Answer (D) is correct.   *(CIA, adapted)*
   REQUIRED: The best protection against viruses.
   DISCUSSION: Software from recognized sources should be tested in quarantine (for example, in a test/development machine or a stand-alone personal computer) because even vendor-supplied software may be infected with viruses. The software should be run with a vaccine program and tested for the existence of logic bombs, etc.
   Answer (A) is incorrect because, if viruses infect a system, the company should restore the system with authorized software, but this procedure does not minimize the likelihood of initial infection. Answer (B) is incorrect because, if viruses infect programs that the company created, it should recompile the programs from source code backups, but this procedure does not minimize the likelihood of initial infection. Answer (C) is incorrect because instituting program change control procedures is good practice but does not minimize the likelihood of the system's being infected initially.

51. Which of the following is an indication that a computer virus is present?

A. Frequent power surges that harm computer equipment.

B. Unexplainable losses of or changes to data.

C. Inadequate backup, recovery, and contingency plans.

D. Numerous copyright violations due to unauthorized use of purchased software.

Answer (B) is correct.   *(CIA, adapted)*
   REQUIRED: The indicator of a computer virus.
   DISCUSSION: The effects of computer viruses range from harmless messages to complete destruction of all data within the system. A symptom of a virus would be the unexplained loss of or change to data.
   Answer (A) is incorrect because power surges are caused by hardware or power supply problems. Answer (C) is incorrect because inadequate back-up, recovery, and contingency plans are operating policy weaknesses. Answer (D) is incorrect because copyright violations represent policy or compliance problems.

52. Which of the following operating procedures increases an organization's exposure to computer viruses?

A. Encryption of data files.

B. Frequent backup of files.

C. Downloading public-domain software from websites.

D. Installing original copies of purchased software on hard disk drives.

Answer (C) is correct.   *(CIA, adapted)*
   REQUIRED: The procedure that increases exposure to viruses.
   DISCUSSION: Viruses are spread through shared data. Downloading public-domain software carries a risk that contaminated data may enter the computer.
   Answer (A) is incorrect because viruses are spread through the distribution of contaminated programs. Answer (B) is incorrect because backing up files does not increase the chances of a virus entering the computer system. Answer (D) is incorrect because original copies of purchased software on hard disk drives should be free of viruses.

53. An organization installed antivirus software on all its personal computers. The software was designed to prevent initial infections, stop replication attempts, detect infections after their occurrence, mark affected system components, and remove viruses from infected components. The major risk in relying on antivirus software is that antivirus software may

A. Not detect certain viruses.

B. Make software installation overly complex.

C. Interfere with system operations.

D. Consume too many system resources.

Answer (A) is correct. *(CIA, adapted)*
REQUIRED: The major risk in relying on antivirus software.
DISCUSSION: Antivirus software designed to identify and remove known viruses is sometimes known as a vaccine. A vaccine works only for known viruses and may not be effective for variants of those viruses or new viruses.
Answer (B) is incorrect because having antivirus software is unlikely to make software installation overly complex.
Answer (C) is incorrect because antivirus software need not interfere with system operations. Its execution can be scheduled in advance so as not to interfere with running programs.
Answer (D) is incorrect because antivirus software can be set to execute at times when it would not consume too many system resources, e.g., at startup.

54. What is the best course of action to take if a program takes longer than usual to load or execute?

A. Test the system by running a different application program.

B. Reboot the system.

C. Run antivirus software.

D. Back up the hard disk files to floppies.

Answer (C) is correct. *(CIA, adapted)*
REQUIRED: The best thing a microcomputer user should do if a program takes longer than usual to load or execute.
DISCUSSION: The described condition is a symptom of a virus. Many viruses will spread and cause additional damage. Use of an appropriate antivirus program may identify and even eliminate a viral infection. Ways to minimize computer virus risk in a networked system include restricted access, regularly updated passwords, periodic testing of systems with virus detection software, and the use of anti-virus software on all shareware prior to introducing it into the network.
Answer (A) is incorrect because running a different program as a test may cause the virus to spread and do additional damage. Answer (B) is incorrect because rebooting the system may cause the virus to spread and do additional damage. Answer (D) is incorrect because backing up hard disk files may cause the virus to spread and do additional damage.

55. Six months after a disgruntled systems programmer was fired and passwords disabled, the company's mainframe computer was brought to a halt when it suddenly erased all of its own files and software. The most likely way the programmer accomplished this was by

A. Returning to the computer center after 6 months.

B. Planting a computer virus through the use of telephone access.

C. Having an accomplice in the computer center.

D. Implanting a virus in the operating system and executing it via a back door.

Answer (D) is correct. *(CIA, adapted)*
REQUIRED: The most likely way the programmer caused the files and software to be erased.
DISCUSSION: Viruses are a form of computer sabotage. They are programs hidden within other programs that have the capacity to duplicate themselves and infect other systems. Sharing of storage media or participation in computer networks creates exposure to viruses. Viruses may result in actions ranging from harmless pranks to erasure of files and programs. A back door is a shortcut created in an operating system that permits a programmer simple access to the system.
Answer (A) is incorrect because the programmer would most likely be denied access to the center. Answer (B) is incorrect because the programmer would not know the necessary passwords. Answer (C) is incorrect because collusion is less likely than individual wrongdoing.

56. Because of competitive pressures to be more responsive to their customers, some organizations have connected their internal personal computer networks through a host computer to outside networks. A risk of this practice is that

A. Viruses may gain entry to one or more company systems.

B. Uploaded files may not be properly edited and validated.

C. Data downloaded to the personal computers may not be sufficiently timely.

D. Software maintenance on the personal computers may become more costly.

Answer (A) is correct. *(CIA, adapted)*
REQUIRED: The risk of connecting internal computer networks to outside networks.
DISCUSSION: Viruses are harmful programs that disrupt memory and processing functions and may destroy data. They spread from network to network, from infected diskettes, or from infected machines. Hence, connecting all networked personal computers through a host computer to outside networks increases the exposure of all of a company's computers to viruses.
Answer (B) is incorrect because whether uploaded files are properly edited and validated is independent of whether external links to other networks exist. Answer (C) is incorrect because whether data downloaded to the personal computers is sufficiently timely is independent of whether external links to other networks exist. Answer (D) is incorrect because whether software maintenance on the personal computers becomes more costly is independent of whether external links to other networks exist.

57. Attacks on computer networks may take many forms. Which of the following uses the computers of innocent parties infected with Trojan horse programs?

    A. A distributed denial-of-service attack.

    B. A man-in-the-middle attack.

    C. A brute-force attack.

    D. A password-cracking attack.

Answer (A) is correct. *(Publisher, adapted)*
REQUIRED: The type of attack on a computer network that uses the computers of innocent parties infected with Trojan horse programs.
DISCUSSION: A denial-of-service attack is an attempt to overload a system (e.g., a network or web server) with false messages so that it cannot function (a system crash). A distributed attack comes from multiple sources, for example, the machines of innocent parties infected by Trojan horses. When activated, these programs send messages to the target and leave the connection open. Many network connections are established to exclude other users, overload primary memory, or corrupt file systems.
Answer (B) is incorrect because a man-in-the-middle attack takes advantage of network packet sniffing and routing and transport protocols to access packets flowing through a network. Answer (C) is incorrect because a brute-force attack uses password cracking software to try large numbers of letter and number combinations to access a network. Answer (D) is incorrect because password-cracking software is used to access a network by using a large number of letter and number combinations.

58. Spoofing is one type of online activity used to launch malicious attacks. Spoofing is

    A. Trying large numbers of letter and number combinations to access a network.

    B. Eavesdropping on information sent by a user to the host computer of a website.

    C. Accessing packets flowing through a network.

    D. Identity misrepresentation in cyberspace.

Answer (D) is correct. *(Publisher, adapted)*
REQUIRED: The nature of spoofing.
DISCUSSION: Passwords, user account numbers, and other information may be stolen using techniques such as Trojan horses, IP spoofing, and packet sniffers. Spoofing is identity misrepresentation in cyberspace, for example, by using a false website to obtain information about visitors.
Answer (A) is incorrect because a brute-force attack uses password cracking software to try large numbers of letter and number combinations to access a network. Answer (B) is incorrect because sniffing is use of software to eavesdrop on information sent by a user to the host computer of a website. Answer (C) is incorrect because a man-in-the-middle attack takes advantage of network packet sniffing and routing and transport protocols to access packets flowing through a network.

59. An organization's computer system should have an intrusion detection system (IDS) if it has external connections. An IDS

    A. Must monitor every call on the system as it occurs.

    B. May examine only packets with certain signatures.

    C. Uses only knowledge-based detection.

    D. Uses only behavior-based detection.

Answer (B) is correct. *(Publisher, adapted)*
REQUIRED: The way in which an IDS functions.
DISCUSSION: A network IDS works by using sensors to examine packets traveling on the network. Each sensor monitors only the segment of the network to which it is attached. A packet is examined if it matches a signature. String signatures (certain strings of text) are potential signs of attack. Port signatures alert the IDS that a point subject to frequent intrusion attempts may be under attack. A header signature is a suspicious combination in a packet header.
Answer (A) is incorrect because a host IDS provides maximum protection only when the software is installed on each computer. It may operate in the following ways: The aggressive response is to monitor every call on the operating system and application as it occurs. A less effective method of preventing attacks is analysis of access log files. A host IDS may also identify questionable processes and verify the security of system files. Answer (C) is incorrect because an IDS is not limited to knowledge-based detection. Knowledge-based detection is based on information about the system's weaknesses and searches for intrusions that take advantage of them. Answer (D) is incorrect because an IDS is not limited to behavior-based detection. Behavior-based detection presumes that an attack will cause an observable anomaly. Actual and normal system behavior (a model of expected operations) are compared. A discrepancy results in an alert.

STUDY UNIT SEVEN
SPECIFIC IT ENGAGEMENTS

(28 pages of outline)

This study unit provides guidance to internal auditors when they perform specific **information technology (IT)** audit engagements. This guidance consists of 5 Practice Advisories that interpret **Standard 2100 – Nature of Work**.

The internal audit activity evaluates and contributes to the improvement of risk management, control, and governance systems.

Except for the Practice Advisory on e-commerce, the materials in this study unit were adopted by The IIA from Guidelines of the **Information Systems Audit and Control Association (ISACA)**.

NOTE: The content outline uses the term "information technology (IT)." However, certain Practice Advisories use the synonym "information systems (IS)."

Core Concepts

- In information systems audits, the IAA addresses risk management, control, and governance.
- All audits should be performed with due professional care.
- Pervasive IS controls are a subset of general controls. They affect the reliability of other controls. Detailed IS controls consist of (1) general controls not classified as pervasive and (2) application controls. The four domains of IS controls are (1) Planning and Organization (PO), (2) Acquisition and Implementation (AI), (3) Delivery and Support (DS), and (4) Monitoring (M). The effectiveness of controls in PO and M influences the effectiveness of controls in AI and DS.
- A primary planning objective is to identify application risks at the system and data levels. Application controls may be in computerized or manual form. If programmed controls are used, the auditor considers relevant general IT controls and controls specific to the audit objective. The general controls may be separately reviewed. General controls may not be reviewed in some cases, e.g., when a package application system is evaluated for acquisition.
- The CAE should determine the extent and adequacy of the right to audit a provider of outsourced services. Legal advice may be needed for this purpose.
- Organizations use the Internet and intranets to gain access to many kinds of applications. These providers affect organizational processes, controls, and control objectives on many levels. Thus, the auditor should evaluate third-party services.
- In an e-commerce audit, the auditor (1) assesses control and whether objectives are achievable, (2) determines risk acceptability, (3) understands information flow, (4) reviews interfaces, and (5) evaluates disaster recovery plans.

7.1 REVIEW OF IS CONTROLS

1.   The Practice Advisory in this subunit covers general controls over the management and monitoring of IS **(pervasive IS controls)** and their interaction with **detailed IS controls** (other general controls and application controls). It also covers IS audit planning, performance, and reporting.

    a.   *PRACTICE ADVISORY 2100-11: EFFECT OF PERVASIVE IS CONTROLS*

        I.   *CONTROLS FRAMEWORK*

        Definition

        Application controls: Refer to the transactions and data relating to each computer-based application system and are therefore specific to each such application. The objectives of application controls, which may be manual or programmed, are to ensure the completeness and accuracy of the records and the validity of the entries made in the records resulting from both manual and programmed processing.

        General computer controls: Controls, other than application controls, that relate to the environment within which computer-based application systems are developed, maintained, and operated. They are therefore applicable to all applications. The objectives of general controls are to ensure the proper development and implementation of applications, the integrity of program and data files, and the integrity of computer operations. Like application controls, general controls may be either manual or programmed.

        Pervasive IS controls: General controls that are designed to manage and monitor the IS environment and therefore affect all IS-related activities.

        Detailed IS controls: Controls over the acquisition, implementation, delivery, and support of IS systems and services. They are made up of application controls plus those general controls not included in pervasive controls.

        For each IS audit, auditors should differentiate between general controls that affect all information systems and operations (pervasive IS controls) and those that operate at a more specific level (detailed IS controls) to focus audit effort on the risk areas relevant to the audit objective. The controls framework described below assists the auditor in achieving this focus.

        Pervasive IS Controls

        *Examples of pervasive IS controls include controls over IS processes defined in COBIT's Planning and Organization domain and Monitoring domain; e.g., "PO1 - Define a Strategic IT Plan" and "M1 - Monitor the Processes." Pervasive IS controls are a **subset of general controls**. They are those general controls that focus on the management and monitoring of IS.*

        NOTE: **COBIT** is the acronym for Control Objectives for Information and Related Technology, an IT control framework copyrighted by the Information Systems Audit and Control Foundation.

        *The effect of pervasive IS controls is not limited to the **reliability of application controls** in the financial systems. Pervasive IS controls also affect the **reliability of the detailed IS controls** over, for example:*

          •   *Program development*
          •   *System implementation*
          •   *Security administration*
          •   *Back-up procedures*

Weak management and monitoring of IS (i.e., weak pervasive IS controls) should alert the auditor to the possibility of a high risk that the controls designed to operate at the detailed level may be ineffective.

Detailed IS Controls

Detailed IS controls are made up of application controls plus those general controls not included in pervasive IS controls. Examples include controls over:

- *Implementation of software packages*
- *System security parameters*
- *Disaster recovery planning*
- *Data input validation*
- *Exception report production*
- *Locking of user accounts after invalid attempts to access them*

Application controls are a subset of detailed IS controls. *Data input validation for example, is both a detailed IS control and an application control. Installing and accrediting systems (AI5) is a detailed IS control, but not an application control.*

*The **relationships among IS controls** are shown in the following outline:*

IS Controls
- *General controls*
  - *Pervasive IS controls*
  - *Detailed IS controls that are not application controls*
- *Application controls*

The auditor should consider the effect of non-IS controls on the scope and audit procedures.

Interaction of Pervasive and Detailed IS Controls

*The COBIT framework divides **IS control processes** into **four domains**:*

- *Planning and Organization*
- *Acquisition and Implementation*
- *Delivery and Support*
- *Monitoring*

The effectiveness of the controls in the Acquisition and Implementation (AI) and Delivery and Support (DS) domains is influenced by the effectiveness of the controls operated in the Planning and Organization (PO) and Monitoring (M) domains. Inadequate planning, organization, and monitoring by management imply that controls over acquisition, implementation, and service delivery and support will be ineffective. Conversely, strong planning, organization, and monitoring can identify and correct ineffective controls over acquisition, implementation, and service delivery and support.

For example, effective detailed IS controls over the process "Acquire and Maintain Application Software" (COBIT process reference AI2) are affected by the adequacy of the pervasive IS controls over processes:

- *"Define a Strategic IT Plan" (COBIT process reference PO1)*
- *"Manage Projects" (COBIT process reference PO10)*
- *"Manage Quality" (COBIT process reference PO11)*
- *"Monitor the Processes" (COBIT process reference M1)*

An audit of an application system acquisition should include the identification of the effect of the IS strategy, the project management approach, quality management, and the approach to monitoring. When, for example, project management is inadequate, the auditor should consider:

- Additional work to provide assurance that the specific project is effectively managed
- Reporting weaknesses in pervasive IS controls to management

A further example is that effective detailed IS controls over the process "Ensure Systems Security" (COBIT process reference DS5) are affected by the adequacy of pervasive IS controls over processes:

- "Define the IT Organization and Relationships" (COBIT process reference PO4)
- "Communicate Management Aims and Direction" (COBIT process reference PO6)
- "Assess Risks" (COBIT process reference PO9)
- "Monitor the Processes" (COBIT process reference M1)

An audit of the adequacy of security parameters in a system, for example UNIX, Windows NT, RACF, should include consideration of management's security policies (PO6), allocation of security responsibilities (PO4), risk assessment procedures (PO9), and procedures for monitoring compliance with its security policies (M1). Even when the parameters do not comply with the auditor's view of "best practice," they may be evaluated as adequate in the light of the risk identified by management and the management policies that direct how that level of risk should be addressed. Audit recommendations should be directed at the risk management or policies, as well as the detailed parameters themselves.

II.   PLANNING

Approach to Relevant Pervasive IS Controls

The Auditing Guideline on Planning the IS Audit states that the auditor should perform a **preliminary assessment of control** over the function being audited. This preliminary assessment should include identifying and evaluating relevant pervasive IS controls. The testing of pervasive IS controls may take place on a cycle different from the specific audit being performed. By their nature, they cover many different aspects of IS usage. The auditor should therefore consider whether any previous audit work in this area could be relied upon to identify and evaluate these controls.

When audit work indicates that **pervasive IS controls are unsatisfactory**, the auditor should consider the effect of this finding on the planned approach to achieving the audit objective:

- Strong pervasive IS controls can contribute to the assurance that may be obtained by an auditor in relation to detailed IS controls.
- Weak pervasive IS controls may undermine strong detailed IS controls or exacerbate weaknesses at the detailed level.

Sufficient Audit Procedures

When pervasive IS controls have a **significant potential effect on the audit objective**, it is not sufficient to plan to audit only the detailed controls. If it is not possible or practical to audit the pervasive IS controls, this **restriction of scope** should be reported. The auditor should plan to test the relevant pervasive IS controls when this will contribute to achieving the audit objective.

Relevant Controls

*Relevant pervasive IS controls are those that have an **effect on the specific audit objectives** for the assignment. For example, if the audit objective is to report on the controls over changes to a specific program library, pervasive IS controls relating to security policies (PO6) will be relevant, but pervasive IS controls relating to determination of the technological direction (PO3) may not be relevant.*

In planning the audit, the auditor should identify which of the total population of pervasive IS controls have an effect on the specific audit objectives and should plan to include these in the audit scope. COBIT's control objectives for the "Planning and Organization" and "Monitoring" domains may help the auditor to identify relevant pervasive IS controls.

Audit Evidence

*Pervasive IS controls may not necessarily be documented, but the internal auditor should plan to obtain **audit evidence** that relevant controls are **operating effectively**. Potential tests are outlined in the Performance of Audit Work section.*

Approach to Relevant Detailed IS Controls

*When audit work indicates **pervasive IS controls are satisfactory**, the auditor should consider reducing the **level of testing** planned for **detailed IS controls** because audit evidence of strong pervasive IS controls contributes to the assurance that may be obtained by an auditor in relation to detailed IS controls. When IS audit work indicates that **pervasive IS controls are not satisfactory**, the auditor should carry out sufficient testing of detailed IS controls to provide audit evidence that they are working effectively despite weaknesses in the relevant pervasive IS controls.*

III. **PERFORMANCE OF AUDIT WORK**

Testing Pervasive IS Controls

The auditor should carry out sufficient testing to provide assurance that relevant pervasive IS controls were operating effectively in the audit period or at a specific point in time. Test procedures may include:

- *Observation*
- *Corroborative inquiries*
- *Review of relevant documentation (policies, standards, meeting minutes, etc.)*
- *Re-performance (using CAATs, for example)*

If the testing of the relevant pervasive IS controls indicates that they are satisfactory, the auditor should proceed with the planned audit of the detailed IS controls that are directly applicable to the audit objective. The level of such testing may be less than would be appropriate if the pervasive IS controls were not operating satisfactorily.

IV.   REPORTING

Pervasive IS Control Weaknesses

If the auditor has identified weaknesses in pervasive IS controls, these should be brought to the attention of management, even when consideration of such areas was not specifically identified in the agreed scope of work.

Restrictions on Scope

*If pervasive IS controls could have a significant effect on the effectiveness of detailed IS controls, and the **pervasive IS controls have not been audited**, the auditor should communicate this situation to management in the final report. The report should include a **statement of the potential effect** on the audit findings, conclusions, and recommendations. For example, when an auditor is reporting on an audit of the acquisition of a package solution, but has not seen the organization's IS strategy, the auditor should include in the report a statement that the IS strategy has not been made available or does not exist. When relevant, the auditor should report the potential effect on the audit findings, conclusions, and recommendations. An example is a statement that it is not possible to say whether the acquisition of the package solution is consistent with the IS strategy or that it will support the future plans of the business.*

PA Summary

- **Application controls** are specific to each such application. They ensure the completeness and accuracy of records and the validity of entries.

- **General controls** are controls, other than application controls, that relate to the environment of computer-based application systems. They ensure the proper development and implementation of applications and the integrity of programs, data files, and computer operations.

- **Pervasive IS controls** are a subset of **general controls**. They manage and monitor the IS environment and affect all IS-related activities. Thus, they affect not only the **reliability of application controls** in the financial systems, but also the **reliability of the detailed IS controls** over, for example, program development, system implementation, security administration, and back-up procedures. Accordingly, weak management and monitoring controls (pervasive IS controls) may indicate that detailed controls are ineffective.

- **Detailed IS controls** address the acquisition, implementation, delivery, and support of IS systems and services. They consist of (1) general controls not classified as pervasive and (2) application controls. For example, accrediting systems is a detailed IS control but not an application control. For each IS audit, auditors should differentiate between pervasive IS controls and those that operate at a more specific level (detailed IS controls) to focus audit effort on the relevant risk areas.

- The four domains of IS controls are (1) Planning and Organization (PO), (2) Acquisition and Implementation (AI), (3) Delivery and Support (DS), and (4) Monitoring (M). The effectiveness of controls in PO and M influence the effectiveness of controls in AI and DS.

- In the **planning** of an IS audit, the **preliminary assessment of control** includes evaluating relevant pervasive IS controls. The testing of pervasive IS controls may occur on a different cycle. The auditor should therefore consider whether previous work can be relied upon to identify and evaluate these controls.

- Pervasive IS controls should be tested if they are **relevant**, i.e., if they may have an effect on the specific audit objective. When pervasive IS controls have a **significant potential effect on the audit objective** and it is not feasible to audit them, the **scope restriction** should be reported.
- **Audit evidence** should be obtained about the operating effectiveness of relevant controls.
- **Satisfactory pervasive IS controls** allow the auditor to consider reducing the audit effort devoted to detailed IS controls. If they are unsatisfactory, the testing of detailed IS controls must provide evidence that they are working effectively despite weaknesses in the relevant pervasive IS controls.
- **Tests of pervasive IS controls** may include observation, inquiries, review of documentation, and reperformance (e.g., with CAATs).
- **Weaknesses** in pervasive IS controls should be reported to management.
- The auditor should report to management when **unaudited pervasive IS controls** significantly affect detailed IS controls. The report should include a **statement of the potential effect** on the audit findings, conclusions, and recommendations.

2.   Stop and review! You have completed the outline for this subunit. Study multiple-choice questions 1 through 3 on page 371.

7.2 APPLICATIONS SYSTEMS REVIEW

1.   The Practice Advisory in this subunit addresses planning, performing, and reporting on an application systems review.

   a.   ***PRACTICE ADVISORY 2100-9: APPLICATIONS SYSTEMS REVIEW***

   *1.   The chief audit executive should determine that the internal audit activity possesses, or has access to, **independent**[1] **and competent auditing resources** to perform an application systems review and to evaluate the associated risk exposures.*

   Planning Considerations

   *2.   An integral part of planning is **understanding** the organization's information system **environment** to a sufficient extent for the auditor to determine the size and complexity of the systems and the extent of the organization's dependence on information systems. The auditor should gain an understanding of the organization's **mission** and **business objectives**, the level and manner in which **information technology and systems** are used to support the organization, and the **risks** and exposures associated with the organization's objectives and its information systems. Also, an understanding of the **organizational structure**, including roles and responsibilities of key information systems (IS) staff and the business process owner of the application system, should be obtained. **Risks** within the **business areas** should also be considered during audit planning.*

---

[1] *Independent – i.e., the auditor was not involved with the development, acquisition, implementation, or maintenance of the application system.*

A **primary objective** of planning is to identify the **application level risks**. The relative level of risk influences the level of audit evidence required. Application level risks at the **system and data level** include such things as:

- System **availability** risks relating to the lack of system operational capability
- System **security** risks relating to unauthorized access to systems or data
- System **integrity** risks relating to the incomplete, inaccurate, untimely, or unauthorized processing of data
- System **maintainability** risks relating to the inability to update the system when required in a manner that continues to provide for system availability, security, and integrity
- **Data** risks relating to its completeness, integrity, confidentiality, privacy, accuracy, and timeliness

Application controls to address the application level risks may be in the form of **computerized** controls built into the system, **manually performed** controls, or a combination of both. Examples include the computerized matching of documents (purchase order, invoice, and goods received report), the checking and signing of a computer generated check, and the review by senior management of exception reports.

Where the option to place reliance on programmed controls is taken, relevant **general information technology (IT) controls** should be considered, as well as controls specifically relevant to the audit objective. General IT controls could be the subject of a **separate review**, which would include such things as physical controls, system level security, network management, data backup, and contingency planning. Depending on the control objectives of the review, the auditor may not need to review general controls, such as when an application system is being evaluated for acquisition.

Application system reviews can be performed (1) when a **package application system** is being evaluated for acquisition, (2) before the application system goes into production (pre-implementation), and (3) after the application system has gone into production (post-implementation). **Pre-implementation application system review** coverage includes the architecture of application level security, plans for the implementation of security, the adequacy of system and user documentation, and the adequacy of actual or planned user acceptance testing. **Post-implementation review** coverage includes application level security after implementation and may cover system conversion if there has been a transfer of data and master file information from the old to the new system.

The objectives and scope of an application systems review usually form part of the engagement plan. The **form and content of the engagement plan** may vary but should include:

- The **objectives and scope** of the application systems review
- **Auditor(s)** performing the review
- A statement regarding the **independence** of the auditor(s) on the project
- When the review will commence and the **timeframe** of the review
- **Reporting arrangements**, including closing meeting arrangements
- **Objectives** should be developed to address the 7 COBIT (Control Objectives for Information and Related Technology) information criteria and then agreed upon by the organization. The 7 COBIT information criteria could include the following:
    - Effectiveness; Efficiency; Confidentiality; Integrity; Availability; Compliance; and Reliability of Information

*When the auditor has been involved previously in the development, acquisition, implementation, or maintenance of an application system and is assigned to an audit engagement, the **independence of the auditor may be impaired**. The auditor should refer to appropriate guidelines to deal with such circumstances.*

Performance of Audit Work

3. **a) Documenting the flow of transactions**

*Information gathered should include both the **computerized and manual aspects** of the system. **The focus** should be on **data input** (whether electronic or manual), **processing, storage, and output** that are of significance to the audit objectives. The auditor may find, depending upon the business processes and the use of technology, that **documenting the transaction flow** may not be practical. In that event, the auditor should prepare a high-level data flow diagram or narrative or use system documentation if provided.*

*Consideration should also be given to documenting **application interfaces with other systems**. The auditor should confirm the documentation by performing procedures such as a **walkthrough** test.*

b) Identifying and testing the application system controls

***Specific controls** to mitigate the application risks may be identified and sufficient audit evidence obtained to assure the auditor that the controls are operating as intended. This can be accomplished through procedures such as inquiry and observation, review of documentation, and testing of the application system controls when programmed controls are being tested (the use of CAATs may be considered).*

*The **nature, timing, and extent of testing** should be based on the level of risk of the area under review and the audit objectives. In the absence of strong **general IT controls**, the auditor may make an assessment of the effect of this weakness on the reliability of the **computerized application controls**. If the internal auditor finds significant weaknesses in the computerized application controls, assurance should be obtained (depending on the audit objective), if possible, from the **manually performed processing controls**.*

The effectiveness of computerized controls is dependent on strong general IT controls. Therefore, if general IT controls are not reviewed, the ability to place reliance on the application controls may be severely limited, and the auditor should consider alternative procedures.

Reporting

4. *Communicating the results of the application systems engagement should clearly describe the **nature of the engagement** and any **limitations, restrictions, or other factors** about which users of the information should be made aware. The auditor should include appropriate **recommendations** to strengthen controls in the report.*

***Weaknesses** identified in the application review either due to an **absence of controls or to non-compliance** should be brought to the attention of the business process owner and to IS management responsible for the support of the application. When weaknesses identified during the application systems review are considered to be significant or material, the **appropriate level of management** should be advised to undertake immediate **corrective action**. Since effective computerized application controls are dependent on general IT controls, weaknesses in this area should also be reported. In the event that **general IT controls were not reviewed**, this fact should be included in the report.*

PA Summary

- The CAE should determine that the IAA has **independent and competent auditing resources** to perform an **application systems review (ASR)** and to evaluate the associated risk exposures.

- In the **planning** phase, the auditor obtains an **understanding** of (1) the IS environment, (2) the entity's mission and business, (3) the level of IT and systems use, (4) risks associated with the organization's objectives and information systems, (5) organizational structure, and (6) business area risks.

- A **primary planning objective** is to identify **application risks. System-level risks** include availability, security, integrity, and maintainability. **Data-level risks** relate to completeness, integrity, confidentiality, privacy, accuracy, and timeliness.

- **Application controls** may be in computerized or manual form.

- If **programmed controls** are used, the auditor considers relevant **general IT controls** and controls **specific to the audit objective**. The general controls also may be separately reviewed. General controls may not be reviewed in some cases, e.g., in an ASR for acquisition of a **package application system**.

- ASRs also may be performed **before or after implementation**.

- The **engagement plan** includes (1) the objectives and scope of the ASR, (2) the reviewers, (3) an auditor independence statement, (4) timing of the review, (5) reporting arrangements, and (6) objectives developed based on COBIT information criteria.

- An auditor whose **independence may be impaired** because of previous involvement with the system should follow appropriate guidelines.

- The auditor gathers information about **manual and computerized** aspects of the system. The focus is on relevant data input, processing, storage, and output. If **documenting transaction flow** is impracticable, the auditor may use system documentation or prepare a data flow diagram or narrative. **Application interfaces** also may be documented. The auditor should confirm the documentation by performing a procedure such as a **walkthrough**.

- The auditor obtains assurances that **specific controls** to application risks are operating effectively.

- The **nature, timing, and extent of testing** depends on risk and audit objectives. For example, the auditor assesses the effect of weak general IT controls on the reliability of **computerized** application controls. Given significant weaknesses in these controls, assurance should be obtained (depending on the audit objective), if possible, from the **manual** processing controls. Failure to review general IT controls limits reliance on application controls.

- The **report** describes (1) the nature of the engagement, (2) any limitations, (3) restrictions, (4) other factors users should be aware of, (5) identified weaknesses due to lack of control or noncompliance, and (6) failure to review general IT controls. Furthermore, when weaknesses identified during the ASR are significant or material, **appropriate management** should be advised to take immediate **corrective action**.

---

2. Stop and review! You have completed the outline for this subunit. Study multiple-choice questions 4 through 9 beginning on page 371.

7.3 OUTSOURCING

1. An alternative to staffing an internal audit activity is to **outsource** internal auditing functions.

    a. To a large organization, the primary advantage of outsourcing is that large **outside service providers** ordinarily have offices in various locations. Thus, engagement requirements in distant locations are more easily accommodated.

    b. One **disadvantage** is that internal auditors tend to be more familiar with the organization. Furthermore, they are more readily available to the organization because they are unaffected by other priorities, such as other clients.

    1) Another disadvantage is that **legal requirements** may prevent the external audit firm from providing internal audit services.

    c. **Cosourcing** is an approach in which the internal audit activity obtains external aid in performing certain activities.

2. The Practice Advisory in this subunit addresses outsourcing in a different context. IS activities are frequently outsourced. However, the Practice Advisory furnishes guidance applicable to audits of all outsourced activities.

    a. ***PRACTICE ADVISORY 2100-12: OUTSOURCING OF IS ACTIVITIES TO OTHER ORGANIZATIONS***

    Considerations Prior to Undertaking the Audit

    1. *The Chief Audit Executive (CAE) should determine that the internal audit activity possesses, or has access to,* **independent[1]** *and* **competent auditing resources** *to perform an audit of Information Systems (IS) activities outsourced to another organization and to evaluate the associated risk exposures.*

    2. *The* **right to audit a provider** *of outsourcing services is often unclear. The* **responsibility for auditing compliance** *is also often not clear. The CAE or designated auditor in cooperation with the legal, contract management, or other responsible department should determine the extent to which the* **outsource agreement** *provides for the audit of the service provider and should consider whether this provision is adequate. If necessary, expert legal advice should be sought.*

    3. *The CAE or designated auditor should also assess the* **potential reliance** *on any IS audit work carried out by either the* **service provider's internal auditors** *or an* **independent third party** *contracted by the service provider. The ability to audit or rely on a another party's work should be determined prior to undertaking the audit.*

---

[1] *Independent – i.e., the auditor was not involved with the planning, selection, or contracting for the outsourced IS activities.*

Planning Considerations

1.   **Fact Finding**

The auditor should **obtain an understanding** of the nature, timing, and extent of the outsourced services. The auditor should establish what **controls the service user** has put in place to address the business requirement "to ensure that roles and responsibilities of third parties are clearly defined, adhered to and continue to satisfy requirements" (COBIT High Level Control Objective DS2).

The **risks** associated with the outsourced services should be identified and assessed.

The auditor should assess the extent to which the service user's controls provide reasonable assurance that business objectives will be achieved, and that undesired events will be prevented or detected and corrected.

2.   **Planning**

The auditor should evaluate any **previous audit report** prepared for the service provider and plan the information systems audit work to address the **audit objectives** relevant to the **service provider's environment**, taking into account the information obtained during planning.

The audit objectives should be agreed upon with the **service user management** before being communicated to the service provider. Any changes requested by the service provider should be agreed with the service user management.

The auditor should plan the information systems audit work to comply with **applicable professional audit standards,** as if the audit were performed in the service user's own environment.

Performing the Audit

1.   **Audit Evidence Requirement**

The audit should be performed as if the service were being provided in the service user's own IS environment.

2.   **Agreement with the Service Provider**

The auditor should consider such things as

- Existence of a **formal agreement** between the service provider and the service user
- Inclusion of a clause in the outsourcing agreement explicitly stating that the service provider is obligated to meet all **legal requirements** applying to its activities and comply with acts and regulations pertaining to the functions it should undertake on behalf of the service user
- Stipulation in the outsourcing agreement that activities performed by the service provider are subject to controls and audits as if they were performed by the service user itself
- Inclusion of audit access rights in the agreement with the service provider
- Existence of **service level agreements (SLAs)** with performance monitoring procedures
- Adherence to the service user's security policies
- Adequacy of the service provider's fidelity insurance arrangements
- Adequacy of the service provider's personnel policies and procedures

3. **Management of Outsourced Services**

The auditor should verify that:

- *Business processes to produce the information used to monitor compliance with the SLAs are appropriately controlled*
- *When SLAs are not being met, the service user has sought remedy, and corrective actions have been considered to achieve the agreed service level*
- *The service user has the capacity and competence to follow up and review the services provided*

4. **Restrictions on Scope**

When the service provider proves unwilling to cooperate with the auditor, the auditor should report the matter to the service user's management as well as to the CAE.

Reporting

The auditor should provide a report in an appropriate form to the intended **service user recipients** *upon the completion of the audit work.*

The auditor should **consider discussing the report** *with the service provider prior to release, but the auditor should not be responsible for issuing the final report to the service provider. If the service provider is to receive a copy, this should ordinarily come from the* **service user's management***.*

The report should specify any **restrictions on distribution** *that the auditor or service user management agree to impose. For example, the service provider should not be able to provide a copy of the report to other users of their service without the permission of the auditor's organization and, when appropriate, the service user. The auditor should also consider including a statement* **excluding liability** *to third parties.*

The audit report should clearly identify a **restriction on scope** *if audit access rights are denied and should explain the effect of this restriction with respect to the audit.*

Follow-up Activities

As if the audit had been performed in the service user's own environment, the auditor should request appropriate information from both the service user and the service provider on **previous relevant findings, conclusions, and recommendations***. The auditor should determine whether appropriate* **corrective actions** *have been implemented in a timely manner by the service provider.*

PA Summary

- The CAE should determine that the IAA has **independent and competent auditing resources** to perform an audit of outsourced IS activities and to evaluate the associated risk. The CAE or designated auditor in cooperation with the responsible department should determine the extent and adequacy of the **right to audit a provider** of outsourced services. Legal advice may be needed.

- The CAE assesses **potential reliance** on the service provider's (1) internal auditors or (2) hired independent third-party auditor.

- The auditor obtains an **understanding** of the outsourced services and the service user's related controls.

- **Risks** and the **service user's controls** should be assessed.

- The auditor should evaluate any **previous audit report** prepared for the provider and plan the work to address the **audit objectives** (1) relevant to the provider's environment and (2) agreed upon with the service user.

- The audit work should be performed in accordance with **professional standards**.

- The audit is performed as if it were conducted in the service user's environment.

- The auditor considers (1) the terms of **a formal agreement** with the provider, including the provider's obligation to meet all **legal requirements** applying to its activities and to permit those activities to be subject to controls and audits as if they were performed by the service user; (2) existence of **service level agreements (SLAs)** with performance monitoring procedures; (3) adherence to the user's security policies; and (4) adequacy of the provider's insurance and personnel policies.

- The auditor verifies that (1) processes to monitor compliance with the **SLAs** are controlled, (2) **corrective actions** have been considered when SLAs are not met, and (3) the **service user** can follow up and review the services provided.

- The provider's **failure to cooperate with the auditor** should be reported to user management and the CAE.

- The auditor provides a report in appropriate form to the intended **service user recipients**. The auditor should **consider discussing the report** with the service provider, but the user is responsible for sending the report to the provider.

- The report specifies any **restrictions on distribution** or **audit scope**.

- The auditor should follow up to determine whether appropriate **corrective actions** have been implemented in a timely manner by the service provider.

3. Stop and review! You have completed the outline for this subunit. Study multiple-choice question 10 on page 373.

7.4 THIRD PARTIES AND CONTROLS

1. The Practice Advisory in this subunit addresses audits of the effect on the organization's IT controls of receiving services from third parties.

    a. ### PRACTICE ADVISORY 2100-13: EFFECT OF THIRD PARTIES ON AN ORGANIZATION'S IT CONTROLS

        1. #### SERVICES OF THIRD-PARTY PROVIDERS

            *Organizations are using the **Internet** and corporate **Intranets** for a variety of purposes. These include providing employees, vendors, and customers access to existing or new human resource, financial, sales, and purchasing applications. This access, in many instances, is provided through one or more **third-party providers**.*

            Third parties may provide such services as:

            -   *Connectivity of internal networks to the Internet*
            -   *Connectivity to the organization's partners through virtual private networks or extranets*
            -   *Connectivity to customers through the use of wireless technology*
            -   *Website development*
            -   *Website maintenance, management, and monitoring*
            -   *Website security services*
            -   *Providing physical location for hardware (known as co-location)*
            -   *Monitoring of system and application access*
            -   *Backup and recovery services*
            -   *Application development, maintenance, and hosting (such as ERP systems and e-commerce systems)*
            -   *Business services, including cash management, credit card, order processing, and call center services.*

        2. #### EFFECT OF THIRD-PARTY PROVIDERS ON AN ORGANIZATION

            *Third-party providers can affect an **organization** (including its partners), its **processes, controls, and control objectives** on many different levels. This includes effects arising from such things as:*

            -   *The economic viability of the third-party provider*
            -   *Third-party provider access to information that is transmitted through their communication systems and applications*
            -   *Systems and application availability*
            -   *Processing integrity*
            -   *Application development and the change management processes*
            -   *The protection of systems and information assets through backup, recovery, contingency planning, and redundancy*

            *Third parties can become a key component in an organization's controls and its achievement of related control objectives. The auditor should **evaluate the services that the third party provides** in relation to the IT environment, related controls, and control objectives.*

An organization that uses third-party providers for **limited purposes**, such as co-location services, may place only **limited reliance** on the third parties' controls as it relates to achieving its control objectives. However, an organization that uses providers for **other purposes**, such as hosting financial accounting systems and e-commerce systems, uses the **third-party provider's controls wholly**, or in conjunction with its own controls, to achieve its control objectives.

Likewise, the ability of the organization to achieve its control objectives can be enhanced or weakened by the **relative effectiveness** or ineffectiveness of the third party's controls. **Weaknesses** can arise from many sources, including:

- Gaps in the control environment arising from the outsourcing of services to the third party
- Poor control design causing controls to operate ineffectively
- Lack of knowledge or inexperience of personnel responsible for control functions
- Over-reliance on the third party's controls (when there are no compensating controls within the organization)

The **lack of controls** or **weakness** in control design, operation, or effectiveness can lead to such **adverse effects** as:

- Loss of information confidentiality and privacy
- Systems not being available for use when needed
- Unauthorized access and changes to systems, applications, or data
- Changes to systems, applications, or data that result in system or security failures, loss of data, loss of data integrity, loss of data protection, or systems unavailability
- Loss of system resources or information assets
- Increased costs incurred by the organization as a result of any of the above

3. **PROCEDURES TO BE PERFORMED BY THE AUDITOR**

Obtaining an understanding

As part of the **planning process**, the auditor should **obtain and document an understanding** of the relationship between the services provided by the third party and the organization's control environment. The auditor should consider reviewing such things as the **contract, service level agreement, policies, and procedures** between the third party and the organization.

The auditor should:

- Document the third party's processes and controls that have a direct effect on the organization's processes and control objectives.
- Identify each control, its location in the combined control environment (internal or external), the type of control, its function (preventive, detective, or corrective), and the organization that performs the function (internal or external).
- Assess the risk of the services provided by the third party to the organization, its controls, and control objectives.
- Determine the significance of third party controls to the ability of the organization to meet its control objectives.
- Confirm the understanding of the control environment by performing such things as inquiry and observation and transaction walk-throughs.

Assessing the role of third-party controls

If the role or effect that the third party has on the organization's control objectives is significant, then the auditor should assess these controls to determine whether they function as described, operate effectively, and assist the organization in achieving its control objectives.

Assessing identified control weaknesses

*Auditors should assess the likelihood (or **control risk**) that weaknesses arising from gaps in control, poor design, or ineffective operation may exist in the IT environment. The auditor should identify where the control weakness exists.*

*The auditor should then assess **whether the control risk is significant** and **what effect it has** on the control environment.*

*When weaknesses are identified, the auditor should determine whether **compensating controls** exist to counter the effect of the identified weaknesses (compensating controls may exist in the organization, the third-party provider, or in both entities). If compensating controls exist, the auditor should determine whether they mitigate the effect of the control weaknesses.*

4. **Contracts with Third-Party Providers**

Roles and responsibilities

*The relationship between the organization and a third-party provider should be **documented in the form of a formal contract**. The contract is a critical element and contains many provisions that govern the actions and responsibilities of each party.*

*The **auditor should review the contract** (possibly with the assistance of the organization's legal counsel) to determine the third party's role and responsibility for assisting the organization in achieving its control objectives. Guidance on how to review a contract is outside the scope of this advisory; however, the following list provides **examples of issues** that should be considered:*

- *Level of service to be provided by the third party (whether to the organization, its partners, or both)*
- *Reasonableness of fees charged by the third party*
- *Responsibilities for data and application privacy and confidentiality*
- *Responsibilities for system, communications, operating system, utility software, data, and application software access controls and administration*
- *Monitoring of assets and related data and response (organization and third-party) and reporting procedures (routine or incident)*
- *Specification of ownership of information assets, including data and domain names*
- *Specification of ownership of custom programming developed by the third-party provider for the organization, including change documentation, source code, and escrow agreements*
- *Provision for systems and data protection, including backup, recovery, contingency planning, and redundancy*
- *Right-to-audit clause (including such things as the ability to meet with third-party provider internal audit personnel and review their audit work papers and reports)*
- *Process for negotiation, review, and approval of changes to the contract and related documents (such as service level agreements and procedures)*

As a minimum, the auditor should review the contract to determine the extent of **responsibility for controls** that the third party undertakes **on behalf of the organization**. This process should assess the sufficiency of identified controls and compliance monitoring/reporting, their design, and operating effectiveness.

Corporate governance

Even when third-party providers are involved, **management is still responsible for the achievement of related control objectives**. As part of this responsibility, management should have a process to govern the relationship with, and the performance of, the third-party provider. **The auditor should identify and review the components of this process**. The auditor should review such things as the process used by management to identify risks associated with the third-party provider, the services provided by the third party, and how management governs the relationship between the two entities.

The auditor's review of the **governance process** should ascertain such things as whether management reviews the third-party providers against the **performance standards or criteria** set forth in the contract and any standards specified by regulatory bodies. The governance process should include review of such things as:

- Financial performance of the third-party provider
- Compliance with terms of the contract
- Changes to the control environment mandated by the third party, its auditors, or regulators
- Results of control reviews performed by others, including the third party's auditors, consultants, or others
- Maintaining adequate levels of insurance

5. **REVIEW OF THIRD-PARTY PROVIDER CONTROLS**

Contract issues

When reviewing third-party provider controls, the auditor should consider the contractual relationship between the organization and the third-party provider and the third-party provider's **evaluation and reporting on their controls**.

Contractual issues may preclude an auditor from reviewing controls at the third-party provider. In these circumstances, the auditor should assess this **limitation of scope** on his or her ability to evaluate the information system control environment.

Independent reports

Third-party providers may provide **reports from independent sources** on their controls. These reports may take the form of service bureau audit reports or other control-based reports. Auditors can use these reports as the **basis for reliance** on controls in the information system control environment.

If the auditor decides to use an independent report as the basis for reliance on information system controls at the third-party provider, then **the auditor should review these reports to determine the following**:

- The independent party is qualified. This can include whether the independent party has an appropriate professional certification or license, has relevant experience, and is in good standing with applicable professional and regulatory authorities.
- The independent party has no relationship with the third-party provider that would impair independence and objectivity.
- The period of coverage of the report.

- *Whether the report is sufficient (i.e., the report covers the applicable systems and controls and includes tests of areas that the auditor would include had he/she performed the work).*
- *Whether the testing of the controls is sufficient to enable the auditor to rely upon the work of the independent party (i.e., the testing of the controls is sufficient as to the nature, timing, and extent of procedures performed).*
- *The report delineates between the responsibilities of the service provider and the responsibilities of the user organization.*
- *The user organization has addressed its responsibilities with respect to proper controls.*

Testing third-party controls

*If the auditor decides to **directly review and test controls at the third-party provider**, then the auditor should do the following:*

- *Work with management and, as applicable or considered appropriate, perform an internal audit of the third-party provider to plan the engagement, set its objectives and scope of review, and determine timing, staffing needs, and other issues.*
- *Address issues such as access to third-party systems and assets and confidentiality.*
- *Develop an audit program, budget, and engagement plan.*
- *Validate control objectives.*

*Once the auditor has completed the fieldwork, a **conclusion on the operating effectiveness** of tested controls should be made. The auditor should review the **effectiveness of the controls within each organization and the interplay of controls** between the organization and the third party. In most situations, controls will overlap between the organization and the third party. The auditor should assess the operating effectiveness of the controls taken together versus individually.*

*Situations may exist in which, for a particular objective, controls in either organization may not exist or do not operate effectively. Additionally, situations may exist in which control strengths in one organization may be partially or completely negated by control weaknesses in the other organization. In these situations, the auditor should **assess the effect these weaknesses have** on the overall control environment and on the extent of their procedures.*

Third-party internal auditors

*The auditor should consider whether the third party has an internal audit department. The presence of **internal auditors can enhance the strength of the control environment**. If an internal audit department exists, the auditor should ascertain the extent of their activities with regard to the systems and controls that affect the organization.*

*If possible, the auditor should **review relevant internal audit reports**. When it is not possible to review these reports, the auditor should discuss the scope of the audits performed, the systems and controls covered, and any significant issues or weaknesses identified. If the third party is unwilling to grant access to the reports, the auditor should **assess this restriction** on the extent of their procedures.*

*The auditor should also consider **assessing the skills and expertise** of the internal audit staff. This can be accomplished through discussions with these individuals and by additional procedures, such as review of their work plans, work papers, and reports.*

6. **SUBCONTRACTORS OF THIRD PARTIES**

    The auditor should **determine whether the third party uses subcontractors** to provide systems and services. When subcontractors are used, the **auditor should review the significance** of these subcontractors to determine the effect they may have on the third party's controls that relate to the organization.

    If the subcontractor does **not have a significant effect** on the controls relevant to the organization, then the auditor should **document** this in the work papers. If it is determined that there is a **significant effect** on the controls relevant to the organization, then the **auditor should evaluate the processes** used by the third party to manage and monitor the **relationship with the subcontractor**. The auditor should consider sections 4 and 5 of this advisory when performing this evaluation.

7. **REPORTING**

    The auditor's report should indicate that the **scope** of the audit extended to controls within both the organization and the third party. The auditor should consider **identifying** the controls, control weaknesses, and compensating controls that exist in each organization. The extent to which **conclusions and recommendations** are communicated should give consideration to the relationship between the organization and the third party. Some third parties may not be willing or able to implement recommendations. In these situations, the auditor should recommend **compensating controls** that the organization could implement to address control weaknesses at the third party.

PA Summary

- Organizations use the **Internet** and **intranets** to gain access to many kinds of applications **provided by third parties**. These providers affect organizational **processes, controls, and control objectives** on many levels. Thus, the auditor should evaluate third-party services.

- An organization may use third-party services for **more than limited purposes**. Such an organization uses the **third party's controls** wholly (or in combination with its own controls) to achieve its control objectives. Thus, **weaknesses** in third-party controls adversely affect the user organization in many ways, such as (1) loss of information confidentiality and privacy; (2) lack of systems availability when needed; (3) unauthorized access and changes to systems, applications, or data; (4) loss of system resources or information assets; and (5) increased costs incurred by the organization as a result of any of the above.

- In the **planning** process, the auditor obtains and documents an **understanding** of the relationship of the third-party services to the **organization's control environment**. The auditor may, for example, review the contract, the service-level agreement, and the procedures for managing the relationship with the third party.

- If **third-party controls** are significant, the auditor assesses their role.

- The auditor also assesses (1) the likelihood that **control risk** exists, (2) where it exists, (3) whether it is significant, (4) what effect it has, and (5) whether compensating controls exist and mitigate the effect of the control weaknesses.

- The relationship with the third party should be documented in a **formal contract** that is reviewed by the auditor, possibly with the help of legal counsel. The review, at a minimum, determines the **third party's responsibility for controls** implemented by the third party for the organization.

- **Management** is still responsible for achieving control objectives. Thus, it should establish a **governance process** for the relationship with, and performance of, the third party. The auditor identifies and reviews the components of the process, e.g., to identify risks associated with the provider, the services provided, and how management governs their relationship. The review also should determine such things as whether management compares the provider's performance with the **standards or criteria** in the contract and any standards of regulations.

- In a **review of third party controls**, the auditor considers contract issues and the third-party's own evaluation. If the review is not permitted, the result is a scope limitation.

- Auditors may rely on reports from **independent** sources on third party controls. The auditor reviews these reports if (s)he decides to rely on them. The review determines the report's period of coverage and whether (1) the independent party is qualified and has no relationship with the provider that would impair independence and objectivity, (2) the report is sufficient, (3) the testing of controls is sufficient, (4) the report defines the responsibilities of the provider and user, and (5) the user has addressed its control responsibilities.

- An auditor who **directly reviews and tests third-party controls** assesses the effectiveness of (1) the separate controls of the organization and the third party and (2) the interplay of those sets of controls. The auditor should (1) work with management and, possibly, perform an internal audit of the third-party provider; (2) address such issues as access to third-party systems and assets and confidentiality; (3) develop an audit program, budget, and engagement plan; and (4) validate control objectives.

- The auditor considers the significance of **third-party internal auditors** to the shared control environment. The auditor determines the extent of their activities with regard to the systems and controls that affect the organization. If possible, the auditor should **review relevant internal audit reports**. The audit should also consider **assessing the skills and expertise** of the internal auditors.

- The auditor reviews the **effect of subcontractors** on the relevant third-party controls. If the effect is significant, the auditor evaluates the processes used by the third party to manage the relationship with the subcontractor.

- The **audit report** (1) indicates the scope of the engagement; (2) may identify controls, weaknesses, and compensating controls; (3) depends on the extent of communication of conclusions and recommendations to the third party; and (4) may recommend compensating controls to be implemented by the organization.

2. Stop and review! You have completed the outline for this subunit. Study multiple-choice questions 11 through 17 beginning on page 374.

7.5 E-COMMERCE

1. The Practice Advisory in this subunit applies to engagements to audit electronic commerce activities.

    a. **PRACTICE ADVISORY 2100-6: CONTROL AND AUDIT IMPLICATIONS OF E-COMMERCE ACTIVITIES**

        1. *Electronic commerce (e-commerce)* is generally defined as "conducting commercial activities over the Internet." These commercial activities can be business-to-business *(B2B)*, business-to-consumer *(B2C)*, and business-to-employee *(B2E)*. The growth of e-commerce has been dramatic and is anticipated to grow even more rapidly in the years ahead. The recent publication by The IIA Research Foundation, **Systems Assurance and Control (SAC)**, and the success of the web-based **www.ITAudit.org** and various email IIA newsletters confirms that technology not only supports e-commerce strategies, but is an integral part. **Web-based and other technology changes** have a dramatic impact on society, governance, economics, competition, markets, organizational structure, and national defense. Clearly, these changes and the dramatic growth of e-commerce create significant control and management challenges that should be considered by internal auditors in developing and implementing their audit plans.

            Understanding and Planning an E-commerce Engagement

        2. Continuous changes in technology offer the internal auditing profession both great opportunity and risk. Before attempting to provide assurance on the systems and processes, an internal auditor should understand the changes in business and information systems, the related risks, and the alignment of strategies with the enterprise's design and market requirements. The internal auditor should **review management's strategic planning and risk assessment processes and its decisions about**

            *   *Which risks are serious*
            *   *Which risks can be insured*
            *   *What current controls will mitigate the risks*
            *   *Which additional compensating controls are necessary*
            *   *What type of monitoring is required*

        3. The major **components of auditing e-commerce activities** are

            *   *Assess the internal control structure, including the tone set by senior management,*
            *   *Provide reasonable assurance that goals and objectives can be achieved,*
            *   *Determine if the risks are acceptable,*
            *   *Understand the information flow,*
            *   *Review the interface issues (such as hardware to hardware, software to software, and hardware to software), and*
            *   *Evaluate the business continuity and disaster recovery plans.*

4.   The Chief Audit Executive's (CAE's) concerns in performing an e-commerce engagement relate to the **competency and capacity** of the internal audit activity. Among the possible factors that may constrain the internal audit activity are the following:

- Does the internal audit activity have sufficient skills? If not, can the skills be acquired?
- Are training or other resources necessary?
- Is the staffing level sufficient for the near term and long term?
- Can the expected audit plan be delivered?

5.   **Internal auditor's questions during risk assessment.** The IIA's SAC publication can assist the internal auditor in audit planning and risk assessment. It includes a list of e-commerce areas that should be of interest to an internal auditor who is undertaking an engagement and assessing risks. The questions for internal auditors to consider are

- Is there a business plan for the e-commerce project or program?
- Does the plan cover the integration of the planning, design, and implementation of the e-commerce system with the strategies of the organization?
- What will be the impact on the performance, security, reliability, and availability of the system?
- Will the functionality meet the end user's needs (e.g., employees, customers, business partners) as well as management's objectives?
- Have governmental and regulatory requirements been analyzed and considered?
- How secure is the hardware and software, and will they prevent or detect unauthorized access, inappropriate use, and other harmful effects and losses?
- Will transaction processing be current, accurate, complete, and indisputable?
- Does the control environment allow the organization to achieve its e-commerce objectives as it moves from concepts to results?
- Does the risk assessment include internal and external forces?
- Have the inherent risks associated with the Internet and Internet provider (such as reliability of basic communications, authentication of users, and who has access) been addressed?
- Have other issues been addressed (for example, disclosures of confidential business information, misuse of intellectual property, violations of copyrights, trademark infringement, libelous statements on Web sites, fraud, misuse of electronic signatures, privacy violations, and reputation damage)?
- If outside vendors are used, has a "going concern" evaluation been conducted by a trusted third party who is qualified to certify the vendor?
- If vendors provide hosting services, do they have a tested business contingency plan? Have they provided a report on activities of service organizations. Such reports can offer valuable information about internal controls to user organizations. Also, have privacy issues been resolved?
- Does the contract include audit rights?

E-commerce Risks and Control Issues

6.   The e-commerce risk and control environment is complex and evolving. **Risk** can be defined as the uncertainty of an event occurring that could have a negative impact on the achievement of objectives. Risk is inherent to every business or government entity. **Opportunity risks** assumed by management are often drivers of organizational activities. Beyond these opportunities may be threats and other dangers that are not clearly understood and fully evaluated and too easily accepted as part of doing business. In striving to **manage risk**, it is essential to have an understanding of **risk elements**. It is also important to be aware of **new threats and changes in technology** that open new vulnerabilities in information security. For management purposes, the seven key questions below can serve to identify organizational risk and target potential ways to control or mitigate the exposures. (Risk practitioners use a variety of different risk management approaches; these questions illustrate one approach.) Risk elements associated with the questions are displayed in brackets.

(a)   **Risk Identification and Quantification**

- What could happen that would adversely affect the organization's ability to achieve its objectives and execute its strategies? **[Threat Events]**
- If it happens, what is the potential financial impact? **[Single Loss Exposure Value]**
- How often might it happen? **[Frequency]**
- How probable are the answers to the first three questions? **[Uncertainty]**

(b)   **Risk Management and Mitigation**

- What can be done to prevent and avoid, mitigate, and detect risks and provide notification? **[Safeguards and Controls]**
- How much will it cost? **[Safeguards and Control Costs]**
- How efficient would that be? **[Cost/Benefit or ROI Analysis]**

7.   Some of the more **critical risk and control issues** to be addressed by the internal auditor are

- General project management risks
- Specific security threats, such as denial of service, physical attacks, viruses, identity theft, and unauthorized access or disclosure of data
- Maintenance of transaction integrity under a complex network of links to legacy systems and data warehouses
- Website content review and approval when there are frequent changes and sophisticated customer features and capabilities that offer around-the-clock service
- Rapid technology changes
- Legal issues, such as increasing regulations throughout the world to protect individual privacy; enforceability of contracts outside of the organization's country; and tax and accounting issues
- Changes to surrounding business processes and organizational structures

Auditing E-commerce Activities

8. The **overall audit objective** should be to ensure that all e-commerce processes have effective internal controls. Management of e-commerce initiatives should be **documented in a strategic plan** that is well developed and approved. If there is a decision not to participate in e-commerce, that decision should be carefully analyzed, documented, and approved by the governing board.

9. **Audit objectives for an e-commerce engagement** may include:

   - Evidence of e-commerce transactions
   - Availability and reliability of security system
   - Effective interface between e-commerce and financial systems
   - Security of monetary transactions
   - Effectiveness of customer authentication process
   - Adequacy of business continuity processes, including the resumption of operations
   - Compliance with common security standards
   - Effective use and control of digital signatures
   - Adequacy of systems, policies, and procedures to control Public Key Certificates (using public key cryptographic techniques)
   - Adequacy and timeliness of operating data and information
   - Documented evidence of an effective system of internal control

10. The **details of the audit program** used to audit e-commerce activities in specific organizations will vary depending on industry, country, and legal and business models. The following is an **outline of a possible e-commerce audit protocol** for key areas.

   (a) **E-commerce organization** – The internal auditor should do the following:

   - Determine the value of transactions
   - Identify the stakeholders (external and internal)
   - Review the change management process
   - Examine the approval process
   - Review the business plan for e-commerce activities
   - Evaluate the policies over Public Key Certificates
   - Review the digital signature procedures
   - Examine service level agreements between buyer, supplier, and certification authority
   - Ascertain the quality assurance policy
   - Assess the privacy policy and compliance in e-commerce activities
   - Assess the incident response capability

   (b) **Fraud** – The internal auditor should be alert for the following **conditions**:

   - Unauthorized movement of money (e.g., transfers to jurisdictions where the recovery of funds would be difficult).
   - Duplication of payments.
   - Denial of orders placed or received, goods received, or payments made.
   - Exception reports and procedures: effectiveness of the follow-up.
   - Digital signatures: Are they used for all transactions? Who authorizes them? Who has access to them?
   - Protections against viruses and hacking activities (history file, use of tools).

- Access rights: Are they reviewed regularly? Are they promptly revised when staff members are changed?
- History of interception of transactions by unauthorized persons.

(c) **Authentication** – *The internal auditor should review the policies for* **authenticating transactions and evaluating controls**.

- Evidence of regular reviews
- Control self-assessment (CSA) tools used by management
- Regular independent checks
- Segregation of duties
- Tools that management should have in place: firewalls (multi-level to partition e-commerce and other activities), password management, independent reconciliation, and audit trails

(d) **Corruption of data** – *The internal auditor should* **evaluate controls over data integrity**.

- Who can amend catalogues and prices or rates? What is the approval mechanism?
- Can someone destroy audit trails?
- Who can approve bulletin board amendments?
- What are the procedures for ordering and recording?
- Is the process of online tendering providing adequate documentation?
- Tools that should be in place include: intrusion management (monitoring software, automatic timeout, and trend analysis), physical security for e-commerce servers, change controls, and reconciliation.

(e) **Business interruptions** – *The internal auditor should review the* **business continuity plan** *and determine if it has been tested. Management should have devised an alternative means to process the transactions in the event of an interruption. Management should have a process in place to address the following* **potential conditions**:

- Volume attacks
- Denial of service attacks
- Inadequacies in interfacing between e-commerce and financial management systems
- Backup facilities
- Strategies to counter: hacking, intrusion, cracking, viruses, worms, Trojan horses, and back doors

(f) **Management issues** – *The internal auditor should* **evaluate how well business units are managing the e-commerce process**. *The following are some relevant topics:*

- Project management reviews of individual initiatives and development projects.
- System Development Life Cycle reviews.
- Vendor selection, vendor capabilities, employee confidentiality, and bonding.
- Post-implementation economic reviews: Are anticipated benefits being achieved? What metrics are being used to measure success?
- Post-implementation process reviews: Are new processes in place and working effectively?

PA Summary

- **Electronic commerce (e-commerce)** means "conducting commercial activities over the Internet." These activities can be business-to-business **(B2B)**, business-to-consumer **(B2C)**, and business to employee **(B2E)**. Technology not only supports these e-commerce strategies but also is an integral part. **Web-based and other technology changes** have had a pervasive impact. Such changes and the dramatic growth of e-commerce create significant control and management challenges.

- In **understanding and planning** an e-commerce engagement, the auditor should understand the changes in business and information systems, the related risks, and the alignment of strategies with design and market requirements. The auditor reviews **strategic planning** and **risk assessment** and management's decisions about risks, controls, and monitoring.

- The auditor (1) assesses **control** and whether there is reasonable assurance that **objectives** are achievable, (2) determines **risk acceptability**, (3) understands **information flow**, (4) reviews **interfaces**, and (5) evaluates **disaster recovery plans**.

- The CAE's concerns are the **competency and capacity** of the IAA. **Limiting factors** are (1) the sufficiency of skills, (2) the need for training and other resources, (3) long-term and short-term staffing levels, and (4) deliverability of the expected audit plan.

- The auditor considers many factors during the **risk assessment**, such as (1) the existence of a **business plan**; (2) its coverage of the integration of the planning, design, and implementation of the e-commerce system with the strategies of the organization; (3) the effect on the **system**; (4) whether **users' needs** will be met; (5) consideration of **regulatory** issues; (6) the **security** of hardware and software and whether they prevent or detect harmful effects and losses; (7) transaction **processing** integrity and accuracy; (8) strength of the **control environment**; (9) **completeness** of the risk assessment; (10) **inherent risks** associated with the Internet and Internet provider; (11) implications of dealing with **outside vendors**, e.g., whether a going concern evaluation has conducted by a trusted, qualified third party, and if vendors provide hosting services, they have a tested business contingency plan; and (12) legal matters, e.g., issues involving taxes, contract enforcement in other countries, privacy, intellectual property, defamation, copyrights, trademarks, fraud, and electronic signatures.

- **Risk** is the uncertainty of an event's occurrence that could adversely affect the achievement of objectives. Risk is inherent. **Opportunity risks** assumed by management are drivers of activities. Beyond them may be threats and other dangers not clearly understood and fully evaluated and too easily accepted. **Managing risk** requires an understanding of **risk elements** and an awareness of **new threats and changes in technology** affecting information security. **Seven key questions** identify organizational risk and possible ways of controlling or mitigating the exposures. The following are the questions and the related risk elements: (1) what adverse events could happen **(threat events)**, (2) what will be the financial effect **(single loss exposure value)**, (3) how often **(frequency)**, (4) how probable are the preceding answers **(uncertainty)**, (5) what can be done by way of risk management **(safeguards and controls)**, (6) what is the cost **(cost of safeguards and controls)**, and (7) how efficient is risk management **(cost/ benefit or ROI analysis)**.

PA Summary continued on next page

PA Summary continued

- The auditor should address the **critical risk and control issues**, such as (1) general project management, (2) specific security threats, (3) transaction integrity in a complex network, (4) website content changes, (5) technology change, (6) legal concerns, and (7) changes in business processes and structures.

- The **overall audit objective** is effective control. Management of e-commerce should be **documented** in an approved **strategic plan**. **Specific audit objectives** for an e-commerce engagement should be defined, for example, (1) evidence of transactions, (2) availability and reliability of security, (3) effective interface with financial systems, (4) security of monetary transactions, (5) effectiveness of customer authentication, (6) adequacy of business continuity processes, (7) compliance with security standards, (8) use and control of digital signatures, (9) adequacy of control of public key certificates, (10) adequacy and timeliness of operating data, and (11) documentation of effective control.

- The **e-commerce audit program** will vary with the organization. The following are the components of a general e-commerce **audit protocol** for key areas: (1) e-commerce organization, (2) fraud conditions (red flags), (3) authentication of transactions and evaluation of controls, (4) evaluation of controls over data integrity, (5) review of the continuity plan for coping with business interruptions, and (6) evaluation of how well business units are managing e-commerce.

---

2. Stop and review! You have completed the outline for this subunit. Study multiple-choice questions 18 through 38 beginning on page 376.

7.6 STUDY UNIT 7 SUMMARY

1. For each IS audit, auditors should differentiate between pervasive IS controls (general controls that affect all systems and operations) and detailed IS controls (application controls and other general controls) to focus audit effort on risks relevant to the audit objective.

2. In an application systems review, the primary planning objective is to identify application risks at the systems and data levels. Performance involves documenting transaction flows and testing controls. The report should make control recommendations, and weaknesses should be communicated.

3. An alternative to staffing an internal audit activity is to outsource internal auditing functions.

4. IS activities are often outsourced. The CAE should determine the extent and adequacy of the right to audit a provider of outsourced services. Legal advice may be needed for this purpose. The CAE assesses potential reliance on the service provider's internal auditors or hired third-party auditor. The agreement with the service provider is crucial.

5. Organizations use the Internet and intranets to gain access to many kinds of applications provided by third parties. These providers affect organizational processes, controls, and control objectives on many levels. Thus, the auditor should evaluate third-party services.

6. In understanding and planning an e-commerce engagement, the auditor reviews strategic planning and risk assessment and management's decisions about risks, controls, and monitoring. The auditor assesses control and whether objectives are achievable, determines risk acceptability, understands information flow, reviews interfaces, and evaluates disaster recovery plans.

QUESTIONS

7.1 Review of IS Controls

1. The two broad groupings of information systems control activities are general controls and application controls. General controls include controls

- A. Designed to assure that only authorized users receive output from processing.
- B. For developing, modifying, and maintaining computer programs.
- C. Relating to the correction and resubmission of faulty data.
- D. Designed to ensure that all data submitted for processing have been properly authorized.

Answer (B) is correct. *(Publisher, adapted)*
REQUIRED: The general controls.
DISCUSSION: General controls are policies and procedures that relate to many information systems applications and support the effective functioning of application controls by helping to ensure the continued proper operation of information systems. General controls include controls over (1) data center and network operations; (2) systems software acquisition and maintenance; (3) access security; and (4) application systems acquisition, development, and maintenance.
Answer (A) is incorrect because control over report distribution (output) is an application control. Answer (C) is incorrect because correction of input errors is an application control. Answer (D) is incorrect because authorization of input is an application control.

2. Application control objectives do not normally include assurance that

- A. Authorized transactions are completely processed once and only once.
- B. Transaction data are complete and accurate.
- C. Review and approval procedures for new systems are set by policy and adhered to.
- D. Processing results are received by the intended user.

Answer (C) is correct. *(CISA, adapted)*
REQUIRED: The assurance not provided by an application control.
DISCUSSION: Application controls provide reasonable assurance that the recording, processing, and reporting of data are properly performed. Review and approval procedures for new systems are among the general controls known as system software acquisition and maintenance controls.
Answer (A) is incorrect because an objective of application controls is that authorized transactions are completely processed once and only once. Answer (B) is incorrect because an objective of application controls is that transaction data is complete and accurate. Answer (D) is incorrect because an objective of application controls is that processing results are received by the intended user.

3. The purpose of input controls is to ensure the

- A. Authorization of access to data files.
- B. Authorization of access to program files.
- C. Completeness, accuracy, and validity of updating.
- D. Completeness, accuracy, and validity of input.

Answer (D) is correct. *(CIA, adapted)*
REQUIRED: The purpose of input controls.
DISCUSSION: Input controls provide reasonable assurance that data received for computer processing have been properly authorized and are in a form suitable for processing, i.e., complete, accurate, and valid. Input controls also relate to rejection, correction, and resubmission of data that were initially incorrect.
Answer (A) is incorrect because access controls authorize access to data files. Answer (B) is incorrect because access controls authorize access to program files. Answer (C) is incorrect because processing controls ensure the completeness, accuracy, and validity of updating.

7.2 Applications Systems Review

4. Which review(s) of a package application system cover(s) system conversion when master file information has been transferred?

I. Post-implementation review
II. Pre-implementation review
III. Evaluation for acquisition

- A. I only.
- B. II only.
- C. I and II only.
- D. I, II, and III.

Answer (A) is correct. *(Publisher, adapted)*
REQUIRED: The review(s) of a package application system covering conversion when master file information has been transferred.
DISCUSSION: Application system reviews can be performed (1) when a package application system is being evaluated for acquisition, (2) before the application system goes into production (pre-implementation), and (3) after the application system has gone into production (post-implementation). Pre-implementation review coverage includes (1) the architecture of application level security, (2) plans for the implementation of security, (3) the adequacy of system and user documentation, and (4) the adequacy of actual or planned user acceptance testing. Post-implementation review coverage includes application level security after implementation. It also may cover system conversion if data and master file information have been transferred from the old to the new system (PA 2100-9).

5. Application level risks of an information system relating to the incomplete, inaccurate, untimely, or unauthorized processing of data are system

   A. Maintainability risks.

   B. Security risks.

   C. Integrity risks.

   D. Availability risks.

Answer (C) is correct. *(Publisher, adapted)*
REQUIRED: The type of risks related to the incomplete, inaccurate, untimely, or unauthorized processing of data.
DISCUSSION: According to PA 2100-9, application level risks at the system and data level include:

- System availability risks relating to the lack of system operational capability
- System security risks relating to unauthorized access to systems or data
- System integrity risks relating to the incomplete, inaccurate, untimely, or unauthorized processing of data
- System maintainability risks relating to the inability to update the system when required in a manner that continues to provide for system availability, security, and integrity
- Data risks relating to its completeness, integrity, confidentiality, privacy, accuracy, and timeliness

Answer (A) is incorrect because system maintainability risks relate to the inability to update the system when required in a manner that continues to provide for system availability, security, and integrity. Answer (B) is incorrect because system security risks relate to unauthorized access to systems or data. Answer (D) is incorrect because system availability risks relate to the lack of system operational capability.

6. The independence of auditors may be impaired if their previous involvement with an application system included

I.   Acquisition
II. Maintenance
III. Development

   A. I only.

   B. II only.

   C. II and III only.

   D. I, II, and III.

Answer (D) is correct. *(Publisher, adapted)*
REQUIRED: The previous involvement with an application system that does not impair the independence of an auditor.
DISCUSSION: When the auditor has been involved previously in the development, acquisition, implementation, or maintenance of an application system and is assigned to an audit engagement, independence may be impaired. The auditor should refer to appropriate guidelines to deal with such circumstances (PA 2100-9).

Answer (A) is incorrect because impairment may occur if involvement also included maintenance and development. Answer (B) is incorrect because impairment may occur if involvement also included acquisition and development. Answer (C) is incorrect because impairment may occur if involvement also included acquisition.

7. In an application systems review, the auditor may document the flow of transactions. The focus of this audit step should be on

   A. Manual data input, processing, access, and output.

   B. Performing a walk-through.

   C. Manual and electronic data input, processing, storage, and output.

   D. Application interfaces with other systems.

Answer (C) is correct. *(Publisher, adapted)*
REQUIRED: The focus of documenting the flow of transactions in an application system.
DISCUSSION: Information gathered should include both the computerized and manual aspects of the system. The focus should be on data input (whether electronic or manual), processing, storage, and output that are of significance to the audit objectives. The auditor may find, depending upon the business processes and the use of technology, that documenting the transaction flow may not be practical. In that event, the auditor should prepare a high-level data flow diagram or narrative or use system documentation if provided. Consideration should also be given to documenting application interfaces with other systems. The auditor should confirm the documentation by performing procedures such as a walk-through test.

Answer (A) is incorrect because manual and electronic data input are documented. Access is not a focus of the flow of transactions. Answer (B) is incorrect because performing a walk-through merely confirms the documentation. Answer (D) is incorrect because documenting application interfaces with other systems should be considered but is not the focus of the documentation of transactions.

8. An auditor performing an application systems review identifies and tests controls. The effectiveness of computerized application controls

    A. Depends on strong general IT controls.

    B. Should not be assessed if general IT controls are weak.

    C. Must be determined by testing manual processing controls.

    D. Should be assessed only if general IT controls are not reviewed.

Answer (A) is correct. *(Publisher, adapted)*
    REQUIRED: The true statement about the audit of application controls.
    DISCUSSION: The effectiveness of computerized controls is dependent on strong general IT controls. Thus, if general IT controls are not reviewed, the ability to place reliance on the application controls may be severely limited, and the auditor should consider alternative procedures.
    Answer (B) is incorrect because, in the absence of strong general IT controls, the auditor may make an assessment of the effect of this weakness on the reliability of the computerized application controls. Answer (C) is incorrect because, if the internal auditor finds significant weaknesses in the computerized application controls, assurance should be obtained (depending on the audit objective), if possible, from the manually performed processing controls. Answer (D) is incorrect because, if general IT controls are not reviewed, the ability to rely on application controls may be severely limited.

9. What should the engagement plan of an application systems review contain?

    A. Recommendations to strengthen controls.

    B. A statement regarding the independence of the auditors.

    C. Advice to take immediate corrective action.

    D. Mission and objectives of the audited organization.

Answer (B) is correct. *(Publisher, adapted)*
    REQUIRED: The item(s) included in the engagement plan of an application systems review.
    DISCUSSION: The specifics of the engagement plan may vary but should contain (1) auditors performing the review, (2) a statement regarding the independence of the auditors, (3) objectives and scope, (4) when the review commences and its time frame, and (5) reporting arrangements (PA 2100-9).
    Answer (A) is incorrect because recommendations to strengthen controls are contained in the report issued at the conclusion of the review. Answer (C) is incorrect because advice to take immediate corrective action when weaknesses are material or significant is contained in the report issued at the conclusion of the review. Answer (D) is incorrect because the mission and objectives of the organization are part of the planning and preparation for the review (not items included in the engagement plan).

7.3 Outsourcing

10. An approach in which the internal audit activity obtains external aid in performing certain activities is

    A. Cosourcing.

    B. Outsourcing.

    C. Joint venture.

    D. Informal consulting.

Answer (A) is correct. *(Publisher, adapted)*
    REQUIRED: The term that best describes an approach in which the internal audit activity obtains external aid in performing certain activities.
    DISCUSSION: Cosourcing is an approach in which the internal audit activity obtains external aid in performing certain activities. It allows an organization to obtain the benefits of both an internal audit activity and outsourcing.
    Answer (B) is incorrect because outsourcing is an alternative to staffing an internal audit activity. Answer (C) is incorrect because a joint venture is a partnership or conglomerate, usually between organizations. Answer (D) is incorrect because informal consulting is a form of engagement that includes routine activities, such as participation on standing committees; limited-life projects; ad-hoc meetings; and routine information exchange.

7.4 Third Parties and Controls

11. What services most likely place the least reliance on a third party's controls?

A. Order processing services.

B. Hosting e-commerce systems.

C. Co-location services.

D. Hosting accounting systems.

Answer (C) is correct. *(Publisher, adapted)*
REQUIRED: The services placing the least reliance on a third party's controls.
DISCUSSION: An organization that uses third-party providers for limited purposes, such as co-location services, may place only limited reliance on the third parties' controls as it relates to achieving its control objectives. However, an organization that uses providers for other purposes, such as hosting financial accounting systems and e-commerce systems, uses the third-party provider's controls wholly, or in conjunction with its own controls, to achieve its control objectives. Co-location provides a physical location for another organization's hardware (PA 2100-13).
Answer (A) is incorrect because order processing is a transactional activity that is a significant part of the business of many organizations. Outsourcing this activity necessarily involves more than a limited reliance on the third party's controls. Answer (B) is incorrect because hosting e-commerce systems involves, at a minimum, using the third party's controls in conjunction with those of the outsourcing organization. Answer (D) is incorrect because hosting accounting systems involves, at a minimum, using the third party's controls in conjunction with those of the outsourcing organization.

12. What action by an organization in relation to services provided by a third party is most likely to strengthen its own controls?

A. Minimal understanding of the third party's controls combined with full reliance on those controls.

B. Reliance on the third party's controls without compensating controls within the organization.

C. Minimal reliance on the third party's controls combined with implementation of compensating controls within the organization.

D. Outsourcing of services without review of possible gaps in the control environment between the organization and the third party.

Answer (C) is correct. *(Publisher, adapted)*
REQUIRED: The action most likely to strengthen the organization's own controls.
DISCUSSION:. The ability of an organization to achieve its control objectives can be enhanced or weakened by the relative effectiveness or ineffectiveness of the third party's controls. Less reliance on the controls of the third party or implementation of compensating controls within the organization will strengthen an organization's overall control system (PA 2100-13).
Answer (A) is incorrect because lack of knowledge of, or experience with, the third party's controls and full reliance on those controls weakens an organization's own controls. Answer (B) is incorrect because reliance on the third party's controls without compensating controls within the organization is over-reliance. The effect is to weaken an organization's own controls. Answer (D) is incorrect because, without a review, the chance of a gap in the control environment is increased. Gaps in the control environment arising from outsourcing are a weakness.

13. What should an auditor do after identifying a gap in the control environment resulting from outsourcing a service to a third party?

A. Review for compensating controls within the organization.

B. Review for compensating controls within both the organization and the third party.

C. Document the weakness without further review.

D. Review for compensating controls within the third party.

Answer (B) is correct. *(Publisher, adapted)*
REQUIRED: The action by an auditor following the discovery of a gap in the control environment from outsourcing a service to a third party.
DISCUSSION: When weaknesses (e.g., gaps in the control environment arising from outsourcing to a third party) are identified, the auditor should determine whether compensating controls exist to counter the effect of the identified weaknesses. Compensating controls may exist in the organization, the third-party provider, or in both entities. If such controls exist, the auditor determines whether they are effective (PA 2100-13).
Answer (A) is incorrect because the auditor should review for compensating controls within both entities. Answer (C) is incorrect because, following the discovery of a weakness, the auditor should review for compensating controls before concluding the engagement. Answer (D) is incorrect because the auditor should review for compensating controls within both entities.

14. When reviewing a contract with a third-party provider, the auditor must determine the

A. Extent of responsibility for controls that the third party undertakes on behalf of the organization.

B. Level of service to be provided by the third party.

C. Specification of ownership of information assets.

D. Process for negotiation, review, and approval of changes to the contract and related documents.

Answer (A) is correct. *(Publisher, adapted)*
   REQUIRED: The necessary procedure in a review of a contract with a third-party provider.
   DISCUSSION: As a minimum, when reviewing contracts with third-party providers, the auditor should review the contract to determine the extent of responsibility for controls that the third party undertakes on behalf of the organization. This process should assess the sufficiency of identified controls and compliance monitoring/reporting, their design, and operating effectiveness (PA 2100-13).
   Answer (B) is incorrect because the level of service to be provided by the third party is an issue that should be considered, not the minimum requirement. Answer (C) is incorrect because specification of ownership of information assets is an issue that should be considered, not the minimum requirement. Answer (D) is incorrect because the process for negotiation, review, and approval of changes to the contract and related documents is an issue that should be considered, not the minimum requirement.

15. Who is ultimately responsible for a third-party service provider's compliance with the terms of a contract?

A. Internal auditors.

B. IT technicians.

C. Third-party service provider

D. Corporate management.

Answer (D) is correct. *(Publisher, adapted)*
   REQUIRED: The individual(s) responsible for ensuring a third-party service provider complies with the terms of a contract.
   DISCUSSION: According to PA 2100-13, even when third-party providers are involved, management is still responsible for the achievement of related control objectives. As part of this responsibility, management should have a process to govern the relationship with, and the performance of, the third-party provider. The governance process should include review of:

● Financial performance of the third-party provider

● Compliance with terms of the contract

● Changes to the control environment mandated by the third party, its auditors, or regulators

● Results of control reviews performed by others, including the third party's auditors, consultants, or others

● Maintaining adequate levels of insurance

   Answer (A) is incorrect because corporate management is responsible for a third-party service provider's compliance with the terms of a contract. Internal auditors review the governance process but do not assume management responsibilities. Answer (B) is incorrect because corporate management is responsible for a third-party service provider's compliance with the terms of a contract. Answer (C) is incorrect because corporate management is responsible for a third party's compliance with the terms of a contract.

16. An auditor may be prevented from reviewing the third-party provider's controls due to contractual issues. In these circumstances, the auditor

A. Has no other obligation in this area.

B. Should treat this limitation of the scope of the engagement as precluding a report on the organization's internal control.

C. Should assess this limitation's effect on his/her ability to evaluate the third party's IS control environment.

D. May assume that no weaknesses exist in the third party's control environment.

Answer (C) is correct. *(Publisher, adapted)*
   REQUIRED: The auditor's response to contractual issues that prevent review of the third-party provider's controls.
   DISCUSSION: Contractual issues may preclude an auditor from reviewing controls at the third-party provider. In these circumstances, the auditor should assess this limitation of scope on his or her ability to evaluate the information system control environment of the organization (PA 2100-13).
   Answer (A) is incorrect because the auditor should assess this limitation of scope on his or her ability to evaluate the information system control environment of the organization. Answer (B) is incorrect because the auditor may use other evidence as a basis for reliance on the third-party controls. Answer (D) is incorrect because the status of weaknesses is unknown. The auditor should assess this limitation's effect on his or her ability to evaluate the organization's IS control environment.

17. Which reports can provide an auditor a basis for reliance on controls in the information system control environment of a third party?

A. Audit reports by the third-party provider's internal auditors.

B. Reports by subcontractors of the third-party provider who furnish systems or services to the organization.

C. Service bureau audit reports presented by the third-party provider.

D. Management reports of the third-party provider.

Answer (C) is correct.   *(Publisher, adapted)*
REQUIRED: The reports that provide auditors a basis for reliance on controls in the IS control environment of a third party.
DISCUSSION: Reports from independent sources (e.g., service bureau audit reports) presented by third-party service providers can be used by the auditor as the basis for reliance on controls in the IS control environment of the third party. To qualify as independent, the source must have no relationship with the third-party provider that would impair independence and objectivity (PA 2100-13).
Answer (A) is incorrect because qualified sources must be independent of the third-party provider. Internal auditors of the third-party provider are not independent. Answer (B) is incorrect because qualified sources must be independent of the third-party provider. Subcontractors of the third-party provider (for systems or services provided to the organization) are not independent. Answer (D) is incorrect because qualified sources must be independent of the third-party provider. Management of the third-party provider is not independent.

7.5 E-Commerce

18. Which of the following is not a major component of an audit of e-commerce activities?

A. Make certain that goals and objectives can be achieved.

B. Assess the internal control structure.

C. Review the interface issues.

D. Evaluate the business continuity and disaster recovery plans.

Answer (A) is correct.   *(Publisher, adapted)*
REQUIRED: The item that is not a major component of an audit of e-commerce activities.
DISCUSSION: Auditing e-commerce activities should provide reasonable assurance – not ensure or make certain – that goals and objectives can be achieved. An auditor cannot be absolutely certain that goals and objectives will be achieved. The following are other major components of an audit of e-commerce activities:

● Assess the internal control structure, including the tone set by senior management,

● Determine whether the risks are acceptable,

● Understand the information flow,

● Review the interface issues (such as hardware to hardware, software to software, and hardware to software), and

● Evaluate the business continuity and disaster recovery plans.

19. ABC Company is a clothing retailer. Greg is an employee of ABC Company and has recently purchased a leather jacket from ABC Company's website. This activity is

A. An e-commerce activity characterized as B2C.

B. An e-commerce activity characterized as B2E.

C. An e-commerce activity characterized as B2B.

D. Not an e-commerce activity because Greg is an employee of ABC Company.

Answer (A) is correct.   *(Publisher, adapted)*
REQUIRED: The true statement about the purchase from a website.
DISCUSSION: Electronic commerce (e-commerce) is generally defined as "conducting commercial activities over the Internet." These commercial activities can be business-to-business (B2B), business-to-consumer (B2C), and business-to-employee (B2E). The activity that took place between Greg and ABC Company is best characterized as a business-to-consumer activity. The transaction was with an individual who was not performing an employee function.
Answer (B) is incorrect because the activity is best characterized as a business-to-consumer e-commerce activity, not a business-to-employee activity. Answer (C) is incorrect because the activity is best characterized as a business-to-consumer activity, not a business-to-business activity. Answer (D) is incorrect because the activity is best characterized as a business-to-consumer activity.

20. When performing an e-commerce engagement, the greatest two concerns about the internal audit activity are

A. Independence and competency.

B. Capacity and objectivity.

C. Competency and objectivity.

D. Capacity and competency.

Answer (D) is correct. *(Publisher, adapted)*
REQUIRED: The greatest concerns about performing an e-commerce engagement.
DISCUSSION: The chief audit executive's (CAE's) concerns about performing an e-commerce engagement are the competency and capacity of the internal audit activity. Among the possible factors that may limit the internal audit activity are the following:

- Does the internal audit activity have sufficient skills? If not, can the skills be acquired?
- Are training or other resources necessary?
- Is the staffing level sufficient for the near term and long term?
- Can the expected audit plan be delivered?

Answer (A) is incorrect because independence is not a primary concern related to the internal audit activity in an e-commerce engagement. Answer (B) is incorrect because objectivity is not a primary concern related to the internal audit activity in an e-commerce engagement. Answer (C) is incorrect because objectivity is not a primary concern related to the internal audit activity in an e-commerce engagement.

21. Which of the following pieces of information is useful to an internal auditor who is conducting a risk assessment for an e-commerce project?

I. The business plan for the e-commerce project

II. The level of functionality required to meet the end user's needs as well as management's objectives

III. The results of a risk assessment performed to evaluate impact of internal and external forces

A. I and II only.

B. I and III only.

C. II and III only.

D. I, II, and III.

Answer (D) is correct. *(Publisher, adapted)*
REQUIRED: The information useful in a risk assessment of an e-commerce project.
DISCUSSION: The IIA's SAC publication can assist the internal auditor in audit planning and risk assessment. It includes a list of e-commerce areas that should be of interest to an internal auditor who is undertaking an engagement and assessing risks. The questions for the internal auditor to consider are listed in PA 2100-6, *Control and Audit Implications of E-commerce Activities*. All of the information given constitutes answers to some of the questions listed.

22. Which type of risks assumed by management are often drivers of organizational activities?

A. Opportunity risks.

B. Inherent risks.

C. General project management risks.

D. Control risks.

Answer (A) is correct. *(Publisher, adapted)*
REQUIRED: The type of risks assumed by management that are often drivers of organizational activities.
DISCUSSION: Risk can be defined as the uncertainty of an event occurring that could have a negative impact on the achievement of objectives. Risk is inherent to every business or government entity. Opportunity risks assumed by management are often drivers of organizational activities. Beyond these opportunities may be threats and other dangers that are not clearly understood or fully evaluated and are too easily accepted as part of doing business.

23. What is the overall audit objective when auditing an e-commerce activity?

A. To ensure that all e-commerce processes have efficient internal controls.

B. To ensure that all e-commerce processes have effective internal controls.

C. To ensure that all e-commerce processes are adequate to fulfill their intended objectives.

D. To ensure that all e-commerce processes meet the functionality requirements of the end users.

Answer (B) is correct. *(Publisher, adapted)*
REQUIRED: The overall audit objective when auditing an e-commerce activity.
DISCUSSION: According to PA 2100-6, when auditing e-commerce activities, the overall audit objective should be to ensure that all e-commerce processes have effective internal controls.
Answer (A) is incorrect because the overall audit objective is not about ensuring the efficiency of internal controls. It is about ensuring the effectiveness of internal controls. Answer (C) is incorrect because adequacy of processes should be considered during the internal auditor's risk assessment. Answer (D) is incorrect because meeting functional requirements should be considered during the internal auditor's risk assessment.

24. An internal auditor is evaluating project management reviews of individual initiatives and development projects and system development life cycle reviews. When performing this service, the internal auditor is addressing which key e-commerce audit area?

- A. Corruption of data.
- B. E-commerce organization.
- C. Management issues.
- D. Business interruptions.

Answer (C) is correct. *(Publisher, adapted)*

REQUIRED: The possible key e-commerce audit area addressed by the internal auditor.

DISCUSSION: According to the outline of a possible e-commerce audit protocol for key areas given in PA 2100-6, the internal auditor should evaluate how well business units are managing the e-commerce process when addressing the possible key audit area of management issues. The following is a list of some relevant topics that the internal auditor should review when doing their evaluation:

- Project management reviews of individual initiatives and development projects.
- System development life cycle reviews.
- Vendor selection, vendor capabilities, employee confidentiality, and bonding.
- Post-implementation economic reviews: Are anticipated benefits being achieved? What metrics are being used to measure success?
- Post-implementation process reviews: Are new processes in place and working effectively?

Answer (A) is incorrect because, when testing for corruption of data, the internal auditor should evaluate controls over data integrity. Answer (B) is incorrect because, when addressing the issue of e-commerce organization, the internal auditor should do a number of things, none of which are asked about in this question. Answer (D) is incorrect because, when testing for business interruptions, the internal auditor should review the business continuity plan and determine if it has been tested.

25. Management has implemented such controls as firewalls, password management, independent reconciliation, and audit trails. These controls should be reviewed and evaluated by the internal auditor when doing testing for which key e-commerce audit area?

- A. Fraud.
- B. Corruption of data.
- C. Business interruptions.
- D. Authentication.

Answer (D) is correct. *(Publisher, adapted)*

REQUIRED: The key e-commerce audit area that should be evaluated and reviewed by the internal auditor.

DISCUSSION: An outline of a possible e-commerce audit protocol for key areas is given in PA 2100-6. In the outline authentication is given as a possible key audit area, and to test for authentication the internal auditor should review the policies for authenticating transactions and evaluating controls. Tools that management should have in place include: firewalls, password management, independent reconciliation, and audit trails.

Answer (A) is incorrect because the management tools discussed in the question are not items that the internal auditor should be alert for when testing for fraud. Answer (B) is incorrect because, when the internal auditor is testing for corruption of data, the tools that should be in place are intrusion management, physical security for e-commerce servers, change controls, and reconciliation. Answer (C) is incorrect because, when the internal auditor is testing for business interruptions, the tools listed in the question would not be items that the internal auditor should be looking for to verify that this risk has some controls.

26. What risk element is management seeking to identify by asking the following question: What could happen that would adversely affect the organization's ability to achieve its objectives and execute its strategies?

- A. Single loss exposure value.
- B. Safeguards and controls.
- C. Threat events.
- D. Frequency.

Answer (C) is correct. *(Publisher, adapted)*

REQUIRED: The risk element that management is seeking to identify.

DISCUSSION: PA 2100-6 poses seven key questions that can identify organizational risk and target potential ways to control or mitigate the exposures. Each question is associated with a risk element. The threat events element is associated with the given question.

Answer (A) is incorrect because the question associated with the single loss exposure value risk element is, "If it happens (the threat event), what is the potential financial impact?" Answer (B) is incorrect because the question associated with the safeguards and controls risk element is, "What can be done to prevent and avoid, mitigate, and detect risks and provide notification?" Answer (D) is incorrect because the question associated with the frequency risk element is, "How often might it happen?"

27. The e-commerce project that an auditor is most likely to assess as having the lowest risk is one that

    A. Has a business plan that covers the integration of the planning, design, and implementation of the e-commerce system with the strategies of the organization.

    B. Considers governmental and regulatory requirements, and other external factors in its risk assessment.

    C. Calls for using outside vendors to provide hosting services.

    D. Addresses the security of the software and the accuracy of transaction processing.

Answer (A) is correct. *(Publisher, adapted)*
    REQUIRED: The e-commerce project that an auditor is likely to assess as having the lowest risk.
    DISCUSSION: The following are a few issues that an internal auditor should consider when undertaking an e-commerce engagement and assessing risks:

- Is there a business plan for the e-commerce project or program?
- Does the plan cover the integration of the planning, design, and implementation of the e-commerce system with the strategies of the organization?
- Have governmental and regulatory requirements been analyzed and considered?
- How secure is the hardware and software, and will they prevent or detect unauthorized access, inappropriate use, and other harmful effects and losses?
- Will transaction processing be current, accurate, complete, and indisputable?
- Does the risk assessment include internal and external forces?
- If outside vendors are used, has a "going concern" evaluation been conducted by a trusted third party who is qualified to certify the vendor?
- If vendors provide hosting services, do they have a tested business contingency plan? Have they provided a recent SAS-70 report? Also, have privacy issues been resolved?

Based on how well the e-commerce project addresses these questions, the project likely to receive the lowest risk assessment is one that has a business plan that covers the integration of the planning, design, and implementation of the e-commerce system with the strategies of the organization.
    Answer (B) is incorrect because the project's business plan should include internal forces in its risk assessment, in addition to external forces, for it to be considered low risk. Answer (C) is incorrect because the use of outside vendors will increase the risk of an e-commerce project, unless assessments such as a "going concern" evaluation have been conducted by a trusted third party who is qualified to certify the vendor, the vendor has a tested business contingency plan, the vendor has provided a recent SAS-70 report, etc. Answer (D) is incorrect because a project's business plan should address hardware security in addition to software security. Moreover, the plan should not only ensure that transaction processing is accurate, but it should also make certain that a processed transaction is current, complete, and indisputable.

28. Electronic commerce (e-commerce) is generally defined as "conducting commercial activities over the Internet." These commercial activities can be all but which of the following?

    A. Business-to-business.

    B. Business-to-consumer.

    C. Business-to-employee.

    D. Consumer-to-business.

Answer (D) is correct. *(Publisher, adapted)*
    REQUIRED: The activity that is not considered part of e-commerce.
    DISCUSSION: These commercial activities can be business-to-business (B2B), business-to-consumer (B2C), and business-to-employee (B2E). Consumer-to-business is not a commercial activity because it does not originate from a business; therefore, it is not considered part of e-commerce.
    Answer (A) is incorrect because business-to-business is a commercial activity that is part of e-commerce. Answer (B) is incorrect because business-to-consumer is a commercial activity that is part of e-commerce. Answer (C) is incorrect because business-to-employee is a commercial activity that is part of e-commerce.

29. With regard to e-commerce, risk is best defined as

- A. The uncertainty of an event occurring that could have a negative impact on the achievement of objectives.

- B. The uncertainty of an event occurring that could positively impact management's ability to safeguard organizational assets.

- C. The uncertainty of an event occurring that could have a positive impact on the achievement of objectives.

- D. The uncertainty of an event occurring that could have an impact on the effective and efficient use of an organization's resources.

Answer (A) is correct. *(Publisher, adapted)*
REQUIRED: The best definition of risk with regard to e-commerce.
DISCUSSION: The e-commerce risk and control environment is complex and evolving. Risk can be defined as the uncertainty of an event occurring that could have a negative impact on the achievement of objectives.
Answer (B) is incorrect because management's objective to safeguard organizational assets is just one of the many management objectives. Answer (C) is incorrect because the impact on the achievement of objectives should be negative, not positive. Answer (D) is incorrect because, although the effective and efficient use of organizational resources is a valid objective, the impact of the uncertain event upon this objective is not strictly negative.

30. Which of the following is not one of the seven elements of risk?

- A. Frequency.

- B. Timing.

- C. ROI analysis.

- D. Uncertainty.

Answer (B) is correct. *(Publisher, adapted)*
REQUIRED: The item that is not one of the seven risk elements.
DISCUSSION: The seven elements of risk are threat events, single loss exposure value, frequency, uncertainty, safeguards and controls, safeguard and control costs, and cost/benefit or ROI analysis. Timing, which is not a risk element, is when a risk may occur. It is different from frequency, which is how often an uncertain event might occur.

31. Which of the following are elements of risk management and mitigation?

I.   Threat events and cost/benefit analysis
II. Safeguards, controls, and ROI analysis
III. Frequency and uncertainty
IV. Safeguard and control costs

- A. I only.

- B. II only.

- C. I and III only.

- D. II and IV only.

Answer (D) is correct. *(Publisher, adapted)*
REQUIRED: The risk elements that are part of risk management and mitigation.
DISCUSSION: The elements relating to risk management and mitigation include safeguards and controls, safeguard and control costs, and cost/benefit or ROI analysis. The other elements of risk – threat events, single loss exposure value, frequency, and uncertainty – comprise risk identification and quantification.

32. A decision not to participate in e-commerce should be carefully analyzed, documented, and approved by whom?

- A. The chief audit executive.

- B. The chief executive officer.

- C. The governing board.

- D. The audit committee.

Answer (C) is correct. *(Publisher, adapted)*
REQUIRED: The entity responsible for analyzing, documenting, and approving e-commerce initiatives.
DISCUSSION: The overall audit objective should be to ensure that all e-commerce processes have effective internal controls. Management of e-commerce initiatives should be documented in a strategic plan that is well developed and approved. If there is a decision not to participate in e-commerce, that decision should be carefully analyzed, documented, and approved by the governing board.

33. Tools that should be in place to ensure data integrity include

I.   Monitoring software
II. Change controls
III. Trend analysis
IV. Automatic timeout

- A. I and III only.

- B. II, III, and IV only.

- C. I, III, and IV only.

- D. I, II, III, and IV.

Answer (D) is correct. *(Publisher, adapted)*
REQUIRED: The tools that should be in place to prevent the corruption of data.
DISCUSSION: The internal auditor should evaluate controls over data integrity. Tools that should be in place in order to ensure data integrity include intrusion management (monitoring software, automatic timeout, and trend analysis), physical security for e-commerce servers, change controls, and reconciliation.

34. Which of the following questions is best associated with the safeguards and controls risk element?

A. What could happen that would adversely affect the organization's ability to achieve its objectives and execute its strategies?

B. What can be done to prevent and avoid, mitigate, and detect risks and provide notification?

C. What is the potential financial impact of the occurrence of an uncertain event?

D. How often might an uncertain event occur?

Answer (B) is correct. *(Publisher, adapted)*
REQUIRED: The question that best incorporates the safeguards and controls risk element.
DISCUSSION: For the purposes of management, there are seven key questions that can serve to identify organizational risk and target potential ways to control or mitigate the exposures. These questions, along with the risk elements associated with them (in brackets), include the following:

● What could happen that would adversely affect the organization's ability to achieve its objectives and execute its strategies? [Threat Events]

● If it happens, what is the potential financial impact? [Single Loss Exposure Value]

● How often might it happen? [Frequency]

● How probable are the answers to the first three questions? [Uncertainty]

● What can be done to prevent and avoid, mitigate, and detect risks and provide notification? [Safeguards and Controls]

● How much will it cost? [Safeguards and Control Costs]

● How efficient would that be? [Cost/Benefit or ROI Analysis]

Answer (A) is incorrect because it is a key question associated with the threat events element of risk. Answer (C) is incorrect because it is a key question associated with the single loss exposure value element of risk. Answer (D) is incorrect because it is a key question associated with the frequency element of risk.

35. Which of the following are critical risk and control issues that an internal auditor must address?

I. Rapid technology changes
II. Maintenance of transaction integrity
III. Website content review and approval
IV. Changes to organizational structures

A. I and II only.

B. I and III only.

C. II and III only.

D. I, II, III, and IV.

Answer (D) is correct. *(Publisher, adapted)*
REQUIRED: The critical risk and control issues that an internal auditor must address.
DISCUSSION: Some of the more critical risk and control issues to be addressed by the internal auditor are

● General project management risks

● Specific security threats, such as denial of service, physical attacks, viruses, identity theft, and unauthorized access or disclosure of data

● Maintenance of transaction integrity under a complex network of links to legacy systems and data warehouses

● Website content review and approval when there are frequent changes and sophisticated customer features and capabilities that offer around-the-clock service

● Rapid technology changes

● Legal issues, such as increasing regulations throughout the world to protect individual privacy; enforceability of contracts outside of the organization's country; and tax and accounting issues

● Changes to surrounding business processes and organizational structures

36. The details of the audit program used to audit e-commerce activities in specific organizations will vary depending on all but which of the following factors?

A. Industry.

B. Organizational culture.

C. Country.

D. Legal and business models.

Answer (B) is correct. *(Publisher, adapted)*
REQUIRED: The factor upon which the details of the audit program used to audit e-commerce activities are not dependent.
DISCUSSION: The details of the audit program used to audit e-commerce activities in specific organizations will vary depending on industry, country, and legal and business models.

37. Security of monetary transactions is one example of an audit objective for an e-commerce engagement. Which of the following is not an audit objective for an e-commerce engagement?

- A. Effective use and control of digital signatures.
- B. Adequacy and timeliness of operating data and information.
- C. Effectiveness of customer authentication process.
- D. Appropriateness of reporting lines.

Answer (D) is correct.   *(Publisher, adapted)*
REQUIRED: The item that is not an audit objective for an e-commerce engagement.
DISCUSSION: Audit objectives for an e-commerce engagement may include:

- Evidence of e-commerce transactions
- Availability and reliability of security system
- Effective interface between e-commerce and financial systems
- Security of monetary transactions
- Effectiveness of customer authentication process
- Adequacy of business continuity processes, including the resumption of operations
- Compliance with common security standards
- Effective use and control of digital signatures
- Adequacy of systems, policies, and procedures to control Public Key Certificates (using public key cryptographic techniques)
- Adequacy and timeliness of operating data and information
- Documented evidence of an effective system of internal control

38. Which of the following e-commerce audit protocol items relates to the area of fraud?

- A. Segregation of duties.
- B. Inadequacies in interfacing between e-commerce and financial management systems.
- C. Examination of service level agreements between buyer, supplier, and certification authority.
- D. Denial of orders placed or received, goods received, or payments made.

Answer (D) is correct.   *(Publisher, adapted)*
REQUIRED: The e-commerce audit protocol item that relates to the area of fraud.
DISCUSSION: With regard to the e-commerce audit protocol in the area of fraud, the internal auditor should be alert for the following conditions:

- Unauthorized movement of money (e.g., transfers to jurisdictions where the recovery of funds would be difficult).
- Duplication of payments.
- Denial of orders placed or received, goods received, or payments made.
- Exception reports and procedures, and effectiveness of the follow up.
- Digital signatures: Are they used for all transactions? Who authorizes them? Who has access to them?
- Protections against viruses and hacking activities (history file, use of tools).
- Access rights: Are they reviewed regularly? Are they promptly revised when staff members are changed?
- History of interception of transactions by unauthorized persons.

Answer (A) is incorrect because segregation of duties is an e-commerce audit protocol in the area of authentication, which includes reviewing the policies for authenticating transactions and evaluating controls. Answer (B) is incorrect because inadequacies in interfacing between e-commerce and financial management systems is an e-commerce audit protocol in the area of business interruptions, which includes reviewing the business continuity plan and determining if it has been tested. Answer (C) is incorrect because examination of service level agreements between buyer, supplier, and certification authority has to do with the area of e-commerce organization.

Use Gleim's *CIA Test Prep* for interactive testing with **over 2,000 additional multiple-choice questions!**

STUDY UNIT EIGHT
STATISTICS AND SAMPLING

(33 pages of outline)

The results of internal auditing work are often characterized by some degree of **uncertainty** because inherent resource limitations require that internal auditors apply **sampling** techniques. The costs of a complete review of records, transactions, events, performance of control procedures, etc., may exceed both the benefits and the available resources. In these cases, sampling must be undertaken. Thus, internal auditors may apply statistical methods that permit a quantitative assessment of the accuracy and reliability of the sample results. In this way, the internal auditors can evaluate their hypotheses about the matters tested and reduce uncertainty to an acceptable level.

Core Concepts

- The probability of an event varies from 0 to 1.
- The joint probability for two events equals the probability (Pr) of the first event multiplied by the conditional probability of the second event, given that the first has already occurred. The probability that either one or both of two events will occur equals the sum of their separate probabilities minus their joint probability. The probabilities for all possible mutually exclusive outcomes of a single experiment must add up to one.
- A probability distribution specifies the values of a random variable and their respective probabilities.
- The normal distribution describes the distribution of the sample mean. About 99% of the area (probability) lies within ±3 standard deviations of the mean. The standard normal distribution has a mean of 0 and a variance of 1.
- For small sample sizes (n < 30) for which only the sample standard deviation is known, the t-distribution provides a reasonable estimate for tests of the population mean if the population is normally distributed.
- A statistic is a numerical characteristic of a sample (taken from a population) computed using only the elements of the sample of the population. A parameter is a numerical characteristic of a population computed using all its elements.
- The mean is the arithmetic average of a set of numbers.
- The variance is the average of the squared deviations from the mean. The standard deviation is the square root of the variance.
- For a sample with the sample mean $\bar{x}$, the population standard deviation (σ) may be estimated from the sample standard deviation, s. The standard error of the mean is the population standard deviation divided by the square root of the sample size. It is the standard deviation of the distribution of sample means.
- The central limit theorem states that, regardless of the distribution of the population from which random samples are drawn, the shape of the sampling distribution of $\bar{x}$ (the mean) approaches the normal distribution as the sample size is increased.

- Precision is an interval about an estimate of a population parameter. The auditor determines the degree of confidence (probability) that the precision interval contains the parameter.
- Hypothesis testing calculates the conditional probability that the hypothesis is true given the sample results.
- Statistical sampling allows quantitative assessment of the precision and reliability of a sample.
- Sampling risk for a test of controls includes the risk of assessing control risk too low and the risk of assessing control risk too high.
- Sampling risk for a substantive test includes the risk of incorrect acceptance and the risk of incorrect rejection.
- If sampling is random, each item in the population has a known and nonzero probability of selection.
- Sample size generally depends on (a) population size, (b) acceptable risk, (c) variability in the population, and (d) the acceptable misstatement or deviation rate.
- Attribute sampling is used to test binary propositions, e.g., whether a control has been performed.
- Variables sampling is used to test whether a stated amount or other measure is materially misstated.
- Probability-proportional-to-size sampling uses a monetary unit as the sampling unit. It systematically selects every nth monetary unit.
- Statistical control charts are graphic aids for monitoring the status of any process subject to acceptable or unacceptable variations.

8.1 PROBABILITY AND PROBABILITY DISTRIBUTIONS

1. Probability is important to management decision making because of the unpredictability of future events. Probability estimation techniques assist in making the best decisions given doubt concerning outcomes.

   a. According to definitions adopted by some writers, decision making under conditions of **risk** occurs when the probability distribution of the possible future states of nature is **known**. Decision making under conditions of **uncertainty** occurs when the probability distribution of possible future states of nature is **not known** and must be subjectively determined.

2. Probability provides a method for mathematically expressing doubt or assurance about the occurrence of a chance event. **The probability of an event varies from 0 to 1.**

   a. A probability of 0 means the event cannot occur. A probability of 1 means the event is certain to occur.

   b. A probability between 0 and 1 indicates the likelihood of the event's occurrence; e.g., the probability that a fair coin will yield heads is 0.5 on any single toss.

3. Basic probability concepts underlie a calculation of **expected value**. The expected value of an action is found by multiplying the probability of each outcome by its payoff and adding the products. It represents the long-term average payoff (mean) for repeated trials.

4. The types of probability are objective and subjective. They differ in how they are calculated.

   a. **Objective probabilities** are calculated from either logic or actual experience. For example, in rolling dice one would logically expect each face on a single die to be equally likely to turn up at a probability of 1/6. Alternatively, the die could be rolled many times, and the fraction of times each face turned up could then be used as the frequency or probability of occurrence.

   b. **Subjective probabilities** are estimates, based on judgment and past experience, of the likelihood of future events. In business, subjective probability can indicate the degree of confidence a person has that a certain outcome will occur, e.g., future performance of a new employee.

5. **Basic Terms**

   a. Two events are **mutually exclusive** if they cannot occur simultaneously (e.g., heads and tails cannot both occur on a single toss of a coin).

   b. The **joint probability** for two events is the probability that **both** will occur.

   c. The **conditional probability** of two events is the probability that one will occur given that the other has already occurred.

   d. Two events are **independent** if the occurrence of one has no effect on the probability of the other (e.g., rolling two dice).

      1) Two events are **dependent** if one event has an effect on the other event.

      2) Two events are **independent** if their joint probability equals the product of their individual probabilities.

      3) Two events are **independent** if the conditional probability of each event equals its unconditional probability.

6. **Combining Probabilities**

   a. The **joint probability for two events** equals the probability (Pr) of the first event multiplied by the conditional probability of the second event, given that the first has already occurred.

      1) EXAMPLE: If 60% of the students at a university are male, Pr(male) is 6/10. If 1/6 of the male students have a B average, Pr(B average given male) is 1/6. Thus, the probability that any given student (male or female) selected at random, is **both** male **and** has a B average is

      $$Pr\,(male) \times Pr\,(B|male) = Pr\,(male \cap B)$$
      $$6/10 \times 1/6 = 1/10$$

         a) Pr(male ∩ B) is .10; that is, the probability that the student is male **and** has a B average is 10%.

   b. The **probability that either one or both of two events will occur** equals the sum of their separate probabilities minus their joint probability.

      1) EXAMPLE: If two fair coins are thrown, the probability that at least one will come up heads is Pr(coin #1 is heads) plus Pr(coin #2 is heads) minus Pr(coin #1 and coin #2 are both heads), or

      $$(.5) + (.5) - (.5 \times .5) = .75$$

      2) EXAMPLE: If in the earlier example 1/3 of all students, male or female, have a B average [Pr(B average) is 1/3], the probability that any given student is male and has a B average is 2/10 [(6/10) × (1/3) = 2/10]. Accordingly, the probability that any given student either is male or has a B average is

      $$Pr\,(male) + Pr\,(B\,avg.) - Pr\,(B \cap male) = Pr\,(male\ or\ has\ B\ avg.)$$
      $$6/10 + 1/3 - 2/10 = .73\ 1/3$$

         a) The term Pr(B ∩ male) must be subtracted to avoid double counting those students who belong to both groups.

c.   The **sum of the probabilities of all possible mutually exclusive outcomes** of a single experiment is one.

1)   EXAMPLE: If two coins (H = heads, T = tails) are flipped, four outcomes are possible:

If Coin # 1 is	If Coin #2 is	Probability of This Combination
H	H	.25
H	T	.25
T	H	.25
T	T	.25
		1.00 (certainty)

7.   A **probability distribution** specifies the values of a **random variable** and their respective probabilities. Certain standard distributions seem to occur frequently in nature and have proven useful in business. These distributions may be classified according to whether the random variable is discrete or continuous.

a.   If the relative frequency of occurrence of the values of a variable can be specified, the values taken together constitute a **function**, and the variable is a **random variable**. A variable is **discrete** if it can assume only certain values in an interval. For example, the number of customers served is a discrete random variable because fractional customers do not exist. Probability distributions of discrete random variables include the following:

1)   **Uniform distribution.** All outcomes are equally likely, such as the flipping of one coin, or even of two coins, as in the example above.

2)   **Binomial distribution.** Each trial has only two possible outcomes, e.g., accept or reject, heads or tails. This distribution shows the likelihood of each of the possible combinations of trial results. It is used in **quality control**.

a)   The binomial formula is

$$\frac{n!}{r!(n-r)!} \times p^r(1-p)^{n-r}$$

If: p is the probability of the given condition.
n is the sample size.
r is the number of occurrences of the condition within the sample.
! is the factorial, i.e., $1 \times 2 \times 3 \times ...$ n, or $1 \times 2 \times 3 \times ...$ r.

b)   EXAMPLE: The social director of a cruise ship is concerned that the occupants at each dining room table be balanced evenly between men and women. The tables have only 6, 10, or 16 seats, and the population of the ship is exactly 50% male and 50% female [Pr(male) = .5 and Pr(female) = .5].

i)   The probability that exactly three males and three females will be seated randomly at a **table for 6** is

$$\frac{6!}{3!(6-3)!} \times .5^3(1-.5)^{6-3} = .3125$$

ii)   For the tables with 10 and 16 seats, the probabilities are .2461 and .1964, respectively. The social director will have to assign seats.

3) The **Poisson distribution** is useful when the event being studied may happen more than once with random frequency during a given period.

   a) The Poisson formula is

   $$f(k) = \frac{\lambda^k e^{-\lambda}}{k!}$$

   If: k is the number of occurrences.
   e is the natural logarithm (2.71828...).
   λ = mean and variance.

   b) When sample size is large and λ (lambda) is small (preferably less than 7), the Poisson distribution approaches the binomial distribution. In that case, λ is assumed to equal np.

   If: n = number of items sampled
   p = probability of a binomial event's occurrence

   c) EXAMPLE: A trucking firm has established that, on average, two of its trucks are involved in an accident each month. Thus, $\lambda = 2$.

   i) The probability of zero crashes in a given month is

   $$f(0) = \frac{\lambda^0 e^{-\lambda}}{0!} = \frac{1e^{-2}}{1} = e^{-2} = .135 \ (Note: \ 0! = 1)$$

   ii) The probability of four crashes in a given month is

   $$f(4) = \frac{\lambda^4 e^{-\lambda}}{4!} = \frac{2^4 e^{-2}}{4!} = .09$$

b. A random variable is **continuous** if no gaps exist in the values it may assume. For example, the weight of an object is a continuous variable because it may be expressed as an unlimited continuum of fractional values as well as whole numbers. Probability distributions of continuous random variables include the following:

   1) **Normal distribution.** The most important of all distributions, it describes many physical phenomena. In sampling, it describes the distribution of the **sample mean** regardless of the distribution of the population. It has a symmetrical, bell-shaped curve centered about the mean (see the diagram on the next page). For the normal distribution, about 68% of the area (or probability) lies within plus or minus 1 standard deviation of the mean, 95.5% lies within plus or minus 2 standard deviations, and 99% lies within plus or minus 3 standard deviations of the mean.

   a) A special type of normal distribution is called the **standard normal distribution**. It has a mean of 0 and variance of 1. All normal distribution problems are first converted to the standard normal distribution to permit use of standard normal distribution tables.

b)   Normal distributions have the following fixed relationships concerning the area under the curve and the distance from the mean.

Distance (±) in Standard Deviations (confidence coefficient)	Area under the Curve (confidence level)
1.0	68%
1.64	90%
1.96	95%
2.0	95.5%
2.57	99%

c)   EXAMPLE: Assume the population standard deviation, which is represented by the Greek letter σ (sigma), is 10.

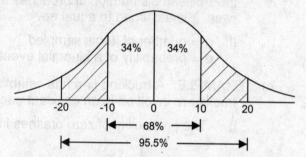

d)   The standard deviation is explained in the next subunit.

2)   The **t-distribution** (also known as Student's distribution) is a special distribution used with small samples, usually fewer than 30, with unknown **population variance**.

a)   For **large sample sizes** (n > 30), the t-distribution is almost identical to the standard normal distribution.

b)   For **small sample sizes** (n < 30) for which only the **sample standard deviation** is known, the t-distribution provides a reasonable estimate for tests of the **population mean** if the population is normally distributed.

c)   The t-distribution is useful in business because large samples are often too expensive. For a small sample, the t-statistic (from a t-table) provides a better estimate of the **standard deviation** than that from a table for the normal distribution.

3)   The **Chi-square distribution** is used in testing the fit between actual data and the theoretical distribution. In other words, it tests whether the sample is likely to be from the population, based on a comparison of the **sample variance** and the **population variance**.

a)   The **Chi-square statistic** (χ^2) is the sample variance (s^2) multiplied by its degree of freedom (n – 1) and divided by the hypothesized population variance (σ^2), if n is the number of items sampled.

b)   A calculated value of the Chi-square statistic greater than the **critical value** in the χ^2 table indicates that the sample chosen comes from a population with greater variance than the hypothesized population variance.

c)   The Chi-square test is useful in business for testing hypotheses concerning populations. If the variance of a process is known and a sample is tested to determine whether it has the same variance, the Chi-square statistic may be calculated.

     d)   EXAMPLE: A canning machine fills cans with a product and has exhibited a long-term standard deviation of .4 ounces, (σ = .4). A new machine is tested, but because the tests are expensive, only 15 cans are examined. The following is the result:

            Sample standard deviation (s) = .311

        i)   The Chi-square statistic is calculated as follows:

$$\chi^2 = \frac{(n-1)s^2}{\sigma^2} = \frac{(15-1).311^2}{.4^2} = 8.463$$

        ii)   Assume the hypothesis is that the new machine has a variance lower than or equal to the variance of the old machine, and that a probability of error (α) of .05 is acceptable. The χ^2 statistic for a probability of alpha error of .05 and 14 degrees of freedom is 23.68 in the χ^2 table. This critical value is much greater than the sample statistic of 8.463, so the hypothesis cannot be rejected. Alpha (α) error is the error of incorrectly rejecting the true hypothesis.

8.   Stop and review! You have completed the outline for this subunit. Study multiple-choice questions 1 through 8 beginning on page 416.

8.2 STATISTICS

1.   The field of statistics concerns information calculated from sample data. The field is divided into two categories: descriptive statistics and inferential statistics. Both are widely used.

    a.   **Descriptive statistics** includes ways to summarize large amounts of raw data.

    b.   **Inferential statistics** draws conclusions about a population based on a sample of the population.

    c.   A **statistic** is a numerical characteristic of a **sample** (taken from a population) computed using only the elements of the sample of the population. For example, the mean and the mode are statistics of the sample.

    d.   A **parameter** is a numerical characteristic of a **population** computed using all its elements. For example, the mean and the mode are parameters of a population.

    e.   **Nonparametric**, or distribution-free, statistics is applied to problems for which **rank order** is known, but the specific distribution is not. Thus, various metals may be ranked in order of hardness without having any measure of hardness.

2.   **Descriptive statistics** summarizes large amounts of data. Measures of central tendency and measures of dispersion are such summaries.

    a.   **Measures of central tendency** are values typical of a set of data.

        1)   The **mean** is the arithmetic average of a set of numbers.

            a)   The mean of a **sample** is often represented with a bar over the letter for the variable ($\bar{x}$).

            b)   The mean of a **population** is often represented by the Greek letter μ (mu).

        2)   The **median** is the halfway value if raw data are arranged in numerical order from lowest to highest. Thus, half the values are smaller than the median and half are larger. It is the 50th percentile.

        3)   The **mode** is the most frequently occurring value. If all values are unique, no mode exists.

4)   **Asymmetrical Distributions**

   a)   The following is a frequency distribution that is **asymmetrical to the right** (positively skewed). The mean is greater than the mode.

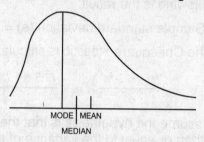

   b)   **Accounting distributions** tend to be asymmetrical to the right. Recorded amounts are zero or greater. Many low-value items are included, but a few high-value items also may be recognized.

   c)   The following is a distribution that is **asymmetrical to the left**. The median is greater than the mean.

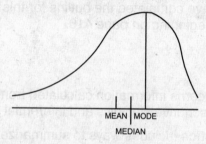

5)   In **symmetrical distributions**, the mean, median, and mode are the same, and the tails are identical. Hence, there is no skew. The **normal and t-distributions** are symmetrical.

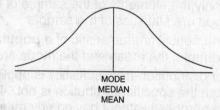

b.   **Measures of dispersion** indicate the variation within a set of numbers.

   1)   An important operation involved is **summation**, represented by the uppercase Greek letter Σ (sigma). The summation sign means to perform the required procedure on every member of the set (every item of the sample) and then add all of the results.

   2)   The **variance** is the average of the squared deviations from the mean. It is found by subtracting the mean from each value, squaring each difference, adding the squared differences, and then dividing the sum by the number of data points. The variance of a **population** is represented by σ^2 (the lowercase Greek letter sigma squared).

a)   The formula for the variance of a set is

$$\sigma^2 \;=\; \sum_{i=1}^{N} \frac{(x_i - \mu)^2}{N}$$

      If: N = the number of elements in the population.
                μ = the population mean
                x_i = the ith element of the set

    i)   If a **sample** is used to estimate the population variance, n – 1 is used instead of N, s^2 instead of σ^2, and $\bar{x}$ instead of μ.)

3)   The **standard deviation** is the square root of the variance.

$$\sigma \;=\; \sqrt{\sum_{i=1}^{N} \frac{(x_i - \mu)^2}{N}}$$

a)   The population standard deviation (σ) may be estimated from the **standard deviation**, s, of a **pilot sample** with the sample mean $\bar{x}$.

$$s \;=\; \sqrt{\sum_{i=1}^{n} \frac{(x_i - \bar{x})^2}{n - 1}}$$

b)   The population standard deviation and the sample standard deviation are always expressed in the **same units as the data**.

c)   The **standard error of the mean** is the population standard deviation divided by the square root of the sample size ($\sigma \div \sqrt{n}$). It is the standard deviation of the distribution of sample means.

4)   The **coefficient of variation** equals the standard deviation divided by the expected value of the dependent variable.

a)   For example, assume that a stock has a 10% expected rate of return with a standard deviation of 5%. The coefficient of variation is .5 (5% ÷ 10%).

b)   Converting the standard deviation to a percentage permits comparison of numbers of different sizes. In the example above, the riskiness of the stock is apparently greater than that of a second stock with an expected return of 20% and a standard deviation of 8% (8% ÷ 20% = .4).

5)   The **range** is the difference between the largest and smallest values in a group.

6)   **Percentiles and quartiles** are other types of location parameters (the mean and median are special cases of these parameters). A percentile is a value of X such that p% of the observations is less and (100 – p)% is greater. Quartiles are the 25th, 50th, and 75th percentiles. For example, the 50th percentile (second quartile) is the median.

c.   A **frequency distribution** summarizes data by segmenting the possible values into equal intervals and showing the number of data points within each interval.

3. **Inferential statistics** provides methods for drawing conclusions about populations based on **sample** information.

    a. Inferential statistics applies to

        1) Estimating population parameters
        2) Testing hypotheses
        3) Examining the degree of relationship between two or more random variables

    b. **Sampling** is important in business because measuring the entire population is usually too costly, too time-consuming, impossible (as in the case of destructive testing), and error-prone. Sampling is used extensively in auditing, quality control, market research, and analytical studies of business operations.

    c. The **central limit theorem** states that, regardless of the distribution of the population from which random samples are drawn, the shape of the **sampling distribution** of $\bar{x}$ (the mean) approaches the normal distribution as the sample size is increased.

        1) Given simple random samples of size n, the **mean** of the sampling distribution of $\bar{x}$ will be μ (the population mean), its **variance** will be $\sigma^2 \div n$, and its **standard deviation** will be $\sigma \div \sqrt{n}$ (the standard error of the mean).

        2) Thus, whenever a process includes the average of independent samples of the same sample size from the same distribution, the **normal distribution** can be used as an approximation of that process even if the underlying population is not normally distributed. The central limit theorem explains why the normal distribution is so useful.

    d. **Population parameters** may be estimated from **sample statistics**.

        1) Every statistic has a sampling distribution that gives every possible value of the statistic and the probability of each of those values.

        2) Hence, the point estimate calculated for a population parameter (such as the sample mean, $\bar{x}$) may take on a **range of values**.

        3) EXAMPLE: From the following population of 10 elements (N), samples of three elements may be chosen in several ways. Assume that the population is normally distributed.

Population	Sample 1	Sample 2	Sample 3
4	4	7	6
7	5	6	9
9	3	5	5
5	$\Sigma x_i = 12$	$\Sigma x_i = 18$	$\Sigma x_i = 20$
6	n = 3	n = 3	n = 3
5			
3	$\bar{x} = 12 \div 3$	$\bar{x} = 18 \div 3$	$\bar{x} = 20 \div 3$
5	= 4	= 6	= 6.67
6			
6			

$$\Sigma x_i = 56 \qquad \mu = 56 \div 10 = 5.6$$
$$\sigma = 1.562 \text{ [based on the formula in Subunit 8.2, item 2.b.3)]}$$

        NOTE: This sample population was chosen for computational convenience only. The population in this example is so small that inference is not required, and the samples are so small that the t-distribution would be more appropriate than the normal distribution.

    e. The quality of the estimates of population parameters depends on two things: the sample size and the variance of the population.

f. **Precision** or the **confidence interval** incorporates the sample size and the population standard deviation along with a probability that the interval includes the true population parameter.

1) For the population mean, precision is

$$\overline{x} \pm z(\sigma \div \sqrt{n})$$

If: $\overline{x}$ = the sample mean, a point estimate of the population mean
z = the standard deviations ensuring a specified confidence level
σ = the standard deviation of the population
n = the sample size
$\sigma \div \sqrt{n}$ = the standard error of the mean (square root of the variance of the sampling distribution of $\overline{x}$)

a) The **assumptions** are that (1) the variance (σ^2) of the population is known, (2) the sample means are normally distributed with a mean equal to the true population mean (μ), and (3) the variance of the sampling distribution is $\sigma^2 \div n$.

b) In the more realistic case in which the **population variance is not known**, and a sample is being evaluated, the distribution is a **t-distribution** with mean equal to μ and variance equal to $s^2 \div n$, when s^2 is the sample variance.

c) Precision for the mean of the population may be estimated given the sample mean and standard deviation. In the preceding example, the mean ($\overline{x}$) of Sample 2 is 6 and the sample size is 3. Thus, the **sample standard deviation** based on the formula in Subunit 8.2, item 2.b.3)a) is

$$s = \sqrt{\frac{(7-6)^2 + (6-6)^2 + (5-6)^2}{3-1}} = 1.0$$

d) To compute precision, the z-value is found in a **table for the standard normal distribution**. If a **two-tailed test** is desired and the confidence level is set at 95%, 2.5% of the area under the normal curve will lie in each tail. Thus, the entries in the body of the table will be .9750 and .0250. These entries correspond to z-values of 1.96 and −1.96, respectively. Accordingly, 95% of the area under the standard normal distribution lies within 1.96 standard deviations of the mean. Hence, precision at a 95% confidence level is $6 \pm 1.96(\sigma \div \sqrt{n})$. Because the population standard deviation is not known, the sample standard deviation (s = 1.0) is used. Precision then becomes

$$6 \pm 1.96 \ (1.0 \div \sqrt{3}) = 6 \pm 1.13 = 4.87 \ to \ 7.13$$

i) Consequently, the probability is 95% that this interval contains the population mean.

4. Stop and review! You have completed the outline for this subunit. Study multiple-choice questions 9 through 13 beginning on page 418.

8.3 HYPOTHESIS TESTING

1. A **hypothesis** is a preliminary assumption about the true state of nature. Hypothesis testing calculates the **conditional probability** that the hypothesis is true given the sample results. The following are the steps in testing a hypothesis:

    a. A hypothesis is formulated to be tested.
    b. Sample evidence is obtained.
    c. The probability that the hypothesis is true, given the observed evidence, is computed.
    d. If that probability is too low, the hypothesis is rejected.

       1) Whether a probability is too low is a subjective measure dependent on the situation. A probability of .6 that a team will win may be sufficient to place a small bet on the next game. A probability of .95 that a parachute will open is too low to justify skydiving.

2. The hypothesis to be tested is the **null hypothesis** or H_0. The alternative hypothesis is denoted H_a.

    a. H_0 may state an equality (=) or indicate that the parameter is equal to or greater (less) than ($\geq$ or $\leq$) some value.
    b. H_a contains every other possibility.

       1) It may be stated as not equal to ($\neq$), greater than (>), or less than (<) some value, depending on the null hypothesis.

3. Hypothesis tests may be **one-tailed** or **two-tailed**.

    a. A one-tailed test results from a hypothesis of the following form:

       H_0: parameter $\leq$ or $\geq$ the hypothesized value
       H_a: parameter > or < the hypothesized value

       1) **One-tailed test, upper tail**

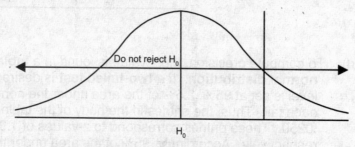

       H_0: parameter $\leq$ the hypothesized value
       H_a: parameter > the hypothesized value

       2) **One-tailed test, lower tail**

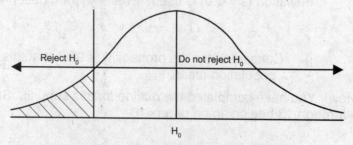

       H_0: parameter $\geq$ the hypothesized value
       H_a: parameter < the hypothesized value

    b.   A **two-tailed test** results from a hypothesis of the following form:

        H_0: parameter = the hypothesized value
        H_a: parameter ≠ the hypothesized value

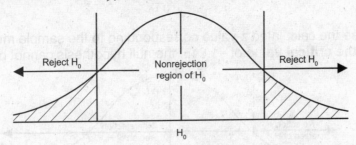

4.   The **probability of error** in hypothesis testing is usually labeled as

State of Nature	Decision	
	Do not reject H_0	Reject H_0
H_0 is true	Correct	Type I Error $P(I) = \alpha$
H_0 is false	Type II Error $P(II) = \beta$	Correct

    a.   These are the same α**(alpha) and** β**(beta) errors** familiar to auditors.

5.   EXAMPLE: The **hypothesis** is that a component fails at a pressure of 80 or more pounds on the average; i.e., the average component will not fail at a pressure below 80 pounds. For a sample of 36 components, the average failure pressure was found to be 77.48 pounds. Given that n is 36, $\bar{x}$ is 77.48 pounds, and σ is 13.32 pounds, the following are the hypotheses:

        H_0: The average failure pressure of the population of components is ≥ 80 pounds.
        H_a: The average failure pressure is < 80 pounds.

    a.   If a 5% chance of being wrong is acceptable, α (Type I error or the chance of incorrect rejection of the null hypothesis) is set equal to .05 and the confidence level at .95. In effect, 5% of the area under the curve of the standard normal distribution will constitute a rejection region. For this **one-tailed test**, the 5% rejection region will fall entirely in the left-hand tail of the distribution because the null hypothesis will not be rejected for any values of the test statistic that fall in the right-hand tail. According to standard tables, 5% of the area under the standard normal curve lies to the left of the **z-value of –1.645**.

    b.   The following is the **formula for the z-statistic**:

$$z = \frac{\bar{x} - \mu_0}{\sigma \div \sqrt{n}}$$

        If: σ = given population standard deviation
             μ_0 = hypothesized true population mean
             n = sample size
             z = standard deviations ensuring the specified confidence level
             $\bar{x}$ = the sample mean

c. Substituting the hypothesized value of the population mean failure pressure ($\mu_0 = 80$ pounds) determines the **z-statistic**.

$$z = \frac{77.48 - 80}{13.32 \div \sqrt{36}} = -1.135$$

d. Because the calculated z-value corresponding to the sample mean of 77.48 is **greater than the critical value** of –1.645, the null hypothesis cannot be rejected.

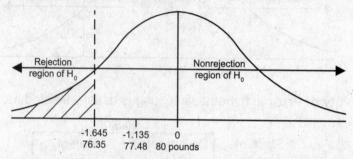

1) The **lower limit** (X) of the 95% nonrejection area under the curve corresponds to the critical z-value. It is calculated as follows:

$$\frac{X - 80 \ pounds}{13.32 \div \sqrt{36}} = -1.645$$

$$X = 80 \ pounds - 1.645(13.32 \div \sqrt{36})$$

$$X = 76.35 \ pounds$$

2) Because a sample average of 77.48 pounds (a z of –1.135) falls within the **nonrejection region** (i.e., > 76.35 pounds), the null hypothesis that the average failure pressure of the population is $\geq$ 80 pounds cannot be rejected. The null hypothesis is rejected only if the sample average is equal to or less than the **critical value** (76.35 pounds).

6. A **failure to prove H_0 is false does not prove that it is true**. This failure simply means that H_0 is not a rejectable hypothesis. In practice, however, auditors often use acceptance as a synonym for nonrejection.

7. Given a small sample (less than 30) and an unknown population variance, the t-statistic (t-distribution) must be used.

a. The **t-distribution** requires a number called **the degrees of freedom**, which is (n – k) for k parameters. When **one parameter** (such as the mean) is estimated, the number of degrees of freedom is (n – 1). The degrees of freedom is a correction factor that is necessary because, given k parameters and n elements, only (n – k) elements are free to vary. After (n – k) elements are chosen, the remaining k elements' values are already determined.

1) EXAMPLE: Two numbers have an average of 5.

$$\bar{x} = \frac{(x_1 + x_2)}{2} = 5$$

a) If x_1 is allowed to vary but the average remains the same, x_1 determines x_2 because only 1 degree of freedom (n – 1) or (2 – 1) is available.

If: $x_1 = 2, x_2 = 8$
     $x_1 = 3, x_2 = 7$

b.   The t-distribution is used in the same way as the z or normal distribution. Standard texts have **t-distribution tables**. In the example about failure pressure of a component, if the sample size had been 25 and the sample standard deviation had been given instead of the population value, the **t-statistic** would have been

$$t = \frac{\overline{x} - \mu_o}{s \div \sqrt{25}} = \frac{77.48 - 80}{13.32 \div \sqrt{25}} = -.946$$

1)   At a confidence level of 95% (rejection region of 5%) and 24 degrees of freedom (sample of 25 − 1 parameter estimated), the t-distribution table indicates that 5% of the area under the curve is to the left of a **t-value of −1.711**. Because the computed value is greater than −1.711, the null hypothesis cannot be rejected in this **one-tailed test**.

2)   As the number of degrees of freedom increases, the t-distribution approximates the **z-distribution**. For degrees of freedom > 30, the z-distribution may be used.

8.   Stop and review! You have completed the outline for this subunit. Study multiple-choice questions 14 through 21 beginning on page 420.

8.4 SAMPLING FUNDAMENTALS

1.   The following Practice Advisory on sampling serves as a useful introduction to the subject. It contains "a recommended core set of high level auditor responsibilities to complement detailed audit planning efforts."

a.   *PRACTICE ADVISORY 2100-10: AUDIT SAMPLING*

1.   *PERFORMANCE OF AUDIT WORK*

Audit Sampling

When using statistical or nonstatistical sampling methods, the auditor should design and select an audit sample, perform audit procedures, and evaluate sample results to obtain sufficient, reliable, relevant, and useful audit evidence. In forming an audit opinion auditors frequently do not examine all of the information available as it may be impractical and valid conclusions can be reached using audit sampling.

*Audit sampling is defined as the **application of audit procedures to less than 100% of the population** to enable the auditor to evaluate audit evidence about some characteristic of the items selected to form or assist in forming a conclusion concerning the population. **Statistical sampling** involves the use of techniques from which mathematically constructed conclusions regarding the population can be drawn.*

Nonstatistical sampling is not statistically based and results should not be extrapolated over the population because the sample is unlikely to be representative of the population.

Design of the Sample

When designing the size and structure of an audit sample, auditors should consider the specific audit objectives, the nature of the population and the sampling and selection methods. The auditor should consider the need to involve appropriate specialists in the design and analysis of samples.

*Sampling Unit - The sampling unit will depend on the purpose of the sample. For **compliance testing of controls, attribute sampling** is typically used, where the sampling unit is an event or transaction (e.g., a control such as an authorization on an invoice). For **substantive testing, variable or estimation sampling** is frequently used where the sampling unit is often monetary.*

Audit objectives - *The auditor should consider the specific audit objectives to be achieved and the **audit procedures** that are most likely to achieve those objectives. When audit sampling is appropriate, consideration should be given to the nature of the **audit evidence** sought and possible error conditions.*

Population - *The population is the entire set of data from which the auditor wishes to sample in order to reach a conclusion on the population. Therefore, the population from which the sample is drawn has to be appropriate and verified as complete for the specific audit objective.*

Stratification - *To assist in the efficient and effective design of the sample, stratification may be appropriate. Stratification is the process of dividing a population into subpopulations with similar characteristics explicitly defined so that each sampling unit can belong to only one stratum.*

Sample size - *When determining sample size, the auditor should consider the sampling risk, the amount of the error that would be acceptable, and the extent to which errors are expected.*

Sampling risk - *Sampling risk arises from the possibility that the auditor's conclusion may be different from the conclusion that would be reached if the entire population were subjected to the same audit procedure. There are two types of sampling risk:*

- *The **risk of incorrect acceptance** - the risk that material misstatement is assessed as unlikely, when in fact the population is materially misstated*

- *The **risk of incorrect rejection** - the risk that material misstatement is assessed as likely, when in fact the population is not materially misstated*

Tolerable error - *Tolerable error is the maximum error in the population that auditors are willing to accept and still conclude that the audit objective has been achieved. For **substantive tests**, tolerable error is related to the auditor's judgment about materiality. In **compliance tests**, it is the maximum rate of deviation from a prescribed control procedure that the auditor is willing to accept.*

Expected error - *If the auditor expects errors to be present in the population, a larger sample than when no error is expected ordinarily has to be examined to conclude that the actual error in the population is not greater than the planned tolerable error. Smaller sample sizes are justified when the population is expected to be error free. When determining the expected error in a population, the auditor should consider such matters as error levels identified in previous audits, changes in the organization's procedures, evidence available from an internal control evaluation, and results from analytical review procedures.*

Selection of the Audit Sample

There are four commonly used sampling methods:

Statistical Sampling Methods

- ***Random sampling*** - *ensures that all combinations of sampling units in the population have an equal chance of selection.*

- **Systematic sampling** - involves selecting sampling units using a fixed interval between selections, the first interval having a random start. Examples include Monetary Unit Sampling or Value-Weighted selection that gives each individual monetary value (e.g., $1) in the population an equal chance of selection. Because the individual monetary unit cannot ordinarily be examined separately, the item that includes the monetary unit is selected for examination. This method systematically weights the selection in favor of the larger amounts but still gives every monetary value an equal opportunity for selection. Another example includes selecting every 'nth unit.

Nonstatistical Sampling Methods

- **Haphazard sampling** - in which the auditor selects the sample without following a structured technique, but avoiding any conscious bias or predictability. However, analysis of a haphazard sample should not be relied upon to form a conclusion on the population.

- **Judgmental sampling** - in which the auditor places a bias on the sample (e.g., all sampling units over a certain value, all for a specific type of exception, all negatives, all new users, etc.). It should be noted that a judgmental sample is not statistically based and results should not be extrapolated over the population. The sample is unlikely to be representative of the population.

The auditor should select sample items in such a way that the sample is expected to be **representative of the population regarding the characteristics being tested** (i.e., using statistical sampling methods). To maintain audit independence, the auditor should ensure the population is complete and control the selection of the sample.

For a sample to be representative of the population, all sampling units in the population should have an equal or known probability of selection (i.e., statistical sampling methods). There are two commonly used **selection methods**: selection on **records** and selection on **quantitative fields** (e.g., monetary units).

For selection on records, common methods are:

- Random sample (statistical sample)
- Haphazard sample (nonstatistical)
- Judgmental sample (nonstatistical; high probability to lead to a biased conclusion)

For selection on quantitative fields, common methods are:

- Random sample (statistical sample on monetary units)
- Fixed interval sample (statistical sample using a fixed interval)
- Cell sample (statistical sample using random selection in an interval)

Documentation

The audit workpapers should include **sufficient detail** to describe clearly the **sampling objective** and the **sampling process** used. The workpapers should include the source of the population, the sampling method used, sampling parameters (e.g., random start number or method by which random start was obtained, sampling interval), items selected, details of audit tests performed and conclusions reached.

Evaluation of Sample Results

*Having performed, on each sample item, audit procedures appropriate to the particular audit objective, the auditor should **analyze any possible errors detected** in the sample to determine whether they are actually errors and, if appropriate, their nature and cause. Those assessed as errors should be projected as appropriate to the population, if the sampling method used is statistically based.*

*Any possible errors detected should be reviewed to determine **whether they are actually errors**. The auditor should consider the **qualitative aspects** of the errors. These include the nature and cause of the errors and the possible effect of the errors on the other phases of the audit. Errors that are the result of the breakdown of an automated process ordinarily have wider implications for error rates than human error.*

*When the expected audit evidence regarding a specific sample item cannot be obtained, the auditor may be able to obtain sufficient audit evidence through performing **alternative procedures** on the item selected.*

*The auditor should consider **projecting the results** of the sample to the population with a method of projection consistent with the method used to select the sample. The projection of the sample may involve estimating probable errors in the population and estimating errors that might not have been detected because of the imprecision of the technique together with the qualitative aspects of errors found.*

*The auditor should consider whether errors in the population might **exceed the tolerable error** by comparing the projected population error to the tolerable error, taking into account the results of other audit procedures relevant to the audit objective. When the projected population error exceeds the tolerable error, the auditor should reassess the sampling risk. If that risk is unacceptable, (s)he should consider extending the audit procedure or performing alternative audit procedures.*

PA Summary

- When using statistical or nonstatistical sampling, the auditor designs and selects a sample, performs procedures, and evaluates results. Valid conclusions can be reached about some characteristic of the population using sampling.
- Sampling applies audit procedures to **less than 100%** of the population.
- **Statistical sampling** techniques permit the auditor to draw **mathematically-constructed conclusions**. However, **nonstatistical sampling** does not permit extrapolation of results to the population because samples are unlikely to be representative.
- **Design** of the sample considers specific audit objectives, nature of the population, and sampling and selection methods. The **sampling unit** depends on the purpose of the sample. For **compliance testing of controls**, **attribute sampling** is used, and the sampling unit is an event or transaction. For **substantive testing**, **variable or estimation sampling** is used, and the sampling unit is often monetary.
- The auditor considers the **audit procedures** most likely to achieve the objectives, the **audit evidence** sought, and possible error conditions.
- The **population** is the set of data from which the auditor samples to reach a conclusion on the population. It must be appropriate and complete for the specific audit objective.

- **Stratification** divides a population into subpopulations with similar characteristics. Each sampling unit belongs to one stratum.
- **Sample size** considers sampling risk, the acceptable error, and the expected error.
- **Sampling risk** is the possibility that the auditor's conclusion may differ from that reached if the entire population is tested. The **risk of incorrect acceptance** is that material misstatement is assessed as unlikely when the population is materially misstated. The **risk of incorrect rejection** is that material misstatement is assessed as likely when the population is not materially misstated. **Tolerable error** is the maximum error in the population consistent with achieving the audit objective. For **substantive tests**, tolerable error relates to judgments about materiality. For **compliance tests**, it is the maximum acceptable rate of deviation from a control.
- Determining **expected error** in a population involves considering error levels in previous audits, changes in the organization's procedures, evidence from a control evaluation, and results of analytical reviews. A sample ordinarily is larger when expected error is greater.
- The most common **statistical sampling methods** are random sampling and systematic sampling. **Random sampling** ensures that all combinations of sampling units have an equal chance of selection. **Systematic sampling** involves selecting sampling units using a fixed interval between selections after a random start. An example is monetary unit sampling. It gives each monetary value an equal chance of selection. The item that includes the monetary unit is selected, thus, weighting the selection in favor of larger amounts. The most common nonstatistical methods are haphazard sampling and judgment sampling. **Haphazard sampling** selects the sample without a structured technique, but avoiding conscious bias or predictability. **Judgmental sampling** places a bias on the sample (e.g., all sampling units over a certain value). For the sample to be **representative** regarding the characteristics tested, statistical methods must be used. Accordingly, all sampling units in the population should have an equal or known probability of selection.
- The most common selection methods define sampling units as **records** or **quantitative fields** (e.g., monetary units).
- The **sampling objective** and **process** should be **documented** in detail.
- **Possible errors** detected should be analyzed. **Projection** of errors to the population is possible if statistical sampling is used. Errors detected are reviewed to determine **whether they are actually errors**, and the auditor considers the **qualitative aspects** of the errors. When the expected audit evidence regarding a specific sample item cannot be obtained, the auditor may be able to perform **alternative procedures**. The auditor should consider **projecting the results** to the population with a method consistent with the method used to select the sample. The auditor should consider whether errors in the population might **exceed tolerable error** by comparing the projection with the tolerable error. When the projection exceeds tolerable error, the auditor should reassess sampling risk.

2. **Sampling** applies an engagement procedure to fewer than 100% of the items under review for the purpose of drawing an inference about a characteristic of the population.

    a. **Judgment (nonstatistical) sampling** is a subjective approach to determining the sample size and sample selection. This subjectivity is not always a weakness. The internal auditor, based on other work, may be able to test the most material and risky transactions and to emphasize the types of transactions subject to high control risk.

    b. **Statistical (probability or random) sampling** is an objective method of determining sample size and selecting the items to be examined. Unlike judgment sampling, it provides a means of quantitatively assessing **precision** or the allowance for sampling risk (how closely the sample represents the population) and reliability or **confidence level** (the probability the sample will represent the population).

        1) Statistical sampling is applicable to **tests of controls** (attribute sampling) and **substantive testing** (variables sampling).
        2) For example, testing controls over sales is ideal for random selection. This type of sampling provides evidence about the quality of processing throughout the period. However, a sales cutoff test is an inappropriate use of random selection. The auditor is concerned that the sales journal has been held open to record the next period's sales. The auditor should select transactions from the latter part of the period and examine supporting evidence to determine whether they were recorded in the proper period.

3. The internal auditor's expectation is that a **random sample is representative** of the population. Thus, the sample should have the same characteristics (e.g., deviation rate or mean) as the population.

4. **Sampling risk** is the probability that a properly drawn sample may not represent the population. Thus, the conclusions based on the sample may differ from those based on examining all the items in the population. The internal auditor controls sampling risk by specifying the acceptable levels of its components when developing the sampling plan.

    a. For **tests of controls** (an application of attribute sampling), sampling risk includes the following:

        1) The **risk of assessing control risk too low** is the risk that the actual control risk is greater than the assessed level of control risk based on the sample. This risk relates to engagement **effectiveness** (a Type II error or Beta risk).

            a) **Control risk** is the risk that controls do not prevent or detect material misstatements on a timely basis.

        2) The **risk of assessing control risk too high** is the risk that actual control risk is less than the assessed level of control risk based on the sample. This risk relates to engagement **efficiency** (a Type I error or Alpha risk).

            a) The internal auditor's overassessment of control risk may lead to an unnecessary extension of the substantive tests.

    b. For **substantive tests** (an application of variables sampling), sampling risk includes the following:

        1) The **risk of incorrect acceptance** is the risk that the sample supports the conclusion that the amount tested is not materially misstated when it is materially misstated. This risk relates to engagement **effectiveness** (a Type II error or Beta risk).

        2) The **risk of incorrect rejection** is the risk that the sample supports the conclusion that the amount tested is materially misstated when it is not. This risk relates to engagement efficiency (a Type I error or Alpha risk).

            a) If the cost and effort of selecting additional sample items are low, a higher risk of incorrect rejection may be acceptable.

c.   The **confidence level**, also termed the reliability level, is the complement of the applicable sampling risk factor. Thus, for a **test of controls**, if the risk of assessing control risk too low is 5%, the internal auditor's confidence level is 95% (1.0 − .05).

1)   For a **substantive test** conducted using classical variables sampling, if the risk of incorrect rejection is 5%, the auditor's confidence level is 95% (1.0 − .05).

5.   **Nonsampling risk** concerns all aspects of engagement risk not caused by sampling.

6.   **Basic Steps in a Statistical Plan**

a.   **Determine the objectives of the test.**

b.   **Define the population.** This step includes defining the sampling unit and considering the completeness of the population.

1)   For tests of controls, it includes defining the period covered.
2)   For substantive tests, it includes identifying individually significant items.

c.   **Determine acceptable levels of sampling risk** (e.g., 5% or 10%).

d.   **Calculate the sample size** using tables or formulas.

1)   **Stratified sampling** minimizes the effect of high variability by dividing the population into subpopulations. **Reducing the variance** within each subpopulation allows the auditor to sample a smaller number of items while holding precision and confidence level constant.

e.   **Select the sampling approach.**

1)   In **random (probability) sampling**, each item in the population has a known and nonzero probability of selection. Random selection is usually accomplished by generating random numbers from a random number table or computer program and tracing them to associated documents or items.

a)   In **simple random sampling**, every possible sample of a given size has the same probability of being chosen.

b)   Efficient use of random number tables often requires that constants be subtracted from the sample items to create a population that more closely matches the numbers in the table. After an acceptable number is found in the table, the constant is added back. Randomness of selection is not impaired by this technique.

2)   **Systematic sampling** selects every nth item after a random start. The value of n equals the population divided by the number of sampling units. The random start should be in the **first interval**. Because the sampling technique only requires counting in the population, no correspondence between random numbers and sampled items is necessary. A systematic sampling plan assumes the items are arranged randomly.

3)   **Block sampling** (cluster sampling) randomly selects groups of items as the **sampling units**. For this plan to be effective, variability within the blocks should be greater than variability among them. If blocks of homogeneous samples are selected, the sample will be biased.

f.   **Take the sample,** i.e., select the items to be evaluated.

g.   **Evaluate the sample results.**

h.   **Document the sampling procedures.**

7. In general, all **sample sizes** are dependent on

    a. The **population size**. As the population size increases, the required sample increases but at a decreasing rate.

    b. The **acceptable risk** (1 – the required confidence level). The smaller the acceptable risk, the larger the sample size.

    c. The **variability in the population**. The more variability in the population, measured by the standard deviation for variables sampling (or the expected deviation rate for attribute sampling), the larger the required sample size.

    d. The **tolerable misstatement** in variables sampling (or **tolerable deviation rate** in attribute sampling). The smaller the acceptable misstatement amount or deviation rate, the larger the required sample size.

8. **The primary methods of variables sampling.** Variables sampling applies to monetary amounts or other quantities in contrast with the binary propositions tested by attribute sampling.

    a. **Unstratified mean-per-unit sampling** calculates the mean and standard deviation of the observed amounts of the sample items. It then multiplies the mean by the number of items in the population to estimate the population amount. **Precision** is determined using the mean and standard deviation of the sample.

        1) Unstratified MPU results in large sample sizes compared with stratified MPU. It is appropriate when unit carrying amounts are unknown or the total is inaccurate.

            a) MPU is most often used with **stratification**, and significant items are usually excluded from the sampled population and evaluated separately.

    b. **Difference estimation** of population misstatement determines differences between the observed and recorded amounts for items in the sample. It calculates the mean difference, and multiplies the mean by the number of items in the population.

        1) Thus, per-item carrying amounts and their total should be known. Moreover, stratification is not necessary when (a) many nonzero differences exist, (b) they are not skewed toward over- or understatements, and (c) their amounts are relatively uniform.

        2) **Precision** is calculated using the mean and standard deviation of the differences.

    c. **Ratio estimation** estimates the population misstatement by multiplying the recorded amount of the population by the ratio of the total observed amount of the sample items to their total recorded amount.

        1) The requirements for efficient difference estimation also apply to ratio estimation. However, ratio estimation also requires **carrying amounts** to be **positive**.

        2) Ratio estimation is **preferable to unstratified MPU** when the standard deviation of the distribution of ratios is less than the standard deviation of the sample item amounts.

        3) Ratio estimation is **preferable to difference estimation** when differences are not relatively uniform.

    d. **Probability-proportional-to-size (PPS) or dollar-unit sampling (DUS).** This approach uses attribute sampling methods to reach a conclusion about the probability of overstating an account balance by a specified amount. PPS sampling (also called dollar-unit, monetary-unit, cumulative-monetary-amount, or combined-attribute-variables sampling) is based on the **Poisson distribution**, which is used in attribute sampling to approximate the binomial distribution.

9. Stop and review! You have completed the outline for this subunit. Study multiple-choice questions 22 through 32 beginning on page 422.

8.5 ATTRIBUTE SAMPLING

1. Attribute sampling applies to binary, yes/no, or error/nonerror propositions. It tests the effectiveness of controls because it can estimate a **rate of occurrence** of control deviations in a population. Attribute sampling requires the existence of evidence indicating performance of the control being tested.

2. **Steps for Testing Controls**

   a. **Define the objectives of the plan.** The internal auditor should clearly state what is to be accomplished, for example, to determine that the deviation rate from an approval process for a transaction is at an acceptable level.

   b. **Define the population.** The population is the focus of interest. The internal auditor wants to reach conclusions about all the items in the population.

      1) The **sampling unit** is the individual item that will be included in the sample. Thus, the population may consist of all the transactions for the fiscal year. The sampling unit is each document representing a transaction and containing the required information that a control was performed.

   c. **Define the deviation conditions.** The characteristic indicator of performance of a control is the attribute of interest, for example, the supervisor's signature of approval on a document.

   d. **Determine the sample size** using tables or formulas. Four factors determine the necessary sample size.

      1) The **allowable risk of assessing control risk too low** has an inverse effect on sample size. The higher the acceptable risk, the smaller the sample. The usual risk level specified by internal auditors is 5% or 10%.

      2) The **tolerable deviation rate** is the maximum rate of deviations from the prescribed control that the internal auditor is willing to accept without altering the planned assessed level of control risk.

         a) If the internal auditor cannot tolerate any deviations, the concept of sampling is inappropriate, and the whole population must be investigated.

      3) The **expected population deviation rate** is an estimate of the deviation rate in the current population. This estimate can be based on the prior year's findings or a pilot sample of approximately 30 to 50 items.

         a) The expected rate should be **less than the tolerable rate**. Otherwise, tests of the control should be omitted, and control risk should be assessed at the maximum.

      4) The **population size** is the total number of sampling units in the population. However, the sample size is relatively insensitive to changes in large populations. For populations over 5,000, a standard table can be used. Use of the standard tables for sampling plans based on a smaller population size is a conservative approach because the sample size will be overstated. Hence, the risk of assessing control risk too low is not affected.

         a) A change in the size of the population has a very small effect on the required sample size when the population is large.

      5) The basic **sample size formula for an attribute sample** is

$$n = \frac{C^2 pq}{P^2}$$

         a) C is the **confidence coefficient** (e.g., at a 95% confidence level, it equals 1.96), p is the **expected deviation rate**, q is (100% − p), and P is the **precision** (per item).

e. **Perform the sampling plan.** A random sample should be taken. Each item should have an equal and nonzero chance of being selected. A random number table can be used to identify the items to be selected if a correspondence is established between random numbers and the sampling units.

1) A statistical consideration is whether to use sampling **with or without replacement**, but the tables are designed for sampling with replacement. The result is a slightly larger sample size than needed. However, in practice, auditors normally sample without replacement. Choosing the same item twice provides no additional evidence.

2) Sampling without replacement means that a population item cannot be selected again after it is selected in the sampling process.

f. **Evaluate and document sample results.** The steps include calculating the sample deviation rate and determining the achieved upper deviation limit.

1) **Sample deviation rate.** The number of deviations observed is divided by the sample size to determine the sample deviation rate. This rate is the best **estimate of the population deviation rate**. However, because the sample may not be representative, the internal auditor cannot state with certainty that the sample rate is the population rate. However, (s)he can state that the rate is not likely to be greater than a specified upper limit.

2) The **achieved upper deviation limit** is based on the sample size and the number of deviations discovered. Again, a standard table is ordinarily consulted. In the table, the intersection of the sample size and the number of deviations indicates the upper achieved deviation limit.

   a) For example, given three deviations in a sample of 150, the sample rate is 2% (3 ÷ 150). At a 95% confidence level (the complement of a 5% risk of assessing control risk too low), a standard table indicates that the true occurrence rate is not greater than 5.1%. The difference between the achieved upper deviation limit determined from a standard table and the sample rate is the **achieved precision**, or 3.1% (5.1% – 2%).

   b) When the sample rate exceeds the **expected population deviation** rate, the achieved upper deviation limit will exceed the tolerable rate at the given risk level. In that case, the sample does not support the planned assessed level of control risk.

3. **Other Attribute Sampling Concepts**

a. **Discovery sampling** is a form of attribute sampling that is appropriate only when a single deviation would be critical. The occurrence rate is assumed to be at or near 0%, and the method cannot be used to evaluate results statistically if deviations are found in the sample. Hence, discovery sampling may be used for testing controls. The sample size is calculated so that the sample will include at least one example of a deviation if it occurs in the population at a given rate.

b. The objective of **stop-or-go sampling** is to reduce the sample size. The internal auditor examines only enough sample items to be able to state that the deviation rate is below a prespecified rate at a prespecified level of confidence. Sample size is not fixed, so the internal auditor can achieve the desired result, even if deviations are found, by enlarging the sample sufficiently. In contrast, discovery sampling and acceptance sampling have fixed sample sizes.

c. **Acceptance sampling for attributes** is useful in **quality control applications** when products are available in lots, are subject to inspection, and can be classified as acceptable or not. Items are selected randomly without replacement, and the results indicate whether the lots are accepted or rejected. To use this method, the internal auditor must specify the lot size, the acceptable quality level, the sampling plan (number of samples), and the level or extent of inspection needed.

1) **Acceptance sampling for variables** is used when the characteristic tested is measurable on a continuous scale and is likely to follow a specific probability distribution. Thus, the sampling plan used may be based on such measures as the sample mean and standard deviation. For example, a lot of ball bearings may be accepted or rejected depending on whether the mean of the sizes of the sample items is within the tolerance limits.

4. Stop and review! You have completed the outline for this subunit. Study multiple-choice questions 33 through 41 beginning on page 426.

8.6 CLASSICAL VARIABLES SAMPLING

1. Sampling for variables usually applies to monetary amounts but may be used for other measures. It attempts to provide information about whether a stated amount, for example, the balance of accounts receivable, is materially misstated. This stated amount is expected to represent the true balance, a number that is not known (and will never be known without a 100% audit). By taking a sample and drawing an inference about the population, the internal auditor either supports or rejects the conclusion about the reported number.

2. **Steps for Testing Variables**

   a. **Define the objectives of the plan.** The internal auditor intends to estimate the recorded amount of the population, for example, an accounts receivable balance.

   b. **Define the population and the sampling unit.** For example, the population might consist of 4,000 accounts receivable with a reported recorded amount of $3.5 million. Each customer account is a **sampling unit**.

   c. **Determine the sample size.** The sample size formula for **mean-per-unit variables sampling** is given below. The same equation may be used for difference and ratio estimation, although σ will be the estimated standard deviation of the population of differences between audit and recorded amounts.

$$n_1 = \frac{C^2 \sigma^2}{P^2}$$

If: n_1 = **sample size** given sampling with replacement

C = **confidence coefficient** or number of standard deviations related to the required confidence level (1 – the risk of incorrect rejection)

σ = **standard deviation of the population** (an estimate based on a pilot sample or from the prior year's sample)

P = **precision** or the allowance for sampling risk. This allowance is on a per-item basis. The precision also may be stated in the denominator as a total, and the number of items in the population (N) is included in the numerator. Achieved precision may be calculated as equal to the confidence coefficient (C) times the standard error of the mean ($\sigma \div \sqrt{n_1}$).

1) **Precision** (confidence interval) is an interval around the sample statistic that is expected to include the true amount of the population at the specified confidence level. In classical variables sampling, precision is calculated based on the normal distribution.

   a) It is a function of the **tolerable misstatement**.

   b) C in the formula is based on the risk of incorrect rejection, but the more important risk is the **risk of incorrect acceptance**.

   i) Precision equals the product of tolerable misstatement and a **ratio determined from a standard table**. This ratio is based on the allowable risk of incorrect acceptance and the risk of incorrect rejection, both specified by the internal auditor.

    ii)   For example, at a confidence level of 90% (10% risk of incorrect rejection) and a risk of incorrect acceptance of 5%, the ratio of the desired precision (allowance for sampling risk) to tolerable misstatement is .500.

2)   The confidence coefficient, C, is based on the **risk of incorrect rejection**:

Risk of Incorrect Rejection	Confidence Level	Confidence Coefficient
20%	80%	1.28
10%	90%	1.64
5%	95%	1.96
1%	99%	2.58

3)   EXAMPLE: The number of sampling units is 4,000 accounts receivable, the estimated population standard deviation is $125 based on a pilot sample, and the desired confidence level is 90%. Assuming tolerable misstatement of $100,000 and a planned risk of incorrect acceptance of 5%, the desired precision can be determined using a ratio from a standard table. As stated above, the ratio for a 10% risk of incorrect rejection and 5% allowable risk of incorrect acceptance is .500. Multiplying .500 by the $100,000 tolerable misstatement results in precision of $50,000. On a per-item basis, it equals $12.50 ($50,000 ÷ 4,000). Thus, the sample size is

$$n_1 = \frac{1.64^2 \times \$125^2}{\$12.50^2}$$

$$= 269 \ (rounded)$$

4)   **Finite population correction factor.** In the basic formula, n_1 is the sample size assuming **sampling with replacement**. It can be adjusted by a correction factor to allow for sampling without replacement. An approximation of the adjusted sample size is

$$n = \frac{n_1}{1 + (n_1 \div N)}$$

   a)   n equals the modified sample size, n_1 equals the sample size determined in the basic formula, and N is the population. The **FPCF** is usually omitted when the initial estimate of the sample size is a very small (less than 5%) proportion of the population.

d. **Select the sample, execute the plan, and evaluate and document the results.**

1)   Randomly select and examine the accounts, e.g., send confirmations.

2)   Calculate the average confirmed accounts receivable amount (assume $880).

3)   Calculate the sample standard deviation (assume $125) to use as an estimate of the population amount.

4)   Evaluate the sample results.

   a)   The best estimate of the population amount is the average accounts receivable from the sample times the number of items in the population. Thus, the amount estimated is

$$Estimate = Average \ sample \ amount \times Number \ of \ items$$

$$= \$880 \times 4,000$$

$$= \$3,520,000$$

b) The **achieved precision** (calculated allowance for sampling risk) is determined by solving the sample-size formula for P.

$$P = \frac{1.64 \times \$125}{\sqrt{269}}$$

$$= \$205 \div 16.4 = \$12.50$$

c) The population size, confidence coefficient, and the standard deviation are the same used to calculate the original sample size. Hence, the precision, P, will be the same as planned, or $12.50. P will be different only when the standard deviation of the sample differs from the estimate used to calculate n_1. Such a difference can result in changes in the levels of risk faced by the internal auditor. However, these issues are beyond the scope of the materials presented here.

d) The **engagement conclusion** is that the internal auditor is 90% confident that the true amount of the population is $3,520,000 plus or minus $50,000 (4,000 × $12.50 per-item precision), an interval of $3,470,000 to $3,570,000. If management's recorded amount was $3.5 million, the internal auditor cannot reject the hypothesis that the recorded amount is not materially misstated.

3. Stop and review! You have completed the outline for this subunit. Study multiple-choice questions 42 through 48 beginning on page 429.

8.7 PROBABILITY-PROPORTIONAL-TO-SIZE (PPS) SAMPLING

1. The **classical approach** uses items (e.g., invoices, checks, etc.) as the **sampling units**. PPS sampling uses a **monetary unit** as the sampling unit, but the item containing the sampled monetary unit is selected for examination.

a. PPS sampling is appropriate for account balances that may include only a few overstated items, such as may be expected in inventory and receivables. Because a **systematic selection method** is used (every nth monetary unit is selected), the larger the transactions or amounts in the population, the more likely a transaction or an amount will be selected. Thus, this method is not used when the primary engagement objective is to search for **understatements**, e.g., of liabilities. Moreover, if many misstatements (over- and understatements) are expected, classical variables sampling is more efficient.

b. In contrast, the classical approach to variables sampling is not always appropriate.

1) When only a **few differences** between recorded and observed amounts are found, difference and ratio estimation sampling may not be efficient.

2) Mean-per-unit estimation sampling also may be difficult in an **unstratified** sampling situation.

2. The following simplified **sample size formula** is used when **anticipated misstatement is zero**:

$$n = \frac{RM \times RF}{TM}$$

If: n = sample size
RM = the recorded amount, e.g., of inventory or accounts receivable
RF = risk or reliability factor based on the Poisson distribution and the internal auditor's specified risk of incorrect acceptance
TM = tolerable misstatement

a. **Tolerable misstatement (TM)** must be specified by the internal auditor. It is the maximum misstatement in an account balance or class of transactions that may exist without causing the financial statements to be materially misstated.

b. The **risk or reliability factor (RF)** is a multiplier, the amount of which is determined by a Poisson factor found in a standard table. RF is always determined for zero misstatements, regardless of the misstatements actually anticipated.

1) The table below is a simplified version quoted by Ratliff, *Internal Auditing: Principles and Techniques*, 2nd edition (1996), page 653, from the AICPA Audit and Accounting Guide, *Audit Sampling* (1992).

Reliability Factors for Overstatements

Number of	Risk of Incorrect Acceptance				
Overstatements	1%	5%	10%	15%	20%
0	4.61	3.00	2.31	1.90	1.61
1	6.64	4.75	3.89	3.38	3.00
2	8.41	6.30	5.33	4.72	4.28

3. EXAMPLE: An organization's inventory balance is expected to have few if any errors of overstatement. The following information relates to an examination of the balance using PPS sampling and the formula and risk factors given above:

Tolerable misstatement...$15,000
Anticipated misstatement...$0
Risk of incorrect acceptance.......................................5%
Recorded amount of accounts receivable....................$300,000

Overstatements discovered:

	Recorded Amount	Observed Amount
1st	$ 400	$ 320
2nd	500	0
3rd	6,000	5,500

a. Accordingly, the **sample size** is 60 items.

$$n = \frac{RM \times RF}{TM} = \frac{\$300,000 \times 3.0}{\$15,000} = 60 \ dollar \ items$$

b. Alternatively, the **dollar sampling interval** can be determined by dividing the TM by the RF ($15,000 ÷ 3.0 = $5,000).

c. **Sample selection.** The items selected correspond to every 5,000th dollar [($300,000 ÷ 60)] in a list of cumulative inventory subtotals.

Description	Inventory on Hand	Unit Cost	Amount	Cumulative Amount
Item A	90	$105	$9,450	$ 9,450
B	30	16	480	9,930
C	70	40	2,800	12,730
D	46	111	5,106	17,836
E	300	7	2,100	19,936
F	390	2	780	20,716
G	450	10	4,500	25,216
•	•	•	•	•
•	•	•	•	•
•	•	•	•	•
				$300,000

1) Given a **random start** at the 1,992nd dollar, the sample will consist of the following:

   a) The first dollar will be $1,992.
   b) The next dollar will be $6,992 ($1,992 + $5,000).
   c) The next dollar will be $11,992 ($6,992 + $5,000).
   d) The next dollar will be $16,992 ($11,992 + $5,000).
   e) Each subsequent dollar equals the prior dollar plus $5,000.

2) Accordingly, the **physical units** selected will include two of item A, one of item C, one of item D, one of item G, etc. They will be inspected, measured, and otherwise audited.

d. If **no misstatements** are found in the 60 items, the internal auditor concludes that the engagement client's balance has a maximum overstatement of $15,000 at the specified risk of incorrect acceptance.

e. **If misstatements occur**, the **average amount of misstatement** must be projected to the entire population.

1) A **tainting percentage** [(recorded amount – observed amount) ÷ recorded amount] is calculated for each misstatement in a sample item when the item is smaller than the sampling interval. This percentage is then applied to the interval to estimate the projected misstatement or taint (population misstatement in that interval).

2) The **sum of the projected misstatements** is the total estimated misstatement in the population.

3) If the sample item is **greater than the sampling interval**, the difference between the carrying amount and audited amount is the projected misstatement for that interval (no percentage is computed).

4) The **total projected misstatement** based on the information in the example is $6,500.

Recorded Amount	Observed Amount	Tainting %	Sampling Interval	Projected Misstatement
$ 400	$ 320	20%	$5,000	$1,000
500	0	100%	5,000	5,000
6,000	5,500	--	--	500
				$6,500

5) The calculation of the **upper misstatement limit (UML)** based on the preceding information is more complex. The first component of the UML is **basic precision**: the product of the sampling interval ($5,000) and the risk factor (3.00) for zero misstatements at the specified risk of incorrect acceptance (5%). The second component is the **total projected misstatement** ($6,500). The third component is an **allowance for widening the precision gap** as a result of finding more than zero misstatements.

   a) This allowance is determined only with respect to logical sampling units with recorded amounts **less than the sampling interval**. If a sample item is equal to or greater than the sampling interval, the degree of taint for that interval is certain, and no further allowance is necessary.

   b) The first step in calculating this allowance is to determine the **adjusted incremental changes in the reliability factors** (these factors increase, and precision widens, as the number of misstatements increases). The factors are from the 5% column in the table. However, amounts already included in (1) basic precision, (2) projected misstatement, and (3) the adjustments for higher-ranked misstatements must not be counted twice. Thus, the **preceding reliability factor plus 1.0** is subtracted from each factor.

c)   The projected misstatements are then ranked from highest to lowest, each adjusted incremental reliability factor is multiplied by the related projected misstatement, and the products are summed. In this case, the UML is found to exceed TM. (Recall that one misstated item exceeded the sampling interval. Hence, no additional allowance is needed for that item.)

Basic precision (3.00 × $5,000)		$15,000
Total projected misstatement		6,500
Allowance for precision gap widening:		
(4.75 – 3.00 – 1.00) × $5,000 = $3,750		
(6.30 – 4.75 – 1.00) × $1,000 =	550	4,300
UML		$25,800

f.   Because the sample size formula was based on a presumed 0% misstatement rate, the **sample size** may have to be increased.

1)   The following is the modified sample size formula when **anticipated misstatement** is not zero:

$$n = \frac{RM \times RF}{TM - (AM \times EF)}$$

If: AM = anticipated misstatement
     EF = an expansion factor derived from the following table
          (Source: AICPA Audit and Accounting Guide, *Audit Sampling*):

	Risk of Incorrect Acceptance				
	1%	5%	10%	15%	20%
Factor	1.9	1.6	1.5	1.4	1.3

4.   Stop and review! You have completed the outline for this subunit. Study multiple-choice questions 49 through 57 beginning on page 432.

8.8 STATISTICAL QUALITY CONTROL

1.   Statistical quality control is a method of determining whether a shipment or production run of units lies within acceptable limits. It is also used to determine whether **production processes** are out of control.

a.   Items are either good or bad, i.e., inside or outside of control limits.
b.   Statistical quality control is based on the **binomial distribution**.

2.   **Acceptance sampling** is a method of determining the probability that the rate of defective items in a batch is less than a specified level.

a.   EXAMPLE: Assume a sample is taken from a population of 500. According to standard acceptance sampling tables, if the sample consists of 25 items and none is defective, the probability is 93% that the population deviation rate is less than 10%. If 60 items are examined and no defectives are found, the probability is 99% that the deviation rate is less than 10%. If two defectives in 60 units are observed, the probability is 96% that the deviation rate is less than 10%.

3.   **Statistical control charts** are graphic aids for monitoring the status of any process subject to acceptable or unacceptable variations during repeated operations. They also have applications of direct interest to auditors and accountants, for example, (a) unit cost of production, (b) direct labor hours used, (c) ratio of actual expenses to budgeted expenses, (d) number of calls by sales personnel, or (e) total accounts receivable.

4. A control chart consists of three lines plotted on a horizontal **time scale**. The center line represents the overall mean or average range for the process being controlled. The other two lines are the **upper control limit (UCL)** and the **lower control limit (LCL)**. The processes are measured periodically, and the values (X) are plotted on the chart. If the value falls within the control limits, no action is taken. If the value falls outside the limits, the process is considered **out of control**, and an investigation is made for possible corrective action. Another advantage of the chart is that it makes **trends** and **cycles** visible.

   a. **P charts** are based on an **attribute** (acceptable/not acceptable) rather than a measure of a variable. Specifically, it shows the percentage of defects in a sample.

   b. **C charts** also are **attribute** control charts. They show defects per item.

   c. An **R chart** shows the range of dispersion of a **variable**, such as size or weight. The center line is the overall mean.

   d. An **X-bar chart** shows the sample mean for a **variable**. The center line is the average range.

   e. EXAMPLE:

   Unit Cost ($)   X   Out of control
   1.05   .... UCL
   1.00   _____X_____
   0.95   ....X...LCL
           _____

           March   April   May

5. **Variations in a process parameter** may have several causes.

   a. **Random variations** occur by chance. Present in virtually all processes, they are not correctable because they will not repeat themselves in the same manner. Excessively narrow control limits will result in many investigations of what are simply random fluctuations.

   b. **Implementation deviations** occur because of human or mechanical failure to achieve target results.

   c. **Measurement variations** result from errors in the measurements of actual results.

   d. **Model fluctuations** can be caused by errors in the formulation of a decision model.

   e. **Prediction variances** result from errors in forecasting data used in a decision model.

6. Establishing control limits based on **benchmarks** is a common method. A more objective method is to use the concept of expected value. The limits are important because they are the decision criteria for determining whether a deviation will be investigated.

7. **Cost-benefit analysis using expected value** provides a more objective basis for setting control limits. The limits of controls should be set so that the cost of an investigation is less than or equal to the benefits derived.

   a. The expected costs include **investigation cost** and the **cost of corrective action**.

   $$
   \begin{array}{l}
   (\textit{Probability of being out of control} \times \textit{Cost of corrective action}) \\
   + \ (\textit{Probability of being in control} \times \textit{Investigation cost}) \\
   \hline
   \textit{Total expected cost}
   \end{array}
   $$

   b. The **benefit** of an investigation is the avoidance of the costs of continuing to operate an out-of-control process. The **expected value of benefits** is the probability of being out of control multiplied by the cost of not being corrected.

8. Stop and review! You have completed the outline for this subunit. Study multiple-choice questions 58 through 61 beginning on page 435.

8.9 STUDY UNIT 8 SUMMARY

1. Probability provides a method for mathematically expressing doubt or assurance about the occurrence of a chance event. The probability of an event varies from 0 to 1. The types of probability are objective and subjective. They differ in how they are calculated.

2. The joint probability for two events is the probability that both will occur. The conditional probability of two events it the probability that one will occur given that the other has already occurred. Probability may be combined.

3. If the relative frequency of occurrence of the values of a variable can be specified, the values taken together constitute a function and the variable is a random variable. A variable is discrete if it can assume only certain values in an interval. The uniform, binomial, and Poisson distributions are among those based on discrete random variables.

4. A random variable is continuous if no gaps exist in the values it may assume. The normal, standard normal, t-, and Chi-square distributions are continuous.

5. Descriptive statistics summarizes large amounts of data. Measures of central tendency and measures of dispersion are such summaries. Measures of central tendency are values typical of a set of data. These measures include the mean, median, and mode.

6. Measures of dispersion indicate the variation within a set of numbers. These measures include (a) the variance, (b) the square root of the variance (the standard deviation), (c) the standard error of the mean, and (d) the coefficient of variation.

7. Inferential statistics provides methods for drawing conclusions about populations based on sample information. A concept crucial to sampling is the central limit theorem. It states that the distribution of the sample mean approaches the normal distribution as the sample size increases. Thus, whenever a process includes the average of independent samples of the same sample size from the same distribution, the normal distribution can be used as an approximation of that process even if the underlying population is not normally distributed. The central limit theorem explains why the normal distribution is so useful.

8. Precision or the confidence interval incorporates the sample size and the population standard deviation along with a probability that the interval includes the true population parameter. Given that z equals the number of standard deviations ensuring a specified confidence level, precision for the population mean is $\overline{x} \pm z\,(\sigma \div \sqrt{n}\,)$.

9. In hypothesis testing, the assertion to be tested is the null hypothesis (H_0). Every other possibility is contained in the alternative hypothesis (H_a). H_0 may state an equality (=) or indicate that the parameter is equal to or greater (less) than ($\geq$ or $\leq$) some value. The types of errors are alpha (incorrect rejection of H_0) and beta (incorrect failure to reject H_0). Hypothesis testing uses the standard normal distribution to compute z-values that define rejection and nonrejection regions under the curve.

10. The t-distribution (also known as Student's distribution) is a special distribution used with small samples, usually fewer than 30, with unknown population variance. For large sample sizes (n > 30), the t-distribution is almost identical to the standard normal distribution. For small sample sizes (n < 30) for which only the sample standard deviation is known, the t-distribution provides a reasonable estimate for tests of the population mean if the population is normally distributed. The t-distribution requires a number called the degrees of freedom, which is (n − k) for k parameters. When one parameter (such as the mean) is estimated, the number of degrees of freedom is (n − 1).

11. Sampling applies audit procedures to less than 100% of the population.

12. Statistical sampling techniques permit the auditor to draw mathematically-constructed conclusions. However, nonstatistical sampling does not permit extrapolation of results to the population because samples are unlikely to be representative.

13. Design of the sample depends on whether the purpose is control testing (attribute sampling) or substantive testing (variable or estimation sampling).

14. Other design considerations are (a) audit objectives and procedures, (b) the desired evidence, (c) whether the sample population is appropriate and complete, (d) whether the population should be stratified, and (e) the sample size. The sample size is a function of acceptable sampling risk, tolerable error, and expected error. The elements of the audit risk model are inherent, control, and detection risk.

15. The most common statistical sampling methods are random sampling and systematic sampling. The most common nonstatistical methods are haphazard sampling and judgment sampling. For the sample to be representative (i.e., sampling units have a nonzero and equal or known probability of selection), statistical methods must be used.

16. The most common selection methods define sampling units as records or quantitative fields.

17. The sampling objective and process should be documented in detail.

18. Possible errors detected should be analyzed. Projection of errors to the population is possible if statistical sampling is used.

19. The primary means of variables sampling are unstratified (mean) per-unit, difference and ratio estimation, and probability-proportional-to-size sampling.

20. Attribute sampling applies to binary, yes/no, or error/nonerror propositions. It tests the effectiveness of controls because it can estimate a rate of occurrence of control deviations in a population.

    The basic sample size formula for an attribute sample is

    $$n = \frac{C^2 pq}{P^2}$$

    C is the confidence coefficient (e.g., at a 95% confidence level, it equals 1.96), p is the expected deviation rate, q is (100% − p), and P is the precision (per item).

21. The sample size formula for mean-per-unit variables sampling is given below. The same equation may be used for difference and ratio estimation, although σ will be the estimated standard deviation of the population of differences between audit and recorded amounts.

    $$n_1 = \frac{C^2 \sigma^2}{P^2}$$

22. The classical approach uses items (e.g., invoices, checks, etc.) as the sampling units. PPS sampling uses a monetary unit as the sampling unit, but the item containing the sampled monetary unit is selected for examination. PPS sampling is appropriate for account balances that may include only a few overstated items, such as may be expected in inventory and receivables. Because a systematic selection method is used (every nth monetary unit is selected), the larger the transactions or amounts in the population, the more likely a transaction or an amount will be selected.

23. Statistical quality control is a method of determining whether a shipment or production run of units lies within acceptable limits. It is also used to determine whether production processes are out of control. Statistical quality control is based on the binomial distribution. Control charts identify conditions for investigation and corrective action. They also make trends and cycles visible.

QUESTIONS

8.1 Probability and Probability Distributions

1. A warehouse contains records from both the retail and the wholesale divisions of the client company. Upon inspecting the contents of one randomly selected box, the internal auditor discovers that they do not match the label. On average, errors of this kind have occurred in 6% of retail boxes and 2% of wholesale boxes. Unfortunately, the part of the label indicating the division of origin is illegible. The internal auditor does know that two-thirds of the boxes in this warehouse come from the wholesale division and one-third from the retail division. Which of the following can be concluded?

    A. The box is more likely to have come from the retail division.

    B. The box is more likely to have come from the wholesale division.

    C. The proportion of retail boxes in the warehouse is probably much larger than the internal auditor thought.

    D. The proportion of wholesale boxes in the warehouse is probably much larger than the internal auditor thought.

Answer (A) is correct. *(CIA, adapted)*
    REQUIRED: The true probabilistic statement.
    DISCUSSION: Two-thirds of the boxes are from the wholesale division. Of these, 2% are mislabeled. Hence, about 1.33% (66 2/3% × 2%) of all the boxes are mislabeled and originated in the wholesale division. One-third of the boxes are from the retail division. Of these, 6% are mislabeled. Hence, about 2% (33 1/3% × 6%) of all the boxes are mislabeled and originated in the retail division. The probability is therefore about 60% [2% ÷ (1.33% + 2%)] that the box came from the retail division.
    Answer (B) is incorrect because the box is more likely to have come from the retail division. Answer (C) is incorrect because the content of one box is an insufficient basis for a conclusion about the proportion of retail boxes in the warehouse. Answer (D) is incorrect because the content of one box is an insufficient basis for a conclusion about the proportion of wholesale boxes in the warehouse.

2. Which of the following is an attribute of a probability distribution?

    A. The total probability associated with all possible occurrences equals zero.

    B. It can be modeled by means of a formula or graph that provides the probability for every possible outcome.

    C. Only one outcome is possible.

    D. It concerns a discrete random variable only.

Answer (B) is correct. *(Publisher, adapted)*
    REQUIRED: The attribute of a probability distribution.
    DISCUSSION: In a probability distribution, the probability of any random event is bounded by 0 (no chance) and 1 (certainty). The total probability of all possible random events must sum to 1. Also, a probability distribution models a random variable through the use of a formula or graph that provides the probability associated with the occurrence of certain values of the random variable.
    Answer (A) is incorrect because the total probability equals 1.0. Answer (C) is incorrect because, if only one outcome is possible, the variable is not random but constant and known with certainty. Answer (D) is incorrect because the random variable may be discrete or continuous.

3. An organization uses two major material inputs in its production. To prepare its manufacturing operations budget, the organization has to project the cost changes of these material inputs. The cost changes are independent of one another. The purchasing department provides the following probabilities associated with projected cost changes:

Cost Change	Material 1	Material 2
3% increase	.3	.5
5% increase	.5	.4
10% increase	.2	.1

The probability that there will be a 3% increase in the cost of both Material 1 and Material 2 is

    A. 15%

    B. 40%

    C. 80%

    D. 20%

Answer (A) is correct. *(CIA, adapted)*
    REQUIRED: The probability of joint increases.
    DISCUSSION: The joint probability of occurrence of two independent events equals the product of their individual probabilities. The probability that the cost of Material 1 will increase by 3% is .3. The probability that the cost of Material 2 will increase by 3% is .5. The probability that both will occur is .15 (.3 × .5).
    Answer (B) is incorrect because 40% is the average of the probabilities of a 3% increase in the costs of Material 1 and Material 2. Answer (C) is incorrect because 80% is the sum of the probabilities of a 3% increase in the costs of Material 1 and Material 2. Answer (D) is incorrect because 20% is the difference between the probabilities of an increase in the costs of Material 1 and Material 2.

4. What is the primary difference between a discrete and a continuous distribution?

   A. One is not a legitimate probability distribution.

   B. Continuous distributions are always symmetric, but discrete distributions are not.

   C. Continuous distributions describe ranges in which any possible value has a probability of occurrence, whereas discrete distributions attribute probabilities only to a finite number of values within a range.

   D. Continuous distributions model finite random variables only, whereas discrete distributions may model any variable.

Answer (C) is correct. *(Publisher, adapted)*
   REQUIRED: The primary difference between a discrete and a continuous distribution.
   DISCUSSION: A continuous distribution describes a random variable that may take an infinite number of values. It is described by an area under a graph such that the total area bounded by its curve and the x axis equals 1.0 and the area between any two points equals the probability that the random variable is between those points. Discrete distributions model only random variables that take on a finite number of values, for example, the number of customers entering a store during a time period.
   Answer (A) is incorrect because both are legitimate probability distributions. Answer (B) is incorrect because continuous probability distributions need not be symmetric. Answer (D) is incorrect because continuous probability distributions model random variables that may take on an infinite amount of values.

5. A Poisson distribution is best described as one used

   A. To assess the probability that a certain event will occur a certain number of times in a given interval of time or space.

   B. To assess the probability of observing an occurrence at least as long (in time, e.g., life of a fuse, engine, etc.) as a specified time interval.

   C. When small samples of less than 30 are examined and the underlying population is assumed to be normal.

   D. To test the fit between the actual data and the theoretical distribution.

Answer (A) is correct. *(Publisher, adapted)*
   REQUIRED: The best description of a Poisson distribution.
   DISCUSSION: A Poisson distribution models the number of times a specified event occurs over a period of time, or over a certain area or volume. It is similar to the binomial distribution when the sample is large and the probability of observing a desired event (p) times the sample size (n) is small, usually $np \leq 7$.
   Answer (B) is incorrect because an exponential distribution is used to assess the probability of observing an occurrence at least as long (in time, e.g., life of a fuse, engine, etc.) as a specified time interval. Answer (C) is incorrect because the t-distribution is used when small samples of less than 30 are examined and the underlying population is assumed to be normal. Answer (D) is incorrect because the Chi-square distribution tests the fit between the actual data and the theoretical distribution.

6. Management of a large computer manufacturer has been much concerned about the consistency across departments in adhering to new and unpopular purchasing guidelines. An internal auditor has a list that rank-orders all departments according to the percentage of purchases that are consistent with the guidelines and indicates which division the department is from. The internal auditor performs a t-test for differences in means on the average rank of departments in divisions A and B to determine whether there is any difference in compliance with the policy and finds that division A (which has more departments) has a significantly higher (i.e., better) average rank than division B. Which one of the following conclusions should be drawn from this analysis?

   A. Division A is complying better with the new policy.

   B. A random sample of departments should be drawn and the analysis recalculated.

   C. A t-test is not valid when the tested groups differ in size.

   D. A t-test is inappropriate for this data, and another type of analysis should be used.

Answer (D) is correct. *(CIA, adapted)*
   REQUIRED: The true statement about application of a t-test to rank-ordered data.
   DISCUSSION: The t-distribution is used for small samples but in the same way as the normal distribution. A t-test is not valid when used with ordinal-level data. A t-test by definition is an application of parametric statistics. Nonparametric (distribution-free) statistics is applied to problems for which rank order but not a specific distribution is known.
   Answer (A) is incorrect because a t-test is not valid in this case. Answer (B) is incorrect because the auditor already has a list of the entire population and no sampling is needed. Answer (C) is incorrect because a t-test can be used with groups that differ in size.

7. An internal auditor is interested in determining whether there is a statistically significant difference among four offices in the proportion of female versus male managers. A Chi-square test is being considered. A principal advantage of this test compared with a t-test in this circumstance is that

A. Generally available software exists for the Chi-square test.

B. The Chi-square can both detect a relationship and measure its strength.

C. The Chi-square can be applied to nominal data.

D. The Chi-square is a parametric, and therefore stronger, test.

Answer (C) is correct. *(CIA, adapted)*
REQUIRED: The principal advantage of the Chi-square test over the t-test.
DISCUSSION: The Chi-square test is used in determining the goodness of fit between actual data and the theoretical distribution. In other words, it tests whether the sample is likely to be from the population, based on a comparison of the sample variance and the population variance. The Chi-square test is appropriately applied to nominal data. Nominal data simply distinguish one item from another, as male from female. The Chi-square statistic equals the product of the sample variance and the degrees of freedom (number in the sample − 1), divided by the population variance. This calculated value is then compared with the critical value in the Chi-square table.
Answer (A) is incorrect because software for the t-test is widely available. Answer (B) is incorrect because the Chi-square test cannot measure the strength of a relationship. Answer (D) is incorrect because the Chi-square test is nonparametric; thus, it is applied to problems in which a parameter is not calculated.

8. The internal auditor is attempting to evaluate the potential dollar effect of a control breakdown in the sales cycle. Two controls are involved. The probability that control A will fail is 10%, and the probability that control B will fail is 5%. The controls are independent such that the failure of one does not affect the failure of the other. In evaluating the potential exposure to the organization, the internal auditor determines that the cost of control A's failure is $10,000, the cost of control B's failure is $25,000, and the cost of failure of both control procedures at the same time is an additional $200,000. If the control procedures are not made more effective, the expected cost to the organization is

A. $1,000

B. $32,250

C. $2,250

D. $3,250

Answer (D) is correct. *(CIA, adapted)*
REQUIRED: The expected cost to the organization.
DISCUSSION: The expected value is the sum of the products of the possible outcomes and their respective probabilities. Moreover, the joint probability that independent events will occur simultaneously is the product of their probabilities. Accordingly, the expected cost is $3,250 {($10,000 × 10%) + ($25,000 × 5%) + [$200,000 × (10% × 5%)]}.
Answer (A) is incorrect because $1,000 is the cost of a simultaneous failure. Answer (B) is incorrect because $32,250 assumes that the joint probability is .15, not .005. Answer (C) is incorrect because $2,250 omits the cost of a simultaneous failure.

8.2 Statistics

9. An organization with 14,344 customers determines that the mean and median accounts receivable balances for the year are $15,412 and $10,382, respectively. From this information, the internal auditor can conclude that the distribution of the accounts receivable balances is continuous and

A. Negatively skewed.

B. Positively skewed.

C. Symmetrically skewed.

D. Evenly distributed between the mean and median.

Answer (B) is correct. *(CIA, adapted)*
REQUIRED: The conclusion drawn from information about the mean and median of accounts receivable.
DISCUSSION: The mean is the arithmetic average, and the median corresponds to the 50th percentile; that is, half the values are greater and half are smaller. The auditor can conclude that the distribution is positively skewed because the mean is greater than the median and the distribution is continuous.
Answer (A) is incorrect because the mean is greater than the median and the distribution is continuous, so the distribution is positively skewed. Answer (C) is incorrect because the distribution would be symmetrically skewed if the mean, median, and mode (the most frequently occurring value) were equal. Answer (D) is incorrect because distributions spread evenly between two values are uniform distributions.

10. Which of the following statements is true concerning the appropriate measure of central tendency for the frequency distribution of loss experience shown below?

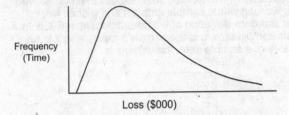

A. The mean, median, and mode are equally appropriate because the distribution is symmetrical.

B. The mode is the most appropriate measure because it considers the dollar amount of the extreme losses.

C. The median is the most appropriate measure because it is not affected by the extreme losses.

D. The mean is the best measure of central tendency because it always lies between the median and mode.

Answer (C) is correct. *(CIA, adapted)*
REQUIRED: The appropriate central tendency measure.
DISCUSSION: Measures of central tendency are the mode, the median, and the mean. The mode is the most frequently occurring value, the median is the value above and below which half of the events occur, and the mean is the average or the arithmetic mean. The median is the best estimate of the central tendency for this distribution because it is not biased by extremes. The given frequency distribution of loss is skewed by the extremely high losses. The median, which consists of absolute numbers of events, is unaffected by the magnitude of the greatest losses.
Answer (A) is incorrect because the example is an asymmetrical distribution. When the distribution is perfectly symmetrical, these three values are identical. Answer (B) is incorrect because the mode does not consider the extreme losses. It is simply the most frequently occurring value. Answer (D) is incorrect because, in this situation, the median lies between the mean and the mode. This distribution is skewed to the right because of the very high loss values. Consequently, the mean is to the right of both the mode and the median.

11. An internal auditor has taken a large sample from a population that is skewed in the sense that it contains a large number of small balances and a small number of large balances. Given this, the internal auditor can conclude

A. The sampling distribution is not normal; thus, PPS sampling based on the Poisson distribution more accurately defines the nature of the population.

B. The sampling distribution is normal; thus, the Z score value can be used in evaluating the sample results.

C. The sampling distribution is not normal; thus, attribute sampling is the only alternative statistical tool that can appropriately be used.

D. None of the answers are correct.

Answer (B) is correct. *(CIA, adapted)*
REQUIRED: The auditor's conclusion about a skewed population.
DISCUSSION: The central limit theorem states that, regardless of the distribution of the population from which random samples are taken, the shape of the sampling distribution of the means approaches the normal distribution as the sample size increases. Hence, Z values (the number of standard deviations needed to provide specified levels of confidence) can be used. Z values represent areas under the curve for the standard normal distribution.
Answer (A) is incorrect because the sampling distribution is deemed to be normal (a continuous distribution). The Poisson distribution approaches the binomial distribution (a discrete distribution) for large samples and thus is related to attribute sampling. Answer (C) is incorrect because the sampling distribution can be normally distributed if a large enough sample size is taken. Moreover, attribute sampling is not appropriate for estimating population values. Answer (D) is incorrect because the sampling distribution is normal.

12. A 90% confidence interval for the mean of a population based on the information in a sample always implies that there is a 90% chance that the

A. Estimate is equal to the true population mean.

B. True population mean is no larger than the largest endpoint of the interval.

C. Standard deviation will not be any greater than 10% of the population mean.

D. True population mean lies within the specified confidence interval.

Answer (D) is correct. *(CIA, adapted)*
REQUIRED: The meaning of a confidence interval.
DISCUSSION: The confidence level, e.g., 90%, is specified by the auditor. A confidence interval equals the sample statistic plus or minus an allowance for sampling risk. If the population is normally distributed and repeated simple random samples of size n are taken, assuming a 90% confidence level, the probability is that 90% of the confidence intervals constructed around the sample results will contain the population value.
Answer (A) is incorrect because computation of a confidence interval permits a statement of the probability that the interval contains the population value. Answer (B) is incorrect because two-sided confidence intervals are more common. The area in each tail of a two-sided, 90% interval is 5%. Answer (C) is incorrect because the confidence interval is based on the standard deviation, but it has no bearing on the size of the standard deviation.

13. The measure of variability of a statistical sample that serves as an estimate of the population variability is the

   A. Basic precision.

   B. Range.

   C. Standard deviation.

   D. Confidence interval.

Answer (C) is correct. *(CIA, adapted)*
   REQUIRED: The measure of variability of a statistical sample.
   DISCUSSION: Variability (dispersion) is measured by the variance, standard deviation, quartile deviations, range, etc., of a sample or population. The sample standard deviation (s) is used when one is working with a sample data set and wishes to estimate the standard deviation of the parent population. Given that N equals sample size, μ is the sample's mean, and x_i is an observed value of a sample item, the formula is

$$s = \sqrt{\frac{\sum_{i=1}^{N}(x_i - \mu)^2}{N - 1}}$$

   Answer (A) is incorrect because basic precision is the range around the sample value that is expected to contain the true population value. Answer (B) is incorrect because the range is the difference between the largest and smallest values in a sample. It is a crude measure of variability but is not used to estimate population variability. Answer (D) is incorrect because confidence interval is a synonym for precision.

8.3 Hypothesis Testing

Questions 14 through 20 are based on the following information. The ABC Organization has specified that the mean number of calories in a can of its diet soda is 1 or less. A consumer testing service examined nine cans with the following amounts of calories: .9, .95, 1.0, 1.05, .85, 1.0, .95, .95, and .9. The mean of these observations is .95. The sum of the squared deviations from the mean is .03. Assume the underlying population is approximately normal.

14. What is the sample standard deviation?

   A. .0577

   B. .0612

   C. .0316

   D. .00375

Answer (B) is correct. *(Publisher, adapted)*
   REQUIRED: The sample standard deviation.
   DISCUSSION: The sample mean is the sum of the observations divided by the sample size. The sample mean is typically denoted as $\bar{x}$. The following is the sample variance (s^2):

$$\sum(x_i - \bar{x})^2 \div (n - 1)$$

The sample standard deviation (s) is the square root of the variance. Thus, the sample variance is .00375 [.03 ÷ (9 – 1)], and the sample standard deviation is .0612 ($\sqrt{.00375}$).
   Answer (A) is incorrect because .0577 results from using n, not n–1, in the denominator. Answer (C) is incorrect because .0316 equals .03 divided by .95. Answer (D) is incorrect because .00375 is the variance.

15. Let μ denote the true mean calories of all diet sodas produced by ABC. What hypothesis should be tested to determine whether ABC's claim is valid?

   A. H_0: $\mu = 1$
        H_a: $\mu < 1$

   B. H_0: $\mu \leq 1$
        H_a: $\mu > 1$

   C. H_0: $\mu = 1$
        H_a: $\mu > 1$

   D. H_0: $\mu = 0$
        H_a: $\mu < 1$

Answer (B) is correct. *(Publisher, adapted)*
   REQUIRED: The hypothesis to be tested to determine whether the advertising claim is valid.
   DISCUSSION: ABC asserts that its diet soda has, on the average, 1 calorie or less. Thus, a possible null hypothesis is H_0: $\mu \leq 1$. The alternative hypothesis is that the mean is greater than 1, that is, H_a: $\mu > 1$. Because the null hypothesis cannot be rejected if the test statistic falls in the left-hand tail of the distribution, the test is one-tailed.

16. The appropriate means for testing this hypothesis is

A. A z-statistic.

B. A t-statistic.

C. An F-statistic.

D. A Q-statistic.

Answer (B) is correct. *(Publisher, adapted)*
REQUIRED: The appropriate statistic to test the hypothesis.
DISCUSSION: The t-statistic is appropriate for tests of hypotheses based on small samples. It measures how the sample mean differs from the hypothesized true mean in terms of standard deviations. The formula is

$$t = \frac{\bar{x} - \mu}{s \div \sqrt{n}}$$

If: $\bar{x}$ = sample mean
μ = hypothesized true mean
s = sample standard deviation
n = sample size

Answer (A) is incorrect because the z-statistic is appropriate when the standard deviation of the population is known or a large sample ($n > 30$) permits a reasonable approximation of the population standard deviation. Answer (C) is incorrect because the F-statistic tests differences in variances. Answer (D) is incorrect because Q-statistic is a nonsense term.

17. The value of the t-statistic is

A. −2.45

B. −.05

C. 2.45

D. 7.35

Answer (A) is correct. *(Publisher, adapted)*
REQUIRED: The value of the t-statistic.
DISCUSSION: Given that $\bar{x}$ equals .95, the hypothesized value of the true mean is 1, the sample standard deviation equals .0612, and the sample size is 9, the value of the t-statistic is

$$t = \frac{.95 - 1}{.0612 \div \sqrt{9}} = \frac{-.05}{.0612 \div 3} = \frac{-.05}{.0204} = -2.45$$

Answer (B) is incorrect because −.05 is the difference between the sample mean and the hypothesized true mean. Answer (C) is incorrect because the value is negative. Answer (D) is incorrect because the calculation requires that the denominator equals the standard deviation times the square root of the sample size.

18. The appropriate number of degrees of freedom for this t-statistic is

A. 8

B. 9

C. 0

D. 1

Answer (A) is correct. *(Publisher, adapted)*
REQUIRED: The appropriate number of degrees of freedom for the t-statistic.
DISCUSSION: The degrees of freedom associated with the test statistic equals the sample size minus the number of parameters being tested. Measurements of calorie content were made for nine cans of diet soda; i.e., nine distinct observations were included in the sample. The only parameter tested is μ, the mean calorie content of the diet sodas, so the number of degrees of freedom is 8 ($9 - 1$).
Answer (B) is incorrect because 9 is the sample size. Answer (C) is incorrect because one parameter is tested. Answer (D) is incorrect because 1 is the number of parameters being tested.

19. The following data are from a table of critical values of t:

d.f.	$t_{.10}$	$t_{.05}$	$t_{.025}$
5	1.476	2.015	2.571
6	1.440	1.943	2.447
7	1.415	1.895	2.365
8	1.397	1.860	2.306
9	1.383	1.833	2.262

The value of t defining the rejection region for testing the hypothesis that ABC's soda has 1 calorie or less per can, assuming a 95% confidence level, is

A. 2.306

B. 1.86

C. 1.833

D. 2.262

Answer (B) is correct. *(Publisher, adapted)*
REQUIRED: The value of t defining the rejection region for testing the hypothesis at a 95% confidence level.
DISCUSSION: The rejection region is determined by the value of t at the appropriate degrees of freedom and the specific level of confidence. Choosing a 95% level of confidence means that the value of t will restrict the probability of a Type 1 error (rejecting the null hypothesis when the null hypothesis is true) to 5%. The rejection region is bounded by this value. Hence, the null hypothesis will be rejected if the t-statistic calculated from the formula is equal to or greater than the t-value from a table of t-values. The t-value correlates the appropriate degrees of freedom ($n - 1$) and the appropriate probability of making a Type 1 error (.05). In this case, with 8 degrees of freedom, the appropriate rejection region is defined by a t-value of 1.86. Thus, a calculated t-statistic equal to or greater than 1.86 permits rejection of the null hypothesis H_0: $\mu \leq 1$.
Answer (A) is incorrect because 2.306 is for a confidence level of 97.5%. Answer (C) is incorrect because 1.833 is for 9 degrees of freedom. Answer (D) is incorrect because 2.262 is for 9 degrees of freedom and a confidence level of 97.5%.

20. Refer to the information on the preceding page(s). Given a critical value of t of 1.86, what conclusion can be drawn with 95% confidence?

A. The manufacturer's claim can be rejected.

B. The manufacturer's claim cannot be rejected.

C. No decision is possible based on current information.

D. All sodas have at most 1 calorie.

Answer (B) is correct.   *(Publisher, adapted)*
REQUIRED: The conclusion with 95% confidence.
DISCUSSION: Given a critical value of t of 1.86, the calculated t-statistic is −2.45.

$$t = \frac{\text{mean of sample} - \text{mean of population}}{\text{std. dev. of sample} \div \sqrt{\text{sample size}}}$$

$$t = \frac{.95 - 1}{\sqrt{.03 \div (9-1)} \div \sqrt{9}}$$

$$t = -2.45$$

Accordingly, the 5% rejection region includes, and lies to the right of, the t-value of 1.86. Because the computed value is less than (to the left of) 1.86 in this one-tailed test, the null hypothesis cannot be rejected.
    Answer (A) is incorrect because the null hypothesis cannot be rejected. Answer (C) is incorrect because the current information provides a basis for a decision. Answer (D) is incorrect because some sodas have more than 1 calorie.

21. An examination of accounts payable was made to determine if the error rate was within the stated policy of 0.5%. One hundred of the 10,000 accounts payable transactions were randomly selected using a 95% confidence level. No errors were found. With 95% certainty, one can conclude that the sample results

A. Indicate another sample is needed.

B. Prove there are no errors in accounts payable.

C. Indicate the null hypothesis is false.

D. Fail to prove the error rate is above 0.5%.

Answer (D) is correct.   *(CIA, adapted)*
REQUIRED: The sound conclusion if a sample contained no errors.
DISCUSSION: The null hypothesis is that the error rate is equal to or less than 0.5%. Given that no errors were found, no basis for disproving the null hypothesis is presented.
    Answer (A) is incorrect because the sample is adequate. Answer (B) is incorrect because even an examination of all 10,000 transactions would not necessarily prove that there are no errors in accounts payable. Answer (C) is incorrect because the null hypothesis has not been disproved.

8.4 Sampling Fundamentals

Questions 22 through 24 are based on the following information. An internal auditor has obtained the following data by selecting a random sample from an inventory population:

	Number of Items	Audited Value	Carrying Amount
Sample	200	$220,000	$ 200,000
Population	5,000		$5,200,000

22. The estimate of the population dollar value using mean-per-unit sampling is

A. $5,000,000

B. $5,420,000

C. $5,500,000

D. $5,720,000

Answer (C) is correct.   *(CIA, adapted)*
REQUIRED: The estimate of the population dollar value using mean-per-unit sampling.
DISCUSSION: MPU sampling averages the audit values of the sample items and multiplies by the number of items in the population. Hence, the MPU population value is $5,500,000 [($220,000 audited value ÷ 200 items in the sample) × 5,000 items in the population].
    Answer (A) is incorrect because $5,000,000 uses the mean of the carrying amount of the sample. Answer (B) is incorrect because $5,420,000 adds the audit value of the sample to the carrying amount of the population. Answer (D) is incorrect because $5,720,000 is based on ratio estimation.

23. The estimate of the population dollar value using difference estimation sampling is

 A. $4,700,000

 B. $5,500,000

 C. $5,680,000

 D. $5,700,000

Answer (D) is correct. *(CIA, adapted)*
 REQUIRED: The estimate of the population dollar value using difference estimation sampling.
 DISCUSSION: Difference estimation of population error entails determining the differences between the audit and carrying amounts for items in the sample, adding the differences, calculating the mean difference, and multiplying the mean by the number of items in the population. An allowance for sampling risk is also calculated. The mean difference per sample item is $100 [($220,000 audit value – $200,000 carrying amount) ÷ 200 items]. Thus, the estimated difference between the population value and the population carrying amount is $500,000 ($100 × 5,000 items), and the estimated population value is $5,700,000 ($500,000 + $5,200,000 population carrying amount).
 Answer (A) is incorrect because $4,700,000 results from subtracting the $500,000 estimated difference. Answer (B) is incorrect because $5,500,000 is based on MPU sampling. Answer (C) is incorrect because $5,680,000 results from subtracting the 200 units in the sample from the 5,000 units in the population.

24. The estimate of the population dollar value using ratio estimation is

 A. $4,727,273

 B. $5,500,000

 C. $5,700,000

 D. $5,720,000

Answer (D) is correct. *(CIA, adapted)*
 REQUIRED: The estimate of the population dollar value using ratio estimation.
 DISCUSSION: Ratio estimation is similar to difference estimation except that it estimates the population error by multiplying the carrying amount of the population by the ratio of the total audit value of the sample items to their total carrying amount. It has been demonstrated that ratio, or difference estimation, is both reliable and efficient when small errors predominate and the errors are not skewed. The ratio is 1.1 ($220,000 ÷ 200,000), so the estimated population value is $5,720,000 (1.1 × $5,200,000).
 Answer (A) is incorrect because $4,727,273 is based on the ratio of carrying amount to audit value. Answer (B) is incorrect because $5,500,000 is based on MPU sampling. Answer (C) is incorrect because $5,700,000 is based on difference estimation.

25. The size of a given sample is jointly a result of characteristics of the population of interest and decisions made by the internal auditor. Everything else being equal, sample size will

 A. Increase if the internal auditor decides to accept more risk of incorrectly concluding that controls are effective when they are in fact ineffective.

 B. Double if the internal auditor finds that the variance of the population is twice as large as was indicated in the pilot sample.

 C. Decrease if the internal auditor increases the tolerable rate of deviation.

 D. Increase as sampling risk increases.

Answer (C) is correct. *(CIA, adapted)*
 REQUIRED: The true statement about the effect on the sample size resulting from a change in a relevant variable.
 DISCUSSION: To determine the sample size for a test of controls, the internal auditor considers (1) the tolerable rate of deviations from the internal control being tested, (2) the expected actual rate of deviations, and (3) the allowable risk of assessing control risk too low (the complement of the confidence level). The tolerable rate is inversely related to sample size. If it is increased, sample size will decrease.
 Answer (A) is incorrect because an increase in allowable risk decreases sample size. Answer (B) is incorrect because doubling the variability of the population will cause the sample size to more than double. Answer (D) is incorrect because sampling risk increases as the sample size decreases.

26. In internal auditing sampling applications, Type I and Type II errors may occur. These risks

    A. Result directly from the chance that the sample obtained by the internal auditor is unrepresentative of the population.

    B. Can be decreased by using more reliable, albeit more expensive, audit procedures.

    C. Have a magnitude based only on the economic consequences of incorrect sample-based conclusions.

    D. Refer respectively to the risks that (1) internal controls will fail and (2) the resultant error will go undetected.

Answer (A) is correct. *(CIA, adapted)*
    REQUIRED: The true statement about Type I and Type II errors.
    DISCUSSION: Sampling risk arises from the possibility that the auditor's conclusions may differ from the conclusions reached if the test were applied in the same way to all items. Hence, a sample may contain proportionately more or fewer misstatements or deviations than exist in the population. Type I and Type II errors are aspects of sampling risk. A Type I or alpha error is an incorrect rejection of a value or an assessment of control risk that is too high. A Type II or beta error is an incorrect acceptance of a value or an assessment of control risk that is too low. Type II errors are the more serious.
    Answer (B) is incorrect because nonsampling risk is dependent on the quality of engagement procedures. Answer (C) is incorrect because these risks do not inherently depend on economic consequences. Answer (D) is incorrect because audit risk includes control risk and detection risk.

27. In preparing a sampling plan for an inventory pricing test, which of the following describes an advantage of statistical sampling over nonstatistical sampling?

    A. Requires nonquantitative expression of sample results.

    B. Provides a quantitative measure of sampling risk.

    C. Minimizes nonsampling risk.

    D. Reduces the level of tolerable error.

Answer (B) is correct. *(CIA, adapted)*
    REQUIRED: The statement describing an advantage of statistical sampling over nonstatistical sampling.
    DISCUSSION: Statistical and nonstatistical sampling are both used to project the characteristics of a population. However, statistical sampling permits the internal auditor to make a quantitative assessment of how closely the sample represents the population for a given level of reliability.
    Answer (A) is incorrect because statistical sampling provides quantified results. Answer (C) is incorrect because nonsampling risk exists in both statistical and nonstatistical sampling. Answer (D) is incorrect because tolerable error is related to materiality and auditor judgment.

28. An internal auditor wants to select a statistically representative sample from a population of 475 inventory control sheets. Each sheet lists the description, physical count, bar code, and unit cost for 50 inventory items. The auditor uses a random number table to construct the sample; the first two columns are listed below. 14326 is the randomly chosen starting point; the sample's first item is found on page 143, line 26. (The route used by the internal auditor is down Column A to the top of Column B.)

Column A	Column B
75233	06852
14326	42904
76562	64854
28123	04978
64227	33150
80938	04301
22539	41240
29452	69521

Where is the fifth item in the sample located?

    A. Page 809, line 38.

    B. Page 429, line 04.

    C. Page 331, line 50.

    D. Page 068, line 52.

Answer (C) is correct. *(CIA, adapted)*
    REQUIRED: The fifth usable number in a random number table.
    DISCUSSION: The fifth usable number is on page 331, line 50. The numbers 75233, 76562, 64227, 80938, 29452, 06852, 64854, and 04978 are not usable because each of the 475 sheets has 50 lines per page.
    Answer (A) is incorrect because page 809, line 38 is the fifth random number but not the fifth usable number. Answer (B) is incorrect because page 429, line 04 is the fourth usable number. Answer (D) is incorrect because page 068, line 52 is not usable since each page has only 50 lines.

29. An internal auditor is designing a stratified, mean-per-unit variables sampling plan. To which one of the following strata should the internal auditor allocate the largest proportion of the overall sample size?

	Number of Items	Expected Mean	Expected Standard Deviation	Total Dollar Value
A.	2,000	$100	$9	$200,000
B.	2,250	$200	$4	$450,000
C.	3,000	$80	$2	$240,000
D.	3,100	$150	$1	$465,000

Answer (A) is correct. *(CIA, adapted)*
REQUIRED: The stratum to be allocated the largest proportion of the overall sample size.
DISCUSSION: Sample size increases as the variability of the population increases. The objective of stratifying a sample is to reduce variation within each stratum in order to be able to use a smaller sample than would be required without stratification. Accordingly, the stratum with the largest expected standard deviation should be allocated the largest proportion of overall sample size. Allocating more selections to strata with larger standard deviations decreases the standard error of the mean (the standard deviation of the distribution of sample means), which results in a smaller confidence interval.

30. For which of the following sample results is sampling risk the smallest?

	Sample Size	Tolerable Deviation Rate	Sample Deviation Rate
A.	40	5%	2%
B.	60	5%	1%
C.	80	4%	3%
D.	100	1%	1%

Answer (B) is correct. *(CIA, adapted)*
REQUIRED: The results for which sampling risk is the smallest.
DISCUSSION: Compared with the other responses to this question, the percentage of deviations in sample B is small relative to the tolerable rate.
Answer (A) is incorrect because the sample size is smaller, the deviation rate is larger, and the tolerable rate is the same as in (B). Answer (C) is incorrect because the sample deviation rate is very large compared with the tolerable rate. Answer (D) is incorrect because the sample rate equals the tolerable rate.

31. If an internal auditor is sampling to test compliance with a particular company policy, which of the following factors should not affect the allowable level of sampling risk?

A. The experience and knowledge of the auditor.

B. The adverse consequences of noncompliance.

C. The acceptable level of risk of making an incorrect audit conclusion.

D. The cost of performing auditing procedures on sample selections.

Answer (A) is correct. *(CIA, adapted)*
REQUIRED: The factor not affecting the allowable level of sampling risk.
DISCUSSION: Sampling risk is the possibility that engagement conclusions based on a sample may differ from those reached if the test were applied to all items in the population. Engagement risk may be defined as composed of two components: sampling risk and nonsampling risk (all aspects of engagement risk not due to sampling). The allowable level of sampling risk is the acceptable risk that a conclusion based on the sample may be incorrect. That risk is a function of the circumstances of the engagement, not the auditor's experience and knowledge.
Answer (B) is incorrect because, as the adverse consequences of noncompliance increase, the allowable level of sampling risk tends to decrease. Answer (C) is incorrect because the acceptable level of sampling risk is one element of the acceptable level of risk of making an incorrect audit conclusion. The other element is nonsampling risk. Answer (D) is incorrect because the cost of performing procedures on sample selections is weighed against the benefit of minimizing the chance of making an incorrect decision.

32. A company is simulating the actions of a government agency in which 50% of the time a recall of a product is required, 40% of the time only notification of the buyer about a potential defect is required, and 10% of the time no action on its part is required. Random numbers of 1 to 100 are being used. An appropriate assignment of random numbers for the recall category would be

A. 1-40

B. 40-90

C. 61-100

D. 11-60

Answer (D) is correct. *(CMA, adapted)*
REQUIRED: The appropriate random numbers to be assigned to an alternative possibility.
DISCUSSION: Given a 50% chance of a recall, 50 different numbers should be assigned to that alternative. This answer is the only alternative with 50 numbers (11-60).
Answer (A) is incorrect because 1-40 is an appropriate assignment of random numbers for the notification category. Answer (B) is incorrect because 40-90 includes 51 numbers. Answer (C) is incorrect because 61-100 is an appropriate assignment of random numbers for the notification category.

8.5 Attribute Sampling

33. An internal auditor is planning to use attribute sampling to test the effectiveness of a specific internal control related to approvals for cash disbursements. In attribute sampling, decreasing the estimated occurrence rate from 5% to 4% while keeping all other sample size planning factors exactly the same would result in a revised sample size that would be

A. Larger.

B. Smaller.

C. Unchanged.

D. Indeterminate.

Answer (B) is correct. *(CIA, adapted)*
REQUIRED: The sample size effect of decreasing the estimated occurrence rate.
DISCUSSION: If C is the confidence coefficient, p is the expected error rate, q is 100% minus p, and P is the desired precision, the basic sample-size formula for attribute sampling is

$$\frac{C^2 pq}{P^2}$$

Accordingly, if the expected error rate (a numerator item) decreases while other factors are held constant, the sample size decreases. For example, the product of 5% and 95% (1.0 − .05) is .0475, but the product of 4% and 96% (1.0 − .04) is .0384.
Answer (A) is incorrect because increasing the expected error rate increases the sample size. Answer (C) is incorrect because changing one variable while holding all other factors constant changes the sample size. Answer (D) is incorrect because decreasing the expected error rate while holding all other factors constant decreases the sample size.

34. If all other sample size planning factors were exactly the same in attribute sampling, changing the confidence level from 95% to 90% and changing the desired precision from 2% to 5% would result in a revised sample size that would be

A. Larger.

B. Smaller.

C. Unchanged.

D. Indeterminate.

Answer (B) is correct. *(CIA, adapted)*
REQUIRED: The sample size effect of decreasing the confidence level and widening the desired precision interval.
DISCUSSION: If C is the confidence coefficient, p is the expected error rate, q is 100% minus p, and P is the desired precision, the basic sample-size formula for attribute sampling is

$$\frac{C^2 pq}{P^2}$$

Thus, if the confidence level is reduced (the numerator item C is lower) and precision is widened (the denominator item P is greater), sample size will be smaller.
Answer (A) is incorrect because increasing C and narrowing P would result in a larger sample size. Answer (C) is incorrect because decreasing C and widening P decreases the sample size. Answer (D) is incorrect because the revised sample size is determinable.

35. Which of the following must be known to evaluate the results of an attribute sample?

A. Estimated dollar value of the population.

B. Standard deviation of the sample values.

C. Actual size of the sample selected.

D. Finite population correction factor.

Answer (C) is correct. *(CIA, adapted)*
REQUIRED: The item necessary to evaluate the results of an attribute sample.
DISCUSSION: Sample size is used to evaluate the actual occurrence rate of the attribute of interest, such as a control deviation (number of a particular attribute identified ÷ actual sample size).
Answer (A) is incorrect because dollar values are irrelevant to attribute sampling. Answer (B) is incorrect because the standard deviation is an element in the variables sampling formula. Answer (D) is incorrect because the finite population correction factor is used to adjust an initial computed sample size.

36. When an internal auditor's sampling objective is to obtain a measurable assurance that a sample will contain at least one occurrence of a specific critical exception existing in a population, the sampling approach to use is

A. Random.

B. Discovery.

C. Probability proportional to size.

D. Variables.

Answer (B) is correct. *(CIA, adapted)*
REQUIRED: The sampling approach used to obtain a measurable assurance that a sample will contain at least one occurrence of a specific critical exception.
DISCUSSION: Discovery sampling is a form of attribute sampling used to identify critical deviations in a population. The occurrence rate is assumed to be at or near 0%, and the method cannot be used to evaluate results statistically if deviations are found in the sample. Hence, discovery sampling is used for tests of controls, but it is appropriate only when one deviation is critical. The sample size is calculated so that the sample will contain at least one example of a deviation if it occurs in the population at a given rate.
   Answer (A) is incorrect because random sampling is a method used to choose the sample. Answer (C) is incorrect because PPS (dollar-unit) sampling is a modified version of attribute sampling that relates deviation rates to dollar amounts. Answer (D) is incorrect because variables sampling is used to estimate the value of a population.

37. A test of 200 invoices randomly selected by the internal auditor revealed that 35 had not been approved for payment. At the 95% confidence level, what precision can be assigned?

A. 6.9%

B. 5.3%

C. 9.1%

D. 3.5%

Answer (B) is correct. *(CIA, adapted)*
REQUIRED: The achieved precision.
DISCUSSION: The following sample-size formula for an attribute sampling application can be solved for precision:

$$n = \frac{C^2 pq}{P^2}$$

C is the confidence coefficient, p is the deviation rate, q is $1 - p$, P is the specified precision, and n is the sample size.

$$P^2 = \frac{(1.96)^2 \times (35 \div 200) \times \left[1 - (35 \div 200)\right]}{200}$$

$$P^2 = .0028$$
$$P = .053 \text{ or } 5.3\%$$

Questions 38 through 41 are based on the following information.

Confidence Level	Deviation Rate	Field Size	Sample Sizes for Precision of							
			+1%	+2%	+3%	+4%	+5%	+6%	+8%	+10%
95%	10%	200					82	65		
		400			196	140	103	77		
		500			217	151	108	81		
		1,000		464	278	178	121	88	51	50
		2,000		604	322	195	129	92	53	51
99%	10%	200						91	64	
		400				193	149	117	76	52
		500				214	162	124	79	53
		1,000			399	272	193	142	85	56
		2,000		854	498	314	213	153	89	58

38. You have decided to use attribute sampling to test the effectiveness of a control over a file of 1,000 purchase orders. You expect a 10% deviation in the population and would like to select a sample sufficiently large to provide a precision of 10% with a 99% level of confidence. What sample size is needed?

A. 50

B. 56

C. 121

D. 193

Answer (B) is correct. *(CIA, adapted)*
REQUIRED: The sample size given the population, expected deviation rate, precision, and confidence level.
DISCUSSION: For a population of 1,000, an expected deviation rate of 10%, a confidence level of 99%, and a precision of 10%, the attribute sampling table specifies a minimum sample size of 56.
Answer (A) is incorrect because 50 is the minimum sample size for a confidence level of 95%. Answer (C) is incorrect because 121 is the minimum sample size for a confidence level of 95% and a precision of 5%. Answer (D) is incorrect because 193 is the minimum sample size for a population of 400 and a precision of 4%.

39. You have decided to use attribute sampling to test the effectiveness of a control over a file of 1,000 purchase orders. You expect a 10% deviation rate in the population and would like your sample results to vary by no more than 40 purchase orders. If you selected a sample size of 178, how reliable would you conclude your sample results to be?

A. 90%

B. 95%

C. 96%

D. 99%

Answer (B) is correct. *(CIA, adapted)*
REQUIRED: The reliability given the population, expected deviation rate, precision, and sample size.
DISCUSSION: For a population of 1,000, an expected deviation rate of 10%, a precision of 4% (40 ÷ 1,000), and a sample size of 178, the attribute sampling table specifies a 95% confidence level or reliability.
Answer (A) is incorrect because the table gives no values for a confidence level of 90%. Answer (C) is incorrect because the table gives no values for a confidence level of 96%. Answer (D) is incorrect because 272 is the sample size for a population of 1,000, precision of 4%, and a 10% deviation rate.

40. You used attribute sampling to test a population of 1,000 purchase orders, and the results showed a deviation rate of 9%. If your sample size was 85 and your confidence level was 99%, what was the upper occurrence limit?

A. 17%

B. 9%

C. 8%

D. 1%

Answer (A) is correct. *(CIA, adapted)*
REQUIRED: The upper occurrence limit given the population size, deviation rate, sample size, and confidence level.
DISCUSSION: For a population size of 1,000, a confidence level of 99%, and a sample size of 85, the precision is +8%. Given the deviation rate of 9%, the upper occurrence limit is 17% (8% + 9%).
Answer (B) is incorrect because 9% is the deviation rate. Answer (C) is incorrect because 8% is the precision. Answer (D) is incorrect because 1% is the difference between the precision and the deviation rate, which has no relevance.

41. You used attribute sampling to test a population of 2,000 purchase orders. Using a reliability level of 99%, an expected deviation rate of 10%, and a sample size of 195, the precision is

    A. More than 5%.

    B. More than 3 but less than 5%.

    C. More than 6 but less than 8%.

    D. Indeterminable from the data given.

Answer (A) is correct. *(CIA, adapted)*
    REQUIRED: The precision given the population size, the reliability level, the expected deviation rate, and the sample size.
    DISCUSSION: At the 99% confidence level and population size of 2,000, the attribute sampling table shows that a sample size of 195 has a precision of between 5% and 6%.
    Answer (B) is incorrect because, at the 95% confidence level and a population size of 2,000, a sample size of 195 has a precision of 4%. Answer (C) is incorrect because a sample of 195 has a precision of less than 6% for all values in the table. Answer (D) is incorrect because the precision is determinable from the data given.

8.6 Classical Variables Sampling

42. An internal auditor used a mean-per-unit sampling plan to estimate the average cost of repairing photocopy machines. The sample size was 50, and population size was 2,000. The mean of the sample was $75. The standard deviation was $14, and the standard error of the mean was $2. What is the confidence interval at a 95% confidence level (Z = 2)?

    A. $47 to $103.

    B. $71 to $79.

    C. $61 to $89.

    D. $73 to $75.

Answer (B) is correct. *(CIA, adapted)*
    REQUIRED: The confidence interval for a given confidence level.
    DISCUSSION: If C is the confidence coefficient and σ is the standard deviation, the following is the basic variables sampling formula solved for precision (P):

$$P = \frac{C\sigma}{\sqrt{n}}$$

If C is given as 2 (Z = 2), the confidence interval equals the mean plus or minus two times the standard error of the mean ($\sigma \div \sqrt{n}$ = $2). Thus, the confidence internal equals $75 ± $4, or $71 to $79.
    Answer (A) is incorrect because $47 to $103 equals two standard deviations above and below the mean. Answer (C) is incorrect because $61 to $89 equals one standard deviation above and below the mean. Answer (D) is incorrect because $73 to $75 equals one standard error below the mean.

43. Which of the following techniques could be used to estimate the standard deviation for a sampling plan?

    A. Difference estimation.

    B. Pilot sample.

    C. Regression.

    D. Discovery sampling.

Answer (B) is correct. *(CIA, adapted)*
    REQUIRED: The means used to estimate the standard deviation for a sampling plan.
    DISCUSSION: Auditors may use the standard deviation of a pilot sample to estimate the standard deviation of a population. An estimate of the population standard deviation, the desired confidence level, and the specified precision are needed to calculate the sample size for a variables sampling application.
    Answer (A) is incorrect because difference estimation is a type of variables sampling plan that calculates the mean difference between audit and recorded amounts in the sample and then multiplies by the number of items in the population. It is not a technique for estimating the standard deviation. Answer (C) is incorrect because auditors use regression (an extension of correlation analysis) to project balances of accounts or other populations. Answer (D) is incorrect because discovery sampling is a type of attribute sampling plan used for detection of critical deviations.

Questions 44 through 47 are based on the following information. Using mean-per-unit sampling to estimate the value of inventory, an internal auditor had the following results:

Projected inventory value	$3,000,000
Confidence level	95%
Confidence interval	$2,800,000 to $3,200,000
Standard error	$100,000
(Standard error = standard deviation ÷ square root of sample size)	
Z-value (approximately)	2.0
Precision	$200,000

The recorded value of inventory was $3,075,000.

44. Which of the following is a logical conclusion from the sample?

A. There is a 95% chance that the misstatement of inventory is less than $100,000.

B. There is a 5% chance that inventory is misstated by $200,000 or more.

C. Inventory is materially misstated.

D. There is a 2.5% chance that inventory is greater than $3,200,000.

Answer (D) is correct. *(CIA, adapted)*
REQUIRED: The logical conclusion from the sample.
DISCUSSION: The internal auditor has specified a 95% confidence level. Thus, the confidence interval should encompass 95% of the area under the curve for the standard normal distribution. Because the possible inventory values may be greater or less than the projected amount, the 5% of the area not included in the confidence interval is divided equally (2.5% each) between the two tails of the distribution. Hence, the probability that the true population value exceeds the upper limit of the confidence interval ($3,200,000) is 2.5%.
Answer (A) is incorrect because the probability is 95% that the confidence interval ($2,800,000 to $3,200,000) contains the true value of the population. Answer (B) is incorrect because the probability is 5% that the true value of the inventory is not contained in the confidence interval. Answer (C) is incorrect because the information given does not permit a conclusion that inventory is materially misstated.

45. Which of the following changes will result in a narrower confidence interval?

A. An increase in the confidence level from 95% to 99%.

B. A decrease in the confidence level from 95% to 90%.

C. A decrease in the allowable risk of incorrect rejection.

D. An increase in the precision.

Answer (B) is correct. *(CIA, adapted)*
REQUIRED: The change resulting in a narrower confidence interval.
DISCUSSION: Assuming the standard error is constant, the confidence interval (the mean ± precision) will narrow if the confidence level decreases from 95% to 90%. Precision equals the standard error times the z-value (the number of standard deviations from the mean of the standard normal distribution corresponding to the desired confidence level). As the desired confidence level decreases, the z-value and the confidence interval must also decrease.
Answer (A) is incorrect because increasing the confidence level increases the z-value and results in a wider confidence interval if the standard error is constant. Answer (C) is incorrect because decreasing the allowable risk of incorrect rejection (the complement of the confidence level) increases the confidence level and results in a wider confidence interval if the standard error is constant. Answer (D) is incorrect because increasing the precision makes the confidence interval wider.

46. The standard error of $100,000 reflects the

A. Projected population error based on errors in the sample.

B. Average rate of error in the sample.

C. Degree of variation in the dollar amount of sample items.

D. Error in the population that the auditor can accept.

Answer (C) is correct. *(CIA, adapted)*
REQUIRED: The meaning of the standard error.
DISCUSSION: The standard error of the mean is the standard deviation of the distribution of sample means and is calculated as population standard deviation (sigma or σ) divided by the square root of n (sample size). The standard error is used to compute precision (the confidence interval). The larger the standard error, the wider the interval.

Answer (A) is incorrect because the standard error is not a projection of error in the population. Answer (B) is incorrect because the standard error is not a measurement of the errors in the sample. Answer (D) is incorrect because the error in the population that the auditor can accept is called tolerable misstatement. It is determined based on the auditor's judgment.

47. If the internal auditor had used nonstatistical sampling instead of statistical sampling, which of the following would be true?

A. The confidence level could not be quantified.

B. The precision would be larger.

C. The projected value of inventory would be less reliable.

D. The risk of incorrect acceptance would be higher.

Answer (A) is correct. *(CIA, adapted)*
REQUIRED: The effect of using nonstatistical instead of statistical sampling.
DISCUSSION: Judgment (nonstatistical) sampling uses the auditor's subjective judgment to determine the sample size (number of items examined) and sample selection (which items to examine). This subjectivity is not always a weakness. The auditor, based on other audit work, may be able to test the most material items and to emphasize the types subject to high control risk. Probability (random) sampling (statistical sampling) provides an objective method of determining sample size and selecting the items to be examined. Unlike judgment sampling, it also provides a means of quantitatively assessing precision (how closely the sample represents the population) and reliability (confidence level, the percentage of times the sample will reflect the population).

Answer (B) is incorrect because, unless the auditor uses statistical sampling, (s)he cannot quantify precision. Answer (C) is incorrect because nonstatistical sampling does not always result in less reliable estimates. However, reliability cannot be quantified. Answer (D) is incorrect because the risk of incorrect acceptance is not quantified in nonstatistical sampling.

48. An internal auditor is performing a test to determine whether a gas and electric appliance manufacturer should move its service center from one location to another. The service center houses the service trucks that are used to drive to the customers' locations to service their appliances. The internal auditor wants to determine the reduction in average miles driven as a result of moving to the other location. Which of the following statistical sampling methods would be most appropriate for this test?

A. Attribute sampling.

B. Discovery sampling.

C. Probability-proportional-to-size (dollar-unit) sampling.

D. Mean-per-unit sampling.

Answer (D) is correct. *(CIA, adapted)*
REQUIRED: The most appropriate statistical sampling method.
DISCUSSION: Mean-per-unit sampling is the only variables sampling method designed to estimate a variable for which individual carrying amounts of items in a population are not available.

Answer (A) is incorrect because attribute sampling will not produce a quantitative value. Answer (B) is incorrect because discovery sampling is used to uncover an attribute that exists in the population with a low rate of occurrence, not to estimate a variable. Answer (C) is incorrect because individual carrying amounts adding up to a total carrying amount are required for PPS sampling to be used.

8.7 Probability-Proportional-to-Size (PPS) Sampling

49. An internal auditor is using dollar-unit sampling with a fixed interval to test an account with a balance of $750,000. The sample size is 50. The internal auditor started the selection process with a random start of 04719. Which of the following items is the third sample item selected?

	Invoice Amount	Cumulative Amount
A.	$7,985	$31,374
B.	$4,108	$35,482
C.	$12,305	$47,787
D.	$456	$48,243

Answer (B) is correct. *(CIA, adapted)*
REQUIRED: The third sample item selected.
DISCUSSION: The selection interval is $15,000 ($750,000 ÷ 50). The randomly selected start was the 4,719th dollar. Consequently, the second item must contain the 19,719th dollar, and the third item must contain the 34,719th dollar. Of the choices given, invoice amount $4,108 (cumulative amount $35,482) must be the third item selected because it includes the 31,375th through 35,482nd dollars.

50. An internal auditor applied dollar-unit sampling to select a sample of costs charged by a contractor. The sample design and results were as follows:

Contract costs charged	$10,000,000
Number of invoices in population	2,000
Tolerable misstatement	1%
Risk of incorrect acceptance	5%
Reliability factor	3.0
Sampling interval	$33,333
Sample size	300
Expected misstatement	None
Detected misstatement	None

Which of the following is true about this sample?

A. The probability of selecting any particular invoice is 15% (300 ÷ 2000).

B. There is a 1% chance that the contract invoices contain significant misstatements.

C. The sampling risk is acceptable if misstatements do not exceed $33,333.

D. The costs are not overstated more than $100,000 (1% of $10,000,000) given a 5% risk of incorrect acceptance.

Answer (D) is correct. *(CIA, adapted)*
REQUIRED: The true statement about the results of a dollar-unit sample.
DISCUSSION: No misstatements were detected in the sample. Thus, at the specified risk of incorrect acceptance, the maximum overstatement of costs charged is 1%. If misstatements had been found, the upper misstatement limit would have to be increased.

Answer (A) is incorrect because the probability of selecting any particular invoice is proportional to the dollar amount of the invoice. Answer (B) is incorrect because the chance is 5% that misstatements are more than 1% of $10,000,000. Answer (C) is incorrect because sampling risk is determined as a matter of auditor judgment. It is a measure of the reliability of the result, not of the result itself.

51. In which of the following situations will monetary-unit sampling be more effective and efficient than ratio estimation?

A. The population contains a large number of differences between the recorded amount and the actual amount.

B. The population is expected to contain few differences between the recorded amount and the actual amount.

C. The population has a high degree of variability in dollar amount.

D. The population has a low degree of variability in dollar amount.

Answer (B) is correct. *(CIA, adapted)*
REQUIRED: The situation in which monetary-unit sampling is preferable to ratio estimation.
DISCUSSION: Monetary-unit (dollar-unit) sampling is especially efficient and effective given few differences. However, variables sampling approaches (e.g., ratio estimation) tend to be more efficient (samples are smaller) as the amount of misstatement increases. Monetary-unit sampling is also inefficient when understatements and negative amounts are expected.

Answer (A) is incorrect because monetary-unit sampling is inefficient compared with classical variables sampling when many differences exist. Answer (C) is incorrect because a high degree of variability in the dollar amount of items in the population is not a basis for preferring one of these methods to another. Answer (D) is incorrect because a low degree of variability in the dollar amount of items in the population is not a basis for preferring one of these methods to the other.

52. An internal auditor is planning to use monetary-unit sampling for testing the dollar value of a large accounts receivable population. The advantages of using monetary-unit sampling (MUS) include all of the following except

A. It is an efficient model for establishing that a low error rate population is not materially misstated.

B. It does not require the normal distribution approximation required by variables sampling.

C. It can be applied to a group of accounts because the sampling units are homogenous.

D. It results in a smaller sample size than classical variables sampling for larger numbers of misstatements.

Answer (D) is correct. *(CIA, adapted)*
    REQUIRED: The item not an advantage of MUS.
    DISCUSSION: MUS is also known as probability-proportional-to-size (PPS) sampling or dollar-unit sampling. It is a modified version of attribute sampling that relates deviation rates to dollar amounts. It uses the dollar as the sampling unit. MUS is appropriate for testing account balances, such as those for inventory and receivables, in which some items may be far larger than others in the population. In effect, it stratifies the population because the larger account balances have a greater chance of being selected. MUS is most useful if few misstatements are expected. Moreover, it is designed to detect overstatements. It is not effective for estimating understatements because the greater the understatement, the less likely the item will be selected. Furthermore, as the number of expected misstatements increases, MUS requires a larger sample size than classical variables sampling.
    Answer (A) is incorrect because MUS is efficient when few misstatements are expected. Answer (B) is incorrect because MUS does not assume normally distributed populations. Answer (C) is incorrect because MUS uses dollars as sampling units.

53. When an internal auditor uses dollar-unit statistical sampling to examine the total value of invoices, each invoice

A. Has an equal probability of being selected.

B. Can be represented by no more than one dollar unit.

C. Has an unknown probability of being selected.

D. Has a probability proportional to its dollar value of being selected.

Answer (D) is correct. *(CIA, adapted)*
    REQUIRED: The effect of using dollar-unit sampling to examine invoices.
    DISCUSSION: Dollar-unit sampling results in the selection of every nth dollar; thus, a $1,000 item is 1,000 times more likely to be selected than a $1 item. The probability of selection of a sampled item is directly proportional to the size of the item.
    Answer (A) is incorrect because each dollar, but not each invoice, has an equal probability of being selected unless all invoices are for the same amount. Answer (B) is incorrect because it is possible for two or more dollars to be selected from the same item; e.g., a $4,500 item will be represented by four dollars if every 1,000th dollar is selected. Answer (C) is incorrect because the probability of selection can be calculated using the dollar value of the item and the dollar value of the population.

54. Monetary-unit sampling (MUS) is most useful when the internal auditor

A. Is testing the accounts payable balance.

B. Cannot cumulatively arrange the population items.

C. Expects to find several material misstatements in the sample.

D. Is concerned with overstatements.

Answer (D) is correct. *(CIA, adapted)*
    REQUIRED: The circumstances in which monetary-unit sampling is most useful.
    DISCUSSION: MUS is also known as probability-proportional-to-size (PPS) sampling or dollar-unit sampling. It is a modified version of attribute sampling that relates deviation rates to dollar amounts. It uses the dollar as the sampling unit. MUS sampling is appropriate for testing account balances, such as those for inventory and receivables, in which some items may be far larger than others in the population. In effect, it stratifies the population because the larger account balances have a greater chance of being selected. MUS is most useful if few misstatements are expected. Moreover, it is designed to detect overstatements. It is not effective for estimating understatements because the greater the understatement, the less likely the item will be selected. Special design considerations are required if the auditor anticipates understatements or zero or negative balances.
    Answer (A) is incorrect because an audit of accounts payable is primarily concerned with understatements.
Answer (B) is incorrect because the items in the population must be arranged by cumulative dollar total. The first dollar is chosen randomly, the second equals the random start plus the sample interval in dollars, etc. Answer (C) is incorrect because, as the expected amount of misstatement increases, the MUS sample size increases. MUS may also overstate the upper misstatement limit when misstatements are found. The result might be rejection of an acceptable balance.

Questions 55 and 56 are based on the following information.

An internal auditor has been assigned to take a dollar-unit sample of a population of vouchers in the purchasing department. The population has a total carrying amount of $300,000. The internal auditor believes that a maximum misstatement of $900 is acceptable and would like to have 95% confidence in the results. (The reliability factor at 95% and zero misstatements = 3.00.) Additional information is provided in the opposite column.

Table of First 10 Vouchers in Population		
Voucher #	Balance	Cumulative Balance
1	$100	$ 100
2	150	250
3	40	290
4	200	490
5	10	500
6	290	790
7	50	840
8	190	1,030
9	20	1,050
10	180	1,230

55. Given a random start of $50 as the first dollar amount, what is the number of the fourth voucher to be selected, assuming that the sample size will be 1,000?

A. 4

B. 6

C. 7

D. 8

Answer (D) is correct. *(CIA, adapted)*
REQUIRED: The number of the fourth voucher selected using dollar-unit sampling.
DISCUSSION: The vouchers have a carrying amount of $300,000 and 1,000 items are to be sampled, so every 300th dollar will be chosen. Given a random start of $50, the vouchers containing the 50th, 350th, 650th, and 950th dollars will be selected. The cumulative amount of the first eight vouchers is $1,030. Accordingly, voucher 8 is the fourth voucher audited. It contains the 950th dollar.
Answer (A) is incorrect because voucher 4 contains the 350th dollar and is the second voucher selected. Answer (B) is incorrect because voucher 6 contains the 650th dollar and is the third voucher selected. Answer (C) is incorrect because voucher 7 is not selected.

56. In examining the sample, one overstatement was detected causing an extension of $270 to the tolerable misstatement. Assuming that the sample size was 1,000 and that the maximum dollar amount of overstatement if no misstatements were found was established to be $900 before the sampling analysis, what conclusion should the internal auditor now draw from the sampling information?

A. The auditor is 95% confident that the dollar amount of overstatement in the population of vouchers is between $900 and $1,170.

B. The auditor is 95% confident that the dollar amount of overstatement in the population of vouchers exceeds $1,170.

C. The auditor is 95% confident that the dollar amount of overstatement in the population of vouchers is less than $1,170.

D. An insufficient number of misstatements were detected to warrant a conclusion.

Answer (C) is correct. *(CIA, adapted)*
REQUIRED: The conclusion from the audit evidence given an extension of tolerable misstatement.
DISCUSSION: Had the internal auditor detected no misstatements in the sample, the auditor could have been 95% confident that the dollar amount of overstatement in the balance was less than $900. Given discovery of an overstatement causing an extension to the tolerable misstatement of $270, the internal auditor could conclude with 95% confidence that the overstatement is less than $1,170 ($900 + $270).
Answer (A) is incorrect because the internal auditor cannot draw a conclusion involving a range with both upper and lower limits. Answer (B) is incorrect because the internal auditor is 95% confident that the overstatement is less than $1,170. Answer (D) is incorrect because a conclusion would have been warranted even if no misstatements had been found.

57. The use of probability-proportional-to-size sampling is inefficient if

A. Bank accounts are being examined.

B. Statistical inferences are to be made.

C. Each account is of equal importance.

D. The number of sampling units is large.

Answer (C) is correct. *(CIA, adapted)*
REQUIRED: The inefficient use of probability-proportional-to-size (PPS) sampling.
DISCUSSION: Probability-proportional-to-size sampling gives greater weight to larger, more significant items. If all items are of the same importance, PPS is inappropriate.
Answer (A) is incorrect because PPS sampling could be appropriate in an examination of bank accounts if larger items are more important than smaller items (which is usually true in variables sampling). Answer (B) is incorrect because PPS sampling permits statistical inferences to be made. Answer (D) is incorrect because PPS sampling could be appropriate with a large number of sampling units if larger items are more important than smaller items.

8.8 Statistical Quality Control

58. Statistical quality control often involves the use of control charts whose basic purpose is to

   A. Determine when accounting control procedures are not working.

   B. Control labor costs in production operations.

   C. Detect performance trends away from normal operations.

   D. Monitor internal control applications of information technology.

Answer (C) is correct. *(CMA, adapted)*
   REQUIRED: The purpose of statistical quality control charts.
   DISCUSSION: Statistical control charts are graphic aids for monitoring the status of any process subject to random variations. The chart consists of three horizontal lines plotted on a horizontal time scale. The vertical scale represents the appropriate quantitative measure. The center line represents the average range or overall mean for the process being controlled. The other two lines are the upper control limit and the lower control limit. The processes are measured periodically, and the values are plotted on the chart. If the value falls within the control limits, no action is taken. If the value falls outside the limits, the process is considered "out of control," and an investigation is made for possible corrective action. Another advantage of the chart is that it makes trends visible.
   Answer (A) is incorrect because quality control concerns product quality, not controls over accounting procedures. Answer (B) is incorrect because quality control concerns product quality, not costs. Answer (D) is incorrect because quality control concerns product quality, not information technology.

59. The statistical quality control department prepares a control chart showing the percentages of defective production. Simple statistical calculations provide control limits that indicate whether assignable causes of variation are explainable on chance grounds. The chart is particularly valuable in determining whether the quality of materials received from outside vendors is consistent from month to month. What is the best term for this chart?

   A. C chart.

   B. P chart.

   C. R chart.

   D. X-bar chart.

Answer (B) is correct. *(CIA, adapted)*
   REQUIRED: The statistical quality control chart described.
   DISCUSSION: A P chart is based on an attribute (acceptable/not acceptable) rather than a measure of a variable, specifically, the percentage of defects in a sample.
   Answer (A) is incorrect because a C chart is also an attribute control chart. It shows defects per item. Answer (C) is incorrect because an R chart displays the range of dispersion of a variable, such as size or weight. Answer (D) is incorrect because an X-bar chart plots the sample mean for a variable.

60. A health insurer uses a computer application to monitor physician bill amounts for various surgical procedures. This program allows the organization to better control reimbursement rates. The X-bar chart below is an example of the output from this application.

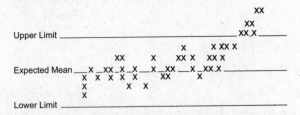

Select the interpretation that best explains the data plotted on the chart.

   A. Random variation.

   B. Abnormal variation.

   C. Normal variation.

   D. Cyclic variation.

Answer (B) is correct. *(CIA, adapted)*
   REQUIRED: The interpretation that best explains the data plotted on the chart.
   DISCUSSION: Statistical quality control charts are graphic aids for monitoring the status of any process subject to random variations. For example, an X-bar chart depicts the sample means for a variable. If the values fall within the upper and lower control limits, no action is taken. Accordingly, values outside these limits are abnormal and should be investigated for possible corrective action.
   Answer (A) is incorrect because random variations should fall within realistically determined control limits. Answer (C) is incorrect because normal variations should fall within realistically determined control limits. Answer (D) is incorrect because, in time series analysis, cyclic variation is the fluctuation in the value of a variable caused by change in the level of general business activity.

61. The most important component of quality control is

A. Ensuring goods and services conform to the design specifications.

B. Satisfying upper management.

C. Conforming with ISO-9000 specifications.

D. Determining the appropriate timing of inspections.

Answer (A) is correct. *(CIA, adapted)*
REQUIRED: The most important component of quality control.
DISCUSSION: The intent of quality control is to ensure that goods and services conform to the design specifications. Whether the focus is on feedforward, feedback, or concurrent control, the emphasis is on ensuring product or service conformity.
Answer (B) is incorrect because quality control is geared towards satisfying the customer, not upper management. Answer (C) is incorrect because ensuring the conformance with ISO-9000 specifications is a component of a compliance audit, not quality control. Answer (D) is incorrect because determining the appropriate timing of inspections is only one step towards approaching quality control. Consequently, it is not the primary component of the quality control function.

Use Gleim's *CIA Test Prep* for interactive testing with **over 2,000 additional multiple-choice questions**!

STUDY UNIT NINE
OTHER ENGAGEMENT TOOLS

(20 pages of outline)

This study unit discusses specific engagement tools not covered in the other study units in Part II. The use of engagement tools for the accumulation of engagement information (evidence) is a pervasive theme of Part II.

Core Concepts

- Flowcharting uses a system of standard symbols to create diagrams of operating processes and procedures.
- Data flow diagrams are graphic illustrations of a system's processes and data flows using four basic symbols.
- Auditors should be able to use graphical methods for planning and controlling the audit, interpret graphic depictions of data when gathering evidence, and produce graphic analyses for documentation and reporting purposes.
- Interviewing is a means of obtaining testimonial evidence from engagement clients, other members of the organization who have contact with them, and independent parties. Good interviewing requires skill in dealing with people and communicating effectively, an understanding of human relations, and the ability to maintain satisfactory relations with clients.
- One common use of formal questionnaires is obtaining an understanding of internal control.
- Systematic problem solving includes four general steps: (a) defining the problem, (b) formulating solutions, (c) choosing a solution, and (d) implementing and evaluating the solution.

9.1 PROCESS MAPPING - FLOWCHARTS

1. Flowcharting is a diagrammatic method of analyzing and understanding the processes and procedures involved in operations, whether manual or computerized.

    a. **Functions.** Flowcharting is applied in the **preliminary survey** and in obtaining an **understanding of internal control**. It is also helpful in systems development.

    b. Flowcharting is based on **standard symbols**.

        1) However, different systems of symbols have been devised. Thus, the internal auditing activity's usage should be consistent.

            a) The internal auditors also should coordinate their methods with those of the **external auditors**.

2.   Flowcharts may be horizontal or vertical.

    a.   **Horizontal flowcharts** (sometimes called **systems flowcharts**) depict areas of responsibility (departments or functions) arranged horizontally across the page in vertical columns or areas.

        1)   Accordingly, activities, controls, and document flows that are the responsibility of a given department or function are shown in the same column.

        2)   The following are typical horizontal flowcharting symbols given in Ratliff, et al., *Internal Auditing: Principles and Techniques*, 2nd edition (1996), page 123:

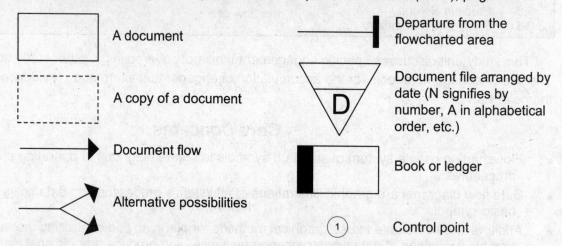

    b.   **Vertical flowcharts** present successive steps in a top-to-bottom format. Ratliff (page 124) suggests the following symbols:

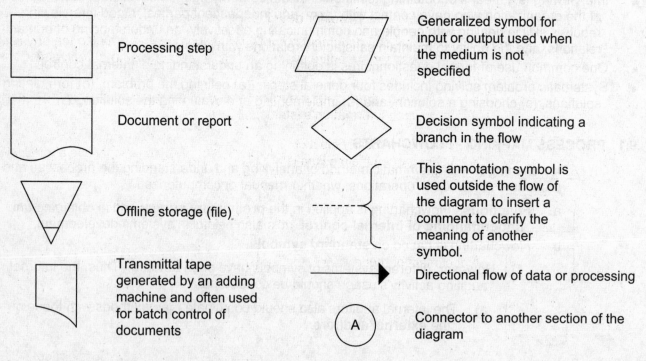

3. Sawyer, Dittenhofer, and Scheiner in *Sawyer's Internal Auditing*, 5th edition, page 210, give the following somewhat different set of flowcharting symbols:

Starting point in the flow of documents

Document

Direction in the flow of a document

Control point

Direction in the flow of information

Permanent file of documents, **A**lphabetically, **N**umerically, and by **D**ate

Temporary file of documents, **A**lphabetically, **N**umerically, and by **D**ate

Operation or action

Document destroyed

Document signed

Document initialed

Punch card

Report or computer printout

Book or ledger

Source of postings to general ledger

4. Flowcharting is still employed as a tool for **developing information systems**.

   a. A **systems flowchart** can document not only manual processes but also the physical design specifications for the entire system, including all input, output, processing steps, important files, and documents.

      1) The following are **input-output symbols** commonly found in systems flowcharts used to develop information systems:

Generalized symbol for input or output used when the medium is not specified

Punched card

A document or report

Punched paper tape

Manual input into a terminal or other online device

Display on a video terminal

Keying operation

Floppy disk

Alternative possibilities

2)   The following are common **processing symbols**:

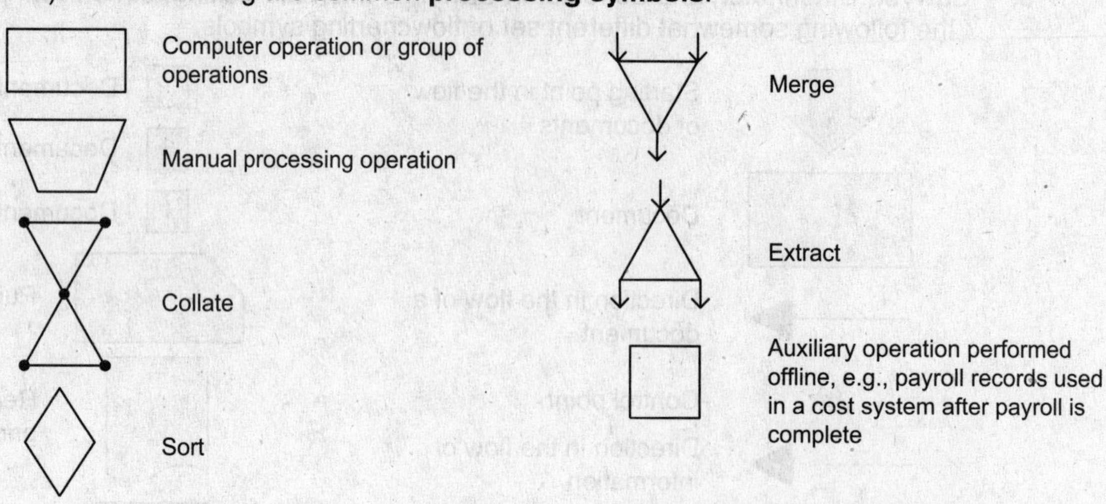

Computer operation or group of operations

Manual processing operation

Collate

Sort

Merge

Extract

Auxiliary operation performed offline, e.g., payroll records used in a cost system after payroll is complete

3)   The following are **other common symbols** used in systems flowcharts:

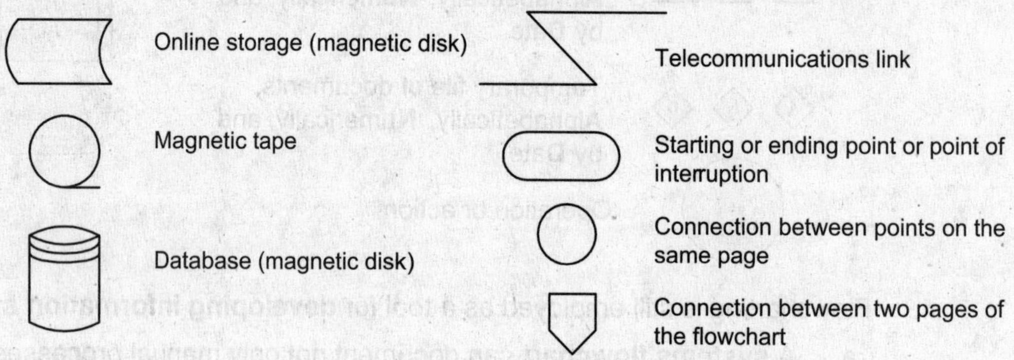

Online storage (magnetic disk)

Magnetic tape

Database (magnetic disk)

Telecommunications link

Starting or ending point or point of interruption

Connection between points on the same page

Connection between two pages of the flowchart

4) The following is an example of a system flowchart, including the document flow, for a computerized purchases-payables application:

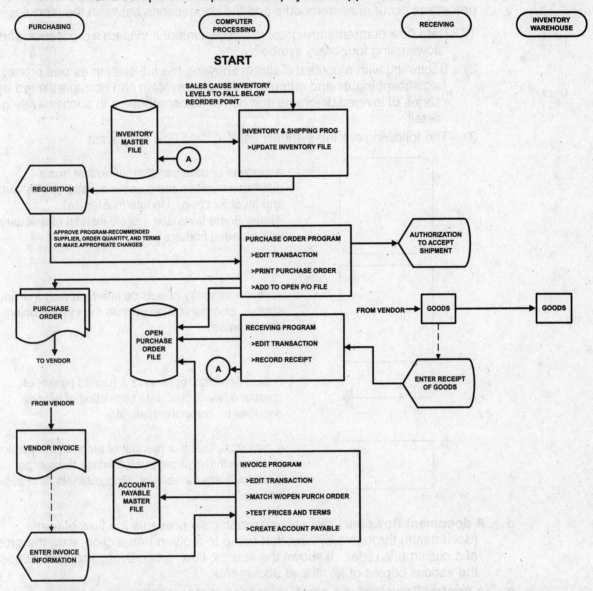

b. A **program flowchart** depicts the specific steps within a program and the order in which they will be executed. However, program flowcharting is no longer viewed as a good program design technique because other methods are more effective for **modular development**.

1) Program flowcharting symbols include some of those mentioned previously (computer operation, general input-output, terminal point, connectors, and direction arrows). They also include

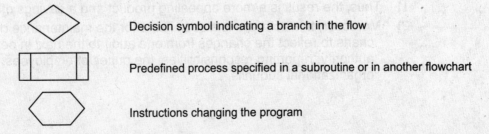

Decision symbol indicating a branch in the flow

Predefined process specified in a subroutine or in another flowchart

Instructions changing the program

c.   **Data flow diagrams** are employed in structured systems analysis, a top-down methodology that divides a system into levels of modules and specifies what processes occur in each module and the connections between the modules.

1)   Data flow diagrams are graphic illustrations of a system's processes and data flows using four basic symbols.

2)   Beginning with a context diagram showing the full system as one process with its significant inputs and outputs, a complex system can be represented by a series of leveled diagrams that depict its components in successively greater detail.

3)   The following are the symbols used in data flow diagrams:

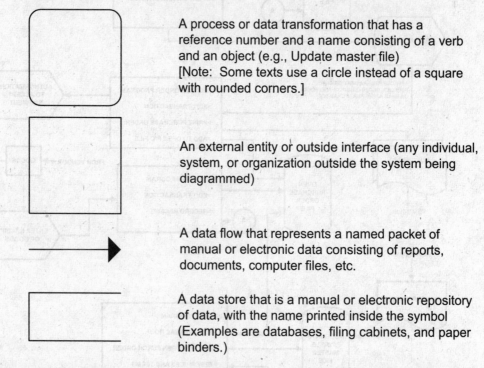

A process or data transformation that has a reference number and a name consisting of a verb and an object (e.g., Update master file) [Note: Some texts use a circle instead of a square with rounded corners.]

An external entity or outside interface (any individual, system, or organization outside the system being diagrammed)

A data flow that represents a named packet of manual or electronic data consisting of reports, documents, computer files, etc.

A data store that is a manual or electronic repository of data, with the name printed inside the symbol (Examples are databases, filing cabinets, and paper binders.)

d.   A **document flowchart** (not shown) graphically presents the flow of forms (documents) through a system that relate to a given transaction, e.g., the processing of a customer's order. It shows the source, flow, processing, and final disposition of the various copies of all related documents.

e.   A **control flowchart** is a graphical means of representing the sequencing of activities and information flows, with related control points. It provides an efficient and comprehensive method of describing relatively complex activities, especially those involving several departments.

5.   **Software** is available to improve the convenience of flowcharting.

a.   Computerized editing permits the easy addition, deletion, or movement of symbols; redrawing of lines; automatic fitting of text within symbols; etc.

1)   Thus, the result is a more appealing product and a savings of audit time.

2)   Moreover, this software is also suitable for the maintenance of organizational charts to reflect the changes from one audit to the next in personnel, lines of authority, reporting responsibilities, the duties of employees, and functions of organizational subunits.

b. Flowcharting is just one form of **graphics analysis** that may be performed by software.

   1) For example, a word-processing package should provide for the presentation of information in the form of tables, pictures, diagrams, bar charts, pie charts, etc.

      a) Another example is the generation of floor plans for analysis of work flows, location of equipment, and potential fire hazards.

6. Stop and review! You have completed the outline for this subunit. Study multiple-choice questions 1 through 24 beginning on page 457.

9.2 PROCESS MAPPING - GRAPHS

1. Auditors should be able to

   a. Use graphical methods for planning and controlling the audit,
   b. Interpret graphic depictions of data when gathering evidence, and
   c. Produce graphic analyses for documentation and reporting purposes.

2. **PERT** (Program Evaluation and Review Technique) and **CPM** (Critical Path Method) are similar techniques that use network diagrams to plan and control complex projects, such as internal audits, in which the proper sequencing of activities is crucial.

   a. A **Gantt chart** is a simpler project control device. It does not depict the interrelationships of activities and omits calculations of activity times and costs.

      1) Instead, the activities are listed on the vertical axis, dates are plotted on the horizontal axis, and the duration of each activity is depicted by a horizontal line.

      2) The following is a simple Gantt chart:

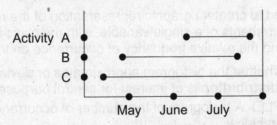

      3) A modern Gantt chart typically displays the degree of completion of each activity. For example, different colors may be used for completed and planned work.

3. Internal auditors may plot points on a **scatter diagram**, a graphical technique used in **regression analysis**. It permits the auditors to identify misstated data, relationships among variables, and unusual operating results.

   a. When the points have a systematic relationship, the **independent (x) variable** and **dependent (y) variable** are likely to be correlated. Thus, the value of one variable is a predictor of the value of the other.

   b. For example, in the scatter diagram on the left, the variables are **uncorrelated**. In the scatter diagram on the right, the variables have a strong **negative correlation**.

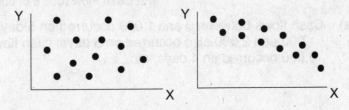

4.   Also related to regression analysis are **statistical control charts**, which are graphic aids for monitoring the status of any process subject to random variations.

    a.   The horizontal axis represents time and the vertical axis the measurement scale.

        1)   Three horizontal lines are drawn on the chart: (a) center line, such as the overall mean for an x-bar chart or the average range for an R chart; (b) upper control limit; and (c) lower control limit. As a result, a visual determination can be made as to whether the plotted points are within control limits.

5.   **Cause-and-effect diagrams** (also called fishbone diagrams or Ishikawa diagrams) provide a problem-solving technique that assists internal auditors in systematically searching for the causes of adverse conditions and therefore in developing findings and recommendations.

6.   **Bar charts** (bar graphs) are a two-dimensional (variables plotted on x and y axes) graphic means of quantitative comparison. They use bars or rectangles with lengths proportional to the measure of the data or things being compared.

    a.   Bar charts may be vertical (column charts) or horizontal.

    b.   **Pareto diagrams** are bar charts in which the frequencies of the various **types of adverse conditions** that may occur in a given process are depicted.

        1)   For example, an internal auditor might construct a Pareto diagram of the types and numbers of control deviations found in the receiving department.

            a)   The tallest (or longest) bar signifies the most common type of problem.

        2)   **Pareto analysis** is based on the 80:20 pattern. In many circumstances, a minority of people or events (roughly 20%) account for most effects (roughly 80%).

    c.   A **histogram** is a bar chart used to depict a **frequency distribution**.

        1)   It is used to create a graphic representation of the results of repeated measurements of a single variable, with the class intervals on the horizontal axis and the relative frequency of occurrence on the vertical axis.

            a)   Whether the histogram approximates or deviates from a **normal distribution** is of interest for control purposes.

        2)   EXAMPLE: A histogram of the number of occurrences of various net cash flows is given below.

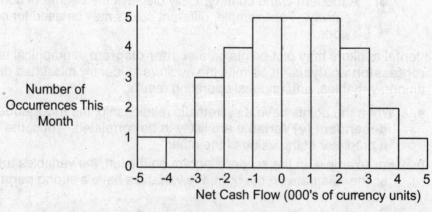

            a)   Cash flows between 0 and 1,000 occurred on 5 days; cash flows between 1,000 and 2,000 also occurred on 5 days; cash flows between 2,000 and 3,000 occurred on 4 days, etc.

7. **Time series or trend analysis** reflects past experience.

   a. These techniques use **line charts** (also called run charts) to display the frequency or amount of a variable (vertical axis) over time (horizontal axis).

      1) A **multiple-line chart** compares items, such as sales of several products over a period of years.

   b. The dependent variable (e.g., sales) is regressed on **time** (the independent variable).

   c. Changes in a variable over time may have several possible **components**.

      1) The **secular trend** is the long-term change that occurs in a series. It is represented by a straight line or curve on a graph.

      2) **Seasonal variations** are common in many businesses. Many methods include seasonal variations in a forecasting model, but most use a seasonal index.

      3) **Cyclical fluctuations** are variations in the level of activity in business periods. Although some fluctuations are beyond the control of the firm, they must be considered in forecasting. They are usually incorporated as index numbers.

      4) **Irregular or random variables** are any variations not included in the categories above. Business can be affected by random happenings (e.g., weather, strikes, fires, etc.).

8. Stop and review! You have completed the outline for this subunit. Study multiple-choice questions 25 through 30 beginning on page 465.

9.3 INTERVIEWING

1. **Interviewing** operating personnel and other individuals, identifying standards for performance evaluation, assessing operational risks, and other data-gathering activities are usually performed during the **preliminary survey** phase of an audit engagement.

2. Interviewing is a means of obtaining **testimonial evidence** from engagement clients, other members of the organization who have contact with them, and independent parties.

   a. An interview allows auditors to ask questions clarifying initial testimony. Thus, auditors may deepen their understanding of operations and seek reasons for unexpected results and unusual events and circumstances.

   b. An interview is a secure and personal form of communication compared with, for example, email or paper-based documents.

3. **Practice Advisory 1210-1: Proficiency** states, "Internal auditors should be skilled in dealing with people and in communicating effectively." Furthermore, "internal auditors should understand human relations and maintain satisfactory relationships with engagement clients."

   a. These skills are the basis of good interviewing.

4. One fundamental **human relations problem** faced by the internal auditor-interviewer is that people dislike being evaluated.

   a. Engagement clients may resent even the most constructive criticism and fear the possibly adverse consequences of an audit report.

   b. Consequently, the internal auditor must gain the confidence of clients by demonstrating self-assurance, persuasiveness, fairness, empathy, and competence.

      1) The internal auditor also may be able to gain the clients' willing **cooperation** by explaining how the engagement may be helpful and by emphasizing that all parties are members of a team pursuing the same objectives.

2) Moreover, the internal auditor must avoid the pitfall of **over-criticism**.

    a) An internal auditor who finds no major problems may be insecure about the result. (S)he may therefore resort to excessive criticism of minor matters, an approach that may alienate engagement clients and management and not be cost beneficial.

5. **Nonfinancial engagements** rely heavily on interviews because of the relative absence of standards and the greater need of the internal auditor to obtain an understanding of unfamiliar and complex operations.

6. Effective **planning** of an interview involves

    a. **Preparing** by reading operations manuals, organizational charts, prior engagement communications, results of questionnaires, etc.

        1) The internal auditor should understand not only the engagement client's functions, procedures, and terminology but also the psychological traits of auditee managers.

    b. **Formulating basic questions**

        1) An internal auditor may use a directive approach emphasizing narrowly focused questions.

        2) An alternative is a nondirective approach using broad questions that are more likely to provide clarification and to result in unexpected observations.

        3) A combination of these approaches is often recommended.

7. The following are issues related to **scheduling** the interview:

    a. Except when **surprise** is needed (e.g., in a review of cash or a fraud engagement), an appointment should be made well in advance for a specific time and place.

    b. The meeting should be in the engagement client's office, if feasible.

    c. The interview's duration should be set in advance.

    d. People tend to be less inhibited in their responses if the interview is one-to-one.

    e. Except in fraud engagements, the purpose should be explained to the client.

    f. If possible, interviews should not be scheduled very late in the day, just before or after a vacation, or just before or after a meal.

8. The following are suggestions for **opening** the interview:

    a. The internal auditor should be punctual, and prompt notice should be given if delay is unavoidable.

    b. Engaging in initial, brief pleasantries may put the engagement client at ease.

    c. The purpose of the interview should be explained.

    d. The internal auditor should be cordial, helpful, and nonthreatening.

    e. Confidentiality should be assured if feasible.

9. **Conducting** the interview is its most important element.

    a. Interviewing requires an understanding of basic **communications theory**:

        1) A **sender** transmits an idea through a message.

        2) This message is **encoded** in a writing, in a verbal statement, or in body language.

        3) The encoded message is **transmitted** through a **channel or medium** to a receiver.

            a) **Barriers** in the channel may interrupt or distort the message.

        4) The **receiver decodes** the message and interprets the message in accordance with his/her experience and knowledge.

            a) Technical jargon should be avoided so as to increase the chance that the message will be accurately decoded.

5) The receiver may then undertake **action** or respond to the message.

6) The words or actions of the receiver provide **feedback** to the sender.

   a) Feedback is vital because it tells the sender whether the message has been understood and acted upon.

7) **Nonverbal communication** (body language) consists of facial expressions, vocal intonations, posture, gestures, appearance, and physical distance. Thus, by its nature, nonverbal communication is much less precise than verbal communication but sometimes may convey more information than verbal communication. However, it is not necessarily more truthful.

   a) Nonverbal communication is heavily influenced by culture. For example, a nod of the head may have opposite meanings in different cultures.

b. The interviewer should be tactful, objective, reasonable, and interested.

   1) (S)he also must avoid an accusatory tone and avoid statements not yet supported by evidence.

   2) The interviewer should not react adversely to the hostility of the interviewee. (S)he should carefully explain the situation and provide an opportunity for the interviewee to calm down and continue the interview.

c. The interview should follow the **agenda** developed in the planning phase.

   1) Nevertheless, the agenda should not be adhered to blindly. Unexpected but worthwhile lines of inquiry may open up during the interview.

d. **Active (effective) listening** includes observing interviewee behavior (body language, such as eye contact), reserving judgment about what is said, asking clarifying questions, and allowing for periods of silence. An effective listener also enhances the communication process by sending appropriate nonverbal signals to the speaker. Thus, even though a person can probably listen and do some routine work, a listener who wishes to convey a positive and encouraging message should stop other activities and focus complete attention on the speaker.

   1) **Reflecting** what is said, that is, summarizing or rephrasing an answer, is a means of stimulating additional comments.

   2) Furthermore, the interviewee should be encouraged to ask relevant questions.

      a) These questions should be heard respectfully and duly included in the record of the interview.

   3) **Empathy** is a sensitive awareness of the speaker's feelings, thoughts, and experience. An empathic listener understands what the speaker wants to communicate rather than what the listener wants to understand.

   4) **Listening with intensity** involves concentrating on the speaker's message and disregarding distractions.

   5) **Attentiveness** is promoted by use of active listening techniques. For example, changing the wording of the questions and the sequence in which they are asked may eliminate some of the tedium associated with a series of interviews. The interviewer also may be able to refine the technique during the process.

e. **Anticipation** is one approach the interviewer can use to maintain focus during a far-ranging discussion. It assumes that the interviewer has done some preparation and is ready to listen intelligently. Active listening permits anticipation because the mind can process information more rapidly than most people speak. Thus, the listener has time to analyze the information and determine what is most important.

f. **Leading questions** (questions suggesting the answer) should be avoided.

g. Loaded questions (questions with self-incriminating answers) also should be avoided.

h. Questions requiring an **explanatory response** are usually preferable to those of the yes/no variety.

    i.   An interviewer should be suspicious of answers that (1) are too smoothly stated, (2) fit too neatly with the interviewer's own preconceptions, (3) consist of generalizations, or (4) contain unfamiliar technical terminology.

         1)   Thus, the interviewer must ask for greater specificity or other clarifications.

    j.   Care should be taken to differentiate statements of **fact** from statements of **opinion**.

    k.   The interviewer should understand what the interviewee regards as **material**.

    l.   Debate and disagreement with the interviewee should be avoided.

10. The interview should be **recorded**.

    a.   Good **note taking** during the interview is essential.

         1)   Notes should be sufficiently readable and thorough to permit a full reconstruction of the information gathered. This write-up step should occur as soon as possible after the interview.

         2)   The interviewee should be informed about the need for note taking.

         3)   Notes should be properly dated and labeled, and the names and positions of interviewees should be included.

         4)   The amount of time spent not looking at the interviewee should be minimized, and questions should not be asked while jotting notes.

    b.   The notes and the **memorandum** prepared with their help are part of the **working papers** and therefore the documentation of the engagement used to prepare communications.

         1)   The memorandum should include significant events during the interview, such as interruptions or emotional outbursts.

         2)   The internal auditor must be careful to use information in its proper context.

11. The interview should be **evaluated**.

    a.   This step is especially important if a follow-up interview is contemplated, but it is useful as a means of internal auditor self-improvement.

    b.   The internal auditor should consider whether objectives were appropriate, whether they were attained, and, if not, why not.

    c.   The internal auditor also should consider whether the planning was efficient, the interviewee was cooperative, and the interviewer made errors.

12. Interviews tend to be of four types:

    a.   A **preliminary interview** is to (1) promote the value of internal auditing, (2) understand the interviewee, (3) gather general information, and (4) serve as a basis for planning future interview strategies.

    b.   A **fact-gathering interview** is oriented to the specific details that can be provided by a particular interviewee.

         1)   Elaboration can be sought in a nondirective manner.

    c.   A **follow-up interview** is intended to answer questions raised during the analysis of the fact-gathering interview. It also tests the interviewee's acceptance of new ideas generated by the auditor.

    d.   An **exit interview** helps to ensure the accuracy of conclusions, findings, and recommendations in the final engagement communication by discussing it with the interviewee.

13. Stop and review! You have completed the outline for this subunit. Study multiple-choice questions 31 through 37 beginning on page 467.

9.4 OTHER DATA-GATHERING TECHNIQUES

1. **Questionnaires** are an efficient way of preparing for an interview.

   a. Formal questionnaires may be sent to the client prior to the auditor's visit.

   b. A **formal questionnaire**, properly prepared and transmitted in advance,

      1) Involves the engagement client's **supervisors and employees** in the engagement and thereby minimizes their apprehension

      2) Provides an opportunity for engagement client **self-evaluation**

      3) May result in a more economical engagement because the information it generates is prepared by those most familiar with it

         a) The internal auditor must still ask clarifying questions and verify responses. However, only those answers that appear inappropriate should be pursued by asking for clarification or explanation. In this way, problems may be isolated and either compensating controls identified or extensions to the engagement procedures planned.

   c. One use is to obtain an **understanding of the client's controls**. But auditors need not fill out standard control questionnaires. The information they document may be found in other working papers, such as flowcharts, checklists, and narratives.

      1) An internal control questionnaire is often very structured and detailed and is drafted in a yes/no or short answer format.

      2) Filling out the questionnaire during an interview with the person who has responsibility for the area that is being reviewed, constructing the questionnaire so that a "no response" requires attention, and supplementing the completed questionnaire with a narrative description or flowchart are appropriate uses of an internal control questionnaire.

      3) **Disadvantages** of these questionnaires are that

         a) They are difficult to prepare.

         b) They are time-consuming to administer.

         c) Engagement clients may be able to anticipate the preferred responses and therefore may not be truthful or give sufficient consideration to the task.

         d) All circumstances cannot be addressed.

         e) They are less effective than interviewing.

   d. The **sequence and format** of questions have many known effects. For example, questions should be in a logical order, and personal questions should be asked last because of the emotions they may evoke. One method for reducing these effects is to use the questionnaire variations that cause these biases to average out across the sample.

      1) Many types of questions may be used, e.g., multiple-choice, checklists, fill-in-the-blank, essay, or options indicating degrees of agreement or disagreement.

      2) Questions must be reliably worded so that they measure what was intended to be measured.

      3) The questionnaire should be short to increase the response rate.

   e. The best approach for obtaining feedback from engagement clients on the **quality of internal audit work** is to provide a questionnaire to the client at the beginning of an engagement, either routinely or periodically, to complete after the engagement. The quality measures being used by the internal audit activity and the internal auditor are then clearly understood by the client, and specific requirements and expectations can be noted by the internal auditor before the engagement begins. The client can then assess the quality of the internal audit work during the engagement and complete the questionnaire after the engagement. This procedure also encourages a continuous process of monitoring quality and feedback by the client throughout the engagement.

2. **Checklists** increase the uniformity of data acquisition. They ensure that a standard approach is taken and minimize the possibility of omitting consideration of factors that can be anticipated.

    a. Disadvantages of checklists include

        1) Providing a false sense of security that all relevant factors are addressed

        2) Inappropriately implying equal weight to each item on the checklist

        3) The difficulty of translating the observation represented by each item on the checklist

        4) Treating a checklist as a rote exercise rather than part of a thoughtful understanding of the unique aspects of the audit

    b. Checklists may be used to control administrative details involved in executing the engagement, to prepare for opening and closing conferences, etc.

3. **Other data sources.** Data can be gathered in many different ways, including

    a. Online sources such as Lexis-Nexis or the National Automated Accounting Research System (NAARS).

    b. Authoritative and technical literature relevant to the issue being researched.

    c. **Surveys.**

        1) **Mail questionnaires** are relatively low in cost, eliminate interviewer bias, and gather large amounts of data. However, they tend to be inflexible, to have a slow response time, and to be prone to nonresponse bias.

            a) The sample will not be truly random if respondents as a group differ from nonrespondents. Thus, people may choose not to respond for reasons related to the purpose of the questionnaire.

        2) **Telephone interviews** are a flexible means of obtaining data rapidly and controlling the sample. However, they introduce interviewer bias, are more costly, and gather less data than mail surveys.

    d. **Observation.** By watching the physical activities of the employees in the organization to see how they perform their duties, the internal auditor can determine whether written policies have been put into practice. Moreover, observing a phenomenon in its natural setting eliminates some aspects of experimental bias.

        1) Observation is limited because employees who know they are being observed may behave differently while being observed. Accordingly, unobtrusive measures may be indicated. The possibility of observing unexpected or unusual behavior makes such measures useful for exploratory investigations.

        2) Moreover, observation is more persuasive for the **existence or occurrence** assertion (whether assets or liabilities exist and whether transactions have occurred) than for the **completeness** assertion (whether all transactions that should be reported are reported).

        3) Lack of experimental control and measurement precision are other weaknesses of observational research. Another is that some things, such as private behavior, attitudes, feelings, and motives, cannot be observed.

    e. **Rating scale. Rating scales** are used to allow people to rate things such as service. The scale represents a continuum of responses.

        1) EXAMPLE: Rate the service you received on a scale of 1 to 10, 10 being the best. Circle the appropriate number.

            1 2 3 4 5 6 7 8 9 10

4. Stop and review! You have completed the outline for this subunit. Study multiple-choice questions 38 through 48 beginning on page 470.

9.5 PROBLEM SOLVING

1.   Problem solving in the organizational setting necessitates systematic approaches because of the importance, difficulty, and unfamiliarity of the situations encountered.

a.   Problem solving has been defined as "the conscious process of bringing the actual situation closer to the desired situation" [Kreitner, *Management*, 9th ed. (2004), p. 268].

2.   The **problem-solving process** includes four general steps:

a.   Defining the problem
b.   Formulating solutions
c.   Choosing a solution
d.   Implementing the solution, measuring results, and evaluating the solution

3.   The most common difficulty in problem solving is **defining the problem**.

a.   A problem solver must first ask the right questions before the right answers (solutions) can be determined. Thus, the problem must be thoroughly understood.

b.   Consistent with the definition above, problem definition has three phases:

1)   Determining the actual situation
2)   Visualizing the desired situation
3)   Isolating the cause of the **variance** of the actual from the desired situation

c.   Difficulties in defining a problem include

1)   Defining the problem in terms of a **given solution**

a)   This process tends to eliminate consideration of alternatives that may have greater merit. For example, if a company is plagued by poor customer service, a manager who defines the issue as a problem with employee motivation may distract attention from the true cause, such as inadequate training, confusing policies, or poor technological support.

2)   Addressing relatively **insignificant matters** at the expense of high-priority items

a)   An organization-wide effort to establish goal congruence helps managers to focus on material matters. Thus, formal organizational objectives and goals should be established and promulgated.

3)   Considering **symptoms** instead of causes

a)   A cause is a factor the presence or absence of which is responsible for the gap between the actual and desired situations. Hence, removing or introducing that factor closes the gap.

b)   However, treating the symptom does not eliminate the gap. For example, higher pay for a discontented employee may not close the gap if the reason for his/her low morale is a need for flexible hours.

4)   **Bounded rationality**, or the inability to see all aspects of the situation (tunnel vision)

a)   Imperfect perception may preclude seeing that a problem exists.

i)   People tend to see what they expect to see.
ii)   People tend to see what they are trained to see.
iii) Personal needs influence what is observed.
iv)   Group pressure may influence what problems are perceived or how they are defined.

d.   A **fishbone diagram** (also called a cause-and-effect diagram or an Ishikawa diagram) is a total quality management process improvement technique used to study **causation** (why the actual and desired situations differ). It organizes the analysis of causation and helps to identify possible interactions among causes.

1)   The head of the skeleton represents the statement of the problem.

2)   The principal classifications of causes are represented by lines (bones) drawn diagonally from the heavy horizontal line (the spine).

3)   Smaller horizontal lines are added in their order of probability in each classification.

4)   Example:

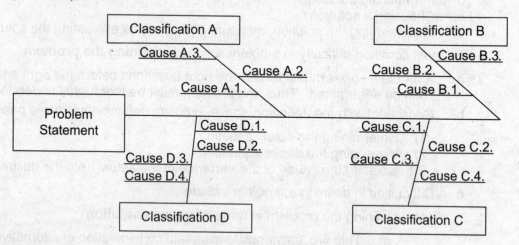

4.   **Formulating solutions** in terms of acceptable levels of risk requires a risk analysis. It is also the step in problem solving that requires the most creativity.

a.   One pitfall during this phase of the problem-solving process is the tendency to limit consideration to one solution.

1)   This mistake occurs because of reluctance to devote the time, mental energy, and other resources needed to make a comprehensive search.

b.   This search for solutions may be a **primary or direct process**.

1)   For example, it may involve surveys, samples, or questionnaires.

c.   The search for solutions may be a **secondary or indirect process**.

1)   For example, it may involve hiring a consultant or reading research studies.

d.   Many techniques have been developed to promote creativity by individuals and groups engaged in problem solving. The following are some of these methods:

1)   **Brainstorming** is an unstructured approach that relies on the spontaneous contribution of ideas from all members of a group. Criticism is not permitted, and all ideas are recorded for later evaluation.

a)   This technique reduces broad problems to their essentials.

b)   Software ("groupware") has been developed to permit brainstorming on a computer network.

2)   **Synectics** is a highly structured group approach to problem statement and solution based on creative thinking. It involves free use of analogies and metaphors in informal exchanges within a carefully selected small group of individuals of diverse personality and areas of specialization.

3) The **Delphi technique** is an approach in which the manager solicits opinions on a problem from experts, summarizes the opinions, and feeds the summaries back to the experts (without revealing any of the participants to each other). The process is reiterated until the opinions converge on an optimal solution.

4) **Value analysis** is a methodical approach primarily designed to optimize performance of an activity at a minimum cost. Emphasis is on the cost-benefit criterion.

5) **Free association** is an approach to idea generation that reports the first thought to come to mind in response to a given stimulus, for example, a symbol or analogy pertaining to a product for which an advertising slogan is sought. The objective is to express the content of consciousness without censorship or control.

6) **Forced relationship** is a structured adaptation of free association. The elements of a problem are analyzed and the associations among them are identified so as to detect patterns that may suggest new ideas.

7) **Blast! then refine** is a U.S. Navy problem-solving methodology. It completely disregards (blasts out of one's consciousness) any existing approach. An entirely new problem solution is then sought that will attain the original objectives.

8) The **Edisonian approach** is a trial-and-error experimental method inspired by famous inventor Thomas Edison. It should usually not be applied unless other approaches have been unsuccessful.

9) **Morphological matrix analysis** is a structured technique that plots decision variables along the axes of a matrix. The relationships of these variables are found in the squares within the chart.

10) **Attribute listing** is applied primarily to improve a tangible object. It lists the parts and essential features of the object and systematically analyzes modifications intended as improvements.

11) The **scientific method** is a rigorous method for finding optimal solutions using classical concepts such as statistics, simulation, logical thinking, and other scientific and mathematical techniques to develop and test hypotheses.

12) **Creative leap** is a process that formulates an ideal solution and then works back to a feasible one.

e. Research suggests the prevalence of two **styles of information processing** for problem solving.

1) The **thinking** or analytic style is objective, deductive, precise, detailed, logical, and repetitive. It is appropriate for dividing a problem into its components and addressing them in sequence.

   a) It tends to prevail in the traditional, pyramidal organization.

   b) This thinking style is most useful for detailed, routine tasks and systematic implementation of plans.

2) The **intuitive** style is subjective, inductive, nonroutine, and unstructured. Intuitive people may rely on hunches and reach decisions without explicitly applying a formal process.

   a) Intuitives may flourish in nontraditional organizations. In these settings, their capacity for viewing the whole of a problem and then arriving at creative solutions through intuition may be more appreciated than in a culture dominated by the thinking style.

3) These information-processing styles are the extremes of a continuum. Many people combine these approaches to varying degrees.

4) The thinking and intuitive styles are complementary. Because organizations need both types of skills, they should encourage both thinkers and intuitives and provide appropriate assignments for them.

f. **The limiting factor principle** states that the crucial factor in problem solving is the one that limits or prevents achievement of the desired goal. The mass of alternative solutions can be reduced if managers can identify the limiting factors.

1) EXAMPLE: If an organization directs a division to turn a loss into a profit, the immediate means might be purchasing new equipment, and a limiting factor might be lack of cash or good credit.

a) Seeking alternative sources for the equipment may reveal someone willing to swap, to take a lien, etc.

b) Alternatives calling for purchases can be discarded.

g. Modern management theorists stress an **open-systems approach**.

1) The organization is viewed as a subsystem of a larger social, political, legal, and economic context.

2) The open-systems view also emphasizes the innumerable interactions of the organization with its environment.

3) One implication of the complex and dynamic open-systems model for problem solving is that searching out all possible solutions is likely to be impossible.

a) A second implication is that every member of the organization needs to develop skills for detecting and creatively solving problems.

5. **Choosing a solution** rarely means adopting the best solution in an absolute sense.

a. The existence of resource constraints, political factors, and other intangibles results in the choice of a solution that is best only in a relative sense.

b. The solution should have the best available balance of **effectiveness** (the degree to which objectives are achieved) and **efficiency** (the ratio of resources consumed to results obtained, that is, input to output).

c. According to Russell Ackoff, the solution chosen may resolve, solve, or dissolve the problem.

1) Resolving a problem is **satisficing**, the selection of an adequate solution rather than the best solution possible, at least in relative terms.

a) Satisficing (satisfying and sufficing) is often justified on grounds of expedience, but it is criticized as antithetical to **continuous improvement**.

2) Solving a problem results from an **optimizing** approach.

a) Optimizing means searching systematically and creatively for the best available solution.

3) **Dissolving** a problem means changing the context so that it cannot occur.

a) The principle is that what cannot go wrong will not go wrong.

i) For example, automating a production process dissolves employee relations problems.

6. **Implementing and evaluating the solution** requires that sufficient time elapse to provide evidence of its success.

    a. The solution should close **the gap between the actual and the desired**.

    b. If the problem still exists, the options are to

        1) Try other solutions
        2) Redefine the problem and the solutions

    c. **Human aspects of the solution** must be considered. A solution is useful only if it can be sold to those responsible for its implementation.

        1) An otherwise optimal solution may fail if the opinion and attitudes of the people involved are not considered in the problem-solving process.

        2) The process must be followed when making **organizational changes**.

            a) Implementing change is a critical part of the problem-solving process because employees can prevent effective change.

    d. The **effects of the action taken** should be followed up. The solution must be implemented with the proper delegation of authority to the individuals responsible. Performance measurement must also be undertaken.

        1) This process puts the solution into a workable framework, which assures it will be carried out.

        2) The failure to provide for practical implementation is the reason many otherwise effective solutions fail to produce the desired results.

        3) Solutions are not fully implemented until they are effectively communicated.

7. **Role of Information in Problem Solving**

    a. The **costs and benefits** involved in obtaining information must be understood.

        1) The better the information, the more it costs.
        2) The optimal value of information should be determined.

    b. Information is never 100% perfect.

    c. The **quality** of the information should be evaluated.

        1) The problem-solving process is dependent on the **quality of information**.

        2) Relatively little information may suffice to generate adequate solutions. Information may cost more than it is worth.

8. Stop and review! You have completed the outline for this subunit. Study multiple-choice questions 49 through 57 beginning on page 474.

9.6 STUDY UNIT 9 SUMMARY

1.   Horizontal flowcharts (sometimes called systems flowcharts) depict areas of responsibility (departments or functions) arranged horizontally across the page in vertical columns or areas. A systems flowchart can document not only manual processes but also the physical design specifications for the entire system, including all input, output, processing steps, and important files. Vertical flowcharts present successive steps in a top-to-bottom format.

2.   Data flow diagrams are employed in structured systems analysis, a top-down methodology that divides a system into levels of modules and specifies what processes occur in each module and the connections between the modules.

3.   Internal auditors use PERT, CPM, and Gantt charts to plan and control the audit.

4.   Internal auditors may use many graphical methods for interpreting and evaluating data, for example, (a) scatter diagrams, (b) statistical control charts, (c) cause-and-effect diagrams, (d) bar charts, (e) Pareto analysis, (f) histograms, and (g) time series (trend) analysis.

5.   Interviewing is a means of obtaining testimonial evidence. An interview allows auditors to ask questions clarifying initial testimony. Thus, auditors may deepen their understanding of operations and seek reasons for unexpected results and unusual events and circumstances.

   a.   Interviews should be effectively planned. This process involves gaining an understanding of the client's operations, etc., and formulating basic questions.

   b.   Conducting the interview is its most important element. The interviewer should understand communications theory, follow the planned agenda, and be an effective listener. Moreover, the interview should be recorded and evaluated.

6.   Other data-gathering techniques include (a) formal and informal questionnaires, (b) checklists, (c) surveys, (d) observation, and (e) rating scales.

7.   Problem solving has been defined as "the conscious process of bringing the actual situation closer to the desired situation" [Kreitner, Management, 9th ed. (2004), p. 268]. Problem definition involves determining the actual situation, visualizing the desired situation, and isolating the cause of the variance. Problem solvers should avoid (a) defining the problem in terms of a given solution, (b) addressing insignificant matters, (c) considering symptoms instead of causes, and (d) failing to see all aspects of the problem.

   a.   Formulating solutions is the step requiring the most creativity, which may be aided by the use of various techniques. A key to identifying solutions is to determine the factors that limit achievement of the desired objective.

   b.   The chosen solution is often best only in a relative sense because of constraints that prevent optimization. The solution should have the best available balance of effectiveness and efficiency.

   c.   Implementing and evaluating the solution requires that sufficient time elapse to provide evidence of its success.

QUESTIONS

9.1 Process Mapping - Flowcharts

1. Which method of evaluating internal controls during the preliminary survey provides the internal auditor with the best visual grasp of a system and a means for analyzing complex operations?

- A. A flowcharting approach.
- B. A questionnaire approach.
- C. A matrix approach.
- D. A detailed narrative approach.

Answer (A) is correct. *(CIA, adapted)*
REQUIRED: The method of evaluating internal controls during the preliminary survey that provides the best visual grasp of a system and a means for analyzing complex operations.
DISCUSSION: Flowcharts are graphical representations of the step-by-step progression of transactions, including document (information) preparation, authorization, flow, storage, etc. Flowcharting allows the internal auditor to analyze a system and to identify the strengths and weaknesses of the purported internal controls and the appropriate areas of audit emphasis.
Answer (B) is incorrect because a questionnaire approach provides only an agenda for evaluation. Answer (C) is incorrect because a matrix approach does not provide the visual grasp of the system that a flowchart does. Answer (D) is incorrect because a detailed narrative does not provide the means of evaluating complex operations that a flowchart does.

2. An internal auditor reviews and adapts a systems flowchart to understand the flow of information in the processing of cash receipts. Which of the following statements is true regarding the use of such flowcharts? The flowcharts

- A. Show specific control procedures used, such as edit tests that are implemented and batch control reconciliations.
- B. Are a good guide to potential segregation of duties.
- C. Are generally kept up to date for systems changes.
- D. Show only computer processing, not manual processing.

Answer (B) is correct. *(CIA, adapted)*
REQUIRED: The use of a systems flowchart.
DISCUSSION: Systems flowcharts are overall graphic analyses of the flow of data and the processing steps in an information system. Accordingly, they can be used to show segregation of duties and the transfer of data between different segments in the organization.
Answer (A) is incorrect because a program flowchart will identify the specific edit tests implemented. Answer (C) is incorrect because the flowcharts are usually not kept up to date for changes. Thus, the auditor will have to interview key personnel to determine changes in processing since the flowchart was developed. Answer (D) is incorrect because a systems flowchart should show both manual and computer processing.

3. The internal auditor wishes to develop a flowchart of (1) the process of receiving sales order information at headquarters, (2) the transmission of the data to the plants to generate the shipment, and (3) the plants' processing of the information for shipment. The internal auditor should

- A. Start with management's decisions to set sales prices. Gather internal documentation on the approval process for changing sales prices. Complement documentation with a copy of the program flowchart. Prepare an overview flowchart that links these details.
- B. Start with a shipment of goods and trace the transaction back through the origination of the sales order as received from the sales representative.
- C. Start with the receipt of a sales order from a sales representative and "walk through" both the manual and computerized processing at headquarters and the plant until the goods are shipped and billed.
- D. Obtain a copy of the plants' systems flowchart for the sales process, interview relevant personnel to determine if any changes have been made, and then develop an overview flowchart which will highlight the basic process.

Answer (C) is correct. *(CIA, adapted)*
REQUIRED: The appropriate flowcharting procedure.
DISCUSSION: The survey during the engagement planning phase helps the internal auditor to become familiar with activities, risks, and controls and to identify areas for audit emphasis. Flowcharting is a typical survey procedure, and the walk-through is a means of gathering information to be reflected in the flowchart.
Answer (A) is incorrect because the issue is the processing of sales orders, not the system for making changes in the sales price data. Answer (B) is incorrect because starting with the completed transaction does not identify processing steps in which documents or data were diverted and processed separately. Answer (D) is incorrect because processing steps that occur other than at the plant level must also be considered.

4. Graphical notations that show the flow and transformation of data within a system or business area are called

    A. Action diagrams.

    B. Program structure charts.

    C. Conceptual data models.

    D. Data flow diagrams.

Answer (D) is correct. *(CIA, adapted)*
    REQUIRED: The graphical notations that show the flow and transformation of data within a system or business area.
    DISCUSSION: Data flow diagrams show how data flow to, from, and within the system and the processes that manipulate the data. A data flow diagram can be used to depict lower-level details as well as higher-level processes. A system can be divided into subsystems, and each subsystem can be further subdivided at levels of increasing detail. Thus, any process can be expanded as many times as necessary to show the required level of detail.
    Answer (A) is incorrect because action diagrams are process logic notations that combine graphics and text to support the definition of technical rules. Answer (B) is incorrect because program structure charts are graphical depictions of the hierarchy of modules or instructions in a program. Answer (C) is incorrect because conceptual data modules are independent definitions of the data requirements that are explained in terms of entities and relationships.

5. The diamond-shaped symbol is commonly used in flowcharting to show or represent a

    A. Process or a single step in a procedure or program.

    B. Terminal output display.

    C. Decision point, conditional testing, or branching.

    D. Predefined process.

Answer (C) is correct. *(CIA, adapted)*
    REQUIRED: The meaning of the diamond-shaped symbol used in flowcharting.
    DISCUSSION: Flowcharts illustrate in pictorial fashion the flow of data, documents, and/or operations in a system. Flowcharts may summarize a system or present great detail, e.g., as found in program flowcharts. According to the American National Standards Institute, the diamond-shaped symbol represents a decision point or test of a condition in a program flowchart, that is, the point at which a determination must be made as to which logic path (branch) to follow. The diamond is also sometimes used in systems flowcharts.
    Answer (A) is incorrect because the rectangle is the appropriate symbol for a process or a single step in a procedure or program. Answer (B) is incorrect because a terminal display is signified by a symbol similar to the shape of a cathode ray tube. Answer (D) is incorrect because a predefined processing step is represented by a rectangle with double lines on either side.

6. Which one of the following best reflects the basic elements of a data flow diagram?

    A. Data sources, data flows, computer configurations, flowchart, and data storage.

    B. Data source, data destination, data flows, transformation processes, and data storage.

    C. Data flows, data storage, and program flowchart.

    D. Data flows, program flowchart, and data destination.

Answer (B) is correct. *(CMA, adapted)*
    REQUIRED: The best description of the basic elements of a data flow diagram.
    DISCUSSION: Structured analysis is a graphical method of defining the inputs, processes, and outputs of a system and dividing it into subsystems. It is a top-down approach that specifies the interfaces between modules and the transformations occurring within each. Data flow diagrams are used in structured analysis. The basic elements of a data flow diagram include data source, data destination, data flows, transformation processes, and data storage.
    Answer (A) is incorrect because computer configuration is not an element of a data flow diagram. Answer (C) is incorrect because a program flowchart is not an element of a data flow diagram, and data source, data destination, and transformation processes are elements. Answer (D) is incorrect because a program flow chart is not an element of a data flow diagram, and data source, data storage, and transformation processes are elements.

Questions 7 and 8 are based on the following information.

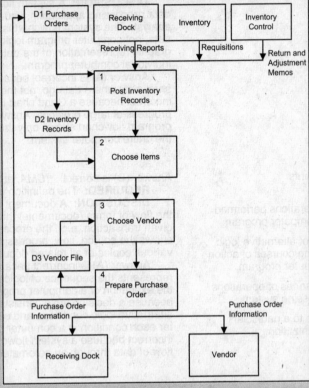

---

7. This figure shows how

A. Physical media are used in the system.

B. Input/output procedures are conducted.

C. Data flow within and out of the system.

D. Accountability is allocated in the system.

Answer (C) is correct. *(CIA, adapted)*
REQUIRED: The nature of the figure.
DISCUSSION: Structured analysis is a systems development methodology. It defines inputs, processes, and outputs and divides systems into modules that depict manageable amounts of detail. Structured analysis relies on diagrams rather than narrative. A typical tool used in structured analysis is the data flow diagram, which shows how data flow to, from, and within the system and the processes that manipulate the data.
Answer (A) is incorrect because the figure does not show physical media or input-output procedures (manifestations of how the system works rather than what it accomplishes). Flowcharts depict these matters. Answer (B) is incorrect because the figure, a data flow diagram, does not show how input/output procedures are conducted (a manifestation of how the system works rather than what it accomplishes). Flowcharts show how input/output procedures are conducted. Answer (D) is incorrect because the figure does not show how accountability is allocated in the system. Accountability transfers are usually shown in flowcharts.

8. This figure could be expanded to show the

A. Edit checks used in preparing purchase orders from stock records.

B. Details of the preparation of purchase orders.

C. Physical media used for stock records, the vendor file, and purchase orders.

D. Workstations required in a distributed system for preparing purchase orders.

Answer (B) is correct. *(CIA, adapted)*
REQUIRED: The result that can be achieved by expanding the figure.
DISCUSSION: A data flow diagram can be used to depict lower-level details as well as higher-level processes. A system can be divided into subsystems, and each subsystem can be further subdivided at levels of increasing detail. Thus, any process can be expanded as many times as necessary to show the required level of detail.
Answer (A) is incorrect because a data flow diagram does not depict edit checks. Answer (C) is incorrect because flowcharts, not data flow diagrams, show the physical media on which data such as stock records, the vendor file, and purchase orders are maintained. Answer (D) is incorrect because flowcharts, not data flow diagrams, show the workstations through which data pass and the sequence of activities.

9. The graphic portrayal of the flow of data and the information processing of a system, including computer hardware, is best displayed in a

A. Data flow diagram.

B. System flowchart.

C. Gantt chart.

D. Program flowchart.

Answer (B) is correct. *(CMA, adapted)*
REQUIRED: The best method of displaying the flow of data and the information processing of a system.
DISCUSSION: A system flowchart is a graphic analysis of a data processing application, usually prepared by a systems analyst. The system flowchart is general and stresses flows of data, not computer program logic. A program flowchart is a graphic representation of the detailed steps and logic of an individual computer program.
Answer (A) is incorrect because a data flow diagram would show only where data go, not the total system. Answer (C) is incorrect because a Gantt chart is a bar chart used to monitor the progress of large projects. Answer (D) is incorrect because a program flowchart shows only the details of a single program, not the entire computer system.

10. A document flowchart represents

A. The sequence of logical operations performed during the execution of a computer program.

B. The possible combinations of alternative logic conditions and corresponding courses of action for each condition in a computer program.

C. The flow of data through a series of operations in an automated data processing system.

D. The flow of forms that relate to a particular transaction through an organization.

Answer (D) is correct. *(CMA, adapted)*
REQUIRED: The definition of a document flowchart.
DISCUSSION: A document flowchart graphically presents the flow of forms (documents) through a system that relate to a given transaction, e.g., the processing of a customer's order. It shows the source, flow, processing, and final disposition of the various copies of all related documents.
Answer (A) is incorrect because a program flowchart represents the sequence of logical operations performed during the execution of a computer program. Answer (B) is incorrect because a decision table consists of the possible combinations of alternative logic conditions and corresponding courses of action for each condition in a computer program. Answer (C) is incorrect because a system flowchart is used to represent the flow of data through an automated data processing system.

11. The symbol employed to represent the printing of the employees' paychecks by the computer is

A.

B.

C.

D.

Answer (C) is correct. *(CMA, adapted)*
REQUIRED: The flowchart symbol for the printing of paychecks by a computer.
DISCUSSION: The printing of paychecks by the computer is an operation depicted by the general processing symbol, which is a rectangle.
Answer (A) is incorrect because a trapezoid depicts a manual operation. Answer (B) is incorrect because a square is an auxiliary operation performed by a machine other than a computer. Answer (D) is incorrect because this symbol indicates manual input, e.g., entry of a proper code through a computer console.

12. The symbol employed to represent the employees' checks printed by the computer is

A.

B.

C.

D.

Answer (D) is correct. *(CMA, adapted)*
REQUIRED: The symbol used to represent employee checks printed by a computer.
DISCUSSION: Employee checks printed by the computer are depicted by the document symbol, which resembles the top of a grand piano.
Answer (A) is incorrect because a parallelogram is the general symbol for input or output. Answer (B) is incorrect because a trapezoid indicates a manual operation. Answer (C) is incorrect because this symbol indicates manual input.

13. The correct labeling, in order, for the flowchart symbols is

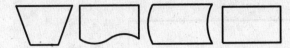

- A. Document, display, online storage, and entry operation.
- B. Manual operation, processing, offline storage, and input-output activity.
- C. Display, document, online storage, and entry operation.
- D. Manual operation, document, online storage, and entry operation.

Answer (D) is correct. *(CMA, adapted)*
REQUIRED: The correct sequence of labels of four flowchart symbols.
DISCUSSION: The first symbol indicates a manual operation, which is an offline process. The second symbol represents a document, while the third symbol indicates online storage (e.g., a disk drive). The final symbol represents an operation. An operation is defined as a process resulting in a change in the information or the flow direction. In other words, it can be an entry operation.
Answer (A) is incorrect because the first symbol, a trapezoid, is for a manual operation. Answer (B) is incorrect because the third symbol is for online storage. Answer (C) is incorrect because the first symbol does not represent display.

14. The symbol employed to determine whether an employee's wages are above or below the maximum limit for FICA taxes is

A.

B.

C.

D.

Answer (B) is correct. *(CMA, adapted)*
REQUIRED: The symbol to determine if an employee's wages are within a limit.
DISCUSSION: The question implies a decision, for which a diamond is the flowcharting symbol.
Answer (A) is incorrect because a rectangle is the general symbol for a process or operation. Answer (C) is incorrect because a trapezoid symbolizes a manual operation. Answer (D) is incorrect because a square represents an auxiliary operation performed by a machine other than a computer.

15. Which of the following symbolic representations indicates that a sales invoice has been filed?

A.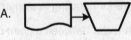

B.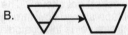

C.

D.

Answer (D) is correct. *(CPA, adapted)*
REQUIRED: The symbols indicating filing of a document.
DISCUSSION: The arrow from the document symbol to the triangle with the mid-line parallel to its base indicates that a document has been stored in an offline file.
Answer (A) is incorrect because the arrow from the document symbol to the trapezoid indicates manual (offline) processing of the document. Answer (B) is incorrect because the arrow from offline storage to the manual operation symbol signifies manual (offline) processing of an offline file. Answer (C) is incorrect because the arrow from the trapezoid to the triangle with a mid-line indicates that manual (offline) processing is followed by offline file storage of the result.

Questions 16 through 20 are based on the following information. This flowchart depicts the processing of daily cash receipts for Rockmart Manufacturing.

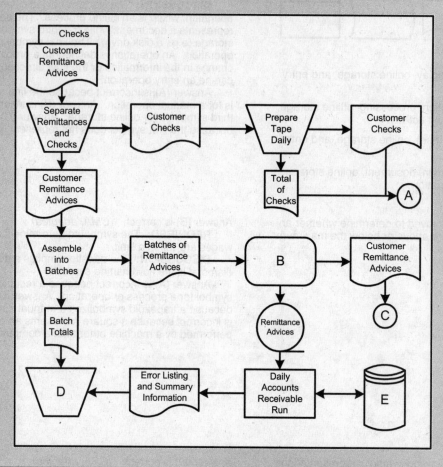

16. The customer checks accompanied by the control tape (refer to symbol A) are

A. Forwarded daily to the billing department for deposit.

B. Taken by the mail clerk to the bank for deposit daily.

C. Forwarded to the treasurer for deposit daily.

D. Accumulated for a week and then forwarded to the treasurer for deposit weekly.

Answer (C) is correct. *(CMA, adapted)*
REQUIRED: The proper procedure for handling customer checks and the related control tape.
DISCUSSION: Symbol A is a connector between a point on this flowchart and another part of the flowchart not shown. The checks and the adding machine control tape should flow through symbol A to the treasurer's office. The treasurer is the custodian of funds and is responsible for deposit of daily receipts.
Answer (A) is incorrect because record keepers perform functions that should be separate from custody of assets. Answer (B) is incorrect because the mail clerk should prepare a list of checks received before they are forwarded to the treasurer for deposit. Answer (D) is incorrect because daily receipts should be deposited intact daily and then reconciled with the bank deposit records. Prompt deposit also safeguards assets and avoids loss of interest income.

17. The appropriate description that should be placed in symbol B is

A. Keying and verifying.

B. Error correction.

C. Collation of remittance advices.

D. Batch processing.

Answer (A) is correct. *(CMA, adapted)*
REQUIRED: The appropriate description for symbol B.
DISCUSSION: Because the figure below symbol B signifies magnetic tape, the operation represented by symbol B must be keying the information onto the tape. Verifying the keyed data would also occur at this step.
Answer (B) is incorrect because error correction would occur subsequently except for keying errors. Answer (C) is incorrect because collation has already occurred. Answer (D) is incorrect because batch processing describes the entire system.

18. The next action to take with the customer remittance advices (refer to symbol C) is to

A. Discard them immediately.

B. File them daily by batch number.

C. Forward them to the internal audit department for internal review.

D. Forward them to the treasurer to compare with the monthly bank statement.

Answer (B) is correct. *(CMA, adapted)*
REQUIRED: The action taken with the customer remittance advices at symbol C.
DISCUSSION: All activity with respect to the paper documents most likely ceases at symbol C. Thus, the batched documents must be filed.
Answer (A) is incorrect because the documents should be kept for reference and review. Answer (C) is incorrect because internal auditors cannot feasibly review all documents regarding transactions even in an engagement. Answer (D) is incorrect because comparison by the treasurer is inappropriate. (S)he has custody of cash.

19. The appropriate description that should be placed in symbol D is

A. Attach batch total to report and file.

B. Reconcile cash balances.

C. Compare batch total and correct as necessary.

D. Proof report.

Answer (C) is correct. *(CMA, adapted)*
REQUIRED: The appropriate description for symbol D.
DISCUSSION: This flowcharting symbol indicates a manual operation or offline process. Because the input to this operation consists of an adding machine tape containing batch totals and a document containing summary information about the accounts receivable update and an error listing, the operation apparently involves comparing these items.
Answer (A) is incorrect because no filing symbol is given. Answer (B) is incorrect because the flowchart concerns daily receipts, not the reconciliation of cash balances. Answer (D) is incorrect because symbol D indicates a comparison, not output in the form of a report.

20. The appropriate description that should be placed in symbol E is

A. Accounts receivable master file.

B. Bad debts master file.

C. Remittance advice master file.

D. Cash projection file.

Answer (A) is correct. *(CMA, adapted)*
REQUIRED: The appropriate description of symbol E.
DISCUSSION: The flowcharting figure at symbol E indicates magnetic disk storage. Because it is an input and output for the daily computer processing of accounts receivable, it must be the accounts receivable master file.
Answer (B) is incorrect because bad debts are not a part of processing daily receipts. Answer (C) is incorrect because the remittance advice master file was not used for the daily accounts receivable run. Answer (D) is incorrect because the cash projection file was not used for the daily accounts receivable run.

21. The symbol used to represent the physical act of collecting employees' time cards for processing is

A.

B.

C.

D.

Answer (A) is correct. *(CMA, adapted)*
REQUIRED: The symbol used to represent the physical act of collecting employees' time cards for processing.
DISCUSSION: Collecting employees' time cards is a manual operation represented by a trapezoid with equal nonparallel sides.
Answer (B) is incorrect because this symbol represents manual input. Answer (C) is incorrect because a rectangle is the general symbol for processing. Answer (D) is incorrect because a parallelogram is the general symbol for input or output.

22. The symbol used to represent the employees' payroll records stored on magnetic tape is

A. ▽

B. ▢

C. ▢

D. ○

Answer (D) is correct.   *(CMA, adapted)*
REQUIRED: The symbol representing employees' payroll records stored on magnetic tape.
DISCUSSION: The magnetic tape symbol (a circle with a tangent at its base) indicates storage on magnetic tape.
Answer (A) is incorrect because a triangle with a mid-line parallel to its base depicts offline storage. Answer (B) is incorrect because this symbol represents online storage. Answer (C) is incorrect because this symbol represents punched paper tape.

23. The symbol used to represent the weekly payroll register generated by the computer is

A. ○

B. ▽

C. ▢

D. ▢

Answer (D) is correct.   *(CMA, adapted)*
REQUIRED: The symbol used to represent a weekly payroll register printed by a computer.
DISCUSSION: The weekly payroll register on a computer printout is represented by a document symbol, which resembles the top of a grand piano.
Answer (A) is incorrect because a circle with a tangent at its base represents magnetic tape input-output or storage.
Answer (B) is incorrect because a triangle with a mid-line parallel to its base depicts offline storage. Answer (C) is incorrect because a rectangle is the general symbol for a process.

24. The symbol used to represent the file of hard-copy, computer-generated payroll reports kept for future reference is

A. ○

B. ▽

C. ▢

D. ▱

Answer (B) is correct.   *(CMA, adapted)*
REQUIRED: The symbol used to represent the kept file of hard-copy, computer-generated payroll reports.
DISCUSSION: Hard-copy, computer-generated payroll reports are kept in offline storage, which is symbolized by a triangle with a mid-line parallel to its base.
Answer (A) is incorrect because a circle with a tangent at its base represents a magnetic tape. Answer (C) is incorrect because this symbol represents online storage. Answer (D) is incorrect because a parallelogram is the general symbol for input or output.

9.2 Process Mapping - Graphs

25. A bank is designing an on-the-job training program for its branch managers. The bank would like to design the program so that participants can complete it as quickly as possible. The training program requires that certain activities be completed before others. For example, a participant cannot make credit loan decisions without first having obtained experience in the loan department. An appropriate scheduling technique for this training program is

A. PERT/CPM.

B. Linear programming.

C. Queuing theory.

D. Sensitivity analysis.

Answer (A) is correct. *(CIA, adapted)*
REQUIRED: The appropriate scheduling technique.
DISCUSSION: PERT/CPM is a network technique for scheduling interrelated time series activities and identifying any critical paths in the series of activities. The critical path is the longest path through the network.
Answer (B) is incorrect because linear programming is a mathematical technique for maximizing or minimizing a given objective function subject to certain constraints. Answer (C) is incorrect because queuing theory is used to minimize the costs of waiting lines when items arrive randomly at a service point and are serviced sequentially. Answer (D) is incorrect because sensitivity analysis is a method for studying the effects of changes in one or more variables on the results of a decision model.

26. A Gantt chart

A. Shows the critical path for a project.

B. Is used for determining an optimal product mix.

C. Shows only the activities along the critical path of a network.

D. Does not necessarily show the critical path through a network.

Answer (D) is correct. *(CMA, adapted)*
REQUIRED: The true statement about a Gantt chart.
DISCUSSION: A Gantt or bar chart is sometimes used in conjunction with PERT or CPM to show the progress of a special project. Time is shown on the horizontal axis, the length of a bar equals the length of an activity, and shading indicates the degree of completion. However, the Gantt chart is not as sophisticated as PERT or CPM in that it does not reflect the relationships among the activities or define a critical path.
Answer (A) is incorrect because the critical path is not shown on a Gantt chart. Answer (B) is incorrect because linear programming is used to determine an optimal product mix. Answer (C) is incorrect because a Gantt chart shows the activities to be completed but not their sequencing.

27. The Gantt chart shows that the project is

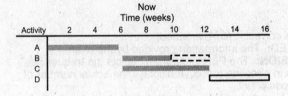

A. Complete.

B. Ahead of schedule.

C. On schedule.

D. Behind schedule.

Answer (B) is correct. *(CIA, adapted)*
REQUIRED: The status of a project according to the Gantt chart.
DISCUSSION: The time at which the evaluation is being made (now) is 8 weeks. Assuming that each of the bars represents the expected time necessary to complete an activity and that the shaded regions represent the portions completed, activity A was completed as scheduled. Activity B is ahead of schedule, and activity C was completed ahead of schedule. Consequently, the project is ahead of schedule.

28. Quality control programs employ many tools for problem definition and analysis. A scatter diagram is one of these tools. The objective of a scatter diagram is to

A. Display a population of items for analysis.

B. Show frequency distribution in graphic form.

C. Divide a universe of data into homogeneous groups.

D. Show the vital trend and separate trivial items.

Answer (A) is correct. *(CIA, adapted)*
REQUIRED: The objective of a scatter diagram.
DISCUSSION: The objective of a scatter diagram is to demonstrate correlations. Each observation is represented by a dot on a graph corresponding to a particular value of X (the independent variable) and Y (the dependent variable).
Answer (B) is incorrect because the objective of a histogram is to show frequency distribution in graphic form. Answer (C) is incorrect because the objective of stratification is to divide a universe of data into homogeneous groups. Answer (D) is incorrect because regression analysis is used to find trend lines.

Questions 29 and 30 are based on the following information. An organization has collected data on the complaints made by personal computer users and has categorized the complaints.

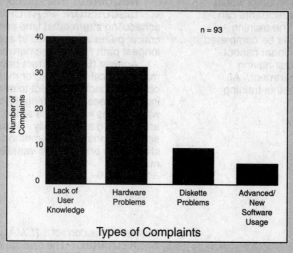

29. Using the information collected, the organization should focus on

A. The total number of personal computer complaints that occurred.

B. The number of computer complaints associated with diskette problems and new software usage.

C. The number of computer complaints associated with the lack of user knowledge and hardware problems.

D. The cost to alleviate all computer complaints.

Answer (C) is correct. *(CIA, adapted)*
REQUIRED: The organization's focus based on the data.
DISCUSSION: Complaints based on lack of user knowledge and hardware problems are by far the most frequent according to this chart. Consequently, the organization should devote its resources primarily to these issues.
Answer (A) is incorrect because more detailed information is not available. The Pareto diagram does not focus on the total quantity of computer complaints. Answer (B) is incorrect because complaints about diskettes and software are infrequent. Answer (D) is incorrect because cost information is not provided.

30. The chart displays

A. The arithmetic mean of each computer complaint.

B. The relative frequency of each computer complaint.

C. The median of each computer complaint.

D. The absolute frequency of each computer complaint.

Answer (D) is correct. *(CIA, adapted)*
REQUIRED: The information provided by the chart.
DISCUSSION: The Pareto diagram depicts the frequencies of complaints in absolute terms. It displays the actual number of each type of complaint.
Answer (A) is incorrect because the chart does not display arithmetic means. Answer (B) is incorrect because the chart does not display relative frequencies. Answer (C) is incorrect because the chart does not display medians of each type of complaint.

9.3 Interviewing

31. The current engagement relating to disbursement activities shows a significant number of errors made during the accounts payable vouchering process that have resulted in lost discounts and an extraordinary number of adjustments and credit memos. To date, the causes have not been fully identified for all types of errors noted. The most appropriate course of action for the internal auditor to take related to these problems is to

A. Interview accounts payable clerks and those involved in processing these transactions.

B. Expand sample sizes for attributes already tested in transactions entered by accounts payable and purchasing.

C. Concentrate on audit program requirements for cash disbursements testing to discover any related information from those tests.

D. Describe the transaction-related problems identified to date in a special report to management without expressing a cause or an auditor's conclusion about the situation.

Answer (A) is correct. *(CIA, adapted)*
REQUIRED: The most appropriate action by the internal auditor to determine the causes of the errors noted in the engagement relating to disbursement activities.
DISCUSSION: The three methods of gathering feedback include observing, analyzing, and questioning. Interviewing the personnel and others involved in the accounts payable vouchering process is the most appropriate action.
Answer (B) is incorrect because expanding sample sizes will generate more factual information about error rates in these attributes, but it will not provide feedback on the causes of the errors. Answer (C) is incorrect because cash disbursements testing will show results of transaction processing after the vouchering process has been performed and corrections have been posted to the system. This information will not provide additional feedback on the causes of the errors. Answer (D) is incorrect because the internal auditor is interested in gathering feedback on the causes of the errors.

32. When conducting interviews during the early stages of an internal auditing engagement, it is more effective to

A. Ask for specific answers that can be quantified.

B. Ask people about their jobs.

C. Ask surprise questions about daily procedures.

D. Take advantage of the fact that fear is an important part of the engagement.

Answer (B) is correct. *(CIA, adapted)*
REQUIRED: The most effective way to conduct interviews during the early stages of an engagement.
DISCUSSION: To improve internal auditor-engagement client cooperation, the internal auditor should, to the extent feasible, humanize the engagement process. For example, individuals feel more important being asked people-type questions, such as asking people about their jobs, rather than control-type questions.
Answer (A) is incorrect because later field work will cover information that can be quantified. Building rapport is more important in the early interviews. Answer (C) is incorrect because, unless fraud is suspected or the engagement concerns cash or negotiable securities, the more effective approach is to defuse the engagement client anxiety that results from anticipating the engagement. Answer (D) is incorrect because, although engagement client fear is a natural part of anticipating the engagement, the internal auditor should keep it from playing an important role by using good interpersonal skills to build a positive participative relationship with the engagement client.

33. During an interview with a data input clerk to discuss a computerized system used to track employee training requirements and compliance, an internal auditor identifies a potentially significant weakness in the system. The internal auditor should

A. Not mention the weakness, directly or indirectly, to avoid making the clerk uncomfortable.

B. Ask indirect questions that will help get more factual information relating to the potential weakness.

C. Ask the clerk about the weakness and determine immediately whether the observation should be communicated.

D. Conduct a second interview after determining whether the weakness actually exists.

Answer (B) is correct. *(CIA, adapted)*
REQUIRED: The interview technique for obtaining information from a data input clerk about a control weakness in a computerized tracking system.
DISCUSSION: Indirect questions may allow the internal auditor to obtain some information without making the clerk feel accused. An interviewee who has been put at ease and does not feel threatened is more likely to be cooperative.
Answer (A) is incorrect because the internal auditor has an obligation to obtain information. The weakness may compromise the security of the company, so the internal auditor should not simply avoid the issue. Answer (C) is incorrect because the clerk is not likely to provide sufficient information to permit the internal auditor to determine whether the observation should be communicated immediately. Answer (D) is incorrect because a second interview is probably inefficient. The internal auditor should learn as much as possible from the first interview, speak to others who may have additional information, and return to this clerk only if needed to clarify something specific about his/her duties.

34. When an internal auditor is interviewing to gain information, (s)he will not be able to remember everything that was said in the interview. The most effective way to record interview information for later use is to

A. Write notes quickly, trying to write down everything in detail as it is said; then highlight important points after the meeting.

B. Tape record the interview to capture everything that everyone says; then type everything said into a computer for documentation.

C. Hire a professional secretary to take notes, allowing complete concentration on the interview; then delete unimportant points after the meeting.

D. Organize notes around topics on the interview plan and note responses in the appropriate area, reviewing the notes after the meeting to make additions.

35. As part of an engagement to evaluate safety management programs, an internal auditor interviews the individual responsible for writing, issuing, and maintaining safety procedures. While the internal auditor's primary interest is to identify the controls ensuring that procedures are kept current, the individual has a tremendous amount of information and seems intent on telling the internal auditor most of it. What might the internal auditor do to guard against missing what is important?

A. Write down everything the individual says. If the internal auditor gets behind, ask for a pause and catch up. After the interview, the internal auditor can sift through the notes and be confident of finding the key information.

B. Tape record the interview and later extract the relevant information.

C. Do not sort through extraneous information. Revisit the topic with the individual's supervisor and obtain any needed information at that time.

D. During the conversation, make an effort to anticipate the approach of a point of critical interest.

Answer (D) is correct. *(CIA, adapted)*
    REQUIRED: The most effective way to record interview information.
    DISCUSSION: Preparing for the interview is crucial. The internal auditor should have learned as much as possible about the engagement client, determined the engagement objectives, and prepared questions. During the interview, the internal auditor should record notes on a split page, which lists the questions on one side and contains space for responses on the other. After the interview, the internal auditor should expand on the notes while the material is still fresh.
    Answer (A) is incorrect because extensive note taking may interfere with communication with the respondent. Maintaining eye contact and observing nonverbal signals is difficult if the interviewer is preoccupied with his/her notes. Answer (B) is incorrect because tape recording might be used for controversial material, but it usually will not elicit positive feelings from the respondent. For most organizational purposes, exact quotes are unnecessary. Answer (C) is incorrect because, aside from cost, this option is unworkable given the loss of confidentiality and the probable negative reaction from the respondent.

Answer (D) is correct. *(CIA, adapted)*
    REQUIRED: The internal auditor's approach to interviewing an individual who intends to communicate a large amount of information.
    DISCUSSION: Anticipation is one approach the internal auditor can use to maintain focus during a far-ranging discussion. It assumes that the internal auditor has done some homework and is prepared to listen intelligently. Active listening permits anticipation because the mind can process information more rapidly than most people speak. Thus, the listener has time to analyze the information and determine what is most important.
    Answer (A) is incorrect because the internal auditor will probably miss important points in the effort to record everything. Answer (B) is incorrect because recording the entire interview is inefficient. Answer (C) is incorrect because this procedure would be a waste of everyone's time, and the internal auditor still may not obtain the information sought.

36. During an interview to identify controls over the quality of wastewater discharge, the responsible employee refers only to a department procedure when asked about controls to ensure that samples are collected and analyzed. In the internal auditor's experience, such operations should maintain a log to record all samples, the types of analyses performed, and whether results should be reported to management or regulatory agencies. For some reason, this employee is reluctant to discuss detailed responsibilities in this area. The best thing for the internal auditor to do in this case is

A. Continue the interview and discuss other elements of the employee's duties, returning periodically to the samples and analytical results.

B. Relate what the internal auditor has seen at other facilities and tell the employee that the log is necessary.

C. Accept the information as given and record an observation finding that adequate controls are in place.

D. Interview the supervisor of the employee and discuss the auditee's duties in detail.

Answer (A) is correct. *(CIA, adapted)*
REQUIRED: The best approach to interviewing an individual who is reluctant to provide information.
DISCUSSION: The internal auditor may wish to return to the issue of controls over the samples after the employee has been put at ease. Nonjudgmental questioning, good listening habits, and a cooperative approach may lower the employee's defenses and elicit the desired information.
Answer (B) is incorrect because the employee need not be lectured about what is in place at another facility. However, at the conclusion of an engagement, including such information about best management practices in the final engagement communication is appropriate. Answer (C) is incorrect because, if an internal auditor strongly suspects that a control is not in place, accepting the employee's first, unsupported representation is an insufficient basis for an observation that will ultimately be challenged. Answer (D) is incorrect because interviewing the supervisor will not extract additional information from the employee.

37. The current internal auditing engagement to evaluate disbursements activities shows a significant number of errors made during the accounts payable vouchering process that have resulted in lost discounts and an extraordinary number of adjustments and credit memos. Engagement hours are already over budget in this section because of the number of exceptions to be analyzed. Internal auditing staff has had time to observe the operations performed by each of the voucher clerks; sample and analyze transaction documents in the accounts payable, purchasing, and receiving departments; and obtain system statistics on transaction volume, error-correction transactions, and lost-discount summaries. To date, the causes for all types of errors noted during detail testing, observation, and analysis of exceptions have not been fully identified in any of the three departments. The most appropriate course of action for the lead internal auditor to determine the causes of these errors is to

A. Question and get the opinions of the accounts payable clerks and those involved in processing these transactions.

B. Expand sample sizes for attributes already tested in transactions entered by accounts payable, purchasing, and receiving.

C. Concentrate on engagement work program requirements for cash disbursements testing to discover any related information from those tests.

D. Describe the transaction-related problems identified to date in a special engagement communication to management without expressing a cause or an internal auditor's conclusion about the situation.

Answer (A) is correct. *(CIA, adapted)*
REQUIRED: The most appropriate action by the lead internal auditor to determine the causes of the errors.
DISCUSSION: The methods of gathering feedback include observing, analyzing, and questioning. Questioning (interviewing) the personnel of the engagement clients and others affected within the organization is the method that has not yet been used.
Answer (B) is incorrect because expanding sample sizes will generate more factual information about error rates in these attributes, but it will not provide feedback. Answer (C) is incorrect because cash disbursements testing provides information about transaction processing after the vouchering process has been performed and corrections have been posted to the system. This information will not provide additional feedback. Answer (D) is incorrect because an engagement communication to management will not generate additional information about the causes of the problem.

9.4 Other Data-Gathering Techniques

38. An internal auditing team developed a preliminary questionnaire with the following response choices:

I.   Probably not a problem
II.   Possibly a problem
III. Probably a problem

The questionnaire illustrates the use of

    A. Trend analysis.

    B. Ratio analysis.

    C. Unobtrusive measures or observations.

    D. Rating scales.

Answer (D) is correct. *(CIA, adapted)*
    REQUIRED: The technique illustrated by the questionnaire.
    DISCUSSION: A rating scale may be used when a range of opinions is expected. The scale represents a continuum of responses. In this case, it reflects probability statements.
    Answer (A) is incorrect because trend analysis extrapolates past and current conditions. Answer (B) is incorrect because ratio analysis considers the internal relationships of financial data. Answer (C) is incorrect because use of rating scales requires the participant to participate actively. Thus, it is not unobtrusive.

39. An internal auditing manager is conducting the annual meeting with manufacturing division management to discuss proposed engagement plans and activities for the next year. After some discussion about the past year's activity at 12 plants in the division, the divisional vice president agrees that all significant recommendations made by the internal auditing staff refer to key controls and related operating activities that are correctly described for local management within the volume of standard operating procedures for the division. The vice president proposes to transcribe key control activities from the division's extensive written procedures to a self-assessment standard operating procedure (SOP) questionnaire. What significance should the internal auditing manager attach to such SOP questionnaires in relation to the proposed engagement schedule for the next year?

    A. The SOP questionnaires should improve control adequacy, but the internal auditors need to verify that controls are working as documented in the SOP.

    B. Adding this control should eliminate significant engagement recommendations in the coming year, so the scope of engagement activities can be reduced accordingly.

    C. Engagement activity can be reduced if the vice president agrees to require the internal audit activity's approval of all divisional standard operating procedures.

    D. SOP questionnaires must be mailed and controlled by the internal audit activity to be considered in relation to the proposed engagement schedule.

Answer (A) is correct. *(CIA, adapted)*
    REQUIRED: The significance of SOP questionnaires for the proposed engagement schedule.
    DISCUSSION: A specific advantage of an SOP questionnaire is that it may be used by local management to periodically ensure that employee practices remain current with relevant, valid, and up-to-date standard operating procedures. The overall level of control and the control environment improve when follow-up activities are performed to determine that controls are being implemented as intended.
    Answer (B) is incorrect because SOP questionnaires have no impact on inherent risk, and the internal auditors have no information that such a control will be effective. Answer (C) is incorrect because standard operating procedures, as described, provide directive controls that appear to be adequate. IAA approval does not affect the operation of these controls. Answer (D) is incorrect because control of SOP questionnaires by the IAA would not affect the information obtained. Such information must be verified to be considered objective.

40. An internal auditor must weigh the cost of an engagement procedure against the persuasiveness of the evidence to be gathered. Observation is one engagement procedure that involves cost-benefit trade-offs. Which of the following statements regarding observation as an engagement technique is (are) true?

I. Observation is limited because individuals may react differently when being observed.

II. When testing financial statement balances, observation is more persuasive for the completeness assertion than it is for the existence assertion.

III. Observation is effective in providing information about how the organization's processes differ from those specified by written policies.

A. I only.

B. II only.

C. I and III only.

D. I, II, and III.

Answer (C) is correct. *(CIA, adapted)*
REQUIRED: The true statement(s) regarding observation as an audit technique.
DISCUSSION: Observation consists of watching the physical activities of the employees in the organization to see how they perform their duties. The internal auditor can determine whether written policies have been put into practice. Observation is limited because employees who know they are being observed may behave differently while being observed. Moreover, observation is more persuasive for the existence or occurrence assertion (whether assets or liabilities exist and whether transactions have occurred) than for the completeness assertion (whether all transactions that should be reported are reported).

41. Management answered "yes" to every question when filling out an internal control questionnaire and stated that all listed requirements and control activities were part of their procedures. An internal auditor retrieved this questionnaire from management during the preliminary survey visit but did not review the responses with management while on site. The internal auditor's supervisor should be critical of the above procedure because

A. Engagement information must be corroborated in some way.

B. Internal control questionnaires cannot be relied upon.

C. The internal auditors were not present while the questionnaire was being filled out.

D. The questionnaire was not designed to address accounting operations and controls.

Answer (A) is correct. *(CIA, adapted)*
REQUIRED: The criticism of the internal auditor's procedure.
DISCUSSION: Self-assessment questionnaires provide indirect information. Because this information is provided by engagement client personnel and not by independent sources, it must be confirmed.
Answer (B) is incorrect because the adaptability of general-purpose ICQs to different organizational units, personnel, and functional units is one of their strengths. Answer (C) is incorrect because ICQs can be designed so that the engagement client can answer the questions without the internal auditor's presence. Answer (D) is incorrect because an ICQ does not need to address accounting information to ensure integrity.

42. A questionnaire consists of a series of questions relating to controls normally required to prevent or detect errors and fraud that may occur for each type of transaction. Which of the following is not an advantage of a questionnaire?

A. A questionnaire provides a framework that minimizes the possibility of overlooking aspects of internal control.

B. A questionnaire can be easily completed.

C. A questionnaire is flexible in design and application.

D. The completed questionnaire provides documentation that the internal auditor become familiar with internal control.

Answer (C) is correct. *(Publisher, adapted)*
REQUIRED: The statement not considered an advantage of a questionnaire.
DISCUSSION: Questionnaires are designed to be inflexible in that the responses to certain questions are expected. Questionnaires are not easily adapted to unique situations. The approach that offers the most flexibility is a narrative memorandum describing internal control. The next most flexible approach is a flowchart.
Answer (A) is incorrect because a questionnaire provides a framework to assure that control concerns are not overlooked. Answer (B) is incorrect because a questionnaire is relatively easy to complete. For the most part, only yes/no responses are elicited from management and employees. Answer (D) is incorrect because the completed questionnaire can become part of the working papers to document the internal auditor's becoming familiar with the engagement client's activities, risks, and controls.

Questions 43 through 46 are based on the following information. An internal auditing team has been assigned to review "the customer satisfaction measurement system" that the Industrial Products Division implemented 2 years ago. This system consists of an annual mail survey conducted by the division's customer service office. A survey is sent to 100 purchasing departments randomly selected from all customers who made purchases in the prior 12 months. The survey is three pages long, and its 30 questions use a mixture of response modes (e.g., some questions are open-ended, some are multiple-choice, and others use a response scale). The customer service office mails the survey in September and tabulates the results for questionnaires returned by October 15. Only one mailing is sent. If the customer does not return the questionnaire, no follow-up is conducted. When the survey was last conducted, 45 of the questionnaires were not returned.

43. Many questionnaires are made up of a series of different questions that use the same response categories (e.g., strongly agree, agree, neither, disagree, strongly disagree). Some designs will have different groups of respondents answer alternative versions of the questionnaire that present the questions in different orders and reverse the orientation of the endpoints of the scale (e.g., agree on the right and disagree on the left or vice versa). The purpose of such questionnaire variations is to

A. Eliminate intentional misrepresentations.

B. Reduce the effects of pattern response tendencies.

C. Test whether respondents are reading the questionnaire.

D. Make it possible to get information about more than one population parameter using the same questions.

Answer (B) is correct. *(CIA, adapted)*
REQUIRED: The purpose of questionnaire variations.
DISCUSSION: The sequence and format of questions have many known effects. For example, questions should be in a logical order, and personal questions should be asked last because of the emotions they may evoke. One method for reducing these effects is to use questionnaire variations that cause these biases to average out across the sample.
Answer (A) is incorrect because questionnaire variations cannot eliminate intentional misrepresentations. Answer (C) is incorrect because questionnaire variations cannot test whether respondents are reading the questionnaire. Answer (D) is incorrect because questionnaire variations cannot make it possible to get information about more than one population parameter using the same questions.

44. Several of the internal auditing team members are concerned about the low response rate, the poor quality of the questionnaire design, and the potentially biased wording of some of the questions. They suggest that the customer service office might want to supplement the survey with some unobtrusive data collection such as observing customer interactions in the office or collecting audiotapes of phone conversations with customers. Which of the following is not a potential advantage of unobtrusive data collection compared to surveys or interviews?

A. Interactions with customers can be observed as they occur in their natural setting.

B. It is easier to make precise measurements of the variables under study.

C. Unexpected or unusual events are more likely to be observed.

D. People are less likely to alter their behavior because they are being studied.

Answer (B) is correct. *(CIA, adapted)*
REQUIRED: The item not an advantage of unobtrusive data collection.
DISCUSSION: Lack of experimental control and measurement precision are weaknesses of observational research. Another is that some things, such as private behavior, attitudes, feelings, and motives, cannot be observed.
Answer (A) is incorrect because observing the phenomenon in its natural setting eliminates some aspects of experimental bias. Answer (C) is incorrect because the possibility of observing unexpected or unusual behavior makes unobtrusive measures useful for exploratory investigations. Answer (D) is incorrect because, if research subjects are unaware of being studied, they are less likely to do what they think the researcher wants, censor their comments, etc.

45. Nonresponse bias is often a concern in conducting mail surveys. The main reason that nonresponse bias can cause difficulties in a sample such as the one taken by the customer service office is that

- A. The sample means and standard errors are harder to compute.
- B. Those who did not respond may be systematically different from those who did.
- C. The questionnaire is too short.
- D. Confidence intervals are narrower.

Answer (B) is correct. *(CIA, adapted)*
REQUIRED: The reason that nonresponse bias reduces the validity of a sample.
DISCUSSION: The sample will not be truly random if respondents as a group differ from nonrespondents. Thus, people may choose not to respond for reasons related to the purpose of the questionnaire.
Answer (A) is incorrect because formulas are as easy to use with bad data as with good data. Answer (C) is incorrect because longer questionnaires increase nonresponse bias. Answer (D) is incorrect because nonresponse decreases sample size, so confidence intervals would be wider rather than narrower.

46. Which of the following is not an advantage of face-to-face interviews over mail surveys?

- A. The response rate is typically higher.
- B. Interviewers can increase a respondent's comprehension of questions.
- C. Survey designers can use a wider variety of types of questions.
- D. They are less expensive because mailing costs are avoided.

Answer (D) is correct. *(CIA, adapted)*
REQUIRED: The item not an advantage of face-to-face interviews.
DISCUSSION: One of the principal advantages of mail surveys is their cost efficiency. Mailing costs are lower than the costs of telephone interviews and still lower than the costs of face-to-face interviews.
Answer (A) is incorrect because mail surveys often have low response rates. Answer (B) is incorrect because the interviewer's ability to interpret responses and rephrase questions increases response quality. Answer (C) is incorrect because audiovisual aids, complex sequences, and other varieties of questions are made possible by the interactive nature of interviews.

47. A well-designed internal control questionnaire should

- A. Elicit "yes" or "no" responses rather than narrative responses and be organized by department.
- B. Be a sufficient source of data for assessment of control risk.
- C. Help evaluate the effectiveness of internal control.
- D. Be independent of the objectives of the internal auditing engagement.

Answer (C) is correct. *(CIA, adapted)*
REQUIRED: The function of an internal control questionnaire.
DISCUSSION: An internal control questionnaire consists of a series of questions about the organization's controls designed to prevent or detect errors or fraud. Answers to the questions help the internal auditor to identify specific controls relevant to specific assertions and to design tests of controls to evaluate the effectiveness of their design and operation.
Answer (A) is incorrect because yes/no question formats and question sequence by department may facilitate administering the questionnaire, but other formats and methods of question organization are possible. Answer (B) is incorrect because the questionnaire is a tool to help understand and document internal control but is not sufficient as the sole source of information to support the assessment of control risk. Answer (D) is incorrect because the internal control questionnaire must be designed to achieve the engagement objectives.

48. Which of the following statements indicates the wrong way to use an internal control questionnaire?

- A. Clarifying all answers with written remarks and explanations.
- B. Filling out the questionnaire during an interview with the person who has responsibility for the area that is being reviewed.
- C. Constructing the questionnaire so that a no response requires attention.
- D. Supplementing the completed questionnaire with a narrative description or flowchart.

Answer (A) is correct. *(CIA, adapted)*
REQUIRED: The statement indicating the wrong way to use an internal control questionnaire.
DISCUSSION: Only those answers that appear inappropriate should be pursued by asking for clarification or explanation. In this way, problem areas may be pinpointed and either compensating controls identified or extensions to the engagement procedures planned.
Answer (B) is incorrect because filling out the questionnaire during an interview with the person who has responsibility for the area that is being reviewed is an appropriate use of an internal control questionnaire. Answer (C) is incorrect because constructing the questionnaire so that a no response requires attention is an appropriate use of an internal control questionnaire. Answer (D) is incorrect because supplementing the completed questionnaire with a narrative description or flowchart is an appropriate use of an internal control questionnaire.

9.5 Problem Solving

49. As part of the decision-making process, alternative solutions ordinarily should be screened for the most appealing balance of effectiveness and efficiency in view of relevant constraints and intangibles. When a problem is resolved by selecting a course of action that meets the minimum constraints, a manager is said to be

A. Satisficing.

B. Optimizing.

C. Idealizing.

D. Maximizing.

Answer (A) is correct. *(CIA, adapted)*
REQUIRED: The term for resolving a problem by selecting a course of action that meets the minimum constraints.
DISCUSSION: Satisficing is the decision-making process in which the decision maker uses a minimal amount of information in an effort to reduce to a minimum the amount of time it takes to make a decision. The result is a decision that is not the best but is good enough to give satisfactory resolution.
Answer (B) is incorrect because optimizing means selecting the best possible solution. Answer (C) is incorrect because idealizing involves changing the situation so that the problem no longer exists. Answer (D) is incorrect because maximizing is a synonym for optimizing and involves selecting the best solution.

50. An organization wishes to determine what advertising mix of radio, television, and newspapers offers the optimal desired result in increased sales and improved public image. Which of the following techniques is most appropriate to use?

A. Synectics.

B. Value analysis.

C. Brainstorming.

D. Forced relationship.

Answer (B) is correct. *(CIA, adapted)*
REQUIRED: The technique to determine the optimal advertising mix.
DISCUSSION: Value analysis is a methodical approach primarily designed to optimize performance of an activity at a minimum cost. Emphasis is on the cost-benefit criterion.
Answer (A) is incorrect because synectics is a highly structured group approach to problem statement and solution based on creative thinking. It involves free use of analogies and metaphors in informal exchange within a carefully selected small group of individuals of diverse personality and areas of specialization. Answer (C) is incorrect because brainstorming breaks down broadly based problems into their essentials. Answer (D) is incorrect because forced relationship is a structured adaptation of free association. The elements of a problem are analyzed and the associations among them are identified so as to detect patterns that may suggest new ideas.

51. Costs of a specific department must be cut by 40% and quality must improve or it cannot compete in the marketplace. This drastic charge was recently given to your department. You do not have time for more traditional techniques. You must come up with something quickly. Conventional cost-cutting techniques have been attempted but to no avail. You decide to employ a radical new production arrangement. Which of the following techniques is most appropriate to use?

A. Blast! then refine.

B. Edisonian.

C. Morphological matrix analysis.

D. Operations research.

Answer (A) is correct. *(CIA, adapted)*
REQUIRED: The technique that quickly implements a radical new production arrangement.
DISCUSSION: "Blast! then refine" is a U.S. Navy problem-solving methodology. It completely disregards (blasts out of one's consciousness) any existing approach. An entirely new problem solution is then sought that will attain the original objectives.
Answer (B) is incorrect because the Edisonian approach is a trial-and-error experimental method. It should usually not be applied unless other approaches have been unsuccessful. Answer (C) is incorrect because morphological matrix analysis is a structured technique that plots decision variables along the axes of a matrix. The relationships of these variables are found in the squares within the chart. Answer (D) is incorrect because operations research attempts to find optimal solutions using classical concepts such as statistics, simulation, logical thinking, and other scientific and mathematical techniques to develop and test hypotheses.

52. An organization is about to introduce a new service and wishes to develop a new slogan and logo to be used in advertising and on organizational publications. You have been chosen to participate in this process and to look at past slogans, logos, and suggestions given by the advertising agency. You are not limited to the suggested ideas and have been encouraged to suggest original ideas of your own. Which of the following techniques is most appropriate to use?

    A. Brainstorming.

    B. Value analysis.

    C. Free association.

    D. Attribute listing.

Answer (C) is correct. *(CIA, adapted)*
    REQUIRED: The technique that considers suggested ideas but also encourages original thinking.
    DISCUSSION: Free association is an approach to idea generation that reports the first thought to come to mind in response to a given stimulus, for example, a symbol or analogy pertaining to a product for which an advertising slogan is sought. The objective is to express the content of consciousness without censorship or control.
    Answer (A) is incorrect because brainstorming breaks down broadly based problems into their essentials. It is an unstructured approach that relies on the spontaneous contribution of ideas from all members of a group. Answer (B) is incorrect because value analysis is a methodical approach primarily designed to optimize performance of an activity at a minimum cost. Answer (D) is incorrect because attribute listing is applied primarily to improve a tangible object.

53. An organization has a computer that it no longer needs because of a discontinued operation. Currently, there are several computer projects that may be able to use the machine, but some modification will be necessary if such new application is to be successful. Which of the following techniques is most appropriate to use?

    A. Attribute listing.

    B. Operations research.

    C. Morphological matrix analysis.

    D. Synectics.

Answer (A) is correct. *(CIA, adapted)*
    REQUIRED: The technique useful in developing new uses for a computer.
    DISCUSSION: Attribute listing is applied primarily to improve a tangible object. It lists the parts and essential features of the object and systematically analyzes modifications intended as improvements.
    Answer (B) is incorrect because operations research attempts to find optimal solutions using classical concepts such as statistics, simulation, logical thinking, and other scientific and mathematical techniques to develop and test hypotheses. This application closely fits the problem and charge given.
    Answer (C) is incorrect because morphological matrix analysis is a structured technique that plots decision variables along the axes of a matrix. The relationships of these variables are found in the squares within the chart. Answer (D) is incorrect because synectics is a highly structured group approach to problem statement and solution based on creative thinking. It involves free use of analogies and metaphors in informal exchange within a carefully selected small group of individuals of diverse personality and areas of specialization.

54. An organization has experienced numerous complaints because a passenger door has not opened smoothly. All attempts to repair the door have failed. The item is no longer under warranty, and the manufacturer has informed the company that a very expensive new door must be purchased and installed to solve the problem. You have been asked to supervise an attempt by your engineering department to come up with less expensive alternative solutions. Which of the following techniques is most appropriate to use?

    A. Free association.

    B. Operations research.

    C. Blast! then refine.

    D. Edisonian.

Answer (D) is correct. *(CIA, adapted)*
    REQUIRED: The technique that would be applied by an engineering department to come up with less expensive alternative solutions.
    DISCUSSION: The Edisonian approach is a trial-and-error experimental method. It should usually not be applied unless other approaches have been unsuccessful.
    Answer (A) is incorrect because free association is an approach to idea generation that reports the first thought to come to mind in response to a given stimulus, for example, a symbol or analogy pertaining to a product for which an advertising slogan is sought. The objective is to express the content of consciousness without censorship or control. Answer (B) is incorrect because operations research attempts to find optimal solutions using classical concepts such as statistics, simulation, logical thinking, and other scientific and mathematical techniques to develop and test hypotheses. This application closely fits the problem and charge given. Answer (C) is incorrect because "blast! then refine" is a U.S. Navy problem-solving methodology. It completely disregards (blasts out of one's consciousness) any existing approach. An entirely new problem solution is then sought that will attain the original objectives.

55. An organization is concerned that spare parts inventories are too large. It has attempted to keep critical parts for its fleet in stock so that equipment will have minimal downtime. Management wants to know what the optimal spare parts inventory should be if downtime is estimated to cost $150 per day. Carrying cost and order cost have not been measured. You have been asked to make a formal recommendation on spare parts stocking levels. Which of the following techniques is most appropriate to use?

A. Operations research.

B. Value analysis.

C. Attribute listing.

D. Brainstorming.

Answer (A) is correct. *(CIA, adapted)*
REQUIRED: The technique for determining the optimal spare parts inventory.
DISCUSSION: Operations research attempts to find optimal solutions using classical concepts such as statistics, simulation, logical thinking, and other scientific and mathematical techniques to develop and test hypotheses. This application closely fits the problem and charge given.
Answer (B) is incorrect because value analysis is a methodical approach primarily designed to optimize performance of an activity at a minimum cost. Emphasis is on the cost-benefit criterion. Answer (C) is incorrect because attribute listing is applied primarily to improve a tangible object. It lists the parts and essential features of the object and systematically analyzes modifications intended as improvements. Answer (D) is incorrect because brainstorming breaks down broadly based problems into their essentials. It is an unstructured approach that relies on the spontaneous contribution of ideas from all members of a group.

56. A chief executive officer (CEO) believes that a major competitor may be planning a new campaign. The CEO sends a questionnaire to key personnel asking for original thinking concerning what the new campaign may be. The CEO selects the best possibilities then sends another questionnaire asking for the most likely option. The process employed by the CEO is called the

A. Least squares technique.

B. Delphi technique.

C. Maximum likelihood technique.

D. Optimizing of expected payoffs.

Answer (B) is correct. *(CIA, adapted)*
REQUIRED: The process employed by the CEO to encourage original thinking.
DISCUSSION: The Delphi technique is a forecasting or decision-making approach that attempts to avoid groupthink (the tendency of individuals to conform to what they perceive to be the consensus). The technique allows only written, anonymous communication among group members. Each member takes a position on the problem at hand. A summary of these positions is communicated to each member. The process is repeated for several iterations as the members move toward a consensus. Thus, the Delphi technique is a qualitative, not quantitative, technique.
Answer (A) is incorrect because least squares refers to regression analysis and involves specified variables. Answer (C) is incorrect because the maximum likelihood technique is a complex alternative to least squares. Answer (D) is incorrect because optimizing expected payoffs is used in the analysis of decision-making alternatives, which relies on historical information.

57. An organization's executive committee, meeting to solve an important problem, spent 30 minutes analyzing data and debating the cause of the problem. Finally, they agreed and could move on to the next step. Possible steps in the creative problem-solving process are listed below. Which step should the committee perform next?

A. Select a solution.

B. Generate alternative solutions.

C. Identify the problem.

D. Consider the reaction of competitors to various courses of action.

Answer (B) is correct. *(CIA, adapted)*
REQUIRED: The next step in the creative problem-solving process.
DISCUSSION: Kreitner states that "managerial problem solving consists of a four-step sequence: (1) identifying the problem, (2) generating alternative solutions, (3) selecting a solution, and (4) implementing and evaluating the solution." In the first step, management determines what the actual situation is, what the desired situation is, and the reason for the difference.
Answer (A) is incorrect because selecting a solution is the third step in the process. Answer (C) is incorrect because identifying the problem is the first step in the process. Answer (D) is incorrect because considering the reaction of competitors is part of the fourth step of implementing and evaluating the solution.

STUDY UNIT TEN
ETHICS AND FRAUD

(28 pages of outline)

The ethics outline in this study unit is important to internal auditors both personally and professionally. All professionals have ethical responsibilities: (1) objectivity, (2) integrity, (3) confidential and disinterested use and protection of information, and (4) competence. They are stated in The IIA Code of Ethics, a document that is heavily tested. It is reproduced in full in the second subunit of this study unit. The first subunit provides a useful perspective on ethics.

The second major topic in this study unit is fraud. The scope of work of internal auditors extends to the examination and evaluation of the organization's system of internal control. Internal control is the primary means of deterring and detecting fraud. Moreover, the internal audit activity should evaluate the design, implementation, and effectiveness of the organization's ethics-related objectives, programs, and activities. Consequently, internal auditors play an important role in minimizing the effects of fraud on the organization.

Core Concepts

- An organization's code of ethics is the established general value system the organization wishes to apply to its members' activities by communicating organizational purposes and beliefs and establishing uniform ethical guidelines for members.

- The purpose of The IIA Code of Ethics is to promote an ethical culture in the profession of internal auditing.

- Internal auditors must uphold four principles:

  a. Integrity
  b. Objectivity
  c. Confidentiality
  d. Competency

- Fraud is characterized by intentional deception. It may be perpetrated for the benefit, or to the detriment, of the organization. The perpetrators may be persons outside or inside the organization.

- Control is the principal method of deterring fraud. Internal auditors primarily deter fraud by evaluating the adequacy and effectiveness of control.

- When fraud is suspected, the appropriate authorities in the organization should be informed. The auditor recommends whatever investigation is necessary and follows up.

- The CAE must report significant fraud to the board and senior management.

- Detection of fraud consists of identifying indicators of fraud sufficient to warrant an investigation.

- Performance of audit procedures does not guarantee fraud detection.

- The objective of internal auditing in fraud detection is to provide analyses, appraisals, recommendations, counsel, and information.

- Management is responsible for establishing and maintaining effective control at reasonable cost. Auditors promote effective control at reasonable cost.

- With regard to fraud detection, auditors must exercise due professional care.
- An internal auditor involved in a fraud investigation may risk hindering the investigation by not conducting it professionally. An internal auditor risks giving cause for legal action by an employee-suspect (whether or not guilty) against the auditor and the organization. Legal liability may arise for violation of rights provided by law.

10.1 PERSPECTIVE ON ETHICS

1. **Definitions**

   a. **Business ethics** are an organization's policies and standards established to ensure certain kinds of behavior by its members.

   b. **Individual ethics** are the moral principles and standards of conduct adhered to by an individual.

2. **Issues in Business Ethics**

   a. General business understanding of ethical issues
   b. Compliance with laws (tax, securities, antitrust, environmental, privacy, labor, etc.)
   c. External financial reporting
   d. Conflicts of interest
   e. Entertainment and gift expenses
   f. Relations with customers and suppliers (Should gifts or kickbacks be given or accepted?)
   g. Social responsibility

3. **Factors That May Lead to Unethical Behavior**

   a. In any normal population, some people behave unethically. If these people hold leadership positions, they may have a bad influence on subordinates.

   b. **Organizational Factors**

      1) Pressures to improve short-run performance may promote unethical behavior.
      2) Emphasis on strict adherence to chain-of-command authority may provide excuses for ignoring ethics when following orders.
      3) Informal work-group loyalties may subvert ethical behavior.
      4) Committee decision processes may make it possible to abstain from or avoid ethical obligations.

   c. **External Factors**

      1) Pressure of competition may compromise ethics in the interest of survival.
      2) Wrongful behavior of others may force a compromise of ethics.
      3) Definitions of ethical behavior may vary from one culture to another. For instance, bribes to officials or buyers may be consistent with some countries' customary business practices.

4. **General Guides to Ethics**

   a. The **Golden Rule** states, "Do unto others as you would have them do unto you."
   b. **Fairness.** Individuals and businesses should act in ways that are fair or just to all.
   c. **General respect.** Individuals and businesses should act to respect the planet and the rights of others because business decisions have widespread effects.
   d. **Law.** Another view is that adherence to legal codes satisfies ethical obligations.

e. However, most people believe that law embodies **ethical precepts** but is not synonymous with them. Thus, what is unethical may not be illegal, and nonlegal sources of ethical guidance must be considered.

1) For example, the philosopher Immanuel Kant devised the **categorical imperative**. It is an approach to any ethical decision that asks what the consequences would be if all persons in the same circumstances (category) behaved similarly.

2) **Natural law** concepts are a source of ethical standards because they assert that certain human rights are fundamental, such as the life, liberty, and pursuit of happiness rights mentioned in the U.S. Declaration of Independence. Under this view, a business decision should be evaluated based on how it affects the rights of groups, e.g., consumers or employees.

3) According to **utilitarian ethics**, a decision is good if it maximizes social utility, that is, provides the greatest good for the greatest number of people.

4) Various concepts of the **social responsibility** of business have evolved from a greater awareness of ethical obligations.

a) The economist **Milton Friedman** took a limited view. He argued that a business must stay "within the rules of the game." Thus, it should engage in "open and free competition without deception or fraud," but it is otherwise obligated only to earn profits.

b) A second view is that businesses must consider the interests of all **stakeholders**. In a given situation, some may have interests superior to the interest of shareholders.

c) A third view is that major corporations have **citizenship** responsibilities, for example, to protect the environment or promote human rights.

5. **Simplified Criteria for Evaluating Ethical Behavior**

a. "Would this behavior be acceptable if people I respect knew I was doing this?"

b. "What are the consequences of this behavior for myself, other employees, customers, and society?"

6. Ethics are **individual and personal**, influenced by

a. Life experiences (rewards for doing right, punishment for doing wrong)
b. Friendship groups (professional associations, informal groups)
c. Organizational pressures (responsibilities to superiors and the organization)

7. **Codes of Ethics**

a. An organization's code of ethics is the **established general value system** the organization wishes to apply to its members' activities by

1) Communicating organizational purposes and beliefs and
2) Establishing uniform ethical guidelines for members.

a) This guidance extends to decision making.

b. Because laws and specific rules cannot cover all situations, organizations benefit from having an established code of ethics. The code effectively **communicates acceptable values** to all members, including recruits and subcontractors. For example, a code may

1) Require compliance with the law
2) Prohibit conflicts of interest, such as accepting anything from customers and vendors, using organizational information for personal gain, or having financial dealings with those who also deal with the organization

3) Provide a method of **policing and disciplining members** for violations through

   a) Formal review panels
   b) Group pressure (informal)

4) Set high **standards** against which individuals can measure their own performance

5) Communicate to those **outside the organization** the value system from which its members must not be asked to deviate

c. A typical code for auditors or accountants in an organization requires

   1) **Independence** from conflicts of economic or professional interest

      a) They are responsible for **presenting information fairly** to shareholders or owners rather than protecting management.

      b) They are responsible for presenting appropriate information to **all managers**. They should not favor certain managers or conceal unfavorable information.

      c) They are responsible for **maintaining an ethical presence** in the conduct of professional activities.

         i) They should do what they can to ensure organizational **compliance** with the spirit as well as the letter of pertinent laws and regulations.

         ii) They should conduct themselves according to the highest moral and legal **standards**.

         iii) They should report to appropriate internal or external authority any **illegal or fraudulent** organizational act.

   2) **Integrity** and a refusal to compromise professional values for the sake of personal goals

   3) **Objectivity** in presenting information, preparing reports, and making analyses

8. **Role of the Internal Auditor**

   a. *2130*   *Governance* – *The internal audit activity should assess and make appropriate recommendations for improving the governance process in its accomplishment of the following objectives:*

      • *Promoting appropriate ethics and values within the organization.*

      • *Ensuring effective organizational performance management and accountability.*

      • *Effectively communicating risk and control information to appropriate areas of the organization.*

      • *Effectively coordinating the activities of and communicating information among the board, external and internal auditors, and management.*

      2130.A1 – The internal audit activity should evaluate the design, implementation, and effectiveness of the organization's ethics-related objectives, programs, and activities.

      2130.C1 – Consulting engagement objectives should be consistent with the overall values and goals of the organization.

b. This section is taken from *Practice Advisory 2130-1: Role of the Internal Audit Activity and Internal Auditor in the Ethical Culture of an Organization*.

    1. This Practice Advisory **underscores the importance of organizational culture** in establishing the ethical climate of an enterprise and suggests the role that internal auditors could play in improving that ethical climate. Among other things, the Practice Advisory states that all people associated with the organization, and specifically internal auditors, should assume the role of **ethics advocates**.

    4. *All people* associated with the organization share some *responsibility* for the state of its ethical culture. Because of the complexity and dispersion of decision-making processes in most enterprises, each individual should be encouraged to be an **ethics advocate**, whether the role is delegated officially or merely conveyed informally. *Codes of conduct* and *statements of vision and policy* are important declarations of the organization's values and goals, the behavior expected of its people, and the strategies for maintaining a culture that aligns with its legal, ethical, and societal responsibilities. A growing number of organizations have designated a *chief ethics officer* as counselor of executives, managers, and others and as champion within the organization for "doing the right thing."

    5. *Internal auditors and the internal audit activity* should take an active role in support of the organization's ethical culture. They possess a high level of trust and integrity within the organization and the skills to be effective advocates of ethical conduct. They have the competence and capacity to appeal to the enterprise's leaders, managers, and other employees to comply with the legal, ethical, and societal responsibilities of the organization.

    6. *The internal audit activity may assume one of several different **roles as an ethics advocate**. Those roles include chief ethics officer (ombudsperson, compliance officer, management ethics counselor, or ethics expert), member of an internal ethics council, or assessor of the organization's ethical climate. In some circumstances, the role of chief ethics officer may conflict with the independence attribute of the internal audit activity.*

    7. *At a minimum*, the internal audit activity should **periodically assess** the state of the ethical climate of the organization and the effectiveness of its strategies, tactics, communications, and other processes in achieving the desired level of **legal and ethical compliance**. Internal auditors should evaluate the effectiveness of the following features of an enhanced, highly effective ethical culture:

- *Formal Code of Conduct*, which is clear and understandable, and related statements, policies (including procedures covering fraud and corruption), and other expressions of aspiration.
- Frequent communications and demonstrations of expected ethical attitudes and behavior by the **influential leaders** of the organization.
- *Explicit strategies* to support and enhance the ethical culture with regular programs to update and renew the organization's commitment to an ethical culture.
- Several easily accessible ways for people to **confidentially report** alleged violations of the Code, policies, and other acts of misconduct.
- *Regular declarations* by employees, suppliers, and customers that they are aware of the requirements for ethical behavior in transacting the organization's affairs.

- ***Clear delegation of responsibilities*** to ensure that ethical consequences are evaluated, confidential counseling is provided, allegations of misconduct are investigated, and case findings are properly reported.
- ***Easy access to learning*** opportunities to enable all employees to be ethics advocates.
- ***Positive personnel practices*** that encourage every employee to contribute to the ethical climate of the organization.
- ***Regular surveys*** of employees, suppliers, and customers to determine the state of the ethical climate in the organization.
- ***Regular reviews*** of the formal and informal processes within the organization that could potentially create pressures and biases that would undermine the ethical culture.
- ***Regular reference and background checks*** as part of hiring procedures, including integrity tests, drug screening, and similar measures.

PA Summary

- Because of their skills and position in the organization, auditors should actively support the ethical culture. **Roles** may include chief ethics officer, member of an ethics council, or assessor of the ethical climate.

- The **minimum IAA role** is assessor of the ethical climate and the effectiveness of processes to achieve legal and ethical compliance. Internal auditors should evaluate the effectiveness of the following features of an enhanced, highly effective ethical culture: (1) a **formal Code of Conduct**; (2) frequent communications by **influential leaders**; (3) **explicit strategies** to enhance the ethical culture with regular programs; (4) easily accessible ways to **confidentially report** alleged violations; (5) **regular declarations** by employees, suppliers, and customers about the requirements for ethical behavior; (6) **clear delegation of responsibilities** for providing counsel, investigation, and reporting; (7) **easy access to learning** opportunities; (8) **positive personnel practices** that encourage every employee to contribute; (9) **regular surveys** to determine the state of the ethical climate; (10) **regular reviews** of the processes that undermine the ethical culture; and (11) **regular reference and background checks**.

---

9. Stop and review! You have completed the outline for this subunit. Study multiple-choice questions 1 through 7 beginning on page 504.

10.2 THE IIA CODE OF ETHICS

1. CIA examination candidates should know the four **Principles** and twelve **Rules of Conduct**. The full text, including the Introduction and Applicability and Enforcement sections, appears at the end of this subunit.

2. The IIA Code of Ethics should be read with the **International Standards for the Professional Practice of Internal Auditing**.

3. The IIA Code of Ethics applies to **individuals and entities**, including members of The Institute, CIAs, and candidates for certification. However, it also furnishes guidance to **anyone who provides internal auditing services**.

THE INSTITUTE OF INTERNAL AUDITORS
CODE OF ETHICS

INTRODUCTION: The purpose of The Institute's <u>Code of Ethics</u> is to promote an ethical culture in the profession of internal auditing.

Internal auditing is an independent, objective assurance and consulting activity designed to add value and improve an organization's operations. It helps an organization accomplish its objectives by bringing a systematic, disciplined approach to evaluate and improve the effectiveness of risk management, control, and governance processes.

A code of ethics is necessary and appropriate for the profession of internal auditing, founded as it is on the trust placed in its objective assurance about risk management, control, and governance. The Institute's <u>Code of Ethics</u> extends beyond the definition of internal auditing to include two essential components:

1. Principles that are relevant to the profession and practice of internal auditing.

2. Rules of Conduct that describe behavior norms expected of internal auditors. These rules are an aid to interpreting the Principles into practical applications and are intended to guide the ethical conduct of internal auditors.

The <u>Code of Ethics</u> together with The Institute's <u>Professional Practices Framework</u> and other relevant Institute pronouncements provide guidance to internal auditors serving others. "Internal auditors" refers to Institute members, recipients of or candidates for IIA professional certifications, and those who provide internal auditing services within the definition of internal auditing.

APPLICABILITY AND ENFORCEMENT: This <u>Code of Ethics</u> applies to both individuals and entities that provide internal auditing services.

For Institute members and recipients of or candidates for IIA professional certifications, breaches of the <u>Code of Ethics</u> will be evaluated and administered according to The Institute's Bylaws and Administrative Guidelines. The fact that a particular conduct is not mentioned in the Rules of Conduct does not prevent it from being unacceptable or discreditable, and therefore, the member, certification holder, or candidate can be liable for disciplinary action.

Principles

Internal auditors are expected to apply and uphold the following principles:

Integrity

The integrity of internal auditors establishes trust and thus provides the basis for reliance on their judgment.

Objectivity

Internal auditors exhibit the highest level of professional objectivity in gathering, evaluating, and communicating information about the activity or process being examined. Internal auditors make a balanced assessment of all the relevant circumstances and are not unduly influenced by their own interests or by others in forming judgments.

Confidentiality

Internal auditors respect the value and ownership of information they receive and do not disclose information without appropriate authority unless there is a legal or professional obligation to do so.

Competency

Internal auditors apply the knowledge, skills, and experience needed in the performance of internal auditing services.

RULES OF CONDUCT

1. **Integrity**
   Internal auditors:

   1.1 Shall perform their work with honesty, diligence, and responsibility.

   1.2 Shall observe the law and make disclosures expected by the law and the profession.

   1.3 Shall not knowingly be a party to any illegal activity, or engage in acts that are discreditable to the profession of internal auditing or to the organization.

   1.4 Shall respect and contribute to the legitimate and ethical objectives of the organization.

2. **Objectivity**
Internal auditors:

2.1 Shall not participate in any activity or relationship that may impair or be presumed to impair their unbiased assessment. This participation includes those activities or relationships that may be in conflict with the interests of the organization.

2.2 Shall not accept anything that may impair or be presumed to impair their professional judgment.

2.3 Shall disclose all material facts known to them that, if not disclosed, may distort the reporting of activities under review.

3. **Confidentiality**
Internal auditors:

3.1 Shall be prudent in the use and protection of information acquired in the course of their duties.

3.2 Shall not use information for any personal gain or in any manner that would be contrary to the law or detrimental to the legitimate and ethical objectives of the organization.

4. **Competency**
Internal auditors:

4.1 Shall engage only in those services for which they have the necessary knowledge, skills, and experience.

4.2 Shall perform internal auditing services in accordance with the <u>International Standards for the Professional Practice of Internal Auditing</u>.

4.3 Shall continually improve their proficiency and the effectiveness and quality of their services.

4. Stop and review! You have completed the outline for this subunit. Study multiple-choice questions 8 through 41 beginning on page 507.

10.3 FRAUD RESPONSIBILITIES OF INTERNAL AUDITORS

1. This subunit concerns the duty of internal auditors to deter, detect, investigate, and communicate information about fraud. Fraud is a form of **white-collar crime**, a term that applies to numerous nonviolent offenses that have cheating and dishonesty as their main characteristic. Other examples are insider trading, embezzlement, and forgery. These matters are covered in one Assurance Implementation Standard and two Practice Advisories. The foregoing pronouncements are related to the specific Attribute Standard on proficiency.

2. *1210.A2* – *The internal auditor should have sufficient knowledge to identify the indicators of fraud but is not expected to have the expertise of a person whose primary responsibility is detecting and investigating fraud.*

   a. <u>**PRACTICE ADVISORY 1210.A2-1: AUDITOR'S RESPONSIBILITIES RELATING TO FRAUD RISK ASSESSMENT, PREVENTION, AND DETECTION**</u>

   WHAT IS FRAUD?

   Fraud encompasses a range of irregularities and illegal acts characterized by intentional deception or misrepresentation, which an individual knows to be false or does not believe to be true. Throughout this practice advisory, and in PA1210.A.2-2, the guidance may refer to certain actions as "fraud," which may also be legally defined and/or commonly known as corruption. Fraud is perpetrated by a person knowing that it could result in some unauthorized benefit to him or her, to the organization, or to another person, and can be perpetrated by persons outside and inside the organization.

1. **Fraud perpetrated to the detriment of the organization** is conducted generally for the direct or indirect benefit of an employee, outside individual, or another organization. Some examples are

   - Acceptance of bribes or kickbacks
   - Diversion to an employee or outsider of a potentially profitable transaction that would normally generate profits for the organization
   - Embezzlement, as typified by the misappropriation of money or property, and falsification of financial records to cover up an act, thus making detection difficult
   - Intentional concealment or misrepresentation of events, transactions, or data
   - Claims submitted for services or goods not actually provided to the organization
   - Intentional failure to act in circumstances where action is required by the company or by law
   - Unauthorized or illegal use of confidential or proprietary information
   - Unauthorized or illegal manipulation of information technology networks or operating systems
   - Theft

2. **Fraud designed to benefit the organization** generally produces such benefit by exploiting an unfair or dishonest advantage that also may deceive an outside party. Perpetrators of such acts usually accrue an indirect personal benefit, such as management bonus payments or promotions. Examples of fraud designed to benefit the organization include:

   - Improper payments, such as illegal political contributions, bribes, and kickbacks, as well as payoffs to government officials, intermediaries of government officials, customers, or suppliers.
   - Intentional and improper representation or valuation of transactions, assets, liabilities, and income, among others.
   - Intentional and improper transfer pricing (e.g., valuation of goods exchanged between related organizations). By purposely structuring pricing techniques improperly, management can improve their operating results to the detriment of the other organization.
   - Intentional and improper related-party activities in which one party receives some benefit not obtainable in an arm's-length transaction.
   - Intentional failure to record or disclose significant information accurately or completely, which may present an enhanced picture of the organization to outside parties.
   - Sale or assignment of fictitious or misrepresented assets.
   - Intentional failure to act in circumstances where action is required by the company or by law.
   - Intentional errors in tax compliance activities to reduce taxes owed.
   - Prohibited business activities, such as those that violate government statutes, rules, regulations, or contracts.

In addition to the above, different ways of classifying or categorizing fraud exist. The auditor may want to explore information published by professional accounting or fraud investigation firms and associations to determine which classification method is most appropriate for his or her organization.

WHY DOES FRAUD OCCUR?

There are generally three factors that influence the commission of fraud. These are opportunity, motive, and rationalization.

1.   **Opportunity**

-   *A process may be designed properly for typical conditions. However, a window of opportunity may arise for something to go wrong or create circumstances for the control to fail.*
-   *An opportunity for fraud may exist due to poor control design or lack of controls. For example, a system can be developed that appears to protect assets but which is missing an important control. Anyone aware of the gap can take what they want without much effort.*
-   *Persons in positions of authority can create opportunities to override existing controls, because subordinates or weak controls allow them to circumvent the rules.*

2.   **Motive** (also called incentive or pressure)

-   *While people can rationalize their acts, there needs to be a motive to make them behave that way.*
-   *Power is a great motivator. Power can be simply gaining esteem in the eyes of family or coworkers. For instance, many computer frauds are done to show the hacker has the power to do it rather than to cause intentional harm.*
-   *Another motivator is the gratification of a desire, such as greed, or an addiction.*
-   *The third motivator is pressure, either from physical stresses or from outside parties.*

3.   **Rationalization**

-   *Most individuals consider themselves good persons, even if they occasionally do something bad. To convince themselves they are still good persons, they may rationalize or deny their acts. For example, these individuals might consider that they were entitled to the stolen item or that if executives break the rules, it must be alright for others to do so as well.*
-   *Some people will do things that are defined as unacceptable behavior by the organization, yet are commonplace in their culture or were accepted by previous employers. As a result, these individuals will not comply with rules that don't make sense to them.*
-   *Some people may have periods of financial difficulty in their lives, have succumbed to a costly addiction, or are facing other pressures. Consequently, they will rationalize that they are just borrowing the money and, when their lives improve, they will pay it back. Others may feel that stealing from a company is not bad, thereby depersonalizing the act.*

*Although auditors may not be able to know the exact motive or rationalization leading to fraud, they are expected to understand enough about internal controls to **identify opportunities for fraud**. Auditors also should **understand fraud schemes** and scenarios, as well as be aware of the **signs that point to fraud and how to prevent them**. Information available from The IIA and other professional associations or organizations should be reviewed to ensure that the auditor's knowledge is current.*

FRAUD AND MISCONDUCT RISK ASSESSMENT

*All organizations are exposed to a degree of fraud risk in any process where human input is required. The degree to which an organization is exposed relates to the **fraud risks inherent in the business**, the extent to which effective **internal controls** are present either to prevent or detect fraud, and the **honesty and integrity** of those involved in the process.*

*__Fraud risk__ is the **probability** that fraud will occur and the potential severity or **consequences** to the organization when it occurs. The probability of a fraudulent activity is based, typically, on how easy it is to commit fraud, the motivational factors leading to fraud, and the company's fraud history. **Fraud management** includes limiting or eliminating consequences, which is more than limiting or eliminating financial loss. For example, for some organizations, loss of reputation may have considerable impact on their ability to attract and retain skilled employees or customers for their products, as well as to obtain facilities and licenses necessary for the business' growth and sustainability.*

*__To assess fraud risk__, internal auditors should use the organization's **enterprise risk management model** if one is in use. Otherwise, auditors could use the following guidelines:*

1. *Understand the **specific fraud schemes** that could threaten the organization. Use a **risk model** to map and assess the organization's vulnerability to these fraud schemes, which covers all inherent risks to the organization. The risk model also should use **consistent categories** (i.e., there should be no overlap between risk areas) and be detailed enough for a risk assessment to identify and cover anticipated high-risk areas.*

   *The **Committee of Sponsoring Organizations** of the Treadway Commission's (COSO's) Enterprise Risk Management framework provides a useful model that includes sections on:*

   - *__Event identification__, such as brainstorming activities, interviews, focus groups, surveys, industry research, and event inventories*
   - *__Risk assessments__ that include probabilities and consequences*
   - *__Risk response strategies__, such as treating, transferring, tolerating, or terminating risk*
   - *__Control activities__, such as linking risks to existing anti-fraud programs and control activities, and validating their effectiveness*
   - *__Monitoring__, including audit plans and programs that consider residual fraud and risk due to misconduct*

2. *When evaluating controls to prevent or reduce fraud risks to an organization, the internal auditor should consider **costs and benefits**. The evaluation should consider whether fraud could be committed by an individual or requires **collusion**. In practice, 100-percent fraud prevention is neither possible nor cost effective. The internal auditor also should consider the negative effects of unjustly suspecting employees or giving the appearance that employees are not trusted.*

ELEMENTS OF FRAUD PREVENTION OR DETERRENCE

Fraud prevention involves those actions taken to discourage the commission of fraud and limit fraud exposure when it occurs. The principal mechanism for preventing fraud is **internal control**. Primary responsibility for establishing and maintaining internal control should rest with **management**.

The following are some control elements of a **fraud prevention program** presented within the **COSO control framework** as an example. Each element would be a valid consideration, regardless of which control framework the auditor uses.

1. **Control environment.** Companies must establish an appropriate control environment that includes:

    - A code of conduct, ethics policy, or fraud policy to set the appropriate tone at the top
    - Ethics and whistleblower hotline programs to report concerns
    - Hiring and promotion guidelines and practices
    - Oversight by the audit committee, board, or other oversight body
    - Investigation of reported issues and remediation of confirmed violations

2. **Fraud risk assessment.** Organizations should identify and assess fraud-related risks, including assessing the potential for fraudulent financial reporting, asset misappropriations, improper receipts and expenditures, or financial misconduct by management and others. Companies also should assess whether adequate segregation of duties exists.

3. **Control activities.** Companies should establish and implement effective control practices, including actions taken by management to identify, prevent, and mitigate fraudulent financial reporting or misuse of the organization's assets, as well as prevent override of controls by management. In addition, companies should establish an affirmation or certification process to confirm employees have read and understood corporate policies and are in compliance with them.

4. **Information and communication.** Companies must establish effective fraud-related information and communication practices, including documentation and dissemination of policies, guidance, and results; opportunities to discuss ethical dilemmas; communication channels; training for personnel; and considerations of the impact and use of technology for fraud deterrence, such as the use of continuous monitoring software.

5. **Monitoring.** Organizations should conduct ongoing and periodic performance assessments and identify the impact and use of computer technology for fraud deterrence.

Internal Auditor's Role

Internal auditors are responsible for assisting in fraud prevention by examining and evaluating the **adequacy and effectiveness of their internal controls' system**, commensurate with the extent of a potential exposure within the organization. When meeting their responsibilities, internal auditors should consider the following elements:

1. **Control environment.** Assess aspects of the control environment, conduct proactive fraud audits and investigations, communicate results of fraud audits, and provide support for remediation efforts. In some cases, internal auditors also may own the whistleblower hotline.

2. **Fraud risk assessment.** Evaluate management's fraud risk assessment, in particular, their processes for identifying, assessing, and testing potential fraud and misconduct schemes and scenarios, including those that could involve suppliers, contractors, and other parties.

3. **Control activities.** Assess the design and operating effectiveness of fraud-related controls; ensure that audit plans and programs address residual risk and incorporate fraud audits; evaluate the design of facilities from a fraud or theft perspective; and review proposed changes to laws, regulations, or systems, and their impacts on controls.

4. **Information and communication.** Assess the operating effectiveness of information and communication systems and practices, as well as provide support to fraud-related training initiatives.

5. **Monitoring.** Assess monitoring activities and related computer software; conduct investigations; support the audit committee's oversight related to control and fraud matters; support the development of fraud indicators; and hire and train employees so they can have the appropriate fraud audit or investigative experience.

FRAUD DETECTION

Management and the internal audit activity have different roles with respect to fraud detection. Here is a description of each:

Management's Role in Fraud Detection

Management is responsible for **establishing and maintaining an effective control system** at a reasonable cost. This includes designing some controls to indicate when other controls are not working effectively. Following up on these indicators may result in the determination that fraud may have occurred.

One example of a **monitoring control** is the establishment and communication of a hotline or similar system customers or employees can use to make complaints or identify concerns. Other monitoring and detection controls include

- Installing alarm systems on facility doors and windows
- Installing surveillance cameras
- Designing edit checks into information systems
- Performing inventory counts
- Auditing
- Reviewing and approving invoices and cost center charges
- Reconciling accounts

Internal Auditor's Role in Fraud Detection

To the degree that fraud may be present in activities covered in the normal course of audit work, internal auditors have a responsibility to exercise **due professional care** as specifically defined in Standard 1220 of the International Standards for the Professional Practice of Internal Auditing with respect to fraud detection.

However, most internal auditors are not expected to have knowledge equivalent to that of a **person whose primary responsibility is detecting and investigating fraud**. Also, audit procedures alone, even when carried out with due professional care, do not guarantee that fraud will be detected.

A well-designed internal control system should not be conducive to fraud. Tests conducted by auditors improve the likelihood that any existing fraud indicators will be detected and considered for further investigation.

In conducting engagements, the **internal auditor's responsibilities for detecting fraud** are to:

- *Consider fraud risks* in the assessment of control design and determination of audit steps to perform. While internal auditors are not expected to detect fraud and irregularities, internal auditors are expected to obtain reasonable assurance that business objectives for the process under review are being achieved and material control deficiencies– whether through simple error or intentional effort–are detected.

- Have **sufficient knowledge of fraud to identify red flags** indicating fraud may have been committed. This knowledge includes the characteristics of fraud, the techniques used to commit fraud, and the various fraud schemes and scenarios associated with the activities reviewed.

- *Be alert to opportunities that could allow fraud,* such as control weaknesses. If significant control weaknesses are detected, additional tests conducted by internal auditors should be directed at identifying other fraud indicators. Some examples of indicators are unauthorized transactions, sudden fluctuations in the volume or value of transactions, control overrides, unexplained pricing exceptions, and unusually large product losses. Internal auditors should recognize that the presence of more than one indicator at any one time increases the probability that fraud has occurred.

- *Evaluate the indicators of fraud* and decide whether any further action is necessary or whether an investigation should be recommended.

- *Notify the appropriate authorities* within the organization to recommend an investigation if a determination is made that fraud has occurred.

PA Summary

- **Fraud encompasses an array of irregularities and illegal acts characterized by intentional deception or misrepresentation.** It can be perpetrated for the benefit, or to the detriment, of the organization and by persons outside or inside the organization. Fraud perpetrated to the **detriment of the organization** generally is for the direct or indirect benefit of an employee, outside individual, or another organization. Fraud designed to **benefit the organization** generally produces such benefit by exploiting an unfair or dishonest advantage that also may deceive an outside party.

- The **factors** that influence the commission of fraud are **opportunity, motive (incentive or pressure), and rationalization.** Internal auditors should know enough about **internal control** to identify opportunities, understand fraud schemes and how to prevent them, and recognize fraud signs. An **opportunity** for fraud may exist due to (1) occurrence of abnormal conditions, (2) poor control design, (3) lack of controls, or (4) override of existing controls by persons in positions of authority. **Motives** are (1) power, (2) gratification of a desire, and (3) pressure. **Rationalization** is finding some justification for fraudulent actions.

- The **degree of fraud exposure** depends on inherent risk, the effectiveness of controls (detective or preventive), and the honesty and integrity of the people involved.

- **Fraud risk** has two elements: (1) the probability of fraud and (2) the consequences if it occurs. Probability is based on how easy it is to commit fraud, motives leading to fraud, and the entity's fraud history.

- **Fraud management** limits or eliminates financial and nonfinancial consequences.
- **Fraud risk assessment** should be based on an **ERM model** if one is in use. Otherwise, auditors should understand specific schemes and use a **risk model** to assess vulnerability. This model should cover all inherent risks, use **consistent categories**, and be detailed enough for a risk assessment to identify high-risk areas. The **COSO's model** has sections on (1) event identification, (2) risk assessments, (3) risk response strategies, (4) control activities, and (5) monitoring. An **evaluation of controls** considers the **costs and benefits** of prevention and whether fraud requires **collusion**. Complete fraud prevention is neither possible nor cost effective.
- **Fraud prevention** discourages the commission of fraud and limits exposure when it occurs. The principal mechanism for preventing fraud is **control**. Primary responsibility for establishing and maintaining control rests with **management**.
- The **elements** of the **COSO control framework** provide an example of the control elements of a **fraud prevention program**: (1) control environment, (2) fraud risk assessment, (3) control activities, (4) information and communication, and (5) monitoring.
- **Internal auditors** are responsible for assisting in the **prevention** of fraud by examining and evaluating the **adequacy and effectiveness** of the system of internal control, in proportion to the extent of the potential exposure in the organization. To meet their responsibilities, internal auditors consider their specific duties with respect to the five elements of the fraud prevention program in the COSO control framework.
- **Management's responsibility** for **fraud detection** is to establish and maintain effective control at a reasonable cost.
- The internal auditor's role in **fraud detection** includes exercising **due professional care**. The exercise of due professional care does **not** guarantee detection of fraud.
- Auditors need not have the **fraud knowledge** of a specialist.
- **Well-designed controls** are not conducive to fraud. Audit tests improve the likelihood that **fraud indicators** will be detected.
- Internal auditors should consider **fraud risk** when assessing control design and selecting audit procedures. Auditors should obtain reasonable assurance that objectives are achieved and material control deficiencies are detected.
- Internal auditors also must (1) have sufficient **knowledge of fraud** to identify **red flags** (characteristics, techniques used, and schemes), (2) be alert to opportunities (e.g., control weaknesses) that could allow fraud, (3) **evaluate** the indicators, and (4) **notify appropriate authorities** if necessary.

b. ### PRACTICE ADVISORY 1210.A2-2: AUDITOR'S RESPONSIBILITIES RELATING TO FRAUD INVESTIGATION, REPORTING, RESOLUTION, AND COMMUNICATION

INVESTIGATING FRAUD

This section of the practice advisory does **not refer to the activity known as "auditing for fraud,"** defined as "an audit designed to proactively detect indications of fraud in those processes or transactions where analysis indicates the risk of fraud to be significant." This guidance refers to investigations initiated when a **concern over control failures or suspicion of wrongdoing is raised within the organization**. Suspicions can result from a formal complaint process, informal tips, or an audit, including an audit designed to test for fraud.

A **fraud investigation** consists of gathering sufficient information about specific details and performing those procedures necessary to determine whether fraud has occurred, the loss or exposures associated with the fraud, who was involved in it, and the fraud scheme (how it happened). An important outcome of investigations is that innocent persons are cleared of suspicion.

Investigations should be designed to discover the **full nature and extent of the fraudulent activity**, not just the event that may have initiated the investigation. **Investigation work** includes preparing workpapers/file documentation sufficient for a legal proceeding.

Internal auditors, lawyers, investigators, security personnel, and other **specialists** from inside or outside the organization are the parties that usually conduct or participate in fraud investigations.

Investigations and the **related resolution activities** need to be carefully managed in consideration of **local law**. Laws may direct how and where investigations are conducted, disciplinary and recovery practices, and communications. It is in the best interests of an auditor, both professionally and legally, to work effectively with the organization's legal counsel and to become familiar with the relevant laws. The guidance provided here is directed at an international audience and is therefore general in nature.

Management's Role

Management is responsible for developing **controls over the investigation process**, including developing policies and procedures for effective investigations and standards for handling the results of investigations, reporting, and communications. Such standards are often documented in a **fraud policy**, and internal audit may be involved in developing the policy.

Such policies and procedures must consider the **rights of individuals** involved, the **qualifications** of those authorized to conduct investigations, and the **relevant laws** of the countries and local governments where the frauds occurred or were investigated. The policies should consider the extent to which management will **discipline** employees, suppliers, or customers, including taking legal measures to recover losses and civil or criminal prosecution. It is important for management to clearly define the **authority and responsibilities of various roles** within an investigation, especially the relationship between the investigator and legal counsel. It is also important for management to design and comply with **procedures that minimize internal communications about an ongoing investigation**, especially in the initial phases.

*The policy should specify the **role the investigator will have in making a determination that fraud has been committed**. Management should consider whether the investigator or management reaches a conclusion of fraud, or whether the company refers the facts to outside authorities for their conclusion. A judgment that fraud has occurred may, in some jurisdictions, only be made by law enforcement or judicial authorities. The investigation may simply result in a conclusion that company policy was violated.*

Internal Audit's Role

*The role of internal audit in investigations should be defined in the **internal audit charter** as well as the fraud policies. For example, internal audit may have the primary responsibility for fraud investigations, may act as a resource for investigations, or must refrain from involving itself in investigations (because they are responsible for assessing the effectiveness of investigations). Any of these roles can be acceptable, as long as the impact of these activities on internal audit's independence is recognized and handled appropriately.*

***To maintain proficiency**, fraud investigation teams have a responsibility to obtain sufficient knowledge of fraud schemes, investigation techniques, and laws. There are national and international programs that provide training and certifications for investigators and forensic specialists.*

***If internal audit is responsible** for ensuring that investigations are conducted, it may conduct an investigation using in-house staff, **outsourcing**, or a combination of both. In some cases, internal audit may also use nonaudit employees of the organization to assist.*

*It is often important to assemble the investigation team without delay. If the organization needs **external experts**, the chief audit executive should consider **prequalifying the service provider(s)** so that the external resources are available quickly.*

*In companies where primary responsibility for the investigation function is not assigned to internal audit, auditors may still be asked to help **gather information and make recommendations for internal control improvements**.*

NOTE: An internal auditor's engagement to conduct a fraud investigation is an example of **forensic auditing**.

Investigator's Role (whether assigned to internal auditing or elsewhere)

*An **investigation plan** must be developed for each investigation, following the organization's investigation procedures or protocols. The lead investigator should determine the **knowledge, skills, and other competencies** needed to carry out the investigation effectively and assign competent, appropriate people to the team. This process should include assurance that there is no potential **conflict of interest** with those being investigated or with any of the employees of the organization.*

The plan should consider methods to:

- *Gather evidence, such as surveillance, interviews, or written statements*
- *Document the evidence, considering legal rules of evidence and the business uses of the evidence*
- *Determine the extent of the fraud*
- *Determine the scheme (techniques used to perpetrate the fraud)*
- *Evaluate the cause*
- *Identify the perpetrators*

At any point in this process, the investigator may conclude that the complaint or suspicion was unfounded and follow a process to **close the case***.*

Activities should be coordinated *with management, legal counsel, and other specialists, such as human resources and insurance risk management, as appropriate throughout the course of the investigation.*

Investigators must be knowledgeable and cognizant of the **rights of persons** *within the scope of the investigation and the* **reputation of the organization itself***.*

The **level and extent of complicity** *in the fraud throughout the organization should be assessed. This assessment can be critical to ensuring that crucial evidence is not destroyed nor tainted, and to avoid obtaining misleading information from persons who may be involved.*

REPORTING ON FRAUD

Fraud reporting consists of the various **oral or written, interim or final, communications** *to senior management and/or the board of directors regarding the status and results of fraud investigations. Reports can be preliminary and ongoing throughout the investigation. A written report may follow any oral briefing made to management and the board of directors to document the findings.*

Section 2400 of the International Standards for the Professional Practice of Internal Auditing provides information applicable to engagement communications. Additional interpretive guidance on fraud reporting internally follows:

- *A draft of the proposed final communications on fraud should be submitted to* **legal counsel for review***. In cases where the organization is able to invoke* **client privilege** *and has chosen to do so, the report must be addressed to legal counsel.*

- *When the* **incidence of significant fraud or erosion of trust** *have been established to a reasonable certainty, senior management and the board of directors should be notified immediately.*

- *The* **results of a fraud investigation** *may indicate that fraud may have had a previously undiscovered adverse effect on the organization's financial position and its operational results for one or more years for which* **financial statements** *have already been issued. Senior management and the board of directors should be informed of such a discovery.*

- *A written report or other* **formal communication should be issued at the conclusion of the investigation phase***. It should include the basis for beginning an investigation, time frames, observations, conclusions, resolution, and corrective action taken (or recommendations) to improve controls. Depending on how the investigation was resolved, the report may need to be written in a manner that provides* **confidentiality** *to some of the people involved. The content of this report is sensitive, and it must meet the needs of the board of directors and management while complying with legal requirements and restrictions and company policies and procedures.*

RESOLUTION OF FRAUD INCIDENTS

Management is responsible for resolving fraud incidents, *not the internal auditor nor the investigator. Resolution consists of determining what actions will be taken by the organization once a fraud scheme and perpetrator(s) have been fully investigated and evidence has been reviewed.*

Internal auditors *should assess the facts of investigations and advise management relating to* **remediation of control weaknesses** *that lead to the fraud. Auditors should* **design additional steps in routine audit programs** *or develop "auditing for fraud" programs to help disclose the existence of similar frauds in the future.*

Management's fraud policies and procedures *(mentioned earlier in the practice advisory) should define who has authority and responsibility for each process.* **Internal auditors may be involved** *as* **advisors** *in the following processes, as long as the impact of these activities on internal audit's* **independence** *is recognized and handled appropriately. Resolution may include all or some of the following:*

- *Providing closure to persons who were initially under suspicion but were found to be innocent*
- *Providing closure to those who reported a concern*
- *Disciplining an employee in accordance with company standards, employment legislation, or employment contracts*
- *Requesting voluntary financial restitution from an employee, customer, or supplier*
- *Terminating contracts with suppliers*
- *Reporting the incident to law enforcement, regulatory bodies, or similar authorities, and cooperating with their investigation*
- *Entering into civil litigation or similar legal processes*
- *Filing an insurance claim*
- *Filing a complaint with the perpetrator's professional association*

In addition to advising clients, internal auditors may become involved in:

- *Monitoring the investigation process to help ensure that the organization follows relevant policies, procedures, and applicable laws and statutes (where internal auditing was not responsible for conducting the investigation)*
- *Locating and/or securing the misappropriated or related assets*
- *Supporting the organization's legal, insurance, or other recovery actions*
- *Evaluating and monitoring the organization's internal and external post-investigation reporting and communication plans and practices*
- *Monitoring the implementation of recommended control improvements to help ensure timeliness, effectiveness, and efficiency*

COMMUNICATIONS

To limit the risk of the unofficial dissemination of inappropriate and/or inaccurate information, the internal auditor can advise management in the **design of a communication strategy and tactical plan** *as early in the investigation as possible.*

In addition to fraud reporting mentioned above, there are two types of communications that may result from an investigation: **public communications** *that may arise and* **planned internal communications***.*

Any **comments made by management** *to the press, law enforcement, or other external parties are best coordinated through legal counsel. Comments should be made only by authorized spokespersons.*

Internal communications are a strategic tool used by management to reinforce its position relating to **integrity**, to demonstrate that it takes appropriate action when company **policy is violated**, and to show why **internal controls** are important. Such communications may take the form of a newsletter article or a memo from management, or the situation may be used as an example in the organization's integrity training program. These communications generally take place **after the case has been resolved internally**, and they do not specify the names of perpetrators or other specific investigation details that are not necessary for the message or that contravene laws.

An investigation and its results may cause **significant stress or morale issues** that may disrupt the organization, especially when the fraud becomes public. Management may plan interactive employee sessions and/or team-building strategies for this contingency.

FORMING AN OPINION ON THE SYSTEM OF INTERNAL CONTROL RELATED TO FRAUD

The internal auditor may be asked by management or the board to issue an opinion on the organization's system of internal control related to fraud. Auditors should refer to various practice advisories in the 2410 series and other IIA practice aids, such as "Practical Considerations Regarding Internal Auditing Expressing an Opinion on Internal Controls," to determine whether they have sufficiently considered related information before expressing an opinion.

PA Summary

- The **fraud investigation** described in PA 1210.A2-2 (as opposed to an audit for fraud) is begun when (1) concern about **control failures** or (2) suspicion of wrongdoing is raised within the organization. An investigation should be designed to determine whether fraud has occurred, the loss or exposures, who was involved, and the fraud scheme. It should discover the **full nature and extent** of the fraud. The investigation and resolution activities must be in accordance with local law, and the auditor should work effectively with legal counsel and become familiar with the relevant laws.

- **Management** should develop **controls over the investigation process**, including policies, procedures, and standards. Such standards are often documented in a **fraud policy**, and internal audit may be involved in developing the policy. Policies and procedures must consider (1) the rights of individuals, (2) the qualifications of investigators, (3) relevant laws, (4) the extent of discipline, (5) the authority and responsibilities of the persons involved in the investigation, and (6) compliance with procedures for minimizing internal communication about an ongoing investigation. The policy should specify the **role the investigator will have in making a determination that fraud has been committed**.

- The **role of internal audit** should be defined in the **charter**. Moreover, fraud investigation teams must be **proficient** regarding fraud schemes, investigation methods, and the law. If internal audit is responsible for the investigation, use of **external experts** (possibly pre-qualified) or nonaudit employees of the organization may be necessary. If auditors do not have primary responsibility for the investigation, they may be asked to **gather information and make recommendations for control improvements**.

- An **investigation plan** should be developed, and the lead investigator should assign people to the team. **Conflicts of interest** should be avoided. Furthermore, investigators should (1) assess the probable level and extent of **complicity in the fraud**; (2) determine **competencies** required; (3) design procedures; (4) **coordinate activities** with management, counsel, and other specialists; and (5) be aware of the **rights** of all persons and the organization's **reputation**.

- **Reporting of fraud** consists of the various oral or written, interim, or final communications to management or the board regarding the status and results of fraud investigations. A draft of the final communication should be submitted to **legal counsel for review**. To invoke **client privilege**, the report must be addressed to counsel. Internal audit has the responsibility to report immediately any **incident of significant fraud or erosion of trust** to senior management and the board. If the investigation's results indicate that **previously issued financial statements** may have been adversely affected, senior management and the board also should be informed. A formal communication is issued at the **end of the investigation**. The report may need to protect the **confidentiality** of some people and comply with the law and organizational policy.

- Management is responsible for **resolving fraud incidents**. Resolution consists of actions to be taken after completion of the investigation and review of the evidence. **Internal auditors** assess the facts and provide advice about remediation of control weaknesses. In addition, they should include procedures in **routine audit programs** or **design specific programs** for detecting fraud. **Management's fraud policies** should define who has authority and responsibility for each process. Internal auditors may be **advisors** in many parts of the process, but the effect on internal audit's **independence** should be handled appropriately.

- The internal auditor may give advice about designing a **communication strategy and tactical plan**. Communications may include public communications and planned internal communications. **Comments by management** are best coordinated through legal counsel and made only by authorized spokespersons.

- An internal auditor asked to **express an opinion** on the system of internal control related to fraud should consult The IIA practice aids.

3. Stop and review! You have completed the outline for this subunit. Study multiple-choice questions 42 through 60 beginning on page 520.

10.4 FRAUD INDICATORS

1. Professional literature has devoted considerable attention to the **red flags** that may signal fraudulent conduct. The internal auditor should be alert to red flags and investigate any conditions that might indicate potential fraud. Red flags do not need to be documented unless the auditor conducts a fraud investigation or the red flags are pertinent to a particular engagement observation.

2. An internal auditor's **responsibilities for the detection of fraud** include having sufficient knowledge to identify indicators that fraud may have been committed, identifying control weaknesses that could allow fraud to occur, and evaluating the indicators of fraud sufficiently to determine whether a fraud investigation should be conducted.

3.   **Factors Contributing to or Permitting Fraud**

    a.   Ineffective internal control, for example,

        1)   Not separating the functional responsibilities of authorization, custodianship, and record keeping, e.g., failing to segregate users and computer functions, such as by access controls, or not segregating duties within the computer function

        2)   Unlimited access to assets

        3)   Failure to record transactions, resulting in lack of accountability

        4)   Not comparing existing assets with recorded amounts

        5)   Transaction execution without proper authorizations

        6)   Not implementing prescribed controls because of

            a)   Lack of personnel

            b)   Unqualified personnel

        7)   Lack of computer expertise by supervisors

        8)   Ability to bypass controls with utility programs

        9)   Unrestricted access to computer disks

        10)   Location of computer terminals off-site without compensating controls

        11)   Use of untested off-the-shelf vendor software

    b.   Collusion among employees over whom little control is exercised

    c.   Existence of liquid assets, such as cash, bearer securities, or highly marketable merchandise

4.   **Danger Signs Pointing toward the Possibility of Embezzlement**, *Sawyer's Internal Auditing*, 5th ed. [L.B. Sawyer, et al., The Institute of Internal Auditors, 2003 (p. 1183)]

    a.   *Borrowing small amounts from fellow employees*

    b.   *Placing personal checks in change funds -- undated, postdated -- or requesting others to "hold" checks*

    c.   *Personal checks cashed and returned for irregular reasons*

    d.   *Collectors or creditors appearing at the place of business and excessive use of telephone to "stall off" creditors*

    e.   *Placing unauthorized IOUs in change funds or prevailing on others in authority to accept IOUs for small, short-term loans*

    f.   *Inclination toward covering up inefficiencies by "plugging" figures*

    g.   *Pronounced criticism of others so as to divert suspicion*

    h.   *Replying to questions with unreasonable explanations*

    i.   *Gambling in any form beyond ability to stand the loss*

    j.   *Excessive drinking and nightclubbing or associating with questionable characters*

    k.   *Buying or otherwise acquiring through "business" channels expensive automobiles and extravagant household furnishings*

    l.   *Explaining a higher standard of living as money left from an estate*

    m.   *Getting annoyed at reasonable questioning*

    n.   *Refusing to leave custody of records during the day; working overtime regularly*

    o.   *Refusing to take vacations and shunning promotions for fear of detection*

    p.   *Constant association with, and entertainment by, a member of a supplier's staff*

    q.   *Carrying an unusually large bank balance or heavy buying of securities*

    r.   *Extended illness of self or family, usually without a plan of debt liquidation*

    s.   *Bragging about exploits and/or carrying unusual amounts of money*

    t.   *Rewriting records under the guise of neatness in presentation*

5. **Common Forms of Fraud**, *Sawyer's Internal Auditing*, 5th ed. [L.B. Sawyer, et al., The Institute of Internal Auditors, 2003 (pp. 1181-1182)]

   a. *Pilfering stamps*

   b. *Stealing merchandise, tools, supplies, and other items of equipment*

   c. *Removing small amounts from cash funds and registers*

   d. *Failing to record sales of merchandise and pocketing the cash*

   e. *Creating overages in cash funds and registers by underrecording*

   f. *Overloading expense accounts or diverting advances to personal use*

   g. *Lapping collections on customers' accounts*

   h. *Pocketing payments on customers' accounts and issuing receipts on scraps of paper or in self-designed receipt books*

   i. *Collecting an account, pocketing the money, and charging it off; collecting charged-off accounts and not reporting*

   j. *Charging customers' accounts with cash stolen*

   k. *Issuing credit for false customer claims and returns*

   l. *Failing to make bank deposits daily or depositing only part of the money*

   m. *Altering dates on deposit slips to cover stealing*

   n. *Making round-sum deposits -- attempting to catch up by end of month*

   o. *Carrying fictitious extra help on payrolls, or increasing rates or hours*

   p. *Carrying employees on payroll beyond actual severance dates*

   q. *Falsifying additions to payrolls; withholding unclaimed wages*

   r. *Destroying, altering, or voiding cash sales tickets and pocketing the cash*

   s. *Withholding cash sales amounts by using false charge accounts*

   t. *Recording unwarranted cash discounts*

   u. *Increasing amounts of petty cash vouchers and/or totals in accounting for disbursements*

   v. *Using personal expenditure receipts to support false paid-out items*

   w. *Using carbon copies of previously used original vouchers or using a properly approved voucher of a prior period by changing the date*

   x. *Paying false invoices, either self-prepared or obtained through collusion with suppliers*

   y. *Increasing the amounts of suppliers' invoices through collusion*

   z. *Charging personal purchases to the company through the misuse of purchase orders*

   aa. *Billing stolen merchandise to fictitious accounts*

   ab. *Shipping stolen merchandise to an employee or relative's home*

   ac. *Falsifying inventories to cover thefts or delinquencies*

   ad. *Seizing checks payable to the company or to suppliers*

   ae. *Raising canceled bank checks to agree with fictitious entries*

   af. *Inserting fictitious ledger sheets*

   ag. *Causing erroneous footings of cash receipts and disbursements books*

   ah. *Deliberately confusing postings to control and detail accounts*

   ai. *Selling waste and scrap and pocketing the proceeds*

   aj. *"Selling" door keys or combinations to safes or vaults*

   ak. *Creating credit balances on ledgers and converting to cash*

   al. *Falsifying bills of lading and splitting with carrier*

   am. *Obtaining blank checks (unprotected) and forging the signature*

   an. *Permitting special prices or privileges to customers, or granting business to favored suppliers, for "kickbacks"*

   ao. *Improper use of access cards, such as credit, retail, telephone, and smart cards*

6. **Management fraud** usually occurs because of the ease with which management can circumvent the system of internal control. *Sawyer's Internal Auditing* lists eight reasons behind management fraud:

    a. *Executives sometimes take rash steps from which they cannot retreat.*
    b. *Profit centers may distort facts to hold off divestment.*
    c. *Incompetent managers may deceive to survive.*
    d. *Performance may be distorted to warrant larger bonuses.*
    e. *The need to succeed can turn managers to deception.*
    f. *Unscrupulous managers may serve interests that conflict.*
    g. *Profits may be inflated to obtain advantages in the marketplace.*
    h. *The one who controls both the assets and their records is in a perfect position to falsify the latter.*

7. **Fraud danger signals.** Even the most effective internal control can sometimes be circumvented -- perhaps by collusion of two or more employees. Thus, an auditor must be sensitive to certain conditions that might indicate the existence of fraud, including

    a. High personnel turnover
    b. Low employee morale
    c. Paperwork supporting adjusting entries not readily available
    d. Bank reconciliations not completed promptly
    e. Increases in the number of customer complaints
    f. Deteriorating income trend when the industry or the organization as a whole is doing well
    g. Numerous audit adjustments of significant size
    h. Write-offs of inventory shortages with no attempt to determine cause
    i. Unrealistic performance expectations
    j. Rumors of conflicts of interest
    k. Use of duplicate invoices to support payments to suppliers
    l. Use of sole-source procurement contracts

8. **Organizational-Level Red Flags** (*Tone at the Top*, The IIA, November 2003)

    a. Abnormally rapid growth or profits, particularly relative to the industry
    b. Financial results excessively better than those of competitors absent significant operational differences
    c. Unexplained changes in trends or financial statement relationships
    d. Accounts or operations located in tax-haven countries without a good business rationale
    e. Decentralized operations coupled with a weak internal reporting system
    f. Earnings growth combined with a lack of cash
    g. Excessively optimistic public statements about future growth
    h. Use of accounting principles that conform with the letter (form) of requirements, not the substance, or that vary from industry practice
    i. A debt ratio that is too high or difficulty in paying debt
    j. Excessive sensitivity to interest rate fluctuations
    k. End-of-period transactions that are complex, unusual, or significant
    l. Nonenforcement of the organization's ethics code
    m. Material related-party transactions not in the ordinary course of business
    n. Potential business failure in the near term

o.   Use of unusual legal entities, many lines of authority, or contracts with no obvious
     business reason

p.   Business arrangements that are difficult to understand and do not seem to have any
     practical applicability to the entity

9.   Stop and review! You have completed the outline for this subunit. Study multiple-choice
     questions 61 through 75 beginning on page 526.

10.5 ENGAGEMENT PROCEDURES RELATED TO FRAUD

1.   The nature and extent of the specific procedures performed to detect and investigate fraud
     depend on the circumstances of the particular engagement, including the internal auditor's
     risk assessment.

     a.   Accordingly, an outline of specific procedures relative to fraud is beyond the scope of
          this text. However, **analytical procedures** are routinely performed in many
          engagements. They may provide an early indication of fraud.

2.   Internal auditors should have an awareness of the circumstances in which their own
     procedures and expertise may be insufficient. Thus, they may need to make use of
     specialists.

     a.   For example, **forensic experts** may supply special knowledge regarding authenticity
          of documents and signatures, mechanical sources of documents (printers,
          typewriters, computers, etc.), paper and ink chemistry, and fingerprint analysis.

3.   **Forensic auditing** is the use of accounting and auditing knowledge and skills in matters
     having civil or criminal legal implications. Engagements involving fraud, litigation support,
     and expert witness testimony are examples.

4.   Stop and review! You have completed the outline for this subunit. Study multiple-choice
     questions 76 through 92 beginning on page 531.

10.6 CONTROLS RELATED TO FRAUD

1.   Like engagement procedures, specific controls are too diverse to be within the scope of this
     text.

2.   Part I of *CIA Review* (13-1), Study Units 5 and 6, contains extensive guidance on control
     concepts, vocabulary, and techniques. They apply to the design and implementation of
     controls that are relevant to, among many other things, the prevention and detection of
     fraud.

3.   Stop and review! You have completed the outline for this subunit. Study multiple-choice
     questions 93 through 100 beginning on page 538.

10.7 LEGAL HAZARDS OF FRAUD INVESTIGATIONS

1.   An internal auditor involved in a **fraud investigation** may risk hindering the investigation by
     not conducting it professionally.

2.   An internal auditor risks giving cause for legal action by an employee-suspect (whether or
     not guilty) against the auditor and the organization. Legal liability may arise for violation of
     rights provided by law. The following are common grounds for a civil suit:

     a.   **Defamation** is the unjustifiable communication (publication) to a third party of a false
          statement by the employer or an agent of the employer that injures the employee-
          plaintiff's reputation and holds him or her up to hatred, contempt, or ridicule. Oral
          defamation is **slander**. Defamation published in more permanent form (newspaper,
          letter, film) is **libel**.

b.   The tort of **malicious prosecution** of a **criminal or civil action** involves proof of the first three elements below:

1)   The prosecution by the employer-defendant was without probable cause,

2)   The proceedings ended favorably for the person bringing the malicious prosecution suit, and

3)   The initiator of the proceedings acted with malice (for an improper purpose).

4)   In a suit based on the defendant's malicious prosecution of a civil action, the employee-plaintiff also must prove that (s)he suffered actual harm.

c.   **False imprisonment** (or arrest) is the intentional and unjustifiable restraint or confinement of a person. The restraint need not be an actual physical confinement.

d.   **Compounding a felony** is another form of possible wrongdoing by the employer (and internal auditor) in fraud cases. It is an agreement for a consideration (such as restitution of stolen funds) not to prosecute a felony. Compounding a felony is treated as a crime because only the state has such a prerogative.

3.   A **confession** obtained from a suspect may not be the most competent evidence. It may be tainted if the suspect was under any form of duress.

a.   Thus, a confession must be voluntary and after the fact, and no reasonable inference other than the suspect's culpability should be capable of being made from it.

b.   An **admission** by a suspect is a statement of a probative fact, not a statement of guilt.

4.   Because of the legal hazards and their lack of expertise in **criminal interrogation**, internal auditors should often defer to **security specialists**.

a.   Internal auditors should apply many of the interviewing methods used in other circumstances.

1)   "Internal auditors should be skilled in dealing with people and in communicating effectively" (PA 1210-1). One important communications skill is the ability to conduct an effective **interview**. For example, initial questions in a fraud interview should be broad. In contrast with a directive approach emphasizing narrowly focused questions, this nondirective approach is more likely to elicit clarifications and unexpected observations from employees who are under suspicion.

b.   The approach should be unemotional and nonthreatening, and the interviewee should be presumed innocent.

c.   The interview should be performed by two persons, with one serving as a witness.

d.   Interviewers should not interrupt the interviewee (except for clarification) and should attempt to gain his or her confidence.

e.   Interviewers must be certain of their facts before proceeding with an interview of a suspect.

5.   Stop and review! You have completed the outline for this subunit. Study multiple-choice questions 101 through 106 beginning on page 541.

10.8 STUDY UNIT 10 SUMMARY

1. Codes of ethics may be viewed from an organizational or an individual perspective.

2. Issues in business ethics include compliance, external reporting, conflicts of interest, relations with customers and suppliers, and social responsibility.

3. Many organizational and external factors may lead to unethical behavior.

4. General guides to ethics are diverse: (a) the Golden Rule, (b) fairness, (c) general respect, (d) law, (e) Kant's categorical imperative, (f) natural law, (g) utilitarian ethics, and (h) various concepts of social responsibility.

5. A code of ethics communicates acceptable values to members and people outside the organization, provides a method of policing and disciplining members, and sets high standards.

6. An internal auditor must follow The IIA Code of Ethics. According to its Rules of Conduct, an internal auditor must

   a. Perform work with honesty, diligence, and responsibility
   b. Observe the law and make proper disclosures
   c. Not knowingly be a party to an illegal activity or engage in discreditable acts
   d. Respect and contribute to appropriate organizational objectives
   e. Avoid activities or relationships, including conflicts of interest, that presumably impair unbiased assessment
   f. Accept nothing that impairs professional judgment
   g. Disclose material facts so that reports are not distorted
   h. Use and protect information prudently
   i. Not use information for personal gain or in a way contrary to law or appropriate organizational objectives
   j. Perform services only if (s)he has the needed competencies
   k. Perform services in accordance with the Standards
   l. Improve proficiency continually

7. Fraud encompasses an array of irregularities and illegal acts characterized by intentional deception. It can be perpetrated for the benefit or to the detriment of the organization and by persons outside as well as inside the organization. Fraud designed to benefit the organization generally produces such benefit by exploiting an unfair or dishonest advantage that also may deceive an outside party. Fraud perpetrated to the detriment of the organization generally is for the direct or indirect benefit of an employee, outside individual, or another organization.

8. The principal mechanism for deterring fraud is control. Primary responsibility for establishing and maintaining control rests with management. Internal auditors are responsible for assisting in the deterrence of fraud by examining and evaluating the adequacy and the effectiveness of the system of internal control, commensurate with the extent of the potential exposure/risk in the various segments of the organization's operations.

9. An auditor who suspects wrongdoing (a) informs appropriate authorities, (b) recommends any necessary investigation, and (c) follows up to see that IAA responsibilities are met.

10. Investigation of fraud consists of performing extended procedures necessary to determine whether fraud, as suggested by the indicators, has occurred. Internal auditors and other specialists usually conduct fraud investigations. Auditors (a) assess the probable level and extent of complicity in the fraud; (b) determine competencies required; (c) design procedures; (d) coordinate activities with management, counsel, and other specialists; and (e) must be aware of the rights of all parties.

11. Reporting of fraud consists of the various oral or written, interim or final, communications to management regarding the status and results of fraud investigations. The chief audit executive has the responsibility to report immediately any incident of significant fraud to senior management and the board. The report should include the internal auditor's conclusion as to whether sufficient information exists to conduct a full investigation.

12. The objective of internal auditing in fraud detection is to assist members of the organization by providing appraisals, recommendations, etc. The objective also includes promoting effective control at reasonable cost. Thus, deterrence and detection both depend on the system of control established by management.

13. Internal auditors must exercise due professional care regarding fraud detection.

14. Professional literature has devoted considerable attention to the red flags that may signal fraudulent conduct. The internal auditor should be alert to red flags and investigate any conditions that might indicate potential fraud. Red flags do not need to be documented unless the auditor conducts a fraud investigation or the red flags are pertinent to a particular engagement observation.

15. Forensic auditing is the use of accounting and auditing knowledge and skills in matters having civil or criminal legal implications. Engagements involving fraud, litigation support, and expert witness testimony are examples.

16. An internal auditor involved in a fraud investigation may incur legal liability based on defamation, malicious prosecution, false imprisonment, or compounding a felony.

QUESTIONS

10.1 Perspective on Ethics

1. A code of conduct was developed several years ago and distributed by a large financial institution to all its officers and employees. What is the internal auditor's best approach to providing the board with the highest level of comfort about the code of conduct?

A. Fully evaluate the comprehensiveness of the code and compliance with it and report the results to the board.

B. Fully evaluate organizational practices for compliance with the code, and report to the board.

C. Review employee activities for compliance with provisions of the code, and report to the board.

D. Perform tests on various employee transactions to detect potential violations of the code of conduct.

Answer (A) is correct. *(CIA, adapted)*
REQUIRED: The approach that provides the highest level of comfort about the code of conduct.
DISCUSSION: The internal audit activity should evaluate the design, implementation, and effectiveness of the organization's ethics-related objectives, programs, and activities (Standard 2130.A1). When evaluating a code of conduct, it is important to consider comprehensiveness and compliance. The code should address the ethical issues that the employees are expected to encounter and provide suitable guidance. The internal auditor also must consider the extent to which employees are complying with the standards established.
Answer (B) is incorrect because evaluating practices and reporting to the board is not the best approach. Answer (C) is incorrect because reviewing employee activities does not provide as much comfort about the code of conduct as evaluation of comprehensiveness. Answer (D) is incorrect because performing tests on employee transactions is not the best approach.

2. A primary purpose of establishing a code of conduct within a professional organization is to

    A. Reduce the likelihood that members of the profession will be sued for substandard work.

    B. Ensure that all members of the profession perform at approximately the same level of competence.

    C. Promote an ethical culture among professionals who serve others.

    D. Require members of the profession to exhibit loyalty in all matters pertaining to the affairs of their organization.

Answer (C) is correct. *(CIA, adapted)*
    REQUIRED: The primary purpose of establishing a code of conduct within a professional organization.
    DISCUSSION: The IIA Code of Ethics is typical. Its purpose is "to promote an ethical culture in the profession of internal auditing." The definition of internal auditing states that it is "an independent, objective assurance and consulting activity." Moreover, internal auditing is founded on "the trust placed in its objective assurance about risk management, control, and governance." The IIA Code of Ethics further emphasizes that it provides guidance to internal auditors "serving others."
    Answer (A) is incorrect because, although this result may follow from establishing a code of conduct, it is not the primary purpose. To consider it so would be self-serving. Answer (B) is incorrect because a code of conduct may help to establish minimum standards of competence, but it would be impossible to legislate equality of competence by all members of a profession. Answer (D) is incorrect because, in some situations, responsibility to the public at large may conflict with, and be more important than, loyalty to one's organization.

3. An accounting association established a code of ethics for all members. What is one of the association's primary purposes of establishing the code of ethics?

    A. To outline criteria for professional behavior to maintain standards of integrity and objectivity.

    B. To establish standards to follow for effective accounting practice.

    C. To provide a framework within which accounting policies could be effectively developed and executed.

    D. To outline criteria that can be used in conducting interviews of potential new accountants.

Answer (A) is correct. *(CIA, adapted)*
    REQUIRED: The primary purpose of establishing a code of ethics.
    DISCUSSION: The IIA Code of Ethics includes Principles and Rules of Conduct. Internal auditors are expected to apply and uphold four principles: integrity, objectivity, confidentiality, and competence.
    Answer (B) is incorrect because national standard-setting bodies, not a code of ethics, provide guidance for effective accounting practice. Answer (C) is incorrect because a code of ethics does not provide the framework within which accounting policies are developed. Answer (D) is incorrect because the primary purpose is not for interviewing new accountants.

4. A review of an organization's code of conduct revealed that it contained comprehensive guidelines designed to inspire high levels of ethical behavior. The review also revealed that employees were knowledgeable of its provisions. However, some employees still did not comply with the code. What element should a code of conduct contain to enhance its effectiveness?

    A. Periodic review and acknowledgment by all employees.

    B. Employee involvement in its development.

    C. Public knowledge of its contents and purpose.

    D. Provisions for disciplinary action in the event of violations.

Answer (D) is correct. *(CIA, adapted)*
    REQUIRED: The element that enhances the effectiveness of a code of conduct.
    DISCUSSION: Penalties for violations of a code of conduct should enhance its effectiveness. Some individuals will be deterred from misconduct if they expect it to be detected and punished.
    Answer (A) is incorrect because periodic review and acknowledgment would ensure employee knowledge and acceptance of the code, which are not at issue. Answer (B) is incorrect because employee involvement in development would encourage employee acceptance, which is not at issue. Answer (C) is incorrect because public knowledge might affect the behavior of some individuals but not to the same extent as the perceived likelihood of sanctions for wrongdoing.

5. In analyzing the differences between two recently merged businesses, the chief audit executive of Organization A notes that it has a formal code of ethics and Organization B does not. The code of ethics covers such things as purchase agreements, relationships with vendors, and other issues. Its purpose is to guide individual behavior within the firm. Which of the following statements regarding the existence of the code of ethics in A can be logically inferred?

I. A exhibits a higher standard of ethical behavior than does B.

II. A has established objective criteria by which an individual's actions can be evaluated.

III. The absence of a formal code of ethics in B would prevent a successful review of ethical behavior in that organization.

   A. I and II.

   B. II only.

   C. III only.

   D. II and III.

Answer (B) is correct. *(CIA, adapted)*
REQUIRED: The inference(s) regarding the existence or absence of a formal code of ethics.
DISCUSSION: A formal code of ethics effectively communicates acceptable values to all members, provides a method of policing and disciplining members for violations, establishes objective standards against which individuals can measure their own performance, and communicates the organization's value system to outsiders.

6. The best reason for establishing a code of conduct within an organization is that such codes

   A. Are typically required by governments.

   B. Express standards of individual behavior for members of the organization.

   C. Provide a quantifiable basis for personnel evaluations.

   D. Have tremendous public relations potential.

Answer (B) is correct. *(CIA, adapted)*
REQUIRED: The best reason for an organizational code of conduct.
DISCUSSION: An organization's code of ethical conduct is the established general value system the organization wishes to apply to its members' activities by communicating organizational purposes and beliefs and establishing uniform ethical guidelines for members, which include guidance on behavior for members in making decisions. Because laws and specific rules cannot cover all situations, organizations can benefit from having an established ethical code. It effectively communicates acceptable values to all members, including recruits and subcontractors. It also provides a method of policing and disciplining members for violations through formal review panels and group pressure (informal). A code establishes high standards against which individuals can measure their own performance and communicates to those outside the organization the value system from which its members must not be asked to deviate.
Answer (A) is incorrect because governments typically have no such requirement. Answer (C) is incorrect because codes of conduct provide qualitative, not quantitative, standards. Answer (D) is incorrect because other purposes of a code of conduct are much more significant.

7. Which of the following statements is not appropriate to include in a manufacturer's conflict of interest policy? An employee shall not

   A. Accept money, gifts, or services from a customer.

   B. Participate (directly or indirectly) in the management of a public agency.

   C. Borrow from or lend money to vendors.

   D. Use organizational information for private purposes.

Answer (B) is correct. *(CIA, adapted)*
REQUIRED: The item not included in a manufacturer's conflict of interest policy.
DISCUSSION: A prohibition on public service is ordinarily inappropriate. Public service is a right, if not a duty, of all citizens.
Answer (A) is incorrect because a conflict of interest policy should prohibit the transfer of benefits between an employee and those with whom the organization deals. Answer (C) is incorrect because a conflict of interest policy should prohibit financial dealings between an employee and those with whom the organization deals. Answer (D) is incorrect because The IIA Code of Ethics prohibits use of information for personal gain (Rule of Conduct 3.2).

10.2 The IIA Code of Ethics

8. In applying the Rules of Conduct set forth in The IIA Code of Ethics, internal auditors are expected to

    A. Not be unduly influenced by their own interests in forming judgments.

    B. Compare them with standards of other professions.

    C. Be guided by the desires of the engagement client.

    D. Use discretion in deciding whether to use them.

Answer (A) is correct. *(CIA, adapted)*
    REQUIRED: The responsibility of internal auditors under The IIA Code of Ethics.
    DISCUSSION: According to the objectivity principle stated in The IIA Code of Ethics, internal auditors exhibit the highest level of professional objectivity in gathering, evaluating, and communicating information about the activity or process being examined. Internal auditors make a balanced assessment of all the relevant circumstances and are not unduly influenced by their own interests or by others in forming judgments.
    Answer (B) is incorrect because standards of other professions are not intended to provide guidance to internal auditors serving others. Answer (C) is incorrect because auditors should be independent of the engagement client. Answer (D) is incorrect because internal auditors must follow The IIA Code of Ethics.

9. The Rules of Conduct set forth in The IIA Code of Ethics

    A. Describe behavior norms expected of internal auditors.

    B. Are guidelines to assist internal auditors in dealing with engagement clients.

    C. Are interpreted by the Principles.

    D. Apply only to particular conduct specifically mentioned.

Answer (A) is correct. *(CIA, adapted)*
    REQUIRED: The true statement about The IIA Code of Ethics.
    DISCUSSION: A code of ethics is necessary and appropriate for the profession of internal auditing, founded as it is on the trust placed in its objective assurance about risk management, control, and governance. The Institute's Code of Ethics extends beyond the definition of internal auditing to include two essential components: (1) Principles that are relevant to the profession and practice of internal auditing and (2) Rules of Conduct that describe behavior norms expected of internal auditors. These rules are an aid to interpreting the Principles into practical applications and are intended to guide the ethical conduct of internal auditors.
    Answer (B) is incorrect because the Rules of Conduct provide guidance to internal auditors in the discharge of their responsibility to all those whom they serve. Engagement clients are not the only parties served by internal auditing. Answer (C) is incorrect because the Rules of Conduct are an aid in interpreting the Principles. Answer (D) is incorrect because the conduct may be unacceptable or discreditable although not mentioned in the Rules of Conduct.

10. The Code of Ethics requires internal auditors to perform their work with

    A. Honesty, diligence, and responsibility.

    B. Timeliness, sobriety, and clarity.

    C. Knowledge, skills, and competencies.

    D. Punctuality, objectivity, and responsibility.

Answer (A) is correct. *(CIA, adapted)*
    REQUIRED: The qualities internal auditors should exhibit in the performance of their work.
    DISCUSSION: Four rules are stated under the integrity principle. According to Rule of Conduct 1.1 of The IIA Code of Ethics, "Internal auditors shall perform their work with honesty, diligence, and responsibility."
    Answer (B) is incorrect because timeliness, sobriety, and clarity are not mentioned in the Code. Answer (C) is incorrect because knowledge, skills, and competencies are mentioned in the *International Standards for the Professional Practice of Internal Auditing.* Answer (D) is incorrect because punctuality is not mentioned in the Code.

11. Which of the following is permissible under The IIA Code of Ethics?

A. Disclosing confidential, engagement-related, information that is potentially damaging to the organization in response to a court order.

B. Using engagement-related information in a decision to buy an ownership interest in the employer organization.

C. Accepting an unexpected gift from an employee whom the internal auditor has praised in a recent engagement communication.

D. Not reporting significant observations and recommendations about illegal activity to the board because management has indicated it will address the issue.

Answer (A) is correct. *(CIA, adapted)*
REQUIRED: The action permissible under The IIA Code of Ethics.
DISCUSSION: Under Rule of Conduct 1.2, "Internal auditors shall observe the law and make disclosures expected by the law and the profession." Thus, the requirement not to use information in any manner detrimental to the legitimate and ethical objectives of the organization (Rule of Conduct 3.2) does not override the legal obligation to respond to a court order.
Answer (B) is incorrect because Rule of Conduct 3.2 prohibits internal auditors from using information for personal gain. Answer (C) is incorrect because Rule of Conduct 2.2 prohibits internal auditors from accepting anything that may impair or be presumed to impair their professional judgment. Answer (D) is incorrect because Rule of Conduct 1.3 prohibits knowingly being a party to any illegal activity. Internal auditors must also disclose all material facts known to them that, if not disclosed, might distort the reporting of activities under review (Rule of Conduct 2.3).

12. An internal auditor, working for a chemical manufacturer, believed that toxic waste was being dumped in violation of the law. Out of loyalty to the organization, no information regarding the dumping was collected. The internal auditor

A. Violated the Code of Ethics by knowingly becoming a party to an illegal act.

B. Violated the Code of Ethics by failing to protect the well-being of the general public.

C. Did not violate the Code of Ethics. Loyalty to the employer in all matters is required.

D. Did not violate the Code of Ethics. Conclusive information about wrongdoing was not gathered.

Answer (A) is correct. *(CIA, adapted)*
REQUIRED: The ethical implication of failing to gather information about the organization's illegal act.
DISCUSSION: Rule of Conduct 1.3 prohibits knowingly being a party to any illegal activity. Internal auditors must also disclose all material facts known to them that, if not disclosed, might distort the reporting of activities under review (Rule of Conduct 2.3). The internal auditor apparently also failed to perform his/her work with diligence (Rule of Conduct 1.1).
Answer (B) is incorrect because The IIA Code of Ethics does not impose a duty to the general public. Answer (C) is incorrect because an internal auditor may not use information in any manner detrimental to the legitimate and ethical objectives of the organization (Rule of Conduct 3.2) and must respect and contribute to such objectives (Rule of Conduct 1.4). However, illegal dumping of toxic waste is neither legitimate nor ethical. Answer (D) is incorrect because the internal auditor should have collected and reported such information in accordance with the SPPIA.

13. An internal auditor discovered some material inefficiencies in a purchasing function. The purchasing manager is the internal auditor's next-door neighbor and best friend. In accordance with The IIA Code of Ethics, the internal auditor should

A. Objectively include the facts of the case in the engagement communications.

B. Not report the incident because of loyalty to the friend.

C. Include the facts of the case in a special communication submitted only to the friend.

D. Not report the friend unless the activity is illegal.

Answer (A) is correct. *(CIA, adapted)*
REQUIRED: The proper internal auditor action given a conflict between professional duty and friendship.
DISCUSSION: Under Rule of Conduct 2.3, "Internal auditors shall disclose all material facts known to them that, if not disclosed, may distort the reporting of activities under review." Furthermore, under Rule of Conduct 1.4, "Internal auditors shall respect and contribute to the legitimate and ethical objectives of the organization."

14. The chief audit executive (CAE) has been appointed to a committee to evaluate the appointment of the external auditors. The engagement partner for the external accounting firm wants the CAE to join him for a week of hunting at his private lodge. The CAE should

    A. Accept, assuming both their schedules allow it.

    B. Refuse on the grounds of conflict of interest.

    C. Accept as long as it is not charged to employer time.

    D. Ask the comptroller whether accepting the invitation is a violation of the organization's code of ethics.

Answer (B) is correct. *(CIA, adapted)*
    REQUIRED: The CAE's response to a social invitation by an external auditor who is subject to evaluation by a committee on which the CAE serves.
    DISCUSSION: Under Rule of Conduct 2.1, "Internal auditors shall not participate in any activity or relationship that may impair or be presumed to impair their unbiased assessment. This participation includes those activities or relationships that may be in conflict with the interests of the organization." Furthermore, under Rule of Conduct 2.2, "Internal auditors shall not accept anything that may impair or be presumed to impair their professional judgment."
    Answer (A) is incorrect because the auditor should not accept. Answer (C) is incorrect because not changing the time to the company is not sufficient to eliminate conflict-of-interest concerns. Answer (D) is incorrect because the auditor should know that accepting the invitation raises conflict of interest issues.

15. An internal auditor for a large regional bank was asked to serve on the board of directors of a local bank. The bank competes in many of the same markets as the regional bank but focuses more on consumer financing than on business financing. In accepting this position, the internal auditor

    I. Violates The IIA Code of Ethics because serving on the board may be in conflict with the best interests of the internal auditor's employer

    II. Violates The IIA Code of Ethics because the information gained while serving on the board of directors of the local bank may influence recommendations regarding potential acquisitions

    A. I only.

    B. II only.

    C. I and II.

    D. Neither I nor II.

Answer (C) is correct. *(CIA, adapted)*
    REQUIRED: The possible violation(s), if any, of The IIA Code of Ethics.
    DISCUSSION: Under Rule of Conduct 2.1, "Internal auditors shall not participate in any activity or relationship that may impair or be presumed to impair their unbiased assessment. This participation includes those activities or relationships that may be in conflict with the interests of the organization." Accordingly, service on the board of the local bank constitutes a conflict of interest and may prejudice the internal auditor's ability to carry out objectively his or her duties regarding potential acquisitions.

16. Which of the following concurrent occupations could appear to subvert the ethical behavior of an internal auditor?

    A. Internal auditor and a well-known charitable organization's local in-house chairperson.

    B. Internal auditor and part-time business insurance broker.

    C. Internal auditor and adjunct faculty member of a local business college that educates potential employees.

    D. Internal auditor and landlord of multiple housing that publicly advertises for tenants in a local community newspaper listing monthly rental fees.

Answer (B) is correct. *(CIA, adapted)*
    REQUIRED: The concurrent occupations that could create an ethical issue.
    DISCUSSION: Under Rule of Conduct 2.1, "Internal auditors shall not participate in any activity or relationship that may impair or be presumed to impair their unbiased assessment. This participation includes those activities or relationships that may be in conflict with the interests of the organization." As a business insurance broker, the internal auditor may lose his or her objectivity because (s)he might benefit from a change in the employer's insurance coverage.
    Answer (A) is incorrect because the activities of a charity are unlikely to be contrary to the interests of the organization. Answer (C) is incorrect because teaching is compatible with internal auditing. Answer (D) is incorrect because, whereas dealing in commercial properties might involve a conflict, renting residential units most likely does not.

17. Internal auditors should be prudent in their relationships with persons and organizations external to their employers. Which of the following activities will most likely not adversely affect internal auditors' ethical behavior?

A. Accepting compensation from professional organizations for consulting work.

B. Serving as consultants to competitor organizations.

C. Serving as consultants to suppliers.

D. Discussing engagement plans or results with external parties.

Answer (A) is correct.   *(CIA, adapted)*
REQUIRED: The external relationship most likely not to involve an ethics violation.
DISCUSSION: Professional organizations are unlikely to be employees, clients, customers, suppliers, or business associates of the organization. Hence, the consulting fees are not likely to impair or be presumed to impair the internal auditors' professional judgment (Rule of Conduct 2.2). Moreover, relationships with professional organizations are not likely to create a conflict of interest or impair or be presumed to impair internal auditors' unbiased judgment (Rule of Conduct 2.1). Also, the consulting engagement should not result in the improper use of information (Rule of Conduct 3.2).
Answer (B) is incorrect because serving as a consultant to competitors might create a conflict of interest. Answer (C) is incorrect because serving as a consultant to suppliers might create a conflict of interest. Answer (D) is incorrect because internal auditors should "be prudent in the use and protection of information acquired in the course of their duties" (Rule of Conduct 3.1). Furthermore, such discussion might be "detrimental to the legitimate and ethical objectives of the organization" (Rule of Conduct 3.2).

18. An internal auditor has been assigned to an engagement at a foreign subsidiary. The internal auditor is aware that the social climate of the country is such that "facilitating payments" (bribes) are an accepted part of doing business. The internal auditor has completed the engagement and has found significant weaknesses relating to important controls. The subsidiary's manager offers the internal auditor a substantial "facilitating payment" to omit the observations from the final engagement communication with a provision that the internal auditor could revisit the subsidiary in 6 months to verify that the problem areas have been properly addressed. The internal auditor should

A. Not accept the payment because such acceptance is in conflict with the Code of Ethics.

B. Not accept the payment, but omit the observations as long as a verification visit is made in 6 months.

C. Accept the offer because it is consistent with the ethical concepts of the country in which the subsidiary is doing business.

D. Accept the payment because it has the effect of doing the greatest good for the greatest number; the internal auditor is better off, the subsidiary is better off, and the organization is better off because there is strong motivation to correct the deficiencies.

Answer (A) is correct.   *(CIA, adapted)*
REQUIRED: The proper action an internal auditor should take when offered a bribe.
DISCUSSION: Rule of Conduct 2.2 states, "Internal auditors shall not accept anything that may impair or be presumed to impair their professional judgment."
Answer (B) is incorrect because Rule of Conduct 2.3 requires internal auditors to "disclose all material facts known to them that, if not disclosed, may distort the reporting of activities under review." Answer (C) is incorrect because the profession's standards, not the customs of individual countries or regions, should guide the internal auditor's conduct. Answer (D) is incorrect because the action is explicitly prohibited by the Code of Ethics.

19. An internal auditor engages in the preparation of income tax forms during the tax season. For which of the following activities will the internal auditor most likely be in violation of The IIA Code of Ethics?

- A. Writing a tax guide intended for publication and sale to the general public.

- B. Preparing the personal tax return, for a fee, for one of the organization's division managers.

- C. Teaching an evening tax seminar, for a fee, at a local university.

- D. Preparing tax returns for elderly citizens, regardless of their associations, as a public service.

Answer (B) is correct.   *(CIA, adapted)*
REQUIRED: The activity most likely a violation of The IIA Code of Ethics.
DISCUSSION: Rule of Conduct 2.2 states, "Internal auditors shall not accept anything that may impair or be presumed to impair their professional judgment." Preparing a personal tax return for a division manager for a fee falls under this prohibition.

20. An internal auditing team has made observations and recommendations that should significantly improve a division's operating efficiency. Out of appreciation of this work, and because it is the holiday season, the division manager presents the in-charge internal auditor with a gift of moderate value. Which of the following best describes the action prescribed by The IIA Code of Ethics?

- A. Not accept it prior to submission of the final engagement communication.

- B. Not accept it if the gift is presumed to impair the internal auditor's judgment.

- C. Not accept it, regardless of other circumstances, because its value is significant.

- D. Accept it, regardless of other circumstances, because its value is insignificant.

Answer (B) is correct.   *(CIA, adapted)*
REQUIRED: The action prescribed by The IIA Code of Ethics when an engagement client makes a gift to an internal auditor.
DISCUSSION: Rule of Conduct 2.2 states, "Internal auditors shall not accept anything that may impair or be presumed to impair their professional judgment."
Answer (A) is incorrect because the timing of the gift is irrelevant. Answer (C) is incorrect because, according to Rule of Conduct 2.2, the decision whether to accept a gift should be based on the potential impairment of the auditor's judgment. Answer (D) is incorrect because the gift's acceptance should be based on whether the internal auditor's professional judgment will be impaired or be presumed to be impaired.

21. A CIA is working in a noninternal-auditing position as the director of purchasing. The CIA signed a contract to procure a large order from the supplier with the best price, quality, and performance. Shortly after signing the contract, the supplier presented the CIA with a gift of significant monetary value. Which of the following statements regarding the acceptance of the gift is true?

- A. Acceptance of the gift is prohibited only if it is not customary.

- B. Acceptance of the gift violates The IIA Code of Ethics and is prohibited for a CIA.

- C. Because the CIA is no longer acting as an internal auditor, acceptance of the gift is governed only by the organization's code of conduct.

- D. Because the contract was signed before the gift was offered, acceptance of the gift does not violate either The IIA Code of Ethics or the organization's code of conduct.

Answer (B) is correct.   *(CIA, adapted)*
REQUIRED: The true statement about acceptance of a gift from a supplier.
DISCUSSION: Members of The Institute of Internal Auditors and recipients of, or candidates for, IIA professional certifications are subject to disciplinary action for breaches of The IIA Code of Ethics. Rule of Conduct 2.2 states, "Internal auditors shall not accept anything that may impair or be presumed to impair their professional judgment."
Answer (A) is incorrect because acceptance of the gift could easily be presumed to have impaired the CIA's professional judgment. Answer (C) is incorrect because the CIA is still governed by The IIA's code of conduct. Answer (D) is incorrect because the timing of signing the contract is irrelevant.

22. In some countries, governmental units have established audit standards. For example, in the United States, the Government Accountability Office has developed standards for the conduct of governmental audits, particularly those that relate to compliance with government grants. In performing governmental grant compliance audits, the auditor should

    A. Be guided only by the governmental standards.

    B. Be guided only by The IIA Standards because they are more encompassing.

    C. Be guided by the more general standards that have been issued by the public accounting profession.

    D. Follow both The IIA Standards and any additional governmental standards.

Answer (D) is correct. *(CIA, adapted)*
    REQUIRED: The standards an auditor follows when performing governmental grant compliance audits.
    DISCUSSION: Rule of Conduct 4.2 of The IIA Code of Ethics states, "Internal auditors shall perform internal auditing services in accordance with the *International Standards for the Professional Practice of Internal Auditing.*" Furthermore, an internal auditor observes the law (Rule of Conduct 1.2).

23. An organization has recently placed a former operating manager in the position of chief audit executive (CAE). The new CAE is not a member of The IIA and is not a CIA. Henceforth, the internal audit activity will be run strictly by the CAE's standards, not The IIA's. All four staff internal auditors are members of The IIA, but they are not CIAs. According to The IIA Code of Ethics, what is the best course of action for the staff internal auditors?

    A. The Code does not apply because they are not CIAs.

    B. They should comply with the Standards for the Professional Practice of Internal Auditing.

    C. They must respect the legitimate and ethical objectives of the organization and ignore the Standards.

    D. They must resign their jobs to avoid improper activities.

Answer (B) is correct. *(CIA, adapted)*
    REQUIRED: The best course of action when the CAE is not a member of The IIA and not a CIA but the staff are members of The IIA.
    DISCUSSION: Rule of Conduct 4.2 of The IIA Code of Ethics states, "Internal auditors shall perform internal auditing services in accordance with the *International Standards for the Professional Practice of Internal Auditing.*" Because the internal auditors are members of The Institute, The IIA Code of Ethics is enforceable against them even though they are not CIAs.
    Answer (A) is incorrect because The IIA Code of Ethics may be enforced against IIA members and recipients of, or candidates for, IIA professional certifications. Answer (C) is incorrect because internal auditors should respect and contribute to the legitimate and ethical objectives of the organization, but an IIA member, a holder of an IIA professional certification, or a candidate for certification may be liable for disciplinary action for failure to adhere to the Standards. Answer (D) is incorrect because The IIA Code of Ethics says nothing about resignation to avoid improper activities.

24. A new staff internal auditor was told to perform an engagement in an area with which the internal auditor was not familiar. Because of time constraints, no supervision was provided. The assignment represented a good learning experience, but the area was clearly beyond the internal auditor's competence. Nonetheless, the internal auditor prepared comprehensive working papers and communicated the results to management. In this situation,

    A. The internal audit activity violated the Standards by hiring an internal auditor without proficiency in the area.

    B. The internal audit activity violated the Standards by not providing adequate supervision.

    C. The chief audit executive has not violated The IIA Code of Ethics because it does not address supervision.

    D. The Standards and The IIA Code of Ethics were followed by the internal audit activity.

Answer (B) is correct. *(CIA, adapted)*
    REQUIRED: The effect of failing to supervise an internal auditor who lacks proficiency in the area of the engagement.
    DISCUSSION: Although The IIA Code of Ethics does not address supervision directly, it does require that the Standards be followed (Rule of Conduct 4.2). The Standards require engagements to be performed with proficiency and due professional care (Standard 1200). They also should be properly supervised to ensure that objectives are achieved, quality is assured, and staff is developed (Standard 2340).
    Answer (A) is incorrect because all internal auditors need not be proficient in all areas. The internal audit activity should have an appropriate mix of skills. Answer (C) is incorrect because the Code requires compliance with the Standards, and the Standards require proper supervision. Answer (D) is incorrect because the Standards and the Code were not followed.

25. Which situation most likely violates The IIA Code of Ethics and the Standards?

    A. The chief audit executive (CAE) disagrees with the engagement client about the observations and recommendations in a sensitive area. The CAE discusses the detail of the observations and the proposed recommendations with a fellow CAE from another organization.

    B. An organization's charter for the internal audit activity requires the chief audit executive (CAE) to present the yearly engagement work schedule to the board for its approval and suggestions.

    C. The engagement manager has removed the most significant observations and recommendations from the final engagement communication. The in-charge internal auditor opposed the removal, explaining that (s)he knows the reported conditions exist. The in-charge internal auditor agrees that, technically, information is not sufficient to support the observations, but management cannot explain the conditions, and the observations are the only reasonable conclusions.

    D. Because the internal audit activity lacks skill and knowledge in a specialty area, the chief audit executive (CAE) has hired an expert. The engagement manager has been asked to review the expert's approach to the assignment. Although knowledgeable about the area under review, the manager is hesitant to accept the assignment because of lack of expertise.

Answer (A) is correct. *(CIA, adapted)*
REQUIRED: The situation most likely to be considered a violation of The IIA Code of Ethics.
DISCUSSION: According to Rule of Conduct 3.1 of The IIA Code of Ethics, "Internal auditors shall be prudent in the use and protection of information acquired in the course of their duties." According to Rule of Conduct 3.2, "Internal auditors shall not use information for any personal gain or in any manner that would be contrary to the law or detrimental to the legitimate and ethical objectives of the organization." Consequently, discussion of sensitive matters with an unauthorized party is the situation most likely to be considered a Code violation. The information conveyed might be used to the detriment of the organization.
    Answer (B) is incorrect because approval of the engagement work schedule by the board and senior management is required (Standard 2020). Answer (C) is incorrect because information must be sufficient to achieve engagement objectives (Standard 2300). Answer (D) is incorrect because the Standards allow use of experts when needed.

26. During the course of an engagement, an internal auditor discovers that a clerk is embezzling funds from the organization. Although this is the first embezzlement ever encountered and the organization has a security department, the internal auditor decides to interrogate the suspect. If the internal auditor is violating The IIA Code of Ethics, the rule violated is most likely

    A. Failing to exercise due diligence.

    B. Lack of loyalty to the organization.

    C. Lack of competence in this area.

    D. Failing to comply with the law.

Answer (C) is correct. *(CIA, adapted)*
REQUIRED: The ethics rule most likely violated.
DISCUSSION: Rule of Conduct 4.1 under the competency principle states, "Internal auditors shall engage only in those services for which they have the necessary knowledge, skills, and experience." Internal auditors may not have and are not expected to have knowledge equivalent to that of a person whose primary responsibility is to detect and investigate fraud.
    Answer (A) is incorrect because the requirement to perform work with diligence does not override the competency Rules of Conduct or the need to use good judgment. Answer (B) is incorrect because loyalty is better exhibited by consulting professionals and knowing the limits of competence. Answer (D) is incorrect because the internal auditor may violate the suspect's civil rights as a result of inexperience.

27. Which of the following actions taken by a chief audit executive (CAE) could be considered professionally ethical under The IIA Code of Ethics?

    A. The CAE decides to delay an engagement at a branch so that his nephew, the branch manager, will have time to "clean things up."

    B. To save organizational resources, the CAE cancels all staff training for the next 2 years on the basis that all staff are too new to benefit from training.

    C. To save organizational resources, the CAE limits procedures at foreign branches to confirmations from branch managers that no major personnel changes have occurred.

    D. The CAE refuses to provide information about organizational operations to his father, who is a part owner.

Answer (D) is correct. *(CIA, adapted)*
    REQUIRED: Ethical actions under The IIA Code of Ethics.
    DISCUSSION: According to Rule of Conduct 3.1 of The IIA Code of Ethics, "Internal auditors shall be prudent in the use and protection of information acquired in the course of their duties." According to Rule of Conduct 3.2, "Internal auditors shall not use information for any personal gain or in any manner that would be contrary to the law or detrimental to the legitimate and ethical objectives of the organization." Thus, such use of information by the CAE might be illegal under insider trading rules.
    Answer (A) is incorrect because, according to Rule of Conduct 1.1, "Internal auditors shall perform their work with honesty, diligence, and responsibility." Answer (B) is incorrect because, according to Rule of Conduct 4.3, "Internal auditors shall continually improve their proficiency and the effectiveness and quality of their services." Answer (C) is incorrect because, according to Rule of Conduct 4.2, "Internal auditors shall perform internal auditing services in accordance with the Standards for the Professional Practice of Internal Auditing." The Standards require supporting information to be sufficient, reliable, relevant, and useful.

28. Which of the following situations is a violation of The IIA Code of Ethics?

    A. An internal auditor was ordered to testify in a court case in which a merger partner claimed to have been defrauded by the internal auditor's organization. The internal auditor divulged confidential information to the court.

    B. An internal auditor for a manufacturer of office products recently completed an engagement to evaluate the marketing function. Based on this experience, the internal auditor spent several hours one Saturday working as a paid consultant to a hospital in the local area that intended to conduct an engagement to evaluate its marketing function.

    C. An internal auditor gave a speech at a local IIA chapter meeting outlining the contents of a program the internal auditor had developed for engagements relating to electronic data interchange (EDI) connections. Several internal auditors from major competitors were in the audience.

    D. During an engagement, an internal auditor learned that the organization was about to introduce a new product that would revolutionize the industry. Because of the probable success of the new product, the product manager suggested that the internal auditor buy an additional interest in the organization, which the internal auditor did.

Answer (D) is correct. *(CIA, adapted)*
    REQUIRED: The violation of The IIA Code of Ethics.
    DISCUSSION: According to Rule of Conduct 3.2, "Internal auditors shall not use information for any personal gain or in any manner that would be contrary to the law or detrimental to the legitimate and ethical objectives of the organization."
    Answer (A) is incorrect because, according to Rule of Conduct 1.2, "Internal auditors shall observe the law and make disclosures expected by the law and the profession." Failure to comply with a court order is illegal. Answer (B) is incorrect because the hospital is not a competitor or supplier of the internal auditor's employer. Hence, no conflict of interest is involved. Answer (C) is incorrect because giving a speech is not a violation of The IIA Code of Ethics. In fact, The IIA's motto is "progress through sharing."

29. A chief audit executive (CAE) learned that a staff internal auditor provided confidential information to a relative. Both the CAE and staff internal auditor are CIAs. Although the internal auditor did not benefit from the transaction, the relative used the information to make a significant profit. The most appropriate way for the CAE to deal with this problem is to

A. Verbally reprimand the internal auditor.

B. Summarily discharge the internal auditor and notify The IIA.

C. Take no action because the internal auditor did not benefit from the transaction.

D. Inform the Institute's Board of Directors and take the personnel action required by organizational policy.

Answer (D) is correct. *(CIA, adapted)*
REQUIRED: The CAE's appropriate action after learning that a staff internal auditor has provided confidential information to a relative.
DISCUSSION: The staff internal auditor has violated Rule of Conduct 3.2 regarding use of information. A violation of The IIA Code of Ethics is the basis for a complaint to the International Ethics Committee, which is responsible for receiving, interpreting, and investigating all complaints against members or CIAs on behalf of the Board of Directors of The IIA, and making recommendations to the Board on actions to be taken (Administrative Directive 5). In addition, organizational policy must be followed.
Answer (A) is incorrect because the internal auditor has violated Rule of Conduct 3.2 regarding use of information. The IIA should be notified. Answer (B) is incorrect because summary discharge may not be in accordance with company personnel policies. Answer (C) is incorrect because the auditor improperly used information and violated The IIA Code of Ethics. Some action is warranted.

30. During an examination of grants awarded by a nonprofit organization, an internal auditor discovered a number of grants made without the approval of the grant authorization committee (which includes outside representatives), as required by the organization's charter. All the grants, however, were approved and documented by the president. The chair of the grant authorization committee, who is also a member of the board of directors, proposes that the committee meet and retroactively approve all the grants before the engagement communication is issued. If the committee meets and approves the grants before such issuance, the internal auditor should

A. Not report the grants in question because they were approved before the issuance of the engagement communication.

B. Discuss the matter with the chair of the grant committee to determine the rationale for not approving the grants earlier. If the grants are routine, discussion of the grant committee's inaction should be omitted from the engagement communication.

C. Include the items in the communication as an override of the organization's controls. Details about each grant should be reported, and the internal auditor should investigate further for fraud.

D. Report the override of control to the board.

Answer (D) is correct. *(CIA, adapted)*
REQUIRED: The action by an internal auditor if the committee retroactively authorizes certain grants.
DISCUSSION: Rule of Conduct 2.3 states, "Internal auditors shall disclose all material facts known to them that, if not disclosed, may distort the reporting of activities under review." The management override of an important control over approval of grants created a material risk exposure. Thus, the internal auditor is ethically obligated to report the matter to senior officials charged with performing the governance function.
Answer (A) is incorrect because the control override should be reported. Answer (B) is incorrect because the routine nature of the grants is irrelevant to the issue of the violation of the charter. Answer (C) is incorrect because details about each grant need not be included unless the internal auditor believes that fraud may have occurred. Moreover, the appropriate organizational authorities should be informed if wrongdoing is suspected.

31. In a review of travel and entertainment expenses, a certified internal auditor questioned the business purposes of an officer's reimbursed travel expenses. The officer promised to compensate for the questioned amounts by not claiming legitimate expenses in the future. If the officer makes good on the promise, the internal auditor

A. Can ignore the original charging of the non-business expenses.

B. Should inform the tax authorities in any event.

C. Should still include the finding in the final engagement communication.

D. Should recommend that the officer forfeit any frequent flyer miles received as part of the questionable travel.

Answer (C) is correct. *(CIA, adapted)*
REQUIRED: The internal auditor's action when an officer agrees to compensate for questionable expenses by not claiming legitimate expenses in the future.
DISCUSSION: Rule of Conduct 2.3 states, "Internal auditors shall disclose all material facts known to them that, if not disclosed, may distort the reporting of activities under review."
Answer (A) is incorrect because the possibly fraudulent behavior of the officer is a material fact that should be reported regardless of whether the questioned expenses are reimbursed. Answer (B) is incorrect because the Standards require the CAE to disseminate results to the appropriate individuals (Standard 2440). However, communication of results outside the organization is not required in the absence of a legal mandate. Answer (D) is incorrect because management should determine what constitutes just compensation.

32. An internal auditor, nearly finished with an engagement, discovers that the director of marketing has a gambling habit. The gambling issue is not directly related to the existing engagement, and the internal auditor is under pressure to complete it quickly. The internal auditor notes the problem and passes the information on to the chief audit executive but does no further follow-up. The internal auditor's actions

A. Are in violation of The IIA Code of Ethics for withholding meaningful information.

B. Are in violation of the Standards because the internal auditor did not properly follow up on a red flag that might indicate the existence of fraud.

C. Are not in violation of either The IIA Code of Ethics or the Standards.

D. Are in violation of The IIA Code of Ethics for withholding meaningful information and are in violation of the Standards because the internal auditor did not properly follow up on a red flag that might indicate the existence of fraud.

Answer (C) is correct.   *(CIA, adapted)*
   REQUIRED: The true statement(s) about an internal auditor's communication of personal information about an engagement client.
   DISCUSSION: There is no violation of either The IIA Code of Ethics or the Standards. The internal auditor did not withhold information, but rather, properly followed up upon learning of the information.

33. An engagement at a foreign subsidiary disclosed payments to local government officials in return for orders. What action does The IIA Code of Ethics suggest for an internal auditor in such a case?

A. Refrain from any action that might be detrimental to the organization.

B. Report the incident to appropriate regulatory authorities.

C. Inform appropriate organizational officials.

D. Report the practice to the board of The Institute of Internal Auditors.

Answer (C) is correct.   *(CIA, adapted)*
   REQUIRED: The internal auditor's action after learning of payments to foreign officials in return for orders.
   DISCUSSION: Such payments may be illegal. Rule of Conduct 2.3 states, "Internal auditors shall disclose all material facts known to them that, if not disclosed, may distort the reporting of activities under review."
   Answer (A) is incorrect because informing organizational officials is not detrimental to the organization. Answer (B) is incorrect because the Code does not require that the incident be reported to regulatory authorities. Answer (D) is incorrect because the Code does not require reporting to The IIA.

34. During an engagement, an employee with whom you have developed a good working relationship informs you that she has some information about senior management that is damaging to the organization and may concern illegal activities. The employee does not want her name associated with the release of the information. Which of the following actions is considered to be inconsistent with The IIA Code of Ethics and the Standards?

A. Assure the employee that you can maintain her anonymity and listen to the information.

B. Suggest that the employee consider talking to legal counsel.

C. Inform the employee that you will attempt to keep the source of the information confidential and will look into the matter further.

D. Inform the employee of other methods of communicating this type of information.

Answer (A) is correct.   *(CIA, adapted)*
   REQUIRED: The action inconsistent with The IIA Code of Ethics and the Standards.
   DISCUSSION: An internal auditor cannot guarantee anonymity. Information communicated to an internal auditor is not subject to a testimonial privilege. Moreover, Rule of Conduct 2.3 states, "Internal auditors shall disclose all material facts known to them that, if not disclosed, may distort the reporting of activities under review." The identity of the informant may be such a material fact.
   Answer (B) is incorrect because suggesting that the person seek expert legal advice from a qualified individual is appropriate. Answer (C) is incorrect because promising merely to attempt to keep the source of the information confidential is allowable. This promise is not a guarantee of confidentiality. Answer (D) is incorrect because the employee could be directed to other methods of communicating the information in order to maintain her anonymity.

35. During an engagement performed at a manufacturing division of a defense contractor, the internal auditor discovered that the organization apparently was inappropriately adding costs to a cost-plus governmental contract. The internal auditor discussed the matter with senior management, which suggested that the internal auditor seek an opinion from legal counsel. Upon review, legal counsel indicated that the practice was questionable but was not technically in violation of the government contract. Based on legal counsel's decision, the internal auditor decided to omit any discussion of the practice in the final engagement communication sent to senior management and the board. However, the internal auditor did informally communicate legal counsel's decision to senior management. Did the internal auditor violate The IIA's Code of Ethics?

A. No. The internal auditor followed up the matter with appropriate personnel within the organization and reached a conclusion that no fraud was involved.

B. No. If a fraud is suspected, it should be resolved at the divisional level where it is taking place.

C. Yes. It is a violation because all important information, even if resolved, should be reported to the board.

D. Yes. Internal legal counsel's opinion is not sufficient. The internal auditor should have sought advice from outside legal counsel.

Answer (A) is correct. *(CIA, adapted)*
REQUIRED: The reason, if any, for a violation of The IIA's Code of Ethics.
DISCUSSION: Although an argument can be made that the internal auditor should report the matter to the board and senior management, there is no indication that the internal auditor is deliberately withholding material facts that, if not disclosed, may distort reports of activities under review (Rule of Conduct 2.3). Hence, no violation of the Code occurred.

Answer (B) is incorrect because material fraud, if suspected, should be brought to the attention of management. However, in this case, the internal auditor gathered sufficient information to dispel the suspicion of fraud. Answer (C) is incorrect because the internal auditor did not deliberately withhold important information. Answer (D) is incorrect because the internal auditor has gathered sufficient information. Internal legal counsel's opinion appears to be sufficient.

36. The chief audit executive is aware of a material inventory shortage caused by internal control deficiencies at one manufacturing plant. The shortage and related causes are of sufficient magnitude to affect the external auditor's report. Based on The IIA Code of Ethics, what is the CAE's most appropriate course of action?

A. Say nothing; guard against interfering with the independence of the external auditors.

B. Discuss the issue with management and take appropriate action to ensure that the external auditors are informed.

C. Inform the external auditors of the possibility of a shortage but allow them to make an independent assessment of the amount.

D. Communicate the shortages to the board and allow them to communicate it to the external auditor.

Answer (B) is correct. *(CIA, adapted)*
REQUIRED: The most appropriate action, given awareness by the CAE of a matter affecting the external auditor's report.
DISCUSSION: The IIA's Code of Ethics calls for compliance with the Standards (Rule of Conduct 4.2). The CAE should share information and coordinate activities with other internal and external providers of relevant assurance and consulting services (Standard 2050). In addition, all material facts known by the internal auditors should be disclosed (Rule of Conduct 2.3). Because the shortage affects the external auditor's work, in which the internal auditors are participating, the situation must be divulged.

Answer (A) is incorrect because the shortage is a material fact that could distort a report of activities under review if not revealed. Answer (C) is incorrect because the condition is known and the external auditors should be told more than that a possibility of a shortage exists. Answer (D) is incorrect because information should be shared and activities coordinated with the external auditor.

37. Through an engagement performed at the credit department, the chief audit executive (CAE) became aware of a material misstatement of the year-end accounts receivable balance. The external auditors have completed their engagement without detecting the misstatement. What should the CAE do in this situation?

A. Inform the external auditors of the misstatement.

B. Report the misstatement to management when the external auditors present a report.

C. Exclude the misstatement from the final engagement communication because the external auditors are responsible for expressing an opinion on the financial statements.

D. Perform additional engagement procedures on accounts receivable balances to benefit the external auditors.

Answer (A) is correct. *(CIA, adapted)*
REQUIRED: The proper action by the CAE after discovery of a material misstatement not found by the external auditor.
DISCUSSION: Rule of Conduct 2.3 states, "Internal auditors shall disclose all material facts known to them that, if not disclosed, may distort the reporting of activities under review."
Answer (B) is incorrect because the CAE should share information and coordinate activities with the external auditors (Standard 2050). Answer (C) is incorrect because, although the internal audit activity's main focus may be on risk management, control, and governance processes, a material misstatement must be communicated. Answer (D) is incorrect because, when performing an audit, the external auditors should determine what work should be performed by the internal auditor.

38. Which of the following most likely constitutes a violation of The IIA Code of Ethics?

A. Auditor A has accepted an assignment to perform an engagement at the electronics manufacturing division. The auditor has recently joined the internal audit activity. But the auditor was senior auditor for the external audit of that division and has audited many electronics organizations during the past 2 years.

B. Auditor B has been assigned to perform an engagement at the warehousing function 6 months from now. Auditor B has no expertise in that area but accepted the assignment anyway. Auditor B has signed up for continuing professional education courses in warehousing that will be completed before Auditor B's assignment begins.

C. Auditor C is content with the career of an internal auditor and has come to look at it as a regular 9-to-5 job. Auditor C has not engaged in continuing professional education or other activities to improve effectiveness during the last 3 years. However, Auditor C feels the quality of work performed is the same as always.

D. Auditor D discovered an internal financial fraud during the year. The books were adjusted to properly reflect the loss associated with the fraud. Auditor D discussed the fraud with the external auditor when the external auditor reviewed working papers detailing the incident.

Answer (C) is correct. *(CIA, adapted)*
REQUIRED: The violation of The IIA Code of Ethics.
DISCUSSION: Rule of Conduct 4.3 states, "Internal auditors shall continually improve their proficiency and the effectiveness and quality of their services."
Answer (A) is incorrect because no professional conflict of interest exists per se, especially given that the internal auditor was previously in public accounting. However, the internal auditor should be aware of potential conflicts. Answer (B) is incorrect because, according to Rule of Conduct 4.1, "Internal auditors shall engage only in those services for which they have the necessary knowledge, skills, and experience." Thus, Auditor B may perform this service if he has the necessary knowledge, etc. Answer (D) is incorrect because the information was disclosed as part of the normal process of cooperation between the internal and external auditor. Because the books were adjusted, the external auditor was expected to inquire as to the nature of the adjustment.

39. An internal auditor has uncovered facts that could be interpreted as indicating unlawful activity on the part of an engagement client. The internal auditor decides not to inform senior management and the board of these facts because of lack of proof. The internal auditor, however, decides that, if questions are raised regarding the omitted facts, they will be answered fully and truthfully. In taking this action, the internal auditor

    A. Has not violated The IIA Code of Ethics or the Standards because confidentiality takes precedence over all other standards.

    B. Has not violated The IIA Code of Ethics or the Standards because the internal auditor is committed to answering all questions fully and truthfully.

    C. Has violated The IIA Code of Ethics because unlawful acts should have been reported to the appropriate regulatory agency to avoid potential "aiding and abetting" by the internal auditor.

    D. Has violated the Standards because the internal auditor should inform the appropriate authorities in the organization if fraud may be indicated.

Answer (D) is correct. *(CIA, adapted)*
    REQUIRED: The effect of not reporting a suspected irregularity.
    DISCUSSION: The internal auditor should inform the appropriate authorities in the organization if the indicators of the commission of a fraud are sufficient to recommend an investigation. Hence, the internal auditor has a duty to act even though the available facts do not prove that an irregularity has occurred. Moreover, Rule of Conduct 2.3 states, "Internal auditors shall disclose all material facts known to them that, if not disclosed, may distort the reporting of activities under review."
    Answer (A) is incorrect because reporting a possible irregularity to the appropriate organizational authorities is not a breach of the duty of confidentiality owed to the organization. Answer (B) is incorrect because the internal auditor has an affirmative duty to report the results of his or her work. Answer (C) is incorrect because the possibility of unlawful activities should be reported to the appropriate personnel within the organization.

40. Internal auditors who fail to maintain their proficiency through continuing education could be found to be in violation of

    A. *The International Standards for the Professional Practice of Internal Auditing.*

    B. The IIA's Code of Ethics.

    C. Both the Standards for the Professional Practice of Internal Auditing and The IIA's Code of Ethics.

    D. None of the answers are correct.

Answer (C) is correct. *(CIA, adapted)*
    REQUIRED: The effect of failing to meet continuing education requirements.
    DISCUSSION: The IIA's Code of Ethics (Rule of Conduct 4.3) states, "Internal auditors shall continually improve their proficiency and the effectiveness and quality of their services." The Code also requires compliance with the SPPIA (Rule of Conduct 4.2). Furthermore, Standard 1230 states, "Internal auditors should enhance their knowledge, skills, and competencies through continuing professional development." Hence, both The IIA's Code of Ethics and the SPPIA are violated by failing to earn continuing education credits.

41. Today's internal auditor will often encounter a wide range of potential ethical dilemmas, not all of which are explicitly addressed by The IIA's Code of Ethics. If the internal auditor encounters such a dilemma, the internal auditor should always

    A. Seek counsel from an independent attorney to determine the personal consequences of potential actions.

    B. Apply and uphold the principles embodied in The IIA Code of Ethics.

    C. Seek the counsel of the board before deciding on an action.

    D. Act consistently with the code of ethics adopted by the organization even if such action is not consistent with The IIA's Code of Ethics.

Answer (B) is correct. *(CIA, adapted)*
    REQUIRED: The action taken when an internal auditor encounters an ethical dilemma.
    DISCUSSION: The Code includes Principles (integrity, objectivity, confidentiality, and competency) relevant to the profession and practice of internal auditing and Rules of Conduct that describe behavioral norms for internal auditors and that interpret the Principles. Internal auditors are expected to apply and uphold the Principles. Furthermore, that a particular conduct is not mentioned in the Rules does not prevent it from being unacceptable or discreditable.
    Answer (A) is incorrect because seeking the advice of legal counsel on all ethical decisions is impracticable. Answer (C) is incorrect because seeking the advice of the board on all ethical decisions is impracticable. Furthermore, the advice might not be consistent with the profession's standards. Answer (D) is incorrect because, if the organization's standards are not consistent with, or as high as, the profession's standards, the internal auditor is held to the standards of the profession.

10.3 Fraud Responsibilities of Internal Auditors

42. After noting some red flags, an internal auditor has an increased awareness that fraud may be present. Which of the following best describes the internal auditor's responsibility?

    A. Expand activities to determine whether an investigation is warranted.

    B. Report the possibility of fraud to senior management and the board and ask them how they would like to proceed.

    C. Consult with external legal counsel to determine the course of action to be taken, including the approval of the proposed engagement work program to make sure it is acceptable on legal grounds.

    D. Report the matter to the audit committee and request funding for outside service providers to help investigate the possible fraud.

Answer (A) is correct. *(CIA, adapted)*
    REQUIRED: The internal auditor's responsibility after noting some fraud indicators.
    DISCUSSION: An internal auditor's responsibilities for detecting fraud include evaluating fraud indicators and deciding whether any additional action is necessary or whether an investigation should be recommended (PA 1210.A2-1).
    Answer (B) is incorrect because the internal auditor should notify the appropriate authorities within the organization if (s)he has determined that the indicators of fraud are sufficient to recommend an investigation. Answer (C) is incorrect because the internal auditor does not have the authority to consult with external legal counsel. Answer (D) is incorrect because the internal auditor should report the matter and request funding for outside service providers only if (s)he has determined that the indicators of fraud are sufficient to recommend an investigation.

43. In the course of their work, internal auditors must be alert for fraud and other forms of white-collar crime. The important characteristic that distinguishes fraud from other varieties of white-collar crime is that

    A. Fraud encompasses an array of irregularities and illegal acts that involve intentional deception.

    B. Unlike other white-collar crimes, fraud is always perpetrated against an outside party.

    C. White-collar crime is usually perpetrated for the benefit of an organization, but fraud benefits an individual.

    D. White-collar crime is usually perpetrated by outsiders to the detriment of an organization, but fraud is perpetrated by insiders to benefit the organization.

Answer (A) is correct. *(CIA, adapted)*
    REQUIRED: The trait distinguishing fraud from other white-collar crimes.
    DISCUSSION: Fraud encompasses an array of irregularities and illegal acts characterized by intentional deception or misrepresentation. It can be perpetrated for the benefit of or to the detriment of the organization and by persons outside or inside the organization (PA 1210.A2-1).
    Answer (B) is incorrect because fraud may be perpetrated internally. Answer (C) is incorrect because fraud may be perpetrated for the organization's benefit or for otherwise unselfish reasons. Answer (D) is incorrect because fraud may be perpetrated by insiders and outsiders, and it may be either beneficial or detrimental to an organization.

44. Which of the following statements is(are) true regarding the prevention of fraud?

I.   The primary means of preventing fraud is through internal control established and maintained by management.

II. Internal auditors are responsible for assisting in the prevention of fraud by examining and evaluating the adequacy of the internal control system.

III. Internal auditors should assess the operating effectiveness of fraud-related communication systems.

    A. I only.

    B. I and II only.

    C. II only.

    D. I, II, and III.

Answer (D) is correct. *(CIA, adapted)*
    REQUIRED: The true statement(s) about the prevention of fraud.
    DISCUSSION: The principal mechanism for preventing fraud is internal control. Responsibility for establishing and maintaining control rests with management. Furthermore, internal auditors are responsible for assisting in the prevention of fraud by examining and evaluating the adequacy and the effectiveness of the system of internal control, commensurate with the extent of the potential exposure within the organization. Internal auditors also should assess the operating effectiveness of fraud-related communication systems and practices and support fraud-related training initiatives (PA 1210.A2-1).
    Answer (A) is incorrect because internal auditors are responsible for assisting in the prevention of fraud by examining and evaluating the adequacy of the internal control system, and internal auditors should assess the operating effectiveness of fraud-related communication systems. Answer (B) is incorrect because internal auditors should assess the operating effectiveness of fraud-related communication systems. Answer (C) is incorrect because the primary means of preventing fraud is through internal control established and maintained by management, and internal auditors should assess the operating effectiveness of fraud-related communication systems.

45. The internal audit activity's responsibility for preventing fraud is to

    A. Establish internal control.

    B. Maintain internal control.

    C. Evaluate the system of internal control.

    D. Exercise operating authority over fraud prevention activities.

Answer (C) is correct. *(Publisher, adapted)*
    REQUIRED: The internal audit activity's responsibility for preventing fraud.
    DISCUSSION: The principal mechanism for preventing fraud is control, and management has the primary responsibility for establishing and maintaining control. Internal auditors are responsible for assisting in the prevention of fraud by examining and evaluating the adequacy and the effectiveness of the system of internal control (PA 1210.A2-1).
    Answer (A) is incorrect because management's responsibility is to establish internal control. Answer (B) is incorrect because management's responsibility is to maintain internal control. Answer (D) is incorrect because the IAA will not be independent if it exercises operating authority.

46. In an organization with a separate division that is primarily responsible for the prevention of fraud, the internal audit activity is responsible for

    A. Examining and evaluating the adequacy and effectiveness of that division's actions taken to prevent fraud.

    B. Establishing and maintaining that division's system of internal control.

    C. Planning that division's fraud prevention activities.

    D. Controlling that division's fraud prevention activities.

Answer (A) is correct. *(CIA, adapted)*
    REQUIRED: The responsibility of the IAA in an organization with a separate fraud prevention division.
    DISCUSSION: Control is the principal mechanism for the prevention of fraud. Management, in turn, is primarily responsible for the establishment and maintenance of control. Internal auditors are primarily responsible for preventing fraud by examining and evaluating the adequacy and effectiveness of control (PA 1210.A2-1).
    Answer (B) is incorrect because establishing and maintaining control is a responsibility of management. Answer (C) is incorrect because planning fraud prevention activities is a responsibility of management. Answer (D) is incorrect because controlling fraud prevention activities is a responsibility of management.

47. An internal auditor who suspects fraud should

    A. Determine that a loss has been incurred.

    B. Interview those who have been involved in the control of assets.

    C. Identify the employees who could be implicated in the case.

    D. Recommend an investigation after determining that fraud has occurred.

Answer (D) is correct. *(CIA, adapted)*
    REQUIRED: The action to be taken by an internal auditor who suspects fraud.
    DISCUSSION: An internal auditor's responsibilities for detecting fraud include evaluating fraud indicators and deciding whether any additional action is necessary or whether an investigation should be recommended. The internal auditor should notify the appropriate authorities within the organization if (s)he has determined that the indicators of fraud are sufficient to recommend an investigation (PA 1210.A2-1).
    Answer (A) is incorrect because determining the loss could alert the perpetrator of the fraud. The perpetrator could then destroy or compromise evidence. Answer (B) is incorrect because interviewing those who have been involved in the control of assets is part of the fraud investigation. Answer (C) is incorrect because identifying the employees who could be implicated in the case is part of the fraud investigation.

48. The internal auditors' responsibility regarding fraud includes all of the following except

    A. Determining whether the control environment sets the appropriate tone at top.

    B. Ensuring that fraud will not occur.

    C. Being aware of activities in which fraud is likely to occur.

    D. Evaluating the effectiveness of control activities.

Answer (B) is correct. *(CIA, adapted)*
    REQUIRED: The item not part of the internal auditors' responsibility regarding fraud.
    DISCUSSION: Control is the principal mechanism for preventing fraud. Internal auditors are responsible for assisting in the prevention of fraud by examining and evaluating the adequacy and the effectiveness of the system of internal control, commensurate with the extent of the potential exposure in the organization. However, management is responsible for establishing and maintaining internal control (PA 1210.A2-1). Moreover, due professional care requires the conduct of examinations and verifications to a reasonable extent but does not require detailed reviews of all transactions. Thus, the internal auditors cannot give absolute assurance that noncompliance or irregularities do not exist (PA 1220-1).
    Answer (A) is incorrect because internal auditing is responsible for evaluating the organization's control environment. Answer (C) is incorrect because the internal auditor should have sufficient knowledge of fraud indicators and be alert to opportunities that could allow fraud. Answer (D) is incorrect because assessing the design and operating effectiveness of fraud-related controls is the responsibility of internal auditing.

49. During an engagement to review payments under a construction contract with a local firm, the internal auditor found a recurring monthly reimbursement for rent at a local apartment complex. Each reimbursement was authorized by the same project engineer. The internal auditor found no provision for payment of temporary living expenses in the construction contract. Discussion with the project engineer could not resolve the matter. The internal auditor should

    A. Evaluate the indicators of fraud.

    B. Call the engineer into a private meeting to confront the situation.

    C. Complete the engagement as scheduled, noting the recurring reimbursement in the working papers.

    D. Wait until the engineer is surrounded by plenty of witnesses and then inquire about the payments.

Answer (A) is correct. *(CIA, adapted)*
    REQUIRED: The action the internal auditor should take when fraud is suspected.
    DISCUSSION: The internal auditor should evaluate the indicators of fraud and decide whether (1) further action is needed or (2) an investigation should be recommended. When fraud has occurred, the internal auditor should inform the appropriate authorities within the organization and recommend an investigation. When incidents of significant fraud or erosion of trust have been established to a reasonable certainty, senior management and the board should be notified immediately (PA 1210.A2-2).
    Answer (B) is incorrect because the project engineer has already been asked about the facts and did not resolve the issue. Answer (C) is incorrect because the unexplained payment may be an indication of fraud. Answer (D) is incorrect because raising this issue in public may expose the internal auditor to liability for defamation.

50. A disgruntled former employee calls the chief audit executive to report misappropriations of funds by the supervisor of cash operations. Engagement tests subsequently verify the allegations. The CAE should proceed with which of the following actions based upon the above information?

    A. Notify local law enforcement authorities.

    B. Confront the supervisor of cash operations with the allegations.

    C. Inform the treasurer and chief financial officer of the suspected fraud.

    D. Notify the bonding agency.

Answer (C) is correct. *(CIA, adapted)*
    REQUIRED: The proper action, given verification of fraud allegations.
    DISCUSSION: The CAE should inform the appropriate authorities within the organization when fraud has occurred and recommend an investigation (PA 1210.A2-1). The treasurer and chief financial officer are the superiors of the suspect and are thus appropriate parties to notify.
    Answer (A) is incorrect because law enforcement authorities should be called only after a discussion with and the concurrence of management. Answer (B) is incorrect because a confrontation with the cash operations supervisor at this moment could not only hinder further investigation but also lead to slander charges. Answer (D) is incorrect because the bonding agency will be notified after discussion with management and legal counsel.

51. During an engagement at a bank, the internal auditors discover that one loan officer had approved loans to a number of related but separate organizations in violation of regulatory policies. The loan officer indicated that it was an oversight and it would not happen again. However, the internal auditors believe it may have been intentional because the officer is related to one of the primary owners of the group that controls the related organizations. The internal auditors should

A. Inform management of the conflict of interest and the violation of the regulatory requirements and suggest further investigation.

B. Report the violation to the regulatory agency because it constitutes a significant breakdown of the bank's controls.

C. Not report the violation if the loan officer agrees to take corrective action.

D. Expand the engagement procedures to determine if there may be fraudulent activity on the part of the loan officer and communicate the observations to management when the follow-up investigation is complete.

Answer (A) is correct. *(CIA, adapted)*
REQUIRED: The internal auditors' responsibility to report a possible conflict of interest.
DISCUSSION: The internal auditor should evaluate the indicators of fraud and decide whether (1) further action is needed or (2) an investigation should be recommended. When fraud has occurred, the internal auditor should inform the appropriate authorities within the organization and recommend an investigation. When incidents of significant fraud or erosion of trust have been established to a reasonable certainty, senior management and the board should be notified immediately (PA 1210.A2-2). Furthermore, The IIA Code of Ethics states, "Internal auditors shall disclose all material facts known to them that, if not disclosed, may distort the reporting of activities under review."
Answer (B) is incorrect because the internal auditors have no obligation to report to authorities outside the organization. Answer (C) is incorrect because all material facts should be reported. Answer (D) is incorrect because an important violation of both bank and regulatory rules should be reported immediately to senior management and the board for corrective action.

52. The chief audit executive (CAE) uncovers a significant fraudulent activity that appears to involve the executive vice president to whom the CAE reports. Which of the following best describes how the CAE should proceed?

A. Conduct an investigation to ascertain whether the executive vice president is involved in the fraudulent activity.

B. Interview the executive vice president to obtain essential evidence.

C. Notify regulatory authorities and police.

D. Report the facts to the chief executive officer and the board.

Answer (D) is correct. *(CIA, adapted)*
REQUIRED: The appropriate action when suspected fraudulent activity involves the CAE's superior.
DISCUSSION: When incidents of significant fraud or erosion of trust have been established to a reasonable certainty, senior management and the board should be notified immediately (PA 1210.A2-2).
Answer (A) is incorrect because management must determine whether an investigation will be carried out. Answer (B) is incorrect because the internal auditor should avoid confronting persons suspected of theft or fraud until the appropriate authorities within the organization have been notified and have determined the appropriate action. Answer (C) is incorrect because the internal auditor's ethical obligations do not include reporting fraudulent activity to outside authorities unless senior management does not take appropriate action.

53. A significant employee fraud took place shortly after an internal auditing engagement. The internal auditor may not have properly fulfilled the responsibility for the prevention of fraud by failing to note and report that

A. Policies, practices, and procedures to monitor activities and safeguard assets were less extensive in low-risk areas than in high-risk areas.

B. A system of control that depended upon separation of duties could be circumvented by collusion among three employees.

C. There were no written policies describing prohibited activities and the action required whenever violations are discovered.

D. Divisional employees had not been properly trained to distinguish between bona fide signatures and cleverly forged ones on authorization forms.

Answer (C) is correct. *(CIA, adapted)*
REQUIRED: The way in which the internal auditor may not have properly fulfilled the responsibility for the prevention of fraud.
DISCUSSION: Management is responsible for establishing and maintaining internal control. Thus, management also is responsible for the fraud prevention program. The control environment element of this program includes a code of conduct, ethics policy, or fraud policy to set the appropriate tone at the top. Moreover, organizations should establish effective fraud-related information and communication practices, for example, documentation and dissemination of policies, guidelines, and results (PA 1210.A2-1).
Answer (A) is incorrect because, for cost-benefit reasons, controls should be more extensive in high-risk areas. Answer (B) is incorrect because even the best system of control can often be circumvented by collusion. Answer (D) is incorrect because forgery, like collusion, can circumvent even an effective control.

54. If there is fraud in the marketing department, which of the following is beyond the scope of the internal auditor's responsibility of an internal auditor involved in the investigation?

- A. Informing the wrongdoer of his or her legal rights.
- B. Determining the extent of the wrongdoing.
- C. Coordinating activities with management.
- D. Including the wrongdoing in a report that will go to the board.

Answer (A) is correct. *(CIA, adapted)*
REQUIRED: The action beyond the scope of the internal auditor's responsibility.
DISCUSSION: In the investigation of fraud, the internal auditor should (1) assess the probable level and the extent of complicity in the fraud; (2) gather and document evidence; (3) identify the perpetrators; and (4) determine the extent of the fraud, the techniques used, and the cause. When the internal auditor suspects wrongdoing, (s)he should inform the appropriate authorities within the organization. Reporting of fraud includes various oral or written, interim or final, communications to management or the board. Also, activities should be coordinated with management, legal counsel, and other specialists (PA 1210.A2-2). However, the criminal investigation is the responsibility of external authorities. The internal auditor does not have the responsibility or the right to inform the wrongdoer of his or her legal rights.
Answer (B) is incorrect because determining the extent of the wrongdoing is a responsibility of the internal auditor. Answer (C) is incorrect because coordinating activities with management is a responsibility of the internal auditor. Answer (D) is incorrect because including the wrongdoing in a report to the board is a responsibility of the internal auditor.

55. An internal auditor has detected probable employee fraud and is preparing a preliminary report for management. This report should include

- A. A statement that an engagement conducted with due professional care cannot provide absolute assurance that irregularities have not occurred.
- B. The internal auditor's recommendation of an investigation.
- C. The results of a polygraph test administered to the suspected perpetrator(s) of the fraud.
- D. A list of proposed engagement tests to help disclose the existence of similar frauds in the future.

Answer (B) is correct. *(CIA, adapted)*
REQUIRED: The content of a preliminary report on probable employee fraud.
DISCUSSION: Fraud reporting consists of various oral or written, interim or final, communications to senior management or the board about the status and results of fraud investigations. When incidents of significant fraud or erosion of trust have been established to a reasonable certainty, senior management and the board should be notified immediately (PA 1210.A2-2). When fraud has occurred, the internal auditor should recommend an investigation (PA 1210.A2-1).
Answer (A) is incorrect because a report on fraud that has been detected should not include this language. Answer (C) is incorrect because the investigation should follow the preliminary report. Answer (D) is incorrect because a report to operating management would not include such details.

56. When conducting fraud investigations, internal auditors should

- A. Clearly indicate the extent of the internal auditors' knowledge of the fraud when questioning suspects.
- B. Assign personnel to the investigation in accordance with the engagement schedule established at the beginning of the fiscal year.
- C. Perform its investigation independently of lawyers, security personnel, and specialists from outside the organization who are involved in the investigation.
- D. Assess the probable level of, and the extent of complicity in, the fraud within the organization.

Answer (D) is correct. *(CIA, adapted)*
REQUIRED: The role of the internal auditors in fraud investigations.
DISCUSSION: When conducting fraud investigations, internal auditors or others should assess the probable level of, and the extent of complicity in, the fraud within the organization. This assessment can be critical to ensuring that (1) crucial evidence is not tainted or destroyed and (2) misleading information is not obtained from persons who may be involved (PA 1210.A2-2).
Answer (A) is incorrect because, by always giving the impression that additional evidence is in reserve, the internal auditors are more apt to obtain complete and truthful answers. Answer (B) is incorrect because fraud investigations usually occur unexpectedly and cannot be scheduled in advance. Also, the fraud investigation must be conducted by individuals having the appropriate expertise, even if another engagement must be delayed. Answer (C) is incorrect because the internal auditors should coordinate their activities with management, legal counsel, and other specialists.

57. Internal auditors are responsible for reporting fraud to the board when

- A. The incidence of significant fraud has been established to a reasonable certainty.
- B. Suspicious activities have been reported to the internal auditors.
- C. Irregular transactions have been identified and are under investigation.
- D. The review of all suspected fraud-related transactions is complete.

Answer (A) is correct. *(CIA, adapted)*
  REQUIRED: The responsibility of internal auditors for reporting fraud to senior management and the board.
  DISCUSSION: Sufficient investigation should take place to establish reasonable certainty that a fraud has occurred before any reporting is done. When the incidence of significant fraud or erosion of trust has been established to a reasonable certainty, senior management and the board should be notified immediately (PA 1210.A2-2).
  Answer (B) is incorrect because no reporting is required merely because suspicious acts have been reported. Answer (C) is incorrect because irregular transactions under investigation would not require reporting until the investigation determines with reasonable certainty that a significant fraud or erosion of trust has occurred. Answer (D) is incorrect because reporting should occur when the incidence of significant fraud or erosion of trust has been established to a reasonable certainty.

58. A fraud report is required

- A. At the conclusion of the detection phase.
- B. At the conclusion of the investigation phase.
- C. At the conclusion of both the detection and the investigation phases.
- D. Neither at the conclusion of the detection phase nor at the conclusion of the investigation phase.

Answer (B) is correct. *(CIA, adapted)*
  REQUIRED: The situation in which a fraud report is required.
  DISCUSSION: A written report or other formal communication should be issued at the conclusion of the investigation phase. It should include (1) the basis for beginning an investigation, (2) time frames, (3) observations, (4) conclusions, (5) resolution, and (6) corrective action taken (or recommendations) to improve controls (PA 1210.A2-2).
  Answer (A) is incorrect because a fraud report may be desirable but is not required at the conclusion of the detection phase. Answer (C) is incorrect because a written report or other formal communication should be issued at the conclusion of the investigation phase. Answer (D) is incorrect because a fraud report is required at the conclusion of the investigation phase but not at the conclusion of the detection phase.

59. Which of the following is the information that must be included in a fraud report at the conclusion of an investigation?

- A. Purpose, scope, results, and, when appropriate, an expression of the internal auditor's overall opinion.
- B. Criteria, condition, cause, and effect.
- C. Background, observations, and recommendations.
- D. Observations, conclusions, recommendations, and corrective action.

Answer (D) is correct. *(CIA, adapted)*
  REQUIRED: The information that must be included in a fraud report.
  DISCUSSION: A written report or other formal communication should be issued at the conclusion of the investigation phase. It should include (1) the basis for beginning an investigation, (2) time frames, (3) observations, (4) conclusions, (5) resolution, and (6) corrective action taken (or recommendations) to improve controls (PA 1210.A2-2).
  Answer (A) is incorrect because the purpose, scope, and results are included in every final engagement communication. Results include conclusions (opinions) (PA 2410-1). This definition does not include corrective action, etc. Answer (B) is incorrect because criteria, condition, cause, and effect are the attributes of observations and recommendations. A fraud report includes more than observations and recommendations. Answer (C) is incorrect because background is recommended but not required for inclusion in a final engagement communication. Furthermore, conclusions, corrective action, etc., are omitted.

60. An internal auditor finds that senior management has given tacit approval to activities that have resulted in prematurely recognizing revenue for goods that were not shipped. A preliminary investigation corroborates the internal auditor's initial observations. As part of the annual financial statement audit, the internal auditor coordinates work with the external auditor, who has asked to review the engagement working papers related to sales activities. Assuming the amounts could be material to the financial statements, the internal auditor should report the observations to

    A. The internal legal counsel to gain an assessment as to whether the action might constitute a fraud.

    B. The audit committee because it is a significant accounting matter that should be addressed before the year-end audit report is issued.

    C. The external auditor as part of the process of sharing working papers.

    D. All of the answers are correct.

Answer (D) is correct. *(CIA, adapted)*
    REQUIRED: The recipient(s) of a report on an irregularity by senior management.
    DISCUSSION: Because the internal auditor is not trained in the law, internal legal counsel should be consulted to provide expert advice about the matter. Given that senior management is involved, the audit committee must be informed about significant fraud. Furthermore, coordination of internal and external audit efforts should extend to sharing of programs, working papers, and reports.
    Answer (A) is incorrect because recipients should include the internal legal counsel. Answer (B) is incorrect because recipients should include the audit committee. Answer (C) is incorrect because recipients should include the external auditor.

10.4 Fraud Indicators

61. Red flags are conditions that indicate a higher likelihood of fraud. Which of the following is not considered a red flag?

    A. Management has delegated the authority to make purchases under a certain value to subordinates.

    B. An individual has held the same cash-handling job for an extended period without any rotation of duties.

    C. An individual handling marketable securities is responsible for making the purchases, recording the purchases, and reporting any discrepancies and gains/losses to senior management.

    D. The assignment of responsibility and accountability in the accounts receivable department is not clear.

Answer (A) is correct. *(CIA, adapted)*
    REQUIRED: The item that is not a red flag.
    DISCUSSION: Delegating the authority to make purchases under a certain value to subordinates is an acceptable and common practice intended to limit risk while promoting efficiency. It is not, by itself, considered a red flag.
    Answer (B) is incorrect because lack of rotation of duties or cross-training for sensitive jobs is a red flag. Such a person may have a greater opportunity to commit and conceal fraud. Answer (C) is incorrect because an inappropriate combination of duties is a red flag. Answer (D) is incorrect because establishing clear lines of authority and accountability not only helps to assign culpability but also has preventive effects.

62. Internal auditors have been advised to consider red flags to determine whether management is involved in a fraud. Which of the following does not represent a difficulty in using the red flags as fraud indicators?

    A. Many common red flags are also associated with situations in which no fraud exists.

    B. Some red flags are difficult to quantify or to evaluate.

    C. Red flag information is not gathered as a normal part of an engagement.

    D. The red flags literature is not well enough established to have a positive impact on internal auditing.

Answer (D) is correct. *(CIA, adapted)*
    REQUIRED: The item not a difficulty in using red flags as fraud indicators.
    DISCUSSION: The state of red flags literature is not a difficulty. It is well established and will be refined in the future as research is done. Thus, it does not preclude consideration of red flags.
    Answer (A) is incorrect because red flags are developed by correlation analysis, not necessarily by causation analysis. Answer (B) is incorrect because many red flags, such as management's attitude, are difficult to quantify. Answer (C) is incorrect because internal auditors should be able to identify fraud indicators and should be alert to opportunities that could allow fraud. However, internal auditors do not normally perform procedures specifically to gather red flag information.

63. Which of the following is an indicator of possible financial reporting fraud being perpetrated by management of a manufacturer?

A. A trend analysis discloses (1) sales increases of 50% and (2) cost of goods sold increases of 25%.

B. A ratio analysis discloses cost of goods sold is 50% of sales.

C. A cross-sectional analysis of common size statements discloses (1) the firm's percentage of cost of goods sold to sales is 40% and (2) the industry average percentage of cost of goods sold to sales is 50%.

D. A cross-sectional analysis of common size statements discloses (1) the firm's percentage of cost of goods sold to sales is 50% and (2) the industry average percentage of cost of goods sold to sales is 40%.

Answer (A) is correct. *(CIA, adapted)*
REQUIRED: The indicator of possible financial reporting fraud being perpetrated by management of a manufacturer.
DISCUSSION: A 50% increase in sales supported by a 25% increase in cost of goods sold is either fortuitous or fraudulent. Increases in sales are usually accompanied by close to proportional increases in cost of goods sold. Examples of situations in which increases in sales can be disproportionately larger than increases in cost of goods sold include (1) operations within the realm of economies of scale (increasing returns to scale) and (2) the introduction of a highly accepted fashion item. Cases in which disproportionately large sales increases indicate fraudulent conduct include (1) collusion by the host firm's sales personnel and the buying firm's purchasing personnel and (2) collusion by members of two departments within the host firm, such as sales and transportation. Because the internal auditor would not know whether the disproportionately large increase in sales is legitimate, the auditor should view this condition as an indicator of possible fraud.
Answer (B) is incorrect because a gross profit margin (GPM) of 50% is not an indicator of fraud. Manufacturers can expect a range of 40-60% for this ratio. Answer (C) is incorrect because these data indicate an industry GPM of 50% and host firm GPM of 40%. The greater GPM realized by the host firm may result from any number of reasonable causes. These include (1) greater efficiencies exercised by the host firm, (2) greater sales effort (or a more highly accepted product), and (3) measurement errors. Answer (D) is incorrect because these data indicate an industry GPM of 40% and a host firm GPM of 50%. The lower GPM realized by the host firm may result from such causes as (1) host firm inefficiencies; (2) less acceptance of host firm product or less sales effort; and (3) measurement errors.

64. An internal auditor should be concerned about the possibility of fraud if

A. Cash receipts, net of the amounts used to pay petty cash-type expenditures, are deposited in the bank daily.

B. The monthly bank statement reconciliation is performed by the same employee who maintains the perpetual inventory records.

C. The accounts receivable subsidiary ledger and accounts payable subsidiary ledger are maintained by the same person.

D. One person, acting alone, has sole access to the petty cash fund (except for a provision for occasional surprise counts by a supervisor or auditor).

Answer (A) is correct. *(CIA, adapted)*
REQUIRED: The reason an internal auditor should be concerned about the possibility of fraud.
DISCUSSION: Paying petty cash expenditures from cash receipts facilitates the unauthorized removal of cash before deposit. All cash receipts should be deposited intact daily. Petty cash expenditures should be handled through an imprest fund.
Answer (B) is incorrect because the monthly bank reconciliation should not be performed by a person who makes deposits or writes checks, but the inventory clerk has no such responsibilities. Answer (C) is incorrect because there is no direct relationship between the transactions posted to the accounts receivable and accounts payable subsidiary ledgers; having the same person maintain both does not create a control weakness. Answer (D) is incorrect because, to establish accountability for petty cash, only one person should have access to the fund.

Questions 65 through 71 are based on the following information.

Randy and John had known each other for many years. They had become best friends in college, where they both majored in accounting. After graduation, Randy took over the family business from his father. His family had been in the grocery business for several generations. When John had difficulty finding a job, Randy offered him a job in the family store. John proved to be a very capable employee. As John demonstrated his abilities, Randy began delegating more and more responsibility to him. After a period of time, John was doing all of the general accounting and authorization functions for checks, cash, inventories, documents, records, and bank reconciliations. (1) *John was trusted completely and handled all financial functions.* No one checked his work.

Randy decided to expand the business and opened several new stores. (2) *Randy was always handling the most urgent problem... crisis management is what his college professors had termed it.* John assisted with the problems when his other duties allowed him time.

Although successful at work, John had (3) *difficulties with personal financial problems.*

At first, the amounts stolen by John were small. John didn't even worry about making the accounts balance. But John became greedy. "How easy it is to take the money," he said. He felt that he was a critical member of the business team (4) *and that he contributed much more to the success of the company than was represented by his salary.* It would take two or three people to replace me, he often thought to himself. As the amounts became larger and larger, (5) *he made the books balance.* Because of these activities, John was able to purchase an expensive car and take his family on several trips each year. (6) *He also joined an expensive country club.* Things were changing at home, however. (7) *John's family observed that he was often argumentative and at other times very depressed.*

The fraud continued for 6 years. Each year, the business performed more and more poorly. In the last year, the stores had a substantial net loss. Randy's bank required an audit. John confessed when he thought the auditors had discovered his embezzlements.

When discussing frauds, the pressures, opportunities, and rationalizations that cause/allow a perpetrator to commit the fraud are often identified. Symptoms of fraud are also studied.

65. Number 1, "John was trusted completely . . ." is an example of a(n)

A. Document symptom.
B. Situational pressure.
C. Opportunity to commit.
D. Physical symptom.

Answer (C) is correct. *(CIA, adapted)*
REQUIRED: The characteristic of which complete trust in an employee is an example.
DISCUSSION: Complete trust in an individual represents an opportunity to commit fraud. John's actions went unscrutinized because of the absence of an appropriate segregation of functions and his ability to override whatever control procedures were in place.

66. Number 2, "Randy was always handling the most urgent . . ." is an example of a(n)

A. Opportunity to commit.
B. Analytical symptom.
C. Situational pressure.
D. Rationalization.

Answer (A) is correct. *(CIA, adapted)*
REQUIRED: The characteristics of which crisis management is an example.
DISCUSSION: When a manager continually handles the most pressing issues of a company, an opportunity for the manager to commit fraud is created. The lack of long-range planning creates a potential for fraud because organizational objectives may have been replaced with individual initiatives.

67. Number 3, "Difficulties with personal financial problems" is an example of a(n)

A. Behavioral symptom.
B. Situational pressure.
C. Rationalization.
D. Opportunity to commit.

Answer (B) is correct. *(CIA, adapted)*
REQUIRED: The characteristic of which personal financial problems are an example.
DISCUSSION: Financial difficulties create situational pressures or temptations that may contribute to fraud. These situational pressures result from high personal indebtedness, extravagant lifestyles, gambling problems, etc.

68. Number 4, "and that he contributed much more. . ." is an example of a

A. Rationalization.
B. Behavioral symptom.
C. Situational pressure.
D. Physical symptom.

Answer (A) is correct. *(CIA, adapted)*
REQUIRED: The characteristic of which an inflated self-worth is an example.
DISCUSSION: Rationalization occurs when one attributes actions to rational and creditable motives without analysis of one's true and especially unconscious motives. Thus, a feeling that one is contributing more than one is paid would be a rationalization for committing fraud.

69. Number 5, "he made the books balance" is an example of a(n)

    A. Physical symptom.

    B. Analytical symptom.

    C. Lifestyle symptom.

    D. Document symptom.

Answer (D) is correct. *(CIA, adapted)*
    REQUIRED: The characteristic of which covering fraud by tampering with company records is an example.
    DISCUSSION: Tampering with the company's books is a document symptom. In other words, the indicator of fraud consists of the changes in actual company records.

70. Number 6, "He also joined an expensive country club" is an example of a

    A. Rationalization.

    B. Lifestyle symptom.

    C. Behavioral symptom.

    D. Physical symptom.

Answer (B) is correct. *(CIA, adapted)*
    REQUIRED: The characteristic of which an extravagant lifestyle is an example.
    DISCUSSION: John was living beyond his means. The change in lifestyle was a symptom that indicated the presence of fraud.

71. Number 7, "John's family observed that he was often argumentative . . ." is an example of a

    A. Rationalization.

    B. Lifestyle symptom.

    C. Behavioral symptom.

    D. Physical symptom.

Answer (C) is correct. *(CIA, adapted)*
    REQUIRED: The characteristic of which an argumentative attitude is an example.
    DISCUSSION: A drastic change in an employee's behavior may indicate the presence of fraud. The guilt and the other forms of stress associated with perpetrating and concealing the fraud may induce noticeable changes in behavior.

72. Which of the following policies is most likely to result in an environment conducive to the occurrence of fraud?

    A. Budget preparation input by the employees who are responsible for meeting the budget.

    B. Unreasonable sales and production goals.

    C. The division's hiring process frequently results in the rejection of adequately trained applicants.

    D. The application of some accounting controls on a sample basis.

Answer (B) is correct. *(CIA, adapted)*
    REQUIRED: The policy most likely to result in an environment conducive to the occurrence of fraud.
    DISCUSSION: Unrealistically high sales or production quotas can be an incentive to falsify the records or otherwise take inappropriate action to improve performance measures so that the quotas appear to have been met.
    Answer (A) is incorrect because participatory budgeting can reduce antagonism to budgets and reduce the likelihood of inappropriate means of meeting the budget. Answer (C) is incorrect because hiring policies should be based on factors other than adequate training, such as the applicants' personal integrity. Furthermore, hiring of all adequately trained applicants is unlikely to be necessary. Answer (D) is incorrect because, under the reasonable assurance concept, the cost of controls should not exceed their benefits. The cost of applying controls to all relevant transactions rather than a sample may be greater than the resultant savings.

73. Internal auditors should have knowledge about factors (red flags) that have proven to be associated with management fraud. Which of the following factors have generally not been associated with management fraud?

    A. Generous performance-based reward systems.

    B. A domineering management.

    C. Regular comparison of actual results with budgets.

    D. A management preoccupation with increased financial performance.

Answer (C) is correct. *(CIA, adapted)*
    REQUIRED: The factor not associated with management fraud.
    DISCUSSION: Regular comparison of actual results to budgets provides feedback and is a normal and necessary part of the control loop. Ineffective control is an indicator of possible fraud.
    Answer (A) is incorrect because generous reward systems provide incentives for management to distort performance. Answer (B) is incorrect because pressure from superiors provides an incentive for management to distort performance. Answer (D) is incorrect because a management preoccupation with increased financial performance provides an incentive for managers to distort performance.

74. When comparing perpetrators who have embezzled an organization's funds with perpetrators of financial statement fraud (falsified financial statements), those who have falsified financial statements are less likely to

- A. Have experienced an autocratic management style.
- B. Be living beyond their obvious means of support.
- C. Rationalize the fraudulent behavior.
- D. Use organizational expectations as justification for the act.

Answer (B) is correct. *(CIA, adapted)*
REQUIRED: The least likely characteristic of those who have falsified financial statements.
DISCUSSION: Living beyond one's means has been linked to employee fraud (embezzlement), not to financial statement fraud. Fraud perpetrated for the benefit of the organization ordinarily benefits the wrongdoer indirectly, whereas fraud that is detrimental to the organization provides immediate, direct benefits to the employee.
Answer (A) is incorrect because autocratic management styles have been linked to management (financial statement) fraud. Answer (C) is incorrect because rationalization is common to all fraud. Answer (D) is incorrect because high expectations are often given as a motivating factor by those who have committed financial statement fraud.

75. The following are facts about a subsidiary:

1. The subsidiary has been in business for several years and enjoyed good profit margins although the general economy was in a recession, which affected competitors.

2. The working capital ratio has declined from a healthy 3:1 to 0.9:1.

3. Turnover for the last several years has included three controllers, two supervisors of accounts receivable, four payables supervisors, and numerous staff in other financial positions.

4. Purchasing policy requires three bids. However, the supervisor of purchasing at the subsidiary has instituted a policy of sole-source procurement to reduce the number of suppliers.

When conducting a financial audit of the subsidiary, the internal auditor should

- A. Most likely not detect 1., 2., or 3.
- B. Ignore 2. since the economy had a downturn during this period.
- C. Consider 3. to be normal turnover, but be concerned about 2. and 4. as warning signals of fraud.
- D. Consider 1., 2., 3., and 4. as warning signals of fraud.

Answer (D) is correct. *(CIA, adapted)*
REQUIRED: The items an internal auditor should consider in a financial audit of a subsidiary.
DISCUSSION: That the organization has reported high profits when competitors have not may indicate a misstatement of the financial statements. Insufficient working capital may indicate such problems as overexpansion, decreases in revenues, transfers of funds to other organizations, insufficient credit, and excessive expenditures. The internal auditor should be alert for the diversion of funds for personal use through such methods as unrecorded sales and falsified expenditures. Rapid turnover in financial positions may signify existing problems with which the individuals feel uncomfortable but that they do not want to disclose. Accountability for funds and other resources should be determined upon termination of employment. Use of sole-source procurement does not encourage competition to ensure that the organization is obtaining the required materials or equipment at the best price. Sole-source procurement, if not adequately justified, indicates potential favoritism or kickbacks.
Answer (A) is incorrect because the items described can be detected through usual procedures in a financial audit. Answer (B) is incorrect because, although the economy suffered a downturn, the change in working capital is unusual in light of the continuing strong profit margins and should be investigated. Answer (C) is incorrect because the working capital ratio, the high employee turnover rate, and the sole-source procurement policy are all warning signals of fraud.

10.5 Engagement Procedures Related to Fraud

76. Contributions to a nonprofit organization have been constant for the past 3 years. The audit committee has become concerned that the president may have embarked on a scheme in which some of the contributions from many sustaining members have been redirected to other organizations. The audit committee suspects that the scheme may involve taking major contributions and depositing them in alternative accounts or soliciting contributions to be made in the name of another organization. Which of the following procedures should be most effective in detecting the existence of such a fraud?

A. Use generalized audit software to take a sample of pledged receipts not yet collected and confirm the amounts due with the donors.

B. Take a sample that includes all large donors for the past 3 years and a statistical sample of others and request a confirmation of total contributions made to the organization or to affiliated organizations.

C. Take a discovery sample of cash receipts and confirm the amounts of the receipts with the donors. Investigate any differences.

D. Use analytical review procedures to compare contributions generated with those of other comparable institutions over the same period of time. If the amount is significantly less, take a detailed sample of cash receipts and trace to the bank statements.

Answer (B) is correct. *(CIA, adapted)*
REQUIRED: The procedure most effective for detecting misdirected contributions.
DISCUSSION: The engagement objective is to determine whether contributions have been wrongly directed to alternate accounts or solicited for other organizations. Consequently, an appropriate procedure is to send confirmation requests to donors. However, testing transactions recorded by the accounting system will not result in sufficient information about solicitation of contributions for other organizations. The internal auditor must therefore make inquiries of the sustaining members about such solicitations.
Answer (A) is incorrect because sampling amounts listed as unpaid does not provide evidence about contributions previously paid or shifted to another organization. Answer (C) is incorrect because sampling cash receipts that have been recorded by the organization provides no evidence about unrecorded receipts or contributions diverted elsewhere. Answer (D) is incorrect because analytical procedures are of limited use. Also, the follow-up procedure only provides evidence that recorded receipts were also deposited.

77. A production manager for a moderate-sized manufacturer began ordering excessive raw materials and had them delivered to a wholesale business that the manager was running on the side. The manager falsified receiving documents and approved the invoices for payment. Which of the following procedures is most likely to detect this fraud?

A. Take a sample of cash disbursements; compare purchase orders, receiving reports, invoices, and check copies.

B. Take a sample of cash disbursements and confirm the amount purchased, purchase price, and date of shipment with the vendors.

C. Observe the receiving dock and count materials received; compare the counts with receiving reports completed by receiving personnel.

D. Perform analytical tests, comparing production, materials purchased, and raw materials inventory levels; investigate differences.

Answer (D) is correct. *(CIA, adapted)*
REQUIRED: The procedure most likely to detect a purchasing fraud.
DISCUSSION: The application of analytical procedures is based on the premise that, in the absence of known conditions to the contrary, relationships among information may reasonably be expected to exist and continue. Examples of contrary conditions include unusual or nonrecurring transactions or events; accounting, organizational, operational, environmental, and technological changes; inefficiencies; ineffectiveness; errors; irregularities; or illegal acts. Hence, the analytical procedures should identify an unexplained increase in materials used.
Answer (A) is incorrect because, given that documents have been falsified, supporting documents exist for each cash disbursement. Answer (B) is incorrect because the vendors will confirm all transactions. Answer (C) is incorrect because, given that the improper orders are shipped to another location, observing receiving dock counts will not detect the fraud.

Questions 78 and 79 are based on the following information.

Jane Jackson had been the regional sales manager for an organization for over 10 years. During this time, she had become very close friends with Frank Hansen, an internal audit manager. In addition to being neighbors, Jane and Frank had many of the same interests and belonged to the same tennis club. They trusted each other. Frank had helped Jane solve some sales problems, and Jane had given Frank some information that led to significant engagement observations during the past three engagements.

Below are selected analytical data from the organization that have led staff internal auditors to believe that there has been a financial statement fraud. The perpetrator appears to have falsified sales information for the past 2 years. Frank is concerned because he recently completed an engagement in the area and accepted Jane's explanation for differences in the analytical data. Frank is now certain that Jane is involved in the fraud.

	Current Year	Last Year	–2 Year	–3 Year	–4 Year
Increase in sales	10%	8%	6%	4%	5%
Inventory turnover	5	4	5	3.5	4
Gross margin	54%	49%	42%	39%	40%
Change in sales returns	8%	6%	3%	2.5%	3%

78. Which combination of the following analytical data provides the strongest indication of the possibility of the fraud?

A. Percentage increase in sales and inventory turnover.

B. Gross margin percentage and change in sales returns.

C. Inventory turnover and change in sales returns.

D. Percentage increase in sales and gross margin percentage.

Answer (B) is correct. *(CIA, adapted)*
REQUIRED: The analytical data that provide the strongest indication of the possibility of fraud.
DISCUSSION: Rapid increases in gross margin percentage are expected if sales are fictitious, that is, if sales are recorded without shipments and a consequent increase in cost of sales. The large increase in returns is also symptomatic of falsified sales.
Answer (A) is incorrect because the increase in percentage change in sales is not unreasonable and, given the constant increase, one might expect increases in inventory that could keep turnover constant. Answer (C) is incorrect because the turnover and return figures, when taken together, are not indications of sales overstatements. Answer (D) is incorrect because, if the increase in sales was due to a market sales price increase, one might expect these results.

79. The current dilemma in which Frank finds himself was least likely caused by

A. Not rotating engagements every year.

B. Accepting an engagement in an area where he was a close personal friend of management.

C. Failing to select the appropriate analytical procedures.

D. Accepting the response of management without additional testing.

Answer (C) is correct. *(CIA, adapted)*
REQUIRED: The least likely cause of the dilemma.
DISCUSSION: The information given suggests that Frank applied the proper analytical procedures but accepted management's explanation of the findings.
Answer (A) is incorrect because failure to rotate engagements seems to have contributed to Frank's decision to accept management's explanation for the analytical findings. Answer (B) is incorrect because Frank's friendship with Jane impaired his objectivity. Answer (D) is incorrect because Frank's acceptance of management's explanations apparently resulted in his failing to obtain sufficient information.

80. The chief of an organization's security has received an anonymous call accusing a marketing manager of taking kickbacks from a media outlet. Thus, the marketing department is on the list of possible engagement clients for the coming year. The internal audit activity is assigned responsibility for investigating fraud by its charter. If obtaining access to outside media outlet records and personnel is not possible, the best action an internal auditor could take to investigate the allegation of marketing kickbacks is to

A. Search for unrecorded liabilities from media outlets.

B. Obtain a list of approved media outlets.

C. Develop a financial and behavioral profile of the suspect.

D. Vouch any material past charge-offs of receivables.

Answer (C) is correct. *(CIA, adapted)*
REQUIRED: The best action an internal auditor can take to investigate an allegation of kickbacks.
DISCUSSION: The best action is to develop a financial and behavioral profile of the marketing manager. A common indicator of fraud by an employee is an unexplained change in his or her financial status. A standard of living not commensurate with the employee's income may signify wrongdoing. The employee's behavior may also be suspicious (for example, constant association with, and entertainment by, a member of the media outlet's staff). The profile may help to corroborate illegal income and thereby provide a basis for tracing illegal payments to the employee.
Answer (A) is incorrect because, if the employee is taking kickbacks, unrecorded liabilities are not being created. Answer (B) is incorrect because a list of approved media outlets would not provide any information about kickbacks. Answer (D) is incorrect because the receipt of kickbacks would have no effect on accounts receivable.

81. During a post-completion engagement related to a warehouse expansion, the internal auditor noted several invoices for redecorating services from a local merchant that were account-coded and signed for payment only by the cost engineer. The internal auditor should

    A. Compare the cost and description of the services with the account code used in the construction project and with related estimates in the construction-project budget.

    B. Consult with the cost engineer for assurance that these purchases were authorized for this construction project.

    C. Obtain a facsimile of the cost engineer's signature from the accounts payable group and compare it with the signature on the invoices.

    D. Recommend reclassifying the expenditure to the appropriate account code for redecorating services.

Answer (A) is correct. *(CIA, adapted)*
    REQUIRED: The action taken when invoices are account-coded and approved by the cost engineer only.
    DISCUSSION: The internal auditor needs to determine the validity of the transaction because the engineer is performing incompatible tasks. Comparing the cost and description of the services with the account code and the budget will verify the transaction. However, normal controls over disbursements need to be established.
    Answer (B) is incorrect because the cost engineer's assurance would not confirm the authorization of these expenditures. Answer (C) is incorrect because the primary focus is the validity of the transaction within this construction project. Answer (D) is incorrect because there is no basis for reclassifying the transaction within this context.

82. The internal auditor reviewed documentation showing that a customer had recently returned three expensive products to the regional service center for warranty replacement. The documentation also showed that the warranty clerk had rejected the claim and sent it to the customer's local distributor. The claim was rejected because the serial numbers listed in the warranty claim were not found in the computer's sales history file. Subsequently, the distributor supplied three different serial numbers, all of which were validated by the computer system, and the clerk completed the warranty claim for replacements. What is the best course of action for the internal auditor under the circumstances?

    A. Determine if the original serial numbers provided by the customer can be traced to other records, such as production and inventory records.

    B. Notify the appropriate authorities within the organization that there are sufficient indicators that a fraud has been committed.

    C. Verify with the appropriate supervisor that the warranty clerk had followed relevant procedures in the processing and disposition of this claim.

    D. Summarize this item along with other valid transactions in the internal auditor's test of warranty transactions.

Answer (A) is correct. *(CIA, adapted)*
    REQUIRED: The action to be taken by the internal auditor in investigating suspicious warranty claims.
    DISCUSSION: The best course of action for the internal auditor is to determine whether the original serial numbers provided by the customer can be traced to other records, such as production and inventory records. The internal auditor should determine whether the related equipment had actually been reported in a sales transaction.
    Answer (B) is incorrect because the internal auditor should pursue additional information before alerting authorities. Answer (C) is incorrect because verifying that the warranty clerk followed procedures does not provide more information about the validity of the warranty claim. Answer (D) is incorrect because the internal auditor should obtain more information about the validity of the transaction.

83. During an engagement relating to purchasing, the internal auditor finds that the largest blanket purchase order is for tires, which are expensed as vehicle maintenance items. The fleet manager requisitions tires against the blanket order for the company's 400-vehicle service fleet based on a visual inspection of the cars and trucks in the parking lot each week. Sometimes the fleet manager picks up the tires but always signs the receiving report for payment. Vehicle service data are entered into a maintenance database by the mechanic after the tires are installed. What is the best course of action for the internal auditor in these circumstances?

A. Determine whether the number of tires purchased can be reconciled to maintenance records.

B. Count the number of tires on hand and trace them to the related receiving reports.

C. Select a judgmental sample of requisitions and verify that each one is signed by the fleet manager.

D. Compare the number of tires purchased under the blanket purchase order with the number of tires purchased in the prior year for reasonableness.

Answer (A) is correct. *(CIA, adapted)*
REQUIRED: The action to be taken by the internal auditor during a purchasing engagement.
DISCUSSION: The best course of action for the internal auditor is to determine whether the number of tires purchased can be reconciled to maintenance records. That the fleet manager both requisitions and receives the tires provides an opportunity for fraud. The internal auditor should verify whether fraud has occurred. A separate receiving function would diminish the possibility of fraud by providing an independent count of items received.
Answer (B) is incorrect because tracing the tires on hand to the receiving reports would not reveal a fraud. The manager signs the receiving report. Answer (C) is incorrect because testing for signed requisitions would not necessarily reveal whether fraud is present. Answer (D) is incorrect because a fraud could have occurred during the prior year also.

Questions 84 through 86 are based on the following information. During an engagement performed at a smaller division, the internal auditor notes the following regarding the purchasing function:

- There are three purchasing agents. Agent 1 is responsible for ordering all large component parts, agent 2 for electric motors, and agent 3 for smaller parts such as fasteners.
- There are separate accounts payable and receiving departments.
- In order to hold vendors more responsible, all invoices are sent to the purchasing agent placing the order. The purchasing agent matches the vendor invoice, receiving slip, and purchase order. If all match, the purchasing agent sends the documents forward to the accounts payable department. Differences are investigated by the purchasing agent.

- Only the accounts payable department has the ability to authorize an item for payment.
- All recorded receipts are immediately recorded into a perpetual inventory record by the department to which the goods are transferred after receipt.

The internal auditor interviewed both management and the purchasing agents. Both groups were very satisfied with the current system because it helps maintain vendor accountability and provides sufficient segregation of duties given that only the accounts payable department can authorize an item for payment.

---

84. Which of the following engagement procedures is most effective in determining whether material fraud was taking place?

A. Take a random sample of cash disbursements and trace to approved purchase orders and receiving slips.

B. Reconcile the perpetual inventory to the general ledger and investigate any differences.

C. Take a random sample of purchase orders. Trace each purchase order to a receiving slip, vendor invoice, and approval by the accounts payable department.

D. Perform an analytical review of inventory by product line to determine whether a particular product line has increased. Inquire of the purchasing agent as to the reason for the inventory increase.

Answer (B) is correct. *(CIA, adapted)*
REQUIRED: The most effective procedure to determine whether material fraud occurred.
DISCUSSION: A fraud could result in an overstatement of inventory in the ledger. However, the perpetual inventory reflects the actual goods received.
Answer (A) is incorrect because cash disbursements are authorized by accounts payable and are not made in the absence of approved documents. Purchasing agents have control of these documents. Hence, if they are falsified by the purchasing agents, merely verifying that documents exist to support payments is ineffective. Answer (C) is incorrect because tracing purchase orders to receiving slips, invoices, and accounts payable approvals verifies only that purchase orders were processed. It would not detect fictitious purchase orders. Answer (D) is incorrect because analytical review of inventory by product line provides limited evidence on the possibility of fraud but would not be as effective as reconciling inventory.

85. The internal auditor is responsible for evaluating internal control to determine whether it allows undetected fraud. Based on the information presented, the most likely undetected fraud, if any, is that the

A. Purchasing agent is purchasing the majority of products from a favorite vendor because rotation among purchasing agents is not mandatory.

B. Purchasing agent is sending fake purchase orders to a dummy vendor, inserting a receiving slip, and having payments made to the dummy vendor.

C. Receiving department is diverting receipts to different locations and failing to create receiving reports.

D. Production department is deflating the price of products purchased and thereby increasing the reported gross margin of sales.

Answer (B) is correct. *(CIA, adapted)*
    REQUIRED: The most likely undetected fraud.
    DISCUSSION: Internal control is unlikely to detect the purchasing agent's fraud because this individual is in a position to perpetrate and conceal irregularities. Receiving documents and vendors' invoices should be sent to accounts payable, not to the purchasing agent.
    Answer (A) is incorrect because purchasing most goods from a particular vendor may be justified. Answer (C) is incorrect because this possible fraud should be detected by the absence of receiving reports to support vendors' invoices. Answer (D) is incorrect because this response is unrelated to the purchasing environment.

86. Which of the following controls, if properly implemented, is most likely to decrease the likelihood of fraud?

A. Require periodic rotation of purchases among different vendors.

B. Require rotation of duties among the three purchasing agents.

C. Require that receiving reports be sent directly to accounts payable.

D. Require that the updates to the perpetual inventory record be made by the receiving department.

Answer (C) is correct. *(CIA, adapted)*
    REQUIRED: The control most likely to decrease the likelihood of fraud.
    DISCUSSION: This change in procedures prevents the purchasing agent from falsifying receiving reports. An even better procedure is to have both the receiving reports and the vendors' invoices sent to accounts payable.
    Answer (A) is incorrect because rotation of vendors might partially alleviate the problem, but the purchasing agent could develop new dummy vendors. Answer (B) is incorrect because rotation of duties will not affect the type of fraud that could occur in this environment. The purchasing agent could develop another dummy vendor for the new product line. Answer (D) is incorrect because this procedure will create an additional opportunity for fraud by the receiving department.

87. During an engagement, the internal auditor found a scheme in which the warehouse director and the purchasing agent for a retail organization diverted a significant amount of goods to their own warehouse, then sold the goods to third parties. The fraud was not noted earlier because the warehouse director forwarded receiving reports (after updating the perpetual inventory records) to the accounts payable department for processing. Which of the following procedures most likely led to the discovery of the missing materials and the fraud?

A. Take a random sample of receiving reports and trace to the recording in the perpetual inventory record. Note differences and investigate by type of product.

B. Take a random sample of purchase orders and trace them to receiving documents and to the records in the accounts payable department.

C. Take an annual physical inventory, reconciling amounts with the perpetual inventory, noting the pattern of differences and investigating.

D. Take a random sample of sales invoices and trace to the perpetual records to see if inventory was on hand. Investigate any differences.

Answer (C) is correct. *(CIA, adapted)*
    REQUIRED: The audit procedure to detect the diversion of the goods.
    DISCUSSION: Taking an annual physical inventory should lead to the identification of systematic shrinkages in the inventory. The pattern of the shrinkages should implicate the warehouse director. At that time, a fraud investigation should be undertaken.
    Answer (A) is incorrect because sampling receiving reports would not have detected the fraud. The warehouse director updates the perpetual inventory records before forwarding the false receiving reports to accounts payable. Answer (B) is incorrect because taking a sample of purchase orders would not have detected the irregularities. All the goods were ordered, and the perpetrators colluded to falsify receiving reports even when the goods were diverted to another location. Answer (D) is incorrect because the warehouse director falsified the inventory records.

88. The internal auditor suspects a disbursements fraud in which an unknown employee(s) is submitting and approving invoices for payment. Before discussing the potential fraud with management, the internal auditor decides to gather additional information. Which of the following procedures is most helpful in providing the additional information?

A. Use software to develop a list of vendors with post office box numbers or other unusual features. Select a sample of those items and trace to supporting documents such as receiving reports.

B. Select a sample of payments made during the year and investigate each one for approval.

C. Select a sample of receiving reports representative of the period under investigation and trace to approved payment. Note any items not properly processed.

D. Take a sample of invoices received during the past month, examine to determine whether properly authorized for payment, and trace to underlying documents.

Answer (A) is correct.   *(CIA, adapted)*
REQUIRED: The most helpful procedure related to a disbursements fraud.
DISCUSSION: A disbursements fraud may be accomplished through the use of fictitious vendors. Investigating vendors with suspicious characteristics appropriately focuses on payees as sources of additional information.
Answer (B) is incorrect because the individual perpetrating the fraud may have been in a position to obtain approvals. Answer (C) is incorrect because the problem is more likely to be with payments for which no valid support exists. Answer (D) is incorrect because sampling invoices for the past month is not as effective as investigating suspicious vendors. It focuses only on a short period of time, and it does not emphasize the items most likely to be fraudulent.

89. The internal auditor finds a situation in which one person has the ability to collect receivables, make deposits, issue credit memos, and record receipt of payments. The internal auditor suspects the individual may be stealing from cash receipts. Which of the following engagement procedures is most effective in discovering fraud in this scenario?

A. Send positive confirmations to a random selection of customers.

B. Send negative confirmations to all outstanding accounts receivable customers.

C. Perform a detailed review of debits to customer discounts, sales returns, or other debit accounts, excluding cash posted to the cash receipts journal.

D. Take a sample of bank deposits and trace the detail in each bank deposit back to the entry in the cash receipts journal.

Answer (C) is correct.   *(CIA, adapted)*
REQUIRED: The engagement procedure most effective in detecting theft from cash receipts.
DISCUSSION: The most effective procedure is to perform a detailed review of debits to customer discounts, sales returns, etc. These accounts could be used to conceal a theft of cash payments without alerting customers. Seeking confirmation from customers and tracing bank balances will not detect the fraud because neither customer statements nor bank records will contain evidence of fraud.

90. While reviewing a division's accounts, an internal auditor becomes concerned that the division's management may have shipped poor quality merchandise to boost sales and profitability and thereby increase the manager's bonus. For this reason, the internal auditor suspects that returned goods are being shipped to other customers as new products without full correction of their defects. Which of the following engagement procedures is the least effective in determining whether such shipments took place?

A. Examine credit memos issued after year-end for goods shipped before year-end.

B. Physically observe the shipping and receiving area for information of returned goods.

C. Interview customer service representatives regarding unusual amounts of customer complaints.

D. Require the division to take a complete physical inventory at year-end, and observe the taking of the inventory.

Answer (D) is correct. *(CIA, adapted)*
REQUIRED: The least effective procedure to determine whether merchandise returned has been reshipped without the correction of defects.
DISCUSSION: Taking a complete year-end inventory is an ineffective engagement procedure. The goods returned and reshipped without the correction of defects would not be on hand to be counted.
Answer (A) is incorrect because examining credit memos issued after year-end for goods shipped before year-end would show that customers are returning inferior goods. Answer (B) is incorrect because physically observing the shipping and receiving area might reveal goods returned that are not yet accounted for. Answer (C) is incorrect because unusual amounts of customer complaints may suggest a condition not explained by normal spoilage rates.

91. An investment portfolio manager has the authority to use financial derivatives to hedge transactions but is not supposed to take speculative positions. However, the manager launches a scheme that includes (1) taking a position larger than required by the hedge, (2) putting the speculative gains in a suspense account, and (3) transferring the funds to a nonexistent broker and from there to a personal account. Which of the following engagement procedures is least effective in detecting this fraud?

A. Examine individual trades to determine whether the trades violate the authorization limit for the manager.

B. Sample individual trades and determine the exact matching of a hedge. Schedule and investigate all differences.

C. Sample all debits to the suspense account and examine their disposition.

D. Sample fund transfers to brokers and determine if the brokers are on the organization's authorized list for transactions.

Answer (A) is correct. *(CIA, adapted)*
REQUIRED: The least effective engagement procedure for detecting the fraudulent use of derivatives.
DISCUSSION: Examining individual trades to determine whether they violate the authorization limit would not detect the fraud. The speculative nature of the transaction, not its amount, is the violation of policy.
Answer (B) is incorrect because sampling individual trades may detect an unauthorized speculation. Answer (C) is incorrect because all debits to the suspense account should be sampled given the potential for using such an account for irregularities. Answer (D) is incorrect because sampling fund transfers to brokers and determining whether the brokers are on the authorized list for transactions may detect a fictitious party.

92. Management has requested that the internal auditor investigate the possibility that a purchasing agent is receiving kickbacks. Which of the following procedures is least effective in addressing management's concern?

A. Confirm all contract terms with vendors.

B. Analyze, by purchasing agent, all increases in cost of procured goods from specific vendors.

C. Take a statistical sample of goods purchased and compare purchase prices for goods with those of other sources of similar goods, such as other organizations or catalogs.

D. Observe any changes in the lifestyles or individual consumption habits of the purchasing agents involved.

Answer (A) is correct. *(CIA, adapted)*
REQUIRED: The least effective procedure to discover whether a purchasing agent is receiving kickbacks.
DISCUSSION: Confirming contract terms is the least useful procedure because the contract terms are already known. The confirmation would have to be expanded to inquire as to whether the purchasing agent has pressured vendors to make kickbacks. That approach is useful only if the kickbacks were initiated by the purchasing agent rather than the vendor.
Answer (B) is incorrect because analyzing increases in the cost of procured goods from specific vendors provides insight as to what products and which purchasing agent may be involved. Answer (C) is incorrect because sampling goods purchased and comparing prices against other sources of similar goods provides information on excess purchase prices. Answer (D) is incorrect because unexplained changes in personal habits of purchasing agents may reveal the purchasing agent involved in receiving the kickbacks.

10.6 Controls Related to Fraud

93. Which of the following controls is the least effective in preventing a fraud conducted by sending purchase orders to bogus vendors?

A. Require that all purchases be made from an authorized vendor list maintained independently of the individual placing the purchase order.

B. Require that only approved vendors be paid for purchases, based on actual production.

C. Require contracts with all major vendors from whom production components are purchased.

D. Require that total purchases for a month not exceed the total budgeted purchases for that month.

Answer (D) is correct. *(CIA, adapted)*
REQUIRED: The control least effective in preventing a fraud involving bogus vendors.
DISCUSSION: Requiring that total purchases for a month not exceed the total budgeted purchases for that month is the least effective procedure. It controls the total amount of expenditures, not whether a purchase has been requested and authorized, with whom the purchase orders are placed, or whether goods purchased are received.
Answer (A) is incorrect because segregating the selection and approval of reputable vendors from placement of actual orders is an effective means of preventing fraud. Answer (B) is incorrect because restricting payment to approved vendors is an effective means of preventing fraud. Answer (C) is incorrect because requiring contracts with major vendors is an effective means of preventing fraud.

94. A potential problem for a manufacturer is that purchasing agents may take kickbacks or receive gifts from vendors in exchange for favorable contracts. Which of the following is the least effective in preventing this problem?

A. A specific organizational policy prohibiting the acceptance of anything of value from a vendor.

B. An organizational code of ethics that prohibits such activity.

C. A requirement for the purchasing agent to develop a profile of all vendors before the vendors are added to the authorized vendor list.

D. The establishment of long-term contracts with major vendors, with the contract terms approved by senior management.

Answer (C) is correct. *(CIA, adapted)*
REQUIRED: The least effective control to prevent purchasing agents from taking kickbacks or gifts from vendors.
DISCUSSION: A requirement for the purchasing agent to develop a profile of all vendors is the least effective approach because it concerns only the authorization of vendors, a function that should be performed independently of the purchasing agent. It does not address the purchasing agent's relationships with approved vendors.
Answer (A) is incorrect because a policy prohibiting kickbacks and gifts from vendors provides guidance and influences behavior. Answer (B) is incorrect because a code of ethics gives direction to the purchasing agents and is helpful in influencing behavior. Answer (D) is incorrect because approval of long-term vendor contracts by senior management is an effective procedure that is increasingly being used by many organizations.

95. A purchasing agent received expensive gifts from a vendor in return for directing a significant amount of business to that vendor. Which of the following organizational policies most effectively prevents such an occurrence?

A. All purchases exceeding specified monetary amounts should be approved by an official who determines compliance with budgetary requirements.

B. Important high-volume materials should regularly be purchased from at least two different sources in order to afford supply protection.

C. The purchasing function should be decentralized so each department manager or supervisor does his/her own purchasing.

D. Competitive bids should be solicited on purchases to the maximum extent that is practicable.

Answer (D) is correct. *(CIA, adapted)*
REQUIRED: The policy that most effectively prevents or detects bribery by a vendor.
DISCUSSION: In the absence of special circumstances, competitive bidding is a legitimate and effective means of obtaining the lowest price consistent with quality. It is a practice that exploits competition in the market place. Competitive bidding also serves as a control over fraud by restricting the ability of a purchasing agent to reward a favored vendor.
Answer (A) is incorrect because the problem is vendor selection, not authorization of purchases. Answer (B) is incorrect because a purchasing agent could still display favoritism to one of the vendors. Answer (C) is incorrect because decentralization creates more opportunities for buyer fraud.

Questions 96 and 97 are based on the following information. A purchasing agent acquired items for personal use with the organization's funds. The organization allowed designated employees to purchase a specified amount per day in merchandise under open-ended contracts. Supervisory approval of the purchases was required, but that information was not communicated to the vendor. Instead of reviewing and authorizing each purchase order, supervisors routinely signed the authorization sheet at the end of the month without reviewing any of the supporting documentation. Because purchases of this nature were not subject to normal receiving policies, the dishonest employee picked up the supplies at the vendor's warehouse. All purchases were for items routinely ordered by the organization. During the past year, the employee amassed enough merchandise to start a printing and photography business.

96. Which of the following controls would have been most effective in preventing this fraud?

   A. Allowing purchases only from a list of pre-approved vendors.

   B. Requiring the use of prenumbered purchase orders for all purchases of merchandise.

   C. Canceling supporting documents, such as purchase orders and receiving reports, at the time invoices are paid.

   D. Establishing separation of duties between the ordering and receiving of merchandise.

Answer (D) is correct. *(CIA, adapted)*
   REQUIRED: The most effective control to prevent a purchasing agent from purchasing items for personal use with the organization's funds.
   DISCUSSION: Separating the purchasing and receiving functions would have improved internal control. If the supplies in question had been sent to the organization and a receiving report had been prepared by an employee other than the one ordering the goods, the fraud could not have occurred. Moreover, the receiving department should not accept goods unless it has a blind copy of a properly approved purchase order for the items.
   Answer (A) is incorrect because the facts do not suggest that the vendor's actions were inappropriate. Answer (B) is incorrect because prenumbering would not have prevented the fraud. The weakness is in the authorization and receiving procedures. Answer (C) is incorrect because canceling supporting documents when invoices are paid prevents the same document from being used to support two identical payments, but that is not the abuse here.

97. Which of the following engagement procedures performed by the internal auditor is most likely to detect this fraud?

   A. Tracing selected canceled checks to the cash payments journal and to the related vendors' invoices.

   B. Performing a trend analysis of printing supplies expenses for a 2-year period.

   C. Tracing prices and quantities on selected vendors' invoices to the related purchase orders.

   D. Recomputing the clerical accuracy of selected vendors' invoices, including discounts and sales taxes.

Answer (B) is correct. *(CIA, adapted)*
   REQUIRED: The engagement procedure most likely to detect the fraud.
   DISCUSSION: Analytical procedures are evaluations of financial information made by a study of plausible relationships among both financial and nonfinancial data. They involve comparisons of recorded amounts or ratios developed from recorded amounts with expectations developed by the internal auditor. A basic premise underlying the application of analytical procedures is that plausible relationships among data may reasonably be expected to exist and continue in the absence of known conditions to the contrary. Thus, performing a trend analysis of printing supplies expenses for a 2-year period should identify an excess use of supplies.

Questions 98 and 99 are based on the following information. A fraud was perpetrated in a moderate-sized organization when the accounting clerk was delegated too much responsibility. During the year, the organization switched suppliers of a service to a new vendor. The accounting clerk continued to submit fraudulent invoices from the "old supplier." Because contracting for services and approval of supplier invoices had been delegated to the clerk, it was possible for the clerk to continue billings from the old supplier and deposit the subsequent checks, which the clerk was responsible to mail, into a new account the clerk opened in the name of the old supplier. The clerk was considered an excellent employee and eventually was improperly given the added responsibility of preparing the department budgets. This added responsibility allowed the clerk to budget for the amount of the fraudulent payments.

98. Which of the following controls would have been least likely to prevent or detect the fraud described?

A. Requiring authorization of payments by someone other than the clerk negotiating the contract.

B. Comparison by the person signing checks of invoices with an independent verification of services received.

C. Budget preparation by someone other than the person signing contracts and approving payment.

D. Mailing of checks by someone other than the person responsible for check signing or invoice approval.

Answer (D) is correct. *(CIA, adapted)*
REQUIRED: The control least likely to prevent or detect the fraud.
DISCUSSION: Once invoices have been approved and checks prepared and signed, the mailing of the check by an independent person provides no means of preventing improper payments. The person responsible for the treasury function should sign the checks, transmit them, and cancel the supporting documents.
Answer (A) is incorrect because separating contracting for services and approval of invoices would have prevented the fraud. Answer (B) is incorrect because an independent verification of services received reviewed by the check signer would have prevented payment for services not received. Answer (C) is incorrect because independent budget preparation would have allowed an actual-with-budget comparison to detect the payments.

99. Which of the following engagement procedures is most likely to detect the fraud?

A. Take a sample of paid invoices and verify receipt of services by departments involved.

B. Trace a sample of checks disbursed to approved invoices for services.

C. Perform a bank reconciliation and account for all outstanding checks.

D. Trace a sample of receiving documents to invoices and to checks disbursed.

Answer (A) is correct. *(CIA, adapted)*
REQUIRED: The engagement procedure most likely to detect the fraud.
DISCUSSION: Confirming with the using department the receipt of services that have been paid for would uncover the fraud.
Answer (B) is incorrect because the fraudulent invoices were approved by the clerk, and each check is therefore supported by an approved invoice. Answer (C) is incorrect because bank reconciliations do not test the validity of the cash payments. Answer (D) is incorrect because beginning with valid receiving reports will not detect the fraud. The direction of testing is inappropriate.

100. A programmer's accumulation of roundoff errors into one account, which is later accessed by the programmer, is a type of computer fraud. The best way to prevent this type of fraud is to

A. Build in judgment with reasonableness tests.

B. Independently test programs during development and limit access to the programs.

C. Segregate duties of systems development and programming.

D. Use control totals and check the results of the computer.

Answer (B) is correct. *(CIA, adapted)*
REQUIRED: The best way to prevent computer fraud.
DISCUSSION: Programmers should not have access to programs used in processing. The accumulation of roundoff errors into one person's account is a procedure written into the program. Independent testing of a program will lead to discovery of this programmed fraud.
Answer (A) is incorrect because reasonableness tests will not detect this irregularity. In this particular type of fraud, all of the amounts will balance. Answer (C) is incorrect because segregation of duties between systems development and programming would not prevent this type of error. The skills required to construct the program are possessed by programmers. Answer (D) is incorrect because this particular fraud will result in balanced entries. Thus, control totals would not detect the fraud.

10.7 Legal Hazards of Fraud Investigations

101. An internal auditor discovered that company checks were missing. The auditor investigated and found a likely employee suspect. At the completion of the investigation, the internal auditor agreed not to inform authorities provided that the suspect returned the missing checks and paid back inappropriate withdrawals. The internal auditor had probable cause to believe the suspected employee stole the checks. The internal auditor is most likely to be legally liable for

A. Malicious prosecution.

B. Compounding a felony.

C. Breach of fiduciary duty.

D. Defamation.

Answer (B) is correct. *(Publisher, adapted)*
REQUIRED: The most likely basis for legal liability of the internal auditor.
DISCUSSION: Compounding a felony is a crime that involves an agreement for consideration not to prosecute a felony. By offering not to prosecute in return for the missing checks and funds, the internal auditor is committing a crime because only the state can decide which crimes to prosecute.
Answer (A) is incorrect because malicious prosecution involves bringing a civil action or filing a criminal complaint for an improper purpose. Answer (C) is incorrect because the internal auditor's fiduciary duty is to do what is in the best interest of the company. Answer (D) is incorrect because defamation is the publication of material injurious to reputation.

102. Which of the following statements is false regarding a valid confession?

A. It must be voluntary.

B. It must be after the fact.

C. Only the suspect's culpability should be inferred from it.

D. It is the same as an admission.

Answer (D) is correct. *(Publisher, adapted)*
REQUIRED: The false statement about a valid confession.
DISCUSSION: A confession must meet several criteria to avoid being tainted. A confession must be voluntary and after the fact, and only the suspect's guilt should be inferred from the confession. Also, the confession may be tainted if the suspect was under any form of duress. An admission by a suspect is a statement of probative fact, not a statement of guilt.
Answer (A) is incorrect because a confession must be voluntary. Answer (B) is incorrect because a person cannot confess to an act that has not yet been committed. Answer (C) is incorrect because a confession is considered tainted if any conclusion other than guilt could reasonably be inferred.

103. Which of the following techniques should an internal auditor avoid when interviewing an employee for information about possible criminal activity?

A. Only the internal auditor should interview the employee to ensure confidentiality.

B. The internal auditor should not interrupt the interviewee except to clarify statements.

C. The interviewer should conduct the interview in a nonthreatening manner.

D. Interviewers should use interviewing methods similar to those used in other situations.

Answer (A) is correct. *(Publisher, adapted)*
REQUIRED: The improper interview technique.
DISCUSSION: Due to the many legal repercussions of conducting an interview in a situation that may involve criminal activity, an internal auditor should be careful not to violate the interviewee's rights. The internal auditor should conduct the interview with two people, one serving as a witness. However, because of a lack of expertise in criminal interrogation, the internal auditor should allow security specialists to conduct such interviews.
Answer (B) is incorrect because an internal auditor should attempt to maintain the interviewee's confidence. If the interviewer interrupts frequently, the interviewee may become defensive and evasive. Answer (C) is incorrect because, if the interview is conducted in a threatening manner, the interviewee may not respond. Answer (D) is incorrect because the interviewer should be comfortable with the process. Using familiar techniques and methods should produce a more productive interview atmosphere.

104. Which of the following is not one of the elements of the tort of malicious prosecution of criminal activity?

A. The initiator of the proceedings acted without probable cause.

B. The proceedings ended favorably for the party claiming malicious prosecution.

C. The initiator of the proceedings acted with improper purpose.

D. The party claiming malicious prosecution suffered actual harm.

Answer (D) is correct.   *(Publisher, adapted)*
    REQUIRED: The item not an element of the tort of malicious prosecution.
    DISCUSSION: There are three elements needed to prove the tort of malicious prosecution of a criminal action: (1) The initiator acted without probable cause, (2) the proceedings ended favorably for the party claiming malicious prosecution, and (3) the initiator of the proceedings acted with improper purpose. For the tort of malicious prosecution of a civil action, there is one additional element: The plaintiff must prove, in addition to the other three elements, that he or she suffered actual harm as a result of the malicious prosecution.
    Answer (A) is incorrect because a defense to malicious prosecution is that the proceedings were brought because the company had proof or reason to believe the employee actually committed a crime. Answer (B) is incorrect because the proceedings must end favorably for the party bringing the lawsuit. If the employee is guilty of the illegal act, the employee was not maliciously prosecuted. Answer (C) is incorrect because improper purpose is an element of the tort of malicious prosecution.

105. Which of the following actions is acceptable for an internal auditor conducting a fraud investigation?

A. Sign an agreement not to prosecute a suspected employee if the employee is willing to return the stolen items.

B. Offer a reward to employees for information leading to a suspect and then formally charge the suspect based only on employee-provided information.

C. Threaten to terminate a suspected employee if he or she does not confess to the illegal act.

D. Interview all employees who may have knowledge of the illegal act regardless of which employees are suspected of committing the illegal act.

Answer (D) is correct.   *(Publisher, adapted)*
    REQUIRED: The acceptable action when conducting a fraud investigation.
    DISCUSSION: Conducting a fraud investigation is risky because an internal auditor's actions during the investigation can lead to litigation against the company if the investigation is not properly carried out. If the internal auditor professionally investigates all employees who may have knowledge of an illegal act, the internal auditor should be able to avoid legal hazards such as defamation and malicious prosecution.
    Answer (A) is incorrect because this arrangement is compounding a felony. Only the government has the power to make such decisions. Answer (B) is incorrect because charging a suspect with only the information provided by employees can lead to malicious prosecution if the employer does not have proof of wrongdoing by the suspect. Answer (C) is incorrect because a confession is considered tainted if it is given under duress. Threatening to terminate an employee may also lead to torts such as malicious prosecution.

106. Which of the following is a red flag that an organization may be engaging in fraudulent activity?

A. Financial statement results that are above the results for the industry and operations are slightly more efficient than the average for the industry.

B. Lack of earnings growth despite large reserves of cash.

C. Existence of complex transactions that are difficult to understand and appear to have little business purpose.

D. Strong internal reporting in a company with decentralized operations.

Answer (C) is correct.   *(Publisher, adapted)*
    REQUIRED: The organizational red flag.
    DISCUSSION: When management engages in fraudulent transactions, management will often use complex legal entities or rules to disguise the fraud. In addition, management may try to engage in transactions that are unrelated to the purpose of the company so that the fraud will be harder to detect. Transactions with little or no apparent business purpose should be scrutinized carefully because fraud may be present.
    Answer (A) is incorrect because more efficient operations may result in higher than average earnings. The internal auditor should be alerted if the earnings are excessive compared to the industry and there are no major operational differences. Answer (B) is incorrect because a lack of earnings growth may indicate that the market is saturated or that no growth opportunities exist. Excessive earnings with a lack of cash is an indicator that fraud may be present. Answer (D) is incorrect because strong internal reporting within a decentralized company is a deterrence to fraud because it makes fraud easier to detect.

APPENDIX A
THE IIA CONTENT SPECIFICATION OUTLINES (CSOs) AND CROSS REFERENCE

For your convenience, we have reproduced verbatim The IIA's Content Specification Outline (CSO), also known as a Content Syllabus, for each CIA exam part from their website (www.theiia.org). We also have provided cross references to the study units and subunits in this book that correspond to The IIA's more detailed CSO coverage. If one entry appears above a list, it applies to all items. Please visit The IIA's website for updates and more information about the exam. Rely on the Gleim materials to pass each part of the exam. We have researched and studied The IIA's CSOs as well as questions from prior exams to provide you with an excellent review program.

PART I – THE INTERNAL AUDIT ACTIVITY'S ROLE IN GOVERNANCE, RISK, AND CONTROL

A. **COMPLY WITH THE IIA'S ATTRIBUTE STANDARDS (15 - 25%)** (proficiency level) (1.2)

1. Define purpose, authority, and responsibility of the internal audit activity. (2.1)

   a. Determine if purpose, authority, and responsibility of internal audit activity are clearly documented/approved.

   b. Determine if purpose, authority, and responsibility of internal audit activity are communicated to engagement clients.

   c. Demonstrate an understanding of the purpose, authority, and responsibility of the internal audit activity.

2. Maintain independence and objectivity.

   a. Foster independence. (2.2, 2.4)

      1) Understand organizational independence.
      2) Recognize the importance of organizational independence.
      3) Determine if the internal audit activity is properly aligned to achieve organizational independence.

   b. Foster objectivity. (2.3, 2.4)

      1) Establish policies to promote objectivity.
      2) Assess individual objectivity.
      3) Maintain individual objectivity.
      4) Recognize and mitigate impairments to independence and objectivity.

3. Determine if the required knowledge, skills, and competencies are available. (1.5, 1.6)

   a. Understand the knowledge, skills, and competencies that an internal auditor needs to possess.

   b. Identify the knowledge, skills, and competencies required to fulfill the responsibilities of the internal audit activity.

4. Develop and/or procure necessary knowledge, skills, and competencies collectively required by internal audit activity. (1.5, 1.6)

5. Exercise due professional care. (1.6)

6. Promote continuing professional development. (1.7)

   a. Develop and implement a plan for continuing professional development for internal audit staff.
   b. Enhance individual competency through continuing professional development.

7. Promote quality assurance and improvement of the internal audit activity. (9.3-9.7)

   a. Establish and maintain a quality assurance and improvement program.

   b. Monitor the effectiveness of the quality assurance and improvement program.

   c. Report the results of the quality assurance and improvement program to the board or other governing body.

   d. Conduct quality assurance procedures and recommend improvements to the performance of the internal audit activity.

8. Abide by and promote compliance with The IIA Code of Ethics. (1.1, 1.5)

B.   **ESTABLISH A RISK-BASED PLAN TO DETERMINE THE PRIORITIES OF THE INTERNAL AUDIT ACTIVITY (15 - 25%)** (proficiency level) (1.3)

1.   Establish a framework for assessing risk. (8.1, 4.1)
2.   Use the framework to: (8.1, 4.1)

   a.   Identify sources of potential engagements (e.g., audit universe, management request, regulatory mandate)
   b.   Assess organization-wide risk
   c.   Solicit potential engagement topics from various sources
   d.   Collect and analyze data on proposed engagements
   e.   Rank and validate risk priorities

3.   Identify internal audit resource requirements. (8.5)
4.   Coordinate the internal audit activity's efforts with: (Intro of 9, 9.1, 9.2)

   a.   External auditor
   b.   Regulatory oversight bodies
   c.   Other internal assurance functions (e.g., health and safety department)

5.   Select engagements. (8.1, 8.2)

   a.   Participate in the engagement selection process.
   b.   Select engagements.
   c.   Communicate and obtain approval of the engagement plan from board.

C.   **UNDERSTAND THE INTERNAL AUDIT ACTIVITY'S ROLE IN ORGANIZATIONAL GOVERNANCE (10 - 20%)** (proficiency level) (1.3)

1.   Obtain board's approval of audit charter. (2.1, 8.4)
2.   Communicate plan of engagements. (8.2)
3.   Report significant audit issues. (8.3)
4.   Communicate key performance indicators to board on a regular basis. (8.3, 8.4)
5.   Discuss areas of significant risk. (8.1, 4.1)
6.   Support board in enterprise-wide risk assessment. (4.1, 5.2, 6.2, 8.1)
7.   Review positioning of the internal audit function within the risk management framework within the org. (4.1)
8.   Monitor compliance with the corporate code of conduct/business practices. (3.2)
9.   Report on the effectiveness of the control framework. (5.1)
10.   Assist board in assessing the independence of the external auditor. (9.2, 8.4)
11.   Assess ethical climate of the board. (3.2)
12.   Assess ethical climate of the organization. (3.2)
13.   Assess compliance with policies in specific areas (e.g., derivatives). (3.3, 4.1)
14.   Assess organization's reporting mechanism to the board. (3.3, 8.4, 5.4)
15.   Conduct follow-up and report on management response to regulatory body reviews. (3.3)
16.   Conduct follow-up and report on management response to external audit. (3.2)
17.   Assess the adequacy of the performance measurement system, achievement of corporate objective. (3.1, 5.5)
18.   Support a culture of fraud awareness and encourage the reporting of improprieties. (5.4)

D.   **PERFORM OTHER INTERNAL AUDIT ROLES AND RESPONSIBILITIES (0 - 10%)** (proficiency level) (1.3)

1.   Ethics/compliance (3.2)

   a.   Investigate and recommend resolution for ethics/compliance complaints.
   b.   Determine disposition of ethics violations.
   c.   Foster healthy ethical climate.
   d.   Maintain and administer business conduct policy (e.g., conflict of interest).
   e.   Report on compliance.

2.   Risk management (4.1)

   a.   Develop and implement an organization-wide risk and control framework.
   b.   Coordinate enterprise-wide risk assessment.
   c.   Report corporate risk assessment to board.
   d.   Review business continuity planning process.

3.   Privacy (4.2)

   a.   Determine privacy vulnerabilities.
   b.   Report on compliance.

4.   Information or physical security (4.2)

   a.   Determine security vulnerabilities.
   b.   Determine disposition of security violations.
   c.   Report on compliance.

E.   **GOVERNANCE, RISK, AND CONTROL KNOWLEDGE ELEMENTS (15 - 25%)**

   1.   Corporate governance principles (awareness level) (3.2)
   2.   Alternative control frameworks (awareness level) (6.2)
   3.   Risk vocabulary and concepts (proficiency level) (1.4, 6.1)
   4.   Risk management techniques (proficiency level) (4.1)
   5.   Risk/control implications of different organizational structures (proficiency level) (6.4)
   6.   Risk/control implications of different leadership styles (awareness level) (6.5)
   7.   Change management (awareness level) (6.6)
   8.   Conflict management (awareness level) (6.7)
   9.   Management control techniques (proficiency level) (6.3)
   10. Types of control (preventive, detective, input, output) (proficiency level) (6.1)

F.   **PLAN ENGAGEMENTS (15 - 25%)** (proficiency level) (1.3)

   1.   Initiate preliminary communication with engagement client. (7.1)
   2.   Conduct a preliminary survey of the area of engagement. (7.2)

   a.   Obtain input from engagement client.
   b.   Perform analytical reviews.
   c.   Perform benchmarking.
   d.   Conduct interviews.
   e.   Review prior audit reports and other relevant documentation.
   f.   Map processes.
   g.   Develop checklists.

   3.   Complete a detailed risk assessment of the area (prioritize or evaluate risk/control factors). (7.2)
   4.   Coordinate audit engagement efforts with (9.1)

   a.   External auditor
   b.   Regulatory oversight bodies

   5.   Establish/refine engagement objectives and identify/finalize the scope of engagement. (7.2, 7.3)
   6.   Identify or develop criteria for assurance engagements (criteria against which to audit). (5.5)
   7.   Consider the potential for fraud when planning an engagement. (10.4-10.7)

   a.   Be knowledgeable of the risk factors and red flags of fraud.
   b.   Identify common types of fraud associated with the engagement area.
   c.   Determine if risk of fraud requires special consideration when conducting an engagement.

   8.   Determine engagement procedures. (7.4, 10.1)
   9.   Determine the level of staff and resources needed for the engagement. (7.3)
   10. Establish adequate planning and supervision of the engagement. (7.1, 7.5)
   11. Prepare engagement work program. (7.4)

PART II – CONDUCTING THE INTERNAL AUDIT ENGAGEMENT

A. **CONDUCT ENGAGEMENTS (25 - 35%)** (proficiency level)

1. Research and apply appropriate standards: (10.1, 10.2)

    a. IIA Professional Practices Framework (Code of Ethics, Standards, and Practice Advisories)
    b. Other professional, legal, and regulatory standards

2. Maintain an awareness of potential for fraud when conducting an engagement. (10.3-10.8)

    a. Notice indicators or symptoms of fraud.
    b. Design appropriate engagement steps to address significant risk of fraud.
    c. Employ audit tests to detect fraud.
    d. Determine if any suspected fraud merits investigation.

3. Collect data. (1.1, 1.2)
4. Evaluate the relevance, sufficiency, and reliability of evidence. (1.1, 1.4, 1.7)
5. Analyze and interpret data. (1.2)
6. Develop workpapers. (1.8)
7. Review workpapers. (1.9)
8. Communicate interim progress. (2.2)
9. Draw conclusions. (2.2)
10. Develop recommendations when appropriate. (2.2)
11. Report engagement results. (2.4)

    a. Conduct exit conference.
    b. Prepare report or other communication.
    c. Approve engagement report.
    d. Determine distribution of report.
    e. Obtain management response to report.

12. Conduct client satisfaction survey. (1.3)
13. Complete performance appraisals of engagement staff. (1.3)

B. **CONDUCT SPECIFIC ENGAGEMENTS (25 - 35%)** (proficiency level)

1. Conduct assurance engagements.

    a. Fraud investigation (10.3-10.8)

        1) Determine appropriate parties to be involved with investigation.
        2) Establish facts and extent of fraud (e.g., interviews, interrogations, and data analysis).
        3) Report outcomes to appropriate parties.
        4) Complete a process review to improve controls to prevent fraud and recommend changes.

    b. Risk and control self-assessment (3.3)

        1) Facilitated approach

            a) Client-facilitated
            b) Audit-facilitated

        2) Questionnaire approach
        3) Self-certification approach

    c. Audits of third parties and contract auditing (4.6, 7.3, 7.4)
    d. Quality audit engagements (4.4)
    e. Due diligence audit engagements (4.3)
    f. Security audit engagements (4.5)
    g. Privacy audit engagements (4.5)
    h. Performance (key performance indicators) audit engagements (4.4)
    i. Operational (efficiency and effectiveness) audit engagements (Intro. SU 3, 4.6)
    j. Financial audit engagements (3.1)
    k. Information technology (IT) audit engagements

        1) Operating systems (5.2)

            a) Mainframe
            b) Workstations
            c) Server

        2) Application development (5.3)

            a) Application authentication
            b) Systems development methodology
            c) Change control
            d) End user computing

        3) Data and network communications/connections (e.g., LAN, VAN, and WAN) (6.1)
        4) Voice communications (6.1)
        5) System security (e.g., firewalls, access control) (5.4)
        6) Contingency planning (5.5)
        7) Databases (6.2)
        8) Functional areas of IT operations (e.g., data center operations) (5.1)
        9) Web infrastructure (6.1)
        10) Software licensing (5.3)
        11) Electronic Funds Transfer (EFT)/Electronic Data Interchange (EDI) (6.3)
        12) E-Commerce (6.3)
        13) Information protection (viruses, privacy) (6.5)
        14) Encryption (5.4)
        15) Enterprise-wide resource planning (ERP) software (e.g., SAP R/3) (6.4)

    l. Compliance audit engagements (4.1)

  2. Conduct consulting engagements. (3.2)

    a. Internal control training (4.6)
    b. Business process review (4.4)
    c. Benchmarking (4.4)
    d. Information technology (IT) and systems development (7.1-7.3)
    e. Design of performance measurement systems (4.4)

C. MONITOR ENGAGEMENT OUTCOMES (5 - 15%) (proficiency level)

  1. Determine appropriate follow-up activity by the internal audit activity (2.5)
  2. Identify appropriate method to monitor engagement outcomes (2.5)
  3. Conduct follow-up activity (2.5)
  4. Communicate monitoring plan and results (2.1, 2.3, 2.5)

D. FRAUD KNOWLEDGE ELEMENTS (5 - 15%)

  1. Discovery sampling (awareness level) (8.5)
  2. Interrogation techniques (awareness level) (9.3, 10.7)
  3. Forensic auditing (awareness level) (10.5)
  4. Use of computers in analyzing data (proficiency level) (5.3)
  5. Red flag (proficiency level) (10.4)
  6. Types of fraud (proficiency level) (10.4)

E. ENGAGEMENT TOOLS (15 - 25%)

  1. Sampling (awareness level) (8.1-8.7)

    a. Nonstatistical (judgmental)
    b. Statistical

  2. Statistical analyses (process control techniques) (awareness level) (8.8)
  3. Data gathering tools (proficiency level) (9.3, 9.4)

    a. Interviewing
    b. Questionnaires
    c. Checklists

  4. Analytical review techniques (proficiency level)

    a. Ratio estimation (1.2, 8.4)
    b. Variance analysis (e.g., budget vs. actual) (1.2)
    c. Other reasonableness tests (1.2)

  5. Observation (proficiency level) (1.6, 9.4)
  6. Problem solving (proficiency level) (9.5)
  7. Risk and control self-assessment (CSA) (awareness level) (3.3)
  8. Computerized audit tools and techniques (proficiency level)

    a. Embedded audit modules (5.1)
    b. Data extraction techniques (5.1)
    c. Generalized audit software (e.g., ACL, IDEA) (5.1)
    d. Spreadsheet analysis (1.8)
    e. Automated workpapers (e.g., Lotus Notes, Auditor Assistant) (1.8)

  9. Process mapping including flowcharting (proficiency level) (9.1, 9.2)

PART III – BUSINESS ANALYSIS AND INFORMATION TECHNOLOGY

A.   BUSINESS PROCESSES (15 - 25%)

1.   Quality management (e.g., TQM) (awareness level) (1.1)

2.   The International Organization for Standardization (ISO) framework (awareness level) (1.3)

3.   Forecasting (awareness level) (1.4)

4.   Project management techniques (proficiency level) (1.5)

5.   Business process analysis (e.g., workflow analysis and bottleneck management, theory of constraints) (proficiency level) (1.6)

6.   Inventory management techniques and concepts (proficiency level) (2.1)

7.   Marketing -- pricing objectives and policies (awareness level) (2.3)

8.   Marketing -- supply chain management (awareness level) (2.2)

9.   Human resources (individual performance management and measurement, supervision, environmental factors that affect performance, facilitation techniques, personnel sourcing/staffing, training and development, and safety) (proficiency level) (2.4)

10.   Balanced scorecard (awareness level) (1.2)

B.   FINANCIAL ACCOUNTING AND FINANCE (15 - 25%)

1.   Basic concepts and underlying principles of financial accounting (statements, terminology, relationships) (proficiency level) (3.1-3.4)

2.   Intermediate concepts of financial accounting (e.g., bonds, leases, pensions, intangible assets, R&D) (awareness level) (3.5-3.8, 4.1-4.9)

3.   Advanced concepts of financial accounting (e.g., consolidation, partnerships, foreign currency transactions) (awareness level) (4.10-4.13)

4.   Financial statement analysis (proficiency level) (5.9)

5.   Cost of capital evaluation (awareness level) (5.3)

6.   Types of debt and equity (awareness level) (5.1, 5.2, 4.8)

7.   Financial instruments (e.g., derivatives) (awareness level) (5.5, 5.6, 5.8, 3.5)

8.   Cash management (treasury functions) (awareness level) (5.4)

9.   Valuation models (awareness level)

    a.   Inventory valuation (3.6)
    b.   Business valuation (5.7)

10.   Business development life cycles (awareness level) (5.10)

C.   MANAGERIAL ACCOUNTING (10 - 20%)

1.   Cost concepts (e.g., absorption, variable, fixed) (proficiency level) (6.2)
2.   Capital budgeting (awareness level) (6.10)
3.   Operating budget (proficiency level) (6.9)
4.   Transfer pricing (awareness level) (6.12)
5.   Cost-volume-profit analysis (awareness level) (6.1)
6.   Relevant cost (awareness level) (6.11)
7.   Costing systems (e.g., activity-based, standard) (awareness level) (6.3-6.8)
8.   Responsibility accounting (awareness level) (6.13)

D.   REGULATORY, LEGAL, AND ECONOMICS (5 - 15%) (awareness level)

1.   Impact of government legislation and regulation on business
2.   Trade legislation and regulations (7.2)
3.   Taxation schemes (7.3)
4.   Contracts (7.6)
5.   Nature and rules of legal evidence (7.5)
6.   Key economic indicators (7.4)

E. **INFORMATION TECHNOLOGY (IT) (30 - 40%)** (awareness level)

    1.   Control frameworks (e.g., SAC, COBIT) (8.4, 8.5)
    2.   Data and network communications/connections (e.g., LAN, VAN, and WAN) (9.3)
    3.   Electronic funds transfer (EFT) (10.1)
    4.   E-Commerce (10.1)
    5.   Electronic data interchange (EDI) (10.1)
    6.   Functional areas of IT operations (e.g., data center operations) (8.1)
    7.   Encryption (9.1)
    8.   Information protection (e.g., viruses, privacy) (10.4)
    9.   Evaluate investment in IT (cost of ownership) (10.2)
    10. Enterprise-wide resource planning (ERP) software (e.g., SAP R/3) (10.3)
    11. Operating systems (8.2)
    12. Application development (8.3)
    13. Voice communications (9.3)
    14. Contingency planning (9.2)
    15. Systems security (e.g., firewalls, access control) (9.1)
    16. Databases (9.4)
    17. Software licensing (8.3)
    18. Web infrastructure (9.3)

PART IV – BUSINESS MANAGEMENT SKILLS

A. **STRATEGIC MANAGEMENT (20 - 30%)** (awareness level)

    1.   Global analytical techniques

        a.   Structural analysis of industries (1.2, 2.4)
        b.   Competitive strategies (e.g., Porter's model) (1.1, 1.3, 1.4)
        c.   Competitive analysis (2.1, 2.2)
        d.   Market signals (2.3)
        e.   Industry evolution (2.5)

    2.   Industry environments (2.4)

        a.   Competitive strategies related to:

            1) Fragmented industries (3.1)
            2) Emerging industries (3.2)
            3) Declining industries (3.3)

        b.   Competition in global industries (3.4)

            1) Sources/impediments
            2) Evolution of global markets
            3) Strategic alternatives
            4) Trends affecting competition

    3.   Strategic decisions

        a.   Analysis of integration strategies (4.1)
        b.   Capacity expansion (4.2)
        c.   Entry into new businesses (4.3)

    4.   Portfolio techniques of competitive analysis (2.2)
    5.   Product life cycles (2.5)

B. **GLOBAL BUSINESS ENVIRONMENTS (15 - 25%)** (awareness level)

    1.   Cultural/legal/political environments

        a.   Balancing global requirements and local imperatives (5.1)
        b.   Global mindsets (personal characteristics/competencies) (5.3)
        c.   Sources and methods for managing complexities and contradictions (5.1-5.3)
        d.   Managing multicultural teams (5.4)

    2.   Economic/financial environments

        a.   Global, multinational, international, and multilocal compared and contrasted (5.1)
        b.   Requirements for entering the global market place (5.1)
        c.   Creating organizational adaptability (5.3)
        d.   Managing training and development (5.4)

C. **ORGANIZATIONAL BEHAVIOR (20 - 30%)** (awareness level)

    1.   Motivation (6.1, 6.2)

        a.   Relevance and implication of various theories
        b.   Impact of job design, rewards, work schedules, etc.

    2.   Communication

        a.   The process (6.3, 6.4)
        b.   Organizational dynamics (6.3)
        c.   Impact of computerization (6.5)

    3.   Performance (7.1, 7.2)

        a.   Productivity
        b.   Effectiveness

    4.   Structure (7.4, 7.5)

        a.   Centralized/decentralized (7.6)
        b.   Departmentalization (7.3)
        c.   New configurations (e.g., hourglass, cluster, network) (7.6)

D. **MANAGEMENT SKILLS (20 - 30%)** (awareness level)

    1.   Group dynamics

        a.   Traits (cohesiveness, roles, norms, groupthink, etc.) (8.1)
        b.   Stages of group development (8.2)
        c.   Organizational politics (8.3)
        d.   Criteria and determinants of effectiveness (8.4)

    2.   Team building (8.4)

        a.   Methods used in team building
        b.   Assessing team performance

    3.   Leadership skills

        a.   Theories compared/contrasted (9.1, 9.2)
        b.   Leadership grid (topology of leadership styles) (9.2)
        c.   Mentoring (9.2)

    4.   Personal time management (10.1)

E. **NEGOTIATING (5 - 15%)** (awareness level)

    1.   Conflict resolution (10.2)

        a.   Competitive/cooperative
        b.   Compromise, forcing, smoothing, etc.

    2.   Added-value negotiating (10.3)

        a.   Description
        b.   Specific steps

APPENDIX B
THE IIA EXAMINATION BIBLIOGRAPHY

The Institute has prepared a listing of references for the CIA exam, reproduced beginning below. These publications have been chosen by the Board of Regents as reasonably representative of the common body of knowledge for internal auditors. However, all of the information in these texts will not be tested. When possible, questions will be written based on the information contained in the suggested reference list. This bibliography is reorganized in an alphabetical listing by part to give you an overview of the scope of each part. The IIA also indicates that the examination scope includes

1. Articles from *Internal Auditor* (The IIA periodical)
2. IIA research reports
3. IIA pronouncements, e.g., The IIA Code of Ethics and SIASs
4. Past published CIA examinations

The IIA bibliography is reproduced for your information only. The texts you will need to acquire (use) to prepare for the CIA exam will depend on many factors, including

1. Innate ability
2. Length of time out of school
3. Thoroughness of your undergraduate education
4. Familiarity with internal auditing due to relevant experience

SUGGESTED REFERENCES FOR THE CIA EXAM

PART I: THE INTERNAL AUDIT ACTIVITY'S ROLE IN GOVERNANCE, RISK, AND CONTROL

Sawyer, et al, *Sawyer's Internal Auditing*, 5th Ed., The Institute of Internal Auditors.

OR Sears, *Internal Auditing Manual*, WG&L Financial Reporting & Management.

The American Institute of Certified Public Accountants, *Internal Control - Integrated Framework*, 1994.

The Institute of Internal Auditors, Inc., *Professional Practices Framework*, 2002.

OR *Other Control and Governance Frameworks*.

Supplemental:

Albrecht, Wernz, and Williams, *Fraud: Bringing Light to the Dark Side of Business*, Irwin Professional Publishing.

Murphy and Parker, *Handbook of IT Auditing*, Warren, Gorham & Lamont.

Reider, *Complete Guide to Operational Auditing*, John Wiley & Sons, Inc.

PART II: CONDUCTING THE INTERNAL AUDIT ENGAGEMENT

Sawyer, et al, *Sawyer's Internal Auditing*, 5th Ed., The Institute of Internal Auditors.

OR Sears, *Internal Auditing Manual*, WG&L Financial Reporting & Management.

The Institute of Internal Auditors, Inc., *Professional Practices Framework*, 2002.

Supplemental:

Kreitner, *Management*, 9th Ed., Houghton Mifflin Co., 2004.

PART III: BUSINESS ANALYSIS AND INFORMATION TECHNOLOGY

Information Systems and Control Foundation, *Cobit: Governance, Control, and Audit for Information and Related Technology*, 3rd Ed., 2000.

International Accounting Standards Committee, *International Accounting Standards*, 2002.

Kieso, Warfield, and Weygandt, *Intermediate Accounting*, 11th Ed., John Wiley & Sons, Inc., 2004.

Kreitner, *Management*, 9th Ed., Houghton Mifflin Co., 2004.

Sawyer, et al, *Sawyer's Internal Auditing*, 5th Ed., the Institute of Internal Auditors.

OR Sears, *Internal Auditing Manual*, WG&L Financial Reporting & Management.

The Institute of Internal Auditors Research Foundation, *Systems Assurance and Control*, 2003.

Weber, *Information Systems Control and Audit*, Prentice Hall, 1998.

PART IV: BUSINESS MANAGEMENT SKILLS

Bruner, Eaker, Freeman, Spelkman, Teisberg, and Venkataraman, *The Portable MBA*, 4th Ed., John Wiley & Sons, 2002.

Fisher, Ury, and Patton, *Getting to Yes, Negotiating Agreement Without Giving In*, Penguin USA.

Hill, *International Business with Global Resource CD, Powerweb and World Map*, 4th Ed., McGraw-Hill/Irwin, 2002.

Kreitner, *Management*, 9th Ed., Houghton Mifflin Co., 2004.

Kotler, *Marketing Management*, 11th Ed., Prentice Hall, 2002.

PUBLICATIONS AVAILABLE FROM THE IIA

The listing on the previous pages presents only some of the current technical literature available. Quantity discounts are provided. Inquiries should be sent to

Customer Service
Institute of Internal Auditors
249 Maitland Avenue
Altamonte Springs, FL 32701-4201

Request a current catalog by mail or call
(407) 830-7600, ext. 1

Book orders can be placed directly by calling (877) 867-4957 (toll-free) or (770) 442-8633, extension 275.

ORDERING TEXTUAL MATERIAL

The IIA does not carry all of the reference books. Write directly to the publisher if you cannot obtain the desired texts from your local bookstore. Begin your study program with *CIA Review*, Parts I through IV, which most candidates find sufficient. If you need additional reference material, borrow books from colleagues, professors, or a library.

Addison-Wesley Publishing Company
Reading, MA 01867

Basic Books, Inc.
Harper & Row Publishers
10 East 53rd Street
New York, NY 10022

Business Publications, Inc.
1700 Alma, Suite 390
Plano, TX 75075

The Dryden Press
One Salt Creek Lane
Hinsdale, IL 60521-2902

Harcourt Brace Jovanovich
1250 Sixth Avenue
San Diego, CA 92101

Harper & Row
10 East 53rd Street
New York, NY 10022

Holt, Rinehart, Winston
383 Madison Avenue
New York, NY 10017

Houghton Mifflin Company
One Beacon Street
Boston, MA 02108

Richard D. Irwin, Inc.
1818 Ridge Road
Homewood, IL 60430

Kent Publishing Company
20 Park Plaza
Boston, MA 02116

McGraw-Hill Book Company
1221 Avenue of the Americas
New York, NY 10020

Mitchell Publishing, Inc.
915 River Street
Santa Cruz, CA 95060

Prentice-Hall, Inc.
Englewood Cliffs, NJ 07632

Reston Publishing Company
11480 Sunset Hills Road
Reston, VA 22090

South-Western Publishing Company
5101 Madison Road
Cincinnati, OH 45227

West Publishing Company
P.O. Box 55165
St. Paul, MN 55101

John Wiley & Sons, Inc.
605 Third Avenue
New York, NY 10016

PRACTICE ADVISORY INDEX

PRACTICE ADVISORY INDEX

INDEX

NOTE: Practice Advisories are listed in the Practice Advisory Index.

The GLEIM CIA System Works!

This is a quick note from a happy and satisfied CIA On-Line Course user. I followed your study program and recommendations, making only a few personal preference changes. As the Gleim team professed, I did pass each part I took, without any need to retake any part. One time through on each part of the CIA and I was done. You have a good product and the program works.

Gregory White

It is my great pleasure to inform you that I have qualified CIA examination with the help of Gleim materials. Gleim materials, especially Online and CDs were really helpful to prepare for the examinations , which helped me to pass all the papers in my first attempt. Once again I thank you for my victory.

Sheji Valiyakath

I would like to share the great news that I passed my CIA exams. I must say that without your wonderful material i.e. both the books and the CDs I would not have achieved this. Thank you all for creating the study material that really helps candidates conquer the challenging CIA exams. Thanks again.

Mohsin Jagani

Dr. Gleim and users: I appreciate the valuable service that Gleim has provided me. I recently passed the CIA Exam, even though the IIA raised the bar for the passing threshold. My confidence in Gleim is absolute, thus passing the more difficult CIA was not problematic. As a matter of fact, I have passed the Gleim offerings of CFM, CMA, and now CIA. For those interested parties who want to pass these tests, buy Gleim and pass!

Stephen Wills

Thanks so much!!!! The complete online course certainly works! I didn't start studying until August and just received notification that I passed all four parts of the exam on my first attempt.

GLEIM
KNOWLEDGE
TRANSFER
SYSTEMS®

Rebecca Neal

572

COMPLETE GLEIM CPA SYSTEM

All 4 sections, including Gleim Online, books*, *Test Prep CD-Rom*,
Test Prep for Pocket PC, Audio CDs, plus bonus book bag.

☐ $989.95

Also available by exam section @ $274.95 (does not include book bag).

*Fifth book: *CPA Review: A System for Success*

$_____

COMPLETE GLEIM CMA SYSTEM

Includes: Gleim Online, books*, *Test Prep CD-Rom*,
Test Prep for Pocket PC, Audio CDs, plus bonus book bag.

☐ $739.95

Also available by exam part @ $213.95 (does not include book bag).

*Fifth book: *CMA Review: A System for Success*

$_____

COMPLETE GLEIM CIA SYSTEM

Includes: Gleim Online, books*, *Test Prep CD-Rom*,
Test Prep for Pocket PC, Audio CDs, plus bonus book bag.

☐ $824.95

Also available by exam part @ $224.95 (does not include book bag).

*Fifth book: *CIA Review: A System for Success*

$_____

GLEIM EA REVIEW SYSTEM

Includes: Gleim Online, books, *Test Prep CD-Rom*,
Test Prep for Pocket PC, Audio CDs, plus bonus book bag.

☐ $629.95

Also available by exam part @ $224.95 (does not include book bag).

$_____

"THE GLEIM SERIES" EXAM QUESTIONS AND EXPLANATIONS

Includes: 5 books and *Test Prep CD-Rom*.

☐ $112.25

Also available by part @ $29.95.

$_____

GLEIM ONLINE CPE

Try a FREE 4 hour course at gleim.com/cpe
- Easy-to-Complete
- Informative
- Effective

Contact
GLEIM PUBLICATIONS
for further assistance:

gleim.com
800.874.5346
sales@gleim.com

SUBTOTAL $_____
Complete your
order on the
next page

GLEIM PUBLICATIONS, INC.

P. O. Box 12848   Gainesville, FL 32604

TOLL FREE:	800.874.5346		Customer service is available (Eastern Time):
LOCAL:	352.375.0772		8:00 a.m. - 7:00 p.m., Mon. - Fri.
FAX:	352.375.6940		9:00 a.m. - 2:00 p.m., Saturday
INTERNET:	gleim.com		Please have your credit card ready,
E-MAIL:	sales@gleim.com		or save time by ordering online!

SUBTOTAL (from previous page) $_____

Add applicable sales tax for shipments within Florida. _____

Shipping (nonrefundable) 25.00

TOTAL $_____

Fax or write for prices/instructions on shipments outside the 48 contiguous states, or simply order online.

NAME (please print) _____

ADDRESS _____ Apt. _____
(street address required for UPS)

CITY _____ STATE _____ ZIP _____

____ MC/VISA/DISC ____ Check/M.O.   Daytime Telephone (____)_____

Credit Card No. _____ - _____ - _____ - _____

Exp. ____/____ Signature _____
   Month / Year

E-mail address _____

1. We process and ship orders daily, within one business day over 98.8% of the time. Call by 3:00 pm for same day service.

2. Please PHOTOCOPY this order form for others.

3. No CODs. Orders from individuals must be prepaid.

4. Gleim Publications, Inc. guarantees the immediate refund of all resalable texts and unopened software and audios if returned within 30 days. Applies only to items purchased direct from Gleim Publications, Inc. Our shipping charge is nonrefundable.

5. Components of specially priced package deals are nonrefundable.

Prices subject to change without notice.
02/08

For updates and other important information, visit our website.

gleim.com

GLEIM
KNOWLEDGE
TRANSFER
SYSTEMS®

CIA Review: Part II, Thirteenth Edition, First Printing
Please complete and mail to us pages 575 and 576 the week following the CIA exam.

575

Please forward your suggestions, corrections, and comments concerning typographical errors, etc., to **Irvin N. Gleim • c/o Gleim Publications, Inc. • P.O. Box 12848 • University Station • Gainesville, Florida • 32604.** Please include your name and address so we can properly thank you for your interest.

1. _____

2. _____

3. _____

4. _____

5. _____

6. _____

7. _____

8. _____

9. _____

10. _____

11. _____

12. _____

13. _____

14. _____

15. _____

16. _____

17. _____

18. _____

Remember, for superior service: Mail, email, or fax questions about our materials.
Telephone questions about orders, prices, shipments, or payments.

Name: _____

Address: _____

City/State/Zip: _____

Telephone: Home: _____   Work: _____   Fax: _____

Email: _____